The Buddhist Visnu

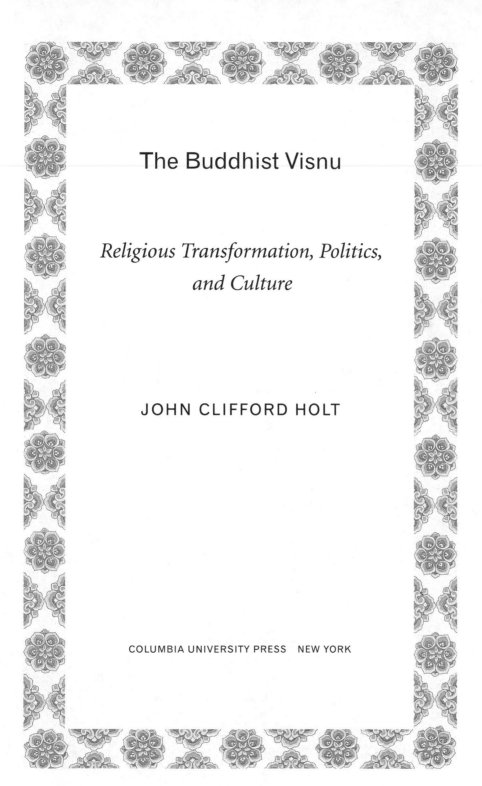

The Buddhist Visnu

Religious Transformation, Politics, and Culture

JOHN CLIFFORD HOLT

COLUMBIA UNIVERSITY PRESS   NEW YORK

Columbia University Press

Publishers Since 1893

New York   Chichester, West Sussex

Copyright © 2004 Columbia University Press

Library of Congress Cataloging-in-Publication Data

Holt, John, 1948–

The Buddhist Visnu : religious transformation, politics, and culture / John Clifford Holt.

p.   cm.

Includes bibliographical references and index.

ISBN 0–231–13322–7 (cloth) — ISBN 0–231–13323–5 (pbk.)

1. Buddhism—Sri Lanka—History. 2. Vishnu (Hindu deity)—Cult—Sri Lanka. 3. Buddhism—
Relations—Hinduism. 4. Hinduism—Relations—Buddhism. 5. Buddhism and politics—
Sri Lanka.   I. Title.

BQ372.H62   2004

294.3′095493—dc22   2003064634

Columbia University Press books are printed on
permanent and durable acid-free paper.

Printed in the United States of America

c 10 9 8 7 6 5 4 3 2 1

p 10 9 8 7 6 5 4 3 2 1

For Sree Padma

Contents

CHAPTER 5
Seeking Protection:
Cultic Life at the *Udarata* Visnu *Devalayas*
160

CHAPTER 6
The *Valiyak Mangalya*:
The Curative Powers of the *Mala Raja*
225

CHAPTER 7
Legacies of the "Buddhist Visnu":
Myth and Cult at the Alutnuvara *Devalaya*
247

CHAPTER 8
Minister of Defense?
The Politics of Deification in Contemporary Sri Lanka
331

CONCLUSION
351

Preface

The religious traditions we study are not boxes of texts, commentaries, and interpretations passed from hand to hand through generations, but dynamic traditions, more like rivers, gushing, rolling, converging, and branching out to water and transforming new lands, or sometimes dying out completely in the desert sands. These traditions have always changed, sometimes gradually and sometimes in ways that would be considered quite revolutionary. (Eck 2000:137)

Indeed, religions do change sporadically or dramatically over the course of history, but not always in the same manner as the natural ebb and flow of water. The trajectories of religious change, more precisely, often stand in reflexive relation to dominant social and political forces in play. Moreover, religious change may be carefully engineered or even consciously contrived, in a manner that may serve the political interests of the state. At other times, religious change may be an unintended consequence of other types of evolving social dynamics, such as shifts in demography or reorientations of political economies.

This study demonstrates how the transformation of Visnu, one of the most important deities of Hindu tradition, became manifest within medieval and modern Sri Lankan Buddhist culture and society, and how a transplanted and integrated Visnu came to be understood within emergent Sinhala Buddhist literature and ritual. It illustrates, moreover, how Visnu's assimilation engendered periodic expressions of resistance. While this resistance may have been a consequence of intermonastic disputes, at least in the contemporary era, such resistance may have been politically inspired. Historically, it is sometimes impossible to separate religion from politics in Sri Lanka. To understand the current controversy in Sri Lanka about whether Buddhists should worship deities, especially deities of Hindu origins, it is important to remember the sometimes incestuous relationship that obtains between religion and politics in this society.

Religions change, and so do the reasons for studying them. The theoretical perspectives that shape our inquiries inevitably vary with the passage of time, eventually becoming historical indices that mark the contingencies of our own intellectual interests. Despite the ebb and flow of often ideologically driven surges and retreats of theory, fundamental patterns of much scholarly practice remain. Thomas Tweed recently described scholarly endeavor this way:

> Scholars continually move back and forth between inside and outside, fact and value, evidence and narrative, the living and the dead, here and there, us and them. (Tweed 2002:270)

Tweed has captured something of my own experience while writing this book. My attempts to study the cult of Visnu in Sri Lanka have been thoroughly engaged in the constant dialectical movements he cites. Indeed, attentive readers will see that the types of materials and issues I have encountered often forced me to shift the locations and perspectives of my inquiries.

This effort has produced only some shades and degrees of understanding, which some critical readers will deem more deeply insightful or more accurate than others. Much of what we discover depends on the nature of the questions we formulate, the types of people we meet, how willing they are to speak to us, how carefully we listen to them, and so on. The Introduction to part I delineates the theoretical rationale and thesis of this study, that political forces are often catalysts for religious change.

This is a study of a dimension of Buddhist religious culture that is not familiar to many readers in the western academy, because the issues, materials, and practices I have studied have not been accessible or examined in depth. The religion of common people is often ignored, its study sometimes sacrificed at the altar of great religious figures, and their lives and writings. Unfortunately, this means that we remain somewhat ignorant of how Buddhist practices and ideals are processed and valued among the vast majority of people who profess to be followers of the Buddha's dharma. Many of us in the field of Buddhist studies, especially in the West, have been adept at dealing with the issues William LaFleur describes in the first of the following paragraphs. However, we have not attended very well to the matters he discusses in the second:

> Early Buddhist doctrinal formulation had usually looked at raw facts of life and death with impassion. In its earliest Indian forms, Buddhism comes across even to the modern readers of texts as a dry-eyed, largely detached and philosophical assessment and acceptance of change, death and decay as inescapable. The three distinguishing marks of all existent things, according to the most basic of Buddhist teachings, is put in a pithy way: "All

things are characterized by impermanence, suffering and the absence of self. . . ."

Common people, however, were not ascetic monks or adept at making such a cold-eye accounting of reality. Their approach to Buddhism was not through a point-by-point analysis of the "constituents of being." Their Buddhism, which had to make sense of life's crises in order to be of any use to them, was a Buddhism that had to mediate the old doctrines through a rich and adaptable store of images and practices connected with folklore. Their concern was not so much to have an objective analysis of "being" as to find, from within the Buddhist tradition, comfort and consolation in their often desperate and miserable lives. (La Fleur 1992:28)

This study aims to show how the cult of Visnu was valorized in Sinhala Buddhist religious culture: how it occupied a revered space with regard to conceptions of political power wielded by elites, how it operated within a field of moral economy (the ethics of social consciousness) understood and articulated especially by Sinhala Buddhistic folk, and how it affected the dynamics of soteriology (religious quest) for the practicing Buddhists who have constituted the vast bulk of the *buddhasasana* (dispensation).

I have severely imposed on many people's time and attention to complete this project. On more than one occasion, I have felt like the conductor of an orchestra because there were so many others contributing simultaneously to the effort. Several people gave of themselves generously at my bidding and accomplished a very significant amount of translation work crucial for the formulation of the manuscript. P. B. Meegaskumbura was a major inspiration of this study. He translated from the original literary Sinhala a number of texts germane to the cults of Visnu, Dadimunda and Mala Raja; these texts appear in chapters 4, 6, and 7, in addition to the *Algama Sannasa*, which appears in chapter 5. He also read through an early version of the manuscript, provided helpful comments. and patiently prepared indices for places mentioned and texts translated or referred to in the final draft; and he was of enormous help to me in understanding the *valiyaka mangalya*, the focus of chapter 6.

Udaya P. Meddegama also provided invaluable assistance. He translated the *yatikas* I collected at the Visnu *devalayas* at up-country and low-country Visnu shrines and also translated significant segments of *sandesaya* literature that have been included in chapter 4. He also translated an important tape recording from the incumbent monk at the Ran Gal Lena Rajamaha Viharaya in Aluthnuvara. Vindya Eriyagama and Kanchuka Dharmasiri were savvy, reliable, and hardworking fieldwork assistants at the Kandy Maha (Visnu) and Aluthnuvara *devalayas* as well as at other up-country and low-country sites.

Vindya Eriyagama translated numerous interviews that were conducted in Sinhala, as well as the "case histories" recorded in chapters 5 and 6. She also translated significant portions of Mudiyanse Dissanayake's *Vimal Valiyak Mangalya* included in chapter 6. Her own experience as a field-worker and her nuanced knowledge of Kandyan culture and society were an enormous help. Kanchuka Dharmasiri also translated interviews from Sinhala to English, as well as portions of secondary historical studies written in Sinhala, and is the talented artist of the drawings found throughout this book. Sunil Goonasekera, Jonathan Walters, Sree Padma, and Gunapala Dharmasiri read through an early draft of the manuscript and each offered constructive comments and advice. As I said, I imposed this project on a lot of very generous people. I sincerely thank each of them.

I am also grateful to Denis Ratwatte, *basnayake nilame* of the Maha Devalaya in Kandy, and the Aluthnuvara Devalaya in Aluthnuvara, who more than tolerated our presence in 2000 and 2001. On many occasions, the *basnayaka nilame* took time out from the demands of his busy schedule to answer what must have seemed to him an endless series of tedious questions, and trusted us with the run of the *devalayas.* I also thank I. G. Sumanasena, who has helped me with my work in Sri Lanka since 1983 and remains a true friend; Rosemary Chunchie, a wonderful support since 1992; and Violet and Maya Perera, for making life in Kandy such a pleasurable and productive experience while I toiled away on this project. Gerald Peiris prepared the map.

A National Endowment of the Humanities Fellowship for College Teachers, a semester appointment as the Numata Chair of Buddhist Studies at the University of Calgary, and a faculty-leave supplement along with a faculty research grant from the Freeman Fund from Bowdoin College provided time and funds for me to undertake the research from 1999 through 2002 leading to this publication. A further grant from Bowdoin College's Faculty Research Fund provided a subvention to help offset publication costs.

I would also like to record my appreciation to Ms. Wendy Lochner, Senior Editor at Columbia University Press for religion, philosophy, and anthropology, for her interest in and support of this project.

Every book of this nature requires a unique and sustained inspiration. Mine has come from the person to whom this book is dedicated: Sree Padma.

The vast bulk of this manuscript was prepared in Sri Lanka on a word-processing program that did not support diacritics. My intention was to add all diacritics by hand when the manuscript moved through the copyediting process. However, I was informed by the Press at that time that the expense of adding the diacritical marks would be prohibitive. I apologize to my readers for their absence. The formally correct *bodhisatva* rather than the conventionally used *bodhisattva* has been used throughout.

Harpswell, Maine

The Buddhist Visnu

PART 1

Introduction

THE HISTORICAL AND THEORETICAL PROBLEMS

"Only unprogressive nations, to hide the sterility of their souls, seek indigenous or supernatural origins for their institutions and culture. Progressive nations borrow cultural elements from everywhere and assert their virile genius in remoulding and re-creating them."
—Martin Wickramasinghe[1]

In many chapters of the history of religions, there are clear and frequent instances in which the myths, rituals, ethics, gods, metaphysics, or symbolism of one religious culture are assimilated, transformed, and subordinated by the devotees of another. In a previous study published a decade ago, I sought to understand how and why the Mahayana Buddhist bodhisatva Avalokitesvara had been absorbed into the predominantly Theravadan Sinhala Buddhist religious culture of Sri Lanka. In that study, I found that many centuries after Avalokitesvara's Mahayana cult had been introduced into Sri Lanka, the bodhisatva had come to be regarded by Sinhala Buddhists as Natha Deviyo, the tutelary god par excellence of up-country Kandyan Theravada Buddhist kingship. Natha's identity, in turn, was then further transformed. After his original identity as Avalokitesvara had been forgotten, he came to be regarded by many as the next Buddha-in-the-making, the bodhisatva Maitreya.[2] My principal thesis in that study of the shifting identities of Avalokitesvara was this: that migrating forms of religious culture are often assimilated into another if they are perceived as functionally efficacious. Moreover, the staying power of such assimilations depends upon the manner in which they can be legitimated convincingly in relation to the *telos*, or ultimate end, of the incorporating religious culture.

In the present study of how the Hindu deity Visnu was incorporated within Sinhala Buddhist religious culture, I am still interested in examining the nuances of this particular pattern of religious change. Much of what follows in this book aims at determining how Visnu's cult has become religiously meaningful for different types of Sinhala Buddhists at various times historically. However, in this current study, additional issues come into play that extend the nature of the theoretical problem: It is often the case that, once elements of a given religious culture are assimilated, transformed, and legitimated by another, counterrreactions in relation to these assimilations may occur. These counterreactions often stimulate attempts to purge or reject precisely what has been previously assimilated. That is, cultural flows leading to the process of assimilation or adaptation may generate significant waves of resistance or patterns of ambivalence in relation to what has been previously absorbed.

Although such reactions belie the means by which a religious culture is engaged in an ongoing process of redefinition, this process of redefinition is often linked to a realpolitik. That is, many assimilations, transformations, or "purifications" occur not only because they are deemed, in general, to be functionally efficacious and soteriologically congenial, but because they are motivated, more precisely, by considerations of political expediency. Religious change occurs not only for religious reasons or rationales per se, but often in relation to the interests of contemporary political forces. Indeed, it is often difficult to separate religious and political forces within the context of social history or in the minds of individual historical players. They are often embedded in one another. This is especially true in the case of Buddhist Sri Lanka.

In pondering this problem theoretically and comparatively, it becomes apparent that this pattern has surfaced in any number of important historical circumstances in relation to a variety of religious and cultural contexts. Ambivalence in reaction to assimilation is often its by-product. Students of East Asian religions, for instance, know how important conceptions of Mahayana Buddhist thought, including dharma and emptiness (*sunyata*), exercised a profound influence upon neo-Confucian thinkers such as Ch'u Hsi and Wang Yang Ming during the tenth and fifteenth centuries c.e. in China, so that understandings of the principle of order and the nature of self-awareness were fundamentally changed.[3]

Simultaneously, however, Buddhist schools of monasticism and their institutions of practice were regarded warily by many Confucian literati and political officials, and sometimes eyed as an intruding or "foreign" presence, never to be fully considered as genuinely Chinese. In the literary circles of the Confucian Chinese elite, Buddhist ideas and institutions, however creative their impact upon Chinese thought and culture, often evoked just such an ambivalent response. Charles Wei-hsyn Fu has put the matter this way: "The neo-Confucian confrontation with Sinitic Mahayana is perhaps the most interesting and significant case of ideological 'love and hate' in the whole history of Chinese philosophy and religion."[4]

A second example is very familiar to students of Islam. This concerns the problem of how Jesus came to be regarded within the context of the Qur'an and later Sufi traditions. Again, the response is profoundly ambivalent. Although the divinity of Jesus as the Son of God, as well as the doctrine of the Trinity, was emphatically repudiated, the virgin birth or immaculate conception of Jesus was reasserted.[5] Such textual ambivalence contains the seeds of what later developed as a historical theory of Islam in which the religions of Moses and Jesus were enfolded into an understanding of a prophetic tradition that commenced with Abraham, and thus antedated the origins of the two rival religious traditions. Such was Islam's own "totalizing" response to the presence of other religious cultures within the regions that came under Muslim political control. Both Moses and Jesus were perceived as genuine prophets who had experienced divine revelations, but their followers were chastised for misunderstanding the truth of their messages. The ambivalence reflected in this interpretation left room for the possibility of valorizing Jesus in subsequent Sufi traditions. Marshall Hodgson (I:402) has described how a prophetic place was preserved for Jesus, but how he was simultaneously subordinated to Muhammad:

> Indeed, many Sufis allotted a special holy place to Jesus as the prophet of the inward life, of the gospel of Love. For among Sufis, as among other mystics, Love of God, and hence tenderness to all His creatures, came to be seen as the heart of inward life, just as reverence for God and justice to all His creatures was the heart of outward life, of the Shari'ah. There remained no doubt, of course, in most Sufis' minds that the revelation to Muhammad was the greatest and purest of the revelations. Sometimes it was put thus: that Moses revealed the majesty of God, and the Law which we must respect out of respect to Him; Jesus revealed the beauty of God, and the Love which we must bear Him when we catch a glimpse of His Reality; but Muhammad came with both Love and Law together, revealing both His majesty and beauty.

A third example, this one more pertinent to the study that follows, is the sometimes intimate and sometimes antagonistic complex of attitudes obtaining between Hindus and Buddhists in India, specifically in relation to how the figure of the Buddha was to be understood. Because this is a massive topic, I am compelled to look specifically, and yet only very briefly and superficially, within the introductory chapter of this book, at the changing manner in which some Hindus have reluctantly absorbed, cleverly subordinated, and then enthusiastically reclaimed the figure of the Buddha for Hinduism. A consideration of this relevant example of the theoretical problem at hand will also help to give some symmetry to a study that is primarily concerned with the Sinhala Buddhist incorporation of Visnu, which is the subject of the chapters that follow. A brief overview of how the Buddha has been regarded in India's Hindu religious culture also provides an opportunity to discuss various dimensions of the religious significance of Visnu within the Hindu context, before observing the nature of his assimilation and transformation among the Sinhala Buddhists of Sri Lanka.

In the study which follows, I will also discuss how Visnu's incorporation into Sinhala Buddhist religious culture has met with various degrees of resistance in late medieval and especially in contemporary times. In particular, I will focus on the significance of a contemporary movement in Sri Lanka led by Theravada monks that aims to discourage Buddhists from venerating the now thoroughly "Buddhist" Visnu. I will discuss the religious and political reasons for why this attempt to remove Visnu from veneration by Buddhists is now taking place.

This, then, is my thesis: that the manner in which deities or prominent sacred aspects of one religious culture are appropriated, legitimated, transformed and/or rejected by another may be, in part, the articulation of carefully considered theological or soteriological innovations invoked by reflective and erudite ecclesiastics; but often, however, some assimilations, and the resistances they frequently engender, are a refraction of social and political dynamics occasioned by a heightened awareness of communal, national, or ethnic consciousness. In the most abstract sense, I am suggesting that social, economic, and political conditions are often refracted in the substance and dynamics of movements for religious reform or innovation, even though the ostensible rationales for these reforms and innovations are usually more formally presented within doctrinal frameworks.

To be clear about my contention: I am not arguing that *all* religious assimilations or religious changes are *always* or *purely* politically inspired or politically expedient. But I am suggesting that many of them are at least partially so, and that we need to explore this possibility historically whenever we attempt to determine why it is that assimilations take place. In the case of the Sinhala Buddhist assimilation and transformation of Visnu, it will be seen in what follows that kingship, both Hindu and Buddhist, played a decisive role in making assimilations and purifications occur. In the contemporary context, Buddhist monks, as successors to the Sinhala kings who understood their own roles as the protectors of the Buddha's *sasana* (dispensation), are playing a similarly protective role. What will be seen is that while kings tend to assimilate, monks more often purge.

After the initial discussion in chapter 1 that analyzes how Hindus have incorporated the Buddha—a discussion that also introduces the major parameters of the cult of the "Buddhist Visnu" and the problems inherent in a study of deity veneration within the Theravada tradition—I shall proceed, in chapter 2, to an overview of how and why elements of Hindu religious culture exercised such a profound influence on aspects of Sinhala Buddhist political history, literature, and architecture from the twelfth through the sixteenth centuries C.E. This is followed by a discussion, in chapter 3, of how the identity of the Sinhala deity Upulvan, variously interpreted by many previous scholars, has come to constitute one of the major aspects of the transformed "Buddhist Visnu"'s mythic profile. In turn, chapter 4 examines late medieval Sinhala Buddhist liturgical poetry and myth to probe further into the evolution of Visnu's religious valorization.

Thus, part 1 of this book is primarily a study that is loosely diachronic in nature, examining mythic and cultic expressions of Sinhala religious culture as they have been evinced in a variety of literary sources: chronicles, inscriptions, poetry, and folk songs.

Part 2 is an examination of the contemporary cult of Visnu in Sri Lanka at the most important venues of its ritualistic expression; and it is a study of a recent movement to purge Buddhism of deity veneration.

THE "HINDU BUDDHA" AND THE "BUDDHIST VISNU"

"Any alien trait can be absorbed and integrated by another culture if it is elastic enough to adjust the new element to its basic pattern."
—Martin Wickramasinghe[1]

This chapter explores very briefly the problem of how Hindus have enfolded the Buddha into their changing religious culture in various historical contexts, as an especially relevant example of the theoretical problem I sketched in the introduction to part 1. The chapter also indicates how some Hindus have adopted a critical stance toward Buddhists and Buddhism. This discussion also provides an opportunity to outline some of the salient features of the cult of Visnu within Hindu religious culture, so that, in later chapters, the nature and significance of Visnu's assimilation into the Buddhist religious culture of Sri Lanka can be more readily understood. The second half of this chapter also introduces the salience of Visnu's cult for Sinhala Buddhists in Theravadan Sri Lanka while noting some of the general issues encountered in a study of deity veneration.

The "Hindu Buddha"

Hindu views of the Buddha and Buddhism have not been constant, nor have they been consistent. Indeed, it is quite artificial to speak of a Hindu view per se, because determining exactly what is "Hindu," in the first place, would be inherently problematic. As with all religious cultures, Hindu practice and Hindu religious ideas have been ever-transforming phenomena, not static entities, throughout a very long history spanning at least three millennia. As such, there is no single, normative view of Hinduism to be ascertained historically, though it is possible to collect various "snapshots" derived from textual distillations generated at a particular moment in history.

Furthermore, it can be quite misleading to refer to "Hinduism" in the ancient period of Indian history as evolving through several centuries into the common era, simply because important characteristics of ritual, mythic, and theological scope, in what is now normally referred to as "Hindu" tradition (a post-Puranic phenomenon), had yet to evolve. When the deities, cultic rites of propitiation, meditative practices, ethical proscriptions, and philosophical or theological schools of thought of what now predominantly constitutes the fundamental structures of Hindu religious culture did finally emerge in the latter half of the first millennium C.E., it was only after Buddhism had exercised a profound influence upon many of them, with Buddhist notions pertaining to karma, the practice of meditation, the nature of the self or nonself, the problematic nature of existence, and the solution to the existential condition, having been incorporated into the ongoing dynamic process. Even the development of what became modern Hindu monasticism, usually traced to the eighth-century activities of the great Hindu philosopher Sankara, was affected by Buddhism.

Yet the historical legacy of Buddhism in India is not limited to its influences upon or its incorporation into the developing tradition we have come to call Hinduism. Buddhism and other *sramana* or heterodox schools were fundamentally distinctive in their origins and remained independent and serious, sustaining challenges to Brahmanical orthodoxy throughout their respective Indian histories. Indeed, it was precisely because they mounted such serious challenges to the Brahmanical tradition that the nature and significance of their teachings had to be contested or reconciled.[2]

Though the accounts of the Pali *suttas* and *Vinaya* usually cast priestly *brahmanas* as spiritual seekers who became enlightened and converted by the Buddha's sermons, these priestly followers of Vedic tradition, both ancient and medieval, must have been generally quite wary of the teachings of the historical Sakyamuni Gautama Buddha from about the sixth century B.C.E., for the Buddha apparently had not been an Aryan kinsman, not a Vedic *rsi* or "seer," nor had he been born into their priestly *brahmin varna,* or caste. If we take the portrayals of early Pali canonical literature seriously, moreover, the Buddha could have been regarded in many circles as an inveterate opponent of Brahmanic public rites, a religious teacher who had opened the ranks of his followers to people of many different castes or ranks, who challenged the verity of Brahmanical metaphysical speculations pertaining to the self (*atman*) and the absolute unchanging ontological reality principle (*Brahman*) while declaring the efficacy of the sacred gods (*deva*s) as irrelevant to the ultimate religious quest.

In addition to these open challenges to Brahmanical conceptions of self, society and cosmos, the Buddha's own *ksatrya* or royal origins made it somewhat difficult, if not impossible, to accommodate him as a teacher in any of the accepted Brahmanical schools (*Vaidika, Vedantika, Srauta, Smarta,* etc.) or theological orientations (*Saiva, Vaisnava, sakta,* or bhakti) that developed formally within the later, more fully evolved, Hindu religious culture. Thus, it is not very surprising, in light of the antithetical stance assumed by the Buddha toward Brahmanical thought and institutions, that in one early medieval Brahmanical text, it is declared that "a *brahmana* who enters a Buddhist temple even in a time of great calamity cannot get rid of the sin by means of hundreds of expiations, since the Buddhists are heretical critics of the sacred *Vedas*."[3]

Vehement rejoinders to the Buddhist critiques of Brahmanical traditions also abound. It is not uncommon to find Buddhists referred to in many other medieval Brahmanical contexts as "outcastes" (*vasalaka*), "devils," or "demons" (*daitya, danava*). Moreover, the fact that the modern Telugu words *lanja dibbalu*, which refer to mounds of earth containing Buddhist archaeological ruins, literally mean "prostitute hill," indicates the degree of hostility and ridicule which Buddhism elicited in some sections of the medieval Hindu community. In light of the Buddha's critique of Brahmanism and the consequent hostility that it provoked, it is remarkable that the image of the Buddha was eventually rehabilitated and incorporated into many Hindu normative constructions, that the Buddha was eventually embraced by some modern Hindus as one of the greatest teachers of humankind, and that some other Hindus would go so far as to say that the Buddha was, in fact, even born a Hindu.

This last claim is frequently asserted in contemporary India, but it has been effectively rebutted by scholars like the late Lal Mani Joshi, a particularly insightful modern Indian historian of religions, who has bluntly rejected the assertion:

> To say that Gautama [the Buddha] was born a Hindu [as some contemporary Hindus and Western observers have claimed] is entirely nonsensical. There is no evidence to think that [Vedic religion] was prevalent among the Sakyas, Mallas, or Licchavis [the pertinent political republics] in the days of the Buddha and Mahavira [the so-called "founder" of Jainism]. On the contrary, there is evidence of the progress and influence of several varieties of Sramanic religion and philosophy which had nothing in common with Brahmanic theism, sacrificialism, and world-affirmation. The ideologies of the *sramanas* cannot be traced to Indo-Aryans . . . Buddhism and numerous other forms of ascetically-oriented soteriologies propounded by *munis* and *sramanas* together with some outstanding teachers of scepticism, materialism, realism, nihilism and eternalism flourished in that small area of modern Uttar Pradesh and Bihar at a time when it had

not been fully aryanized and brahmanized. It is not insignificant that the
anti-Vedic and ascetic tendency of a few Upanisadic texts was inspired by
the teachings of these east Indian *sramanas*.[4] [brackets mine]

Joshi's observation is particularly significant, not only in rebuffing the popular view that the Buddha was born a Hindu and that Buddhism is an offshoot
of Hindu tradition, but it is also important insofar as he is signaling just how
early it was (mid–first millennium B.C.E.) that Buddhist thought seems to have
influenced what are later regarded by many as thoroughly classic Hindu formulations. Specifically, he is referring to passages in several Upanisads that
champion the life of internal meditation over external ritual performance, of
the eremitic wandering ascetic over the domestic priest, and the ethicization
(rather than the ritual mechanization) of the doctrine of karma and its consequences for explaining a theory of rebirth. What Joshi suggests runs against the
grain of speculation offered by many Indian and Western scholars: that Buddhism somehow grew out of Hindu or Brahmanical antecedents that had been
first articulated in the Upanisads. Conversely, what he suggests is that Buddhism may have been a fundamental influence on many Upanisadic discourses
regarding an emergent religious alternative to the sacrificial focus of the *Rg
Veda*.

Buddhistic notions (concentrated meditation, selfless asceticism, and the
ethicization of karma, etc.) were eventually incorporated, in elegant and philo-
sophically precise language, within the poetic syntheses of the *Bhagavad Gita*,
perhaps the most highly revered of all Hindu sacred texts.[5] Within the *Gita*,
Krsna's famous discourse to Arjuna, teaching him the ethic of becoming detached from the fruit of his efforts through the conquering of desire, remains
a classic moment in the history of Indian religions, one that is, no doubt, of
Buddhist inspiration.[6]

Nevertheless, Brahmanical incorporation of Buddhist ideas—what Arnold
Toynbee once called "the philosophical plunder of Buddhism"—was also accompanied later, as I have indicated above, by mean-spirited ridicule. While
the Buddha and some of his selected ideas were eventually regarded most congenially, it can also be said that Buddhism as an institution and community
were rarely accorded the same hospitality from within the Brahmanical ranks,
especially after the eighth century C.E. The Indian cultural historian P. V. Kane
has argued that the assimilation of Buddhist ideas was not a consequence of
Hindu tolerance, nor reflective of a Hindu proclivity for philosophical syncretism.[7] Rather, because institutional Buddhism had become, since the third
century B.C.E., and the days of the emperor Asoka, a pan-Indian, politically significant presence, and Asoka's Buddhistic interpretation of dharma apparently
had become, for a time at least, a matter of implemented public policy, the

Brahmanical community, as a matter of its own survival, had little choice but to adopt a dual strategy: on the one hand, to be congenial to those Buddhist ideas which had become accepted as almost matters of religious common sense, but also, on the other, to undermine, condemn, or chastise rival Buddhists and their institutional communities.

The second part of this strategy became explicit after the eighth century C.E. when the theories and ideologies of kingship in India shifted from Buddhist to Vaisnava and Saiva rationales. Kane's reading of the sociopolitical dynamic between the Brahmanical and Buddhist communities in earlier phases of Indian political history is in accordance with the analyses recently offered by Ronald Inden, which are germane to later medieval historical periods. With reference to the shifting ideology of kingship, Inden writes (1998:67) that

> before the eighth century, the Buddha was accorded the position of universal deity and ceremonies by which a king attained to imperial status were elaborate donative ceremonies entailing gifts to Buddhist monks and the installation of a symbolic Buddha in a stupa. . . . This pattern changed in the eighth century. The Buddha was replaced as the supreme, imperial deity by one of the Hindu gods (except under the Palas of eastern India, the Buddha's homeland) and the performance of *srauta* rites as separate ceremonies was largely abandoned.

The replacement of the Buddha as the "cosmic person" within the mythic ideology of Indian kingship, as we shall see shortly, occurred at about the same time that the Buddha was incorporated and subordinated within the Brahmanical cult of Visnu. That is, before the eighth century, the Buddha and Buddhism enjoyed a sociopolitical status that the Brahmanical community simply could not ignore, and its attacks upon Buddhist institutions were more tempered or muted in fashion as a result. While Buddhism would not disappear from India for several centuries after the eighth, it is clear that royal proclivities for the cults of Visnu and Siva weakened its position within the sociopolitical context and helped to make possible its eventual eclipse and absorption by the priestly Brahmanical community. Inden (55) has elaborated historically on the specific nature and putative significance of this shift:

> The first imperial dynasties that elevate either Visnu or Siva (or Surya, the Sun) to the status of supreme deity (*paramesvara, mahesvara*), equivalent to the Cosmic Man and relegate the Buddha to a secondary position are the short-lived Karkota dynasty of Kashmir and the Gurjara-Pratihara at Kanyakubja in northern India, the Rastrakuta in the Deccan, and the Pallava in south India. This change takes place in the eighth century and is

marked by the building of the first monumental Hindu temples. Previously the Buddha had been accorded imperial-style worship (*puja*). Now as one of the Hindu gods replaced the Buddha at the imperial centre and pinnacle of the cosmo-political system, the image or symbol of the Hindu god comes to be housed in a monumental temple and given increasingly elaborate imperial-style *puja* worship.[8]

In its *Vaisnava* dress, the developing ideology of Indian theories of kingship was undergoing a decisive turn which would also generate a major change in the manner in which the Buddha and Buddhism would be regarded from within a newly regenerated Brahmanical and bhakti (devotional) framework. Within this emergent "full blown" Hindu tradition dominated by the bhakti cults of Visnu (and in some cases Siva), the king was considered a "partial descent" (*amsa*) of the great god Visnu, the preserver of dharma, the natural and moral order, and himself a form of the Cosmic Overlord. Visnu's wife, Laksmi or Sri, the goddess of wealth, prosperity, and good fortune, who worshipfully accompanies her husband in different forms when he descends (*ava-tr*) to earth in one of his various forms, was also considered the consort of the king parallel to and obviously closely connected to the land (Inden 46).

Like the king, the Buddha would also be accorded the status of an avatar within this developing Brahmanical ideological scheme. Inden (71) describes how the new Hindu consecration ceremony, the *abhiseka*, transformed the king into a this-worldly Visnu, an ideal human being of cosmic significance:

The golden water jar, anthropomorphically adorned and dressed, honored and empowered, has itself been made into a microcosmic, immanent image of the Cosmic Man. The waters it contains have in them, by virtue of this act of transubstantiation, the powers of all the gods, beings, and substances that exist in the cosmos. All of these have been generated out of the body of the Cosmic overlord at the beginning of the present cycle of creation. Now, these have all been reconverged and concentrated themselves in the "body" of the water jar, in symbolic reality the microcosm of the Cosmic Man. By transferring its waters—the symbolic 'blood' of the Cosmic Man—or, more precisely, the radiant energy (*tejas*) of Visnu—to the head and body of the king from the jar, the sovereign Visnu, through the agency of the royal astrologer, transmits the 'kingship over kings' to the king and transforms him into a microcosmic and immanent form of the macrocosmic and transcendent Purusa. The ritual enactment of Purusa's creation of the king by drawing together portions of the gods is now completed. The recipient had earlier been made into an independent, regional king by the *vaidika* segment of the rite, the *rajasuhya*; here he has been

made into an imperial, universal king, a replica of Visnu, the Cosmic
Man. . . . Transformed by the *abhiseka* into the image of this Cosmic Sovereign, the king-elect is now ready to be installed (as is the image of a deity
in a temple) in his actual kingdom. As a partial *avatara* or descent of Visnu,
he is ready to descend from the transcendent plane to the immanent world
of his kingdom, to take his place as the microcosmic Purusa, the *axis
mundi* of his domain.

I have quoted at length what Inden has described in detail because this ritual
making-of-a-king provides an excellent portrayal of not only the emergent
"god-king" construction, but also how an avatar was regarded in relation to the
fundamental cosmic being (Visnu). The Buddha's Vaisnava avatar profile was
molded much in the same fashion. Further, this Vaisnava model of kingship
was to exert a concerted impact upon Sinhala Buddhist kingship in Sri Lanka
by the eleventh and twelfth centuries in Polonnaruva (the capital city and imperial ritual center), and with it, curiously, a special accommodation for Visnu
within Buddhist constructions of divine hierarchy.

Haldar has noted a number of structural and substantial similarities between the mythic profiles of Visnu and the Buddha which, he maintains, may
have abetted the assimilation and subordination of the Buddha as an avatar of
Visnu in the Hindu Puranas. Noting the *Visuddhimagga* and *Dhammapada*
commentaries as classic Theravadan sources of cosmogony and cosmology,
Haldar points out that "the Buddha covered the distance of 6,800,000 *yojana*s
in three strides, from the earth to the *Tavatimsa Devaloka*, and reached there
(*Tavatimsa*), setting his right foot down on the top of the Yugandhara and his
left one on Sineru" (Haldar 1970:2–3). He notes how reminiscent this is of the
three strides by which Visnu, in the *Rg Veda*, marks off the cosmic spheres.

Another significant similarity, he notes, may be seen in the fact that Buddhas seem never to be born in the early phases of a *kalpa*, but only after a critical period of decline has set in and there is a need for dharma to be known
among humankind. Haldar sees this as an indication of why "the Buddha may
be regarded as an *avatara*" (Haldar 129) insofar as he functions in the same
way as Visnu—appearing in a period of decline in order to uphold dharma. (It
would be difficult, in fact, to establish the origins of these shared attributes
found within both of the mythic profiles of the Buddha and Visnu, whether
they have evolved from a common source or have their origins exclusively in
one tradition or the other.)

Whatever the origins of these shared attributes, Hindu ambivalence towards the Buddha and Buddhism is no more clearly seen than in the Hindu assimilation and subordination which I wish most to emphasize in this brief
portrayal: By the time of the eighth century C.E., when the political transfor-

mations from Buddhist to Hindu ideology noted above were occurring, the Buddha was being declared an avatar, or an incarnation of Visnu, in not only one Sanskrit Purana, but in no less than four.[9] By this time too, inscriptions in the south, in what is today modern Tamilnadu, at Mahabalipuram, were declaring that the Buddha was the ninth of Visnu's ten incarnations.[10] Eventually, sculpted images of Visnu's ten avatars, including the Buddha, would adorn the columns of the most renowned Visnu temples in South India, with Tiruchchapalli's famous Sri Rangam (Visnu) temple being perhaps the most conspicuous example.[11] The legacy of this formulation was so widespread and enduring that even today in contemporary Sinhala Buddhist Sri Lanka, one can see temple paintings produced in the 1950s at the Visnu *devalaya* in Devinuvara on the southern tip of the island, in which the Buddha is depicted as the ninth avatar of Visnu (see fig. 1.1). Thus the notion gained widespread currency even beyond Hindu India, where one can still hear it enthusiastically asserted by many Hindus even today.

So, what exactly does it mean to be an avatar of Visnu within the context of the Puranas? The Puranas are sometimes referred to as the "fifth *veda*" on account of their great popularity, and hence authority, among common Brahman priests and Hindu devotees of bhakti orientations.[12] Unlike the Vedas, the Brahmanas, and the Upanisads, texts which are substantially sacrificial hymns,

FIGURE 1.1 Painting of the Buddha as the ninth avatar of Visnu, from the 1950s, on the wall of the sanctum sanctorum of the Visnu *devalaya* at Devinuvara

ritual handbooks, and esoteric meditations on the secrets of the self and the cosmos respectively, the Puranas are essentially popular mythic stories detailing the fantastic exploits of the gods, the manner in which they have created the world, how they can reveal its truths, and how they can enter into the worlds of human beings to uphold the order of dharma and to prevent catastrophic worldly destruction by the forces of disorder, usually personified by *asuras*. They also contain many stories about how various places of sacred pilgrimage became hallowed.

Within Vaisnava Hinduism, or the Hinduism that celebrates Visnu as the ontological truth of the fundamental reality of Brahman,[13] Visnu is not only the preserver of dharma or order in the cosmos, which is the manner in which he is popularly portrayed in synthetic understandings of Hinduism; rather, he is also the very creator of the world, the reality behind the beguiling mask of *maya* (variegated illusion), who periodically and benevolently extends his protection to those who seek his refuge. These divine characteristics and prerogatives are the theological and mythic stuff of the Puranas, and Visnu's avatars, or his timely "descents" into the realm of human beings, comprise his most well known attribute and method for intervening within the existential condition. He is a "high god" of personal salvation, as well as a cosmic redeemer of the world.

The myths and doctrine of Visnu's avatars are reflective of two important traits of Hindu *Vaisnava* perspectives. The first trait consists of Visnu's radically transcendent and abstract nature, a transcendence that can be seen to be as ancient as it is abstract. For instance, in an ancient *Rg Veda* hymn[14] (*samhita*), Visnu is referred to, as mentioned above, as the mighty *deva* (god) whose three cosmic strides measured out the tripartite structure of the universe: the celestial, atmospheric, and terrestrial abodes, which become definitive not only for the categorical identities and functions of different types of divinities believed to populate the cosmos, but also, according to some scholars, as mythic projections of the tripartite divisions of society that are hierarchically embedded in the Indo-European social schematization.[15]

While Visnu's transcendence was early on articulated mythically in ancient texts and later represented spectacularly in the doctrine of avatars, his immanence was stressed metaphysically by means of his abstract identification as the fundamental ontological reality of the cosmos. His abstract nature has been reflected in how he has been depicted in the traditions of classical Indian painting and sculpture. For instance, Visnu is sometimes represented as a mist or a cloud, because his abstract philosophical profile makes it difficult to render him suitably in anthropomorphic form (see fig. 1.2). Moreover, the symbol of the footprint (referring to his "three strides") also functions frequently as his preferred nonanthropomorphic representation.[16]

FIGURE 1.2 Brahma, Siva, Indra, a herder, and the Earth-cow ask the enshrouded Visnu to manifest himself. c. 1540 C.E., North India (from Francis Hutchins, *Young Krishna*, 1980).

Visnu's profile in the Puranas, as creator and transcendent savior god par excellence, an analogue to Visnu's equation with Brahma in *Vaisnava* theology, is so utterly abstract that another device, the avatar, abets the process of concretizing his presence and thus renders him accessible to human entreaties as a personal lord. Further, the avatar device, whatever its origins, lends itself quite readily to a religiocultural process of assimilation, since it so obviously implies that Visnu may take on any number of forms to make his power efficacious in the human world.

It is this amenability to assimilation that is the second trait of the Vaisnava Hindu cult that I wish to take note of here. Other scholars have often suggested that the reification of Visnu's avatars, counted as ten, twelve, or twenty-two in various Purana texts,[17] masks a historical process of envelopment in which indigenous religious cults with roots in non-Aryanized India have been enfolded into the Brahmanical *Vaisnava* tradition and thereby subordinated under a Brahmanical *Vaisnava* umbrella. David Kinsley, for instance, argues persuasively that the myths and cult of Krsna were originally religious phenomena peripheral to the later amalgamated cult of Visnu.[18] Thus, the avatar device, a consequence of Visnu's transcendence, provided a handy means by which other deities could be assimilated, subordinated, and legitimated.

I have belabored this discussion relating to Visnu's avatars because this was precisely the device used to assimilate and then to subordinate the figure of the Buddha. Or, to put the matter differently, it was an apt and convenient means to give space to the Buddha, or better, to put the Buddha in his Brahmanical place.

The assimilation of the Buddha as Visnu's ninth avatar was not formulated, however, without an interesting and revealing twist: the *Visnu Purana* states that Visnu's "descent" as the *Buddhavatara* was accomplished so that the wicked and the demonic could be only further misled away from the truth in this current age of degeneracy, the *kali yuga*. That is, through his teachings, the Buddha was regarded as a divinely incarnated purveyor of illusion.

The assimilation of the Buddha as Visnu's avatar and the consequent disingenuous interpretation or rationale for his inclusion aptly articulate the considerable ambivalence characteristic of Hindu attitudes towards Buddhism. One of the effects of rendering the Buddha as an avatar was to undermine his historicity, to make him an appendage of the Vaisnava mythic hierarchy. Another was to assure the traditionally-minded Brahman that the *Buddhavatara* was but a device used by Visnu to further misguide heretics, here the Buddhists in particular. It explained how divine absolute prerogative was actually responsible for the presence of an ancient and annoying rival. Its presence could be chalked up to "God's will"—a necessary evil, as it were.

Furthermore, when one looks into how and to what extent the Buddha was ritually enfolded within Hindu tradition, there is not much to find. Indeed, cultic veneration of the Buddha within Hinduism is virtually absent.

While the Buddha as an avatar of Visnu remained the Buddha's chief claim to fame among many Hindus from the eighth century through colonial times, and even for many in the present, the fortunes of the "Hindu Buddha" took a decidedly different turn in the first half of the twentieth century, during the time of the Indian drive for cultural renaissance and political independence. In this context, a dramatic reclamation project was in the offing. In retrospect, it may be that this reclamation was made possible in light of the disappearance of the Buddha's religion, and its institutionalization, from the land of its birth by the twelfth and thirteenth centuries of the common era.[19] There was no longer any need for the previous expressions of ambivalence that were so characteristic of Hindu stances, since Buddhism as a competitive religion was no longer perceived as a popular rival threat to Brahmanism. From this angle of analysis, the Buddha's reclamation needed only a catalyst for it to gain fruition.

The Buddha's transformation in modern India was first heralded by Swami Vivekananda, one of India's nationalist leaders of religious, cultural, and intellectual "re-awakening." Van der Veer (1999:33) has aptly described Vivekananda's project in the following terms:

The typical strategy of Vivekananda was to systematize a disparate set of traditions, make it intellectually available for a Westernized audience and defensible against Western critique, and incorporate it in the notion of Hindu spirituality carried by the Hindu nation, which was superior to Western materialism, that had been brought to India by an aggressive and arrogant British nation.[20]

Self-proclaimed heir to the inclusive bhakti or devotional religious vision of the nineteenth-century Bengali saint Ramakrsna,[21] the charismatic Vivekananda preached to western and westernized Indian audiences a *Vedanta* philosophy of monism in which the Buddha was eulogized as perhaps the greatest teacher ever of Hindu ideas. Buddhism became one of the "disparate traditions" enfolded into the nationalist Hindu spirituality. Vivekananda proclaimed that the Buddha was basically a reformer and that the Buddhist religion had been nothing more than a "rebel child of Hinduism." Further, he declared that the Buddha was his own *ista devata*, his "chosen deity" for personal worship. Among his many characterizations of the Buddha, what Vivekananda stressed, in harmony with the zeitgeist of his westernized, intellectual, and elitist religious orientation, was that the Buddha was a great rationalist thinker who rose above popular superstitions, a true democrat who preached liberation from caste hierarchy based on the equality of all men, and a great prophet whose selflessness was unparalleled.[22] He felt the Buddha had correctly analyzed the human condition as being one of *dukkha* (or "unsatisfactoriness") and that *dukkha*'s cause was the result of desire. In the following quotation, Vivekananda identifies the Buddha more specifically as the fulfillment of a particular Hindu ideal type:

(The Buddha) is the ideal Karma Yogi, acting entirely without motive, and the history of humanity shows him to have been the greatest man ever born, the greatest combination of heart and brain that ever existed, the greatest soul-power that has ever been manifested.[23]

In identifying the Buddha as the ideal karma yogi, Vivekananda is arguing that the Buddha is the model for one of the basic soteriological strategies articulated within the *Bhagavad Gita*. There is no doubt, as I noted earlier, that this section of the *Gita* is heavily dependent on Buddhistic ideas. So the karma yogi mantel that Vivekananda bestows is, in fact, very apt. But this passage is also very reflective of a specific Hindu assimilation and subordination of the Buddha in another way. Vivekananda has referred to the Buddha as the "greatest soul-power that has ever existed." One of the Buddha's most central arguments against Hindu philosophical constructions is his rejection of the notion of a soul (*anatman*). Yet Vivekananda ignores this important and central argument. Rather, he invokes this very notion of soul to aggrandize the Buddha for his own purposes, and in the process illustrates part of the thesis I have propounded. That is, in this case, the Buddha is assimilated and legitimated exactly by constructing his relation to Hindu soteriology. So what is more significant than Vivekananda's specific karma yogi litany of praise is the more general manner in which Vivekananda unabashedly appropriated the Buddha for his own version of a universalistic Hinduism. To help accomplish this, he linked the teachings of the Buddha to those of Sankara, perhaps the most well-known of all Hindu philosophers and the key proponent of *advaita vedanta*, and explicitly identified the Buddha himself as a promulgator of the Vedanta school of Hindu philosophy per se:

> Buddha was a great Vedantist, and Shankara is often called a hidden Buddhist. Buddha made the analysis, Shankara made the synthesis of it.[24]

This is the dominant image and function of the Buddha sprinkled throughout Vivekananda's collected writings in his attempt to make the case that Vedantic Hinduism, the religion par excellence through which the discipline of knowledge uncovers the hidden universal truth behind all variegated phenomenal existence, is the true philosophical mother of all religions. Notice that Vivekananda's assimilation of the Buddha is framed primarily in doctrinal terms. The Buddha's analysis of existence is congenial to setting up the solution of *jnana yoga* proffered by Sankara. C. D. Sharma, in his *A Critical Survey of Indian Philosophy,* is even more explicit in this regard than Vivekananda. He writes:

> Buddhism and Vedanta should not be viewed as two opposed systems, but one which starts with the Upanisads, finds its indirect support in Buddha, its elaboration in Mahayana Buddhism, its open revival in Gaudapada, (and) which reaches its zenith in Sankara.[25]

Vivekananda's agenda of rehabilitating the image of the Buddha is not without historical precedent, because it is quite evident that Sankara's philosophy was formulated under the heavy influence of Nagarjuna, and perhaps by other Mahayana philosophers as well.[26] Vivekananda actually went further though. His Hindu neo-Vedanta theological agenda was, in general, aimed at promulgating the thesis that while the West was rich in material and scientific accomplishments, it was lacking in genuine spirituality, a spirituality that Eastern religious teachings, in the guise of Vedanta's universal theology, was thoroughly prepared to supply. A refashioned image of the Buddha, whose message was now blended with Victorian sensitivities and Vedantic pretensions to universal truth, was a perfect accomplice for the task, which included converting the intellectual strata of Hindu society in late colonial times.

That Vivekananda eventually succeeded is apparent in the way the Buddha came to be regarded by emerging nationalist leaders at the forefront of India's independence movement in the mid-twentieth century. Consider the following statements by some of its most ardent leaders. First, Mahatma Gandhi:

> I do not consider for one moment that Buddhism has been banished from India. . . . It is impossible to banish Buddha . . . that great Lord, Master and Teacher of mankind. So long as the world lasts, I have not a shadow of doubt that he will rank among the greatest teachers of mankind.[27]

Similarly, here is what Sarvepalli Radhakrishnan, Oxford-educated philosopher and the first president of India, had to say:

> Among the inspiring treasures of the human spirit is the memory of Gautama the Buddha. Its hold over the imagination of millions of our fellow beings is immense; its inspiration to braver and nobler living for centuries is incalculable; its contribution to the refining spirit of man and the humanizing of his social relations is impressive.[28]

Moreover, in another context which speaks directly to the issue at hand, Radhakrishnan wrote this:

> It is an accepted view of the Hindus that the supreme Visnu assumed different forms to accomplish different purposes for the good of mankind. The Buddha was accepted as an avatara who reclaimed Hindus from sanguinary rites and erroneous practices and purified their religion of the numerous abuses which had crept into it. This avatara doctrine helps us to retain the faith of the ancestors while effecting reforms in it. Our Puranas describe the Buddha as the ninth avatar of Visnu.[29]

In the same spirit and yet even more to the specific point I wish to make, the following is what Jawaharlal Nehru, India's first prime minister, and one of India's foremost modern intellectuals and students of history, has to say:

> The conception of the Buddha, to which innumerable loving hands have given shape in carven stone and marble and bronze, *seems to symbolize the whole spirit of Indian thought.* . . . The ages roll by and Buddha seems not so far away after all, his voice whispers in our ears and tells us not to run

away from the struggle but, calm-eyed, to face it . . . *The nation and race which can produce such a magnificent type must have deep reserves of wisdom and inner strength.* . . . His appeal was to logic, reason and experience, his emphasis was on ethics, and his method was psychological analysis.[30] [italics mine]

In his memoirs, Nehru has reported that it was a print of the famous *samadhi* Buddha image from Anuradhapura, Sri Lanka, that adorned his prison cell wall and provided moments of inspiration for him during his extended period of incarceration. In what he has said about the Buddha in the quotation I have cited above, the Buddha has been reclaimed triumphantly as a symbol of indigenous, nationalist understandings of India's history and culture, and its road to modernity.

Finally, consider this last statement about the Buddha by D. C. Sircar, one of India's leading historians in the immediate post-independence period of the 1950s, who saw as his task the recovery of India's indigenous voice:

> Gautama the Buddha and the Maurya emporer Asoka are two of the greatest sons of India and the world, and their lives and achievements stand among India's best contributions to human civilization.[31]

In short, the reclamation of the Buddha in modern India was magnificent and triumphant, and it was perhaps this sensational manner in which it was proclaimed that inspired, in part, B. R. Ambedkar, the framer of India's constitution, to lead members of his depressed *Mahar* caste in a mass conversion to Buddhism.[32]

To summarize briefly, then, the modern Indian acclamation of the Buddha had been preceded by his transformation as an avatar of Visnu, his envelopment within Vivekananda's Vedanta of universal pretensions in response to Westernization, and his being regarded finally as one of modern India's great *bhumiputra*s or "sons of the soil." What should not go unnoticed here is that this modern transformation or reclamation of the Buddha takes place within the context of an evolving rhetoric of nationalist discourse, the secularized successor to the missionary oratories of Vivekananda.[33]

While Vivekananda's message was universalistic, the nationalist discourse was inclusive and historical. That is, India's pre- and post-independent nationalist politicians, like their counterparts in Sri Lanka, sought to create a popular awareness and a historical consciousness of depth and sophistication for their ancient cultures. And in that inclusive understanding, they hoped to generate a great national pride. In reclaiming that history from its most recent colonial past, they also reclaimed the Buddha as a *bhumiputra* with international and modern appeal, a figure who had suddenly become supremely relevant to the nationalist political agenda at hand.

It remains to be seen, with the contemporary eclipse of the Nehru and Gandhi attempt to forge an all-India identity within the context of the Congress Party, whether the Hindu-inspired Bharata Janata Party (BJP), which now heads a coalition government, will sustain such a nationalist regard for the Buddha. Suffice it to say that the Buddha provided earlier nationalists with a symbol to declare that India's civilization was noble, culturally variegated, and intellectually respectable. He served the political forces advocating an all-India inclusive ethic quite well. It is doubtful that he would be as useful to those who are now propounding what seems to be an ethic of exclusivity, though it is possible that a place for a Hindu Buddha may yet be created within politically inspired *hindutva*. In any case, the Buddha's reclamation as a *bhumiputra* occurred because of the construction of an inclusive political consciousness. Visnu's inclusion within a Sinhala Buddhist framework was a product of a similar process.

The "Buddhist Visnu" and the Controversies of Deity Veneration: An Introduction

Sinhala Buddhists, who comprise two-thirds of the current population of Sri Lanka, are exceedingly proud of the fact that their culture is the oldest continuing Buddhist civilization in the world, dating back some 2,300 years. While Visnu is mentioned just once, and that merely in passing, in all of Pali canonical Buddhist literature sacred to the Theravada tradition,[34] modern translations and interpretations of Sri Lanka's fifth-century c.e. Theravada Buddhist quasi-historical monastic chronicle, the *Mahavamsa*, identify Visnu with the sacred role of being the people's and the religions's chief "minister of defense."[35] This identification is derived from a reading of a seminal migration myth recorded in the *Mahavamsa* which explains that the ancient arrival of the progenitors of the Sinhala people, and the subsequent arrival of Buddhism, are in part the result of the protective powers of Visnu.

The identity of Visnu in this specific regard will be discussed thoroughly in the third and fourth chapters. For now, however, I will simply note that a careful study of the *Mahavamsa*, together with a study of inscriptions, and medieval Sinhala literature, shows that Visnu's Buddhistic identity as the island's and the religion's "minister of defense" probably does not antedate the late seventeenth century c.e. Nevertheless, it is now difficult to find any general appraisal of Sinhala religion, or of Sinhala deity propitiation more specifically, in either English or in Sinhala, that does not assume that Visnu has been protecting the Buddhist religion since its inception. There are even some popular folk-loric accounts in Sinhala *kavi* (poetry) that say that Visnu protected the Buddha from Mara, the personification of death, on the night of his enlightenment experience.

Moreover, Visnu *devalaya*s, or shrines to Visnu, are now ubiquitous throughout all Sinhala Buddhist cultural areas in Sri Lanka, especially in rural, village contexts. His integration into popular conceptions and transactions of Buddhist ritual cults has been perhaps as thorough as any other deity in Sinhala Buddhist religious culture. His power is propitiated in invocations at the beginning of virtually every public ritual. Late medieval Sinhala folk literature is also replete with references to his beneficent presence. Indeed, many Sinhalas living in rural areas of the country would be surprised to learn that Visnu is a deity of Brahmanical, Vedic, and Hindu Puranic origins. In the popular mind, Visnu is a very high "god" indeed, one who treads positively on the path leading to nirvana—and eventually to Buddhahood itself. Because of the vast amount of meritorious work he has performed on behalf of those who seek his help, he is popularly regarded as a bodhisatva, or future Buddha.

Here, then, after seeing the assimilation and subordination of the Buddha within a "totalizing" Vaisnava context, we see the general profile of the readapted Visnu within a Buddhist context. Visnu's rationalized legitimacy in this Buddhistic context is effected through the strategy of placing him well along the path to eventual Buddhahood. He, too, in this context, has become an advanced Buddhist seeker after nirvana. Associating his position in relation to the Buddhist soteriological process and goal has thus rendered securely his function and position. This development, then, illustrates the veritable thesis of this study and becomes the central focus of much of what follows in subsequent chapters.

Just as Sinhala villagers would be surprised to learn that Visnu could be anything other than a Buddhist deity, many westerners are surprised to learn that gods have any kind of place in Buddhist cultures at all. The nature and function of the divine in Buddhism seems to be one of the issues least understood by many in the West who are interested in Buddhism. Trade books on the spirituality of Buddhism sold in European and North American bookstores scarcely mention deity veneration at all in their accounts. If deities are mentioned in these more consumer-oriented "spirituality" publications, it is usually negatively or even derisively. In these books, Buddhism is often championed as a religion without gods, a type of spiritual self-help totally dependent upon the will of a determined practitioner, a religion completely oriented toward personal self-attainments, one in which mental, ethical, and emotional proclivities causing existential dissatisfaction can be overcome by the disciplined, intentional assertions generated out of a mind-set of contemplative serenity.[36] Logical rationality and scientific disposition, the pride of the post-enlightenment era, are often emphasized as intrinsic to the Buddhism of these representations, and postmodern versions of this type of literature stress exclusively the spiritual benefits that Buddhism brings to the individual.

Such characterizations, however, are not limited to the bookstore marketplace. Most introductory academic textbooks on comparative religion now in use at North American colleges and universities still present the teachings of the Buddha and the historical development of Buddhist doctrine in this decidedly Eurocentric manner, as if, like Christian Protestantism, Buddhism were primarily a matter of faith or religious belief.[37] Within these presentations, Buddhism is often understood essentially as a timeless religious philosophy, not as a complex and changing religious culture in variegated historical contexts. Buddhism is also sometimes rendered as atheistic, and proudly proclaimed so, insofar as it is not seen as a religious discipline dependent on the power of savior figures or omnipotent gods. My sense of these readings is that the profile of Buddhism has been reconstructed in a culturally sanitized fashion, one dissociated from its Asian cultural contexts and made fit for consumption in the spirituality markets of the West.

On the Sri Lankan side, some scholarly monographs by Buddhist studies academics, while noting the ubiquitous presence of the gods even within the oldest layers of classical literary tradition, assert that divinity is beside the point of the basic Buddhist religious quest.[38] While this position is doctrinally correct, it can lead to the inaccurate portrayal of Buddhism as a religion bereft of the presence of the divine. Indeed, almost all portrayals of the Buddha in Pali canonical literature are replete with supernatural wonders, including virtually every appearance of the Buddha himself as a kind of superhuman being. He is represented, to say the least, as a rare and extraordinary being of cosmic significance. Iconographically, that is why his figure is often portrayed on such a massive scale.

Modern Asian Buddhist apologists to the West, such as Walpola Rahula,[39] have misled the reading public by stressing that the Buddha has been understood within Buddhist tradition simply as a human being. To the contrary, Peter Masefield,[40] I think, was quite correct, when he wrote some years back that

until now Buddhism has tended, consciously or otherwise, to suffer demythologisation at the hands of those ignorant of its mythology including, it may be added, some scholars in the East aping the bad habits of the West, so much so that the time has surely come when the texts should be seen in their own terms. If the Buddhism of ancient India is to be understood, it will have to be remythologized in the sense that there will have to be restored to its technical and metaphorical language all the nuances and associations its terms once had for those who heard them.

Part of the problem of recognizing the significance of the divine in Buddhism, specifically within Theravada Buddhist culture and Sinhala Buddhist society, is rooted in a semantic confusion over the English word "god." Asian and Western scholars have been correct in pointing out that the Judeo-Christian and Muslim meanings of this term have no place in Buddhist worldviews. What Buddhists mean by "god" is quite different from the way the term is construed in Hindu theological frameworks as well. I. B. Horner, who laboriously translated into English a number of Pali canonical texts, including the five-volume *Vinayapitaka*, refused, in fact, to translate the terms *deva* and *devata* (usually translated as "god" and "godling" respectively) into English "because the little we do know of them leads us to suppose that they represent kinds of beings for whom in English there are no acceptable equivalents" (1970 I:lvii). She points out that it is clear that, although *deva*s, *devata*s, and *yakkha*s are nonhuman classes of beings, they continue to have close contact with the human world "as their counterparts are thought to do in India, Burma and Ceylon at the present day" (lviii). She worries that English words like "god," "godling," and "demon" are somewhat misleading with regard to the reality of what is being depicted in Pali literature.

Similarly, David Scott's studies (1994) reveal not only semantic misunderstandings derived from colonial discourses depicting *yaksa* rites in southern Sri Lanka but also conceptual errors of the first order. ("Devil-dancing," as it were, is hardly an accurate rendering of *yaktovil*, a highly nuanced ritual aimed at healing physical and emotional imbalances brought about by a variety of causes, both natural and supernatural.) Moreover, in later discussions, in part 2, about the Sinhala deities Devata Bandara (a.k.a. Dadimunda) and Huniyam, who form an important part of Sinhala religion within the cultic context of Visnu's veneration, it becomes clear that the categories of *devata* and *yaksa* often overlap, so that referring to these beings simply as either "gods" or "devils" obscures, rather than identifies, what they represent more precisely within the constructions of Sinhala religious consciousness.

Within classical canonical Theravada Buddhist literature, the *Mahasamaya Sutta* of the *Digha Nikaya* (II: 253ff) is one of the few texts of the Pali *Tipitaka* where the Buddha addresses the issue of *deva*s and *devata*s directly. While preaching this particular discourse, the Buddha and his followers are visited by *devata*s of the ten thousand world systems. After noting that the presence of *devata*s is not unusual, the Buddha begins to identify categorically divine beings of different types according to an obscure non-Brahmanical classification scheme, the basis of which is very difficult to discern. He begins with a reference to *yakkhas*, then to the four *lokapalas*, and various types of *asuras*. In turn, these are followed by some sixty classes of *devas*, starting with those identified with the four primary elements (water, wind, fire, and earth). Then follows another sixty classes of deities in groups of ten. The Buddha's scheme seems to be presented as a hierarchy, so the deities mentioned first (the *yakkhas*) are lowest in rank and power, and those mentioned last are the highest and most distant gods.

Within this scheme, as I mentioned above, we find the only reference to Visnu in the Pali *Tipitaka*, and a rather innocuous one at that. Indeed, all of the major Brahmanical deities, including Brahma, Siva, Indra, Soma, Varuna, etc., are merely mentioned here in passing, with no specific significance attached to any of them. Each is regarded simply as one among the very many. There are no "high gods" here, but there are many deities indeed. The religious worldview of the *Suttapitaka* is not only many centuries removed from later Hindu *bhakti* constructions of cosmic deities, but it has a somewhat different regard for them in comparison to the Vedic conception of deities as well.

What separates the Pali *Tipitaka* Buddhist from the Brahmanical and later Hindu constructions of the divine is very clearly rooted in ontological assumptions and soteriological strategies or explanations. Unlike Brahmanical or Hindu gods (the term "gods" being more applicable in Hindu rather than in Buddhistic contexts), Buddhist deities are neither salvific nor essential or stable fixtures within the cosmos in any permanent way. There certainly are instances in the Brahmanical Hindu Puranas where the impermanence of the gods, and the fact that they undergo rebirths in the cosmos, is stressed.[41] But Buddhist deities have no fundamental fixed abodes in the cosmos or any essential intrinsic being of any sort whatsoever. Rather, whatever the form or class of their constructions within the spiritual hierarchies of *kama, rupa,* or *arupa lokas*, Buddhist *devas* and *devatas* are simply favorable, instantaneous consequences of karmic retribution. Two complete books of the *Suttapitaka*, the karmic stories comprising the *Vimanavatthu* and the *Petavatthu*, illustrate and stress (very redundantly) this important principle at work.[42] From the early Pali perspective, deities represent modes of being determined by the quality of one's actions as a human being.

Rebirth as a *deva* or *devata* is highly valued in the Buddhist cosmos because these categories of contingent being signal experiences of happiness, or a *sugati* course indicating genuine progress towards *nibbana*. Though such rebirth is valued in this cosmological context, the final course to *nibbana* leads to transcendence of all rebirths. Moreover, what is valued, as I have noted, is what *devas* soteriologically represent.

For instance, within advanced meditative practices of the path, one pursuit is known as *devatanussati*, wherein deities function as objects of meditative concentration:

> the ultimate aim of the recollection (of *devas*) is the attainment of perfect concentration (*samadhi*) in stages. First the meditator has to imagine the existence of all these *devas* and then recollect that it was their faith (*saddha*), morality (*sila*), knowledge (*suta*), liberality (*caga*) and wisdom (*panna*) that secured their birth in the heavenly worlds. Next he has to see that he himself is endowed with those qualities: when he does this, his mind ceases to be overwhelmed by lust, hatred and delusion.[43]

The salience of *devas* and *devatas* for most Buddhists, however, lies in the fact that deities embody symbolically not only progress for their own spiritual (*lokottara*) futures, but they can be appealed to for help in times of anxiety or distress. *Devas* and *devatas* are compassionate. Their own eventual spiritual fates are tied to their continued, well-intentioned responses to human entreaties. That is, their *laukika* (immediate and contemporary) responses to human entreaties for justice, prosperity, and peace in a troubled world assures their own *lokottara* (ultimate soteriological) spiritual destinies. As I will show in later chapters, it is precisely this valorization of divinity that is relevant to Buddhist deity cults in Sri Lanka, particularly the cult of Visnu.

My criticism of characterizations of Buddhism, the Western and Western-educated Sri Lankan alike—characterizations which dismiss the importance of the "gods" or ignore their significance entirely—is that they are basically presented without benefit of social, cultural, historical, and sometimes even textual analyses. They misconstrue and almost totally ignore the manner in which Buddhism is practiced outside of Western intellectual enclaves or urban areas of Asian countries where "aping the bad habits of the West" is sometimes a favored pastime. Contrary to these depictions, historians and anthropologists who have studied aspects of Buddhist religious cultures of South and Southeast Asia in nonurban areas have labored, for the past forty or fifty years, to point out that while the "gods" may not be altogether central to Buddhist doctrine or soteriological strategies, they function as genuine sources of religious consciousness for many Buddhist people, insofar as they signify important cognitive and emotive experiences for those who call themselves Buddhists. Following this tradition of scholarship and demonstrating this fundamental point will be a chief subject of later discussions in this book.

The persistent problem of ignoring or banishing the gods into insignificance has been further compounded for two additional reasons. The first reason for the persistence of this problem is that popular cultural flows from the

West to Asia are sometimes uncritically absorbed, and not the least of these has been, ironically, popular westernized understandings of a culturally sanitized Buddhism.[44] How the West understands Buddhism has had an indelible effect on how some Sri Lankans have come to understand their own religious culture. In the second instance, this one more germane to the specific subject of this book, there is an antipathy for some Hindu deities within the textual and historical traditions of Sri Lanka's monastic Theravada Buddhism itself which periodically erupts, given a relevant social stimulus. There are, indeed, a number of references in the Pali canonical corpus of the Theravadins which verge on ridiculing the perceived efficacy of venerating Brahmanical gods, either within the context of ritual implorations[45] or as impediments to maximizing the cultivation of the ethical life.[46] Moreover, there are clear instances in the history of Theravada Buddhism in Sri Lanka, particularly in the thirteenth, fourteenth, fifteenth, and nineteenth centuries C.E., when learned monks chastised their lay followers for worshipping the gods.[47]

Thus, worshipping the "gods" constitutes an old problem that is not simply a matter manufactured in the contemporary context. It has sometimes seriously divided the Buddhist community in Sri Lanka. I shall explore this problem more fully in the eighth chapter. But it must be pointed out that conservative monastic incumbents who have urged Buddhists not to worship "gods" are by no means representative of the majority views in Buddhist cultures. While monastic concerns about lay deity veneration may be couched in doctrinal terms, I want to raise the question as to whether or not these concerns have been linked or not to a wider sociopolitical context.

In the course of the chapters which follow, I will indicate that a continuing historical controversy about venerating Visnu may run parallel to the public fortunes of Sinhala-Tamil (or Sinhala–South Indian) relations in medieval and modern Sri Lankan history. That is, I want to raise the possibility that monastic reactions against deity veneration, especially against gods of Hindu origins, occur in conjunction with the significant establishment and assimilation of South Indian religious and cultural patterns among the Sinhalese, and that these controversies were not solely matters of intermonastic dispute. While assimilations of Hindu deities belie a Sinhala historical genius for inclusivity, they have been, perhaps, periodically perceived by some as threats to the "indigenous" culture, or even, to push the point a bit further, as a signal of potential political domination. That is, the bifocal penchant of assimilation and antipathy found in the case of the early medieval Hindu encounter with Buddhism would seem to be somewhat mirrored here within the context of the later Buddhist encounter with Hinduism.

For example, sculpted gods of Hindu origins to be venerated by Buddhist worshippers were first placed inside Buddhist image houses at Gadaladeniya and Lankatilaka, two historically important temples built and patronized by the kings and courtiers of the fourteenth-century Gampola period in the up-country region of the island near modern Kandy. The Gampola period witnessed unprecedented migrations of peoples of South Indian origins into this up-country region of Sri Lanka, many from the Malabar coast of India (modern day Kerala). A copious amount of folklore, including epic migration sagas, myths about the goddess, and the introduction of several minor deities are still extant in up-country villages as cultural derivations from this migratory (and sometimes mercenary) experience. (I examine this phenomenon in the second chapter.)

As with the Indian historian Kane's thesis that Hinduism had to absorb Buddhism for reasons of survival (see above), the same pattern holds here with the roles reversed. That is, Buddhist kings found it expedient to include Hindu deities within the religious constructions they sponsored. It is not surprising that, concurrently in the Gampola era, one of Theravada's most outstanding critics of deity veneration, Dharmakirti Thera, the chief monastic incumbent of Gadaladeniya itself, articulates his anti-deity perspective forcefully.[48] In this instance, we see a classic case of orthodox monasticism reacting to the by-products of sociopolitical change, and therefore change in religious culture.

The same pattern might be seen in the fifteenth-century Kotte era, when Sanskritic poetics, the major gods of devotional Hinduism, and caste consciousness became pronounced features in Sinhala literary, religious, and social constructions, but not without a strident voice of monastic dissent coming from the eminent monastic figure of Vidagama Maitreya.[49]

In both of these historical and social contexts, the Buddhist state seems to have sanctioned the religious and cultural traditions of newly arrived South Indians, only to see a subsequent Buddhist monastic attempt to purge the tradition of these same assimilations. Thus, a pattern would seem to be clear: immigrations, followed by assimilations, sometimes prompt attempted purifications.

In general, it could be argued that the reason Sinhala Buddhist religious culture has survived for 2,300 years is more the result of its inclusive spirit, and its ability to adapt and transform, rather than any dogged adherence to the purity of doctrine, as some of Theravada's monastic apologetics have often averred. On the whole, many assimilations seem to have stuck, precisely because they have been given a cultural "fit" or an "orbit," and then valorized as being spiritually meaningful. More specifically, and to the point of my argument, is that during the contemporary period of ethnic strife, especially since 1983, the old issue of Buddhists worshipping "Hindu" gods has arisen once more. As the civil war has unfolded, Sinhala public fears of potential Tamil or Indian political domination, founded or not, have surfaced in some sections of the Sinhala community and have been expressed sometimes in a strident fashion.[50] As the government has tried to broker a peace deal by offering a devolution of power for the benefit and appeasement of the minority Tamil community, Sinhala communal and ethnic consciousness has been articulated dramatically among these sections of the Sinhalese community. Within, there is a great fear of being taken over, a recurrent fear of external domination.[51]

A recent version of this issue as it has been articulated in relation to deity-veneration, specifically veneration of Visnu, is examined in the eighth chapter of this book. That examination documents Sinhala antipathy in tension with historic patterns of inclusion, a tension that manifests and sustains what I have identified as a deeply wrought ambivalence to the Hindu presence throughout Sinhala history. It is the historical pattern of inclusivity in relation to waves of immigrant Hinduism that is the subject of the next chapter.

"UNCEASING WAVES"
Brahmanical and Hindu Influences
on Medieval Sinhala Buddhist Culture in Sri Lanka

"Some of our nationalists resent the assertion that Sinhalese culture is made up of and developed from elements borrowed and adapted. The readaptation of foreign elements is a sign of the originality and the virility of a given culture rather than a weakness."
—Martin Wickramasinghe[1]

Introduction

If Sri Lanka were to be identified on a contemporary world map depicting the geography and history of religions, it would no doubt be shaded categorically, along with Burma, Thailand, Cambodia, and Laos, as a predominantly Theravada Buddhist country. Characterizing Sri Lanka's religious culture exclusively in this way, however, would be quite inaccurate, even less appropriate than categorizing Indonesia, for instance, as a Muslim country. Although the majority (approximately two thirds) of Sri Lankans are indeed Buddhist, as the vast majority of Indonesians are now certainly Muslim, religious and cultural constructions in both countries are extraordinarily complex and multilayered. Deeper inquiries reveal how these two remarkable religious cultures continue to bear the stamp of other religions (particularly Hinduism) having inscribed their influences upon them over many centuries of history.[2]

This chapter makes use of some of the extensive research conducted by various Sri Lankan historians and anthropologists in the recent past to explain how and when Hinduism has made its salutary impacts on Sinhala Buddhist religious culture. It also explores, in general, some of the reasons for why these impacts have taken place and then cites some instances of Sinhala Theravada monastic resistance to their occurrences. Primarily, this general historical review is limited to the period of the twelfth through the sixteenth centuries C.E.—when many communities from the South Indian Coromandel and Malabar coasts were migrating to Sri Lanka. It also provides the general historical background for the focus of the next chapter, which is concerned specifically with the problem of the "Buddhist Visnu"'s origins and identity. While the particular focus of my inquiry is how Visnu came to be absorbed meaningfully into the evolving matrix of Sinhala Buddhist culture, one of the noteworthy processes in the history of religions in Sri Lanka is the manner in which many elements, patterns, and practices of Hindu traditions, in general, have been woven into the fabric of this Buddhist religious culture.[3] This study of Visnu focuses on only one small fragment of a larger historical process of cultural transformation at work.

Generations of immigrants and mercenaries deriving from a profusion of castes in various regions of South India, like the unceasing waves washing up on Sri Lanka's shores, have brought with them a kaleidoscope of religious myths and rites reflective of the Hindu worldviews specific to their original locales. In time, some of these have been found congenial and have been "Buddhacized" or "Sinhalized": accepted into but subordinated to the evolving structures and values, or principles and assumptions, of the Sinhala religious culture that is grounded in the soteriology of the Buddha—at the same time, extending the heterogeneity of the very culture into which they have been absorbed.[4] For instance, Kataragama Deviyo, known in the Sanskrit Puranas as Skanda, the mythic son of Siva and Parvati (a tradition in turn married to the indigenous Tamil ecstatic cult of the mountain god Murugan in South India), remains one of the most powerful and popular deities venerated by Sinhala Buddhists on the island today. His cult has been studied in depth by many scholars.[5] Shrines to the goddess Pattini, the heroine of the Tamil epic *Cilappatikaram*, are also prevalent in most Sinhala cultural areas. Obeyeskere's massive study (1984) of Pattini documents the monumental extent to which her cult was incorporated and further developed within the ritual life of Sinhala villages in various parts of the island.

We have already seen, in the first chapter, that Visnu *devalayas* are ubiquitous in Sinhala Buddhist–culture areas on the island. These three gods of Hindu origin, together with the Mahayana-derived Natha Deviyo (Bodhisatva Avalokitesvara), came to be regarded as the four guardian deities of Sinhaladvipa (the medieval name for Sri Lanka, or "island of Sinhalas") during the late medieval Kandyan period (eighteenth century C.E.), were substituted for another set of guardian gods who had been established a few centuries earlier (fourteenth century).[6] Within the traditional metaphysics or soteriology of emerging Sinhala Buddhist worldviews, all four deities are regarded as bodhisatvas on the path to *nibbana*.[7]

Today, their local temples in the sacred area of the old traditional Kandyan capital in proximity to the Dalada Maligava ("Temple of the Tooth-relic") remain the most important, if not the most conspicuous, foci for Sinhala Buddhist deity veneration in the up-country region of the island. Moreover, since the eighteenth-century reign of the Nayakkar king Kirti Sri Rajasimha (1751–82 C.E.), each of these gods has been accorded a formal place of honor and recognition in the annual ritual processions of Sri Lanka's most famous religio-cultural pageant, the *asala perahera*.[8] As H. L. Seneviratne (1978) demonstrated, one of the primary functions of this royally sponsored public rite was to express, in orderly and symbolic fashion, the hierarchy of divine and social identities constitutive of the Kandyan sociocosmology.

What is interesting about this particular selection of incorporated Hindu deities (and the Mahayana Bodhisatva Avalokitesvara) is that, when regarded as a whole, they represent the major currents (Vaisnava, Saiva, Sakta, and Mahayana) of South Indian religion that have been contemporary in India for most of the history of the Theravada Buddhist tradition in Sri Lanka, at least since the later centuries of the first millenium C.E. Thus, the incorporation of these deities indicates that the Buddhistic culture of Sinhala Sri Lanka has been historically inclusive of the major trajectories of religious development that have occurred in India concomitantly; that is, the empathetic dimension of an ambivalent division over the assimilation of Hindu elements into a predominantly Theravada Buddhist religious culture has usually outweighed the antipathetic. The two dispositions often stand in reflexive relation to each other, in dialectical tension.

What follows is a brief survey of some of the important historical evidence from ideological, literary, and material sources that indicate periodic flows of Brahmanical and Hindu presence among the Sinhalas, primarily from the twelfth through the sixteenth century C.E. In presenting and discussing this evidence, I aim to illustrate why the influence and integration of Hindu constructs in the late medieval period of Sinhala history was very thorough, and that Visnu's incorporation was but a part of a larger process of assimilation. There is also evidence indicating a resistance to Visnu's assimilation in particular.

The Salience of Rhetoric:
Elements of the Vaisnava Ideology of Kingship at Polonnaruva

If there is any traditional literary source that might be expected to mute or deemphasize an acceptable place for and positive influence of the Brahmanical and Hindu presence in the history of a predominantly Sinhala Theravada Buddhist religious culture, it could be the Pali *Mahavamsa* and its continuation, the *Culavamsa*, as it has been dubbed by its translator, Wilhelm Geiger. These traditional sources are essentially an orthodox Buddhist-monastic chronicle of Theravada-minded accounts of how the *Buddhasasana* has fared under the reigns of Sri Lanka's long line of royalty. The narratives of this chronicle, beginning with mythic accounts of the Buddha's three visits, the immigration of the prototypical Sinhalas to the island, and the celebrated arrival of institutional Buddhism, consist almost entirely of either elaborate accounts of what various hero-kings have allegedly accomplished to defend, support, and glorify the religion of the Buddha, or briefer accounts that roundly condemn the damaging effects of others who were judged heretical or hostile to the religion.

This fundamentally apologetic literature articulates an ideal model of *sangha*-state relations,[9] relations deemed primordial, even predestined, as well as enduringly reciprocal (the *sangha* legitimating the king; the king patronizing the *sangha*).[10] The work was written, so it proclaims, "for the serene joy and emotion of the pious." But a close reading of this spectacularly "pro-Theravada," often melodramatic source leaves little doubt that Sri Lankan or Sinhala kings presided over a rather cosmopolitan populace from at least the twelfth through the eighteenth centuries C.E., and that many of these kings seemed disposed to accept and nurture the reality of that cosmopolitan character as part of their kingdoms' cultural make-up. Insofar as kingship often reflects the reality it rules, it is not surprising that Sinhala kingship during this era of increasing social variegation tended to become ever more eclectic in its symbolic expression, more composite or aggregate in its ideology and appeal.

Searching through the *Mahavamasa–Culavamsa* for clues to the presence of Hinduism, however, is a bit like reading Confucian histories to learn about the presence of Taoism. It is a somewhat dubious historical exercise per se, especially since the *Mahavamsa–Culavamsa* that we can read today is, undoubtedly, a compilation that was assembled in at least four different historical settings over a period of some 1,300 years,[11] and it contains much that is legendary and folkloric. It is one source among others, primarily the inscriptional and the artistic, that requires examination.

Among the kings who receive the greatest eulogies in the compilation are three of the four who commissioned the writing of the work during their reigns: Parakramabahu I (1153–86 C.E.), Parakramabahu IV (1302–26 C.E.), and Kirti Sri Rajasimha (1751–82 C.E.). The first part of the chronicle consists of a fifth-century C.E. reading of the previous 1,100 years, the second a twelfth-century reading of the previous 700, the third an early fourteenth-century presentation on the late twelfth through the early fourteenth centuries; and the fourth is an eighteenth-century reading of the previous 400-odd years. In addition, because myth, eulogy, and political history are thoroughly intertwined throughout, the *Mahavamsa–Culavamsa* may be a fascinating source to study in search of cultural meaning, but it is also a source that can strain historical credulity as well. In spite of these caveats, the important point to stress here is that the *Mahavamsa–Culavamsa* contains numerous references to the presence of Hinduism; and among those references, it has constructed profiles of Buddhist kingship which unmistakably reflect accommodation to the operative Hindu conceptions of royalty, especially in relation to Hindu conceptions of the divine.

In his indices to the *Mahavamsa–Culavamsa*, translator Wilhelm Geiger lists exactly 100 references made to gods of Brahmanical or Hindu origins within the 100 chapters that form the completed text.[12] Among the gods who figure in various passages are Brahma, Visnu, Siva, Laksmi, Indra, Kuvera, Skanda, Visvakarman, Brhaspati, and Sarasvati (*Culavamsa* 2: 347–48. (There is much more to say about the specific Visnu references in the next chapter.) The vast majority of these occur in the last three (post–twelfth century c.e.) installments of the text. The implication is readily apparent. Why this is the case takes my inquiry into the heart of the matter.

The *Mahavamsa* (the first 37 chapters attributed to the fifth century c.e.) contains only three references to the royal office of the *brahmin purohita*, an official advisory post in the king's court. The first occurs in the mythic story of Pandukabhaya's consecration (p. 73; 10.79), the second within the context of Devanampiyatissa's consecration in the third century b.c.e. (pp. 78–79; 11.26), and the third in the story about how the passionate, philanderous, and murderous Queen Anula (early first century c.e.), who is credited with poisoning several lover-kings, had made a *brahmana* her temporary king before poisoning him only six months later (pp. 239f; 34.15–31).

While these three instances might indicate that Brahmanical practice and knowledge were accorded some scope during the early centuries of kingship in Sri Lanka, there are also indications that Brahmanical traditions were, at times, rejected and condemned. For instance, King Mahasena, whose reign was disastrous for the Mahavihara *sangha*, and which forms the concluding segment of the text, is said to have completely destroyed temples dedicated to the Brahmanical gods (p. 270; 37.41). While the literary evidence for the ancient pre-Polonnaruva period is scant, it seems to indicate an ambivalent attitude to the presence of Brahmanical tradition: sometimes Brahmans serve the court, sometimes their temples are ransacked.

That *brahmanas* were recognized, supported through royal donations, and served in the courts of various later Sri Lankan kings can be noted in several other places in the second installment of the *Mahavamsa–Culavamsa*. For instance, King Kassapa III (717–24 c.e.) is said to have "encouraged the way of life fitting for laity, *bhikkhus* and *brahmanas*" (1:112; 48.23). Included in the list of his benefactions, King Sena II (851–885 c.e.) is said to have

had a thousand jars of gold filled with pearls and on top of each he placed
a costly jewel and presented it to a thousand *brahmanas* whom he had fed

with milk rice in pure jeweled goblets, as well as golden threads. (1:153; 51.65–66)

What *may be* noteworthy about these last two references, if they can be regarded as roughly accurate references to the royal activities of this era, is that they would appear to indicate the ascendancy of Brahmans at royal courts precisely during the time that, as Inden has indicated (see ch. 1, pp. 12–14 above), the ideology of kingship in many parts of India was shifting away from the cult of the cosmic Buddha to Vaisnava or Saivite orientations. There is, of course, no indication in our text that such a shift actually occurred in Sri Lanka during this time period, only that Brahmans were favorably regarded during specific royal reigns.

Royal rhetoric reflecting the presence of Hindu conceptions of kingship does not seem to appear graphically in the text until the Polonnaruva period (eleventh through thirteenth centuries), and then only after a period of intense military invasions and occupations by South Indian imperial armies.[13] Regarding the *Mahavamsa–Culavamsa*'s characterization of kingship in the twelfth-century Polonnaruva era, however, indications of state-sponsored Hindu cultic practices and Sanskrit literary activity are much more readily apparent.[14] Vikramabahu II (1116–37 c.e.), for instance, is reported to have actually held the ancient Vedic soma sacrifice "performed by the house priest and other *brahmanas* well-versed in the *Vedas* and the *Vedangas*" (1: 234; 62.33). More significantly, he is also depicted as having his son's bodily marks read "by *brahmanas* versed in the lore of bodily marks" (1:234; 62.45–7) to determine if the prince was destined for kingship. This latter instance is very important; for it seems to be a clear signal that Hindu conceptions of kingship had formally come into play in determining royal successions.

Parakramabahu I (1153–86 c.e.), widely remembered in Sinhala history as one of the greatest patrons of Theravada Buddhist tradition, owing in part to the *Culavamsa*'s lengthy and laudatory account of his support for Buddhism, including his restoration and unification of the Buddhist monastic *sangha* under Theravada auspices, is reported to have been given the *upanayana* (thread investiture) ceremony by his uncle, Kirti Sri Megha, assisted "by *brahmanas* versed in the *Veda*" (1:244; 64.13–17). Since the *upanayana* is a Brahmanical rite performed to negotiate the transition in identity from childhood to adulthood, it would appear that Parakramabahu's *ksatriya varna* (warrior caste) was being affirmed in the process of preparing him for his role as an acceptable king according to Brahmanical standards, i.e., at least in a manner that would be clearly understood by Hindu observers.

In describing Parakramabahu's consolidation of rule in Rohana (the south and southeastern swaths of the island), the *Culavamsa* makes analogical allusions to the great mythic victories won in the Sanskrit epics *Mahabharata* and *Ramayana*. Here is one descriptive example:

> Thereupon the best soldiers of the two parties fought a severe action in the middle of the river. Now raged between the two armies a terrible battle like to that of the gods with the *Danavas* (2: 49; 75.54). . . . They fought an exceedingly terrible battle like the monkeys who leapt over the ocean in the combat between Rama and Ravana. (2: 49; 75.59)

Parakramabahu himself is compared to Kama, the god of love, later in the narrative that recounts the wonders of his reign (2:100; 77.106). His chief consort, Queen Rupavati, is said to have loved him "as Sita loved Rama" (2:17; 73.137).

Since the compiler of this section of the *Culavamsa* may have been, according to Kemper (1992:34–47), from the Cola country in India, he would likely have been well-versed in classical Hindu conceptions of kingship and epic literature. It would appear that his appeals to Hindu imagery and practice, which also seem designed to flatter his royal patron (Parakramabahu I), are either a reflection of the religious proclivities of the royal court or the king's own empathy for those Brahmanical traditions; possibly a reflection of the need to present the king's power and accomplishments in as variegated a fashion as might be appropriate to the king's similarly variegated social and political constituencies; or, more bluntly, a measure of propaganda dished out in language that his political and military foes from South India would surely understand. Likely, all of these reasons and perhaps others came into play.[15]

Regardless of what they were exactly at the time, we do know that at least elements of the *Ramayana* were the basis for the creation of poetic literature as early, perhaps, as the sixth century c.e., and that traditions from "tenth-century Tripuri knew of Kumaradasa, the author of the Janakhirana ['Theft of Sita in Sri Lanka']—and in Sinhala tradition, a king of Sri Lanka [King Kumanara Dhatusena, 508–16 c.e.]—and considered him second only to Kalidasa as a poet" (Hallisey 2003:690).

The extent to which Parakramabahu patronized things Hindu—Brahmans, temples, and their gods—arises in relation to how the *Culavamsa* credits him with erecting thirteen *devalayas* (2:117; 79.19) and repairing some seventy-nine more in the *rajarattha* region (2:117; 79:22), while erecting another twenty-four temples to the gods in southern Rohana (2:123; 79:81). From this account, it would appear that the compiler of this section of the *Culavamsa* wanted to record the fact that Parakramabahu supported *both* Hindu and Buddhist constructions within the country's religious culture. The portrayal, therefore, is of a kingship with an inclusive ethic. Or to put the matter bluntly in another way: Parakramabahu was to be regarded as the master patron of both Buddhist and Hindu establishments, the supreme imperial overlord of all communities.

It is likely that several of the temples dedicated to Visnu and Siva at Polonnaruva, shrines studied by historians and archeological teams in the twentieth century, are among those being referred to in the *Culavamsa* account. But as Liyanagamage (1968:121) points out: "the Saiva and Vaisnava *devalas* in Polonnaruva are generally regarded as monuments erected in the [time of] Cola occupation of [the] Rajarattha (1017–70 C.E.). In many cases, this view is confirmed by Tamil inscriptions from the time of the Cola kings, like Rajaraja I and Rajendra I, found at the sites of these monuments"[16] [brackets mine]. While Liyanagamage seems to be correct in this instance and, as such, casts some doubt on the *Culavamsa*'s implication that all of these Hindu temples were built or repaired by Parakramabahu, the fact remains that the *Culavamsa*, though a Theravada-inspired text, is articulating an inclusive or transcendent model of kingship by indicating Parakramabahu's supportive disposition to Hindu cults as well as Buddhist. That is, Parakramabahu lays claim to patronizing all religious establishments—he is to be regarded as their chief support.

Parakramabahu's own inclusive or imperial disposition *may be* reflected in other instances of material culture as well. For example, at Polonnaruva's magnificent *Gal Vihara*, allegedly constructed under the patronage of Parakramabahu I, a seated Buddha in the artificially excavated *Vijjadhara guha* cave is flanked by two figures who, it has been argued, may be either the bodhisatvas Manjusri and Vajrapani, or even less likely, the bodhisatvas Maitreya and Avalokitesvara. Between and above the Buddha (whose identity, according to von Schroeder, may be Aksobhya) and these two respective flanking "bodhisatvas" are two more figures identified as a four-headed Brahma and a four-armed Visnu (von Schroeder 1990:363, 368; see plate 109c). The identification of these Hindu deities was first made by H. C. P. Bell in 1907.

The identification of Visnu in this particular setting is of paramount importance for my own study: it could signal the first attempt, in the evidence of material culture available at this time, to incorporate Visnu into a Buddhistic cosmology. But, unfortunately, there is a possible complication and confusion. Von Schroeder and others before him (Fernando, 1960, for instance) have asserted that the ensemble of sculptures in the *Vijjadhara guha* cave at Gal Vihara is tantric in nature, and thus the assimilation of Visnu, if that identification holds, would have been made in a Mahayana or tantric context of symbol and cosmology, and not Theravadin. However, Mudiyanse (1967:107–119) has rebutted in great detail most of Fernando's observations warranting an identification of tantric symbolism in this sculptural constellation, and seems to have anticipated Von Schroeder's similar observations as well, thus casting some doubt on the matter. Furthermore, in my own previous and extensive research on the cult of the Mahayana bodhisatva Avalokitesvara in Sri Lanka (1991), I did not find any instances of Hindu assimilations of this nature into the Mahayana. Because of that, I am inclined to agree with Mudiyanse, and chiefly for the reason he advances: a tantric construction at the Gal Vihara master site of Parakramabahu I would have run completely counter to the ethos of the king's religious enterprise to purify and unite the Buddhist *sangha* under the Theravada Mahavihara umbrella. That is, it seems unlikely that his "masterpiece" at Gal Vihara would be meant to articulate the rival Mahayana cosmology and soteriology.

Beyond this reason, aside from this specific sculptural "evidence," there is no other indication of the Mahayana in the Polonnaruva archeological complex dating to this general historical period. Moreover, the iconography of the two flanking "bodhisatvas" in question is so indistinct that I have had a difficult time distinguishing them at all from similar types of fly-whisk bearers frequently found in various Buddhist caves throughout Deccan India.

On the other hand, in the absence of any other explanation by Mudiyanse regarding the identity of the two deities in question, Von Schroeder's identification of the two as Brahma and Visnu, confirming A. C. P. Bell's earlier finding, is very much a distinct possibility. The identification of Visnu is based upon the presence of a handheld *sankha* (conch), one of Visnu's four traditional attributes. What makes me hesitant to accept this suggestion as final and conclusive, however, is that in every other instance in which images of Hindu deities have been found within the entire Polonnaruva archeological complex, they were enshrined within specifically identifiable Hindu temples. That is, the cultic practices of Buddhists and Hindus at Polonnaruva seem to have been kept quite consciously separate from one another. There also does not seem to be any evidence unearthed at the massive monastic Alahana Parivena (built by Parakramabahu I) archeological site that indicates the presence of Hindu deities, or Puranic cultic practices in relation to Hindu deities, within the confines of this huge monastic university (Prematilleke 1981).[17] Later literary sources in both Pali and Sinhala depict the presence of Brahma and Visnu at the Buddha's moment of enlightenment. In these instances, they appear with fly whisks and *sankha* (conch shell) respectively. Perhaps the sculpture at Vijadhara was a harbinger of this depiction.

If Visnu is indeed the identity of the sculpture in question, then my sense is that it represents an experimental anomaly, or as I have said, a harbinger at best. The sculpture in question, an attendant deity to the Buddha, would probably not have been an object of worship per se. Indeed, it is an object that only represents a deity worshipping the Buddha (here *devatideva*, "the god beyond the gods"). If the Visnu figure at Gal Vihara is, after all, a Visnu figure, it is a remarkable "find" or "marker." It is still some distance from the thoroughly integrated "Buddhist Visnu" of the sort who appears and is worshipped as a Buddhist deity several centuries later in the up-country regions of the island. But what this Visnu represents in this sculptural constellation, if it is Visnu at all, is a subordinated Hindu presence within a predominantly Theravada Buddhist composition. As such, and beyond its specific religious meaning, it may be taken (and perhaps charitably so) as symbolically characteristic of either the inclusive liberality of Parakramabahu's Polonnaruva kingship or a statement of propaganda, the message of which would be clear: as Visnu worships the Buddha, Cola Hindus venerate a Sinhala Buddhist king. At least this is what might constitute its "political reading."

Such a reading of this material prompts a deeper consideration of the ideology and rhetoric of kingship at Polonnaruva. S. Pathmanathan (1982, 1986), who has written extensively about Hindu influence from India on Sri Lanka in the medieval Polonnaruva (eleventh through thirteenth centuries C.E.) and Kotte (fifteenth and sixteenth centuries C.E.) eras respectively, notes that, in the case of kingship, a significant cultural influence came about due to intensive political contacts with the Cola, the Pandyan, and Kalinga dynasties in South India. Some of this influence was also the direct result of strategic marriage alliances forged by Polonnaruva kings, alliances that had the international effect of creating balances of power and the domestic effect of fostering the presence of various South Indian factions in the Polonnaruva royal court, once it had been established as the post-Cola Sinhala capital.

Before that, Polonnaruva had been a provincial capital city under Cola sovereignty for at least the first seventy years of the eleventh century. The longstanding (thirteen centuries) capital of Anuradhapura to Polonnaruva's northwest had been sacked in the late tenth century by Cola armies. Subsequently, the new Cola imperial center had been established to the east in Polonnaruva, a strategic location that helped to extend control, as much as possible, to the south and east regions of the island, where disestablished Sinhala royalty had fled. It is probable that the archeological remains of the several Visnu and Saiva shrines at Polonnaruva served the cultic proclivities of these South India Cola officials, as Liyanagamage asserts (see above). Later, after the Sinhalas had regained power at Polonnaruva, these shrines served the religious orientations of the South Indian factions at court, who were possibly the relations and courtiers of the king's South Indian queens.

In the first chapter, I noted how, three centuries earlier than the Polonnaruva period, in India, the ideology of kingship began to shift from Buddhist to Vaisnava and Saiva orientations. Pathmanathan (1982:123) mentions how, during the Polonnaruva period, the *Culavamsa* begins to cite the influence of the same types of Puranic Hindu and classical Brahmanical conceptions of kingship at work. Specifically, he notes how the *Culavamsa* refers to Parakram-

abahu I as having mastered Kautilya's *Arthasastra*, the classical Indian treatise
on the dynamics of political power that is sometimes compared to Machi-
avelli's work in the West, and other treatises concerned with military science.
Pathmanathan also cites textual and inscriptional evidence to indicate how the
powerful Sinhala king who closely followed Parakramabahu I, Nissanka Malla
(1187–96 C.E.), seems to have appealed to *dharmasastra* texts to publicly articulate the ideology of his kingship. Moreover, Pathmanathan also points out
how the *Culavamsa* refers to *Manu Smrti* as a treatise frequently consulted by
Vijayabahu II (1186–87 C.E.), Parakramabahu Pandya (1212–15 C.E.) and then
Parakramabahu II (1236–71 C.E.), about whom there will be more to say in the
third and seventh chapters.

At some length (124–26) he explains the increased use of epithets such as
cakravarti and *rajadhiraja* during this time period. He hastens to add that
cakravarti does not signal the revival of the term as it was deployed in the context of the ancient Buddhist ideology of kingship,[18] but rather the fact that Sinhala rulers had been influenced by conceptions of kingship then articulated in
neighboring South Indian states where the term *cakravarti* connoted "supreme
overlord," an emperor-*avatara* who rules by *danda* (power or "the stick"), as
opposed to the Pali Buddhist conception wherein the *cakkavatti* rules by
dhamma. What differentiates its usage here from its ancient Buddhist usage, of
course, is that the cosmology within which it is deployed is thoroughly Puranic
Hindu. This is how the term was also deployed by *aryacakravarttis* in the Tamil
kingdom of fourteenth-century Jaffna as well.

The conception of kingship that emerged in the Polonnaruva period, therefore, "was a consequence of the combined effect of three conceptions, the
dhammic conception rooted in Buddhist idealism, the heroic ideal depicted in
the *Arthasastra* and the epic tradition and the conception of the divinity of
kingship as expressed in the *dharmasastra* literature" (126).[19] This mix is apparent earlier in the Ambagamuva inscription of Vijayabahu I (1059–1114
C.E.):

> He has surpassed the Sun in the majesty inherent
> in him, Mahesvara in prowess, Visnu in
> haughty spirit, the chief of the gods (Indra) in
> kingly state, the lord of riches (Kuvera)
> in exhaustible wealth, Kitisiru in (bestowing)
> happiness to living beings, the preceptor of the
> gods (Brhaspati) in the fertility of wisdom, the
> moon in gentleness, Kandarpa in the richness of
> his beauty and the Bodhisatva in the fullness
> of his benevolence.[20] [parentheses in translation text]

Vijayabahu, of course, is the Sinhala king who overthrew the Cola powers at Polonnaruva and set the stage thirty years later for the magnificent construction activities of Parakramabahu I, which signal a revived efflorescence of Sinhala and Theravada fortunes.

Pathmanathan certifies that the Brahmanic and Hindu rhetoric noted above in relation to Vijayabahu was also used to depict Parakramabahu I in the Devanagala inscription.[21] Even before this, during the reign of Vikramabahu I (1029–41 C.E.)—a Sinhala king in Rohana coping as best as he could with the powerful Cola presence established in Polonnaruva—the ideology of the king as a divine avatar had been articulated. With specific reference to what is clearly the classical conception of the king as an avatar of Visnu, Pathmanathan says:

> The adoption of the terminology expressive of the notion of divinity of kingship in the inscriptions of other rulers of Polonnaruwa may suggest that the expression *rajanarayana* used in connection with Vikramabahu was intended to convey the same idea in a more developed form . . . it should not be ignored as mere metaphor purely on account of the eulogistic manner of the inscription in which it occurs. The expression could be interpreted in a literal sense as referring to the king as Visnu and this idea had become familiar to many Indian rulers long before the tenth century. . . . The connection of a saviour was partly derived from the theory of avatara associated with Vaishnavism and propagated by later versions of the *Ramayana* and the *Purana*s. (139; boldface mine)

Pathmanathan's significant studies of Hindu influence on Buddhist kingship at Polonnaruva are of great salience to my discussion. They not only complement the findings of my own research, but they also provide a warrant in this context for one of the central assertions of my thesis: that religiocultural assimilations or purifications are often the consequence of political dynamics or political expediency. The rhetoric deployed in relation to these Sinhala kings represents a co-option of their rivals' legitimating claims to power. It is language making a claim in the language of the rival's own framework; hence, it is language whose intention would be surely understood.

The Buddhist king, in this medieval Sinhala context, was also often regarded as a kind of microcosmic symbol of his kingdom, or at least of his royal court. Engaging the conceptions of kingship of South India contemporaries and from Cola predecessors at Polonnaruva—conceptions rooted within Vaisnava and Saiva cosmologies—meant that the king could be regarded compositely as a type of *axis mundi cum avatar*. The apparent mix so evident in the rhetoric of kingship ideology articulated in relevant inscriptions and in the *Culavamsa* account I have been noting may also reflect, in fact, the political and cultural plurality of this time and place: a mixture of Hindu and Buddhist peoples whose principles of legitimization and hierarchy were deemed complementary. If the king's constituency was a mix of Hindu and Buddhist peoples, it makes complete political sense, in *Arthasastra* fashion, that his mythic public profile of legitimization be constructed in such a composite manner, to appeal to as many constituents as possible. Or further within the context of the *Arthasastra* mind-set, the rhetoric expresses imperial and absolute power in language clearly understood by the king's Hindu-oriented supporters and/or enemies. The claim that the king was an avatar of Visnu was tantamount to claiming total suzerainty.

That the rhetoric of royalty during the Polonnaruva period registered negatively on some of the *literati* of the Theravada monastic *sangha* in Polonnaruva is evident in the *Amavatura* ("The Flood of Nectar") written by Gurulugomi. This Sinhala text is regarded as "the earliest example of (Sinhala) connected prose writing" (C. Reynolds: 32), having been produced around 1200 C.E. following the reigns of Parakramabahu I and Nissanka Malla and during the apex of Polonnaruva's glories. "The language of the *Amavatura* eschews Sanskrit words almost entirely, and sticks to 'pure' Sinhalese" (32).[22] It is also a thoroughly Buddhistic apologetic piece of religious literature. Here, there is no concession to the Hindu *weltanschaung*.

The substance of one of the major stories comprising the *Amavatura* is especially relevant to my argument regarding the antipathetic side of Sinhala ambivalence to religious assimilations, Hindu ones in particular.[23] It is concerned with how Sakra, king of the gods (the Brahmanic Indra), was approached by Mahamungalan (Mahamoggallana), one of the Buddha's most powerful disciples (known for his cosmological tours of heavens and hells). The setting for the exchange is the splendor of Sakra's heaven. Cleverly, Mahamungalan asks Sakra to preach a sutra which the Buddha had previously made known to him. Sakra's response and Mahamungalan's rejoinder is this:

'My lord, we are very busy. Though my own business be little, great is the business of the gods. Even such things as we learn well truly escape quickly from our memory and are no more seen, as pictures in a darkened room. Therefore I am not able to declare what my lord asks of me.' Then the great elder reflected thus: 'Wherefore does the king of gods remember not this matter?," and he thought 'The gods are very foolish; for they are overcome by the things of the six senses which press upon them by the six doors. They know not whether they have eaten or whether they have not eaten, nor whether they have drunk or whether they have not drunk.' And he saw how the gods were bemused and did forget. (78)

Mahamungalan proceeds to perform a wondrous miracle that so frightens and amazes Sakra and all of the other gods in his assembly that they then beg to hear the sutra they had forgotten. The text clearly represents an attempt to indicate how, from a Theravada Buddhistic perspective, the gods and their activities are subordinate to the Buddha's *dhamma*, and that they, too, are in need of following its realization to gain the final spiritual goal of *nibbana*. Later in the text (88–89), Sakra directly asks the Buddha why it is that the gods are bound to the samsaric world of rebirth. The Buddha's response is:

> 'King of gods! Whatever gods there be, whatever men or asuras or nagas or heavenly musicians, in fine whatever creatures there be, each among them gives gifts and offers worship with earnest resolution, saying "Let us divide whatsoever we can hold in our hands, and thus let us enjoy it without hatred, without violence, without enemies, without ill-will, and without wrath towards any." And yet they live lives with enemies, with ill will; for they are bound to the fetters of envy and avarice.'

The text concludes with this:

> Thus the Buddha is the subjugator of rude mankind, the subdued Sakra the king of gods; and whereas it is spoken of others also, know that he sat also in four and twenty places and preached the Law four and twenty times and subdued a million times a million gods at each time that he became of the ranks of the Worthy, at each time that he entered the Paths, or advanced in the Paths, or attained the Middle of the Paths; and he brought them all to the immortal greatness of nirvana. (89–90)

Ostensibly, this critique of the gods is made precisely on grounds of doctrinal orthodoxy, but it is not difficult to imagine that it also reflects the political sentiments of the monastic literati toward royal aggrandizement occasioned by the Vaisnava ideology of divine kingship.

From Rhetoric to Reality:
Hindu Saturation in the "Drift to the Southwest"

The historical period following the demise of Polonnaruva, wrought by the devastating invasion by Magha from Kalinga and his mercenaries from Kerala in the early thirteenth century, is often referred to by Sri Lankan historians as "the drift to the Southwest." It was an epoch of immense political turmoil. Except for the remarkable reign of Parakramabahu VI in the fifteenth century, when all of Sri Lanka fell under his single sway (the only time of such single rule between the reign of Parakramabahu I in the twelfth century and the Kandyan capitulation to the British in the early nineteenth), the island was frequently invaded from without and divided by sometimes as many as four different rulers within. Sinhala kings often adopted a defensive political posture in these difficult circumstances.

Referring to the substantial transformations occurring within Sinhala Buddhist religious culture during this time of stormy political changes, Pathmanathan (1986:81), in underscoring the legacy of this era, says:

> The period under consideration [the three centuries prior to the Portuguese conquest of the maritime provinces in the early sixteenth century] is of special significance as it was then that Buddhism in the form in which it has come down to modern times attained many of its characteristics. [brackets mine]

To emphasize the more precise nature of these enduring transformations, he quotes the work of Lynn de Silva[24] who says:

> The recourse to the gods is a place where Hinduism has flowed into Buddhism and . . . has given it a new vitality. Indeed, when one sees Buddhism in actual practice one is surprised by the amount of conscious Hinduism which lies within Buddhist ritual and ceremonial practices. There is hardly a place of Buddhist devotion where one will not find images of Hindu gods and shrines.

One conventional interpretation (Ilangasinha's and many others) of this development is that Sinhala kingship was so often in a state of enervation and impoverishment that it simply lacked the means to be able to support the Theravada *sangha* in a manner similar to the backing given it by the state during the Anuradhapura and Polonnaruva periods. While there may be some truth in this assertion, the more likely reality is that kings, understanding their predicaments in terms of power relations, lent their sanction of and support to religious institutions in light of the exigencies of the contemporary realpolitik. Given the increasing number of Hindus living within their kingdoms, it is likely that the awareness of their constituency contributed to their congeniality with Hindu ideologies of kingship.

Rajasimha I, in the late sixteenth century, actually went so far as to banish the Buddhist *sangha* from his capital at Sitavaka and formally embraced Saivism.[25] The practice of kings stylizing themselves as divinely ordained would have held a special appeal to them, especially if they reigned in perilous conditions inducing bouts of personal insecurity. Certainly the epithets deployed by kings in the later Kandyan period (sixteenth through eighteenth century C.E.), in *sannasas* that they had inscribed on copper plates reflect a penchant for an inflated and eclectic rhetoric (in comparison to the reality of their tenuous holds on power).[26]

I have been suggesting that changing sociopolitical conditions from the twelfth through the sixteenth centuries were very important factors contributing to the manner in which elements of Hinduism, especially the cult of Visnu, were incorporated into Sinhala Buddhist religious culture. We have just seen how the manner in which kingship seems to have been conceived and represented during the Polonnaruva period supports this view. In the period of Sinhala history following the demise of Polonnaruva in the thirteenth century until the conversion of King Dharmapala to the Roman Catholicism of the Portuguese in the late sixteenth, conceptions of kingship remain an important port of entry for the increasing Hindu influence in Sri Lanka. But during this later period, Hindu influence becomes much broader in scope and intensity, transcending the rhetoric of Sinhala kingship and court politics while becoming suffused into many other aspects of culture.

We will see that Vaisnava Hinduism remained an important conceptual force in play at the royal courts of the time, but one might also go on to cite its easily discernible presence in some exemplary compositions of classical Sinhala literature, in the design and ornamentation of architecture, and in the popular cultic practices of Buddhist monasticism. I would suggest that Hindu permeation of Sinhala culture during this period was not just a by-product of royal scenarios of legitimization, but also a consequence of the island's changing demography, owing to the nature of the many military campaigns that were waged, and to the transformation of the political economy itself.

As late as the date of Bhuvanekabahu VII (1521–51 C.E.), there is evidence (from the Portuguese in this instance), of Brahman pundits serving as royal advisors to Sinhala kings (Ilangasinha: 196). Indeed, a Brahman advisor is known to have been selected to travel to Portugal on behalf of this particular Sinhala king to represent royal interests in contemporary negotiations with the King of Portugal. Ilangasinha (375) is of the view that with the passing of Parakramabahu VI in the 1460s,

> the influence of the [Buddhist] Sangha on the kings and nobles of Kotte
> [the sixteenth-century capital just southeast of modern Colombo] steadily
> waned, and that of *brahmins* gained ground until by the time of the arrival
> of the Portuguese [early sixteenth century], the upper strata of Sinhalese
> society were more or less becoming Hinduized. [brackets mine]

The trajectory that Ilangasinha identifies had been, in fact, long in the making. As Pathmanathan points out (1986:82): "Documents recording royal grants or proclamations issued in this period refer to Hindu gods along with the [Buddhist] *triratna* ['triple gem'—Buddha, *Dhamma*, and *Sangha*] in their concluding portions" [brackets mine]. That is, gods of Hindu origin were, during the time frame with which I am now concerned, thoroughly integrated in the rhetorical language of power officially proclaimed by a royalty articulating a rhetoric of legitimation. Moreover, the presence and importance of Brahmans at court, from the thirteenth-century reign of Parakramabahu II (1236–71 C.E.) at Dambadeniya until the conversion to Portuguese Christian Catholicism by Dharmapala at Kotte in the latter part of the sixteenth century, is evident from any number of sources, both literary and inscriptional. For example, one could cite Pathmanathan's (1986:99–100) summary description of Parakramabahu II's daily routine as it was recorded in the thirteenth-century *Kandavuru Sirita*:

> The king was met at dawn by the Brahmin *purohita* from whom he received the sacred *kusa* grass, a conch shell filled with sanctified water and blessings. The *purohita*, it is said, made inquiries about his dreams at night and made recommendations for the performance of appropriate ceremonies in case they were considered auspicious.

That more than one type of Brahman attended the king, and that they had attained degrees of speciality beyond their purely ritual roles, is evident in what Pathmanathan adds in commenting on the *Kandavuru Sirita* passage just cited: "Parakramabahu II, who had a concern for the promotion of knowledge and learning is known to have made provision for the maintenance of a brahmin scholar who had a specialized knowledge of Sanskrit and medicine. Brahmins were also consulted on matters relating to astrology. . . ."

There is another compelling reference that occurs in the *Culavamsa*'s description of the events that occurred during Parakramabahu II's long reign at Dambadeniya. The *Culavamsa* (2:151–2; 83:41–51), in describing Prince Virabahu's defeat of Chandrabhanu and his *Javaka* mercenaries,[27] alludes to Virabahu in the following manner: "Going forth to combat like Rama, Prince Virabahu slew a number of Javakas, as Rama (slew) the Rakkhasas [parenthesis in text]." Since Virabahu then repairs to Devinuvara to worship Uppalavanna after his victory, there is some reason to explore further the identity of the god Rama as Upulvan in the next chapter. The royal visit to Devinuvara at this time is also critical, as we shall see, for the establishment of the cult of Visnu at upcountry Aluthnuvara, a development examined in chapter 7.

Brahmanical influence at the Sinhala royal court, moreover the specific presence of a Vaisnava ideology of kingship, is clearly an evident aspect of the Kurunegala reign of Parakramabahu IV (1302–26 c.e.), who, in addition to being a patron of the *Culavamsa*, is depicted in the *Caracotimalai*, a Tamil handbook on astrology, as "the incarnation of Visnu who churned the ocean to obtain the nectar" (Pathmanathan 1986:102). This would be the second documented specific instance, then, that a Sinhala king had been literally referred to as Visnu's avatar (the first being the eleventh-century Vikramabahu I, who had claimed Polonnaruva for Sinhalas following their history-reversing defeat of the Colas). Another later, explicit reference to the application of a Vaisnava Hindu ideology to Sinhala kingship is found in Sri Rahula's fifteenth-century poetic Sinhala *Salalihini Sandesaya*, this time with reference to Parakramabahu VI (1412–67 c.e.):

> There friend, feast your gaze on the great Lord Parakramabahu
> Who is to the Sun's Race as the sun is to the lotus-pond
> In whose bosom Lakshmi the goddess lies always
> Radiant, his beauty unblemished, like Ramba's lord.
> Wearing all sixty-four kingly insignia, including the crown,
> Like Visnu incarnate, he graces the lion throne.
> Bow low at his gracious feet and take leave of this King
> Who came down from Manu in unbroken line.

One interesting pattern that surfaces in the years following Parakramabahu VI's reign is that as the political situation continued to deteriorate for Sinhala rulers, the strength and presence of Brahmans at court, as well as the veneration of Hindu deities, seems to have increased. Ilangasinha observes at length the nature of this peculiar dynamic:

> The latter part of the fifteenth century and the whole of the sixteenth century are marked by political instability, chaos and constant warfare in the country. Preoccupied by these political troubles, the rulers of the country could not extend the necessary patronage to [Buddhist] religious affairs. The growing influences of *brahmin*s not only at the royal court but also on society of this time caused in some ways [to] diminish the relationship between the state and the Sangha. The *Nikayasamgrahaya* records that Virabahu Adipada gave slaves, male and female, cattle, houses, elephants and villages to *brahmin*s. The latter seem to have come in increasing numbers from India to benefit from the liberality of the Sinhalese rulers of the day. This influx of *brahmin*s to Ceylon from India no doubt was due to the

fact that Muslim inroads deprived many of them of their livelihood. A few of these *brahmin*s were converted to Buddhism, but most practised the forms of religion to which they were accustomed, and gained adherents from among the Buddhists. The prestige of *brahmin*s seem to have grown stronger in the course of time. . . . It is perhaps not too wide a guess to suggest that this growing influence of *brahmin*s on the royal court weakened the relationship of the state and Sangha after the reign of Parakramabahu VI. This may be further supported by the fact that after Vidagama Maitreya in the reign of Bhuvanekabahu VI we do not hear any member of the Sangha holding the title of *rajaguru,* 'adviser to the king.'" [Ilangasinha 211–212; brackets mine][28]

In relation to the influence of Hinduism on the literature of the court and of the elite literati of the time, Pathmanathan (1986:82) complements the general view just advanced by Ilangasinha:

Through Hinduism the ruling classes and the *literati* in the Sinhalese kingdoms gained access to the secular branches of learning developed in India. The study of Sanskrit and Tamil languages along with Pali and Sinhalese at the court and some of the monastic establishments tended to promote inter-cultural communication and gave access to several varieties of Indian literature.

Commenting on the profusion of references to Sanskrit myths in the classical Sinhala literature of this era, Pathmanathan continues (1986:105):

The churning of the ocean by Visnu with the aid of the Mandara mountain, Agastya's reduction of the ocean, the extraordinary prowess and feats of Ravana, the piercing of Mount Meru by Skanda . . . are among the most important puranic myths and epic legends alluded to in the Sinhalese poetic works produced during this period.

In the *Gira Sandesaya,* one of the many *duta kavyas,* poems that beseech the powers of various deities for divine assistance, and which were written during the reign of Parakramabahu VI, there is a description (217–27) of the Vijayabahu Pirivena (located between modern Ambalangoda and Hikkaduwa), which was presided over by the famous *gamavasi* poet-monk Sri Rahula. It is quite detailed. From this, it appears that the academic curriculum of this Buddhist educational institution was quite diverse and included not only the teaching of Pali, but also Sanskrit, Tamil, prosody, logic, drama, and astrology. Ilangasinha (40) notes that students at this institution included Brahmans from India who studied the Vedas alongside Buddhist texts, and he speculates that many may have come to the *pirivena* owing to the fame of Sri Rahula's erudition as a master of six languages (239). He adds: "It may be assumed that the famous *brahmin* scholar, Sri Ramacandra Bharati, who learnt Buddhism under Sri Rahula, was a teacher of Sanskrit at the Vijayabahu Pirivena. He composed the Sanskrit *sataka* poem, the *Bhakti-sataka* in honour of the Buddha" (250).

Ilangasinha further cites references in the Pali text from Northern Thailand, the *Jinakalamali*, to note that students were also coming from Southeast Asia in the fifteenth century to study Buddhist texts under the guidance of Sinhalese *mahatheras*. Moreover, to underscore the cosmopolitan character of the era's educational institutions, he cites a variety of sources (250–252) in which it becomes apparent that Buddhist monastic educational institutions during the Kotte period even offered the study of Tamil drama. Summarizing the *Culavamsa*'s distanced account of the royal education of kings during this period, Ilangasinha writes: "The influence which Sanskrit learning exerted on the political and social spheres may be judged from the statements in the chronicles with regard to the education of princes like Parakramabahu (VI) and the references therein to authorities like Kautilya and Manu" (248).[29]

With regard to the production and style of material culture during this same era, some of the Buddhist architectural monuments of this period actually had closer affinities with Hindu architectural forms and conceptions than with Buddhist monuments of the preceding centuries. In architectural form and conception, the *devalayas* built for the guardian deities of the island (more about whom later), were distinctively Dravidian.

Lankatilaka and Gadaladeniya, two temples of immediate concern to me in later chapters of this study, temples where I have conducted some fieldwork on the ritual cult of Visnu, were built in the early years of the Gampola period (1341–1410 c.e.). Their importance, as I indicated briefly in chapter 1, lies in the fact they are the first Buddhist monuments that thoroughly integrate the presence of Hindu deities with the worship of the Buddha. Pathmanathan (1986:108–109) has this to say about the Hindu influence exerted on both:

> The monuments of Lankatilaka and Gadaladeniya in the interior parts of the island, which are representative of the architecture of the period under consideration, provide sufficient evidence of influence exerted by the Hindu tradition on the construction of Buddhist monuments. In the preceding periods the influence of the Hindu tradition on the Sinhalese monuments was marginal . . . with the notable exceptions of Nalanda Gedige and the shrine of Upulvan described as the *galge*. . . . In the Lankatilaka [monument] which was of brick construction except for the base and door frames, the Dravidian influence is remarkable but also restrained. The ex-

terior walls of the *garbhagrha* at Lankatilaka in the niches of which the images of the guardian deities have been accommodated merit attention on account of their resemblances with those of the corresponding architectural components of Hinduism. . . . The Gadaladeniya monument represents a distinct stage in the evolution of the Sinhalese architectural tradition characterised by the architectural design of a Hindu temple with suitable modifications for the purposes of Buddhist religious worship. It is also significant that such a development synchronised with a phase in the development in Buddhism characterized by the incorporation of the cult of guardian gods and *devale* worship into its tradition.[30]

These considerations beg the obvious question: aside from the royal court, from where did these cultural flows originate and by what processes? With regard to how and where the cultural flow from Hindu India was occurring, Pathmanathan says:

> Another noteworthy feature was the prominence attained by coastal towns as centres of constructional activity and cultural interaction. Dynastic capitals lost their pre-eminence as centres of constructional and cultural activities as dynastic power declined and its resources diminished.

One of the major differences in accounting for Hindu influence in the post-Polonnaruva period is that rather than matrimonial alliances being forged with powers based in South India, Sinhala royalty adopted Hindu practices and traditions through the influence of "matrimonial connections made with locally established families of South Indian extraction" (Pathmanathan 1986:83). The Alakesvara family, who dominated Sinhala kingship for about a century, were a primary example of this pattern. Their influence was such that in the last half of the fourteenth century claims to kinship (and therefore the succession of kingship) were sometimes based on principles of matrilineal descent. This societal trait is probably the consequence of heavy migration from Kerala, the place of origin of the Alakesvaras. It is a pattern still discernible in Kerala today[31] and one that lasted for a long era in the Kandyan region of Sri Lanka too.

What also distinguishes this era from the Polonnaruva period is that "Hindu influence on Buddhism operated chiefly through the medium of commerce and emanated mostly from Malabar and the Vijayanagara empire [*ibid.*]. This was an era of intensified seaborne trade, and consequently coastal ports were the most dynamic venues for cultural flows.[32] Pathmanathan writes:

> Native inhabitants and foreigners of diverse ethnic groups and faiths were participants in these enterprises. Some of them established permanent

communities and also fostered craft-production in which artisan communities became permanently involved. Hindus from Southern India and Gujerat and Muslims from India, Persia and Arab countries were among the foreigners involved in the process. Some of them had settled down in some principal towns like Galle, Devinuwara, Colombo, Negombo and Chilaw.

Since one of Visnu's major shrines is located in Devinuvara, the historical and cultic importance of this site, especially, will be discussed in the next chapter and in the conclusion.

Trade and commerce were not the only factors leading to the increasing heterogeneity of Sinhala religious culture. Liyanagamage (1986) points out that Kerala mercenaries formed a large contingent of Parakramabahu's army, which dislodged the Colas from Sri Lanka finally in the late twelfth century, and that some of these mercenaries were quite possibly the *velakkaras* who were charged with guarding the Tooth Relic of the Buddha, which by this time had become the ritual symbol of the Sinhalese kings.

In his assessment of the presence of Keralas from the Malabar coast in medieval Sri Lanka during the period with which I am concerned, Liyanagamage (1986) notes, with irony, how the Keralas had formed the entirety of Magha's contingent, which ransacked Sinhala-ruled Polonnaruva in the mid-thirteenth century, and yet about a hundred years later were enlisted by Sinhala rulers in the Gampola period to defend the kingdom against invasions by the Jaffna Aryacakravartti (68–70). They were probably recruited by the Alakesvaras, who, as I have mentioned, were the dominant political family of the time and whose own origin was clearly in Kerala. Their increasing power during the Gampola period is known from a number of inscriptions and literary texts.[33]

The Alakesvaras' great wealth was derived from merchant activities, chiefly trade between Sri Lanka's southwest coast and Kerala. They had parlayed their position as successful merchants to gain control over vast amounts of land bordered by the ocean on the west and the mountains around modern Ratnapura to the east. Before the Aryacakravartti's invasion, it is clear that the Alakesvaras had established power so deep into the up-country, around the royal capital in Gampola itself, that they had colluded with the Tamil Aryacakravartti in Jaffna in allowing him, in the regions just north of Kandy, to force payment of transport dues to *brahmanas* acting on the Aryacakravartti's behalf (Liyanagamage 1986:72). Whatever terms of collusion had been reached, they must have been abrogated by one party or the other; for the Alakesvaras and the Aryacakravartti were locked in a bitter war towards the end of the fourteenth century. The Alakesvara defeat of the Tamil king not only brought the family enormous prestige, but it underscored their thorough identification with Sinhala economic and political interests.

In discussing the political significance of the Alakesvara family, Liyanagam-age confirms through inscriptional evidence that they were originally from a caste of traders in Kerala (73). He provides an extensive translation of a tract from the *Alakesvara Yuddhaya,* a sixteenth-century text upon which the later *Rajavaliya* seems quite dependent in parts, which details in laudatory fashion the heroic accomplishments especially of Nissanka Alagakkonara, the head of the family credited with the Aryacakravartti's defeat. Liyanagamage has added his own commentary on the revelations and perspectives of this interesting source: how the stature and ability of Nissanka Alagakkonara stands out in con-trast to the weakness and cowardice of the Sinhalese king Bhuvanekabahu; how the latter is portrayed as having deserted his people in the hill country while seeking refuge with the Alaksevaras at Raigama during the peak of hostilities with the Jaffna Aryacakravartti; and how, once the Alakesvaras had defeated the Aryacakravartti, Bhuvanekabahu was able to return to his capital in Gampola. The image proffered is one of a great political savior. On his historical signifi-cance for the political fortunes of Sinhala royalty, Liyanagamage writes:

> Alagakkonara built the fortress of Jayawardhanapura [which eventually became the royal palace in the Kotte era], stored adequate food and other requisites, collected troops and thus created an effective overall defense strategy. . . . It is the fortifications erected by Alagakkonara and the sense of confidence and morale created by him during his stewardship that en-abled Parakramabahu VI, at a later stage, to [entirely] subjugate the Jaffna kingdom thereby effecting the unification of the island, for the last time prior to the arrival of Western nations to the Island. In passing it may be noted that although medieval chroniclers had highlighted the achieve-ments of the Alakesvaras, modern historians, possibly in their enthusiasm to underline the greatness of Parakramabahu, seem to bypass the signifi-cant contributions of the Alakesvaras, but for which the Sinhalese rulers task would have been more difficult, if not impossible. [75; brackets mine]

In addition to this commentary by Liyanagamage regarding the Alakesvara legacy for Sinhala political history, note specifically the symbolism of the Kotte fortification that Alakesvara had erected. On each of the four corners of the fortification wall was located a *devalaya* to the national guardian deities of the time: Vibhisana, Saman, Upulvan, and Skanda.[34]

What I am suggesting is that the Alakesvara family, with its roots in Hindu Kerala, played a significant role in propagating the cosmological idea that four divine guardian deities protected the island from invasion. The idea itself seems to have surfaced for the first time in the mid-fourteenth-century Lankatilaka inscription, when the Alakesvaras had already begun to assert their power over the weakening Sinhala kingship of the Gampola era.

In the conclusion to his article on the place of the Keralas in medieval Sinhala history, Liyanagamage (76) reflects on the ironies of history regarding how various factions of Kerala immigrants, including the Alakesvaras, became acculturated to Tamil or Sinhala culture. Noting how Keralas had been mercenaries for Magha in the thirteenth century and had later fought for the Alakesvaras against the Jaffna Aryacakravartti, Liyanagamage underlines how allegiances and identities can shift so quickly within a brief period of tumultuous history.

It is quite natural that in the face of growing Dravidian settlements in the Jaffna peninsula and adjacent areas, the Sinhalese who were at one time the majority community in those parts, were reduced to a minority and were eventually submerged, retaining but faint traces of their Sinhalese identity. In other words, it may well be said that they had come to be 'Tamilized' in the course of time. Undoubtedly the same process may have taken place in reverse order in the areas further south where the Sinhalese formed the majority. Tamil minorities living among the Sinhalese in those parts of the Island would have been 'Sinhalized' with the passage of time. The Alakesvaras were no exception to this historical process. Though their Kerala origins were not forgotten, for all intents and purposes the Alakesvaras had virtually become Sinhalese. . . . It is the irony of history that when the Sinhalese and Tamils confronted each other in the battlefield, as indeed they did in the fourteenth century, the former would scarcely have known that they were not quite so 'Sinhala' as they thought they were, much as the latter would hardly have known that they were ultimately not quite so 'Damila' either. [75]

Then adding his own twist of irony, since Liyanagamage was writing his piece in the immediate aftermath of the 1983 ethnic pogrom and the militancy it spawned among both Tamil and Sinhala communities, he says: "It is by no means fitting that this knowledge should continue to be the prerogative of the historians."

While Pathmanathan, Ilangasinha, and Liyanagamage have written extensively on the social, political, and historical dynamics contributing to Hinduism's influence on Sinhala Buddhist culture, Obeyesekere's (1983) anthropological studies of the cult of Pattini are very instructive in gaining insight into how domesticated Sinhalas have come to construct an understanding of their migrations from India to Sri Lanka through (Obeyesekere following Eliade) the process known as the "historicization of myth."[35] It bears mentioning specifically in this context what Obeyesekere (1983:361–75) has determined on the basis of his detailed analyses of the Gajabahu "colonization myth." It has great relevance to the central theme of this chapter.

In summary, the Gajabahu myth describes how the second-century Sri Lankan king Gajabahu avenges a moral wrong (the kidnapping of a widow's two sons among 12,000 others) by the king of Soli (Tamil Cola South India). Gajabahu takes with him a giant named Nila, parts the waters of the ocean separating Sri Lanka from Soli, and visits the Soli king while Nila gathers together the elephants of the royal city and kills them by banging them together! Following such an act of intimidation, Gajabahu visits the Soli king, who at first refuses to let the captives go [thus a second "Moses" scene is revisited]. Gajabahu not only demands the 12,000 but another 12,000, or else, he says, he will destroy the city. To make his threat more forceful,

> Nila squeezed out water from sand and showed it; squeezed water from his iron mace and showed that. Having in this way intimidated the king of Soli he received the original number supplemented by an equal number of men, making 24,000 persons in all. He [Gajabahu] also took away the jewelled anklets of goddess Pattini and the insignia of the gods of the four devalas, and also the bowl-relic which had been carried off in the time of king Valagamba; and admonishing the king not to act thus in the future, departed.
>
>   On arrival he landed the captives; sent each captive who owned ancestral property to his inherited estate, and caused the supernumerary captives to be distributed over and settle in these countries, viz., Alutkuruwa, Sarasiya pattuwa, Yatinuwara, Udunuwara, Tumpane, Hewaheta, Pansiya pattuwa, Egoda Tiha, and Megoda Tiha. The king ruled 24 years, and went to the world of the gods. [Obeyesekere 1983:364; Rajavaliya: 40–41]

Obeyesekere has made a number of astute observations regarding the historical, social, and religious significance of this myth. In general, he points out in relation to its many versions (which begin with the thirteenth-century Pujavaliya's imaginative embellishment of the Dipavamsa and Mahavamsa accounts of the historical second-century king and continue through expansions in the sixteenth- and seventeenth-century Rajaratnakara and Rajavaliya), "The Gajabahu myth has been a continually viable one, justifying and explaining the existence of South Indian settlers in Sri Lanka [1983:367]."

It has not only functioned as a myth of origins for a number of migrating communities, but it has also served as a myth of origins for the preeminently significant religio-cultural pageant, the asala perahara. He also suggests that one way to read the Gajabahu story is as a myth of "reversal" generated during the Dambedeniya dynasty in the aftermath of Magha's invasion. Obeyesekere says (371): "If I am right about the fantasy in the myth as the opposite of reality, the period of the depredations of Magha was probably the time when the myth evolved." Further,

> When we compare the Gajabahu myth and the Magha account, we realize again that the former is a myth that is the opposite of the latter 'reality'; Magha invades Sri Lanka with twenty-four thousand (or twenty thousand Kerala troops); Gajabahu brings back twenty-four thousand; Magha plunders and terrorizes the Sinhalas, killing their king; Gajabahu terrorizes the Colas; Magha populates Sinhala villages with Tamil *conquerors*; Gajabahu does it with Tamil *captives*. Even more important than these polarities are the social-psychological functions of the myth, which are to boost the self-esteem of people whose "morale" had sunk low in an era of troubles. (Obeyesekere 1983:372)

This is but a segment comprising Obeyesekere's rich analyses of the myth. Within this context, what needs underscoring relates to two matters. The first is that Obeyesekere has shown that the part of the story about recovering the "insignia of the four *devalayas*" does not occur until the *Rajavaliya*'s version in the seventeenth or eighteenth century (Obeyesekere: 368). This should be emphasized now because it has a bearing on when it is possible to identify the "Buddhist Visnu" per se, an issue to be explored in the next chapter. Second, Obeyesekere's interpretation is completely complementary and congruent with Pathmanathan's and Liyanagamage's historical discussions of how many Kerala peoples were pouring into the up-country and coastal regions of the island from the thirteenth through the fifteenth centuries as mercenaries and traders.

It is very likely that this migration in reality was responsible for the importation and assimilation of many Hindu traditions. While it is impossible to determine with any great degree of accuracy, I would speculate that much of the Hindu *Saiva* presence in Sri Lanka originated with the Tamil Colas from the tenth and eleventh centuries, and much of the Hindu *Vaisnava* presence with the Keralas from the thirteenth and fourteenth. Even to this day, some *salagama* caste peoples who originate from the Malabar Coast (Kerala), in a popular recension of their origin myth, celebrate Visnu as a kind of primordial progenitor.

The Antipathetic Response

In the preceding pages, I have indicated the various ways in which, from the thirteenth through the sixteenth centuries, Sri Lanka was awash in Brahmanical and Hindu influence, and how the monastic prelate at fourteenth-century Gadaladeniya, Dharmakirti, objected to the Hindu influences in his midst. I have also cited the example of the thirteenth-century *Amavatura* in the Polonnaruva period. Here, I briefly want to discuss the fifteenth-century *Budugunalamkaraya*, which contains perhaps the wittiest protest of all.

In opposition to the growing veneration for Hindu deities, the eminent monastic leader and royal tutor of Parakramabahu VI and Prince Sapumal (who became Bhuvanekabahu VI), Vidagama Maitreya, wrote a stinging castigation in his *Budugunalamkaraya* of those who worship the gods. It was, no doubt, a text for the consumption of the educated literati of the court and for the *gamavasi* segment of the monastic fraternity—the likes of Sri Rahula. As Ilangasinha notes (45–46), much of the text is composed to extol the virtues of the Buddha on the one hand and to argue the inferiority of Brahmanical gods and the ineffectuality of Hindu priestcraft on the other. In this respect the work is significant not only because it depicts the attempts by some members of the *sangha* in this period to decry the worship of Hindu deities, a practice which had attracted adherents even among the most distinguished monks of the day, but it also raises the question of the antipathetic dimension of Sinhala ambivalence. It is clear that Vidagama's ruthless and sarcastic condemnation of Brahmanical practice and belief emerged during this period as a result of immense Hindu influence on the royal court and society at large.

The *Budugunalamkaraya* ("Ornament of the Buddha's Virtues"), written in 1470 by Vidagama Maitreya, must have been the author's final work. Peiris and van Geyzel, who have translated a portion of the *Budugunalamkaraya* (C. Reynolds: 269–77) refer to Vidagama Maitreya as

"the author [who] belonged to a strict puritan sect and [who] spends much energy in preaching against brahmins and other worshippers of gods. In the first extract given here, the king has just been advised by one of his counselors to seek aid for the plague-stricken city from Jains. Another counselor now pours scorn on the Jains, and recommends instead the brahmanical offerings to Agni the fire-god. Another counselor pours scorn on this suggestion also, but recommends the worship of Siva. Yet another counselor thinks that Vishnu is a worthier object of worship, but he in turn is attacked by another. All the descriptions are full of sarcasm."

The context of the narrative is a story known first in Sinhala literature through the *Butsarana* (thirteenth century c.e.). It is about a plague that occurred during the time of the Buddha at Vesali.[36] It cannot be taken as definitive evidence for the thriving cults of Brahmanical deities in Sri Lanka on the face of it, because it is referring back purportedly to the time of the Buddha. However, most Sinhala historians (Ilangasinha and Ariyapala, for instance) have read the text in that way. What it certainly does record is Vidagama Maitreya's observations that such worship is fruitless in comparison to veneration of the Buddha. In that sense, it represents an attempt not only to close out deity veneration, particularly of the Hindu gods, but it also seems to represent the assertion that worship of the Buddha is a powerful device for managing *laukika* (this-worldly) matters of grave concern. The specific passage (274) regarding the cult of Visnu has been translated as follows:

'As God of the three Worlds, there is but Vishnu. No other is like him. He alone is worthy of sacrifices,' said the minister. 'Then let rich offerings be made to him.'

When that minister had uttered those words which proclaimed the special power of Vishnu, another minister who stood nearby spoke in the assembly in this fashion:

'You speak as one who fetches salt water for a thirsty man to drink. Is it because there's too little sorrow here that one should add a further mountain of it?

'You fear not mockery in this world, and you say what you will in your ignorance, but have you ever heard that anyone has obtained blessings by making offerings to Vishnu?

'"Vishnu is present everywhere! Never has he been separated from Sita! There was a war on account of this!"—Now to what end has this lying tale been spread?

'Rama, who could not get across a sea which a monkey hopped over, is believed to have built a bridge to get himself here. Could a god's power be so small in this world?

'Listen to my words of truth, for you do not understand! Rama was overtaken by fear, and that is why he started that war with clubs of iron.

'He blew on his conch, and yet could not expel ill-feeling and appetite from his heart. Since he is in terror himself how could he expel the terrors of men?

'The sacrifical rites performed for him with a prayer to win salvation in the future are like striving to obtain sweet ghee by setting camel's milk to curdle!'

The *Budugunalamakaraya* moves on to a praise of the Buddha, emphasizing his mastery over all the worlds, including heavens and hells, and how his followers will not be made to suffer from various calamities:

All deep pain borne by all species that have life,
Human or animal, found in the ten thousand universes
—Of all this, on the day when the Lord
Attained Buddhahood, not even a trace remained. [277]

Two interesting points are raised in these passages. In addition to the obvious general antipathy expressed in relation to things Hindu, the power of the Buddha is now framed in a decidedly more this-worldly (*laukika*) fashion, inadvertently lending support to later Buddhist monastic practices which have not been, traditionally speaking, the wont of the Buddhist *bhikkhu*, e.g., trying to assert, through ritual practices, the powers that traditionally were reserved for the gods.

I mention this now because it is an issue that comes up in a very different, political context in the twentieth century—that is, that the *sangha* can do for the country what was previously thought to be the prerogative of the gods.[37] Second, passages like those from the *Amavatura* and the *Budugunalamkaraya*, and from the *Saddharmaratnavaliya* as well,[38] are frequently cited by historians of a nationalist bent on the one hand to characterize the *sangha* as heroically defending the faith and on the other to marginalize the contributions of assimilated communities.

Thus, antipathetic sentiment within some sections of the Theravada Buddhist Sinhala monastic community is seen by some to have a deep historical vein. It may be possible to see this perspective as somewhat anachronistic, given the trajectories of some nationalistic historians of the modern period. Yet it cannot be denied, at the same time, that the antipathy expressed herein would be more than merely a matter of intermonastic dispute, for it would seem to stand in a reflexive relation to the growing tide of Sinhala assimilation of Hindu elements.

In summary, the period of the twelfth through the sixteenth century in Sri Lanka was one of great political instability and religio-cultural transformation, owing in part to the importation of many Hindu ideas and practices first seen in relation to kingship but also as a by-product of a shifting demography and the burgeoning development of seaborne trade. This Hindu presence is seen not only in the ideology of kingship articulated symbolically by Sinhala kings but also in the literature and architecture of the period. It is a time in which the popularity of deity veneration was on the ascent. Nonetheless, such veneration of Hindu deities by Sinhala Buddhists met with periodic resistance expressed by eminent Buddhist monks of the orthodox Theravada *sangha*. These Hindu deities were eventually "Buddhacized" or "Sinhalized" in the same manner in which migrating Hindus from South India, especially from

Kerala, accommodated themselves to, and were accommodated by, a new culture.

As is so often the case, patterns of change in religion stand in reflexive relation to larger patterns of change taking place in society. The inclusion of Hindu elements in Buddhist cultic practice and the resistance to this inclusion may very well reflect the more general social patterns of immigration, assimilation, and accommodation—and, consequently, reactions to these very processes of social change within the Buddhist religious institutional context.

THE SANDALWOOD IMAGE
Upulvan Deviyo and the Origins of the Visnu Cult
in Sinhala Buddhist Sri Lanka

"In any advanced culture there are not many elements which could be definitely said to have been independently invented by the community which developed that particular culture. Not only the cultures but communities have migrated, and it is not possible to trace to its remote origin the history of a given people and their culture."
—Martin Wickramasinghe[1]

When Wilhelm Geiger published his German and then English translations of the Pali *Mahavamsa* in 1912, his accomplishment created a major and lasting contribution to the study of Buddhism in the West. It also produced, perhaps unwittingly, important effects on how many Theravada Buddhists in twentieth-century Sri Lanka would come to understand various aspects of the nature and legacy of their own religious culture. With Geiger's translation published for the Pali Text Society in London, the *Mahavamsa* was not only available to interested readers in the West, but it also enjoyed an increased popularity among the English-reading Sinhala elite in twentieth-century colonial Ceylon, especially those who were becoming the leaders of the incipient Sinhala Buddhist nationalist movement.[2] Subsequent to Geiger's translation, western and western-educated Sinhalese scholars have analyzed its mythic values[3] while others have mined it for its historical[4] revelations; in turn, public-school educators have used its accounts as sources for English and Sinhala textbooks on Sri Lanka's history. On important Buddhist holidays, such as Poson *poya* (June full moon) or Vesak *poya* (May full moon), Sri Lankan newspapers print articles that report *Mahavamsa* episodes as if they were historical givens;[5] and post-independence politicians have not hesitated to legitimate Sinhala nationalistic ideologies or government initiatives, sometimes for politically hegemonic purposes, by appealing to the text's seemingly unquestionable authority.[6]

While the *Mahavamsa*'s general scope of influence upon historical, cultural, and political understandings in modern Sri Lanka has been as broad as it has been deep, at times producing a "*Mahavamsa* mentality," Geiger's specific translations of crucial passages have also contributed to definitions and perspectives on particular issues that remain, upon closer scrutiny, matters of great complexity and nuance. In this chapter, I will cite some of the implications of Geiger's seemingly innocuous translation of *Mahavamsa* 7.5; 55, where he rendered Pali *devass' uppalavannassa* into English as "the god who is in colour like the lotus" and then added an influential explanatory footnote that reads simply: "that is, Visnu." I will then present and analyze several theories advanced by various scholars about the origins of the Visnu cult in Sri Lanka, in particular the problem of Upulvan's identification as Visnu and its ramifications for this study.

Some modern academic writers on Sinhala culture, mostly anthropologists, seem unaware of the problem involving the identity of Upulvan.[7] They simply report that Visnu is a Hindu god whom Buddhists venerate. Others[8] who are aware have sometimes dismissed the issue as unimportant or merely "academic." What I will demonstrate, however, is that the issues involved in considering the identity and origins of Upulvan are of some significant importance for understanding the nature of religious change and the general accommodation of the Hindu presence in Sinhala Buddhist culture. In examining the specific case of the conflation which occurred between Upulvan and Visnu, I am interested in exactly who and what was transformed in this process. Pondering these issues has led me to offer some new comments regarding an old problem that has received much attention from many an earlier mind.

The *Mahavamsa* passage I have cited is part of a seminal myth that has assumed great importance to the Sinhalese, especially in the twentieth century, when hotly contested ethnic claims to "homelands" or separate states have been advanced by rival communal constituencies. It forms part of the well-known mythic story of how Vijaya, son of the lion-man king Sinhabahu, the progenitor of the Sinhala race, was banished from India for his ignoble conduct and, together with 700 men and their families, put on a ship and sent forth to sea in exile. Vijaya and his retinue landed in Sri Lanka "on the day that the Tathagata lay down between two twinlike sala-trees to pass into nibbana" (*Mahavamsa* 6.47; 54).

When the Guide of the World, having accomplished the salvation of the whole world and having reached the utmost state of blissful rest, was lying on the bed of his nibbana, in the midst of the great assembly of the gods, he, the great sage, the greatest of those who have speech, spoke to Sakka (Indra) who stood near him: "Vijaya, son of king Sihabahu, is come to Lanka from the country of Lala, together with seven hundred followers. In Lanka, O lord of the gods, will my religion be established, therefore carefully protect him with his followers and Lanka.

When the lord of the gods heard the words of the Tathagata, he from respect handed over the guardianship of Lanka to the god who is in colour like the lotus.

And no sooner had the god received the charge from Sakka than he came speedily to Lanka and sat down at the foot of a tree in the guise of a wandering ascetic. And all the followers of Vijaya came to him and asked him: "What island is this sir?" "The island of Lanka," he answered. There are no men here, and here no dangers will arise." And when he had spoken so and sprinkled water on them from his water-vessel, and had wound a thread about their hands he vanished through the air. (*Mahavamsa* 7.8; 55)[9]

This specific passage, together with the narrative in the very first chapter of the *Mahavamsa* in which the Buddha proclaims that Sri Lanka will be a place where his *dhamma* will bear fruition (*Mahavamsa* 1.20; 3), are *Mahavamsa* episodes frequently cited by those Sinhalas who make nationalist primordial claims on Sri Lanka's custody and assert the island's special place in the history of the *Buddhadhamma*'s dispensation. In the Vijaya story, the coming of the proto-Sinhalas to the island is linked to the fate of the Buddha's religion. There it is warranted by the Buddha, the culture-hero of Sinhala Buddhist civilization, that his religion is to take root and endure on this island.

The persistence of the Vijaya myth is affirmed by the fact that is taken very seriously, even literally, by many Sinhalas in modern Sri Lanka, as veritable political and social history and as an ancient, hallowed warrant for the country's continued and undivided political integrity.[10] It is also part of the mythic basis for the important annual Valiyak ritual held at the Maha Devalaya in Kandy immediately following the performance of the *asala perahara*. Indeed, it would be difficult to find anyone who claims to be a Sinhala Buddhist who is not familiar with the Vijaya story and who does not recognize its religio-political import. It is primarily an immigration myth of origins (or better, a colonization myth) that introduces a cycle of related ancient legends about how Vijaya and his three ruling successors (Panduvasadeva, Abhaya, and Pandukabhaya) established a lineage of kingship at Anuradhapura by overcoming the powers of the indigenous *yakkha*s and *yakkhini*s, and by legitimating their reigns through marriage to princesses from Madurai.

The Vijaya story follows another cycle of myths in the *Mahavamsa* that explain the Buddha's three visits to the island, the lineage myth of kingship that begins with the primordial first king Mahasammata (identified also as a direct ancestor of the Buddha *in illo tempore*), and the history of the Buddhist monastic *sangha* including a recounting of the first three monastic councils held in India to determine the true *dhamma* and practice. As these precede the Vijaya cycle of legends, the *Mahavamsa* contains another cycle of myths which follow the Vijaya-related stories and which account for the coming of Theravada Buddhist institutional traditions to the island.[11]

So the Vijaya and related cycle of myths are sandwiched between stories that have to do with establishment of various facets of Buddhism on the island: sacred places, primordial kingship, the *sangha,* the cult of the *bodhi* tree, etc. It is within this network of mythic frameworks that Visnu is now understood to play the sacred role as the island's and the religion's guardian, its chief "minister of defense." Visnu is popularly understood to be the deity in the story who reveals to Vijaya's men that the identity of the island is "Lanka," who assures them that there are no dangers present, and then sprinkles water and ties a *pirith* thread for them to wear, both acts symbolizing a blessing and a protection that aids them in their encounter with the hostile forces of *yakkhas* and *yakkhinis* early on in the story, and is regarded by some Sinhalas in modern Sri Lanka as the origin of the practice of *pirith*.[12]

There are also several late medieval literary tracts that indicate that Visnu's guardianship role was understood widely and popularly from at least the seventeenth century. The deity within the Vijaya story, however, is not actually Visnu. Rather, it is Upulvan, who was later made over or folded into the "Buddhist Visnu," probably by the late seventeenth century. So there is some value in finding out more about Upulvan, determining his mythic profile, and ascertaining his place in Sinhala cultural history. Understanding more about Upulvan's profile and cult means attaining familiarity with a portion of the eventual profile of the "Buddhist Visnu," since the cult of Visnu in Sri Lanka eventually absorbed Upulvan.

As seen in Vijaya's story, Visnu's profile, as it derives from Upulvan, casts him in the role of the defender of the Sinhalas, defending the prosperity of Buddhism in Sri Lanka. This is more important than the mere folkloric accommodation it may seem at first. Why this is so is indicated in a number of ways in the chapters comprising part 2. Just one example from among many in history will suffice for now:

In the mid-nineteenth century, a Kandyan nationalist rebel named Gongalegoda Banda from Matale,[13] leader of one of the two most serious insurrections faced by the British during their political administration of colonial Ceylon, swore an oath in front of the Visnu image at Dambulla claiming that he was, indeed, a descendant of Kirti Sri Rajasinha and that he was determined to wrest power back from the foreign usurpers with the blessings of this deity.[14]

He gained the support, and was urged to lead a rebellion, by Kandyan chieftains who, according a contemporary British official of the time, "were moved by the vague idea of the advantages to be derived from having a King professing Buddhism, who would not only protect but also maintain their religion inviolate [Appuhamy 1995:457]." In this historical instance within the colonial context, the political significance of Visnu in Sinhala claims for political autonomy is clearly articulated as a form of resistance to British power.

Gongalegoda Banda's oath was taken before the impressive "Visnu" image now in the first cave temple at Dambulla. Mythic traditions claim it is the famous Upulvan image first carved out of *kihirali* wood (red sandalwood) at Devinuvara in the reign of an eighth-century c.e. king, Dapul Sen. Over the centuries, Upulvan was accorded the status of *devaraja*, or "king of the gods." In fifteenth-century poetic court literature, he is the object of several pleas, more so than any other deity, to come to the assistance of the king and courtiers for personal and political support. Earlier, as well, in the fourteenth-century Gampola era, he had become formally recognized as one of the "four guardian deities" of Sri Lanka. This, in general, is a significant aspect of the legacy that Visnu inherited from Upulvan, a critical position in relation to defending the interest of the religion and the state throughout history.

It is now difficult to find general appraisals of Sinhala religion, or of Sinhala deity propitiation more specifically, in either English or Sinhala, which do not assume that Visnu is one of the four guardian deities of the island, and that he has been, since ancient times, specifically in charge of protecting the *Buddhasasana*. Moreover, as I have previously written, Visnu *devalaya*s are now ubiquitous throughout all Sinhala cultural areas in Sri Lanka, especially in village contexts. And, as I mentioned in the first chapter, his integration into popular conceptions and transactions of Buddhist ritual culture has been as thorough as any other deity in the country, probably even more so than the very popular Kataragama Deviyo (a.k.a. Murugan, or Skanda). Very recently, a small and inconspicuous Visnu *devalaya* has even been opened within the confines of the Dalada Maligava ("Temple of the Tooth-Relic") in Kandy, the only *devalaya* that has ever been allowed within its premises during the Maligava's long history. What this seems to indicate is that Visnu's intimacy with the Buddha and Buddhism now seems to be as close as any other Sinhala deity, with the possible exception of Natha Deviyo (originally Bodhisatva Avalokitesvara), regarded by many in these modern times as the next Buddha, Maitreya.[15]

It is clear that Visnu has been and continues to remain, an important, intimate, politically significant deity in Sri Lanka, one whose veneration, in fact, is now at the center of partisan political bickering, the topic of the eighth chapter of this study.

Theories About the Identity of Upulvan

Despite the fact that general or related appraisals of Sinhala Buddhist religious culture have simply assumed that Upulvan is Visnu, the identity of Upulvan is actually a question that, during the past fifty years in Sri Lanka, has occupied the attention and research of a number of prominent scholars, whose work seems to have gone unnoticed, especially in the West. A review of the substance and parameters of these inquiries will serve not only as a method of introducing the religio-cultural "depth dimension" of Visnu's cult in Sri Lanka but also as a way to further telescope and refine the historical discussion regarding the introduction of facets of Hindu culture and polity into Sinhala Buddhist traditions that was broadly begun in chapter 2. Unlike the ideology of kingship dealt with there, the religio-cultural processes at work in this instance go beyond eclecticism. While the cult of Upulvan per se was eventually eclipsed in popular culture, his mythic profile became the basis for the transformed identity that Visnu's assumes among the Sinhalas. So the historical focus of this chapter is considerably more narrow, and at the same time it takes my discussion into many details about the cult of Upulvan that serve as helpful background for the literary sources I will consider in the fourth chapter, and for a consideration of the contemporary ritual cult of Visnu in part 2.

Much has been written in various articles and books over the past fifty years by a number of Sri Lankan and Western scholars trying to solve the question of Upulvan's identity. I have noted how Geiger and Barnett, writing in the early years of the twentieth century, indicated in passing that Upulvan was simply Visnu, since that is how he has been popularly conceived. The implication of Geiger's footnote, however, is that Upulvan's identity as the "Buddhist Visnu" is as old as Mahanama's compilation of the first section of the *Mahavamsa* in the fifth century C.E.. In fact, a close reading of the *Mahavamsa* reveals that the word "Visnu" never actually appears throughout the entire text. It is only Upulvan who is mentioned. Barnett's simple instructions to "see Visnu" in the listing for Upulvan within his *Alphabetical Guide to Sinhala Folklore* means that he, too, treated the issue as a matter of fact to be taken without a second thought. Indeed, the conflation between Visnu and Upulvan has "stuck," having been valorized by Sinhala Buddhists for at least the past three centuries or more. The question of Upulvan being any deity other than Visnu seems simply not to have arisen until recently.

Beginning in the 1950s, however, and continuing through the 1990s, other scholars have advanced various and sometimes elaborate theories about Upulvan's ultimate origins and his true identity. There is one school of thought that identifies Upulvan as originally the Mahayana bodhisatva Avalokitesvara, another as the Vedic deity Varuna; still others have argued that Upulvan is none other than Rama or Krsna; and finally, it has even been suggested that Upulvan may be a Zoroastrian deity, perhaps Ahura Mazda. In the end, after reviewing this scholarly literature (and in the process taking into account many of the important features of Upulvan's cult), I suggest that various religious constituencies worshipping Upulvan at different historical moments may have attached some of these specific identities to the god, or at least interpreted his presence as manifest instances of them. But I also argue that a new way of looking at the problem may obviate the need for elaborate and speculative theories regarding his original identity. I suggest that, in the final analysis, Upulvan's original identity may not be recoverable, or that Upulvan be regarded simply as an indigenous Sinhala deity who rose in popularity in the thirteenth and fourteenth centuries in Devinuvara on the southern tip of the island.

What is of greater significance to me, however, is that Upulvan's mythic character has come to color the "Buddhist Visnu"; that is, the conflation between the two deities has provided Visnu with a specifically Sinhala Buddhist personality and character. The important question, then, has not so much to do with which deity Upulvan's identity can be correctly or originally ascribed to, but rather how the cult of Upulvan has provided the mythic, cultic, and theological content for the Buddhist transformation of Visnu. Once this transformation took root, Visnu was no longer a "Hindu god" whose cult was orchestrated by priestly Brahmans, but instead he was blended into the fortunes of Sinhala Buddhist mythico-historical perceptions, and his cult of propitiation was made subject to the patterns constituting the practice of deity veneration within this inclusive religious culture. That is, he ceased to be Hindu and became Buddhist. That much, at least, will be abundantly clear in the next chapter when some relevant medieval Sinhala literature is considered.

The Avalokitesvara Hypothesis

Paranavitana (1928:35–71) was the first scholar to open up discussion on the "mysterious" or problematic identity of Upulvan, within a short passage in his groundbreaking article "Mahayanism in Ceylon." In his brief comments on Upulvan, he argues that the identity of the god is really Bodhisatva Avalokitesvara. He pointed out that it would have been strange indeed if a Chinese, royally sponsored flotilla led by the mighty admiral Cheng Ho in the early 1400s, which landed at Devinuvara (on at least one if not several of his seven epic expeditions into the Indian Ocean during the fifteenth century), would be bearing gifts or paying tribute to a Hindu divinity like Visnu. It would make more sense, he suggested, for them to be venerating Avalokitesvara, the "lord of the sea," who is known in China primarily as the goddess/bodhisatva Kuan Yin. In fact, a historically important stone inscription brought from the Chinese Ming court by Cheng Ho and left in Devinuvara, the so-called "Trilingual Slab" written in Chinese, Tamil, and Persian (now in possession of the National Museum in Colombo), contains the following passage (*Epigraphia Zeylanica* 3:336):

> **All sentient beings** who exist in the world are being protected, in happiness, by the **compassion** of the lord. Men, whomsoever they come hither, have their obstacles to happiness removed through the divine **grace** of the Lord of Tenavari. [boldface mine]

The language and ethos of this inscription, coupled with the fact that it is of Chinese origin, makes it quite suggestive that by "Lord of Tenavari" (Sinhala: "Devinuvara") the Chinese meant Avalokitesvara, insofar as the most well-known trait of this particular bodhisatva is his compassionate protection of all sentient beings, which is given freely out of his selfless grace.

It is difficult to ascertain what the motives were for making this declaration at Devinuvara. From what we know about worship of this deity during this time, it would seem that the local populace did not regard the god as Avalokitesvara (see below). Yet it is somewhat clear that the Chinese were interested in declaring that the god of Devinuvara was known well to them too, and that they had come to register their recognition of his great power and even to solicit his protection. Perhaps their arrival at Devinuvara and their prostration before the island's guardian deity were a subterfuge, for we know that Cheng Ho proceeded subsequently to kidnap Vira Alakesvara, the reigning Sinhala king at Kotte, taking him to the Ming court in China. Then, with the backing of these Chinese naval forces, a scion of a rival court faction was declared Parakramabahu VI.[16] Thus, following their visit to venerate the guardian deity of the island's shrine at Devinuvara, the Chinese orchestrated a coup d'état.

There are several other considerations that have been marshaled in support of identifying Upulvan as Avalokitesvara. Perhaps the most startling material evidence, especially when coupled with a popular mythological tradition, has to do with the iconography of the "Visnu image" in the *devaraja lena* (or Cave I) at Dambulla, the massive and ancient rock temple in central Sri Lanka on the southern plains of the old *rajarata* region (see fig. 3.1). This is the very image I have mentioned at the beginning of this chapter, the one that was apparently made complicit in the 1848 rebellion against the British led by Gongalegoda Banda of Matale. In any case, I quote from Von Schroeder's (1990) three extensive notes on the image, which provide much grist for later discussion:

> Wood sculpture of Avalokitesvara with the effigy of Amitabha in the hair-dress (sic), worshipped as Upulvan deiyo (sic). . . . Possibly copied in the

FIGURE 3.1 Avalokitesvara painted blue and known as Upulvan
or Visnu in Cave #1, Dambulla

12th century from an image dating from the Late Anuradhapura Period.
(Von Schroeder: 356)

Especially enigmatic is the iconography of the blue coloured Upulvan
deiyo, variously identified as Varuna, Rama and Avalokitesvara, but nevertheless worshipped by the common Sinhalese as Visnu. Of the two Upul-
vans at Dambulla, one is represented in the ascetic manner and one is bejewelled [sic]. . . . It is apparent that this sculpture [the image in the
devaraja lena] possesses no similarities with Visnu. What counts most for
the worshippers is the popular identification, which has little regard for the
iconographic symbols representing the intentions of the makers. (Von
Schroeder: 383; brackets mine)

It is a popular belief in Sri Lanka that this image originates from the
Visnu Devale at Dondra (Devundara) from where it had been taken first

to Alutnuvara and then subsequently to the Mahasaman Devale at Ratnapura. . . . The importation of a wooden image of Visnu from India during
the Pallava period is recorded in an Ola manuscript discovered in the
Kegalla district [H. C. P Bell, *Report of the Kegalla District*, pp. 46–48]. In
the year 712 of the Saka Varsa (790 A.D.), a red sandalwood image of
Vishnu was brought across the sea. King Dapulu Sen, after having a vision
of the image, built for it a *devavimanaya* at Devinuvara. Some 183 years
later (973 A.D.), the image known as Sri Visnu Diviya-raja was transferred
to the newly built *devamandiraya* at Alutnuvara. The above mentioned
King Dapulu Sen would be Dappula I (815–831) who is historically related
to a restoration of the stone temple at Dondra. The Saka year 712 (790
A.D.) may refer to the prince whose regnal years as King Dappula II lasted
from c, 815–831 A.D. The present condition of the Upulvan in Cave I is too
excellent by far to date from around 800 A.D., and possibly represents a replacement copied during the Polonnaruva period. It is obvious that this
image, which bears no similarity to Visnu, represents an emanation of
Amitabha. However, the lack of an attribute in the left hand rules out any
precise identification, such as Avalokitesvara Padmapani [von Schroeder:
406; brackets in text].

I will first address some of von Schroeder's comments and then go on to review
the case for Upulvan-as-Avalokitesvara as it has been made by two other scholars in some detail.

Von Schroeder believes that the image in question is of some considerable
antiquity, that it may date to the twelfth century, and may be a copy of another
image from earlier Anuradhapura periods. Avalokitesvara images are, indeed,
very abundant from the seventh through the eleventh centuries in Sri Lanka,
while at the same time there are no contemporary images that can be identified strictly as Upulvan within this same time frame. While von Schroeder is
reluctant to identify the image precisely as Padmapani (which is Perera's
[1971] argument summarized below) on the basis of the lack of a lotus present
in the left hand, he nonetheless identifies the image as Avalokitesvara (306).

I think he is unmistakably correct in this. In my own previous iconographical studies of Avalokitesvara figures in Sri Lanka (1991:72–90), I came across
any number of Avalokitesvara images created in Sri Lanka in which the bodhisatva is not bearing a lotus in the left hand. In any case, the image in question may not be Padmapani in particular, but it is definitely Avalokitesvara. It
is obviously not a Visnu figure, as von Schroeder correctly asserts (383), but
there is a complex mythic tradition regarding a red sandalwood image to
which he alludes (406) that lays claim to the image as Upulvan (and hence
Visnu in the popular mind). Von Schroeder has referred to a recension of the
myth as it has been told within an old *ola* leaf manuscript reported by Bell. Ac-

tually, in that specific version of the myth, the red sandalwood image does *not* make its way to Dambulla.[17] As will become clear in the following pages, there are many other variants to this important myth as well.

That the mythic identification of the "Visnu image" at the *devaraja lena* at Dambulla is identified as the famous red sandalwood image of Upulvan in some popular oral traditions is also attested to by Scott (1994:41–42). He reports the story as he was apparently first told it in Devinuvara and then as he heard it repeated again by the *kapurala* of the Visnu *devalaya* in the *devaraja lena* at Dambulla in 1987. I will quote his entire version of the myth as he has published it because it contains a number of details that are relevant, together with von Schroeder's comments just cited, to this and further evolving discussions.

> In Devinuvara, the King of the Southern Kingdom of Ruhunu, Dapulusen, once offered a reward to any man who could carve, out of the red sandalwood he would make specially available for the purpose, an image of the deity of the town, Uppalavanna. Many tried, and as many failed. In time, however, there appeared a man of humble bearing who made known his desire to try as others had. He shut himself in the room with the sandalwood and remained there for days on end.
>
> At length the King himself, growing curious and impatient, went to inquire as to the progress. He opened the door, and there before him stood a nine-foot sandalwood image of Uppalavanna. The man, however, was nowhere to be seen. Nor was there any evidence, in the way of wood shavings, say, of the sandalwood having actually been worked. All who saw were astonished. The image was then taken to the top of a small hill (the site, it is said, of the original *devale* or shrine-house of this deity), and there installed so that it *looked* directly over the southernmost tip of the island.
>
> In time the Portuguese came and conquered the maritime areas of Lanka. They came to Devinuvara. But try as they might, they could not sail across the line of the deity's eyesight. Enraged, they committed an atrocity upon the image, cutting the legs so that the sight of the deity fell upon the ground. The deity was thus rendered powerless to stop their rampage. Or so the Portuguese thought. Eventually, in retreat from their colonial successors, the Dutch, the Portuguese ransacked the ancient town of Devinuvara. They loaded their ships with the loot. And, of course, they loaded the red sandalwood image of Uppalavanna whose eyesight had so impeded their marauding designs. But in taking flight, their ships sank. And the sandalwood image of Uppalavanna floated around the western coast of Lanka, beaching itself at the town of Chilaw. From there it was taken to the great Rock Temple at Dambulla in the central highlands. And even today it can still be seen there.[18]

The logic of the argument for Avalokitesvara as the true identity of Upulvan would be apparent if this myth were historical and if the image were clearly Avalokitesvara iconographically (which it is). It is more likely, however, that this variant of the mythic story is a comparatively recent invention formulated to explain the image's provenance following a major restoration of the Dambulla *lena*s in the early eighteenth century C.E. It would seem to be a reworking of older versions of the myth, made to fit in with developing circumstances at Dambulla, i.e., to reflect the importance of the "Buddhist Visnu." The simple solution to accommodating Visnu at Dambulla seems to have been to paint the bodhisatva image blue and make a compelling account for the presence of the deity!

In the *Dambuluvihara Tudapata*, dating to the reign of Narendra Sinha in 1726 C.E., the cave is referred to as *devaraja lena* ("temple cave of the 'king of the gods'") (A. Seneviratne 1984b:50). *Devaraja* is a frequently used epithet for Upulvan (though more frequently used in relation to Sakka in Sinhala literature) in many medieval inscriptions and in some literary works, so it is likely a reference to the presence of what was regarded by the early eighteenth century as an image of Upulvan, and by extension at this time, Visnu. Thus, the tradition of identifying this Avalokitesvara image as Upulvan probably dates back to this time, and Scott's revamped version of the myth of the sandalwood image explains its presence.

The earliest literary reference to the myth of the red sandalwood image is found in the fifteenth-century *Parakumba Sirita*, apparently written for the pleasure of Parakramabahu VI's court in Kotte. Precisely when this myth was actually associated with the image at Dambulla is perhaps ultimately unknowable (as unknowable as determining exactly when it was painted blue to signify its identification with Visnu), but it is not beyond reason to speculate that it must have been part of the lore which led Gongalegoda Banda of Matale in 1848 to enlist the powers of the deity at the beginning of his rebellion against the British. It would have certainly bolstered the prestige of his efforts. As Scott tells the myth, the image's powers of protection are considerable, and the Portuguese desecration of the icon, a moral travesty, led karmically to their own destruction. The image, however, survives to protect another day, but now in a new venue.

As I have said, there are other variants of this myth which declare that the "Visnu image" was brought instead to Alutnuvara in the thirteenth century, and then to Kandy (rather than Dambulla) in the seventeenth or eighteenth century (or even to Gadaladeniya or Hanguranketa, depending on which *kapurala* is relating the myth and where it is told). I will show that the story of the red sandalwood image was at first the myth of origins for Upulvan *deviyo*, and has since developed into the root myth explaining the dispensation of the

Visnu cult in Sri Lanka. The variant I have just quoted and discussed functions precisely in this manner to explain the presence and significance of the cult of Visnu at Dambulla.

However, there are other dimensions to the case for Upulvan as Avalokitesvara that need to be examined before we consider other issues connected to Upulvan's conflation with Visnu. Perera (1971) and Wanaratana (1972) have written extensively in support of the Upulvan-as-Avalokitesvara hypothesis. Wanaratana's argument is based partly on a consideration of another summary variant of the sandalwood image myth. He (16 ff.) cites it, as he says it is found (but actually with quite a bit of embellishment), in the fifteenth-century Sinhala panegyric and poetic *Parakumba Sirita*,[19] which I have just referred to above as the myth's first literary reference:

> *Upulvan* took the form of a *kihiri* (sandalwood log) floating in the sea and came ashore at Devinuvara. King Dappula had dreamt of Upulvan Deviyo, who informed him of his impending arrival in the form of sandalwood. The following day, the king waited on the shore for the arrival of the log and then took it to his *maligava* in a grand *perahera*. He had the sandalwood log carved into statues of Upulvan, his wife Sanda Vathi, and his son Dhanurdhara, and kept them safely in Devinuvara. The *kapurala* of the Seenigama *devalaya* (between Hikkaduwa and Telwatte) also dreamt of Upulvan *deviyo* on the same night as the king had, being told that the sandalwood would come to the Seenigama shore. But when the *kapurala* did not appear by the shore in time, the log carried itself to Devinuvara.[20]

The focus of the myth as it is presented here is somewhat different. Instead of emphasizing the dispensation of the Visnu cult, it explains why Devinuvara becomes the cultic site of the god's provenance (rather than some other place, such as Seenigama). Thus, the dispensation dimension has not yet been added. In this version, the king's role in establishing the cult of Upulvan is rather more intimate than in Scott's version. In Wanaratana's version, the sandalwood log produces the form not just of Upulvan, but of his wife and son as well. Indeed, in this version of the myth, the red sandalwood log is a *murti*, or actual form of the god. There are no miracles involved in its carving per se. In the version that Scott tells, what is miraculous is the manner in which the image was carved. Wanaratana's version also serves as a warrant for the performance of the most important ritual, the *perahara*, in honor of the god—a ritual event that I will describe in the conclusion of this study. In both recensions of the myth, however, royalty is seen to play a crucial role in the original establishment of Upulvan's cult, thus implying the deity's role as a guardian of the island.

Wanaratana does not discuss any of this. He is only interested in proving Upulvan's identity as Avalokitesvara. Here follows his case: Citing the fact that *kihiri* was the choice of wood regarded as most auspicious for the carving of Natha *deviyo* (Avalokitesvara) images, and noting that Avalokitesvara is believed to possess the special ability to cure diseases of the skin by means of the medicine derived from *kihiri*,[21] Wanaratne thus begins to build his case for identifying Upulvan as Avalokitesvara. He proceeds to argue circumstantially that Mahayana Buddhism had proliferated during the time of King Dappula (ninth century C.E.), a prince of Rohana who contended for the throne in Anuradhapura.

Since it is known from the *Culavamsa* that Dappula had constructed a bodhisatva image some fifteen feet in height, and that Dappula's brother, King Agbo (Aggabodhi), was the king responsible for the construction of the largest known Avalokitesvara statue in the world, at Maligawila in the southeast quadrant, he speculates that the fifteen-foot-high bodhisatva image must have been made of *kihiri* and in the likeness of Avalokitesvara. He argues (133 ff.) that the identification of Upulvan with Visnu occurred later in the Kotte period during the second half of Parakramabau VI's reign (1412–67 C.E.), after the king had married his daughter to a Tamil prince, and then granted two villages (Naimmana and Veraduwa), according to the an inscription found nearby, to Brahmans who worked at the *devalaya*. That is, the later identification of Upulvan with Visnu was effected, in part or as a whole, by a marriage alliance of political significance. His finding is consistent with what I have argued about how political matters are often an impetus for inclusion or exclusion, in this case the transformation and assimilation of a Hindu deity into a Buddhist culture.

On the whole, Wanaratana's arguments for Upulvan's identity with Avalokitesvara are interesting, but they remain largely circumstantial. He has gathered some interesting "facts" into an entertaining ensemble, but he has not linked them together in a creditably causal fashion, nor do they corroborate with other more solid information that I cite below.

Perera's assessments are not much more persuasive than Wanaratana's, being also quite speculative in nature. At times, Perera is also overly preoccupied with critiquing the views of Paranavitana, who had argued (1953) in an influential book that the identity of Upulvan is really the Vedic deity Varuna. (Since I shall examine Paranavitana's argument for Varuna shortly, I shall forego those parts of Perera's substantial argument that are concerned with his criticisms of the Varuna hypothesis and concentrate, instead, on summarizing his case for Upulvan as Avalokitesvara.) Part of the value of Perera's work is that he has cited many of the references to Upulvan that can be garnered from the *Culavamsa* and from inscriptions. For that reason, in addition to his arguments in favor of the Avalokitesvara hypothesis, his work in this context is worth a close review.

Perera begins his case by arguing for the relative ubiquity of the cult of Upulvan throughout ancient Sri Lanka, in contrast to those scholars, especially Paranavitana, who have stated that the Upulvan cult was largely confined to the southern region of Devinuvara. In an earlier study, when he argues for the identity of Avalokitesvara in the famous "man and horse" rock-carved sculpture at Isurumuniya in Anuradhapura,[22] Perera says he found inscriptions by Kassapa I, the famous king of Sigiriya, which, he asserts, identify the Isurumuniya complex at that time as "Bo-Upulvan." Therefore, he says, "we may surmise that these early inscriptions were evidence to prove that the shrine Isurumuniya was once dedicated in honour of the great divine concept of the Sinhalese Buddhists, namely the god Upulvan" [90].[23]

In reviewing various other notices of Upulvan in history, Perera cites the same *Parakumba Sirita* panegyric that refers to the sculpting of the red sandalwood image by the ninth-century King Dappula II, a reference which he finds corroborated by the *Culavamsa*'s (1:94–95; 45:55–56, 62–63) references to the king's construction of the Khadirali Vihara, presumably in Devinuvara. He then cites the *Culavamsa* passage (2:152; 83:49–50) which reports how Prince Virabahu, nephew of Parakramabahu II of Dambedeniya (1236–70 C.E.), went on a pilgrimage of gratitude to Devinuvara, to worship Upulvan and to establish a *pirivena* (monastic learning center), after he had defeated the Javaka army of the invader, Chandrabhanu, from the peninsula of Southeast Asia.[24]

He notes further that during the reign of Parakramabahu II, the *Culavamsa* (85:85) says that the king had the shrine of Upulvan in Devinuvara renovated, and he instituted the annual procession, *asala perahara*, in honor of the god. Perera also calls attention to the *Dambuluvihara Tudapatas* of the two Kandyan kings, Narendra Sinha (1707–39 C.E.) and Kirti Sri Rajasinha (1751–82 C.E.), within which images to Upulvan at Dambulla, as I have noted above, are mentioned as having been repaired.

Curiously, Perera also refers to the earlier Kandyan king Vimala Dharma Suriya II (1687–1707 C.E.) as transferring a village formerly dedicated to the maintenance of the Upulvan shrine in Kandy to the Dambulla *viharaya*. This reference (which unfortunately he does not clearly footnote) would be the earliest documented indication of an Upulvan or Visnu *devalaya* in Kandy. He goes on to note the existence of another Upulvan shrine in Sitavaka in the mid-sixteenth century[25] and the inscriptional references to Upulvan as the supreme protector of the country at Gadaladeniya and Lankatilaka. His point here (88–94) in rehearsing all of these references to Upulvan is, as I said previously, to prove that the cult of Upulvan was far more widespread than other scholars have led us to believe. In this, he has been quite observant, and his point is well taken, though its significance is relevant to the medieval rather than to the ancient historical period.

Perera then proceeds to build his case for Upulvan as Avalokitesvara. His opening assertion consists of pointing out the functional similarities between the Vijaya legend in the *Mahavamsa* and a well-known Mahayana myth found in many sources about the merchant prince, Simhala, who along with 500 other merchants, comes to Lanka after his ship is wrecked at sea, is duped and seduced by *raksasis*, but finally saved spectacularly by Avalokitesvara in the form of a white-winged horse.[26] Both of these stories, he argues, are colonization myths that probably reflect the reality of a single historical episode of divine assistance, remembered in different ways by the Mahayana and Theravada traditions respectively (94).

The fundamental problem with Perera's interpretation of these two myths is that he has completely historicized them. The Vijaya legend is clearly meant to hallow the presence of the Sinhalas in Lanka for all time under the protection of Upulvan, who is authorized (and hence the Sinhalas too) ultimately by the Buddha's directive. It is a story in which Lanka is regarded as a place where the Sinhalas and the Buddha's dharma will flourish. It is part of the *dhammadipa* charter for the people of this island. The story of Simhala, on the other hand, is one about escape from Lanka, not its domestication. Here Lanka epitomizes the dangers of samsara, instead of a *dhammadipa*. It is a myth of Indian Mahayana origins, and like other stereotypes in Indian myth, Lanka is a dreaded place occupied by *raksasas* and *raksasis*.

The meaning of each, then, is really quite different, and the type of divine help rendered in each is also substantially of different kinds. The Vijaya story is, indeed, a Sinhala colonization myth of Lanka; but the story of the merchant Sinhala is a Mahayana religious allegory about the problematic nature of existence per se: how samsara can be transcended by the compassionate grace of the bodhisatva. Perera's assertion that the two stories reflect a single historical episode remembered subsequently in different ways is thus a good example of how some scholars are prone to historicize myth. Myths of this nature usually function as explanatory devices, but they are primarily a genre of literature about religious and/or political meaning and not primarily reliable for historical facticity.

After postulating how widespread the Mahayana tradition in general had become before the writing of the *Mahavamsa* and *Dipavamsa* in the fifth and fourth centuries C.E., Perera then contends that Upulvan represents Avalokitesvara in his "lotus-bearing aspect." He suggests that in subordinating Upulvan to Sakka [Indra] in the Vijaya legend, "the Theravada *bhikkhu*s of Mahavihara [a monastery in Anuradhapura] had contrived to lessen the importance of Upulvan" [95; brackets mine].

Perera's speculation on this point seems extremely bold, if not far-fetched, to put the matter charitably. The earliest icons of Avalokitesvara found in Sri Lanka are at Situlpahuwa in the jungles of the southwest (now part of Yala National Park), and Tiriyaya (some thirty miles north of Trincomalee on the northeast coast). The images found at these sites do not predate the seventh or eighth century C.E., at the very earliest. While elements of the Mahayana tradition are known and/or may be inferred in earlier periods of Sri Lankan history, there is absolutely no proof of the literary, inscriptional, or iconographic kind that supports a finding for the presence of the Avalokitesvara cult in Sri Lanka before the seventh or eighth century C.E.[27] Therefore, it is not possible for Upulvan to be identified as the bodhisatva's "lotus bearing aspect" three centuries earlier.

I would suggest that Perera's reading of Upulvan's "subordinated" role in the Vijaya legend also involves a mistaken rendering of the intention of the compilers of the chronicles as well. Upulvan's assigned divine role, as the people's, the religion's, and the island's chief protector or "minister of defense," a role sanctioned by the Buddha, doesn't strike me as a subordinate role at all, particularly in what is chiefly a colonization myth. Moreover, the presence of Sakka in the story would seem but a literary device invented to link the Buddha to Upulvan, since nowhere else in all of Pali Buddhist literature is Upulvan mentioned at all.[28] That is, Sakka is but the method of introduction for Upulvan to be ultimately authorized by the Buddha as the island's chief "minister of defense," because he is nowhere else to be found in the sacred scriptures of the Buddhists or the Hindus. Thus, Perera's citations, discussions, and interpretations of the evidence he cites from the first millennium are somewhat dubious in nature.

With regard to the *duta kavya* or *sandesa* literature of the fourteenth and fifteenth centuries, Perera cites numerous quotations reflecting the profile of Upulvan in order to demonstrate affinities with the divine profile of Avalokitesvara in Mahayana literature (95–98). Again, there is a fatal flaw in Perera's reasoning. He first ignores the fact that the god Natha (Avalokitesvara) and Upulvan are regarded as two distinct deities throughout *sandesa* literature, as they are in the inscriptions from Lankatilaka and Gadaladeniya. While he finally acknowledges this (103), his response is extremely weak: "We have already discussed above that by this period of Ceylon's history, much confusion had set in with regard to religious practices and beliefs, and people had forgotten their previous traditions, religious observations, etc." Here Perera seems to be something of a scion of the heritage he describes. Seeing one god where there are actually two needs a better explanation than what he has provided.

The remainder of Perera's study in support of the Avalokitesvara hypothesis mentions the episode of Cheng Ho's visit to Devinuvara, and it further develops the critique of Paranavitana's Varuna hypothesis, speculating that the color of Upulvan was really green, rather than blue, since *nil* in Sinhala can mean either. Therefore, "One could conjecture that the image [of Upulvan at Dambulla] was a reference to a Mahayana Tantric practice centered around the worship of Avalokitesvara or Tara, dressed in green [101; brackets mine]." This last contention is even more preposterous, since it would be based upon a flourishing Mahayana cult at Dambulla in the eighteenth century when it is clear that Mahayana cults had probably vanished from the island by the twelfth or thirteenth centuries. Moreover, he suggests randomly, without any supporting evidence, that the current Natha Devalaya in Kandy was probably the location of an Upulvan shrine. There are other unwarranted speculations that the reader may entertain directly (99–104).

Regarding, then, the "Avalolitesvara hypothesis" for Upulvan's original identity, it would seem that the only creditable conjectures warranted by this discussion are: 1) the Chinese contingent led by Cheng Ho may have indeed regarded the deity at Devinuvara, most likely Upulvan, as Avalokitesvara, for whatever reasons; and 2) the image in what, by the early eighteenth century, was regarded as the *devaraja lena* ("Upulvan's cave") at Dambulla was originally an Avalokitesvara image, but later came to be regarded, as articulated in a variant of the myth of the sandalwood image, as a Visnu icon. As for the general hypothesis that Upulvan is really Avalokitesvara in some variant form, most of the remaining evidence cited by Wanaratana and Perera is either circumstantial in nature or can be interpreted in more likely ways.

But what is intriguing in this discussion are three other points raised by Perera. All are circumstantial and can be hardly asserted with certainty, but all are worth pondering a little further. The first is that it is possible that the Isurumuniya complex at Anuradhapura may have been referred to as some kind of ritual complex in relation to an early cult of Upulvan. I think that this is not as far-fetched as it may seem at first; for, if the Vijaya legend is attributable to the first compilations of the *Dipavamsa* and *Mahavamsa* in the fourth and fifth centuries c.e. at Anuradhapura, it is not unreasonable to expect that some kind of devotional marker would be present for Upulvan, the protector of the Sinhalas, in the decades or the century that followed.

Second, the existence of an Upulvan *devalaya* at the end of the seventeenth or the beginning of the eighteenth century in the sacred area of Kandy during the reign of Vimaladharmasuriya II is very possible indeed. The royal predecessor and father of this king, Rajasimha II (1635–87 c.e.), recovered Devinuvara from Portuguese control late in his reign and is said to have rebuilt the temple there in honor of Visnu (Queryoz: 1057). That another temple to Upulvan or Visnu would be erected at this time in the royal capital, or later and more likely during his son's (Vimaladharmasuriya II) time, in light of the

Culavamsa's lavish but general praise for the construction activities of this latter king in the sacred area, is also not unreasonable to expect. But if an Upulvan *devalaya* was built in Kandy, it should not be confused with the Natha Devalaya. The *devalaya* in question may have been, instead, what is today known as the Maha Devalaya dedicated to Visnu.

Third, Perera's reference to an Upulvan *devalaya* in the Sitavaka region at this time is also warranted. For the *Culavamsa*'s depiction[29] of Parakramabahu IV's construction activities credits him with building a "new town" ("*Alutnuvara*"), and within Alutnuvara, a shrine to *Uppalavanna devaraja*. This final point, as will be shown in chapter 7, has an important bearing on the mythic and historical origins of the Alutnuvara Devalaya and Upulvan's direct connection to those beginnings.

The "Varuna Hypothesis"

With the publication of Paranavitana's *The Shrine of Upulvan at Devundara* in 1953 by Oxford University Press, on the eve of the completion of comprehensive renovations at Devinuvara's Visnu *devalaya*,[30] the prospect of Upulvan's historical importance was signaled to the scholarly community and to the Sinhala elite. It is a remarkable book, folio-sized and containing 24 plates of structures, diagrams, figures, coins, maps, inscriptions, and sculptures. More than half of the written text per se (pp. 19–59 out of 81 pages) is devoted to Paranavitana's brilliant but overly inventive theory that Upulvan was not originally Visnu, but none other than the ancient Vedic and Brahmanical deity Varuna.

In his historical introduction and in a subsequent discussion identifying the archaeological remains of the old *galge* shrine in Devinuvara (1–18), Paranavitana mentions that the oldest document referring to Devinuvara itself is an inscription attributable to the great Polonnaruva king, Nissamka Malla, in the late twelfth century,[31] that the earliest appearance of *Devanagara* (the Pali name for the town) is in the *Culavamsa* record[32] of Vijayabahu I's reign (1059–1114 c.e.), during which time Polonnaruva was taken back from the Colas. What he establishes is that Devinuvara had become a small city worthy of mention by kings and chroniclers by the eleventh or twelfth century.

But he also mentions many other salient issues connected to the history of the cult of Upulvan. I will cite them in passing now as a way to introduce yet more details into the picture and to help contextualize Paranavitana's argument in support of the "Varuna hypthothesis": the *Culavamsa*'s account of Dappula II building his *Khadirali pirivena* at what later apparently becomes Devinunwara; the *Parakumba Sirita*'s fifteenth-century inchoate version of the sandalwood image myth; the visit by the Chinese led by Cheng Ho and the trilingual inscription they left; Upulvan's many references in the poetic *sandesa*s; and the shrine's destruction by Thome de Souza and his Portuguese soldiers in 1588.

He also argues that Upulvan's identity yielded to Visnu as the result of Brahmans arriving in Devinuvara after fleeing the establishment of Muslim power in South India; he points out how Queroz reports that the Kandyan king Rajasimha II erected a Visnu *devalaya* when he evicted the Portuguese in the mid-seventeenth century; he asserts that the original *galge* ("rock house") shrine now in ruins is unrelated to any Dravidian (or for that matter Sinhala) architectural prototypes and dates it to the seventh century before the ascent of Cola power; that the site of the current Devinuvara Visnu *devalaya* and adjacent monastic *viharaya* was the ancient site of the *Khadirali pirivena* built by Dappula; and that the ruins of the *galge*, located about half a kilometer away from the current *devalaya/viharaya* complex, perched on a hill overlooking the sea, was the original shrine of Upulvan Deviyo (see fig. 3.2). Having set the table with these references and interesting findings as a backdrop, Paranavitana proceeds to what becomes the heart of his monograph: the thesis that Upulvan's origins are rooted in the Vedic cult of Varuna.

At the outset of his proof, and after declaring that the name Upulvan has become obsolete and commonly replaced by Visnu, he almost seems to take delight in stating rather wryly (20):

> To those Hindus who regard Visnu as the Supreme Deity, it would come as a shock to be told that in Ceylon he is invited by the average Buddhist to partake of merits earned by meditating on the Buddha, so that he may remain for a long time without falling down from his exalted position in Heaven—which, according to Buddhism, is the fate of every god.

Here, Paranavitana has signaled how the accommodation of Visnu into Sinhala Buddhist culture has been subjected to an understanding of the nature of divinity within the context of the cosmology and soteriology of the Theravada. That is, Visnu has been demoted. (Visnu's position in the Sinhala Buddhist pantheon is shown later to be rationalized as the result of the deity's ethical profile and his perceived ability to produce positive karmic merit.) Insofar as Visnu was identified as Upulvan, he inherited Upulvan's position within the Sinhala pantheon as "king of the gods" (*devaraja*) and protector of the religion and the island. Here, I think Paranavitana is absolutely correct.

Paranavitana notes that it was W. F. Gunawardhana, in his translation of the *Kokila Sandesa* and in his edition of the *Mayura Sandesa*, who first pointed out in the 1920s that Visnu and Upulvan were regarded as two separate deities in the fifteenth-century Sinhala literature of the Kotte period, when Parakram-

FIGURE 3.2 Galge near Visnu *devalaya* in Devinuvara

abahu VI reigned. Sir Baron Jayatilaka, in his critical edition of the *Tisara Sandesa*, a fourteenth-century poem from the Gampola era, and perhaps the first of the *sandesa* genre, supported and confirmed Gunawardhana's finding (1935:ix). Paranavitana also refers to how the Lankatilaka inscription puts the two gods into different classes: Kihireli-Upulvan as a superior guardian deity of the island, along with Vibhisana, Sumana (Saman), and Kanda-Kumara (Kataragama), while Visnu is only mentioned among a number of other gods.[33] To underscore the distinctive identities and the superiority accorded to Upulvan in the *Tisara Sandesa*, Paranavitana quotes verse 18 from the *Tisara's* panegyric on Upulvan:

> When Sri [Visnu's spouse] and Sarasvati [Brahma's spouse] remained con-
> tentedly with this god (Upulvan), would not Brahma, inflamed with the

fire of grief, have turned dark of complexion, as did Visnu, had he (Brahma) not, in that predicament, observed (the vow of) continence with determination and thus avoided suffering from the grief which resulted from the separation (from the beloved)? [parentheses in text, brackets mine]

Having established the fact that Upulvan and Visnu were regarded distinctly in the historical and literary milieu of the fourteenth and fifteenth centuries (20–23), an important point that many observers of Sinhala Buddhist religious culture have missed, Paranavitana proceeds to his lengthy, detailed, and often tangent-filled Varuna hypothesis directly. But first take note here of the characterization of Visnu and Brahma as "continent," or celibate. In the next chapter, this same characterization surfaces in other tracts of Sinhala literature and becomes a marker of Visnu's Sinhala Buddhist identity, in contrast to his Hindu profile.

Because Paranavitana's argument is so detailed, elaborate, and tangential, I will quote only his remarkably concise (given the nature of the argument), yet still somewhat lengthy conclusions (57–58). This approach is more accurate and faithful to the author's intent than any attempt I might make to summarize.[34]

The main conclusions arrived at in this investigation may now be summarized. Up to the fifteenth century, Upulvan was considered to be a god distinct from Visnu with whom he is now identified. The representations of Upulvan which then existed did not show those iconographical features which are peculiar to Visnu [52–54]. The name Upulvan (P. 'Uppala-vanna') need not necessarily be interpreted as a *bahuvrihi* compound, as is usually done. *Upul* (*Uppala*) and *Van* (*Vanna*) may be taken as two distinct names of the god which have been joined in one compound. *Vanna* seems to have been used in the *Spk.* as an equivalent of *Varuna* and is obviously the rendering into Pali of the Old Sinhalese form, *Vana*, which had developed from *Varuna* in accordance with well-known phonological processes [22–25]. Evidence is also found in a very early Brahmi inscription for the existence of Varuna worship among the ancient Sinhalese [24–25]. *Vanna* being equivalent to *Varuna*, the first member of the compound may be explained as the rendering into Pali of an old Sinhalese word equivalent to *Uda-pala*, 'the protector of Waters.' The characteristics of Upulvan, as they are alluded to in Sinhalese poems, are in agreement with those of Varuna [25–28]. Moreover, this identification agrees with the statement in the *Parevi Sandesa* that Upulvan's consort was Sandavan, the name being the periphrasis of *Gauri* (the White or Brilliant Goddess), the appellation of

Varuna's consort according to the Sanskrit epics [29–32]. The identification of Upulvan with Varuna makes it possible to interpret intelligently,
without taking undue liberties with the text, the verse in the *Parevi Sandesa*
eulogizing the goddess Sandavan. It also enables us to understand the next
verse in the same poem, in praise of a subsidiary deity named Dunu-devu-
raja, who is none other than the personification of Varuna's bow mentioned in the epics [32–42].

The Bow-god was honoured at Devundara in the form of Rama, the
best known among the epic heroes who wielded a bow given by Varuna
[41–44]. The *Parevi Sandesa* also affords evidence to support the view that
it was as an incarnation of the Bow-god that Rama was worshipped in ancient Ceylon. The cult of Rama, too, seems to have prevailed among the
ancient Sinhalese [43–44]. This secondary deity, the Bow-god Rama, gradually overshadowed Upulvan and, in accordance with the religious beliefs
which then prevailed in India, was taken to be the same as Visnu [42–46].
But Upulvan still lingers in the guise of the Western God, a term applicable to Varuna [45–47]. The tradition that Upulvan arrived at Devundara
from the sea is also consonant with his being identical with Varuna who, in
post-Vedic times, evolved into a Sea-god [47–52]. It also stands to reason
that the Aryan-speaking immigrants who settled down in Ceylon, originally a sea-faring folk, would have given a prominent place to Varuna
among the gods they worshipped, and it is most appropriate for the Sea-
god to be considered as the protector of an island like Ceylon. The *samka*
and *cakra* are emblems which are as appropriate to Varuna as to Visnu
[52–54]. 'Meghavanna', the throne name of ancient Sinhalese kings, can
also be interpreted as an appellation of Varuna in another and earlier aspect, the bestower of rain [54–57].

If these conclusions are found acceptable, the origins of religious beliefs
which prevailed among the Sinhalese people up to the fifteenth century in
connexion with the cult of Upulvan can be traced back to those which
guided the lives of the Indo-Aryans in the remotest antiquity. Nay, they can
even be traced back to the religious beliefs of Aryan-speaking peoples in
the Indo-Iranian and Indo-European stages. For Varuna figures in the earliest document so far known (c. 1400 B.C.) in which there is mention of an
Aryan God. . . .

As rich and dense as this passage may seem to be at first sight, it is actually remarkably cogent and concise in comparison to the preceding thirty-eight
pages it summarizes, or the two pages of rife speculation with which the chapter then concludes (the nature of which is indicated by the final paragraph of
the extract, which I have intentionally included). There is also more to ponder

in his argument than what I have quoted above, and the following pages refer specifically to Paranavitana's attempt to account for the social process that led to Upulvan's eclipse in favor of Rama at Devinuvara. (This part of his analysis is reasonable and, with the aid of other observations generated by other scholars, may actually help to explain the eventual conflation between Upulvan and Visnu.) I think it is also likely that the provenance of the Hindu epic *Ramayana* was considerable in the medieval period, as evidenced by the manner in which it is alluded to in the ideology of kingship discussed in the previous chapter in relation to the Polonnaruva through Kotte periods. Its influence also may be seen, *perhaps*, in the first set of four guardian deities of the island found at Gadaladeniya and Lankatilaka. These four guardian deities play significant roles in the *Ramayana* (if, for the moment, it is assumed that Upulvan can be identified with Rama and Saman with Laksman).

However, it is difficult to agree with Paranavitana that the Brahmanical epics (*Mahabharata* and *Ramayana*) were part and parcel of the religion of the ancient Sinhalese. Apart from his speculations, there is simply no material, cultural, or literary evidence to indicate that being the case, especially during the time dating back to the sixth century B.C.E.[35] As for his central argument that Upulvan was originally Varuna, it is a case that is replete with serious problems. It is based on a related series of "could be" etymological speculations that give the impression of a house of cards. When one speculation is proven problematic, the entire enterprise is called into question, because one speculation is built upon another *in seriatim*. That is the fault of his method.

That Paranavitana's thesis proved controversial goes without saying. The most trenchant of the many critiques that surfaced was advanced by Obeyesekere (1984:313–19). His critique was aimed at demonstrating how faulty Paranavitana's method had been for arriving at his conclusions.

> The major thrust of Paranvitana's analysis is etymological and phonological. He attempts to trace the history of a cultural complex through shifts in meaning and, more important, through systematic phonological changes. . . . . Most of these phonological changes are highly dubious, at best based on a set of ideal conditions almost never realized in practice. If, for example, Sinhala people were trained philologists, the theory might be justified. Phonological evidence, if it is to be used in cultural analysis, should be predictive, not "post-dictive" as in the present case. . . .
>
> One glaring instance of this is the derivation of the god's name, "Upul." How did this transformation come about? The consensus by Sinhala people that "Upul" meant blue lotus "does not make any sense" (1953, p. 25). The *real* meaning (which incidentally, has never been actually held by Sinhala people) is based on the fact that Varuna is the "lord of the waters."

There are many epithets used to designate this idea in Sanskrit literature. Other epithets are also appropriate, *even though they are not found in extant literature!* "One such possible epithet is *Uda-pala. Uda* as a synonym of *udaka* and *pala* can be used with the same meaning as *pati* (lord). . . . As there are no long vowels in ancient Sinhalese, *Udapala* would have changed to *Udapala.* The loss of the syllable *da* by syncope . . . would also result in *Upala.* It is also conceivable that the vowel in the second syllable of *Uda-pala* was slurred over in pronunciation, giving rise to *Udpala* and *Uppala.* If the origin of the name is as suggested above, the form Upulvan in Sinhalese literature is a natural development from *Upala-vana*" (1953, p. 25). All these changes, it should be noted, are based on an epithet given to Varuna by Paranavitana himself, since he admits it is nowhere found in extant literature. (1984:314–15)

Obeyesekere had said enough at this point to call off the search for the original Upulvan in the supposed Lankan cult of Varuna, especially on the dubious grounds he illustrated above in exposing the inventive character of Paranavitana's argument. But Obeyesekere didn't stop here with his criticism of the Varuna hypothesis. He went on to adduce his own conclusion that, after all, Upulvan is probably just an early Buddhist adaptation of Visnu. Since Obeyesekere's view on this matter is well-considered, his own thesis must be seriously examined.

Noting that the evidence from the *sandesa* literature and the Lankatilaka rock inscription clearly refer to two separate gods, Obeyesekere says, however, "One could have a situation where two distinct gods could on another level become one" (315). What Obeyesekere has actually done here, and admits to, is to having invoked the Puranic conception of *avatara*, i.e., that Visnu and Upulvan are references to the same god, who assumes different forms. For Obeyesekere, Upulvan is an early Buddhist "take" on Visnu, and the other Visnu referred to in inscriptions and in *sandesa* literature is the original god of Hinduism: there is now a "Buddhist Visnu" and a "Hindu Visnu," as it were.

This last part of his analysis is very helpful because, as will be shown in later chapters, there are occasions in myth, art, and ritual when the Hindu cosmology of Visnu may be invoked in lieu of the Buddhist. (In the first chapter, I have mentioned how this is the case with wall paintings adorning the modern Visnu *devalaya* in Devinuvara.) But what is dealt with here in this chapter, much more specifically, is the question of the identity of the Visnu in relation to Upulvan. Is Upulvan's identity, especially before the fifteenth century, traceable to Visnu?

To support his *avatara* thesis, Obeyesekere cites two stanzas from a ritual text he collected at Sinigama, where Upulvan is mentioned along with Visnu as seemingly partaking of one whole divinity. (There will be examples later where this occurs in an important royal *sannasa,* and in the *yatika*s of *kapurala*s at contemporary Visnu *devalaya*s.) Paradoxically, he offers the following:

> I am advocating the thesis that Upulvan and Visnu are different deities and yet the same. Upulvan in the accepted meaning "blue-lotus-hued" makes more sense than Paranavitana's involved phonological excursus. That the early Sinhala who came from northern India worshiped the popular lotus-colored god of that region is more plausible than their worship of Varuna, a deity who never excited the popular imagination. Thus I am inclined to the view that Upulvan was an early Buddhist adaptation of Visnu and was later given the title of Upulvan. [1984:316]

Unfortunately Obeyesekere doesn't give us any proof that Upulvan was an early adaptation of Visnu, and at this point in his commentary he seems to have fallen into the same trap as Paranavitana. There is no evidence of any type, aside from the presence of the rhetoric of Sinhala kings from the Polonnaruva period forward, for a cult of Visnu among the Sinhalas. It has even been indicated that there is very little in the way of support for a cult of Upulvan in the ancient period, let alone the postulation that it somehow can be linked to a Visnu cult among the proto-Sinhalas of some period in the millennium before the common era.

I think it is more likely, as I said at the outset, that Upulvan originated as an indigenous deity in Sri Lanka and was later conflated with Visnu, rather than originating with the identity of an early Sinhala adaptation of Visnu. In other words, I think it is more accurate to invert the process that Obeyesekere has described: Upulvan becomes Visnu rather than the other way around. If Upulvan's origins had to do with Visnu, there would be some traces of such a legacy in the development. But there isn't any iconographic, mythic, or ritual trail to follow to warrant this conclusion. Thus, I think that what has transpired in Sinhala Buddhist religious culture is that a sixteenth- or seventeenth-century conflation between Upulvan and Visnu made possible a later adaptation and transformation of the latter.[36] In the process, Upulvan was largely forgotten, but lives on in the guise of the transformed "Buddhist Visnu." This also makes much more sense than Paranavitana's argument that the successor to Upulvan is the "Western god" (*Basnahira Deviyo*).

And finally, there is no literary, inscriptional, material, or cultural evidence for a cult of Varuna in Sri Lanka. As noted above, Obeyesekere has devastated the linguistic argument supporting Paranvitana's thesis. Therefore, it is difficult to imagine that the cult of Upulvan somehow originated as a Varuna cult.

But Paranavitana collected much of the available material that provides evidence for Upulvan historically. His comments about the architecture of the *galge*, the original Upulvan shrine, are also relevant to my own thesis. If Upulvan's origins are not Hindu, that is, if he were a god indigenous to the Sinhalas, then the fact that his shrine is architecturally unrelated to South Indian, and indeed, to Anuradhapura styles of construction is consonant with my understanding of the rise of his indigenous cult in southern Sri Lanka, rather than in the ancient north central regions of the island in the vicinity of Anuradhapura.

The Rama Hypothesis

Yet another hypothesis in relation to the question of Upulvan's original identity involves the theory that the cults of Rama or Krsna were responsible for the origins of the cult of Upulvan. This possibility was first advanced by M. B. Ariyapala in 1956.

> We have already shown that the confusion between Visnu and Upulvan may have been due to colour, as they are both painted blue. We would here, like to hazard the question whether it was possible that Krsna was worshipped in the form of Upulvan, or was it even Rama who was thus worshipped after his alleged victory over Ravana? Both Rama and Krsna are painted black or blue, and are considered to be *avataras* of Visnu . . . Rama or Ramacandra, the ideal hero of the Hindus and husband of Sita, has been widely worshipped in India, and of his worship in Ceylon, we have direct and definite evidence. The Kokila–sandesa refers to a Rama *kovila* in Jaffna. . . . Here the author refers to the building of the bridge to land Rama's army in Ceylon. This temple was no doubt put up by the Tamils, who occupied the north of the island. The question now is whether this Rama-worship, which was known to the north, spread southwards in some form or other. Can it be in the form of Upulvan? We saw that Rama was black or blue, and black was often confused with blue. We see this in the case of Krsna, who, as his name indicates, is black. But he is often painted blue. If it was not Rama, who was thus worshipped, could it then be Krsna? When we consider how widespread and popular the cult of Krsna was in India, it seems unlikely that it did not leave its impress on the island of Ceylon.
>
> Such being the position, it is not unreasonable to raise the question whether Krsna-worship was not known in Ceylon. If it was known, could it have been in the form of Upulvan? One obvious objection to this view is Upulvan's connexion, according to Buddhist traditions, with Buddhist religion. As for Rama-worship, it is quite likely that he came to be worshipped after his alleged victory over Ravana, and the people may have looked upon him as a protector. [1956:190]

Thus, what Ariyapala has suggested is that it may have been possible that either the cult of Rama or Krsna gave birth to the cult of Upulvan. In the case of Krsna, he adduces absolutely no evidence for his conjecture, save for the issue of color and the fact that his cult was very popular in India. The latter argument is particularly weak, because there are any number of deities who have been popular throughout India who have not found a sustained cultic presence in Sri Lanka. Even Hanuman, who is such an important figure in the *Ramayana*, is not known as a deity who gained much provenance in Sri Lanka. On the other hand, Ganesha's cult is thoroughly established among the Sinhalas.

If Krsna's cult had been introduced to the Sinhalas and taken firm root, there would be a more substantial legacy of evidence reflecting it. But there isn't much at all, or at least it is very faint; allusions to the deity in later seventeenth- to nineteenth-century folklore are the only possible evidence of his cult. So Krsna was probably never seriously domesticated. There are also no affinities between the profiles of Upulvan and Krsna. In light of the fact that beyond some late literary references, there is no other evidence supporting the existence of the Krsna cult in Sri Lanka, and that there are no perceived affinities between Krsna and Upulvan (except possibly color), how could the cult of Krsna be seriously regarded as responsible for the origins of the cult of Upulvan?

As for Rama, there are more compelling reasons to consider the hypothesis more seriously, but not necessarily for the reasons that Ariyapala advances. Speculating that it was from fifteenth-century Jaffna that the cult of Rama may have spread down to the opposite end of the island, including Devinuvara, thereby accounting for the appearance of the Upulvan cult, is completely untenable and inconsistent with many facts that we have previously cited. First, if Upulvan had his origins in the fifteenth century cult of Rama on the northern Jaffna peninsula, why does he appear in the fifth-century *Mahavamsa* as the guardian of the Sinhalas and Buddhism? And what about all of the other references to the god of Devinuvara which predate the fifteenth-century references, some of which Ariyapala himself has previously cited (1956:187–88)?

As for his second suggestion (which contradicts his first), that Sinhalas would have worshipped Rama after his alleged victory over Ravana, this is evidently another example of a Sri Lankan scholar falling victim to the process of the historicization of myth. If Ariyapala wanted to make the case for either of his suggestions, he would have to proceed in one of the following ways: In the first instance, he would have to show, somehow, that Sapumal Kumara, the adopted Tamil son of Parakramabahu VI who conquered Jaffna on the king's behalf in the mid-fifteenth century and then succeeded him as king Bhuvanekabahu VI, was somehow involved in or supported the spread of the cult of Rama, specifically to Devinuvara. There is no evidence in the available historical record to support this. In the second instance, he would have to document the popularity of the *Ramayana* among the Sinhalas in a period earlier than I have indicated was the case. He hasn't attempted to do this, nor do I think he could have been successful had he tried. Thus, if the Rama hypothesis is going to be weighed seriously, it must be supported by better evidence.

Following Ariyapala, Anuradha Seneviratne (1984a) made a bold attempt to identify Rama with Upulvan several years later. Most of the literary material he cites in support of his claim is actually from the period of history *after* the time (before the fifteenth century) with which I have been concerned thus far. That is, he cites several literary tracts[37] that would seem to indicate how Upulvan had been identified with Rama (and hence Visnu) in the popular minds of later (seventeenth through nineteenth century) Kandyan religious culture. (We shall examine literature of this nature in the following chapter.)

But none of his references from history, popular folklore, and ritual provide sufficient warrants to lead me to believe that Upulvan had been identified with Rama or Visnu by the Sinhalas in the period before the fifteenth century, or conclusively, for that matter, before the seventeenth. But curiously, he does cite (1984a:223) the early sixteenth-century northern Thai Buddhist text, the *Jinakalamalini,* as having identified the four guardian deities of Sri Lanka as Sumana (Saman), Rama, Lakkhana (Laksman), and Kattagama (Skanda or Kataragama *deviyo*). This, indeed, is a tantalizing reference, insofar as it is provided by a Siamese Theravada Buddhist monk. But there are some serious problems involved in equating this set of four guardian deities with the early set I've mentioned before, which are based on the fourteenth-century Lankatilaka inscription. In the first place, Vibhisana has not been included. In the second place, the references to Sumana and Lakkhana would seem redundant, since Sumana (Saman) and Lakkhana (Laksman—Saman) appear to be the same deity. It would appear to be a bit of a stretch, then, to agree entirely with Seneviratne when he says, "This evidence proves beyond doubt that the god worshipped at Devundara was none other than Rama."

Seneviratne's other supporting evidence for identifying Upulvan with Rama comes from his consideration of a bas-relief found at Devinuvara, which depicts a royal figure drawing a bow (224–25). Since another sculpted relief depicts a character with five heads, he concludes that the second figure must be Ravana ("the other five heads may be hidden from view. . . ."), though Paranavitana held, I think correctly, that this second figure in question was Skanda. The bulk of the remainder of Seneviratne's study is concerned with what the author sees as thematic parallels between the myth articulated within the extended ritual dance, the *kohomba kankariya,* and the *Ramayana.* In both stories, Seneviratne argues, the theme of Aryan peoples gaining victory over

non-Aryan peoples predominates. With regard to the latter epic, Seneviratne
concludes his article by saying (235–36):

> In light of these accounts we can say that the two characters of Rama and
> Ravana are the heroes of a pre-historical battle between two race groups
> whom we may call Aryans and non-Aryans. Rama, the victorious, in
> course of time was deified by his people and remembered with affection.
> When the Sinhala people came to Lanka from North India they brought
> with them their beliefs. Of them the story of Rama was the most impor-
> tant. As a result the Sinhalese people regarded Rama who was like a blue
> lotus as the guardian of Lanka and her people. The development of this re-
> ligious cult in Sri Lanka underwent several changes because of the inter-
> ference of the orthodox Buddhists whose main task besides their own sal-
> vation was to safeguard and usher the Buddhist dispensation against the
> uprising Hinduism, so that it shall last for five thousand years in the island
> of Sri Lanka.

Again, two familiar problems arise marking the analytical attempts of Sri
Lankan scholars who have reckoned with this specific problem: 1) the histori-
cization of mythic traditions, and 2) the imputation of the presence of the
Ramayana story as a religious artifact of the ancient Sinhalas. However,
Seneviratne's final sentence does suggest that he is aware of how the cult of
Rama has been challenged and also transformed by Sinhala Buddhists over the
centuries.

It is apparent that the cult of Rama formed an important piece of the Visnu
cult historically, as evidenced from the type of literature Seneviratne has cited,
and from a crucially important royal land grant from the Maha Devalaya in
Kandy, which I have recently had translated. Nonetheless, the assumption in
Seneviratne's analysis has been the same as in every other one examined thus
far: that Upulvan was originally a deity other than Upulvan. In this case, the
hypothesis is Rama. Again, it is helpful to invert the main conclusion and assert that Upulvan later became identified with Rama, within the cult of the
"Buddhist Visnu." In other words, there has been a constituency of worshippers who have understood that Rama is Upulvan.

The Zoroastrian Hypothesis

S. D. de Lanerolle (1964:xx) connects not only the origins of Upulvan but those
of Sakra and Saman as well, to Persian origins. Very generally, he sees affinities
between Upulvan and the Zoroastrian high god Ahura Mazda, and briefly spec-

ulates that there was a Persian presence in ancient Sri Lanka. De Lanerolle's view is supported by R. Tundeniya, a locally noted folklorist, formerly an employee of the University of Peradeniya library, with an outstanding reputation for his knowledge of traditional lore in the up-country of Sri Lanka.

I interviewed Mr. Tundeniya at length regarding his views about the identity of Upulvan and Alutnuvara *deviyo*. Mr. Tundeniya remains unconvinced of all the other arguments (Upulvan as Avalokitesvara, Varuna, Krsna, or Rama) we have reviewed in this chapter. His opinion that Upulvan must have been Ahura Mazda is based on two factors: 1) his belief that a Persian community existed in Devinuvara from early medieval times; and 2) that Upulvan's character (and lack of resemblance to any Indic deities) is more closely associated with Ahura Mazda. In particular, Mr. Tundeniya, holds that a review of the Sinhala literature on Upulvan will reveal his consistent association with the forces of light.

When I asked Mr. Tundeniya for any historical evidence of a Persian community in Sri Lanka, he mentioned the Trilingual Slab Inscription and quipped, "Why else would the Chinese have left the inscription in Persian if they didn't expect anyone would read it?" But he conceded that there are no inscriptions left by this Persian community per se in Sri Lanka.

Tundeniya's comments should not be taken lightly. The fact of the matter is that Devinuvara was a very cosmopolitan port in medieval times. Though there is no direct evidence for Tundeniya's speculation, if Upulvan was taken for Avalokitesvara by the Chinese and as Rama by Brahmans, it is possible that a Persian Zorastrian community might have understood the deity regarded as the "king of the gods" at Devinuvara to be Ahura Mazda.

Recently, Pathmanathan (2000) has written an extensive paper on the history of Devinuvara that sheds some very helpful light on the current discussion. His paper, along with some other sources, is the subject of the next section of this chapter. There we attempt a historical reconstruction of the cult of Upulvan, in the process of trying to determine when Upulvan was absorbed into the ongoing cult of Visnu.

Upulvan and Devinuvara: A Historical Analysis

As I have noted in critiquing the analyses offered by other scholars who have worked on the problem of Upulvan's identity, there is a tendency among them to "historicize" myth. It is better to begin this section by explaining more clearly what I have meant by this.

Myths, of course, are of many different types, but their function can be said to be, in general, explanatory in nature. They try to explain how something, usually a revered religio-cultural artifact, deity, condition, or practice came into being. They have their own logic and usually appeal to a moral authority, often divine or ancestral, to explain the "why" or "how" of the issue in focus. They are "true" narratives insofar as they articulate a religious meaning held normatively by a given community.

The relationship between myth and history is thus very complex. On the one hand, myth is a part of history, since its expression takes place in time and it is a construction of culture. And like history, it is explanatory, and a function of memory and creativity. Myth may also be, at times, a retelling of historical events, and actually may contain some historicity.

Myth is, then, seemingly dependent upon history. On the other hand, myths often refer to a primordial time that transcends history (*in illo tempore*); or myth may function as a device designed to introduce historical time per se, bridging the primordial and the existential. This latter sense is how the Vijaya myth and its Upulvan episode seem to function within the *Mahavamsa*. The myth bridges the primordial time of origins (Sinhabahu as the "lion-man" progenitor of the race, and Vijaya, the Sinhala ancestor who comes to Lanka and inaugurates local, linear time).

The myths of the Buddha's visits to the island also function precisely in this fashion. They signal the beginning of "Buddhist time" on the island. Together, these cycles of myth, therefore, within the religious imagination of tradition, articulate and explain the beginnings of "Sinhala Buddhist time" in Sri Lanka. Simply put, they are explanatory devices marking the origins of Sinhala Buddhist civilization in Sri Lanka. The myth of the red sandalwood image is similarly meant to explain the origins of the Upulvan cult in Devinuvara.

The various cultural and religious qualities or values special to "Sinhala Buddhist time" have been articulated within narrative texts such as the *Dipavamsa* and *Mahavamsa-Culavamsa*. Here, the critical moments of history, at least as they have been remembered or judiciously selected, have been situated within a mythic narrative replete with mythic references and a mythic logic. This narrative literature, as with all narrative literature, is written with a motive. The motive of the *Mahavamsa* has been clearly proclaimed: it was "compiled for the serene joy and emotion of the pious." It is clearly, then, a religious text of sacred meaning written as a story to stimulate or inculcate a religious disposition. Or, to put the matter another way, it is an excellent example of a process involving the mythicization of history.[38]

What I have referred to as the "historicization of myth" occurs when literature of this type is understood as a kind of virtual history, with its specific claims interpreted as facticity and therefore with absolute historical certainty. While many events in the *Mahavamsa* may be corroborated by archaeology (the historical accuracy of the text has sometimes proved uncanny), the fact of the matter is that the *Mahavamsa* is primarily a religious and mythic text preoccupied with instilling spiritual values while legitimating Buddhist practices and institutions, especially the *sangha* and Buddhist kingship. It countenances what has been understood as normative by the consensus of the Theravada Buddhist Sinhala community. It is a charter for that religio-political community, a blueprint of what it holds sacred in tradition. It also sanctifies the political rule of exemplary Sri Lankan kings, and condemns others who have been judged as adversarial to Buddhism. As such, it participates in history, insofar as it expresses certain religio-cultural and religio-political sentiments and, in turn, shapes how the world in general and time in particular is viewed by Sinhala Buddhists.

But confusion arises when its many mythic episodes are treated simply as the facts of history. Attempts to date the coming of Vijaya comprise one example of this confusion. How does one really date what is clearly *primordial* time? Or problems arise when the historicity of the Buddha's visits to the island, clearly mythic in nature, is used to authenticate contemporary political claims to Sinhala sovereignty?

To give another example of the point I am trying to make here about the manner in which texts like the *Mahavamsa* have been deployed, simply compare the following statements: 1) Vijaya established the presence of the Sinhalas in Sri Lanka who, since that time, along with Buddhism, have been protected by Visnu; 2) by the fifth century c.e., the Theravada Buddhist monastic chronicle, the *Mahavamsa*, articulated the sentiment that the origins and legacy of a distinctive sense of social, political, and religious identity is reflected in cycles of mythic narratives recounting the coming of Buddhism and the progenitors of the Sinhala people to Lanka, both of which are believed to be sanctioned and protected by divinely ordained power. Respectively, these two statements reflect the historicization of myth (first sentence) and the recognition that myth is part of history, a mode of consciousness that attempts to explain events within a meaningful frame of reference (the second sentence). The second sentence resists the historicization of myth, while the first asserts myth as history.

In the present discussion, I will examine the cult of Upulvan from the perspective reflected in the second of the two statements I have just summarized. It would be appropriate to include in this discussion some relevant examples from Sinhala literature that help to broaden an understanding of Upulvan's divine profile. But we will postpone an examination of Upulvan in the poetic *sandesa* literature from the fourteenth and fifteenth centuries until the next chapter, when we will take up the Sinhala folk and ritual literature of the later Kandyan period.

The point of the present section is to summarize what can be usefully drawn from the previous discussion regarding the problem of Upulvan's identity, and to try to make use of insights derived from other non-narrative sources (inscriptions and old historical descriptions) in order to construct a reasonable statement regarding the time and circumstances in which the cult of Upulvan became the basis for the transformed cult of the "Buddhist Visnu."

Unless the story of Vijaya is an interpolation of the *Mahavamsa* inserted at a date later than Mahanama's fifth-century compilation,[39] it must be regarded as the earliest literary recognition of Upulvan.

I have noted Perera's contention (see above) that the Isurumuniya complex at Anuradhapura was named after Upulvan in the fifth century c.e., though the certainty of this remains somewhat in doubt. Upulvan is not met again until the myth of the sandalwood image, the story of his introduction to Devinuvara, which, is associated with King Dappula, who reigned in the ninth century, and according to the *Culavamsa*, had constructed the Khadirali *viharaya*, and in the process, according to the *Parakumba Sirita*, had established the town of Devinuvara,[40] which some believe was actually Dappula's capital city.[41] The date of the myth of the sandalwood image is not ascertainable, but it must predate its first literary reference in the fifteenth-century *Parakumba Sirita*, in which panegyric it becomes a marker for the significance of Dappula's ninth-century reign. The linking of the myth of the sandalwood image to the *Culavamsa*'s account of Dappula's ninth-century activities is an association that may have occurred earlier than the *Parakumba Sirita.*

Devinuvara was known by many different names: Giriyala, Girihela, Kihirelipura, Devundara, Devanagara, and the Tamil name used by the Chinese, Thenevarai.[42]

In any number of literary references as recent as the eighteenth century, Upulvan is referred to as Kihirelli Upulvan, signaling his intimate connection with the myth of the sandalwood image and the initial establishment of his cult at Devinuvara.

It is difficult to associate the *Mahavamsa* myth of Vijaya's coming to Lanka and the myth of the sandalwood image, for the latter reads as a myth of origins, or a means of explaining the introduction of the cult of the god to Lanka.[43] As in many myths about the origins of particular deities in Sri Lanka, Upulvan comes from the sea. But unlike the deities of these other myths, he is not a banished or an exiled prince from India, but instead comes either as a sculpted *murti* or in the nonanthropomorphic form of a sandalwood log, to be carved into a form suitable for his veneration. In the *Mahavamsa*'s fifth-century telling of the Vijaya story, Upulvan is already figured anthropomorphically as a deity. It seems certain that the two stories represent two independent mythic traditions. The myth of the sandalwood image, which is later extended as the cult of Visnu's diaspora myth, is nowhere mentioned in the monastic chronicles. What is clear, however, is that the *cult* of Upulvan has its historical origins in the south, and precisely in Devinuvara, which takes its very name from the cultic presence of the deity. The historical timing of its origins cannot be established with accuracy. Perhaps the most that can be said is that it came into vogue between the ninth and eleventh centuries C.E.

Upulvan is not directly mentioned after the Vijaya story in *Mahavamsa-Culavamsa* until some seventy-six chapters later, with its account of how Prince Virabahu, following his defeat of Southeast Asian rival Chandrabhanu during the reign of Parakramabahu II in the thirteenth century, went on an extended pilgrimage to Devinuvara to give thanks to Upulvan for his victory. Two chapters later, Parakramabahu II learns that

> in the sacred town of Devanagara which was a mine of meritorious works, the shrine long since erected to the lotus-hued god—the King of the gods, had now fallen into decay . . . [so] he betook himself to the superb town and in rebuilding the dwelling of the King of the gods like to the heavenly mansion of the King of the gods, he made it an abode of all riches. Then the best of men had the town filled with all splendours even as the beauteous city of the gods. Hereupon, he determined to celebrate every year in the town an Asalhi festival for the god [Culavamsa 2:167; 85: 85–89].[44]

There are a number of issues raised in this passage, but I will cite only two in this context. First, this is the first time that *devaraja* ("King of the Gods") is used as an epithet for Upulvan in *vamsa* literature, including its commentary. It is a clear reference to the fact that Upulvan's status became increasingly refined or defined. Second, in this context I would also cite Pathmanathan's discussion (2000:1–5) of the Devundara slab inscription left by Parakramabahu II,[45] which he believes is an indication that this king was then attempting "to consolidate his authority particularly over areas of commercial prosperity and cultural importance" (4), which in turn indicates that the town must have enjoyed previously some degrees of autonomy in its administration. These two observations underscore how and why Upulvan seems to have been given a type of official or state status.

The famous Muslim itinerant, Ibn Battuta, visited Devinuvara several decades later than the time of Parakramabahu II in the 1340s. His account of the town would seem to support Pathmanathan's comment and also lend some insight into the extent to which Upulvan's shrine dominated the local political economy. According to Ibn Battuta,[46]

> Beneath this mountain is a large bay which yields precious stones. Its waters appear extremely blue to the eye. From this spot, we travelled for two

days and reached a large town, Dinur, situated on the sea coast, and inhabited by merchants. There is here a vast temple, the idol in which bears the name of the town. There are in this temple about five-hundred women born of infidel fathers, who sing and dance every night before the idol. The town with its revenues belongs to the idol; all those who live in this temple, and those who visit it are fed therefrom. The idol itself is of gold, and of the height of a man. It has large rubies for eyes, and these, I was told shine like two lamps at night.

Ibn Battuta's description, if it is not also a matter of the historicization of myth or mythicization of history, raises some interesting questions that may not be resolvable. In the first instance, his account may suggest that the shrine at Devinuvara had become a Hindu temple at this time, for the 500 women dancers could suggest a cult of *devadasis*, a type which was prevalent at the famous Jaggannath temple in Orissa. Second, the image he describes is certainly not the sandalwood image of the myth I have frequently referred to throughout this chapter. That means that either the sandalwood image had already disappeared, or that the myth of its origins had yet to be invented. Since the first premise would have to be based upon a historicization of the myth, it would appear to be a tenuous assertion.

Pathmanathan (2000) has pondered the significance of Ibn Battuta's description and approaches the first problem in this way (29–30):

> The besetting difficulty about the description of the temple as recorded by Ibn Battuta pertains to the identity of the temple. There is a certain degree of ambiguity and it is not certain whether he was describing the *devale* of Uppalavanna or a *kovil*, the temple of Visnu. . . . The description is applicable to both types of institutions, as there were basic similarities in the manner in which worship was conducted at them. There is also the possibility that the original character of the *devale* had already been transformed on account of intercultural interactions and such a development could be expected at a port-city inhabited and visited by people of diverse origins and affiliated to a variety of religious traditions. It would appear that the patron deity of Devanagara was supported by kings, Buddhist pilgrims, Hindu merchants and artisans residing in the town. On the other hand, the reference to a *kovil* in an inscription by Parakramabahu II suggests the possibility that the temple described by Ibn Battuta was a Hindu temple of Visnu.

I am unsure about Pathmanathan's comment regarding the basic similarity of worship in a Buddhist *devalaya* and a Hindu *kovil*. There are too many liturgical protocols followed by *brahmanas* which are not attended to by Buddhist *kapuralas* to make this statement with much confidence. (While the basic structure of a sacrifice and petition are present in both, there is a distinctive liturgy in each tradition that specifies the details of worship.)

But the second half of Pathmanathan's statement is quite credible. From all accounts, it would appear that Devinuvara was a veritable crossroads for trade, given its strategic location at the southernmost tip of the South Asian subcontinent. Upulvan was clearly the god of this multicultural city (Devinuvara). While, by the fourteenth century, he was hailed as one of the "four guardian deities" of Lanka" by the Sinhala rulers, it was also possible that, as an iconographically indistinct deity, he was worshipped in any number of ways by various constituencies. Pathmanathan signals this particular understanding himself when he says in the conclusion to his paper (41): "It would appear that the shrine of Uppalavanna was venerated and supported also by Hindu and Chinese merchants who had developed their own beliefs and conceptions in relation to the presiding deity of the city."

Throughout his detailed paper on the cultural history of Devinuvara, Pathmanathan points out, chiefly from inscriptional evidence, that from the thirteenth century onwards, a community of *brahmanas* resided at Devinuvara and received royal patronage from a number of kings, beginning with Parakramabahu II in the thirteenth century and continuing through at least the fifteenth-century reign of Parakramabahu VI. He mentions the possibility that another large Visnu temple existed in Devinuvara, one that coexisted with the Upulvan *devalaya*, and that both may have been ritually administered by this *brahmana* community (41). As for the origins of the Upulvan cult, he speculates that it was a "probably a pre-Buddhist cult which was assimilated by Buddhist tradition" (17). He also cites a commentary to the *Mayura Sandesa* from the seventeenth century in which the author identifies Upulvan as Visnu.[47] In support of the thesis that this was a time when the conflation between Upulvan and Visnu had finally occurred, I cite the Portuguese Roman Catholic priest-historian, Queyroz (1992:441), who describes Devinuvara in the following passage:

> Half a league beyond Mature was a Pagode, which next to that of Triquilemale was one of the greatest resorts in Ceylon, where are found stone pillars which the kings of China ordered to be set up there with Letters of that nation as a token, it seems, of their devotion to those Idols. There was afterwards in that place a church of the Religious of St. Francis transforming the worship of Vixnude Vira Jurica into the worship of the true God. On this spot the Kinglets of times past had their Court, calling it Janura, which means 'City of God.' The Portuguese called it Tanauare from the name of a neighboring village in which lived the dancing girls of that Pagode. The

word Tanauare is also a corruption of the Portuguese, for the proper name must be Natan-uare which means in that language 'come and dance.'

Queyroz goes on to describe the burning and demolition of the temple by Thome de Souza de Arronches, "Captain-major of the sea," who had 120 soldiers accompanying him in 1587 while Rajasimha I of Sitavaka was laying siege to Colombo.[48] Since Queyroz was writing about a century after the events he records, he is reflecting the view that, by at least the late seventeenth century, the shrine at Devinuvara had been nominally identified with Visnu. From Queryoz, it is also reported, as I have mentioned before, that the Kandyan king Rajasimha II (1635–87 C.E.), recaptured the city in the mid-seventeenth century and "rebuilt" the temple of Visnu.

Ilangasinha (336–37) further notes how the *Alutnuvara Devale Karavima*

records that the *brahmins* versed in Vaisnava lore were invited from Ramesvaram to fashion an image of the Devinuvara god. It was just after the red sandal-wood image of Visnu had been washed ashore in the reign of Dapulusen that these exports were brought from Ramesvaram.

The *Alutnuvara Devale Karavima* is dated, according to Ilangasinha and Liyanagamage, to the seventeenth century. Insofar as Visnu has replaced Upulvan as the deity represented by the red sandalwood image who eventually came to up-country Alutnuvara, the identification of Visnu as the "real" god of Alutnuvara already had been accomplished at this time, or at least a change in the myth had been invented (Visnu substituted for Upulvan), to solidify this claim.

From these notices, it can be surmised that the conflation between Upulvan and Visnu occurred somewhere between the fourteenth-century description of Ibn Battuta and the mid-seventeenth century. But since *sandesa* literature consistently refers to two distinct deities and dates to at least mid-fifteenth century, the time frame of the conflation can be narrowed further to this two-hundred-year span (fifteenth to seventeenth centuries C.E.).

Paranavitana's ruminations about this problem are quite suggestive, yet they also remain quite speculative. Speculative as they are, they would seem consonant with Pathmanathan's suggestion that there was a simultaneous cult of Visnu in Devinuvara. Paranavitana, Ilangasinha (336–37), and Pathmanathan argue that it is from the royally supported *brahmanas* at Devinuvara that the identification of Upulvan with Visnu is likely to have occurred, whether as a distinct avatar of Visnu or as Visnu himself (the distinction is, of course, theologically problematic for Puranic tradition).

While Paranavitana (1953:43) believes that the "bow-god" (Dunudeva) at Devinuvara was identified by the Brahman community as Rama and that eventually his cult superceded or eclipsed the cult of Upulvan, and finally turned into a general cult of Visnu, it is also possible that the Brahman community identified Upulvan per se with Rama. This has been Anuradha Seneviratne's (1984a) thesis. There are several references to Rama's bow within folk-ballad literature dedicated to Rama or Upulvan in Kandyan sources. These, indeed, may be shadows of an earlier identification between Upulvan and Rama at Devinuvara. Further, by the early eighteenth century, a land grant made in 1709 by King Narendra Sinha in Kandy, in support of the Maha Devalaya in Kandy, is addressed specifically to Sri Ramacandra, and Khireli Upulvan is given as one of his epithets.[49]

In addition, the *Rama Sandesa*, in the early nineteenth century, addressed to the deity of the Hanguranketa Visnu Devalaya, clearly identifies Rama as the god of the shrine. These pieces of evidence would seem to support a hypothesis that Upulvan was more precisely identified with Rama by *brahmanas* in the later Devinuvara period before the destruction of his temple at the hands of marauding Portuguese in the late sixteenth century c.e. However, the exact truth of the matter may never be known with any degree of certainty. That Upulvan was equated with Rama in later popular Buddhist lore will soon become quite clear. But whether or not this identification actually occurred at Devinuvara only remains a probability.

In conclusion, though comparatively little can be known directly about the cult of Upulvan from the material that has been reviewed in this chapter, it is clear that the very ambiguity of the god's mythic profile lent itself to a variety of interpretations by various religious constituencies: Avalokitesvara, Rama, possibly Ahura Mazda, and finally Visnu. Since Upulvan is not mentioned in any of the sacred, canonical texts of the Sanskrit Hindu or Pali Buddhist traditions, it is impossible to establish his origins within either of these two religions.

Pathmanathan has hazarded the opinion that Upulvan was a "pre-Buddhist deity," but I would modify his suggestion somewhat. It would be difficult to establish that the cult of Upulvan is "pre-Buddhist" per se, as there is no evidence to suggest the presence of his cult before the appearance of Buddhism on the island. It may be more accurate to say that the cult of Upulvan originated amidst Buddhistic people most likely in the southern extremities of the island. What seems clear after Upulvan's introduction is that virtually every notice pertaining to his cult in the Buddhist tradition (the *Mahavamsa-Culavamsa* or the inscriptions left by various Sinhala Buddhist kings) is politically related or politically motivated. He appears as the guardian deity of the Sinhalas and their religion in the *Mahavamsa* colonization myth of Vijaya; he is the patron deity and namesake of an important regional town apparently established in the ninth century by a Buddhist king or contender for the throne; he is thanked by a royal pilgrim (Prince Virabahu) after strategic military victories in the thirteenth century; he is recognized as one of the "four guardian deities" of the island in the fourteenth-century Gampola era; his cult is lavishly patronized by kingship in the fifteenth-century Kotte period; and he is recognized in fifteenth-century *sandesa* literature as perhaps the most powerful of all the gods (*devaraja*), as the one most frequently appealed to for divine assistance to the benefit of the state.

It would therefore not be an exaggeration to suggest that the origins and/or assimilation of the Upulvan cult within Sinhala Buddhist religious culture was politically significant indeed. The myth of the sandalwood image and its extension as an explanatory account of the cult's dissemination from Devinuvara to the central up-country region of the island is linked to the activities of royalty who lent their enthusiasm and resources to establish the cult of Visnu throughout the Kandyan region of the island. This process itself is a good example of the mythicization of history taking place within Sinhala Buddhist religious culture and would seem consonant with the thesis that incorporated additions to a religious tradition are often politically inspired.

The sixteenth-century destruction of the Devinuvara shrine may have been the final blow to Upulvan's cult as a distinctive divinity, at least apart from Visnu. A century later in the mid-seventeenth century, he had been absorbed into the cult of Visnu, as indicated by the fact that when his shrine was rebuilt in Devinuvara, it was dedicated to Visnu. Furthermore, when seventeenth-century texts refer to the dissemination of the Upulvan cult, the god in question is then referred to as Visnu. It could also be said, therefore, that the relative eclipse of the cult of Upulvan, *because* of his high political profile, was also due in part to a singular religio-political act: the desecration and destruction of his shrine at Devinuvara by the politically and religiously hostile Portuguese,[50] and the waning fortunes of Sinhala Buddhist kingship which followed Parakramabahu VI. Since Rajasimha I (1581–93 C.E.) of Sitavaka had converted to Saivism while the Portuguese were destroying the shrine of Upulvan at Devinuvara,[51] it would appear that this is precisely a moment when political support for the cult had either completely evaporated or was deemed incapable of stemming the tide. That does not mean that Upulvan's cult was subsequently completely moribund; for as seen in the next chapter, many references to his divine exploits continue to be told in the later literature of the Kandyan period, although much of it in the name of a "Buddhist Visnu."

It is in the *sandesa* literature of the fifteenth century, in the folk ballads from the seventeenth- through early nineteenth-century Kandyan period, and in the liturgical chants of contemporary ritual specialists that the substance of Upulvan's (and hence the "Buddhist Visnu's") mythic profile becomes much more transparent. Those materials are the focus of the following chapter, an attempt to further an understanding of the content of Visnu's profile within the Sinhala Buddhist religio-cultural context.

TRANSFORMED DEITY

The "Buddhist Visnu" in Sinhala Literature and Liturgy

"Buddhists in a very late stage in their history borrowed the Vishnu image from India, and it found a shrine in their temple. But they do not worship the new god or offer flowers to him [as they do the Buddha]. They merely ask favours and make offerings of tokens, or bribes. To make an immortal god mortal requires, I believe, originality as daring as that required for creating an immortal god for a pantheon, if not more so."
—Martin Wickramasinghe[1]

In several tracts of late medieval Sinhala folk literature dating from the seventeenth through the early nineteenth centuries C.E. and in the contemporary liturgical petitions (*yatika*) chanted by *kapuralas* (shrine priests) recorded recently at important Visnu *devalayas*,[2] Visnu is uniformly praised for his prowess in protecting the *Buddhasasana* ("dispensation") for a period of 5,000 years following the enlightenment of the Buddha. It is his most telling and popular trait in Sinhala Buddhist religious culture. Almost as prevalent are references alluding to Visnu being present and protecting the Buddha from Mara (death personified) along with his forces of fear and seduction during the Buddha's pivotal night of enlightenment. These are two of the especially salient mythic moments, in addition to some others now attributed to Visnu, that derive originally from the cult of Upulvan. The mythic episode of Upulvan's defense of the Buddha, now attributed to Visnu, pushes Visnu's importance for Sinhala Buddhist tradition back to the paradigmatic moment of the life of the Buddha, and hence to the very beginnings of the *Buddhasasana*. It is an event that was later linked to other patriotic deities, including Alutnuvara Deviyo (a.k.a.: Dadimunda, Devata Bandara) and Huniyam, whose cults, as discussed in chapter 7, constitute related subsidiary orientations at the major Visnu *devalayas* in up-country Sri Lanka.

In the present chapter, I will examine mythic references to Upulvan first within the fourteenth- and fifteenth-century early *sandesa* poetic tradition before noting significant references to both Upulvan and Visnu in the Kandyan folk-ballad literature dating from the seventeenth to the nineteenth century. Although I will also examine some other literatures of a liturgical nature as well, in the next chapter I will present and analyze the contemporary *yatikas* (liturgical plaints) of *kapuralas* that I recently recorded in contemporary ritual contexts at important Visnu *devalayas* in up-country Sri Lanka.

In this presentation, what I intend to illustrate follows from what I had indicated in the conclusion to the last chapter's discussion: that the content of the "Buddhist Visnu's" profile derives, in part, from earlier conceptions intrinsic to the Sinhala cult of Upulvan and that the specific identification of Upulvan with Rama, which seems to have originated earlier at Devinuvara, continued to gain in strength in the later Kandyan period before vanishing almost entirely in the twentieth century. I will also indicate how Hindu Puranic traditions were also woven into the evolving Buddhist Visnu cult, producing in the process a truly conflated and transformed deity.

By way of introduction to the general problem of this chapter, however, and before I address the relevant Sinhala literature per se, I will present two *astakas* (eight-versed poems) from a collection of texts used in *bali* rites (of exorcism) that might be observed for virtually any auspicious occasion in Sri Lanka. The first, composed in Sanskrit and very likely the older of the two, is the *Narayana Astaka*. Judging from its orientation, its language, and from a reference within its fourth line, it is apparently a text with a provenance that was traditionally royal. The second, composed in a mix of Sanskrit and Pali, was likely composed much later in time and is clearly of a more popular appeal. When read serially, these two poems are like bookends to the problem at hand, clearly illustrating the types of transitions that Visnu experienced in his adaptation from Hindu to Buddhist cultic orientations. That is, they can be read as "before and after" cameos of his evolving mythic profile. As such, they introduce concisely the fundamental pattern I hope to illustrate in this chapter.

NARAYANA ASATKA[3]

Sri Kanta reposed upon his arm, his body straight and handsome,
Hero of a powerful clan, he glitters in lustrous blue.
Hari! Who subdued the mighty and arrogant Ravana, and mesmerized
   the sagacious Magadhans,
Lord Narayana! Ever-protect our noble commander (*senapati*).

Illustrious son of Dasaratha, dexterous as Drona with weapons, destroyer
   of Dhuryodhana's pride,

Rama, who triumphs over enemies mounting no serious challenge to
    Hanuman's glory,
Hari! Who subdued the mighty and arrogant Ravana, and mesmerized
    the sagacious Magadhans,
Lord Narayana! Ever-protect our noble commander.

Giving us Laksmi, Kaustubha, Parijata, Sura, Dhanvatari, the moon,
The wish-fulfilling cow, the divine elephant, and the heavenly maidens
    led by Rambha,
Hari! Who subdued the mighty and arrogant Ravana, and mesmerized
    the sagacious Magadhans,
Lord Narayana! Ever-protect our noble commander.

Giving us the seven-faced horse, ambrosia, Hari's bow, conch and
    potion,
These are the fourteen jewels, the wishing gems of daily life.[4]
Hari! Who subdued the mighty and arrogant Ravana, and mesmerized
    the sagacious Magadhans,
Lord Narayana! Ever-protect our noble commander!

Sri Rama wears the nine-gemmed ornament! Sri Rama protects this
    world!
Sri Rama is like a thousand rays of sun! Sri Ramachandra is benevolent!
Hari! Who subdued the mighty and arrogant Ravana, and mesmerized
    the sagacious Magadhans,
Lord Narayana! Ever-protect our noble commander!

Sri Rama gives us freedom (*mukti*)! Forever we sing his praise!
Devotion for Sri Ramachandra, the glory of the Raghu clan, who takes
    our fears away.
Hari! Who subdued the mighty and arrogant Ravana, and mesmerized
    the sagacious Magadhans,
Lord Narayana! Ever-protect our noble commander!

O mighty power, threefold power, bearer of the plough and fount of all
    pleasure,
O Narayana of the blessed thirty-three,[5] who chases away the three mis-
    fortunes and three fears,
Hari! Who subdued the mighty and arrogant Ravana, and mesmerized
    the sagacious Magadhans,
Lord Narayana! Ever-protect our noble commander!

Grant us longevity, sons, wealth and glory.

May Sri Lanka be the venue for whatever pleases Lord Rama.

Hari! Who subdued the mighty and arrogant Ravana, and mesmerized
   the sagacious Magadhans,

Lord Narayana! Ever-protect our noble commander![6]

VISNU ASTAKAYA[7]

Selfless giving and moral conduct generated great wisdom,

And by realizing the five great virtues, Visnu shelters us all.

Sri Visnu, Buddha-in-the-making, has realized the ten acts of virtue.

May he assuage all your troubles, heal your illnesses and bring you good
   fortune.

His beautiful body is a resplendent lotus-hue (*utpala varna*).

Lord of this world because of his courage, majesty, wisdom and wealth,

Sri Visnu, Buddha-in-the-making, protects all who petition him.

May he assuage all your troubles, heal your illnesses and bring you good
   fortune.

Like the richly red Mt. Meru that towers above the seven mountain sides

And provides succor and happiness to all people of the Four Great Islands,

Sri Visnu, Buddha-in-the-making, is like the royal wishing-tree of
   Sumeru indeed.

May he assuage all your troubles, heal your illnesses and bring you good
   fortune.

Like Mahesvara's thirty gems that bring prosperity to the Four Quarters,

Like the rain that grows the trees and the creepers,

Sri Visnu, Buddha-in-the-making, sustains this world with his humility
   and compassion.

May he assuage all your troubles, heal your illnesses and bring you good
   fortune.

He dispels the darkness of the three worlds and the Four Great Islands

By cultivating the blue lotus whose color he bears.

Sri Visnu, Buddha-in-the –making, that mighty sun of a thousand rays,

May he assuage all your troubles, heal your illnesses and bring you good
   fortune.

In this world, he protects the auspicious *sasana* of our all-knowing guide,
And his benevolence, virtues, and pleasing qualities permeate the world.
Sri Visnu, Buddha-in-the-making, dispels our delusions.
May he assuage all your troubles, heal your illnesses and bring you good
     fortune.

Casting out *yaksas, pretas, pisacas* and *bhutas*, a harbinger of joy to many,
He safeguards the pure teaching and maintains the *dharma*.
Sri Visnu, Buddha-in-the-making, full of power and majesty,
May he assuage all your troubles, heal your illnesses and bring you good
     fortune.

As the moon opens up the lilies, of the night,
Daily he nurtures happiness and great joy for the wise and virtuous by
     removing their ills and troubles.
Sri Visnu, Buddha-in-the-making, powerful and glorious as the sun,
May he assuage all your troubles, heal your illnesses and bring you good
     fortune.

Early *Sandesa* Literature:
Upulvan Before Visnu

Sandesa literature, though formally a poetic genre, actually provides some detailed information about various aspects of society and culture in Sri Lanka
during the fourteenth and fifteenth centuries. Otherwise known as *duta kavya*,
this poetic genre seems to have been first introduced in Sri Lanka during the
politically precarious fourteenth-century Gampola era, and then further developed significantly in the ensuing fifteenth-century Kotte period. Although
the most noted and accomplished *sandesas* were composed in the fourteenth
and fifteenth centuries, the writing of *sandesas* actually continued into the
nineteenth. H. B. M. Ilangasinha describes the general historical significance of
sandesa literature in the following way:

> The secular outlook of the *sandesas*, in contrast with the exclusively religious
> character of the earlier literary works, allowed more freedom of expression
> for the Sinhalese poets. Thus the poets began to describe contemporary life
> and what they saw around them, the beauties of nature, the forms of wor-
> ship, seats of learning, men of eminence, etc., to an extent never done before.
> These *sandesas* were intended as messages to various gods and distinguished

personalities in the country and they differ in their subjects. They have considerable historical value, for their authors seem to have taken great pains to depict a faithful picture of the society of the time. [35]

It needs to be added that the descriptive perspective cultivated in *sandesa* literature is a perspective that would have been pleasing to the royal patrons of this poetry. That is, *sandesa* poetry seems to have been as politically motivated as it was aesthetically accomplished. But, while comparatively "secularized" in comparison to the literature of the Polonnaruva and Anuradhapura periods, *sandesas* still contain much that is religious in nature.

The *sandesas* are also a pointed example of how Sanskrit literature, as well as the poetry of vernacular languages in South India, had come to influence and enhance the form and content of Sinhala literature by the fourteenth and fifteenth centuries.[8] As with Hindu conceptions of kingship that were generated much earlier in India and then later adapted in Buddhist Sri Lanka, this genre of poetics had been developed in India several centuries earlier, beginning at least in the eighth century C.E. before it began to be cultivated much later in Sri Lanka. A Sinhala translation, with commentary, of Kalidasa's eighth-century C.E. classic, *Meghaduta* ("The Cloud Messenger") had been written by the twelfth-century Polonnaruva era (Godakumbura 1955:140–41). This particularly ornate poem, a Sanskrit literary masterpiece, in which a passing cloud is asked to play an intermediary role in conveying a message of pining love from an exiled *yaksa* to his estranged lover, seems to have become exceedingly paradigmatic in form for Sinhala poetics by the fourteenth and fifteenth centuries. Listening to Sinhala *sandesas* would have constituted a favorite pastime of royalty and courtiers, for its entertaining and sophisticated speech, as well as for its political congeniality.

Godakumbura introduces his chapter on "Sinhalese Sandesa Poems" in his standard work, *Sinhalese Literature* (1955:183), with these words:

The Meghaduta of Kalidasa provided the model for many Sanskrit poets who wrote similar poems. This form of poetical composition, which gave ample opportunity to its author to display his powers of description, had a special appeal to Sinhalese poets. . . . . The Sinhalese Sandesa writers no doubt got the idea of this type of poem from the Meghaduta, but they developed the theme along rather different lines. Later Sanskrit poets used as their message-carriers living beings, chiefly birds, in place of inanimate objects like clouds. The Sinhalese poets did the same, until the very last phase, when some of the Sandesa writers applied the Sinhalese Sandesa and its arrangement differently somewhat from Kalidasa's Meghaduta.

The primary difference between the Kalidasa's Sanskrit *Meghaduta* and the *sandesas* produced by Sinhala poets in the fourteenth and fifteenth centuries lies not so much in the fact that they chose different objects to convey messages. That seems a rather insignificant suggestion by Godakumbura. Instead, the fundamental difference lies in the subject matter and purport: While Kalidasa's work was primarily a poetry of love's emotions at its finest, at many moments aesthetically and subtly suggestive of the erotic, Sinhala *sandesas*, though containing descriptively attractive profiles of divinities, are essentially *political* in intent. They were ostensibly concerned with cultivating divine favor for royal well-being, rather than expressing privately held emotions. To be sure, there are sections in these Sinhala poems in which dancing girls at the temple in Devinuvara, for instance, are described in some alluring detail; but the Sinhala *sandesas* are more formal and "public" in nature than the original *Meghaduta*, and sometimes smack of thinly veiled panegyrics meant to flatter members of the royal family. So, rather than poetics at the service of love's stirring emotions, Sinhala *sandesas* seem to be literary devices wherein a burgeoning aesthetic of language has been enlisted to articulate political aspirations within the state, its administration, and its allied institutions. For instance, as Ilangasinha notes:

> The *Tisara Sandesa* is the oldest of the existing Sinhalese *sandesa* poems, and is attributed to the reign of Parakramabahu V (1344–59) of Dadigama. The purpose of the *Tisara Sandesa* was to convey a message through a swan from Devinuvara to the King (Parakramabahu) at Dadigama to inform him that a monk residing at Devinuvara was in engaged in prayers to Upulvan, that he might be pleased to protect the king and make him victorious over his enemies, and also to bless the royal mother, Sumitra, and to keep watch over his ministers of state [Ilangasinha: 44].

Ilangsinha's summary of the *Tisara*'s intent is quite apt. But a more exact sense of the poem's purpose can be gained by quoting some of its early verses in detail:[9]

> Like a lion who, by the power of his mighty arm shatters the pride of the elephant-like Asuras, Upulvan, the king of the gods of this city, is like the king of the gods in the Tavatimsa heaven.

> The majestic flames of Upulvan have pierced the hearts of enemy kings and have exited through their heads as crest gems. Moreover, those flames pierced the hearts of their wives and were reflected as red rays in their eyes.

When Upulvan's glorious rays spread throughout the world, they
  changed the natural color of all other objects, except for two things: the
  red color in the eyes of enemies' wives and the blue complexion of this
  lord.

Once a *rsi* named Agastya drained the water of the seven seas by cupping
  it within his hands. Although gods and men constantly take in the
  ocean of beauty deriving from the figure of this deity, it never runs dry,
  but continues to grow all the time.

Several verses follow these that continue the description in this manner, including the verse alluded to in the previous chapter, in which Visnu turns dark
as the result of losing Sri Kanta (Laksmi) to Upulvan. What is particularly
striking about this *Tisara* passage is the devastatingly powerful war-like image
of Upulvan that is conjured. At the same time, what the *Tisara Sandesa* seems
to be reflecting is another very interesting and important development in the
history of Sinhala Buddhist religion: an eminent Buddhist monk is portrayed
as appealing to the powers of a divinity in order to insure the protection of
kingship. When the political circumstances of the mid-fourteenth century are
recalled, specifically the precarious situation that Sinhala kings faced in relation to the forces of the Aryacakravarti of Jaffna, it is clear that the intention of
the poem speaks directly to the troubled political context at hand. It would also
seem to signal that the veneration of the gods by Buddhist monks for this-
worldly (*laukika*) political concerns had become regarded, perhaps, as an acceptable or unexceptional practice, at least among a given segment of the
sangha, and therefore quite at variance with the monastic sentiments expressed
in texts like the *Amavatura* and the *Budugunalamkaraya*. The *sandesas* are not
a literature oriented to the religion of renunciation.

Referring more specifically to the popularity and political significance of the
gods, especially Upulvan, in *sandesa* literature, Ilangasinha (328) has written:

Of these [gods], Upulvan seems to have been the most popular god of this
time. His popularity is proved by the fact that the majority of *sandesa*
poems written in this period, namely *Mayura, Kokila, Parevi and Tisara*,
are addressed to him. The functions that this god was requested to carry
out in this period were manifold, but he was specifically expected to grant
political favours to supplicants. [brackets mine]

I am unsure whether or not Upulvan was in reality the most popular Sinhala
deity in the fourteenth and fifteenth centuries, as Ilangasinha suggests. However, I think that what Ilangasinha has alluded to is the very real possibility that

Upulvan was regarded as the most politically significant deity of that time, or that his perceived power (and its function) was regarded as most closely allied to the state's interest. The politically significant profile of Upulvan, of course, is very long-standing, beginning with his warrant to protect Vijaya's men in the *Mahavamsa*, his birth as "king of the gods" as described in the myth of the sandalwood image, and the obvious role he is given in the *Culavamsa*'s account of Prince Virabahu's pilgrimage during the reign of Parakramabau II after the defeat of Chandrabhanu and his mercenary army.

The concluding verses of the poem go even further than what has been indicated thus far in *explicitly* linking the power of the state to Upulvan. In the *Tisara* passage (verse 187) that follows, it can be seen that the specific request being made by the eminent Buddhist monk through his avian messenger is that kingship should be regarded as an extension of divine power aimed at protecting the *Buddhasasana*.

> King of the gods, Upulvan, blessed with all imaginable comforts, although you received your warrant from Sakra, the king of the gods, to protect Sri Lanka, your duty will be much easier if you have the assistance of good kings living in proximity. Kindly protect King Parakramabahu especially as he unites the people of this island of Lanka.

The poem continues on in subsequent verses to ask for Upulvan's protective blessing upon the king's ministers so that they will enjoy glory, wealth, virtue, and longevity.

Upulvan's divine and mythic profile is found in greatest detail within the verses of the *Mayura Sandesa*,[10] which along with the *Tisara Sandesa*, was composed during the politically tenuous Gampola era. These two *sandesas* were paradigmatic for the many other *sandesas*, including the *Hamsa, Parevi, Gira, Kokila,* and *Salalihini*, which followed in the fifteenth-century Kotte period. In the lengthy *Mayura* passage that follows, Upulvan's body and his this-worldly (*laukika*) power are first described in effulgent (and sometimes ingratiating) language, before the clear intention of the poem to invoke Upulvan's protection of the state is finally stated. I quote from the *Mayura* at some length not only to illustrate this fundamental point about the worldly and political character of this poetry, but also to illustrate its uses of language, imagery, and mythic allusion:

133. Worship at the feet of the lord, who directly maintains the happiness of the world, who is like the moon in spreading pure and clear luster, an ocean of the cool waters of compassion, like the rain-cloud-deity who dispels drought.

134. He is Lanka's water-source. Hundreds of moons, and a myriad of red jewels glistening like a coral tree in full bloom, are born in his crown.

135. Can the lightning of the deep blue thunder-cloud be compared with the glittering gold band worn on Upulvan's forehead? Does lightning last as long?

136. Can the brilliance of the sun compare to the glow of round gold ornaments on his lotus-like face, which shine like two discs of the sun? A single sun is not even one three hundred sixtieth as bright!

137. Can the blue lotus compare to the eyes of this lord, which with a single benign glance bestows abundance upon those who call for him?

138. No one knows the whereabouts of Indra's bow which disappeared quietly before the wondrous eyebrows of this lord, eyebrows like fish-hooks attracting the fish-eyes of heavenly *apsaras*.

139. His navel is like a garden in bloom watered by the fertile glances of noble women fascinated by his form, a garden spreading even to his lower line of hair.

140. On his vast breast that contains the waters of compassion is a pearl necklace, like a line of waves on a pond. Like fish swimming about in that pond, the shadowy eyes of heavenly *apsaras* reflect.

141. Even Ananta, the king of the *nagas*, cannot describe his two arms that fall on to the shoulders of heavenly *apsaras* accompanying Lakshmi.

142. Lakshmi prefers to ever-reside close to his lotus-like face, Sarasvati reclines on his breast. Nothing in these three worlds can compare to the arms that possess Sri!

143. Three enticing wrinkles on his slender waist are marks of the heavy weight of the compassion born by his upper torso.

144. The legs of this lord cannot even be compared to the trunks of elephants, for trunks have cavities. Perhaps the neck of a peacock is comparable, if its thinness at the top is disregarded.

145. The toe nails of this god are extremely brilliant, like the *malati*
     flowers worn by Laksmi in her hair, or like pearls cast ashore by the
     waves of the sea, or, like the feather-like specks in the eye lashes of
     Asuras which Brahma forgot to glue at the beginning of time.

146. Two eyes cannot absorb the inconceivable ocean of this god's
     beauty, beauty that makes all who behold him wonder-struck.

147. He is ever foremost in providing prosperity to the world. To all who
     contemplate him, wealth is assured. If he enters dreams, all dangers
     vanish. He dispenses glory, power, wealth and long-life.

148. However poets may describe, the powers of the wishing-gem and
     the heavenly cows are never combined. Yet you, O lord, your
     propensity for charity is but a part of all your other virtues.

148. Goddesses dwelling on Mount Meru, in the Himalayas, those living
     at the foot of wishing-trees in the Nandana garden, and those along
     the shores of the rivers in heaven, sing praises of this lord.

150. Indeed, it would be difficult even for the *naga*-king Ananta with his
     thousand mouths to describe but a fraction of Upulvan's glory,
     glory that has spread throughout the universe for the benefit of
     those many who have called upon him.

151. Contemplating his glory, approach this god who is as brilliant as
     the crown jewels of *asura* kings, who is the great benefactor and
     protector of justice, and offer up the reason for your arrival.

152. Dear friend! Plead in this way: "King Bhuvanekabahu, our lord and
     illustrious ruler of the world, makes this request. 'Since you, lord,
     with your mighty power zealously protect this world and Lanka in
     particular, cast down your compassionate glance and destroy all of
     his enemies from all quarters, quell what is against order in the
     country, and grant him all power to rule with justice so that this
     country will be like the Ocean of Milk turning into the Ocean of
     Gold and vice-versa.'"

152. Further, worship this lord once again and request his protection for
     Queen Chandravati who is pleasant and adorable like Sri Kanta
     [Laksmi], who glorifies the lineage of the sun like a moon shining

over the Ocean of Milk, who benefits the world by her great charity like the wishing creeper, who is always lovable, an unguent on the bodies of all women, who is the foremost in glory, kinship, beauty and virtue. Finally, request that she should be blessed with a son, like a gem, who will perpetuate the royal lineage and become a crowning glory to her.

154. May this deity of Lanka also grant great abundant wealth and prosperity to increase the affluence of the three lords who are like Mount Meru flanked by the sun and moon, namely: Alagakkonara, our lord who is embraced by Laksmi herself, whose ocean of praises are now renown; the heir-apparent [Apa], who is virtuous and glorious, a master of the strategic; and Lord Dev-himi [Devasvami], who in his benevolence and wealth, is like a wishing-tree to the people.

The *sandesa* continues on for several more verses, asking Upulvan to protect specifically the king's Tamil bodyguards (*agampodi*), the battalions of the royal army including its mercenaries, the political and administrative officials at the capital, including the minister in charge of elephants and the minister in charge of the clerical division; and finally, long life is sought for the Ven. Dharmakirti (at Gadaladeniya)[11] as well as the *bhikkhus* and *samaneras* of both the *gamavasi* (village) and *vanavasi* (forest-dwelling) fraternities of monks. It is a remarkable series of verses yielding considerable insight into Upulvan's distinct and overt role as the divine protector of all important aspects of the state's administrative power and its religion. I have quoted it at length not only because it is the most detailed account of Upulvan within the *sandesas*, but also because of the number of important issues it presents for discussion.

The first is the manner in which Upulvan is understood within this passage to be the most eminent of the gods in the divine pantheon. All of the others to which he is compared are, in fact, of Sanskrit and Hindu origins. I have noted in previous discussions that Upulvan is often referred to in the *Culavamsa* and in many royal inscriptions as *devaraja* or "king of the gods," an epithet often used in connection with Sakra, the Buddhist transformation of Indra. Verses 135 and 138 contain allusions to Upulvan's superiority in relation to Indra: verse 135 indicating that the deep-blue thundercloud and its lightning—one of the most frequent ways of depicting the presence of Indra in Vedic literature, can't compare in glory to the shining gold headband of Upulvan; verse 138 indicating that Indra's bow has quietly vanished in the presence of Upulvan. Similarly, the passage implies that Upulvan is beyond comparison or superior to Surya (the sun in verse 135), Visnu, Siva, and Brahma. Ananta, the *naga*-king mentioned in verses 141 and 150, who cannot describe the greatness of Upul-van even with his thousand mouths, is the serpent that Visnu is known to rest upon in between the creation of *yugas* ("world aeons"). While Siva is normally portrayed with a moon in his hair, Upulvan sports hundreds of them in his crown (verse 134). Laksmi and Sarasvati, the traditional spouses or consorts of Visnu and Brahma in Puranic Hinduism, prefer to dwell with Upulvan in a rather intimately described fashion than with their traditional divine mates.

Upulvan, then, is understood in this passage to be the greatest of gods, be-yond the equal of any other, the foremost in providing for the *laukika* welfare of those who call upon him, with happiness, prosperity, and fertility. At the same time, there isn't a hint in these verses of the Puranic Hindu soteriologi-cal concern for *moksa* (transcendence of rebirth). Upulvan appears, instead, as a kind of "super-Vedic" deity prepared to respond with bounty.

More significant for the profile that Upulvan will later bequeath to the even-tual "Buddhist Visnu" is the manner in which he is not only regarded as the great patron of prosperity, but also of the religion, and especially of the state.[12] The last is emphasized to such an extent that it seems as if the most important specific divine favor Upulvan is asked to grant is a male offspring to carry on the royal lineage. Moreover, the appeal made to Upulvan mentions the need to empower the king so that he might rule with justice, a motif that seems to en-noble the *Mayura*'s plea beyond that of the *Tisara*'s, where the appeal is more directly for sheer political power. Similarly, the later *Hamsa* [verse 198] and *Kokila* [verse 289] *sandesas* appeal almost nakedly for power without any men-tion of justice. As Visnu is always so allied with the interests of *dharma* in the Hindu context, Upulvan is so linked here, but the meaning of *dharma* is more thoroughly moral in nature within this *Mayura* context. Within the contem-porary cult of the "Buddhist Visnu," it is often this concern for ethical justice that accounts for Visnu's elevated stature in relation to the lesser deities related to his cult.

Unlike the great gods of Hindu tradition to whom Upulvan is so favorably compared in this passage, and despite all of his resplendent glories described in such an overblown fashion, his power is decidedly *laukika* ("worldly") in character. Unlike Visnu and Siva in the Puranic context, Upulvan is not the kind of deity who is the object of bhakti devotion, or a god who intercedes salv-ifically. There is no element of transcendence in his profile whatsoever.

This is an important point to remember when regarding the character of the "Buddhist Visnu:" in the context of the religious culture of the Sinhala Buddhists—he has been stripped of his direct soteriological importance. He becomes important in relation to, rather than being constitutive of, the sum-mum bonum of the religion. Yet he is a god who assists devotees in their ne-gotiations with the difficulties of existence. Insofar as Buddhism is a religion that is concerned primarily with assuaging the experience of *dukkha* ("unsatisfactoriness") in the human condition, Visnu's profile, understood in this way, can certainly be rationalized on Buddhist soteriological grounds, but there is never a suggestion that the god can provide a means for the final attainment of the religious goal: *nibbana* (nirvana).

That the transformed "Buddhist Visnu" is legitimated in relation to, rather than constitutive of, the final religious goal is clearly illustrated in the early verses (4–5) of the *Mayura Sandesa*, wherein Upulvan is linked to the significance of the Buddha's enlightenment experience:

4.   Living in the "City of the god" [Devinuvara], displaying the power of his bow, with his fame spreading in the four directions, on the day that the recluse Siddhartha gained enlightenment, Upulvan received the warrant so that the country would be prosperous and magnificent.

5.   On the morning of Siddhartha's enlightenment, Mara, appearing in a terrible disguise, approached the Vajrasana with the idea of capturing it. While all the gods fled in fear, Siddhartha sat firmly like a singular kingly lion.

Verse 4 recalls Upulvan's role in the *Mahavamsa*'s myth of Vijaya and the prototypical Sinhalas. In a later seventeenth-century commentary on the fourteenth-century *Mayura Sandesa* (1929:213–18), Ven. Dipankara adds in relation to verse 5 that, while all of the other gods in attendance at the Buddha's enlightenment had fled with the appearance of Mara, *Visnu* (rather than Upulvan) remained behind with the Buddha, protecting him with his mighty bow, so that Mara himself became terrified. Visnu's association with, and hence his legitimation by, this extremely important mythic moment appears, then, to have been well known by this time. Like Geiger in the early twentieth century, Ven. Dipankara justified his identification of Upulvan with Visnu on the basis of his blue color. In the later *Kokila Sandesa* of the fifteenth century, Upulvan is manifestly and specifically identified as having played this role on the night of the Buddha's enlightenment, as part of his larger cosmic role of defeating the forces of chaos. Two verses of the *Kokila*[13] express this understanding directly:

23.   By bravery and might equal to Lord Visnu, expressing anger he defeated the cruel and proud *asuras*. And now, he happily protects the *Buddhasasana*, that good king, Kihirali Upul, who lives here.

30.   As the *bodhisatva* sat on the Diamond-throne, Vasarvarti [Mara]
       rapidly approached to wage war. Fearlessly, this god displayed the
       power of his bow. So, how can I further describe the majesty of his
       power?

Familiarity with this *Kokila* passage may have been the reason why Ven. Dipankara extracted the meaning of *Mayura* verse 5 in the manner that he did.
In any case, the original identity of the deity (later identified in various literary
sources as Visnu, Devata Bandara, or Huniyam) who assists the Buddha
against Mara during his enlightenment experience is clearly Upulvan. In addition, the method by which he conquered Mara, his bow, later becomes the valorized object of a number of folk-ballad sources. The power of Upulvan's (and
hence Visnu's) bow is enlisted to overcome the affects of sorcery or possession.
But what is of signal importance here is that within the century between the
fourteenth-century *Mayura* and the fifteenth-century *Kokila*, the conflation
between Upulvan and Visnu had been effected.

Late Medieval Sinhala Ballads and Liturgies: Upulvan as Visnu

One of the perplexing patterns encountered in exploring the significance of
Visnu in Sinhala Buddhist culture is that, while this important deity is quite
ubiquitous, and therefore conspicuous, within cultic village temple contexts
throughout the countryside, there is a comparative paucity of literature, either
classical or popular in character, in which Visnu figures as a lead mythic player.
In the many myths where he is mentioned, Visnu is often a part-time player,
darting in and out of the lives of other deities who are clearly the protagonists
of the story at hand. The same is true in many ritual contexts where his power,
along with the powers of the other three guardian or "warrant" deities of the
island (warranted by the Buddha or higher gods like Visnu to act within the
human world), is merely propitiated in a formal manner, almost as a matter of
courtesy. In these instances, Visnu remains as a constant, yet something of a
background figure.

Nonetheless, Visnu does appear very often, if only in passing, in a wide body
of folk literature. Sometimes he is clearly embodying the profile he assumed
from Upulvan that has just been elaborated in relation to *sandesa* literature. At
other times, elements of his Sanskrit Hindu Puranic profile predominate. Most
often, elements from both the Upulvan and Puranic profiles are combined in
relation to other concerns of intrinsic importance to popular Sinhala religion.
A review of this genre of literature reveals the fact that Visnu has been reli-

giously valorized very deeply within Sinhala Buddhist culture. That is, while I have argued for and demonstrated the political impetus for Upulvan's identity and Visnu's inclusion within the Buddhist religious culture of the Sinhalas, it does not follow from this that the significance of the "Buddhist Visnu" has been solely political in nature for his subsequent devotees. A study of Visnu's profile within the context of folk-ballad literature and ritual liturgies reveals a myriad of ways in which his divine power was envisaged and entreated once he had been assimilated into popular belief and cultic practice. That is, while political machinations may have figured in the formal recognition or accommodation of his cult, individuals who have personalized his cult clearly have done so for reasons other than political. (This issue will be addressed squarely in chapters 5 through 8).

Neither Neville, in his *Sinhala Kavi* (1954), nor Barnett, in his "Alphabetical Guide to Sinhalese Folklore from Ballad Sources," two major reference works that serve as detailed indices to this genre of popular literature, discriminate between Upulvan and Visnu in their categorically descriptive entries. It is clear, as I have mentioned before, that both Neville and Barnett assumed that Upulvan was simply Visnu; they were not aware of the earlier separate identities of the two gods, nor would the content of much of the literature that they surveyed have provided them with many reasons to suspect such separate origins. For, by the time that these ballads were constructed, the identity of both deities had been confused, or better *conflated*.

Yet, given the nature of the sources at hand and what has been ascertained in the previous chapters, it is now possible to identify two streams of myth that were conflated in the cultic context, producing an image of a deity whose powers have been recognized and deployed (by royalty, shrine priests, poets, devotees) in at least three different ways (see below).

In this section, then, I will try to illustrate how these two mythic streams were compatible with one another and were combined for many purposes. In this process of conflation, particular elements of Upulvan's and Visnu's earlier mythic profiles were both stressed, on the one hand creating a "Buddhist Visnu" more variegated than the earlier Upulvan, and on the other a "Buddhist Visnu" far more entwined in the worldly affairs of his devotees, and much less soteriologically significant, than the Hindu Visnu of Puranic origins. As Wickramasinghe has noted (see chapter epigraph), the Sinhalas succeeded creatively in making a mortal deity out of an immortal one.

That said, it becomes obvious that there exists a number of layers to the divine personality of Visnu as it is portrayed in popular Sinhala Buddhist literature, deriving from the Upulvan and Puranic streams. In the seventeenth-through nineteenth-century folk-ballad literature collected by Neville and summarized by Barnett, Visnu's power, and thus his religious valorization, is, as I have said, invoked in at least three major ways. The first is how he is identified as an intrinsic force related to the mythic creation of ritual objects of central importance to Sinhala cultic practice, or even to the creation of the cosmos itself. The second is the power he is perceived to maintain in relation to problems of preventing or curing illness or sorcery. And finally, there is his mythic profile, his divine personality as a guardian or "boon-conferring" deity, derived from his characterization in a variety of colorful stories explaining how his powerful presence was instrumental in the establishment of a variety of cultic activities. A closer examination of these layers should disclose the evolving character of this conflated god.

Visnu and Origins

A persistent trait of South Asian religious cosmology is seen very clearly in one of the most well-known Brahmanical creation myths, in the *Rg Veda*, hymn X: 90. In this famous passage about the sacrificial dismemberment of the primordial cosmic man, Purusa, the practice of assigning or identifying various elements of Purusa's biological or physical body with natural, social, or cosmic elements, which in turn are further identified with the corresponding powers of various deities, is enshrined. That ancient, priestly, Brahmanical practice is continued in the late medieval Sinhala literature now under consideration. In a series of folk ballads from the seventeenth through the nineteenth centuries, Visnu is identified variously as playing an important role in the origins of various ritual objects or cultural constructions. These specific identifications reflect just how thoroughly his perceived powers were integrated and valorized by the late medieval Sinhalas.

For instance, the *Dalumura Upata Sinhala Kavi* 1:287) is a story explaining the origin of the betel leaf. The offering of betel is one of the most common forms of ritual that convey an attitude of supplication on the part of a sacrificer to an honored receiver. It connotes hierarchy and respect. In this *kavi* (poem), the original betel plant is said to have grown in six different directions associated with six different colors. Gods, in turn, are identified with these directions and colors: Kadawara is identified with the northwest and the color of copper; Pattini with the north and the color of white; Sakra with the east and the color green or blue (*nil*); Natha with the southwest and the color of bronze; while Visnu is associated with the south and, like Sakra, with the color green or blue (*nil*). The mythic theme being articulated here is that betel is inclined to grow in the direction of the gods. It is a sacred plant. Further, the ballad continues its account by noting that on the south side of the leaf (however that could be determined!), *rsi*'s (seers) reside; on the reverse side, the goddess Uma (traditional spouse of Siva); at the stalk, Brahma; and at the very tip of the betel leaf, Visnu is found. The obvious point of the song is that betel leaf is imbued with a sacred presence, including the divinity of Visnu.

The offering of betel is probably the most prevalent form of ritual behavior expressing respect and gratitude. Offering betel to a deity and requesting that the deity be present upon an altar's flower offering for the duration of a ritual proceeding is also one of the most common elements found in virtually all Sinhala ritual liturgies. While Visnu may be present intrinsically in a betel leaf, his powerful presence can only be drawn out for whatever purpose through a direct invocation by means of incantation. In the liturgical example provided below, which consists of a poem sung during the ritual offering of betel to Visnu, Hindu and Buddhist elements of Visnu's popular and conflated mythic profile that signal the type of power being ritually induced, may be clearly seen.

OFFERING OF BETEL TO VISNU[14]

1.   Taking golden bow in hand
     As he gives witness to creation's unfolding,
     Sri Visnu vows to attain Buddhahood.
     Knowing his great powers, I worship him.

2.   They gathered in Jambudipa [India],
     Were sent to Lanka with *pirit*,
     Brought at that time by
     Sri Visnu who came to this land.

3.   Seeing enemy *yaksas*,
     Binding them with *pirit* and throwing them north,
     Subjugating other *yaksas*,
     Did Visnu's incarnations contend.

4.   With his eternal disc of power and rule,
     Custodian of the Buddha's dispensation,
     Protector of land and royalty,
     May god Utpalavan come to this altar.

5.   God Narayana with his ten *avatars* takes charge of all Lanka.
     He comes as a flame with blue rays of diamond brilliance.
     Cruel, wicked and savage *yaksas* are scorched by his flame.
     O Visnu, divine-eyed one, come to this flower altar without
        delay!

6.   Wearing blue floral clothes and a twisted golden necklace, he
             comes!
        Intending to be Buddha, he defeats Mara's army and fulfills the
             *paramita*s.
        His bow, tinkling sonorously throughout the heavens, is taken with
             resolve in hand.
        Do come, O Narayana, to this flower altar! I hear him coming!

7.   With a long holy hand like a deep blue cloud,
        He draws that bow with the tinkling sound in gathering clouds.
        Upul, Rama, appear as incarnations among Narayana's ten *avatar*s.
        Please accept this betel, incense, sandal, and flowers.

8.   "After five thousand years of prosperity, I shall attain Buddhahood.
        Like the moon over the milky ocean, Lanka will remain shining in
             glory."
        The golden curtain of the Vaikuntha mansion opens!
        May your compassion prevail for five thousand years! The *deva* is
             coming!

9.   Seven sable-tail fan bearers holding golden bows and arrows flank
        The blue curtains, canopied bright white parasols in the middle of
             Vaikuntha palace.
        God Pulvan, God Narayana, will become the Buddha in the future.

May you, Narayana, accept our offerings of flowers and betel with affection.

10.[15] Vasudeva, Supreme Brahman, "Thatness" [*tanmurti*], the Highest
             Purusa,
        The unmanifest, beyond qualities [*nirguna*], tranquil,
        I worship you in the name of Sri Visnu.

11.[16] Om, hram, hrim, hrum! May Sri Visnu, highest of the gods,
        Come from East India to this auspicious moment.
        Accept! Accept! Stay! Support! Support! Protect! Be victorious!

This is a remarkably composite summary of many of Visnu's traits now constituting his profile within popular Sinhala Buddhist religion. Here, at least three of his mythic layers are evident: allusions to his relation to the *Buddhasasana* (as Upulvan); his Hindu Puranbic profile; and his role in dispelling *yaksa* forces of potential illness and chaos.

In relation to the first of these, Visnu 1) is said to be destined for Buddha-hood himself in his effort to perfect the *paramitas*; that is, he is a bodhisatva; 2) is identified as Upulvan, the guardian deity who first protected the Buddha from Mara, then provided *pirit* (incantations of sutras, regarded as a form of protective power) to Vijaya's men; and 3) continues to protect the *sasana* for 5,000 years. These are the most obvious Buddhistic elements. In relation to the second, the Hindu elements, he is invoked as Narayana, who appears in the world through his ten avatars. Upulvan and Rama are mentioned especially in this connection. Allusions are made to Visnu's celestial Vaikuntha palace and to his primordial creative act of churning the Ocean of Milk. He is equated with Brahman, here understood as "thatness," a Brahmanic formula for iden-tifying the fundamental reality of the cosmos—a tradition of conceptual spec-ulation that goes back to the earliest Upanisads. He is also referred to as *nir-guna*, "without qualities," signaling his ultimate transcendence of the samsaric world. Sanskrit mantras are deployed to affect the powers of Visnu in the song's conclusion. In relation to the third, Visnu's bow is seen as having power to subdue the malfeasance of *yaksas*, and he is celebrated as a mighty van-quisher of these powerful foes.

What is remarkable is how these three mythic layers are so fully integrated in this brief passage. For instance, the concept of Visnu's avatars is seen as a method by which *yaksas* are subdued. Or Upulvan, the great protector of the *sasana*, is here understood as being one of Visnu's avatars. And finally, Visnu is regarded as a bodhisatva intent on the achievement of nirvana. The interplay of mythic motifs drawn originally from a variety of different sources is thus thoroughly and harmoniously effected.

While the offering of betel, accompanied by ritual chant, is a common pro-cedure in Sinhala deity propitiation, the use of coconuts in a variety of ritual-istic ways is only slightly less common. In the *Pol Upata* (*Sinhala Kavi* 2:103), a story about the origins of the coconut, there is also another series of inter-esting allusions and identifications somewhat similar to what was noted in the discussion of the betel leaf. In this instance, the myth is about how "king co-conuts" (*tambili*) first had to be grown before they could be procured for a rit-ual designed to cure a king of his illness. Ganesa and Visnu are identified with the fruit, or the edible pulp, of the coconut. They are intrinsically present in what is nourishing and medicinal.

With regard to another myth of this specific genre, an account of the origins of the torch used in the *Yak Puda Piliwela* (*Sinhala Kavi* 2:132), a ritual offer-ing meant to placate *yaksas*, it is said that Kanda Kumara (a.k.a. Skanda, Kataragama Deviyo) resides in the body of the torch, Visnu in the oil, and Pat-tini in the flame. As in the two previous cases of the betel leaf and the coconut, wherein Visnu is said to dwell intrinsically, but must also be invoked directly to unharness his powers for specific purposes, Obeyesekere has recorded an excellent example of how the ritual offering of the torch to Visnu, replete with many mythic allusions, attempts to set into motion a number of different types of protective forces.[17]

> Heavy with prosperity, this blessed Sri Lanka!
> The birth of god Visnu in old times [I recount]
> Whose blessings spread wide
> Whose glory o'erspreads the earth
> Like the moon shining o'er the world.
>
> Fathered by King Sundara
> Of Candravati his queen
> From her womb rose a craving
> [That her son to be born]
> Would with filaments of flowers
> Placed on his blessed hands
> [Worship the Buddha]
> And wage war against Mara
> And thereby attain warrant [from the Buddha].
>
> By that queen's wish
> Ten months elapsed
> And she felt birth pains
> On the full moon of Poson [June]
> Under the sign of Aquarius [*kumbha*]
> And the *dasa* [period] of Saturn [*senasuru*].
> Then the Brahman named Jyoti
> Served him with gold milk [ran kiri]
> And named him Great Visnu [Maha Visnu]
> And then with gold ornaments
> He decked the god.
>
> Full seven years went by
> Till the Mara war was won
> And then our Muni with pleasure
> Named his Glorious Visnu [*teda* Visnu]
> In charge of Sri Lanka.
>
> He was asked to measure
> The earth in three steps,
> And take charge of it.

But he couldn't complete it
And was given the title Ada Visnu [half-Visnu]
On the third occasion
At the city of Visala
He banished the demons
And was named Mulu Visnu [complete Visnu]
On the fourth occasion
He was named Sri Visnu
And on the fifth occasion
He was given the title of Maha Visnu.
[Taking the forms of ten avatars
Obtaining *varan* ten times
To protect the Buddha *sasana*].[18]

As instructed [by the Buddha]
We give you merit O king
All of us who live in Sri Lanka
By offering you a torch of time.
From the suffering that has befallen us
Help us cross over to the other shore!
We'll take an emerald[s]
And place it above.

As the goddess Pattini wished
You created a stone raft
For Prince Devol to land
At the shrine of Sinigama.
You gave him a warrant to land there.
In a *gurulu* [eagle] vehicle
The king of the gods was invited (to Sinigama).
From that day it's been told to us
To give prime place to Visnu
And secondarily to the god Devol
To allocate special [coconut] trees from the orchard
And make oil from them and
Make a torch of time
And offer merit to the god as instructed.
Today also to this god, we give
The merit from this [torch] offering.

O god Maha Visnu
I sing about your goodness

Listen with your divine ear
And see with your divine eye
Come down into this dance arena [ranga mandala]
And for the *atura*s here
Ninety-eight types of *roga* [diseases]
And ninety-nine *vyadhi* [pains] banish
And two hundred and three dangers
Banish forever.
May you live long—may your beauty increase. . . .
[all brackets and parentheses in Obeyeskere's text]

Obeyesekere (1984:106) has commented extensively on the significance of this poem for illustrating how Visnu has been "incorporated into a Buddhist framework." He points out: 1) how Visnu's birth to King Sundara and Queen Candravati on the full-moon day of Poson *poya* (the day in June each year when the introduction of the religion to the island is celebrated) indicates that "Visnu's birth [has been] given Sinhala Buddhist legitimacy"; 2) how Visnu is linked to Mara's defeat; 3) how he is given a warrant (*varama*) to protect Lanka; 4) how "an attempt is made to retranslate [Visnu's] ten forms into a Buddhist idiom"; 5) how the famous Vedic myth of the three strides is reworked in a way that demonstrates how "the Buddhists have symbolically cut Visnu down to size . . ." but later he is "given a chance to be whole or complete . . . when he banished the demons of disease . . . thereby performing an exemplary Buddhist deed . . . [by being] linked to the Buddhist mythology of the *Ratana Sutta*"; and 6) how "the concept of the ten avatars is related to the notion of a warrant (*varama*) given by the Buddha to Visnu ten times to protect the Buddhist church (*sasana*)."

Obeyesekere's observations are compelling and supportive of the discussion at hand. Visnu's Puranic profile is accommodated, enlisted, and subordinated. It is conflated with the mythic events associated with Upulvan. His power is put to use to protect the supplicants from illness and disease. In turn, they transfer merit to Visnu to aid him in his quest for *nibbana*. He is linked to a lesser deity (Devol) of the Sinhala pantheon, just as he is linked to Alutnuvara Deviyo and Huniyam. Links of this nature localize his presence and in the process make powerful his immediate significance.

In these three mythic instances discussed so far—the origins and offering of the betel leaf, the coconut, and the ritual torch—it is clear that Visnu has been valorized as a power intrinsic to the wholesome forces of the cosmos in general, and to the well-being made possible by the Buddhist dispensation specifically. But as Wickramasinghe and Obeyesekere have pointed out, Buddhists have "cut him down to size," or transformed Visnu from immortal to mortal.

Perhaps it might be just as accurate to say that Visnu's powers have not been reconceived in this process; rather, they seem to have been reoriented, and placed at the service of the Buddhist worldview and its constitutive social and soteriological values.

Visnu is also connected intimately to yet another myth of origins preserved in the *Visnu Widiya Kavi* (*Sinhala Kavi* 1:341). The same general dynamic suggested by Wickramasinghe and Obeyesekere is even more graphically apparent in this instance. This song begins with verses recounting Vijaya's arrival on the island and Visnu's (by this time replacing Upulvan) giving of the *pirit* thread for protection from *yaksas*. But then the myth takes a decidedly different turn from its *Mahavamsa* version. Following the familiar account of Vijaya's landing and Visnu's reception of his men, Brahma appears and calls upon Visnu to measure the waters of a great flood that is occurring. Visnu dives into the water (reminiscent of his boar incarnation), and plants a lotus seed, which grows into a flower that blossoms with five petals. On each of these five petals, Brahma finds a robe that he keeps—one for each of the five Buddhas who will appear during this *kalpa*. The beginning of the *kalpa* commences from this moment. These robes are given by Brahma to Buddhas on the occasion of their enlightenments. Only one remains at this time—for the future Buddha Maitreya. The song concludes with a reference to Visnu, who then takes his three strides to measure out the cosmos.

This last story of this type, the story of the beginning of this *kalpa* and the concomitant appearance of the Buddhas' robes, is a perfect illustration of how Hindu elements have been combined with Buddhist motifs to produce a specifically "Buddhist Visnu." In this myth, the Buddhist elements stress Visnu's role as the patron of the *Buddhasasana* by not only recalling the *Mahavamsa*'s episode of Upulvan's meeting with Vijaya's men, but also by adding the interesting feature that it is through Visnu's function as a cosmic creator[19] (drawn explicitly from his Hindu Puranic profile and signaled by his diving into the primeval waters and his planting of the lotus seed), and through his role in establishing the order of that creation (again, drawn explicitly from his Vedic profile—the measuring of the cosmos in three strides), that the robes of Buddhas in this *kalpa* are accounted for. That is, the cosmogonic powers of the Hindu Visnu are here enlisted to support the appearance of the symbol par excellence (the robe) of Buddhist soteriology. It is also an obvious example of the conflations that have occurred in the construction of the profile of the "Buddhist Visnu."

Visnu and Exorcism

Among the many allusions to Visnu's ability to cure sickness and to assist in exorcisms—allusions to what becomes a major dimension of the cult of the

"Buddhist Visnu" in contemporary Sri Lanka—there is a cycle of folk ballads which refer to the powers associated with Visnu's "golden bow." Indeed, the first line of the "Offering of Betel to Visnu," quoted in full above, refers to "taking the golden bow in hand." In the previous chapter, it was noted that "the bow god" mentioned in the *Kokila Sandesa* was possibly a subsidiary deity, *possibly* identified with Rama at Devinuvara. But, also with reference to a verse noted in the *Mayura Sandesa*, Upulvan was, like Rama, renowned for the prowess of his golden bow. In Sanskrit literature and Hindu iconography, the bow is not an attribute especially associated with Visnu. It is, however, often an attribute of Rama. Thus, its emphasis in Sinhala folk-ballad literature derives from its associations with either Upulvan or with Rama, or possibly both—the distinction between the two figures having become less and less apparent as the conflation process intensified within the Sinhala cult of the "Buddhist Visnu."

In any case, this cycle of ballads is well worth close scrutiny, as it provides an entrée into a discussion of Visnu's power as it relates to the alleviation of suffering brought about by sorcery, possession, and illness. Moreover, overcoming the deleterious powers of *yaksas* has become almost a sine qua non for all deities in Sri Lanka. If they are not presently entreated for assistance in overcoming the powers of *yaksas,* it is still likely that they have achieved their status mythically in the past by subduing them.

Despite their titles, which would seem to indicate that they might be substantial referents, *Randunu Kavi, Randunu Upata,* and *Ran Dunu Mangalle* (*Sinhala Kavi* 3:172–73 and 1:125] are rather straightforward ballads that invoke the power of the golden bow (*ran dunu*) within the context of exorcisms. The last of these refers to some ten golden bows at play in the sky, an allusion perhaps to each of Visnu's avatars. It also describes the power of the golden bow to combat sorcery, and to break stone and iron. What is also interesting in this *kavi* is that the epithets for Visnu include Rama Raja, Pulvan Surindu, Narayana, and Kihireli Narayana. The mentioning of these four names together signals a complete conflation among Visnu, Rama, and Upulvan.

There are two other ballads, besides these, of a mythically very substantial nature to consider here in detail. The first is the *Randunu Alattiya* (*Sinhala Kavi* 2:136) or "Praise of the Golden Bow." The myth recounted here is a kind of addendum to the story of Visnu protecting the Buddha from Mara on the night of his enlightenment experience. Visnu's sister, Manikpala, was cursed by Mara in an act of revenge, so Visnu set out to find the golden bow which had the power to break Mara's sorcery.

In a related saga (the *Manikpala Sahalla* in *Sinhala Kavi* 2:136), Mara assumes the form of a snake, who entwines itself around the feet of Manikpala and then enters into her womb. (Neville notes that in yet other versions of this story, the entry of the snake occurs only within a dream.) To relieve Manikpala of her distress from the serpent's possession, Visnu heroically searches for the golden bow in all of the world's seas, including the Salt Sea, the Blue Sea, the Blood Sea, and the Deep (Silent) Sea, but to no avail. Finally he discovers the golden bow in the Ocean of Milk, which he proceeds to churn with all of his might. As the golden bow floats up from the ocean's depths to the surface of the milky sea, its brilliance appears as startling as lightning, and hence lightning is said to have been introduced to the world. The golden bow then magically plays about the universe, travelling through the seven seas, the *sura* and Brahma *loka*s (worlds), and the four continents. Visnu finally seizes it with his right hand, and its brilliance becomes even more radiant. *Devas* and *yaksas* sing songs of praise, Dadimunda (a.k.a. Alutnuvara Deviyo, Devata Bandara) fans it, and Huniyam *yakkha* holds a torch for it. It is then ritually bathed in the seven lakes, the seven rivers, and the seven seas, before its powers are harnessed to cure Manikpala by exorcising the serpent curse of Mara's revenge.

There are a number of interesting allusions that are transparent in this myth. It is clearly a myth that explains the provenance of the golden bow in exorcism rituals. Visnu's own sister is the first to be cured, and so the story of her cure in the face of Mara's cunning is meant to be paradigmatic for all that might follow. Of course, the story also reflects a great deal of conflation between Hindu and Buddhist elements. One of Visnu's best-known feats in the Puranas is his churning of the milky ocean that results in the creation of new world eras. Its incorporation here also signals the creation of a new method of curing possessions.

That Visnu's golden bow is a source of great power is indicated by its "orientation tour" of the cosmos, a motif indicating its mastery over its realms and those who dwell therein, including all the *devas* and *yaksas* who sing its praise, as well as the powerful gods Dadimunda and Huniyam, who symbolically accord it great honor. The mention of these two gods in subservient relation to Visnu may also indicate that the origins of the myth come from the ritual contexts of one or more of the Visnu *devalayas* in the Kandyan region, where shrines to all three of these hierarchically related gods constitute the cultic venues of one site. That the myth itself is predicated upon Visnu's protection of the Buddha establishes its Buddhistic base. And, just as sexual seduction is associated with Mara's attack on the Buddha, the imagery of a snake entering the womb of a sacred figure enhances the allusion to sexuality leading to suffering in the world of samsara. While imagery such as this (or of snakes entering into snake holes), within the Hindu context, signals the fertility of the goddess,[20] the converse meaning in a Buddhist context obtains here. It is here a symbol of death's potential. Powerful forces of a sacred origin are needed to combat it. Visnu's golden bow is one such method.

There is a second significant myth, the *Vaikuntha Alankara* (*Sinhala Kavi* 3:218), that further indicates the power of Visnu's golden bow in relation to rites of exorcism. In this particular mythic construction, there are still more in-

dications of Visnu's conflation with Upulvan, or the synchronization of Buddhist and Hindu elements. The myth begins with a description of Visnu's
Vaikuntha giri palace, and then declares that Visnu's bow has great power to resist sorcery. It then shifts focus from Visnu's palace in heaven to the shores of
southern Lanka, where Visnu's mother, the heartwood of the sandalwood tree,
gives birth to his form. Visnu thereby arrives at Devundara bearing the sun and
the moon as his standards, and causes a king to construct his sanctuary there.
In his Devundara temple, his eight-armed image is described as holding the
lotus, the mace, the conch, a sword, a *cakra* (wheel), a bow, and the eighth hand
in *abhaya* ("fear not") *mudra*. He is then described as appearing in the guises
of his ten avatars, taking his three cosmic strides, and then churning the Ocean
of Milk to inaugurate the beginning of a new world aeon.

As in the previous myth just discussed, the churning of the ocean results in
the appearance of powerful divine weapons, just as in the *Visnu Vidiye Kavi* it
was the source of the robes of the cosmic Buddhas of this *kalpa*—except that,
in this case, it is not Visnu's golden bow that surfaces from the depths of the
ocean. Instead, weapons of other important Buddhist deities are obtained
through Visnu's work. Sakra gets his conch, Kanda Kumara receives his spear,
the ancient *rsi*'s obtain their five arrows, Pattini her *halamba* (bangle), and Upulvan his seven golden bows.

This is a myth reflecting almost the full consolidation of motifs associated
with the profile of the "Buddhist Visnu." The Sinhala myth of the sandalwood
image has been enclosed within the Sanskritic Puranic profile of the god, indicated by the description of his heavenly abode (Vaikuntha), by his three cosmic strides, by his churning of the Ocean of Milk, by the presence of attributes
well-known to his standard iconography, and by his appearances in the forms
of his ten avatars. Beyond the declaration of the power of his golden bow and
the fact that the sandalwood image myth has been wedded to his Puranic profile, the primary purpose of this myth appears to be an attempt to establish the
overlordship of Visnu's creative power in relation to other Buddhist deities—
those who receive their own power as a result of Visnu's primordial acts and
are, therefore, understood to be dependent upon Visnu. He is responsible for
having procured their instruments of power. (This is a sign of Visnu's role as a
"warrant deity," which will be examined more fully in the next section.)

There are also two other noteworthy elements in this myth. The first is that
Upulvan is regarded as a deity separate from Visnu, despite the fact that the
sandalwood image myth is so well-known in its association with Upulvan.
Here, it is linked instead to Visnu. The second is the mention of the sun and
moon as Visnu's standards. These are later very clearly incorporated in the cult
of Alutnuvara Deviyo, whose own conflations and associations with Visnu will
be discussed in chapter 7. Mysteriously, the poem concludes by stating that

Upulvan hid his seven bows in the depths of the Ocean of Milk. Does this signify his eclipse?

Finally, in relation to these ballads which take as their prime consideration the power of Visnu's golden bow to assuage the suffering brought about by exorcism, there is a mention of Visnu in the *Satara Waran Mal Yahan* (II) (*Sinhala Kavi* 2:38) as holding Rama's arrow with the golden bow. He is addressed in this *kavi* as "Bosat Narayana," who rides an elephant. This particular notice of the conflated or subordinated Visnu is highly significant, for it very clearly signals his bodhisatva status as the "Buddhist Visnu." Perhaps his *vahana* as the elephant, rather than the *garuda*, is simply a confusion, or more evidence of localization. Elephants, normally, are the *vahanas* of both Saman and Natha.

There is a series of other ballads that refer to Visnu's power in combating sorcery. These include *Diwa Salu Santiya* (*Sinhala Kavi* 3:73), "The Incantation of the Celestial Cloth," and several others, such as the *Sat Adiya Kavi* (*Sinhala Kavi* 1:196), "The Ballad of the Seven Steps," and the *Ansapada Mangalaya* (1:141), "Ode to the Measured Steps," the latter two having to do with a very important and complex ritual of exorcism. The ritual of the "seven steps" consists of serially invoking the powers of gods, or various elements of Buddhism associated with each of "seven steps," as a method of curing possession. The "Incantation of the Celestial Cloth" may have to do with a famous *petikada* tapestry, the legend of which connects the Alutnuvara, Kandy Maha (Visnu), and Hanguranketa Visnu *devalayas*. (The significance of this tapestry may be found in chapter 7.)

The ballad per se, in which the celestial cloth is given by Visnu and other deities, is said to have the power to ward off the sorcery associated with Devol Deviyo.[21] The two ballads that have to do with the ritual of the seven steps do not signal anything of particular significance or relevance to the ritual cult of Visnu, as Visnu is just one of many deities whose powers are invoked in this elaborate proceeding.[22] However, I will quote one version of it as it pertains to Visnu's role in this important ritual procedure. Since this is a ritual that attempts to invoke virtually all powers possible to cure possession, the invocation to Visnu in this ritual represents a summary understanding of his significance as it has been tailored specifically to the needs at hand:

HAT ADIYE DEHI KAPIMA
(CUTTING OF THE LIME IN THE RITUAL OF SEVEN STEPS)[23]
MAL YAHAN KAVI

1.   I worship the Lord Rama,
     The god who holds the arrow in his right hand.

Mention of his name brings fortune and prosperity.
I shall now tell of his virtues.

2.   Shooting powerful arrows,
      Expelling darkness and bringing light,
      Striding but twice over the four sides of Mt. Meru,
      May Rama, majestic lord, arrive.

3.   Bedecked in soft, divine cloth,
      Perfumed with fragrant flowers and sandal scent,
      May Rama arrive without delay
      Through the billowing blue clouds of the sky

4.   Taking his golden bow in hand.
      [The Buddha] surveying with divine eyes
      Saw that Visnu would attain Buddhahood.
      I worship that powerful Visnu with my devotion.

5.   Blue as the ocean,
      Holding bows in both hands,
      You who strive to become a future Buddha
      By fulfilling the ten perfections,

6.   Living in a golden mansion
      Surrounded by curtains,
      You, would-be Buddha,
      I worship as powerful Visnu.

7.   Crowned of gold, divinely ornamented, clothed in blue,
      Crowned of gold, armed powerfully with a golden bow and arrows
      Crowned of gold, gem-netted, golden belted, sounds of war,
      Comes the resplendent King Rama on his *gurulu vahana*.[24]

8.   Send down a sign of the wondrous golden bow,
      Brilliant light flashing from its two ends.
      Assemble the blue hued gods and send down radiant beams.
      Unabashed, descend to this flower altar!

9.   O Vishnu, you who commands all of Sri Lanka,
      Sending out deep blue rays from your gem[25] in all directions,

Incinerating vicious, wicked and dangerous *yaksas*,
Look upon our altar and come without fail!

10.   Like a full moon appears from behind the clouds,
Red sandalwood fragrance pervades all space,
By a gaze the troubles of Lankans disappear,
Now gaze at this flower altar, Sri Visnu, and come!

11.   For company, present the likes of Isuru and Uma.
Endearment, by taking water in your right hand to dip the hair
Of beloved children,
See the betel that I have offered and come without delay.

12.   With a moon-like disc in hand, wearing pleated cloth,
When riding your *vahana,* comes the *kisi-bisi* sound from your
armour
And the tinkling of foot bells. With golden bow and arrows in
hand,
You come to sport on this flower altar.

13.   Wearing a beautiful flower garland necklace,
Like foam breaking over the waves,
Blue pendant, blue turban, and blue body,
Your approach is like an elephant process.

14.[26] Sri Vishnu, completely auspicious,
Who destroys all *bhutas,*
I offer you incense, lamps, and smoke.
I worship Visnu! Prosperity!

15.   With eyes like the two qualities of the moon,
Endowed with manifold power, dark-bodied (*krsna deha*) and
pleasing,
Eminent in the world with tenfold powers fulfilling the ten
perfections,
Completed, dispeller of fear, that Visnu I worship.

What becomes evident in this song are many of the motifs already cited as instances of Visnu's power framed within the Buddhist context. But within its specific ritual context here, what the poet has attempted is a distillation of the nature of Visnu's power, so that, along with power derived from six other sources, it can be put to use in the service of an exorcism. That is, this is a poem meant to summarize the essence of Visnu's relevance to the powers needed to successfully negotiate a ritual exorcism. The power of Visnu's (or more accurately Rama's) golden bow is again stressed within this context. What is particularly novel in the poet's imagination is his identification of Visnu's "tenfold powers" (his avatars) with the fulfillment of the ten perfections (*paramitas*), an interpretation of the significance of Visnu's ten incarnations as the means by which he realizes the path to Buddhahood.

Finally, there are two other relevant ballads in which Visnu's power to counteract sorcery or to facilitate exorcism are mentioned. These are the *Tis Paeye Kima* (*Sinhala Kavi* 3:297), "The Thirty Paeye Story," and the *Pinidiya Alattiya* (3:342), "The Rose-water Sprinkling." In the former, several of Visnu's powerful forms are included among the thirty invocations that take up to half a day to recite. Laksmi is invoked as the fourteenth power, Venuput[27] ("Visnu's son," Kama) is the seventeenth, Rama is the eighteenth, and Venu (which is actually the Pali form of Visnu) assuming the form of the boar is twenty-seventh. In this ballad, Dadimunda (a.k.a. Alutnuvara Deviyo, Devata Bandara), rather than Upulvan or Visnu, is referred to as the deity who protected the Buddha during his night of enlightenment. In the latter ballad, the rose-water sprinkling seems to be an allusion to Sri Visnu blessing Vijaya's men, which in this version of the story causes Visnu's retinue of *yaksas* to dance for joy. There is also an allusion to the power of Visnu's golden bow in this song.

From this brief discussion of Visnu's mythic power in relation to sorcery and exorcism, then, it is clear that these poems refer to an important dimension of his ritual cult in Sinhala Buddhist religious culture. Rather than discussing the specifics of the attendant ritual dynamics involved in sorcery, possession, and exorcism in this chapter, we will defer until chapter 7 addressing those matters in relation to religion in the *devalaya* context. In the present chapter, I am more concerned with articulating the manner in which Visnu has been projected mythically. There is no doubt that these mythical projections come alive within the context of ritual. But for the sake of the problem at hand, to determine the nature of the conflation between Upulvan and Visnu, and hence the mythic profiles of the "Buddhist Visnu," we will continue the examination of other mythic instances related to the cult of Visnu in late medieval Sinhala literature.

The Heroic and Human Rama

There are three mythic cycles, in particular, to be addressed now, which contribute to the heart of Visnu's divine profile in Sinhala literature and Buddhist culture.

The first has to do with the story of Ravana and Rama. There are a number of very abbreviated Sinhala recastings of episodes from the epic *Ramayana* that contain some interesting local interpretations which, in the process, modify the character of Rama and his significance for the Visnu cult in Sri Lanka.[28]

The second is an important myth that has enjoyed a wide dispensation in Sinhala folklore. It is about Visnu as a conqueror of the archetypal *asura*, Bhasma. It reflects a further degree of moral power associated with Visnu.

The third myth does not present Visnu as its protagonist. Rather it is primarily about how Skanda (a.k.a. Kanda Kumara, Kataragama Deviyo, Murugan) came to marry Valliamma; but Visnu figures very significantly in this extremely well-known myth nonetheless. In it, he is cast in a familiar role: the deity behind the scenes who makes possible other divine expressions of love and power.

All of these myths, which go beyond the mythic inheritance that Upulvan has bequeathed to the "Buddhist Visnu," lend considerably more insight into the character of Visnu as it has been refracted within Sinhala Buddhist culture.

The historical importance of the *Ravana Hatana*, the *Ravana Katawa*, the *Ravana Puwata*, the *Palavala Dane* (*Sinhala Kavi* 3:97; 1:205; 3:99; and 1:38), and the significant presence of Rama and Ravana in the roughly contemporary chronicle, the *Rajavaliya* (Gunasekera 1900), lies in the fact that not only do they provide evidence of the relative popularity of the *Ramayana* story from at least the seventeenth century, but they also contain episodes either framed very differently in comparison to its Sanskrit or other Indian recensions, or episodes that are entirely unique.[29]

In the second chapter, I noted how allusions to the *Ramayana* epic are seen in the rhetoric of kingship during the twelfth-century Polonnaruva period. It is, of course, likely that the Pali *Dasaratha Jataka* was a well-known story throughout Sinhala and Theravada history in Sri Lanka from the early Anuradhapura period on, but this *jataka* version of the story is so completely different from the *Ramayana* episodes related in later Sinhala folk-ballad literature that there can be no confusing the two,[30] or any merit in speculating that the latter were derived from the former. They represent two separate appropriations or transformations of the epic. However, there is considerable and very interesting overlap between the *Dasaratha Jataka* and the *Rajavaliya*.

The *Dasaratha Jataka* (Cowell 4:78–82) is named for the righteous king of Benares. In the text his chief queen, the eldest of 16,000 wives, gives birth to two sons and a daughter, the elder son being Rama-pandita ("Rama the wise"), the younger brother being Lakkhana (Laksmana), and the younger daughter being Sita.[31] In time, his chief queen, the mother of Rama, dies, and Dasaratha reluctantly finds another consort to replace her, who subsequently gives birth to Bharata, of whom the king becomes exceedingly fond, and on whose account the king promises his mother a boon, which she accepts but defers for seven years.

After seven years, she approaches Dasaratha to grant her the boon of making her son king, which he refuses angrily. But she repeatedly and insistently makes the request so that Dasaratha, in turn, begins to fear that she may be plotting to kill Rama and Lakkhana. Determining from astrologers that he has twelve years left to live, he summons Rama and Lakkhana and says that, for the sake of their safety, they should repair to a neighboring kingdom, from which, after twelve years, they should return to inherit the kingdom.

With great fanfare, they depart from Benares, and Sita elects to join them, Rama being regarded as a father by the younger Lakkhana and Sita.[32] After nine years (rather than twelve), Dasaratha dies, and the queen attempts to install her son Bharata as king. But the royal courtiers resist her designs and remind her that "the lords of the umbrella are dwelling in the forest." Bharata declares that he will go to find Rama, return with him, "and raise the umbrella over him." When he finds Rama alone (Lakkhana and Sita are out gathering food in the forest, so they do not immediately receive the news of Dasaratha's death). To Bharata's surprise, Rama receives the news without sorrow or emotion. On Lakkhana's and Sita's return, Rama asks them to stand in a pond, and he proceeds to divulge the sad news, to which they react with great lamentations. Rama then preaches to them in *gathas* about the nature of impermanence (*anicca*), which, when understood, allays their grief. Bharata requests them all to return to administer the kingdom, but since Rama had promised his father he would return in twelve (rather than nine) years, he instructs Bharata to rule in his place. After Bharata continues to object, Rama tells him to place his (Rama's) straw slippers on the throne until he returns. Bharata departs with Lakkhana and Sita to the capital, and places the slippers on the throne. Whenever a royal adjudication is needed, the slippers indicate approval or disapproval by either remaining quiet or becoming agitated. In three years, Rama returns with great fanfare, Sita becomes his queen consort, they are anointed with the ceremonial sprinkling (*abhiseka*), and thereupon Rama, as a *mahasattva*, circumambulates the city to begin his reign of righteousness, which lasts some 16,000 years.

This is the ending of the abbreviated story of Rama according to the *Dasaratha Jataka*. The narrative is thus cut short and does not include the bulk of the remaining story as it has come to be known in Sanskrit recensions. As I have noted, however, there are interesting overlaps with the *Dasaratha Jataka* in the *Rajavaliya*'s depiction of Rama, and there are significant Sinhala adaptations to the many further episodes of the *Ramayana* within the Sinhala folk-ballad tradition. We will turn to the *Rajavaliya* first.

After giving an account of the traditional cosmography of the universe, and an account of the Okkaka lineage descending from the first primordial king Mahasammata (Gunasekera: 1–7), the *Rajavaliya* narrative introduces a story about Aritta, the last in the line of the Okkakas, having four sons and five daughters by his chief queen, Hastapala, who subsequently dies and is replaced by another queen, who bears a prince named Jantu, of whom the king is exceedingly fond, and as a result, asks his new queen to request whatever she desires.

When Jantu comes of age, his mother asks the king to abdicate in favor of Jantu. The king at first refuses and points out that his four sons by his previous queen have precedence over Jantu. But the queen persists, and accuses him of lying by reminding him of his former promise to provide anything she desires. Shamed, the king, summons his sons, telling them to go wherever they wish and to take whatever they desire, save the royal paraphernalia. The five princesses declare that they will also depart with their brothers and so, together with great retinues of ministers, brahmans, noblemen, and merchants, set out "to build a city for our Okkaka race" (8) peacefully.

Traveling for several days to the southeast of Benares, they come across the bodhisatva, who is in his incarnation as the hermit Kapila. Kapila is practicing austerities in the forest. He asks the princes what they seek and offers them the area he has been using for his *pansala* (temple) because of its auspicious qualities, on the condition that when their city is complete, they name it after him, "Kapilavastu."

The four princes decide that they should not marry from the families of other kings so as not to "be a scandal to our royal race" (9) and, since they can find no suitable royal partners for their sisters, they marry their four sisters and decide to treat the eldest sister as their mother. Apparently incest is preferable to violating caste *dharma*! The *Rajavaliya* then proclaims:

> Upon hearing that the princes had not united themselves to any other caste, their father was greatly pleased; and three times shouted with joy and declaimed as loud as thunder, saying, "These be *Sakya* princes!" And be it noted that since the time the said Okkaka king thus exclaimed, the title 'Okkaka' dynasty was changed into the title of 'Sakya' dynasty. Thus, 240,770 kings of the Sakya race reigned in the city of Kimbulvatpura. [9]

This would seem to be the end of the mythic account of how the Buddha's city of Kapilavastu and his Sakya family originated, the borrowings or similarities with the *Dasaratha Jataka* and Valmiki's *Ramayana* being quite obvious, the main themes having been enlisted in a different mythic service. But the narrative in the *Rajavaliya* does not end here. Subsequently, the connections with Rama and allusions to Sita only intensify.

The eldest sister, who had "become as a mother" to the four other princesses and princes, contracts leprosy, and as a result, is taken by her brothers a great distance from the new city where she is placed into a pit, along with all the necessary requisites she would need to go on living. Meanwhile, King Rama of Benares also contracts leprosy, abdicates in favor of his son, and retires to the forest, "being resolved to die" (10). He begins to eat the bark and flowers of a certain tree, and builds a loft in the hollow of a *kolom* tree (it is unclear if this is a separate tree), where he survives the difficulties of living in the wild.

One night, Rama hears the screams of the elder princess as a tiger attempts to enter her pit. The next morning, he descends from the *kolom* tree, encounters the princess, inquires who she is, and learns of her similar condition of leprosy. While she bashfully explains that she would rather lose her life than disgrace her family, caste, and race, Rama explains that he is the King of Benares, has suffered from the same disease as she, but has cured himself and will cure her too. She is so cured, and he "lived with her in love. In the course of time she bore the king twins at sixteen births, altogether thirty-two princes" [10].

One day, subsequently, Rama encounters an archer who inquires about the identity of the thirty-two princes. When Rama explains his story, the archer returns to Benares and tells Rama's son, the current king, that his father is alive and living in the forest. Rama's son then proceeds to the forest, finds Rama, and constructs a magnificent city on the site of the *kolom* tree, naming the city "Koliya."

Meanwhile, the four younger brothers and the four younger sisters of the princess [Sita] whom Rama has married have given birth to eight daughters each—thirty-two princesses in all. While at first collectively rejecting a marriage proposal from Rama's [and Sita's] thirty-two sons "because they were born in the hole of a *kolom* tree," they later accept invitations "to attend aquatic sports" and "and during the sports on the river the princes took each princess by the hand and led her into the Koliya city." The story ends with the following denouement:

> The royal fathers of the said princesses laughed, saying, "Our nephews are clever: they have carried off their own cousins." Since that time there were intermarriages between the royalty of Kimbulvat and Koliya cities. It should be noted that the royal families . . . were united into one clan [11].

In such a manner does the late seventeenth-century Sinhala Buddhist *Rajavaliya* transform the story of Rama and turn him into an ancestor of Sinhala kingship. It is from the marriage alliance between Rama and the eldest sister (apparently Sita) that the Sakyas, and hence the Buddha, descend. This also becomes Vijaya's lineage. The narrative then proceeds to tell Vijaya's story in terms very close to those in the *Mahavamsa*.

The Theravada (*Dasaratha Jataka*) and Sinhala (*Rajavaliya*) appropriations of the Rama story involve what is, by now, a familiar pattern: the transformation and subordination of Hindu ideals into a framework that makes accommodation functional. What is also interesting within the context of the *Rajavaliya* is that within the Vijaya story (that commences just after the Rama story here detailed), Upulvan appears as a figure entirely separate from that of Rama, indicating that at least in this context, his conflation with Rama had not been completely effected. Since the *Rajavaliya* itself contains an account of Kandyan kingship through the reign of Rajasimha II (1635–87 C.E.) and in its closing lines mentions that he entrusted the kingdom to his son, Vimaladharmasuriya II (1687–1707), this means that it is likely that the text, as it has now been translated, was redacted during the reign of Vimaladharmasuriya II. It is during this king's reign (1687–1707 C.E.) that the Visnu *devalaya* in Alutnuvara was shifted to Kandy.

In 1709, there is hard evidence (in the form of a land grant to the Maha Devalaya in Kandy, discussed in the next chapter) that the identities of Rama and Upulvan had been precisely conflated by Sinhala royalty (King Narendra Sinha). Thus, it is possible to surmise that the Upulvan/Rama linkage occurred at the end of the seventeenth or the beginning of the eighteenth century in Kandy, if it had not occurred in other locales earlier. In the present context, however, there is more to relate about the Sinhala Buddhist apprehension of the *Ramayana*.

In the midst of the *Rajavaliya*'s subsequent account of King Panduvas's sickness—*divi dos* (a type of curse that causes melancholy or depression), owing to Vijaya's "perjury" in relation to his betrayal of Kuveni, the queen of the *raksasis* with whom he had cohabited, for the sake of a Pandyan queen born of appropriate lineage (*Rajavaliya* 14–19)—Ravana is mentioned twice. At the beginning of the myth, there is the following passage:

> After the war of Ravana, and before the attainment of Buddhahood by our Buddha, the teacher of the three worlds, Lanka had been the abode of demons for 1,844 years [14].

Then at the conclusion of the myth, when divine intervention has resulted in Panduvas being restored to his senses, there is this:

> In former times there was no sea between Tuttukudi and Lanka; but there stood the city of Ravana. Be it known that by his wickedness, his

fortress, 25 palaces, and 400,000 streets, were all overwhelmed by the
sea. [18]

While the *Rajavaliya* mentions Ravana twice, and in the latter instance in a
manner reflecting his villainous portrait in the *Ramayana,* he is not mentioned
specifically in connection with Rama. Unlike the Sanskrit recensions of the
Ramayana, there is no account of the destruction of Ravana's palace and city
and the loss of his life at the hands of Rama. The two are kept quite separate.
Moreover, in the Sinhala folk-ballad versions of the *Ramayana* story, brief as
they are, Ravana is clearly not regarded in such an unequivocal manner as the
embodiment of *adharmic* or evil forces. He is regarded much more ambiva-
lently. Indeed, this is how A. Seneviratne (1984a:235) depicts Ravana, as he is
known from popular Sinhala folklore:

> People speak of [Ravana's] valour and intelligence; ten heads for his learn-
> ing and wisdom. He was also a master of music. The musical instrument
> known as the Ravanahasta or Ravana vina is his invention. His knowledge
> of medicine is highly regarded and respected. The medical texts such as
> *Nadiprakasa, Kumaratantra,* and *Arkaprakasa* are attributed to him. He
> was so powerful and courageous that Rama could kill him only by divine
> intervention.

Seneviratne's final point is all the more interesting, owing to the fact that in
Valmiki's *Ramayana,* Ravana had been given a boon so that he would be invincible in relation to deities and vulnerable only to humans. Here, the situation has been apparently reversed. Be that as it may, there are more hints of this
"other side" of Ravana in the *Sinhala kavi* renditions of the story.

The late medieval Sinhala poetic versions of the story, as noted above, are ti-
tled after Ravana, not Rama. In itself, this is an indication of the fact that Ravana's character is treated with much more empathy. In the *Ravana Katawa*
(*Sinhala Kavi*:205), written in little over a hundred verses, Ravana's ancient city
is described in terms similar to the *Rajavaliya*'s brief account—25 palaces and
400,000 streets, etc. Following Valmiki's Sanskrit recension, Ravana's sister becomes enchanted with Rama and boldly asks Rama, in a manner seemingly
unbecoming of a princess (but in line with her true nature as a *raksasi*), to
marry her.

Rama demurs and suggests that she approach, instead, his brother, Saman
deviyo.[33] Saman also declines. She then returns to Rama and begs him to divorce Sita. In response to this suggestion, Rama slices off her nose. When his
sister reports to Ravana what has happened to her, out of revenge for this act
of cruelty, Ravana abducts Sita, and the stage is set for monkey-king Hanu-

man's famous visit to Ravana's garden in Lanka, where Sita is held captive. Discovered by Ravana's men, Hanuman's tail is set afire by having cloths dipped in oil attached and set ablaze. The strategy backfires as Hanuman springs on to the thatched roofs of the city's houses, and the entire city is set on fire. Hanuman escapes amidst the chaos and returns to Rama, an invasion of Lanka is launched, Rama slays Ravana in a personal duel, and Sita is finally recovered.

This Sinhala version of the story is not quite as melodramatic nor or as defined as Valmiki's Sanskrit version. In the latter, while Rama, Laksman, and Sita are still in the forest following the visit from Bharata, the *raksasi* Surpanakha (Ravana's sister) falls in love with Rama, and, largely in the same manner as in the *Ravana Katawa*, boldly offers herself in marriage to him. When Rama refuses, Surpanakha determines that Sita is the impediment to her desire and makes plans to devour her. In Sita's defense, Laksmana mutilates Surpanakha, who then flees to her brother Ravana to report the cruelty of the two brothers. In addition, she speaks of Sita's extraordinary beauty in such a way that her description excites Ravana's passion. Ravana devises a plan to trick Rama and Laksmana away from their hermitage in pursuit of a deer. While they are gone, he arrives at the scene posing as a wandering mendicant, gains entrance, and manages to carry Sita off to Lanka. Hanuman sneaks off to Lanka on a spy mission and witnesses Ravana's attempted seductions and intimidation of Sita, who staunchly resists his advances and threats.

There is, of course, much more to Valmiki's narrative, but enough has been said to compare the two versions in terms of how the characters are depicted. In the *Ravana Katawa*, while Ravana's sister acts in a manner that is not appropriate for a princess, her behavior does not appear to warrant the response that Rama (not Laksman, as in the Valmiki narrative) gives to her. There is some justification, then, in Ravana's abduction of Sita, since it is seen as an act of revenge for the cruelty that Rama has visited upon his sister. Further, in the *Ravana Katawa*, no mention is made of Ravana's attempted seductions of Sita, nor of his sister's descriptions of her beauty, which incite his passions. The portraits of both Rama and Ravana, therefore, are a good deal more ambivalent that the neat constructions in Valmiki's *Ramayana*.

That ambivalence is further evident in another Sinhala episode of the story which has no provenance in the Sanskrit. The *Palavala Dane* (#1; *Sinhala Kavi* 1:38), which seems to be of later origin than the *Ravana Katawa*, contains a remarkable series of episodes that cast Rama's character in a considerably different light, though in the end he is clearly identified with Upulvan. The 216-verse poem actually begins with the coronation of Kuveni by Vijaya, his perjured repudiation of Kuveni for the Pandyan princess, the *divi dos* that he and Panduvas suffer as a result; and then it relates how Sakra, with thirty-six *vali yaksas* and Veddha (aboriginal) chiefs in the service of Mala Raja (the "flower king"), with the assistance of Rahu disguised as a boar, effects Panduvas's cure. This is followed by a long description of the Himalayan wilderness where Upulvan and Sita are said to dwell in the Vaikuntha palace. Then, as a retrospective, the story is told of Rama's conquest of Ravana, and this contains the episodes I wish to highlight.

One day Sita *devi* painted a picture of Ravana and was detected gazing upon it by Rama. In anger, Rama took her to the forest and instructed Saman *deva* to cut her body in two. Saman, however, took pity on Sita, since she was pregnant with a child, and left her alone in the forest. Soon thereafter, she encountered a *rsi* who gave her shelter in a hut near his own. She fed herself on herbs until the time came for her to deliver her child, which she did successfully. Her son's name was Sandalindu. One day while Sita was out collecting herbs, the child slipped off her bed, fell to the floor, and crawled under the bed.

The *rsi*, whom Sita had asked to watch over the child in her absence, became anxious when he could not locate Sandalindu. Assuming the child had somehow become lost, and not wanting Sita to suffer grief, he created a second child from a flower and laid it asleep on the bed. Sita returned, began suckling the child, while Sandalindu began to cry. Sita assumed that a divine miracle had occurred and doubted the *rsi*'s explanation. To convince her, he took some arrow grass and created yet a third child. The third child was named Kistiri Raja, while the second was named Mala Raja. Hence, the mythic account of the "flower king" who, under Sakra's direction, cured King Panduvas of his *divi dos*.

But the story continues to play out. One day Rama happened to see Sita's three young princes playing and became annoyed when they paid him no respect. So, he shot three arrows at them, but to no avail—they simply glanced away. Bewildered, Rama asked the children about their parents. When he learned of their identity, he was overjoyed that Sita was still alive, and he restored her as his queen.

What I have just outlined above is one of the root myths celebrated in a ritual known as the *valiyak natum* ("ritual dance"), performed annually at the Maha Devalaya in Kandy following the conclusion of the *asala perahara*. The ritual is of such historical importance to the cult of Visnu in Sri Lanka that it is written about extensively in chapter 6. But here, we will continue with the literary analysis of the Sinhala folkloric texts germane to Rama.

In the *Ravana Puwata* and in the *Palavala Dane*, it is fair to say that Rama's profile is much more ambiguous or ambivalent than the image of Rama as the embodiment of dharma usually associated with the figure in Valmiki's *Ramayana*. Not only is there a moral question raised by Rama's treatment of Ravana's sister in the *Ravana Puwata*,[34] but it hardly seems appropriate for an embodiment of dharma to be shooting arrows at three young children simply because they did not pay a formal obeisance, as is the case in the *Palavala Dane.*

My sense is that these portrayals are not accidents, and that what they reflect is something of the ambivalent Sinhala Buddhist disposition signaled by both Obeyesekere's and Martin Wickramasinghe's comments cited above. That is, these instances would seem indicative of attempts to "cut Visnu down to size" or to "make an immortal god mortal." Wickramasinghe's comment is especially relevant here. From these episodes, and here I would also include the depiction of Rama that is offered in the *Rajavaliya* as well, Rama is much more of a human figure than a divine one. Not only does he suffer from moral failures, but he also suffers from physically debilitating diseases. No doubt he remains a royal warrior in the Sinhala mind-set. Indeed, I think this particular casting is what is responsible for the heavy provenance given to the "golden bow" in late medieval *Sinhala kavya,* but he cannot be regarded in the same fashion as he is depicted in the more Hindu-oriented recensions of the story, whether those depictions be dharma-oriented or bhakti-oriented, simply because of the fact that in the Sinhala Buddhist context, the mythic and soteriological frames of reference are very different in nature.

I also would submit that Rama's royal warrior profile is precisely the reason why he was regarded so congenially in relation to Upulvan, the great protector of royal interests in medieval Sri Lanka. This would seem to be substantiated in the *Palavala Dane.* Here, as I have mentioned, Upulvan and Sita are first mentioned as dwelling together in the Vaikuntha palace in the Himalayas, and the *Ramayana* episodes are inserted in a kind of retrospect. They explain the background of how Upulvan and Sita achieved their heavenly conditions as Rama and Sita. The implication is that Rama is understood to be the human king who later becomes a deity, and whose power continues to be associated with the well-being of kingship and righteous rule.

There is one more variant to the *Ramayana* as it is articulated within Sinhala literature that I will briefly explore before attending to other mythic orientations of Visnu. This is found in the *Ravana Puwata* (*Sinhala Kavi* 3:98–99), a poem that is brief, but forty verses in length. Though the poem clearly takes the *Ramayana* as its subject, it is unique in two ways: the first is that Visnu (rather than Rama) is explicitly identified as the protagonist throughout; the second is that it contains a unique episode, one somewhat reminiscent of Krisna in his association with the *gopis* (cow girls) of Vraj. This episode is inserted at the beginning of the poem before referring to the familiar episodes of the story. Visnu goes to bathe in the pond in his park and finds that all the purple lotuses (*upul*) have been picked and that the water has become muddied. Angry at this spoilage, he determines to get to the bottom of this outrage. He conceals himself in the bushes beside the pond and begins to watch.

Shortly, seven goddesses arrive to bathe, leaving their clothes on the pond's bank. Visnu stealthily steals one set of clothes, but is then discovered by the goddesses, who immediately take flight. But one goddess, whose clothes are in Visnu's possession, remains behind, unable to leave without her garments. This is Sita. Visnu approaches her, takes her away, and makes her his wife. Then the poem proceeds to recount other *Ramayana* episodes, including the encounter with Ravana's sister. In this rendition of the encounter, rather than Rama or Laksmana cutting off her nose and/or ears, Visnu, in an angry rage, breaks her leg instead!

Although the *Ravana Puwata* is written skillfully in fine literary Sinhala, it articulates a much coarser conception of episodes in comparison to other Sinhala renditions. Sita is won not by the chivalry or cultivated martial skills of Rama, but by the cunning character of Visnu—a profile evident in other myths to be explored. That Visnu, rather than Rama, is identified explicitly throughout the poem as the protagonist represents, I think, the manner in which the various personalities constitutive of his general cult in Sri Lanka have been eventually submerged or coalesced within the profile of the "Buddhist Visnu."

Finally, in this section dealing with the Rama dimension of the "Buddhist Visnu," one last text is presented that reflects how Rama and Upulvan were conflated in late medieval Sinhala Buddhist culture. This text is not another example of the genre of Sinhala *kavi*, folk ballads, ritual liturgy, or quasi-historical chronicles, such as the *Mahavamsa* and *Rajavaliya*, that have been reviewed in this section. Rather, this text may constitute one of the last expressions of the *sandesa* poetic tradition. Unlike most other examples of this genre which are written in Sinhala, this one, the *Rama Sandesa*, was composed in Pali. It might be regarded as a kind of addendum to the *sandesa* literature that I discussed earlier in this chapter. It is a late eighteenth- or an early nineteenth-century text composed by a Buddhist monk at Sri Jayawardhanapura (Kotte) during the final years of the reign of the last Kandyan king, Sri Vikrama Rajasinha. It is, therefore, an early nineteenth-century text that seems to have been written for a monastic audience. Insofar as the earlier *sandesa* tradition was concerned primarily with asking for divine protection for Lankan kings, the *Rama Sandesa* is no exception. Like the *Tisara* and *Mayura Sandesa*s, it was written during a time of grave threat to royalty. Indeed, within just a few years of its composition, the British had disestablished Kandyan kingship once and for all. Its fundamental importance within the current context of discussion is that it underscores the identity of Visnu/Upulvan as Rama in Kandy and Hanguranketa.

Before its concluding invocation of Rama, which clearly expresses the primary intent of the poem to protect the *Buddhasasana* and King Sri Vikrama Rajasinha, 132 verses describe the sacred capital of Kandy, including the Dalada Maligava ("Temple of the Tooth-relic"), the four *devalayas* of the "four guardian deities," the Ganesa *kovil,* and their illustrious monks, the Malvatta and Asgiriya *viharayas,* including the legacy of the first *sangharaja* of the Siyam *nikaya* (Saranamkara). The poem also provides a flattering eulogy of the king and describes his two victories over the invading British, before it shifts focus to a description of the town of Hanguranketa (some twenty miles southeast of Kandy in the elevated hill country), built as a defensive fortress during the time of Rajasinha II in the seventeenth century. Hanguranketa is also the site of one of the *devalayas* important to the contemporary cult of Visnu in Sri Lanka. Here is the poem's description of Rama and its invocation of his power:[35]

133. In this resplendent city, impenetrable by enemies, full of wealth, Rama, who provides for all desires of the people like the wish-fulfilling tree, prevails.

134. Rama's temple, with its waving banners on the roof protecting it from the sun's heat, glistens like a heavenly mansion, like Mount Meru surrounded by lightning.

135. Its highest pinnacle is like a streak of cloud descending to the earth.

136. Rama appears, in this Mount Meru-like setting, wearing a shining band on his forehead, a crown on his head, arm and ear ornaments; his neck is like the golden *kambu* drum.

137. Rama's glory, in all its purity, spreads like the autumn cloud, or the light of the moon, or like the white water lilies [on the pond].

138. As the lion-king shines among the beasts, the swan among the birds, the moon in the sky, so Rama shines among the gods.

139. Ravana, that king of kings, victor over enemies, ferocious, wicked, difficult to subdue, the kidnapper of the divine Sita, was split in two by Rama's arrows.

140. Rama shines like a shaft of flame above Ananta, the *naga* king who resides in the Ocean of Milk.

141. When he was king, Rama displayed his might by the miraculous power of his sandals. Now that he is a god, his power is inconceivable.

142. "Omniscient One, truly wise, highest of the two-legged, highest of the gods, like the crest gem, may you protect the *sasana* of the Buddha.

143/4. "O Govinda, king of the three worlds, with glory that pervades all directions, destroy the enemies and return in all your glory, with your pearl necklace, golden crown and earrings.

145. "O Lord, you who are like the sun to those sinful ones who are like the owls of the night, and the moon to the righteous, god of the gods, may you protect the *sasana* of the Sugata.

146. "You have protected the Tri-Simhala so well, like a cave protected by the lion-king, by dispelling the *yaksas* and pisacas by the dart of your hand.

147. "O Uppalavanna, of the color of the blue lotus, may you protect in earnest the lion-like king Sri Vikrama, king of kings, truthful and wise.

148. "Rama, may you protect this lord Sri Vikrama Rajasinha, the giver of wealth like the wishing tree, the ruler of the world, born of the race of the sun, forever.

One of the interesting features of this late *sandesa* poem is that there is no messenger conveying the plea. It begins descriptively and ends with an invocation of Rama starting at verse 142. It is, therefore, a direct plea by a Buddhist monk, who tells us that he is Sumangala Thera of Kunkunawa, who works tirelessly in support of the *Buddhasasana* (vs. 149–50). The extremely eclectic nature of this work, an eclecticism reflective of the nature of the cult of the matured "Buddhist Visnu" per se, is seen in the fact that: 1) it is composed in Pali (the formal language of Theravada Buddhist scripture, and thus only accessible and limited to Buddhist monks); 2) it contains allusions to the Rama of the *Ramayana* (conquering Ravana the kidnapper of Sita, and his sandals); 3) Visnu's Puranic profile (reclining on the *naga* king Ananta at the bottom of the Ocean of Milk); 4) a reference to Krsna (Govinda); 5) a comparison to the wish-fulfilling tree of Buddhist apocalyptic imagery; 6) a call (twice) to protect the *Buddhasasana*; and 7) an explicit identification with Upulvan, who is called upon, as he is so frequently in fourteenth- and fifteenth-century *sandesa* literature, to protect Lankan royalty and the state.

As such, it is a fitting summary of how Rama was incorporated into the evolving portrayal of Visnu by the time of the Lankan kingship's disestablishment in the early nineteenth century. That the Upulvan/Rama dimension of the "Buddhist Visnu" would fade in its importance in the nineteenth and twentieth century, and that the protector of the *Buddhasasana* motif would remain important, is indicative of the historical disappearance of Lankan kingship, on the one hand, and the serious threat posed to the *Buddhasasana* by the intruding British and Christian presence on the other.

Guardian or "Warrant" Deity

By the middle of the eighteenth century, Visnu's identity as one of the four "guardian deities" of Lanka had been formally established, as evidenced by his inclusion, along with Natha, Pattini, and Kataragama, in the ritual proceedings of the annual *asala perahara* during the reign of Kirti Sri Rajasinha (1751–82 c.e.). That identification may have been solidified much earlier on, in the late seventeenth-century reign of Vimaladharmasuriya II (1687–1707). In any case, the identification of these four guardian deities sustains the original concept of these deities that was introduced during the fourteenth-century Gampola period, while the specific identities have been changed. A number of folk ballads, which must postdate these times, were written to celebrate the provenance of these four deities. What follows is a discussion of the significance of two of these *kavi*: the *Satara Waran Mal Yahana* (II) (*Sinhala Kavi* 2:38), "Flower Altar of the Four Guardians"; and *Satara Devala Devi Puwata* (*Sinhala Kavi* 2:158), "The Story of the Deities of the Four Temples."

The significance of the first *kavi* lies not so much in the specific details it employs to depict the "Buddhist Visnu," though that is the primary reason I am including it within the present discussion. Its more general importance lies in the fact that it is a poem that is one of the most intoned pieces of liturgy found in Sinhala folklore. That is, it is often sung before the beginning of a variety of types of rituals, ranging from exorcisms to pageants and dramas (such as *sokari*). It is a formal, yet "shorthand" manner of acknowledging the important presence of the four guardian deities on whatever public occasion is deemed appropriate,[36] following on first acknowledging the Buddha, dharma, and *sangha*. I am referring to its contents now, not because they are so extraordinary, but because this *kavi* contains what is likely to be one of the most familiar depictions of Visnu in Sinhala Buddhist culture.

In this *kavi*, Visnu is invoked as holding Rama's arrow in one hand and his golden bow in the other. His body is described as being blue, and he wears a blue robe with a garland of flowers draped around his neck. Most importantly, he is addressed as "Narayana Bosat," signaling his concomitant identity as Visnu Deviyo and his status as a bodhisatva. The depiction is simple, but fully expressive of his contemporary and well-known profile.

The second *kavi*, however, the *Satara Dewala Devi Puvata*, contains a very important myth, rooted in Puranic origins, one well-known as well in Tamil culture. The entire *kavi* is but forty-four verses in length, so verses relevant to each deity are compact and to the point. The section on Visnu begins with a reference to his arrival in Lanka and his binding of the *Demala yaksas* ("Tamil *yaksas*"), an indication of the definite Sinhala provenance of this version of the myth. It then refers to Visnu's Puranic boar incarnation, in which he dived into the primordial waters to spear the earth with his tusk and establish the inhabitable land of this *kalpa*.

This cosmogonic act is followed by a description of his tortoise *avatara*, in which he supported Mount Meru after the chief of the *nagas* had entwined himself around the mountain's base and a fierce wind threatened to topple it over. The verses to Visnu conclude with how, as "Pulvan *deva*," he alone, of all the gods, stood firm beside the Buddha during the paradigmatic struggle with Mara on the night of the enlightenment experience. While there are no mythic instances that are new in this description—instances that haven't been alluded to before as being incorporated into the profile of the "Buddhist Visnu"—the combination of all of these specific attributes within one telling is novel.

Also new are additional verses that allude to a myth of great salience. It is a myth with a fairly common Puranic theme: how an *asura*, either through the practice of austerities or through the acquisition of knowledge, gains great power and threatens to destroy the universe. In this instance, the myth is about how Bhasma Asura had learned a mantra from Siva which, when recited, while placing the hand on the head, would reduce any physical body to ashes. Having discovered this great power, Bhasma began to chase Siva himself with the intention of destroying the great deity and taking over the universe.

While Siva was in flight from Bhasma, he told Visnu of the predicament. Visnu assumed the form of a beautiful young woman in a swing, singing love songs. When Bhasma encountered her, he was overcome with infatuation and began to make passionate overtures to the young woman. Visnu, in the guise of the young woman, enamored him further, and so possessed Bhasma's attention that he became single-minded in his pursuit of her by falling deeply in love. With his bait so hooked, Visnu, as the beautiful young woman, asked Bhasma to swear his undying fidelity to her by reciting an oath with his hand placed upon his head. As he did so, Bhasma was immediately incinerated, and completely reduced to ashes.

In Obeyesekere's account of the main ceremony of the *gammaduva* series of rites chiefly held in honor of Pattini, there is a set of observances known as the *kala pandama,* or the "ritual of the torch of time." He explains the significance of these observances in this way (1984:113):

> The torch of time, according to informants, is meant to avert "bad times." It is planted in honor of three gods: Visnu, time past; Kataragama, time present; and Devata Bandara, time future. . . . Visnu is the head of the pantheon, but he is a benign god; he belongs to the time past. In fact, in the past he was less benign and more involved in the affairs of man. . . . Kataragama is today widely propitiated for overcoming current problems: he belongs to time present, the operative here and now. But according to karmic logic . . . his rise must eventually result in his downfall; when this happens a lesser god like Devata Bandara must take his place. This is in fact what is happening now. Thus, Devata Bandara represents time future.

In chapters 5 and 7, we shall learn how Devata Bandara (a.k.a. Alutnuvara *deviyo,* Dadimunda) is related to Visnu within the cultic contexts observed at Visnu *devalayas,* but Obeyesekere's comments about this ritual context are cited now because it is the venue within which he recorded the following oral continuation of the myth of Visnu and Bhasma. The "torch of time" observances function as a preliminary liturgical invocation somewhat similar to the chanting of the *Satara Dewala Devi Puwata,* although in regard to a different set of deities. In any case, the fascinating continuation of the myth at hand that Obeyesekere (114) has recorded is as follows:

> Bhasma the *asura* was so infatuated that he forgot his hand was charmed. He touched his head and swore fidelity to the beautiful woman and thus was consumed into ashes. Out of those ashes arose Devol Deviyo and Gini Kurumbara.
>
> Isvara [Siva] meanwhile saw no sign of Bhasma, so he came back from hiding. He saw instead the same beautiful woman on the swing. He was also infatuated and wanted to marry her. But the woman [Visnu] asked him: "Are you married?" He said, "Yes." "Then I can't marry you." Go tell Umayangana that there is a beautiful woman on the swing singing love songs, and ask her if you may bring her as your chief queen [*mahesi*]."
>
> Isvara went to his palace and asked Umayangana's permission to bring home the beautiful woman as his queen [*mahesi*]." "Yes, go bring her," said Umayangana.
>
> But when Isvara came back, the beautiful woman was pregnant. She said, "I can't marry you now since I am pregnant. So ask Umayangana's permission to bring home a pregnant woman." Isvara went back to Umayangana, and once again Umayangana agreed. But when he returned

this time the woman had had a child and was once again pregnant. She said, "This cannot be done, you have to ask your wife's permission to bring home a pregnant woman with a child."

This happened six times. Meanwhile, the eldest child was big enough to walk, and he was away picking flowers. When Isvara came for the seventh time he thought that this was a wonder, a miraculous creation, not a normal birth. So Isvara brought Uma to see the woman. Visnu saw them come and shed his female guise. He awaited their arrival with the six children, since the eldest was away picking flowers. Isvara's wife saw the child and said, "*Ane*, my brother has a heap of children [*kanda*, "heap," "mountain," "lot of"]. She embraced the children together saying, "*is kandak*" ["a mountain of heads"]. Thus Skanda [i.e., *Is-kanda*] was born with six faces and twelve arms. The eldest brother escaped this transformation. He was named Aiyanayaka, "eldest brother," "chief brother."[37]

Obeyesekere points out that there is also a Tamil version of this myth. In the Tamil version, only Aiyanar is born, and he is born of a sexual union of Siva and the beautiful woman (Visnu).[38] Obeyesekere (114–115) adds: "The Sinhala myth is their own invention, I suspect. The folk etymology of Skanda as 'Is' *plus* 'Kanda' cannot be justified in Tamil. In the Tamil myth Visnu as female (Mohini) has intercourse with Siva; this would be much too indecorous for the Sri Lankan Visnu."

This continuation of the myth at hand, as well as Obeyesekere's comments, raises a number of interesting issues. Although the provenance of this continuation is somewhat removed from the context of the medieval literature I have been surveying (since it was recorded in the late twentieth century), it still provides an interesting opportunity to ascertain something additional and something unique about the "Buddhist Visnu."

The first point is that the myth has been reworked in such a way that it not only establishes Visnu as the most clever of the deities—the deity with the ingenuity and power to withstand *asura* usurpers—but it also casts him in the role of being responsible for the birth of a number of other deities. In this myth, it is through his creative *maya* that Skanda (Kataragama *deviyo*), Devol, and Aiyanar are all born. Other mythic traditions elaborate upon these "Vaisnava" introductions. The process illustrated within this particular myth would seem to represent a reworking of Visnu's power to be incarnated as avatars—a way of explaining the origins of particular deities in relation to a higher, divinely creative power or principle.

In several other myths about the introduction of deities to the island, Visnu plays the role of the deity who grants them permission to land and to take up residence on the island. That is, he provides a warrant for their presence, a warrant that, in turn, is based on his own warrant derived from the Buddha to protect Lanka. Both of these ways of accounting for the presence of a myriad of deities who become important within the Sinhala cultic context illustrate how the "Buddhist Visnu" occupies such an exalted and powerful position, and why he is regarded as an eventual Buddha. In this mythic retelling, he is the presence of the ethical voice throughout: by means of his guile, saving Siva and the world from the power-crazed Bhasma Asura, and then correctly instructing Siva on what is proper, so that the final end of that benevolent power which is accessible (in the presence of Skanda and Aiyanar) is realized.

Obeyesekere (59) has made the very interesting observation in his discussion about the nature of deities within the Sinhala pantheon that "while the Buddha is made into a kind of god, the god is made into a kind of Buddha." What he is suggesting here is that the Buddha functions as the ultimate legitimator of all benevolent actions in the world. Visnu, for instance, receives his warrant or instructions to act for the benefit of the *Buddhasasana*, and therefore for the benefit of those who understand their existence in light of the *sasana*'s soteriological significance. Furthermore, Buddhist deities are meant to personify Buddhist virtues. They are, in fact, ethical postulations expressed in the mythic mode. The higher the deity, such as Visnu, the more virtue he embodies, and thus the closer he is to nirvana's realization. Visnu's responsibility in introducing powerful and benevolent forces into the world is a virtuous act, part of his guardian or "warrant" deity responsibilities for the benefit of all those in need.

The second point is related to the first and has to do with the manner in which "divine sexuality" is conceptualized in Sinhala Buddhist culture. While there is one instance in *sandesa* literature where Upulvan is seen as an attractive figure for Laksmi and Saravasti (Visnu's and Brahma's traditional consorts or *saktis*), the Sinhala deities *in general*, and Visnu in particular, are decidedly *asexual* in orientation. Kataragama, as I will illustrate shortly, is something of an exception to this in the present. In the past, Visnu may have been sexually impassioned, as indicated in the *Ravana Puwata*, where he hides Sita's clothes, is enamored of her, and marries her. But as Obeyesekere has pointed out, Visnu having intercourse is too "indecorous" for the Sinhalas, or it is too anomalous to be compatible with the image of a deity who is now a bodhisatva and who is, relatively speaking, close to the attainment of nirvana (i.e., the extinguishing of *tanha* or desire). The "Buddhist Visnu"'s profile, then, stands in sharp contrast with his image as it has been cultivated in popular Tamil myth. Shulman (1980:308–316) describes a related cycle of myths that celebrate Visnu's sexual transformations and reproductive powers. Here, for example, is how he briefly retells the myth of Bhasma Asura:

A demon worshipped Siva and was given the power to turn anything to ashes with the touch of his hand. He tried to turn Siva himself to ashes; the god fled from him, and Visnu took the form of Mohini and bewitched the demon into imitating the hand movements of her dance. Mohini put her hand on her head, and the demon followed suit—and turned himself to ash. Siva made love to Mohini, and their son, Aiyanar, was born. [308]

Note that in this myth, Siva's engaging in sexual intercourse with Visnu is reported as almost a matter of fact. In the Sinhala version of the myth, great care is taken to avoid the mention of sex altogether, and the beautiful woman (Visnu) is insistent on propriety in asking for Uma's permission to accept an increasingly ridiculous demand—one that is eventually abandoned. For several pages after retelling the Tamil version of this myth, Shulman proceeds to discuss the meaning of the "widely distributed insistence on Visnu's female capabilities" in the Tamil Saiva Hindu context. He notes that it may reflect a sectarian effort to turn Visnu into Siva's *sakti* and, hence, signal the subordination of Visnu within the context of a Saiva interpretive framework. Or, he muses, perhaps this myth represents, as it is "often seen, as expressing syncretistic or harmonizing tendencies between the two cults of Siva and Visnu" (309).

Whatever may be the sociopolitical origins or significance of this mythic version, the point is that Visnu's sexual transformations are a celebrated, rather than avoided, aspect of his divine personality. On the other hand, in the Sinhala context, the "Buddhist Visnu" is kept at a distance from the sexual act, and the reproduction of the six children who become Kataragama, and the seventh who becomes Aiyanar, are understood to be the products of his magical, rather than sexual, capabilities. This is completely consistent with Visnu's image as it has been cultivated among the Sinhalese. In *devalayas* dedicated to his propitiation, he is never represented iconographically with a *sakti*—consort or spouse. In situ, he is always presented alone, presumably as a celibate deity, yet his reproductive abilities are acknowledged in different ways.

As the Sinhala version of the myth has indicated, Visnu is also linked to the origins of both Kataragama Deviyo and Aiyanar. In a Veddha rendition of how Kataragama married Valliamma, a myth well-known not only in Sri Lanka among the Sinhalas but in Tamilnadu as well, Visnu is also responsible for the birth of Valliamma. But in its "Veddha" expression, his sexuality does form a central episode. Neville (*Sinhala Kavi* 2:188–89) collected this very unique Sinhala translation of the Veddha myth, which, judging from the poem's colophon, dates to 1642 C.E.

The poem begins straightforwardly by relating that a son, Kumaru, was born to the "three-eyed one" (Siva). No explanation is given of the circumstances. Uma went to see him (indicating that she was not his mother?), embraced him, and named him Kanda Kumaru. Kanda Kumaru eventually grew to manhood, defeated all the *yaksas*, and reigned supreme in Sri Lanka. With six faces and twelve hands, and resided in Paelaniya, a town of great beauty.

Meanwhile, Visnu went out one day to the nearby forests to practice austerities and spotted a doe that won his fancy. He assumed the form of a golden stag and won her over as his mate. From their union, a human girl was born, which gave fright to her mother. The doe deserted the girl who, in the meantime, was protected from any harm by the earth goddess. One day, Veddha hunters came across the child and brought her to their king, who adopted her as his own. She was named Valliamma, and by the time she was seven, had grown to be very beautiful. Because of her parentage, all of the wild animals would pay her homage.

One day, the sage Narada saw her and reported her beauty to Kanda Kumaru. Assuming the guise of a Veddha, he presented himself to the young girl, saying that he had lost his way and was famished. Valliamma, however, was not taken in and sent him away. He then created a tree that blocked the local path. When the Veddhas tried to cut it down, blood came forth. The next day, when they were hunting, they left Valliamma alone, and Kanda Kumaru again tried his ruse, but again to no avail. A third time he returned, this time disguised as a recluse from Andhra. The Veddhas had never encountered such a person before, so they showed him hospitality and asked him to guard Valliamma. When they went hunting, Valliamma prepared the recluse some food. He choked on the food and asked for water. As there was none nearby, she proceeded to the forest, followed by the recluse. Finding him water, she offered it to him, and he drank it, looked deeply into her face and then sprinkled the remaining water on her face, much to her consternation.

No matter what form of advances were made, Valliamma rejected Kanda Kumaru. Finally Kanda Kumaru colluded with Ganesa to appear as a full elephant to frighten Valliamma. Once he had done this, Kanda Kumaru assumed his true form, rescued her, and thus finally won over her love. He resumed his disguise as a recluse, and the two of them returned to the Veddha village. There the woman who was overseeing Valliamma, and suspicious of their absence, asked them what they had been doing. The couple decided to elope, but were followed by the woman and persuaded to return. Soon they decided to elope again, and this time they were followed by all the Veddhas who, upon spotting them, shot arrows which magically glanced off them. But Kanda Kumaru shot his own arrows in return and killed most of the Veddhas. Valliamma lamented the loss of her "relations," so Kanda Kumaru instructed her to bring them back to life, which she did. Then he assumed his own form and received the worship of the Veddhas. Thereafter, they were married by the Veddha king, and the deity gave the Veddhas the power to cure ills caused by heat and cold—from *bhutas*, *raksasas*, and *yaksas* (inferior supernatural beings who may cause diseases or mental ills). The couple visited Kataragama and erected a palace, where they continue to dwell. Neville (*Sinhala Kavi* 2:188–89) cites an isolated verse that refers to Uma as the mother of Valliamma, "and we must suppose that Uma had assumed the form of a spotted doe, when Visnu as the golden stag won her love."

This is a very unusual (and sometimes confusing) myth in a number of ways. Not only is Visnu the real father of Valliamma, but it would appear that Uma, who had taken the form of the doe, is regarded as the mother of Valliamma. Thus, her parentage mixes two sectarian traditions. Uma, of course, is always the spouse of Siva, yet Siva's son, Kanda Kumaru, does not appear to be the son of Uma. It may be that the Sinhala or Veddha teller of this myth was unaware of important sectarian divisions within Hinduism, and it is doubtful that this version would represent some attempt at harmonious syncretism.

Be that as it may, the myth also reflects a reluctance to admit Visnu's sexuality directly. It is only in the form of an animal that his procreative powers are noticed. Further, what is accomplished in the story is Visnu's function, again, as the creator of a very significant deity, and as the facilitator of a powerful cultic creation. Indeed, citing the two different mythic cycles just discussed, it is possible to identify Visnu as the progenitor of *both* of these important deities whose cult is now one of the most popular in Sri Lanka among Sinhala Buddhists. Taken together, if there is any sectarian or ethnic consciousness reflected within these respective myths regarding the origins of Kataragama and Valliamma, its significance would be that Visnu, rather than Siva, is the ultimate progenitor of the divine couple, a development that may signal an opposition to Tamil Saiva dominance of the cult which, in fact, is the religio-cultural origin of this now transformed understanding.[39] More abstractly, these transformations reflect the Sinhala Buddhist proclivity for favoring Vaisnava assimilations rather than Saivite.

There is one final Sinhala folk ballad, seemingly of a rather late date, the *Upulwan Asnaya* (*Sinhala Kavi* 3:183), or "the Saga of Upulvan," that I would like to present at the conclusion of this discussion, because it seems to be of such a composite nature, summarizing so many of the details that comprise the evolved mythic profile of the "Buddhist Visnu," and adding a few new elements of its own. It is certainly not a learned poem, but it does represent an attempt to present an almost universal image of Visnu, yet one thoroughly rooted in a Sinhala Buddhist context.

It opens with an enumeration of Visnu's ten names: Sri Visnu, Maha Visnu, Nala Devata, Damora, Govinda, Harihara Raja, and Pulvan Surindu. These names, several of which are totally unfamiliar and which, in fact, number only seven rather than ten, would seem to represent an attempt to account for Visnu's avatars. Upulvan, it is said, has assumed the form of a red-backed woodpecker, a frog, a cormorant, and a boar. If these "incarnations" are taken as constitutive of Upulvan, then the number of Visnu's "appearances" does total ten.

The poem proceeds to say that in the Kreta *yuga*, Visnu was white in color; in the Treta, golden; in the Dvapara, red; and in the Kali *yuga* (at present), he is blue. He was given responsibility for Lanka by the Buddha and is assisted in that task by his brother, Saman Deviyo. At the time of the Buddha's enlightenment, he was also given charge of the *sasana* after defending the Buddha against Mara. He dwells in either the Vaikuntha heaven or at the bottom of the Ocean of Milk. He conquered Ravana, Bali *asura*, and Bhasma *asura*. He is destined to become Rama Buddha. In his four hands, he holds the golden bow and a conch. His main shrines are said to be at Samanala (Adam's Peak), Diva Guha (at the base of Samanala, where the Buddha rested before his climb), the Dalada Mandira, Dambulla, Sri Mahabodhi in Anuradhapura, and Mecca!

The *Upulwan Asnaya*, therefore, truly reflects an attempt to express the various mythic dimensions eclectically gathered to project the character of the "Buddhist Visnu." Eventually, Buddhists expected to see him as "Rama Buddha." In the meantime, he guards Sri Lanka and its Buddhist dispensation through the power of his golden bow, a Hindu deity converted to the bodhisatva path: an immortal deity transformed to mortal being intent on the realization of nirvana.

PART 2

Introduction

THE CULT OF VISNU IN BUDDHIST SRI LANKA

The second part of this study, the fifth through ninth chapters, consists largely of an analysis of the religious and political significance of the cult of the "Buddhist Visnu" in contemporary Sri Lanka. The presentation, however, is not simply synchronic. I have found it necessary to provide a number of historical and literary discussions as well as various theoretical asides in order to frame adequately many of the contemporary expressions of the Visnu cult as they are articulated today.

Much of what follows was initiated by months of fieldwork conducted from late 1999 through mid-2001, mainly at the Maha Devalaya in Kandy, and at the Alutnuvara Devalaya in Alutnuvara, in the up-country (*udarata*) or highland region of Sri Lanka. While most of my time was spent as an observer at these two important ritual venues, I also visited Visnu shrines at Hanguranketa, Lankatilaka, and Gadaladeniya on numerous occasions, in addition to Kande Viharaya in Alutgama, and Devinuvara in the island's southwest. The nature and rationale of my approach to field study will be explained in these chapters.

Chapter 5 focuses on contemporary cultic life at Visnu's Maha Devalaya in Kandy, as it regularly unfolds on *kemmura* days—those Wednesdays and Saturdays of each week when the deities are deemed more likely to be attentive to the plaints of their devotees. Here my concern has been to explain when and why devotees venerate Visnu and his "prime minister," Dadimunda, and how the pleas of these devotees are fielded or anticipated by *kapuralas* (shrine priests). I have also provided an extended discussion of the *devalaya* as a religious and public institution, from the perspective of the *basnayaka nilame* (the temple's lay custodian).

Before any of those issues are addressed, however, I have attempted a reconstruction of the late medieval history of the Kandy Visnu *devalaya* (Maha Devalaya). I have also argued at length that previous attempts to understand the nature of religion at the *devalayas* of Buddhist deities in Sri Lanka, especially those inspired by the work of Max Weber, which assume that this form of religion is a popular accretion and a distortion of Buddhism brought about by the failure of karma to explain misfortune, are somewhat misguided. I have attemped to show, rather, that the logic of karma, consistent with the teachings of the Buddha, is a fundamentally coherent rationale that functions as the basis not only for the moral economy of Sinhala Buddhist religious culture, and thus the hierarchy of the divine pantheon, but also for secondary forms (including astrology, exorcism, and possession) of explanation for misfortune. In my attempt to illustrate the substance and scope of contemporary *devalaya* religious culture, I have provided one case study of an elderly woman who has been a faithful devotee at the Kandy Visnu *devalaya* for many years.

In chapter 6, I have written a brief study and provided important translations intrinsic to the *valiyak mangalya*, an annual ritual performed at the Kandy Visnu *devalaya* for a period of seven days following the performance of the *asala perahera*. The *valiyak* rite is a kind of cultural fossil, an index to the importance formerly associated with Visnu/Rama in popular Sinhala religion. While there is evidence that this ritual at one time may have been quite widespread, practiced at all the *devalayas* that participate in the annual *perahera*, it has been held only at the Kandy Visnu *devalaya* in the memory of today's ritual participants.

Thus, the *valiyak mangalya* is the only rite in Sinhala Buddhist religious culture that is distinctive to the cult of Visnu and to the Kandy Visnu *devalaya*. Its significance reaches back deeply into medieval religious culture and discloses the great importance attached to Visnu's powers of protection and healing. It is within this context that one of the important cycles of myths I discussed in chapter 4—one of them dealing with the birth given to Valiyak princes by Sita—is given ritual life. Here we see how one more important aspect of the cult of Visnu was formally and religiously valorized.

The cultic seat of Visnu shifted from Alutnuvara to Kandy in the late seventeenth century. As a result, Devata Bandara, or Dadimunda Deviyo, replaced Visnu as the deity venerated at the Alutnuvara shrine, and in the process succeeded Visnu as the "Alutnuvara Deviyo." Chapter 7 examines how elements of the cult of Visnu have been appropriated by the cult of Dadimunda, a more martially oriented deity of growing importance to some groups of Sinhala Buddhists. I have also attempted to capture the ethos of the contemporary cult of Dadimunda by noting the shift of importance of this deity from being a power deployed to exorcise *yaksas* to one deeply embedded in the growing prevalence of divine possession, or *disti*.

To illustrate the power and parameters of *disti*, possession by Visnu and Dadimunda, I have provided two exemplary case studies of middle-aged women who currently operate their own private *devalayas* in the up-country Kandyan region. Alutnuvara has been for them, as for many others, the venue for receiving their *varamas*, or "warrants," to practice arts of healing and to communicate with the dead. My aim here is to bear witness to the relative dispersion of the cult of Visnu into the matrix of contemporary popular Sinhala religion.

Chapter 8 shifts the focus of the second part of this study and returns to some of the issues first raised in chapter 1: chiefly, the political significance of the cult of Visnu in contemporary Sri Lanka. In part 1, I endeavored to illustrate the political significance of Upulvan and Visnu to Sinhala kingship and the state. In chapter 8, I show how veneration of Visnu and other deities has been at the center of a contemporary controversy regarding the old issue of the place of deities in Buddhism. What is further revealed in this discussion is that the contemporary incarnation of this problem is largely politically motivated, driven by a section of the Buddhist *sangha* and lay community who have adopted an ethic of exclusivity in their understandings of Buddhism.

This discussion brings me back full circle to the thesis laid out in the introduction to the first part of this study, where it is asserted that assimilations and purifications of Sinhala Buddhist religious culture are often the consequence of concern for political power. Those Buddhists now arguing for the jettisoning of deity veneration do so not so much out of their concern for doctrinal purity, but rather as a reactionary fear that their culture and society will soon be overrun by the influences and practices of Hindus, Muslims, and Christians in Sri Lanka. This discussion sets the stage for the observations made in chapter 9, the conclusion to this study.

5

SEEKING PROTECTION

Cultic Life at the *Udarata* Visnu *Devalayas*

"There are many both Gods and Devils, which they worship, known by particular names which they call them by. They do acknowledge one to be the supreme . . . which they signifieth the Creator of Heaven and Earth; and it is he also who still ruleth and governeth the same. This great Supreme God, they hold, sends forth other Deities to see his Will and Pleasure executed in the World; and these are the petty and inferior gods. These they say are the Souls of good men, who formerly lived upon the Earth. There are Devils also, who are the Inflicters of Sickness and Misery upon them. And these they hold to be the Souls of evil men."
—Robert Knox[1]

Robert Knox was a young Englishman who lived in and around Kandy, held hostage by the Kandyan king, Rajasimha II, in the 1660s and 1670s. His famous account of his capture by the king's men after he was shipwrecked with the captain (his father) and crew off the east coast of the island near Trincomalee, his further account of imprisonment and gradual adjustment to life among the seventeenth-century up-country Sinhalas, and then the details of his dramatic escape through Anuradhapura to Dutch-controlled Mannar (an island off the northwest coast of Sri Lanka) almost twenty years later, are supplemented by his lengthy and thorough depiction of Kandyan Sinhala social customs of those times.

Historically, Knox's description is an invaluable historical portrait, and the earliest European portrayal of Kandyan Sinhala culture now extant. Remarkably, though laden with the late-medieval worldviews and the language of a common Protestant Englishman, one can still read Knox's observations of seventeenth-century life in Kandy and find many rich and varied resonances with contemporary Sinhala social attitudes, ritual practices, and religious beliefs.

In Knox's descriptions of religious practices in Kandy, there are few references to the Buddha and to the religious practices of Buddhist monks. Perhaps monasticism was somewhat moribund during his time, and did not play a large role in the public-ritual life of the people. Otherwise, it would seem strange that Knox did not provide more of such references. In that Rajasimha II, unlike his son Vimaladharmasuriya II, does not seem to have been particularly a religious man, it is not so surprising that Knox does not provide descriptions of the public monastic presence in Kandy. What he has to tell us about the Kandyan practice of religion is confined almost entirely to popular religious practices centered on seeking protection from deities and warding off the afflictions of *yaksas*.

No doubt, Knox's description of the Sinhala "Supreme God," whom he says was also regarded as "Creator of Heaven and Earth," was articulated in part under the influence of his seventeenth-century Christian Protestant conceptions of religion. The language he uses, of course, is somewhat biblical in nature. Nonetheless, upon a closer look, it would appear that Knox was actually quite perceptive in his understanding of several aspects of Sinhala religion. Indeed, in the passage cited above, he has quite aptly referred to the Sinhala Buddhist understanding of how karma explains rebirth as either a *devata* or as a *yaksa*, and how these supernatural forces are perceived to act benevolently or malevolently upon the lives of the people.

But there is some question about the identity of the "Supreme God" that Knox has referred to in this passage. It could be that the "Buddhist Visnu," and the deities that he [Visnu] "sends forth . . . to see his Will and Pleasure executed in the World" are a reference to Visnu's avatars, very loosely understood. Or it could be, but I think less likely, Dadimunda Devata Bandara and those who are sent forth could be construed as the *yaksas* under Dadimunda's command.

In a subsequent passage (to the one I have cited above), Knox, in describing the annual *asala perahara* ritual procession he witnessed in Kandy, has this to say (79):

After these comes an Elephant with two Priests on his back: one whereof is the Priest before spoken of, carrying the painted stick on his Shoulder, who represents *Allout neur Dio*, that is, the *God and Maker of Heaven and Earth*. The other sits behind him, holding a round thing, like an Umbrella, over his head, to keep off Sun or Rain. Then within a yard after him on each hand of him follow two other elephants mounted with two other priests, with a priest sitting behind each, hold Umbrella's as the former, one of them represents *Cotteragom Dio*, and the other *Potting Dio*. These three Gods that ride here in Company are accounted of all other the greatest and the chiefest, each one having his residence in several *Pagoda*. [Knox's italics]

At first reading, it appears that in referring to "Allout neur Dio," Knox was identifying Alutnuvara Deviyo (a.k.a. Devata Bandara or Dadimunda) as the "God and Maker of Heaven and Earth," or the "Supreme God." "[A] priest carrying the painted stick" could well be, indeed, a reference to Devata Bandara's powerful "golden cane," renowned in literary and cultic contexts, as the instrument used by *kapuralas* to beat *yaksas* thought to possess devotees into submission. But during Knox's time in the Kandyan region, Visnu's main shrine in the up-country region was possibly still located in Alutnuvara, a village and temple complex some eleven miles to the west of Kandy; or possibly Visnu's chief shrine had just been moved from Alutnuvara to Kandy around this time.[2] Because Alutnuvara had been the long-standing seat of the cult of Upulvan and the emergent "Buddhist Visnu" in up-country Sri Lanka, a cultic venue which I have indicated could date back to the thirteenth-century reign of Parakramabahu II, it is also quite possible that Visnu was known at this time and in this region as the deity of Alutnuvara. Sometimes, in Sinhala culture, deities take on the name of the town where their main shrine is located, such as at Kataragama where Skanda (a.k.a. Murugan, Kumaraswamy, etc.) has become known throughout the island as Kataragama Deviyo.[3]

As noted in chapter 3, the Sinhala Kandyan king Rajasimha II had rebuilt the shrine of Upulvan in Devinuvara as a Visnu *devalaya* after chasing the Portuguese from the island with the collusion of the Dutch in 1658. Thus, it can be inferred that Rajasimha II was congenial to the cult of Visnu and apparently understood its political importance to his rule, and perhaps its legacy of legitimization for Sinhala Buddhist rulers of Lanka.

Thus, it could well be that Knox's reference to *Allout Nuer Dio* is a confirmation of Visnu's (as Alutnuvara Deviyo's) presence in Kandy, especially in light of his description of the deity as the "Supreme God" who was "Creator and Maker of Heaven and Earth." Dadimunda Devata Bandara, on the other hand, became "Alutnuvara Deviyo" only after Visnu's cultic seat had been shifted to Kandy from Alutnuvara, probably in the mid- to- late seventeenth century. Unlike Visnu, this specific deity is not often referred to in such grandiose cosmic terms. While he is mighty and powerful, the ballads sung in his honor—some of which are presented and discussed in the seventh chapter—celebrate his birth as a son of the *yaksa* Purnaka, born from ash, how he became feared because of his power as the chief of the *yaksas*, and how he has come to be regarded as an ally of the Buddha and the interests of Buddhist religion. Even this last attribute is attached to his mythic profile *after* the "Buddhist Visnu's" departure from Alutnuvara.

Further, there is no doubt that the other deities that Knox refers to in this same passage are Kataragama Deviyo and Pattini Deviyo. Along with Natha and Visnu, these deities became the four "warrant gods" of Kandyan religion

known to us through the traditions of written Kandyan folklore and in surviving oral literature still recited within ritual contexts. They correspond to
what Knox has referred to as the "greatest and chiefest" of the Sinhala deities.

From at least the time of Kirti Sri Rajasimha in the 1750s (some seventy or
eighty years after Knox left Kandy), these same four deities, along with the
Dalada ("Tooth-relic" of the Buddha), have been feted and celebrated within
the formal public processions of the annual *asala perahara* in Kandy. That
Visnu would be grouped with Pattini and Kataragama in Knox's earlier description of the *perahara* procession is thus far more likely than for
Dadimunda to have been referred to as such. For Dadimunda is not only a
deity who has never been known to have been included within the ritual context of the Kandy *perahara*, but he is also categorically regarded as a deity decidedly inferior in divine status to Kataragama and Pattini. That is, he doesn't
"fit in" with these gods. Rather, he is often classed instead as another type: a
bandara-level deity.[4] Indeed, his epithet "Devata Bandara" is an accurate description of his standing within the pantheon: as a *devata* and a *bandara*, he is
not as elevated in the pantheon as Kataragama, Pattini, Natha, or Visnu, all of
whom are *devas*, nor is he regarded as far advanced on the path to *nibbana* as
these four "warrant gods." In fact, he is understood to derive his power and his
right to exercise it from a grant or boon derived from Visnu, Saman, or
Kataragama, depending upon various mythic traditions. As a *bandara* deity,
his origins may be of a euhemeristic nature.[5]

Attributes clearly derived from Upulvan or the "Buddhist Visnu" in the
mythic profile of Dadimunda, or "Alutnuvara Deviyo," as he has been popularly known since the late-seventeenth or early eighteenth century, are in abundant evidence in some of the historical and literary materials to be examined
in chapter 7. These indicate that, once Visnu was succeeded in Alutnuvara by
Dadimunda, the latter deity was the beneficiary of many of the important attributes of the former. From the seventeenth century on, Dadimunda was not
only closely linked to Visnu in Kandy, but eventually became known by some
as Visnu's *adikar*, or "prime minister," a status indicated symbolically by the
fact that his small *devalaya* was located adjacent to the main shrine of Visnu
within the Visnu *devalaya* compound in Kandy (see fig. 5.1).

There remains some uncertainty, as I have indicated before, about exactly
when Visnu's chief *devalaya* was established at its present location in immediate proximity to the Dalada Maligava and royal palace in Kandy, but Knox's
reference may signal the formal ritual presence of Visnu by the 1660s or 1670s
in its present location, although there is no hard documentary evidence to
confirm this.

Whether or not Visnu's cultic seat was shifted from Alutnuvara to Kandy
during the time of Rajasimha II, or during the reign of his son, Vimaladhar-

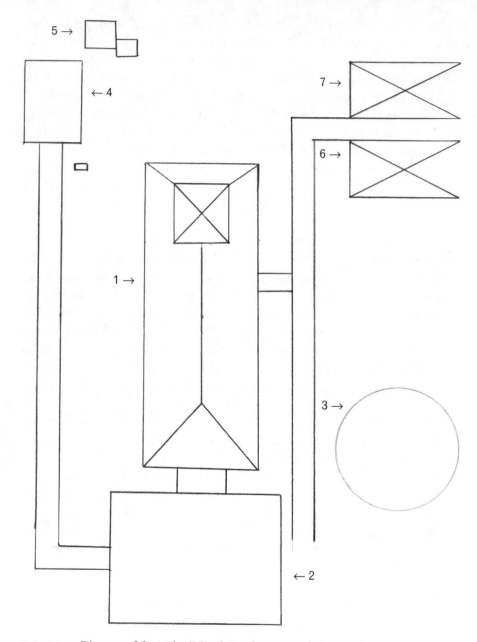

FIGURE 5.1 Diagram of the Maha (Visnu) Devalaya in Kandy by Kanchuka Dharmasiri
1 = Visnu Devalaya; 2 = Portico when the Valiyak Mangalysa is performed; 3 = Bo Tree;
4 = Dadimunda Devalaya; 5 = Huniyam Devalaya; 6 = Murutan kitchen; 7 = Kapuralas'
quarters

masuriya II (1687–1707 c.e.), there is firm documentary evidence for its existence in Kandy in 1709[6] during the reign of Narendra Sinha (1707–1739 c.e.).
In the course of field-study conversations at the Kandy Visnu *devalaya* in the
spring of 2000, I learned of the existence of a gold-plated sheaf, enclosed
within a beautifully carved ivory case, regarded by the current *basnayaka nilame* (temple administrative custodian) as the "*devalaya's sannasa.*"

After several weeks of coaxing, the *basnayaka nilame* finally allowed this
precious cultural artifact to be examined and then translated. Its contents not
only confirm the presence of the Visnu *devalaya* in Kandy in 1709 c.e., but it
also contains a very significant portrayal of the "Buddhist Visnu" in the earliest decade of the eighteenth century—one whose aspects I have identified in
many previous discussions thus far. Here is the *sannasa*, translated into English for the first time:

[THE GOLD PLATED *SANNASA*
OF THE VISNU *DEVALAYA*, KANDY][7]

Hail! Whereas we have appealed to Lord Sri Ramachandra, highest and
holiest supreme being, who bears the name Giri[hela],[8] [and the name]
Khadiradehali,[9] who wears an ornamented garland and whose body glitters like the color of a blue gem, who is the vanquisher of hoards of Mara-
like enemies [including] the Ten-faced One,[10] Kumbhakarna, Somaka,[11]
Bali Asura, Raktabija,[12] Madhukaitabha,[13] Kamsa the Asura,[14] and Hi-
ranya,[15] that he should, in a mind imbued with compassion and love, fulfil all aspirations of the great king who has been entrusted with the responsibilities of protecting the *pratipatti sasana* of the all-knowing lord of
the ten powers and the island of Sri Lanka, tasks to which he [Sri Ra-
machandra] himself has been given charge, so that all royal strategies con-
tending with calamities, impending dangers, and various deeds caused by
envious, partisan, distrustful, wicked adversaries and inimical external enemies, be successfully quashed, completely dispelled, thoroughly eradicated, and totally suppressed, like the mass of darkness expelled by the sun,
while elevating those who are honorable, loyal, obedient, trustworthy, devoted and adoring to his retinue, thereby further enhancing his great
power, fame, authority, accomplishments, valor, longevity and prosperity;
therefore, this present decree grants [this *devalaya*] twelve villages in Algama of Hatarakorale, including all lands, cultivated fields, highlands, low-
lands, tanks, reservoirs, lands not-cultivated, as well as services attendant
to them, on this Saturday, the third day of the waxing moon in Durutu,[16]
in the year of Virodhi, One Thousand, Six Hundred and Thirty-one of the

Saka Era;[17] may all intentions declared herein be fulfilled in every way; this is the compassionate decree proclaimed by His Great Majesty Sri Vira-parakrama Narendrasimha.

This beautifully preserved gold-plated *sannasa* issued by Narendra Sinha in the second year of his reign is, in fact, the record of a massive grant of land (including twelve villages in Algama)[18] made by the king to the *devalaya* in order to endow income and services for its ceremonial needs and physical maintenance.[19] It is a critical piece of evidence for this study, not only insofar as it establishes without doubt the formal presence and royal support for the Kandy Visnu *devalaya* in the first decade of the eighteenth century, but it completely confirms public recognition of a preserved composite character of the "Buddhist Visnu" that is so clearly depicted in various earlier sources.

What is so compelling about the *sannasa*'s description is not only that the supreme deity addressed is identified as Rama, but also that there are straightforward references to the early Sinhala name for Devinuvara (Girihela), and to the myth of the sandalwood image (Khadiradehali), so closely associated with the old Sinhala cult of Upulvan. Moreover, Visnu's Hindu Puranic prowess in conquering various *asuras* through the appearances of his *avataras* (including no less than Krsna, indicated by the reference to the defeat of Kamsa) is associated in kind with Rama's defeat of Ravana ("the Ten-faced One"). All of these divine enemies are referred to, in a Buddhist-inspired fashion, as "Mara-like" in nature.

And finally, the fundamental political function of Visnu within Sanskrit Puranic ideology, and of Upulvan in Sinhala *sandesaya* and *vamsa* literature, is asserted with great emphasis: to empower the righteous Buddhist king, so that the well-being of the Buddhist *sasana* in particular, and Lanka in general, will be sustained in triumphant fashion. What the *sannasa* reveals, therefore, is that primary aspects of the "Buddhist Visnu's" mythic profile arrived in Kandy basically intact by the end of the seventeenth or by the beginning of the eighteenth century, and that it had been well preserved and distilled from the earlier disparate formulations constituting the stratigraphy of its history.

It has also been surmised that Visnu's cultic presence as a deity central to the fortunes of Sinhala kingship had made its impact upon the expressive symbolism of Kandy's cultural geography by the seventeenth century as well. Duncan (74) quotes the *Kavmini Kondola*, a text which he says was written during the seventeenth century, as saying: "large walls that were seen in the city . . . are like the huge waves that surrounded the Ocean of Milk when the god Vishnu stirred it at the time of creation." In Duncan's study of the semiotics of "the politics of landscape interpretation in the Kandyan kingdom," he frequently refers to the symbolism of these wave-shaped walls as "synecdoches" (cosmological references within a consciously contrived, allegorically symbolized landscape) of the presence of royal Hindu discourses, which, in addition to Buddhist discourses,[20] informed the ideology of Sinhala Buddhist kingship. This would be a legacy of the process begun as early as the Polonnaruva period, a legacy unpacked in chapter 2 of this study. In writing about the spatial symbolism of the sacred "temple square" complex of Kandy, Duncan (114) says this in particular about the symbolism of the Visnu *devalaya*:

> To the north of the eastern rectangle lay the Vishnu Devale, surrounded by a moat, a wave swell and a cloud drift wall, all synecdoches standing for the heavenly Ganges flowing down from Mount Meru. Post-Vedic mythology places Vishnu's paradise, which is called Vaikuntha, on the *northern* peak of Mount Meru. The *devale*'s location, when considered in light of the fact that a road leading to it was at that time named Vaikuntha Vidiya, strongly suggests that the Visnu Devale was thought of as the northern peak of Mount Meru. . . . To the west of the Vishnu Devale lay a small *devale* to Dedimunda (Devata Bandara), a godling who serves as Vishnu's *adikar*, and commander in chief. Here we see the world of the gods mirroring the world of the king's court. This is an interesting reversal which reinforced the liminality of the city by further blurring the line between the world of the gods and the world of humans, for not only could the king emulate the gods, but the gods could also emulate the king.

Of further relevance to the symbolic place of the Visnu *devalaya* in relation to Kandyan kingship, Duncan (122) goes on to note that the last of the Kandyan kings, Sri Vikrama Rajasimha, (1798–1815 C.E.)

> during his consecration, first marched out of the palace and north, the direction that the cakravartin marches at the start of his reign, to the Visnu Devale and after receiving the blessing of Visnu, who was himself a *bodhisatva*, head of the Buddhist pantheon and entrusted by Sakra to protect Buddhism in Lanka, the king marched south to the Natha Devale [where he was to formally receive his royal name]. [brackets mine][21]

While Knox's late-seventeenth-century observations, the *devalaya*'s early-eighteenth-century *sannasa* of Narendra Sinha, and Duncan's interpretations of the semiotics of public-landscape symbolism provide an image of how Visnu's presence was understood as being cosmologically functional in late-medieval Kandy, these sources also contain harbingers of how Visnu (and Dadimunda, Visnu's "prime minister") would function in popular Sinhala religion in the centuries to come. Knox, in particular, had other "descriptions" to offer, regarding the popular forms of religion he observed during his twenty years of up-country captivity. The following is one of his most remarkable passages (83), and I quote it below in full as a way of introducing the general substance and parameters of "*devalaya* religion," with which the next three chapters are concerned:

> There are few or none zealous in their worship, or have any great matter of esteem for their Gods. And they seldom busie themselves in matters of the Religion, until they come to be sick or very aged. They debar none that would come to see their Ceremonies of their worship; and if a stranger should dislike their way, reprove or mock at them for their Ignorance and Folly, they would acknowledge the same, and laugh at the superstitions of their own Devotion, but withall tell you that they are constrained to do what they do, to keep themselves safe from the malice and mischiefs that the evil spirits would otherwise do them, with which, they say, their Country swarm.
>
> Sometimes in their Sickness they go to the House of their Gods with an Offering, with which they present him, intreating his favour and aid to restore them to health. Upon the recovery whereof they promise him not to fail but to give unto his Majesty (for they entitle him) far greater Gifts or Rewards. . . .
>
> It is a usual saying, and very frequent among them (if their *Gerahah*, which is their fortune, be bad), "What can God do against it?": Nay, I have often heard them say, "Give him no Sacrifice, but shit in his Mouth; what kind of God is He?"

Knox's observations, as I mentioned, are colored by his late-medieval Protestant Christian dispositions and categorical understandings. For example, his reading of the functional character of Sinhala religion led him to believe that the Sinhalas were not "zealous" in their worship of deities, or did not hold them in the highest "esteem." Guided by his Christian standards of piety, Knox, in his own mind, observed that popular religion among the Sinhalas was not then (nor is it now) a matter of a private meditative spiritual dialogue between creator and created (as it is within Christian Protestant tradition), but rather a ritualistic manner of religion, in the tradition of the ancient Brahmanical Vedas, of seeking immediate help in despairing conditions of sickness or fear, or in aligning oneself with divine or cosmic forces that can have an influence on the power dynamics of the immediate situation.

Indeed, it is still true today that most people who visit *devalayas* do so with particular and practical reasons in mind. They seek divine favors of power in exchange for the modest sacrifices they make. If they perceive their requests to be granted, they return to offer a ritual of gratitude. Thus, one of the general patterns of popular Sinhala religion consists of making a vow before a deity in the deity's shrine and then returning later to perform a subsequent *puja* of gratitude, should the deity's power be perceived as effective. Most people do not come to the *devalaya* as a matter of worship per se, to glorify the deity of the shrine, or to confess sins and to ask forgiveness. Rather "*devalaya* religion" is, as Wickramasinghe notes in the epigraph for chapter 4, a very functional type of religiosity. If a petition to the deity fails, it is because the deity is understood not to have the necessary power to grant it. These are fallible deities, not omnipotent forces.

I think Knox was incisive in a number of other ways too. The first is that, as I have just noted, deities are not regarded as all-powerful. They may not be able to overcome the forces of karmic retribution that have caused a present experience of misfortune (*dosa*). Indeed, deities are also subject to the inexorable forces of karma. Moreover, if sickness or misfortune is attributed to a *yaksa,* then the only possible means of warding off the danger is through a different type of karmic action; that is, correct ritual technology. In a manner similar to the mechanics of ritual as described in the Vedic *Sathapatha Brahmana*, this involves identifying and enlisting a specific supernatural force superior to and more powerful than the one causing affliction.

Yaksas were perceived more often in Knox's time than they are now as the causes of illness and danger. But there is still a sense, even if that sense is now somewhat secularized, that the country still "swarms" with a *yaksa* presence. This phenomenon will be discussed more fully in chapter 7. For now, it's sufficient to indicate that the popularity of a deity is largely based on the perceived efficacy of its power to solve thoroughly worldly (*laukika*) types of problems.

Some deities, of course, are perceived as being much more appropriate or more adept at this than others, and some types of problems are regarded as "specialty areas" relevant to a particular deity. Thus, many women visit Pattini's shrine in Kandy if they are hopeful of having children, especially without complications. Men seeking vocational promotions are apt to turn up at the shrines of Kataragama or Dadimunda.[22] Businessmen or traders also prefer Kataragama in overwhelming numbers to any of the other gods at the four *devalayas* in Kandy.[23] The specialty of Visnu in contemporary Sri Lanka may be, for some individuals, his continued political significance, but more widely, it also includes his association with just causes and his ability to provide a kind of "blessing" (*santiya*) of general well-being for those experiencing difficulties due to planetary configurations. Knox has pointed out how the deities are enlisted primarily in a defensive posture, as a means of cure but also as means of sustaining hope.

Another aspect of Sinhala religion that Knox observed was (and until recently has been) its relative tolerance and liberality with regard to other religions, or those who hold alien religious worldviews. Indeed, unlike the exclusivity of many Hindu temples or Brahmanical contexts in India, Buddhist *viharayas* and *devalayas* in Sri Lanka are never off-limits to non-Sinhalas or non-Buddhists. This does not mean that there is no concern with aspects of purity and pollution. Indeed, as I shall indicate shortly, proscriptions regarding purity and pollution abound, especially for *kapuralas*, the ritual functionaries at *devalayas*. But there is very little in the way of sectarian consciousness that prohibits the presence of outsiders in the midst of any ritual performance.

This relative tolerance or liberality can also be perceived in various historical circumstances too. Probably one of the most graphic illustrations of this aspect of the Sinhala religion occurred during the late-seventeenth- and eighteenth-century reigns of Kandyan kingship, when the colonial Dutch were in control of the southern and western littorals of the island. Because of hostilities between the Protestant Dutch and Sinhala Roman Catholics, it was not uncommon for the Buddhist king in Kandy to provide refuge for Sinhala Catholics who were enduring various forms of discrimination at the hands of the Protestant Dutch. It is thus an irony of history that a Buddhist political regime came to afford protection to Christians suffering at the hands of their fellow Christians.

Working on the basis of observations made by Knox some 350 years ago, enough has been said to set the scene for an overview of the kind of religion that is practiced at the Visnu *devalayas* in the Kandyan cultural area today.

Devalaya Religion: An Introduction

Before describing religious life at the Kandy Maha (Visnu) Devalaya in detail, I should set the context for understanding this type of religiosity within Sinhala Buddhist religious culture in general. Normally, a *devalaya* (literally "abode of the deity") is located within or attached to a Buddhist *viharaya* (monastic complex or temple). The *devalaya* proper may be a small, separate, and simple building, or an adjacent cave or *puja* room next to the main shrine hall meant for worshipping the Buddha (*buduge*). In either case, a typical *devalaya* contains just two rooms, or one room with two sections—one housing the image of the deity (the *sanctum sanctorum*), separated by a curtain from the second area, which is often the *digge*, or audience hall, where devotees present themselves and their petitions to the *kapurala* or shrine priest.

Sometimes, there is a verandah attached at the front of free-standing *devalayas*, where ritual drumming occurs during *pujas* offered by the *kapurala* to the deity. Generally, drumming accompanies *puja*s only at those *devalayas* endowed by *rajakariya* services of the drumming caste. All of the Visnu *devalayas* in the Kandy region where I conducted a field study had been royally endowed. Alternatively, it is more often the case that images of deities are simply located within *buduges* per se. In these instances, there is no separate endowment for the purpose of venerating deities.

While Visnu *devalayas* are located within the same building complex as the *buduges* at Lankatilaka and Gadaladeniya *viharayas*, the Visnu *devalayas* in Kandy and Hanguranketa, and the Dadimunda *devalaya* in Alutnuvara, are separate structural entities altogether. That is, whereas it is usually the case that *devalayas* are somehow "attached" to *viharayas* or physically located within monastic *viharaya* compounds, in the three locations mentioned the situation is almost reversed. There are Buddhist monks living in the vicinity of these major *devalayas*, but their temples are clearly derivative of the *devalayas'* wealth and fame. All of the five Visnu *devalayas* in the Kandyan culture area where I made ritual observations were originally endowed royally. In any case, the sheer physical proximity of *viharayas* and *devalayas* begs fundamental questions between the relationship of religious activities that are performed within the contexts of both types of shrines. To restate a fundamental question raised in the very first chapter of this study: how are the deities related to the Buddha or "Buddhism"?

Kitsiri Malalagoda, writing from a social historian's perspective, tempered by a Weberian theoretical framework, has attempted to explain the presence of what he, and a number of others,[24] have regarded as religious practices by Sinhala Buddhists that seem to have no origins in the normative literary traditions of the Theravada Buddhist Pali canon. These are the very religious practices that constitute most of the cultic activities at *devalayas*. Malalgoda, in an echo of Weber's attempt to explain how Buddhism became a "religion of the masses," says this about the "vital motivational factors that lay behind sustained adherence to seemingly contradictory belief and ritual systems" (23) that can be "traced to 'non-Buddhist' sources: pre-Buddhist, Hindu and Mahayanist"(!):

> Basic among the 'plebian religious needs' . . . was the need for 'emergency aid in external and internal distress.' Hence the crucial dilemma for Buddhism at the plebian level was the inadequacy of its basic concepts—as embodied in karma and rebirth—to explain *all* external and internal distress, and the inefficiency of its prescriptions—as embodied in merit-making—as a means of alleviating all such external and internal distress.
>
> In addition to karmic causality, circumstances of good and bad fortune were also explained in terms of two other forms of causality: planetary influences and the benevolent or malevolent actions of different types of supernatural beings. In accordance with these beliefs, magical "technologies" were resorted to in order to control the underlying causal processes: to

ward off disaster and to bring good fortune. . . . The supernatural beings, in whom the Sinhalese believed, were broadly divided into two main categories: the higher deities (*devas*), who were gradually incorporated into the great tradition, and the lesser spirits, or demons (*yaksas*), who were manipulated by the magicians to take back the diseases that they had inflicted on human beings. . . .

It is necessary to note, however, that these beliefs and practices did not have an independent existence. The Buddhist great tradition exercised deep and pervasive influence over the beliefs and practices of the non-Buddhist little tradition, and through the intermixture of these two traditions was formed the Sinhalese Buddhist religious system. All the 'non-Buddhist' supernatural beings derived their legitimacy through warrants (*varam*) received from the 'god above the gods' (*devatideva*), that is, the Buddha, and thereby they were 'converted' and incorporated into the Sinhalese-Buddhist pantheon. . . . [22–24]

Even early Buddhism assumed the existence of supernatural beings, but considered them irrelevant to the attainment of salvation. Since at this early stage, Buddhism was a radical form of other-worldly salvation-striving, propitiatory rituals designed to invoke supernatural beings for this-worldly benefits were depreciated as irrelevant and vulgar practices. [24–25]

Malalgoda is quoted at such length because of the manner in which he has so admirably and succinctly summarized in general the nature and presence of important popular Sinhala Buddhist religious assumptions and practices found at *devalayas*, while simultaneously articulating how these specific practices have come to be understood in relation to "Buddhism" per se. Malalgoda's Weberian interpretation seems to be somewhat congenial to the attitude toward popular religious practices developed by many Sinhala "modern Buddhists," or urban middle-class Buddhists today (Buddhists who Malalgoda himself dubs as "Protestant Buddhists" later in his book).[25]

This particular understanding of popular religious practices in Sinhala Buddhist culture is, in part, the consequence of lay-oriented religious reforms that were promulgated assiduously early in the twentieth century by the ever-popular and still revered Anagarika Dharmapala,[26] reforms in which the practices of purity in ethical conduct, diligence in work, and pride in national origins and customs ("superstitious" rituals excepted), were emphasized to the exclusion of participation in rites of deity propitiation, merit-gaining, healing, vow-taking, protection, etc.—precisely the types of religious practices that often occur at *devalayas*. These latter types of practices were roundly denigrated by the Anagarika Dharmapala and his reform-minded followers. They were regarded, as Malalgoda has noted, as "irrelevant and vulgar,"[27] since the reformers sought to reestablish the religion in its original pristine purity.

In his own otherwise laudable study, Malalgoda implies through his various descriptions and emphases that he, too, shares this perspective. It is a perspective that should be critiqued for its liabilities in order to present a somewhat different understanding of this type of religiosity, as well as its relation to "Buddhism", before the religious context per se at the Kandy Maha (Visnu) and other Visnu *devalayas* in the Sinhala up-country region of Sri Lanka can be described.

The language (for example: "demons," "magicians," "plebian religious needs," "this-worldly," "other-worldly," etc.) that Malalgoda has enlisted to describe popular or lay Sinhala Buddhist practices is loaded with Weberian assumptions about the nature of religion. His interpretation is also reliant upon the theoretical approach advanced by Redfield and later deployed by a long list of others[28] who have argued for a distinctive type of relationship that obtains between so-called "great and little traditions."

With regard to the former, Weber's understanding of Buddhism, as it is presented in his *The Religion of India* (1958) and here adopted entirely uncritically by Malalgoda, was based on a reading of "ancient Buddhism" that Weber had derived solely from a reading of translated Pali canonical texts published in English and German. Weber never set foot in Asia. Therefore, his perspective was necessarily abstract, devoid of any cultivated cultural sensitivities to the continuing religion as it is practiced within the lives of contemporary devotees. His reading is probably one of the most intellectually sophisticated renderings of Buddhist thought ever produced by a westerner, yet, as a result, is also probably about as far removed from the manner in which a common Buddhist in South Asia would understand the nature and significance of his own traditions. Insofar as Weber frequently alluded to the "unmusicality of the masses," "plebian religious needs," etc., his understanding of Buddhism appears to be unquestionably elitist in orientation. Moreover, and consequently, Weber's interpretation seems to put undue emphasis on the role of religious ideas per se as generating specific religious dispositions that, in turn, produce types of social behavior or practices.

In short, Weber has invoked an understanding of Buddhism based exclusively upon religious ideas articulated by ecclesiastical authorities written and edited in ancient, canonical, and textual traditions. It is assumed that this interpretation is the equivalent of the essential nature of Buddhism: religious *thoughts* are at the core of religion's significance. Thus, according to Weber, the genuine religious significance of religious behavior performed by the religious can be measured against, or understood as a by-product of, religious doctrines finely honed by ancient, intellectual, religious specialists. Here, religious be-

liefs, as defined by religious specialists of old, are identified as the causes of religious dispositions, and religious dispositions give rise to religious or other
forms of social behavior.[29] Moreover, practices or behavior not traceable to
doctrine would be regarded as deviant from orthodox norms.

Brilliant and enduring as Weber's thesis has been, there are some serious potential consequences and liabilities involved in applying his approach to Sinhala Buddhist culture. These include: 1) the fact that the structure of Weber's
approach is derived from his earlier studies, aimed specifically at understanding links between doctrinal ideas (such as predestination) in Protestant Christianity, the sociopsychological conditions (e.g., anxiety) that doctrine can create, and the consequent socioeconomic behavior ("inner-worldly asceticism")
of Christians who hold those doctrines; it is an approach that assumes that religious ideas hold the same relative importance and causal efficacy in every
religious culture; 2) his approach fails to recognize that religious practices
or religious experiences, rather than religious ideas, may be occasions within
which religious dispositions are generated; Weber has identified religious ideas
as a source for religious experience when, in fact, religious ideas may be more
accurately understood as *expressions* of religious dispositions ultimately derived from religious experience; 3) his approach restricts an understanding of
what constitutes religious life to that which institutional ecclesiastics have declared it to be, and thereby precludes any attempt to ascertain the nature of religiosity among the great majority of religious adherents.

These theoretical shortcomings actually indicate why Weber's attempt to
find an analogue to the Protestant ethic and the spirit of capitalism failed in his
investigations of Hinduism, Buddhism, Taoism, and Confucianism: no such
premium was likewise placed on the authority or importance of religious doctrine in those religious traditions. What Weber really proved in his studies is
that Protestant Christianity is unique among the major religions of the world
in stressing the importance of holding certain religious beliefs, in that its religious ideas are emphasized to such an extent that they may have a causative or
affective influence on emotion and behavior. If this is the case, as I believe it is,
then trying to understand one religion by means of another's yardstick necessarily leads to confusion. In short, Sinhala Buddhist religious culture, I would
contend, is not really "creedal" in its emphases.

Furthermore, Malalgoda, in following Weber so closely, has asserted that the
"unmusical masses" came to adopt the "irrelevant and vulgar" practices of a religion because of the "inefficiency of its [doctrinal] prescriptions as a means of
alleviating all such external and internal distress." That is, Weber and Malalgoda assume that the doctrine of karma was found insufficient to explain all
causes of misfortune, and so Buddhists invented or adopted other means of explaining and coping with the existence of suffering. These "new" inventions or

adaptations (or "little traditions" according to Malalgoda or as interpreted by Redfield) are then understood to have been somehow grafted onto or "incorporated" into the orthodox doctrinal (here read Redfield's "great") tradition, in the process becoming "converted" and "legitimized." In turn, "all" of these newly invented associations were contrived to receive their warrants of legitimacy from the Buddha.

First, Weber and Malalgoda do not seem to have discerned the manner in which karma functions in relation to "other" (astrological and "*yaksa*") explanations of suffering or misfortune in Sinhala Buddhist religious culture. Karma, in fact, consists not simply of "merit-making" rites (as Malalgoda has implied), nor is it simply just one insufficient "theodicy" or explanation for the cause of suffering among others (effects caused by planetary influences or *yaksas*). Rather, karma is the bedrock assumption of the operative Sinhala moral economy that explains why people are reborn as they are, and encounter various fortunate or unfortunate circumstances, *including* the reasons for their conditions resulting from various astrological configurations, or their propensity to suffer from the malevolence of *yaksa* possession as well. There is no perceived "inefficiency of its prescriptions" from the perspective of Buddhists themselves. Indeed, as I have said, karma is understood to be inexorable, implacable, inescapable, and the ultimate cause explaining all circumstances. To be clearer about this crucial point, I refer to Obeyesekere's analysis of this very issue.

In his study of the Pattini cult as a medical system in traditional Sinhala culture, Obeyesekere has explained the significance of karma this way:

> The several causation theories of *dosa* [misfortune, trouble] are conceptually *interrelated*, a "smaller" theory of disease causation generally "contained" in a larger, and the more concrete contained in the more abstract. Ritual specialists agree that *dosa,* whether arising out of physical causes or through the agency of spirits, is subsumed under two larger "laws" of causation. First, *dosa* arises because of bad planetary influences that can be detected by reading the horoscope. Second, these irrevocable planetary movements are indicators of a person's karma, that is, his good or bad actions in previous rebirths. Thus, planets merely chart a person's karma.
>
> How can the theory of supernatural incursions be related to all this? The view is that when a person's *kala*, or time (i.e., astrological "time") is bad the demons can easily inflict *dosa.* Gods can also cause *dosa* because of bad karma of the individual or the group; they are also instruments of karma, rewarding people or punishing them with *dosa.* They are ineffectual if a person's karma as manifest in his horoscope is good; however, the theory of karma is such that no one can have an entirely good karma.

Hence, anyone can be afflicted with *dosa* by supernatural beings. Thus the *immediate* cause of all illness and misfortunes may be physiological or due to the action of external spirits; the *ultimate* cause is simply the bad karma or the person or groups concerned. In fact, the deities themselves are products of karma—the gods as superior beings have been born in their present state owing to their accumulated good karma, whereas inferior beings are products of bad karma; the general rule is that the lesser the status of the deity, the greater the load of his bad karma, or *karma dosa*. [Obeyesekere 1983:47]

Obeyesekere concludes his discussion by pointing out that even the failure of ritual procedures to produce a cure or amelioration for the condition of suffering is explained by karma: its force being recognized as perhaps too great to be overcome. No doubt that is also why Knox, as well, said, "It is a usual saying, and very frequent among them (if their *Gerahah*, which is their fortune, be bad), "What can God do against it?"

From this discussion, it is possible to see clearly the problem with Malalgoda's (and Weber's) explanation (the insufficiency of karma) for the inclusion or "conversion" of "pre-Buddhist," "non-Buddhist," or "Mahayana Buddhist" practices in Sinhala Buddhist culture. Indeed, rather than being "insufficent," karma is what actually proves the case in point and provides the (Sinhala) cultural logic for all the causes of misfortune thought to come about by planetary influence and by supernatural incursion into the human condition. As Obeyesekere points out, the causes need to be understood as interrelated (*immediate* [*laukika*] and *ultimate* [*lokottara*]). And, awareness of karma is what creates the sense of resignation that Knox has referred to.

Karma, I think, need not be understood only as a "doctrine" either. It literally means "action." In virtually all strands of Hindu and Buddhist thought, it is not rendered so much as a "belief" to depend upon, but rather as an inevitable and ongoing process of causes and conditions, the result of physical and mental dispositions from which its effects are produced. When deities are propitiated to act benevolently on one's behalf, they are actually being induced to act out of their own cultivated compassion—the type of compassion that has motivated those previous actions that have propelled them to their own relatively positive positions within the social structure of the cosmos. It is by the power of their own karma that they have been positioned in such ways to command authority over other powers or to intercede benevolently in the lives of those who suffer.

Therefore, the deities, and their positions of authority, are themselves products of the moral economy of karma. Their hierarchical status within the pantheon of deities in Sinhala religious culture is a reflection of their perceived goodness and compassion. That is, deities themselves are indices of positive karmic production. Ultimately, their relative status is morally derived. The same is said about *yaksas* and their own situation within the field of play.[30] They are what they are because of what they have done, and are therefore likely to do. Understood in this way, the practices in question are not in any way "contradictory." Rather, they are completely consistent with the logic of karma.

Two further points remain to be rebutted. The first is the assertion that these practices have nothing to do with attaining an "other-worldly salvation." This assertion, at best, can only be regarded as partly true, depending upon assumptions brought to it. It is partly true insofar as the existence of planetary inclinations bearing on the life of an individual, the warding off the powers of *yaksas* or *asvaha* (the "evil eye"), or the petitioning of deities for their compassionate benevolence, does not result in the immediate experience of an "other-worldly" *nibbana*. However, the problem with this assumption, to begin with, is that *nibbana* is here understood exclusively as an "other-worldly" rather than an existential realization. To the contrary, in many of the Pali canonical formulations, *nibbana* is understood precisely as an existential realization.[31]

Nibbana is often characterized, for instance, as the *absence* of *raga* ["passion"], *dosa* ["hatred"], and *moha* ["delusion"]—dispositional mental states [*asavas*] that condition the quality of action [karma, *cetana*]. Furthermore if the proximate aim of the Buddha's teachings, as embodied in his famous *Dhammacakka Pavattana Sutta*,[32] wherein he made known the "Four Noble Truths" and the "Noble Eightfold Path," is to assuage the condition of *dukkha* ("unsatisfactoriness" or "suffering"; here, *dosa* certainly qualifies), through the cultivation of *sila* (ethical or moral conduct), *samadhi* (concentration and meditation), and *panna* (wisdom and insight), then whatever practices are consistent with these acts of cultivation may be regarded, at least theoretically, as consonant with Buddhism's ultimate soteriological aims. Appealing to the ethical consciousness of a deity would not seem contradictory at all in this view. Extending the logic of karma at work here, the deities who are being appealed to for "this-worldly" assistance are regarded as eager to help, insofar as the exercise of their bodhisatvic compassion propels them further in their own quest for ultimate spiritual realization.

Moreover, Malalgoda's (and Weber's) assumptions seem to belie an unnecessary dichotomy between "this-worldly" and "other-worldly." As I have discussed at some length elsewhere,[33] the Sinhala categories of *laukika* and *lokottara* do not accurately connote a clear divide between "this-worldly" and "other-worldly." Rather, they are best understood as two ends of a temporal continuum indicating *immediate* and *ultimate* realizations. *Lokottara*, often misunderstood as "other-worldly," actually means "pre-eminent in the world."[34]

Insisting on a rigid distinction between "this-worldly" practices and "other-worldly" attainments completely ignores Buddhist theories of time (as a seamless flow from one occasion to another) and karma per se, insofar as whatever might be attained in any "other-worldly" context is totally dependent upon "this-worldly" action. That is, any nirvana realization occurring in a future *then* (*lokottara*) is dependent upon what conditioning (or "unconditioning") is occurring *now* (*laukika*). If practices leading to amelioration of the *now* are conducive to the absence of *raga, dosa*, and *moha*, that is, if they generate moral consciousness and behavior, peace of mind, and clarity of understanding, then these are certainly not contradictory to the path, nor should they be regarded as simply "irrelevant" and "vulgar."

Second, as for understanding deities, *yaksas*, and ritual actions associated with their cults as local "little" traditions grafted onto the transcendent "great" traditions (symbolized by textual canons and the soteriologies articulated therein) and then legitimated by them, I see little to be gained and much possible distortion in holding on to these hermeneutical (interpretative) constructions. Actually, the so-called "great tradition" does not, in fact, really exist *anywhere*. It is only a scholarly abstraction that transcends cultural space and time. It is impossible to locate any of its constituent elements except in relation to "on the ground," so-called "local" or "little traditions." Where, for instance, is there to be found a temple complex, monastery, or sacred place of any kind, anywhere, that does not participate in the semiotics of localized situations? Is there ever any kind of religious life that is not somehow in situ? Are there ever any religious ideas that exist apart from individuals or groups who hold them and interpret them? Obeyesekere (1963) has argued in his extensive discussion of the "great-little" interpretative device that Sinhala Buddhist religious culture exists as a "unitary system" in the minds of its practitioners. Why, then, impose an artificial distinction where, in fact, none exists in the first place?

Third, there is some question about just how "little" the so-called "little tradition" may be. As Alan Babb (1996:174–95 and Sree Padma (2001:115–18) have pointed out, the elements (goddess veneration, propitiation of "spirits" or ancestors, exorcism, astrology, etc.) in various religious cultures that are usually identified as local, "little" traditions, are actually quite ubiquitous throughout South and Southeast Asia. So they turn out to be not so local at all and may constitute what Babb has called a "pan South Asian ritual culture" found wherever religious communities have systematically observed a regimen of familially oriented or calendrically determined cultic rites. In a sense, elements of the so-called "little tradition" may turn out to be not so "little" at all. Indeed, they are undoubtedly much more widely held than the formulaic subtleties of much religious doctrine. Each of these considerations calls into question the theoretical costs of understanding the nature of these religious phenomena exclusively according to Malalgoda's Weberian scheme.

But what is of value in Malalgoda's summary portrayal is his pointing the way to how various religious phenomena are legitimized in Sinhala Buddhist culture. While he has exaggerated the fact that *all* "non-Buddhist" deities receive their warrants from the Buddha,[35] he has indicated that there is some type of mechanism, or some type of association, that brings these supernatural beings into the sphere of a homologized Sinhala Buddhist religious worldview.

In this study of Visnu, the thesis is that this association occurs often when it is politically expedient. More specifically, the rationalization and positioning of what is included (Visnu and related deities being the focus here) in the religious culture is grounded thoroughly in the operative moral economy of karma. The "Buddhist Visnu" occupies his elevated position within the pantheon precisely because of the intrinsic goodness of his perceived actions—actions that have perpetuated the well-being of the *sasana*, the cultural instrument that houses or provides the means for living what is regarded as a truly religious life.

What legitimates the "Buddhist Visnu," then, is the nature of his perceived moral action. Since the Buddha, as the undisputed "culture hero" of this civilization, is the embodiment of the moral standard, Visnu's actions, which are understood to defend this standard, are intrinsically and categorically of a moral nature. And like the Buddha, Visnu's ultimate religious significance is to be found in his compassionate efforts to assuage the conditions of suffering (*dukkha*) and misfortune (*dosa*) in this world.

At the Maha (Visnu) Devalaya in Kandy, it might be said that virtually all petitions made by devotees to Visnu are made with this kind of understanding in mind: in the simplest formulaic terms, an existential situation conditioned by karmic forces may be ameliorated by appealing to the possibility of other karmic forces being induced to help. This is not a "non-Buddhist" formula. It is completely consistent with, for example, one of the most basic of *Dhammapada* maxims (vs. 183):

> *Sabbapapassa akaranam*
> *Kusalassa upasampada*
> *Sacittapariyodapanam*
> *Etam buddhana sasanam.*

> The non-production of all that is evil,
> The initiation of all that is wholesome,
> The purification of mind,
> This is the Buddha's teaching.

With the substance of this lengthy digression in mind, we may now proceed to a presentation and analysis of contemporary religious practice observed at the chief cultic seat of Visnu in Sri Lanka, the Kandy Maha (Visnu) Devalaya. In what follows, I will organize my comments around the various expressions (religious or not) that I have seen enacted by the *basnayaka nilame, kapuralas,* and devotees; and finally, in the chapter that immediately follows, in relation to the annual ritual performance known as *valiyaka natuma,* the most conspicuous ritual proceeding unique to cultic life at the Kandy Visnu *devalaya,* and the most germane to the substance of this inquiry. I begin with the *basnayaka nilame,* as his comments drawn from informal conversations and formal interviews—numerous occasions for which he was gracious enough to extend—help to set the context for the establishing the significance of what I observed about ritual officiants and participants.

The Basnayaka *Nilame*

When I had previously engaged in fieldwork in the early 1980s, at Natha *devalayas* in Kandy (including the famous Natha *devalaya* located adjacent to the present Visnu *devalaya* in the "sacred square" dominated by the Dalada Maligava) and in outlying villages in the up-country area, I found most *basnayaka nilames* to be rather distracted from *devalaya* affairs. They were also somewhat indifferent to my inquiries, or perhaps just unable to answer many of my questions, so my interactions with them were usually restricted to a formal interview. Moreover, more often than not, I sometimes sensed a muted antipathy toward *basnayaka nilames* among *kapuralas* and village devotees, which I then attributed to the vast differences between them in class and wealth.

While I could have been misled, I sensed none of that kind of scenario during the several months in 2000 and 2001 of my fieldwork at the Kandy Visnu and Alutnuvara *devalayas.* On the contrary, I was impressed, in general, with the *devalaya* esprit de corps and grateful for the very congenial welcome that I (and my assistants) received, not only by the incumbent *basnayaka nilame* but also by members of his staff and attendant *kapuralas.* They patiently answered our questions, voluntarily pointed out interesting occasions as they arose, and, in general, did far more than merely tolerate our presence. The more days and weeks that we were present, the more were we made to feel as if we were an accepted part of the scene, and so the more we were gradually told, despite the fact that I, as a late middle-aged American Westerner of Scandinavian ancestry, was definitely an eye-catching, almost albino-like anomaly in these social contexts.

Mr. Denis Ratwatte was the *basnayaka nilame* of the Kandy Maha (Visnu) Devalaya during those days and months of fieldwork from late 1999 through the 2001 *asala perahara* in August (see fig. 5.2). Members of his family, including his father, grandfather, and granduncle, were former *basnayaka nilames* of the Maha (Visnu) *Devalaya* during the past seventy-five years. For various periods adding up to only about twenty years of that time, someone other than a

FIGURE 5.2 Mr. Denis Ratwatte, *basnayaka nilame* of the
Maha (Visnu) and Aluthnuvara *devalayas*, 2001

member of the current *basnayaka nilame*'s family has occupied this administrative position, overseeing the daily public and business affairs of the *devalaya*. Administration of the *devalaya* has become, obviously, something of a
legacy within his family, and he has been hopeful that in the future, one of his
nephews or sons will take up the task, once he has finally retired completely.

The then current *basnayaka nilame* and his family were extremely well-
connected politically in Sri Lanka. His first cousin was Mrs. Sirima Ratwatte
Bandaranaike, the world's first woman prime minister, who enjoyed several
turns in that office until her death on the day of general elections in November of 2000. The *basnayaka nilame*'s and Mrs. Bandaranaike's fathers were
brothers, and so they shared as a common ancestor the grandfather mentioned
above, who was a previous *basnayaka nilame* of the Kandy Visnu *devalaya*.

Mrs. Bandaranaike's husband, S. W. R. D. Bandaranaike, had been elected in 1956 as the country's prime minister on a platform of "Sinhala only" and Buddhism as the state religion. Since that definitive watershed election in 1956, the family has since been identified with staunch Sinhala Buddhist interests, and they have remained the perennial leaders of the Sri Lanka Freedom Party (SLFP). They aver to be representative of the masses, and the propaganda of their political party constantly reminds supporters that their family stands for the core of traditional Sinhala society: the *sangha* (Buddhist monks), the *veda mahattaya* (*ayurvedic* physicians), the *guru* (teachers), the *govi* (peasants), and the *kamkaru* (the laborers). Moreover, the current President of Sri Lanka (elected in 1994), Chandrika Bandaranaike Kumaratunga, now serving her second term in office, is the daughter of S. W. R. D. and Sirima Ratwatte Bandaranaike, and is therefore the *basnayaka nilame*'s "niece" (though, whenever he referred to her, he respectively called her "madam" in deference to her eminent position). The then Speaker of the House in Parliament, Anura Bandaranaike, was the president's brother and the *basnayaka nilame*'s "nephew." Finally, the then Deputy Minister of Defense and Minister for Power and Energy, General Anuruddha Ratwatte, was the *basnayaka nilame*'s younger brother, and was the undisputed dynamo of SLFP interests in the Kandy area. As mentioned, the *basnayaka nilame* was extremely well-connected politically.

The position of the *basnayaka nilame* in any of the four great *devalayas* (for Visnu, Natha, Pattini, and Kataragama) in Kandy constitutes a relatively high public profile. Each year, during the annual *asala perahara* pageant, the *basnayaka nilames*, dressed in regal, late-medieval Kandyan costumes (see fig. 5.3), lead the contingents of their *devalayas* through the streets of Kandy for ten consecutive nights, along with the contingent of the Dalada Maligava (the "Palace of the Tooth-Relic"), in full view of a huge local and international audience. The *asala perahara* has been given a "play-by-play" broadcast for several years on national television, and can now even be followed on the Internet. This is Sri Lanka's most famous public pageant, a veritable national event of Sinhala Buddhist public culture, or civil religion, in resplendent display, and its history has been studied in depth by many for its religious, sociopolitical, and cultural significance.[36] Because of its prestigious public profile, and symbolic associations with traditional conceptions of Sinhala state power and religion, the *basnayaka nilame* is a position that may be sought after, even campaigned for aggressively, by those with political aspirations.

I had learned about how *basnayaka nilames* are elected back in the early 1980s, but the *basnayaka nilame* of the the Kandy Visnu *devalaya* explained many matters in much greater detail to me. The election of a *basnayaka nilame* for any of the thirteen *devalayas* involved in the *asala perahara* and related rites[37] is conducted by a body of twenty-six officials: thirteen assistant govern-

FIGURE 5.3 President Chandrika Bandaranaike Kumaratunga (first row, fourth from right), the *diyavadana nilame* of the Dalada Maligava (fourth from left), the *basnayaka nilame* of the Kandy Maha (Visnu) *Devalaya* (third from right), and the remaining *basnayaka nilame*s of *devalaya*s represented in the *asala perahara.*

ment agents (formerly known as district revenue officers) and thirteen *basnakaya nilames* of ritual-sharing *devalayas* in the Kandyan area.[38] The term is for five years. No one is supposed to serve after the age of 70, and, like *kapuralas* and the monks of the monastic *Siyam Nikaya*, they must be born into the *goyigama* (higher-caste) community.[39]

The *basnayaka nilame* is not especially pleased with this current system, he said, because the assistant government agents often behave as if they are totally indifferent to the needs of the *devalayas*. He said that he hasn't "seen one A.G.A. set foot in a *devalaya*" since he began serving his tenure as *basnayaka nilame* four to five years ago. Assistant government agents, he said, are purely political appointees with no special religious interests. Because of this, whoever becomes a *basnayaka nilame* is almost totally dependent upon whichever political party is in power, since half the votes electing individuals to the position will come from political partisans. The *basyanayake nilame* believes that this partisanship is not healthy and has not necessarily always been the norm. But it is definitely the case now that many *basnayaka nilames* occupy these positions not out of dedication to the religion or the culture, but for the political recognition derived, and possibly even for control over the vast lands owned by the heavily endowed *devalayas.*

The *basnayaka nilame* often talked about the mounting expenses incurred now in running the Visnu *devalaya.* He had taken on the *devalaya* administration after retiring as a tea-plantation executive, and my impression was that he administered the *devalaya* and its interests in a manner befitting a general manager or chief executive of a large company, or an alert head of a department of government. Although I did not ask to examine any of the *devalaya*'s contemporary and voluminous past records, I did learn from the *basnayaka nilame* that the Kandy Visnu *devalaya* legally owns some 32,000 acres of land, including 7,000 acres of coconut-cultivated estates.[40] This is an astounding amount of land to own in Sri Lanka, where laws are in effect restricting ownership of individual plots to no more than fifty acres each.

The *basnayaka nilame* said that the Kandy Visnu *devalaya* has a good deal of land leased out in Kurunegala (a large district town of about 75,000 people, located about twenty-five miles northwest of Kandy), including what is now the heart of the downtown area. It also owns much land in Kegalle (another large district town located twenty miles to the west), and tracts as far away as Avissawella, located about fifty miles west of Kandy and about twenty-five miles east of Colombo, on the very western borders of the old Kandyan kingdom. The *basnayaka nilame* supervises about 10–15 *vidanes*, who are charged to act as his representatives in trying to keep track of the status and revenues of all of these extensive and far-flung properties. His is almost a full-time job, he argues, to keep tabs on the *devalaya* and to run its business affairs. He employs a full-time clerk in his office to assist him.

The amounts of money remitted by lessees of this vast amount of land, originally donated to the *devalaya* by various Kandyan kings to enhance temple income, is, unfortunately, according to the *basnayaka nilame*, usually a very paltry sum. Rent of some tracts can be as little as three rupees a year (about US $.04). Obviously, some of the *devalaya*'s lands are now extremely valuable real estate, including extensive rice-paddy lands in Alutnuvara and prime commercial locations in Kurunegala and Kegalle. And because rent is such a tiny amount, if there is a choice between paying the rent or performing *rajakariya*[41] service to the *devalaya* for ritual services or for the upkeep of its maintenance, lessees opt for the nominal payment.

"Besides", said the *basnayaka nilame*, "the younger people these days don't like to come to the temple or carry torches for the *perahera.*" So now, instead, he hires people to perform various aspects of the public rituals that used to be taken care of by *rajakariya* responsibilities. He says that it used to be the case, for example, that some people would donate an elephant for the various ritual proceedings and only a small payment would be due the elephant's *mahout*.[42] But attitudes have changed. During one of our conversations, the *basnayaka nilame* stated that it takes about Rs. 850,000 (then US $12,000) in expenses for the *devalaya* to meet its annual *perahara* responsibilities alone,[43] but many revenues from lands have been frozen due to long term leases of 30–40 years given out for practically nothing under previous *basnayaka nilames* (here, obviously not referring to his own relations).

He added that some very wealthy people in Sri Lanka rent out *devalaya* lands for a "mere pittance" and have thus capitalized enormously as a result. The *basnayaka nilame* has suggested to his niece that all the lands should be sold at fair market value, and that the proceeds be used to endow the *devalaya* in perpetuity. But according to current Sri Lankan law, *viharaya* and *devalaya* lands cannot be sold, since the original royal declarations granting their ownership state that they shall remain in the possession of the temples "for as long as the sun and the moon shall shine." It would literally "take an act of Parliament to change this situation."

From what the *basnayaka nilame* reported about the financial holdings and income of the Kandy Visnu *devalaya,* it is clear that the position of *basnayaka nilame* holds great potential for rewarding friends and political associates, especially when new leases on land become available for negotiation. Historically, land grants were a means by which royalty publicly demonstrated their benevolence and insured the income for the continuing ritual life of temples. It was also a means of maintaining control over vast tracts of lands, and of rewarding and insuring loyalty to kings within the ranks of the nobility who usually held these positions. These lands were not taxable. They were given out in exchange for services and rewards, bound by *rajakariya* understandings.[44] Use of these lands included much more then in the way of obligation than today.

The *basnayaka nilame* stated that the income that the *devalaya* makes from money deposited into its donation boxes is now about Rs. 5,000 (US $60) per month, down from its average of Rs. 15,000 (US $175), before all of the government security forces (police and army) were installed to protect the "sacred square."[45] Since that amounts to only about Rs. 60,000 per year, it means that the *basnayaka nilame* must somehow raise the remaining estimated Rs. 800,000 for *perahara* expenses from other sources.

He says that keeping the *devalaya* out of debt is a very serious challenge to whoever administers it. He also says it has been a serious challenge to protect the sanctity of the *devalaya* from the intrusions of army personnel stationed at the large army camp located directly to the north of the *devalaya* compound. Indeed, the *basnayaka nilame* has installed a large fence in the back and on the sides of the *devalaya* compound "so that the army fellows don't disturb what goes on in the *devalaya*." (Indeed, I often sighted armed soldiers peering and sometimes leering into the *devalaya* compound from their positions on higher ground, the type of intrusion, no doubt, in addition to the thorough body-searches required to gain entrance into the "sacred square" area, which would discourage many devotees, male and female, from visiting the *devalaya*).

When the *basnayaka nilame* gave me my initial tour of the *devalaya* premises,[46] I was impressed with what I first saw. When I had seen the *devalaya*'s premises back in the 1980s, conditions were rather ramshackle. But under this *basnayaka nilame*'s stewardship, a lot of effort had gone into cleaning up and relandscaping the grounds entirely. The roof of the *devalaya* had been repaired, and in general, the entire complex had been given a face-lift. The interiors of both the Visnu and Alutnuvara Deviyo (a.k.a. Dadimunda) *devalayas* were now meticulously maintained, draped with beautiful batiks. The *sancta sanctora* for both Visnu and Dadimunda contain beautiful bronze images of Visnu and Dadimunda respectively, the latter said to be a replica of the original in Alutnuvara.

The Visnu image inside the sanctum sanctorum of the Visnu *devalaya*, which has recently been refurbished by the *basnayaka nilame*'s younger brother, is certainly not the famous red sandalwood image of mythic lore (nor was there a local mythic source that I could find which made that claim). It is a small and delicate, elegantly articulated bronze, approximately 12 inches in height, and with somewhat indistinct but standard Kandyan iconographic nobility features, quite king-like in appearance (see fig. 5.4). Judging from its style, it seems to date from the eighteenth or nineteenth centuries. I was not allowed to photograph it.[47] On the basis of seeing the image on many occasions, it is safe to say that here there is no evidence of Hindu iconographic attributes or features that are traditionally associated with the "Hindu Visnu."

Inside the Visnu *devalaya digge* (the worshipping hall where the *kapuralas* receive devotees), the *randoli*, or "queen's palanquin," that holds the "weapons" of the deity (traditionally paraded in the *asala perahara* processions), is kept. It has an ornate and intricate ivory border with Laksmi figures meticulously carved on each end. It is said, according to the *basnayaka nilame*, to have been made during the time of the first Kandyan king, Vimaladharmasuriya I (1592–1604 C.E.). I mention this reference to Laksmi now because one of the interesting features of the cult of the "Buddhist Visnu," in comparison those of the Hindu counterpart, is the *absence* of Laksmi. Visnu is always portrayed alone in Sinhala art, and Laksmi is rarely mentioned in Sinhala literature, especially in relation to Visnu. Mallikarachchi (1998:240) reports that in his survey of about 250 Buddhist traders in Kandy, he frequently found pictures of Laksmi, symbolizing wealth and the aspiration for such, in the shrines found

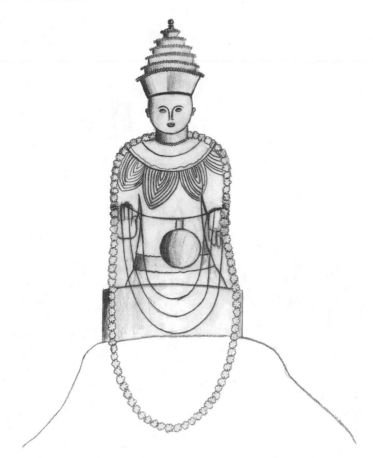

FIGURE 5.4 Sketch of Visnu image in sanctum sanctorum of Maha (Visnu) *Devalaya* in Kandy (Kanchuka Dharmasiri)

inside the traders' shops, but rarely pictures of Visnu. Indeed, in all of the popular depictions of Visnu sold on the pavement, or at small shops in Kandy and Alutnuvara selling various religious "souvenirs," Visnu is figured alone (see fig. 5.5), without his famous spouse.[48] Aside from this one cultural artifact, there is no hint of the presence of Laksmi at the contemporary Kandy Visnu *devalaya*, nor at any of the other Visnu *devalayas* that I frequented during my fieldwork.

The spatial layout of the Kandy Visnu *devalaya* compound (see fig. 5.1) reflects, I would argue, the ethical hierarchy of the deities who are worshipped therein. The Visnu *devalaya* proper dominates the premises in its size and stature. Here, Visnu is duly feted with three *pujas* a day, the vegetarian meals prepared by the *murutan kapurala*. These *pujas* are replete with half an hour of

FIGURE 5.5 Popular portrait of Visnu riding *garuda* (eagle)

drumming before the serving of the three full meals, including *kiribath* ("milk-rice") in the morning at 6 a.m., and then rice and vegetable curries at 10:30 a.m. and 7:30 p.m. After the performance of these *pujas*, the *devalaya* is opened for devotees to present their plaints to the *kapuralas* in the *digge*. *Murutan* is also offered to Dadimunda, but none to *Huniyam*, whose small shrine, about the size of a large kitchen cupboard, lurks behind the Dadimunda *devalaya*. The *devalaya* of Dadimunda, located just to the west of the Visnu *devalaya*, is itself only about thirty-percent the size of the Visnu *devalaya*. The Huniyam *devalaya* was only recently established by the *basnayaka nilame*, a sign that the popularity of this god continues to grow in Buddhist Sri Lanka.

The doors providing entry into the respective sancta sanctora of the Visnu and Dadimunda *devalayas* are draped tastefully with contemporary batik paintings of Visnu and Dadimunda, provided by one of the *devalayas'* most regular visitors, a long-time Kandy business woman devotee who, according to the *basnayaka nilame*, has successfully run a batik boutique for a number of decades.[49]

When the *basnayaka nilame* first showed me the Dadimunda *devalaya* (see fig. 5.6) after the Visnu *devalaya*, he proudly introduced the deity to me as "Visnu's Prime Minister." The *basnayaka nilame* is also the *devalaya* adminis-trator for the chief cultic seat of Dadimunda located at Alutnuvara. This dual role, he says, has been a historical arrangement which, he understands, has been in place since the Visnu *devalaya* shifted to Kandy. The Alutnuvara *dev-alaya*, according to the *basnayaka nilame*, is especially lucrative. It "owes" two months' worth of donations each year to the Visnu *devalaya* in Kandy. That revenue comes to about Rs. 550,000 (US $6,600): it is the money that makes it possible to continue with the ritual obligations of the Visnu *devalaya* in Kandy and keeps it from falling into debt. The *basnayaka nilame* says that what the *kapuralas* at Alutnuvara make is far more than this, since donation boxes typ-ically take in far less than what is offered on the *puja* plate offerings of devo-tees. In the Visnu *devalaya* in Kandy, Rs. 50 is a fairly standard offering.

Every month, the *kapuralas* for both the Vishnu and Dadimunda *devalayas* (including the *kapuralas* for the Alutnuvara *devalaya* in Alutnuvara) come to the *basnayaka nilame*'s office to register their service for various time periods. On this occasion, in addition to individual interviews, I was able to engage them collectively in their views about the three deities (Visnu, Dadimunda, and Huniyam) who are worshipped within the Visnu *devalaya* complex. From their various responses, I was able to piece together what seemed to be a con-sensus among them regarding the relative importance of each and the rela-tionships perceived to be existing between them.

I have already noted that the spatial symbolism of the *devalaya* complex re-flected a clear hierarchical relationship between these deities. According to the

FIGURE 5.6 Sketch of the Dadimunda Devalaya in the Kandy Maha (Visnu) Devalaya compound (Kanchuka Dharmasiri)

basnayaka nilame and the *kapuralas,* Visnu is definitely regarded as a *bosat* (Sinhala for bodhisatva) and therefore a future Buddha. He is a "mild god who likes to do good for all people," "to alleviate their sufferings" (*dukkha* and *dosa*), to "provide a blessing" (*santiya*), etc. While Dadimunda "works for Visnu," he also "does the kinds of things that Visnu does not really want to do. Visnu will not do anything bad." Dadimunda is "a very powerful god and people often come to get things done quickly" and decisively. If the cause is genuinely just, Dadimunda will assist in getting justice or even revenge, but he will not harm or punish a morally good person—so they say. In fact, no deity will do this; so people cannot expect to come to the *devalaya* and ask the deity to punish those they don't like, unless the cause is just. Dadimunda also wants to be a Buddha, but he is behind the queue of Natha, Visnu, Pattini, and Kataragama (see fig. 5.6).

As for Huniyam, he will do things that even Dadimunda would refrain from doing. If, for instance, a devotee comes and seeks revenge from Visnu, the *kapurala* might actually ask the devotee if he wants to ask the deity for help in forging a reconciliation instead. But this also depends on the *kapurala*. It is more likely that the devotee will try to get assistance from Dadimunda rather than asking Visnu to do something that may involve violence or force. Dadimunda is often asked to break up plans or to execute them. From the point of view of one of the Visnu *kapuralas*, Huniyam is something of a "hit man." One of the Dadimunda *kapuralas* referred to Huniyam as a "bodyguard" of Dadimunda.

From these kinds of conversations, I first began to see clearly the ethical hierarchy implicit in how these deities were conceived to operate. While Visnu is regarded as benevolent and a beacon of justice, Dadimunda is regarded as the deity who "can get things done." The *basnayaka nilame* recalled that, despite the fact that he ultimately has become a Kataragama devotee (!), his mother used to advise him and his younger brother to always seek the assistance of Dadimunda in times of great difficulties. While Visnu is viewed unambiguously as a moral being, Dadimunda is, on the whole, also seen as just, though clearly there is some ambivalence characterizing his power. It is said that he will not inflict punishment on anyone who does not deserve it. People fear his power.

In terms of earlier discussions, Visnu, as a *deva*, is both *laukika* and *lokottara*-oriented, with an emphasis on the *lokottara* end of the continuum. Dadimunda is also both but, born as a *yaksa* and known as *Devata Bandara*, is more heavily oriented toward *laukika*, since he is usually petitioned to "get things done quickly." Huniyam is almost exclusively, though not entirely *laukika*, but a supernatural who is clearly the most ambiguous in nature, especially in comparison to the other two. His cult is heavily *yaksa*-entwined. (There is much more about these two deities in the seventh chapter.)

What I most wish to note here is that not only did these three deities appear in a hierarchical relationship at the Visnu *devalaya* in Kandy, but the spatial symbolism and cultic activities of *kapuralas* that I observed at a number of other Visnu *devalayas* in the Kandy area also reflected this very same basic arrangement: a major shrine to the high god Visnu, a smaller, more humble shrine located to the side or behind the Visnu *devalaya* for Dadimunda, and a rather crude and out-of-the-way cultic area or small shrine for Huniyam. While specific *kapuralas* are assigned to ritual duties at the Visnu and Dadimunda *devalayas*, only the Dadimunda *kapuralas* will officiate for Huniyam, and then only when requested specifically by a devotee to do so. At the Visnu *devalaya* in Kandy, Huniyam is not offered *murutan pujas* like those offered to Visnu and Dadimunda respectively. Rather, he is offered scented burning coals.

It was from the *basnayaka nilame* and the *kapuralas* at the Kandy Visnu *devalaya* that I first learned about the historic relationship between the Visnu *devalaya* in Kandy and the Dadimunda *devalaya* in Alutnuvara, a relationship that I subsequently spent much time researching (as is evident from the present, previous, and following chapters). Moreover, I also learned how other *devalayas* in the Kandyan region were ritually linked to the Kandy Visnu *devalaya* as well. The *basnayaka nilame* told me that the Lankatilaka and Gadaladeniya *viharas* are regarded formally, for purposes of the annual *asala perahara*, as Visnu *devalayas*, and therefore form part of his Visnu contingent in the nightly processions of the pageant. Since Hanguranketa is now regarded as part of Nuwara Eliya district, he said, it no longer participates in the Kandy *perahara* and thus is no longer represented within the Visnu contingent. Rather, it is the featured *devalaya* of the Hanguranketa *perahara* itself, which is held a month after Kandy's.

With these comments and perspectives in mind, the discussion now turns away from the *basnayaka nilame* and the administration of the Visnu *devalaya* in Kandy to the religious and ritual worlds of the priestly *kapuralas*. I shall begin with a brief summary of what I found at the Gadaladeniya, Lankatilaka, and Hanguranketa Visnu *devalayas*, before turning in greater detail to the traditions of the Kandy Visnu *devalaya*.

THE *KAPURALAS*

Having learned from the *basnayaka nilame* about the ritual linkage between the Kandy Visnu *devalaya* and the Visnu *devalayas* at Gadaladeniya, Lankatilaka, and Hanguranketa, I spent several days visiting, observing, recording *yatikas* (liturgical prayers), and interviewing *kapuralas* and devotees at these important cultic venues in the Kandy cultural area. As I've mentioned above, I found the same ritual practices and spatial symbolism at work at these *devalayas* as I had first seen at the Kandy Visnu *devalaya*. Within the course of various conversations, each of the *kapuralas* of these Visnu *devalayas* also alluded to their kinship with *kapuralas* in Alutnuvara. At first, I mistakenly assumed that these familial references were to the two families who provide *kapuralas* for ritual services at the Alutnuvara *devalaya*. It was only later that I discovered that the Gadaladeniya, Lankatilaka, and the Hanguranketa *kapuralas* were related to the *kapuralas* of the Kandy Visnu *devalaya*, who actually live in Alutnuvara on lands originally given to them by Kandyan kings, though the Alutnuvara Visnu *kapuralas* (at least the four I came to know) claimed no knowledge of this.

Becoming aware of this set of possible kinship relations provided me with a social and historical raison d'être for the emergence of the similarity in religious, cultic, and symbolic expression at these four *devalayas*—a gestalt and dynamic forming a coherent slice of the Sinhala Buddhist religious culture domiciled and shared in these historically important and related up-country Visnu venues. It would have made perfect sense, for the kings who endowed these Visnu *devalayas,* to have appointed *kapuralas* for them from the extended families of those performing the service at the Kandy Visnu *devalaya.* There are those with memories of this having been precisely the case at Hanguranketa. While small, independent Visnu *devalayas* have proliferated throughout Buddhist Sri Lanka, these four, linked by history, royal support, and the familial traditions of *kapurala* lineages, represent not just a slice, but the historical core of the disseminated cult of Visnu in Sri Lanka.

Gadaladeniya remains a fascinating historical site on all accounts. In previous chapters, I have referred to its architectural significance as reflecting Hindu-Buddhist conflations of the fourteenth century, and as the temple that was home to the famous Theravada *bhikkhu,* Ven. Dharmakirti, a veritable spokesperson of orthodoxy, who vociferously critiqued the worship of deities in Theravada tradition during that time. These days, Gadaladeniya is frequently visited by schoolchildren on field trips, and by local and foreign tourists, as well as by its nearby village clientele. In addition to the various Hindu and Buddhist motifs found within its design, the pillars holding up the canopy over the main entrance contain descending mythic scenes of Krsna, Natharaja (Siva), and Parvati on one side, and descending aniconic (nonanthropomorphic) references to a bird, a lotus blossom, and another floral design on the other ("Buddhist") side.

The *kapurala* who serves both the Visnu and Dadimunda *devalayas* at Gadaladeniya said that he chants *yatikas* for about 50 people on each *kemmura* day, an equal number each to Visnu and Dadimunda. Local people attend largely for the same reasons as in Kandy. Occasionally, he does have to deal with *yaksa* possession. Normally, he refers such cases to Alutnuwara, if they are serious. He lives on land royally endowed to the Visnu *devalaya,* claims ancestors from Devinuwara, protects his purity religiously, and states that the Visnu image ensconced in the Gadaladeniya Visnu *devalaya* is the famous red sandalwood image.[50]

At Lankatilaka, I interviewed a seventy-five-year-old *kapurala* who had been serving the *devalaya* ritually for fifty-two years. I recorded his *yatikava* (see appendix 2) too. He said that he was the twelfth generation in a line of Brahman ancestors who went back 600 years to the origins of the *devalaya* during the reign of Bhuvanekabahu IV, in the fourteenth-century Gampola era. He also lives on *devalaya* land.[51] Though Visnu is the main god of this *devalaya,* there are also images to Kataragama, Ganesa, Saman, Vibhisana, and Kumara Bandara, believed by the *kapurala* to be the most powerful and potentially dangerous deity.[52] A small Dadimunda *devalaya* flanks the Lankatilaka shrine, and a ritual area for Huniyam is at the rear of the Dadimunda *devalaya.* The *kapurala* estimates that about fifty people come on *kemmura* days, and largely for the same set of reasons I had ascertained in Kandy.

At Hanguranketa, I found the *kapurala* tradition in confusion and disarray. The *kapurala's yatikava* was almost completely unintelligible and he claimed to own little knowledge of ritual traditions, having recently inherited the position from an uncle. But I interviewed a former *basnayaka nilame* at some length (who referred to a court case between rival *kapuralas* and the deleterious effect this has had on the *devalaya*). From the former *basnayaka nilame,* I learned about ritual connections with and *devalaya* land endowments in far away Alutnuvara, as well as the existence of an ancient *petikada* (cloth painting) said to have come from Kandy,[53] a marvelous cultural artifact I was able to examine on a subsequent visit to the *devalaya.*[54]

With regard to *kapuralas* at the Kandy Visnu *devalaya*, I should repeat that I found relations between the *kapuralas* and the *basnayaka nilame* at both the Kandy Visnu and the Alutnuvara *devalayas* to be congenial and businesslike, characterized by mutual respect in general. The *kapuralas* have little reason to fear the *basnayaka nilame* as long as they perform their ritual duties. While *basnayaka nilames* are elected for given time frames, and thus "come and go," the familial ancestors of these *kapuralas* have been serving the cult of Upulvan and the "Buddhist Visnu" for many centuries. They live on lands in Alutnuvara given to the *devalaya* by Kandyan kings and assigned to them specifically to cultivate. Their positions are tenured and relatively secure.

According to the *basnayaka nilame*, there is considerable incentive in being a *kapurala* at the Visnu *devalaya* in Kandy because "the post" is fairly lucrative. It is even more so for the *kapuralas* at the shrine in Alutnuvara. The *basnayaka nilame* estimates that the *kapuralas* in Kandy make in one month what they would make farming their Alutnuvara lands in five. The income that the *kapuralas* get is what has been placed on the devotees' *puja* plates. There are five different families of *kapuralas* who rotate their duties at the Kandy Visnu *devalaya*. Each period of duty lasts for a month. The *devalaya* maintains modest living quarters for the *kapuralas*, and a kitchen for the *murutan pujas* is located there as well.

The *basnayaka nilame* once made the comment that the younger *kapuralas* do not know the traditions as the older men do. But the problem seems to be deeper to him than just a matter of ritual knowledge. Indeed, he said, it has become necessary each month to have the younger ones sign an agreement which assures that the moneys they will be making will be shared with their families, and not just kept for themselves. (Following this lead, I later learned just how deeply the *kapurala* vocation is an embedded family concern, and not just a vocational option to be considered and easily rejected by individuals born into a "*kapurala* family.") While the *basnayaka nilame* almost always talked about the *kapuralas* in formal and financial terms, he also added that there are also some spiritual rewards in being a *kapurala*. It was clear that he respected their positions.

The *kapuralas* who are drawn from the five families in Alutnuvara trace their lineage of service to the *devalaya* of some 400 years ago, they say, to the time of the first Kandyan king Vimaladharmasuriya I (1592–1604 c.e.) They credit this king with the building of the *devalaya*.[55] They believe that their ancestors were Brahmans who had first served at the Devinuvara temple to Visnu (Upulvan is only another name for Visnu to them) before it was sacked by the *Parangi* (Portuguese).

The *kapuralas* were eager to attach great importance to preventing *kili*, or "pollution," which they understood as a kind of deleterious contamination of their purity, the effects of which would render their ritual performances ineffective. They say that they must stay pure for a period of three months before assuming their duties as *kapuralas*. That means staying away from all funerals especially, even if it means the death of a father or mother. Every day, they begin their mornings with worship of the Buddha, and then purify themselves with ablutions consisting of turmeric and water. Indeed, they sprinkle themselves with turmeric water, and the interior of the *devalaya* before and after it receives devotees every day. They are pure vegetarians during the time of their service, but may eat Maldive fish at other times.

It was not uncommon to hear from the Visnu *kapuralas* that performing the ritual duties at the *devalaya* gave them the feeling that they were becoming better persons. By this, they specifically referred to growing more compassionate with people who have serious problems, and gaining a measure of personal peace due to contact with Visnu. Practice makes for piety. One of the *kapuralas* for the Dadimunda *devalaya* made the same comment. If his power works, it "makes people happy" and he "gains respect like monk."

None of the *kapuralas* claim to have had dramatic visions of Visnu or Dadimunda, or tumultuous, life-changing religious experiences. Their powers, they insist, stand in direct relation to their observances in the inhibiting of *kili* (pollution). One of the younger *kapuralas* at the Dadimunda *devalaya* in Kandy says that he cannot undertake any other job because it would be so polluting.

Whereas five families share the duties at the Visnu *devalaya*, only one is in charge at the Kandy Dadimunda *devalaya*. This family, like the Visnu *kapuralas*, lives in Alutnuvara, but not on any *devalaya* land since the Dadimunda *devalayas* were not royally endowed. The *kapuralas* of the Kandy Dadimunda *devalaya* are relations of one of the two families who serve as *kapuralas* for the Alutnuvara Devalaya. None of the Dadimunda *kapuralas* gave me permission to record their *yatikas* (liturgical prayers). They said it would be a dangerous practice.

On the whole, these *kapuralas*, unlike those I had come to know in the 1980s who officiate at Natha *devalayas*, are well-to-do members of the *goyigama* ("rice-cultivating") caste, supervising their revenue-producing activities on land formally owned by the *devalaya* (if they are Visnu *kapuralas*). Some have parlayed their earnings to purchase considerable tracts of land of their own, including lucrative rubber and coconut estates.

When I formally interviewed all of the *kaparulas* who served at the Visnu and Dadimunda shrines in Kandy, I asked them the same set of questions and asked them to record their *yatikas*. These are the questions that I put to each:

How long have you been a *kapurala*? What other job do you regularly have? What are the benefits, aside from money, that you enjoy from being a *kapurala*? Can you describe your own religious encounters with the deity? What kinds of help do most of the people who come to this *devalaya* ask for? Do you see a relationship between times of trouble in the country and the frequency of petitions you receive to ask for the deity's help? Do most of the people who come to the *devalaya* visit both Dadimunda and Visnu? How do you (and they) perceive the relation between these two gods? Do many people come to ask for Huniyam's help? Is there a special *kapurala* for Huniyam or do you also act as *kapurala* for Huniyam as well? Is there a different *yatikava*? What do you think of Ven. Soma's argument that Buddhist people should not worship the deities?[56]

My questions indicate the types of information I had hoped to obtain from them. So what they actually told me was dependent upon the nature of these questions and what they volunteered in the elaborations I encouraged, or in other casual conversations that arose from time to time. I have already referred in passing to some of the answers that the *kapuralas* provided to me, and I have incorporated, for the most part, their responses to questions about Huniyam *yaksa* and to the Ven. Soma's antideity campaign in chapters 7 and 8 respectively. Here, I will simply note how the *kapuralas*, in general, described the importance of the deities for themselves and for their clientele.

All of the *kapuralas*, including those at Gadaladeniya and Lankatilaka, reacted animatedly to the question about Ven. Soma's assertion that Buddhists should not worship the gods. Although asking this specific question of these particular people in these contexts is something like asking a Roman Catholic priest at the Vatican if he believes in papal infallibility, their responses were varied in defense of their professions. Even though none of the *kapuralas* have had a dramatic religious experience (possession, vision, or conversion), they all speak of the positive effect they have seen in the lives of those who come to petition Visnu and Dadimunda. Indeed, they say that it is by seeing how these deities have helped so many people that they themselves have come to feel as if they are doing something important and worthwhile.

As I remarked earlier, most of the *kapuralas* also talked about how coming into contact with the deities' powers to help people has made them better people, more compassionate in nature, and calmer in disposition. A *kapurala* at the Visnu *devalaya* offered that his job was directly in line with the aspirations of traditional Buddhism: to assuage the experience of *dukkha*. So, if the gods have these positive effects, why shouldn't people come for help? In addition to this response, some of the *kapuralas* also referred to the traditional role of Visnu as a protector of the Buddha *sasana*. If Visnu has protected Buddhism, why shouldn't he be praised?

The *kapuralas* say that most people coming to the Visnu *devalaya* are asking for help in dealing with everyday problems that arise: counteracting the ill effects of planetary positions, or of *paligahima* (cursing) and *huniyam* (sorcery), in order to get help in stopping domestic violence, to gain or retain prosperity, to find a good marriage match, to pray for a good harvest, to cure illness, to bless their babies and protect pregnancies, or, if they do not get justice from the police, to seek divine retribution.

The numbers of the *devalaya*'s clientele, they say, stand in direct relationship to troubles at large in Kandy. During a recent epidemic of measles in Kandy, many people came to solicit Visnu's healing powers. "God is like a doctor," said one *kapurala*. Devotees ask for help and, in turn, make promises. A number of people come to ask protection for their sons who are in the army. But people also come when they are desperate. That is usually the case when they want to approach Huniyam. Many come at night, when they are less likely to be observed petitioning this *devata/yaksa*.

So, the reason why devotees come to the *devalaya* varies. But the proximity to the Kandy district courts means that some come to seek the justice that has been denied to them there. Given the security arrangements around the "sacred square," the entrance to the courts is now a path that passes directly in front of the Visnu *devalaya*. People from out of town are likely to visit the Visnu *devalaya* as part of their visit to Dalada Maligava and all of the other *devalayas* (Natha, Pattini, and perhaps Kataragama). They simply seek a general blessing (*santiya*). They are more likely to come in the morning for the 10:30 *puja*, which is done after the *darsan* of the Dalada at the Maligava. Devotees coming at night are likely to be from town, stopping by after work. One point emphasized by *kapuralas* from both the Dadimunda and Visnu *devalayas* is that they place a high premium on the "faith" (*bhakti*) of the devotees, as well as their own conditions of purity. These two factors seem to be the most important prerequisites for successful appeals to the deities.

The *kapuralas* say that ninety to ninety-five percent of the people who come to the Visnu *devalaya* are Buddhists, although a few Hindus in the Kandy business community also show up regularly to venerate Visnu. There are even some Christians and Muslims who come for help, especially at the Dadimunda *devalaya*. They don't come out of their own "faith," but because a Buddhist friend has told them about the power of the god "to get things done quickly." People will often come to the Dadimunda *devalaya* in Kandy when they can't go to Alutnuvara. It serves as a type of surrogate.

On various occasions during field study at the Kandy Visnu *devalaya*, I was able to record the *yatikas* (petitionary prayers) of *kapuralas* from four of the five families providing ritual service. *Yatikas* form the heart of the liturgies at *devalayas* in Sri Lanka. They consist of a chant sung in a style unique to each *kapurala*: from, on one hand, rapid-fire types of rants that positively demand a response from the deity, to rather soft, lyrical, and endearing types of poetic entreaties, on the other. They comprise the formula that the *kapuralas* use to petition the deity on behalf of devotees, and they are uniformly and rather simply structured.

The first part consists of calling upon the deity and offering praise. It contains epithets and brief descriptive allusions to the specific fame of the deity. The second contains the petition itself and indicates what powers are to be tapped, as well as the specific request of the supplicant. The nature of the particular request is inserted into the *yatika* at the appropriate place in the second part.[57] Often *yatikas* contain many archaic words that even some of the *kapuralas* cannot translate. All the *kapuralas* say that their *yatikas* never change. They are regarded as sacred words that each has inherited from his or her predecessors. In effect, they are believed to function as elaborate mantras.

In all, I recorded nine *yatikas* for Visnu at various Visnu *devalayas*. Each are presented in English translations in appendix 2 at the end of this chapter. The first four (1–4) were recorded at the Kandy Visnu *devalaya*, the next three (5–7) were recorded at Alutnuvara, Gadaladeniya, and Lankatilaka in the Kandyan culture area, and the final two (8–9) at Devinuvara, at the southern tip of the island. I have referred to them in these three different ways (Kandy Visnu *devalaya*, Kandyan culture area, and Devinuvara) because they relate to three separate groups of *kapurala* traditions or lineages. But *yatikas* numbered 1–7 form what I would call, in general, the "Kandyan tradition." I label them thus because these *devalayas* are linked by ritual proceedings and the kinship of their *kapuralas*.

Numbers 8–9 form the "Devinuvara tradition." No *kapurala* from either the Kandy up-country region or from Devinuvara knew of any surviving or contemporary links between the two traditions. Neither did the *basnayaka nilames*. (I will discuss the ritual traditions of Devinuvara in the final, concluding chapter.) My collection of *yatikas*, however, is less than perfect. I failed to collect a fifth *yatikava* from the Visnu *devalaya* in Kandy; that is, from one *kapurala* representative of the fifth family that ritually serves that *devalaya*. Further, despite two attempts, the *yatikava* from the Hanguranketa Visnu *devalaya* was unintelligible to my expert translator.[58]

With these limitations in mind, the significance of these *yatikas* will be discussed in two ways: first, how various specific references in the first part of the *yatikas* are indications of the surviving elements of the "Buddhist Visnu's" mythic profile (that is, what mythic elements previously noted in textual analyses have been preserved within the liturgies of contemporary *kapuralas*, and thus what seems to have been de-emphasized or lost as well); second, how the *yatikas* anticipate the types of requests, and therefore the religious or worldly needs, of the devotees who ask the *kapuralas* to chant on their behalf.

With regard to what mythic elements of the "Buddhist Visnu" have survived and are emphasized within the contemporary liturgical *yatika*, the most outstanding feature is the complete absence of references to Rama. Because there is such a rich tradition of allusion to Rama in medieval Sinhala literature and because Rama is addressed specifically in the Kandy Visnu *devalaya sannasa*, this absence is stunning. What this must mean is that either this aspect of the "Buddhist Visnu" has been completely dropped during the past 300 years from the liturgical traditions, or that it was an emphasis never stressed by the *kapurala* traditions in the first place, and an aspect stressed only by royally supported traditions now long defunct. Related to this is the complete absence of any *yatika* references to the traditional role of the "Buddhist Visnu" as a protector of the Sinhala state, a feature that was so prominent in medieval *sandesaya* literature and stressed in the *devalaya*'s early eighteenth-century *sannasa*.

In short, this finding indicates the contemporary eclipse of an important dimension of the cult of the "Buddhist Visnu" in Sri Lanka: its public political significance. It could be argued, for instance, that such a reference would be irrelevant to the private petitions of individual devotees, but there are other references to the "Buddhist Visnu's" traditional "public" profile that are not absent, but on the contrary, conspicuous in these *yatikas*. So, that argument is somewhat spurious. Thus, what seems to be the case in the abstract is that while Visnu may have originally found a place within Sinhala Buddhist culture for political reasons, the reasons for his "staying power" have become quite different. That is, he has been valorized for reasons other than political.

While there is no reference in any of these *yatikas* to the mythic moment of Visnu's protection of the Buddha during his confrontation with Mara on the night of his enlightenment, eight of the nine *yatikas* (except the first of those of the Kandy Visnu *devalaya*) mention the expectation that Visnu will become a Buddha in (or for) 5,000 years. This emphasis underscores the general nature and importance, and the extremely high regard, of his continuing Buddhist significance. It is his future as a *buddha*, rather than his prowess in protecting the state, that has survived and continues to receive emphasis. Moreover, four of the *yatikas* (all from the Kandyan culture area, but not found in either of the Devinuvara specimens) refer to his well-known role as the protector of the *Buddhasasana*, a function in which he has gained enormous merit, and which propels him along the bodhisatvic path.

Five of the *yatikas* (three from the Kandy Visnu *devalaya* and two from Devinuvara) contain references to Visnu's identity as Upulvan, thus reflecting a memory of the deity's earlier mythic and historical legacy. Eight of the nine (including all from the Kandy culture area) refer to him as *devaraja*, or "king of the gods," his best-known epithet throughout myth and history. Six of the *yatikas* formally address him as "Sri Visnu," while another six (those from the Kandy Visnu *devalaya* and Devinuvara) indicate his mythic and historic presence at Devinuvara. His heavenly abode in the Himalayas, Vaikuntha, is mentioned in only two of the up-country *yatikas*.

While a string of epithets in some of the Kandyan *yatikas* may reflect an attempt to articulate the presence of Visnu's proclivity to take on numerous forms, only the Devinuvara *yatikas* explicitly mention his ten avatars. In addition, the Devinuvara traditions contain two other details absent from any of the Kandyan: the epithet *Devanarayana* and Visnu's relation to the *kadira* family of deities. What is unique to the Kandyan and absent from the Devinuvara traditions is Visnu's role as protector of the *Buddhasasana*, and allusions to the mythic and heavenly Vaikuntha. All of the other motifs I have mentioned are shared by both traditions.

In sum, the contemporary "Buddhist Visnu," as known in the liturgical traditions of *kapuralas* now serving at Visnu's most important cultic seats, is most uniformly still known as *devaraja* ("king of the gods"), a bodhisatvic Buddha-in-the-making, and is clearly connected historically to the legacy of Upulvan *deviyo* at Devinuvara. What, in general, is noteworthy about these findings is the almost exclusive Buddhist emphases given to Visnu in the Kandyan culture area, while telling aspects of the Hindu background (especially the explicit references to the ten avatars) remain in the Devinuvara *yatika*. In the Kandyan culture area, Visnu is emphatically proclaimed as the protector of the *Buddhasasana*.

While this last motif, in addition to his bodhisatva status, may remain his best-known attribute and account for his exalted status within the ranks of the divine hierarchy, Visnu means more than the substance of his surviving public profile to his devotees. How, specifically, is he expected to respond to those devotees who invoke his name and power?

Devotees

From a reading of the *kapuralas' yatikas* in appendix 2 to this chapter, several dimensions of Visnu's perceived protective power are clearly evident, at least those that are anticipated within the *kapurala*'s liturgical chants. It is clearly powers of protection and prosperity that devotees seek from Visnu, but it is protection from a variety of potential difficulties caused by an equally variable number of potential malefic sources.

In seven of the recorded *yatikas*, the *kapuralas* seek Visnu's protection from the possible misfortunes that can arise from planetary positions. Indeed, in some popular pictoral portrayals of Visnu, he is positioned in the center of the nine planetary deities (*nava graha*) who seem to be in rotation around him (see fig. 5.7).[59] He is "in charge" of these deities, or their powers appear to be devolving from his own cosmic position as creator. Visnu can be petitioned to intervene in order to ward off, but not completely eliminate, misfortunes that arise from the influences of these planets and their changing relations to one another. This is the primary reason that motivates most people to come to the *devalaya* for *santiya* (blessing). Many have been referred to the *devalaya* by local or personal astrologers who have warned them of the commencement of a dangerous period in their lives, according to their astrologically determined horoscopes.

By coming to the *devalaya* and by petitioning Visnu or making a vow to him, devotees are engaging the powers of a defensive posture. Petitioning Visnu to influence the forces of the planetary deities may be just one of any number of measures taken during times determined to be potentially dangerous or malefic. These forces, as I noted in a previous discussion earlier in this chapter, are ultimately determined by a person's karma. They are articulated, in part, through planetary configurations that cannot be eradicated, much in the same way that one cannot eradicate the fact that one has been born into a family within a particular set of socioeconomic conditions. The forces produced by planetary positions can only be coped with more or less effectively, not avoided. In describing the problems of *dosa* caused by planetary influence, Obeyeskere (1983:46) has this to say:

> A person's *graha* is irrevocably determined at birth: each individual is born under the auspices of a particular planet. Right through his life-span his fortunes are determined to a great extent by his stars. The *dosa* that come from planets are the most difficult to eradicate, and hence all types of misfortunes that are generally inexplicable or cannot be eliminated by normal ritual means are classed as *graha dosa*.

Because Visnu is the most cosmically oriented of the four warrant deities, no doubt because of the legacy of his Puranic profile as creator and preserver, he,

FIGURE 5.7 Popular portrait of Visnu surrounded by the *nava graha* (nine planetary deities)

more than any other deity, is associated with the powers of planetary deities and petitioned to exercise his compassion in ameliorating their possible deleterious effects. That is, the force of Visnu's own divine glance may be enlisted to counteract forces that have been unleashed orginally as a result of one's own doing (karma). This is the most general function attributed to Visnu in providing protection. He is thus a deity who is often appealed to as a last resort, when other ritual techniques may have failed and the only possible remaining cause of misfortune is attributed to the stars.

Also mentioned in seven of the nine *yatikas* is the formula of providing protection against the 98 diseases (*rogas*), 99 serious diseases (*vyadhis*), and 203 minor afflictions (*antaras*). These are all regarded as physical ailments or sicknesses brought about by the imbalance of the three basic humors: air, bile, and phlegm. So, whereas the misfortunes of the astrological type require a kind of cosmic realignment, these illnesses require a bodily realignment, or rebalancing. Obeyesekere (1983:44) notes that these types of illnesses are classified *atul pantiye dosa* ("the internal class of *dosa*"), which are caused by natural factors, as opposed to those caused by external sources (planets, *yaksas*, *pretas*, sorcery, etc.). While these "internal" sicknesses are normally treated by *ayurvedic* physicians, Visnu seems to have been given a significant role in aiding the process of healing. Health is one of the major motivating factors in generating devotee visits to his shrines. What is sought is a restoration of balance between the three humors which, in this instance, have been upset not through some kind of external agent, but internally through what Obeyesekere has called the "anger (*kopavima*) of the three humours." From this, it might be adduced that what Visnu is being called upon to do is to assist in the quieting of the agitation causing the imbalance. This is a plea for peace of body and mind.

Dosas may also be caused by a number of other sources as well. Among these, the most prominent in the *kapuralas' yatika* seem to be those that occur as the result of the external malignant forces of *yaksas* or *pretas*, which are mentioned formulaically in five of the nine *yatikas*, or by human beings through the so-called "evil-eye" (*asvaha*), which is mentioned in six. Indeed, the dimensions of Sinhala Buddhist religious culture associated with *yaksas* are enormously complex and have been studied in great detail by many others.[60]

The matter is taken up in general fashion in chapter 7, which focuses on Dadimunda's cult, and the significance of *dos* in the *valiyaka natuma* rite is discussed in chapter 6. For now, to put it simply, though *yaksas* are regarded as one of the traditional sources of *dosa* causing mild or serious illnesses, depending on the particular *yaksa* causing the affliction, I saw not a single case of *yaksa* possession or devotees claiming to be afflicted by *yaksas* during my fieldstudy time at the Kandy Visnu *devalaya*. Moreover, the *kapuralas* reported that it would be regarded as an extremely uncommon experience at the Kandy Visnu *devalaya* for such an event to occur.

Despite the fact, as was noted in the last chapter, that there is considerable folk-ballad literature (the cycle of "golden bow" ballads) linking Visnu to this dimension of religion in Buddhist Sri Lanka, that dimension seems to have largely disappeared in the contemporary cult. If Visnu is invoked at all in ritual proceedings (*tovil*) aimed at alleviating *dosa* caused by *yaksas*, it is only in a preliminary and perfunctory manner.[61] Therefore, it would seem that in the present, at least in the Kandy culture area, Visnu is associated only in a very limited way with the cult of *yaksas*.[62] Insofar as Dadimunda, his "prime minister," is widely regarded as "chief of the *yaksas*," it may be that Visnu's function in this regard is no longer really needed, since another powerful deity has so clearly emerged as a decisive force to meet this particular need.

Dealing with *yaksa* possession is more formally Dadimunda's domain. But Visnu can be generally appealed to as well, insofar as he might provide some measure of protection from *Huniyam yaksa*, whose small shrines, as I have noted, are also to be found inconspicuously within Visnu *devalaya* compounds. But even here, it is more often the case than not that Visnu would be in a positive league with Huniyam, who functions as a *devata* during the bright half of the lunar month.

As mentioned, *pretas* (spirits of departed kin) are also regarded as sources of affliction, but again, I think that like *yaksas*, the mention of these two sources of *dosa* in the *yatikas* of these *kapuralas* is largely a historical legacy, one that rarely seems to come into play these days at contemporary Visnu *devalayas*. *Pretas* are still part of contemporary Buddhist folklore, as they have been since the inception of Buddhism in Lanka,[63] but again, I saw virtually no signs of concern about them at the Kandy Visnu *devalaya*. That Visnu is thought to have some power over them is probably simply a cultural legacy, now "boilerplate" for the various *yatikas*.

Pretas are often ancestors who, as a result of greed, have been reborn in pitiable conditions usually revealed to their surviving relatives in dreams. They are, perhaps, the closest Sinhala analogue to ghosts in the West, though even this would be misleading. They are usually placated through *dana* and *pirit*. Chapter 7, focused on Dadimunda, provides an account of a contemporary female medium who communicates regularly with departed relatives of clients. every Saturday and Wednesday at her own private *devalaya* in rural Kandy.

The almost complete absence of problems associated with *yaksas* and *pretas* at the Kandy Visnu *devalaya* may signal a number of changes, in addition to the continued rise in provenance of Dadimunda. In the first instance, most of the devotee clientele at the Kandy Visnu *devalaya* is from Kandy itself, and not from villages or rural Sri Lanka. This is one of the major differences between the clientele profile of this *devalaya* and the one at Alutnuvara, or the clientele at Hanguranketa, Gadaladeniya, and Lankatilaka. That is, many of the devotees in Kandy are middle-class, and thus more thoroughly secularized in this urbanized context. They are, therefore, more alienated, removed, or simply unfamiliar with the legacy of some of the folk traditions examined in the previous chapter, and specifically with the *yaksa* dimensions of Sinhala religion. Consequently, they do not associate Visnu with a command over *yaksa* forces, for *yaksas* have largely ceased to be regarded seriously as a real force to be reckoned with in their lives.

Another factor may be the diminishing knowledge of the *kapuralas* themselves. Many of those I interviewed were quite apologetic about their limited knowledge of Visnu. They see themselves as largely fulfilling a familial duty and making a living as best as they can. Unfortunately, they do not really regard themselves as experts in the lore of Visnu. (If not them, who?) Disappointingly, none of them were aware of the traditions associated with Visnu's "golden bow."

While I found little in the way of *yaksa* or *preta* concerns at the Kandy Visnu *devalaya*, I did find a number of instances that had to do with protection against the "evil eye," many more so at the Dadimunda *devalaya* in Kandy than at the Visnu *devalaya* per se. Protection from the "evil eye" is mentioned in six of the nine *yatikas* I collected. Scott (1994:38–66) has written a cogent essay on the nature and power of "malign glances" thought to originate from *yaksas*, which he refers to as *disti*, and are associated with the "evil eye."[64] But the term I found deployed in these various *yatikas* and in interviews with various *devotees* was not *disti*, but *asvaha* (literally: "eye poison"). At the Visnu *devalaya* in Kandy, perhaps the most conspicuous concern for this matter of the "evil eye" was evident in the number of small children brought to the *kapuralas* by parents to receive protection from Visnu's compassionate glance, thought to be an antidote for whatever malignant powers might derive from the "evil eye." As is shown later in this chapter and again in chapter 7, *disti* can also be interpreted as a constructive power, and many individuals have enlisted it to set up their own businesses as healers or as communicators with the dead.

Finally, the *yatikas* I recorded, in addition to these various types of protection, also appeal to Visnu for reasons of prosperity. In seven of the nine *yatikas*, specific appeals are made in this regard. Visnu's power is especially relevant at the time of Alut Avurudu (the Sinhala New Year in April), but my sense is that similar appeals are made to any number of other deities as well, not only at this time but throughout the year.

In addition to the Visnu *kapuralas'* *yatikas*, I also came across the following texts from the *Sarva Deva Kannalawa*, a printed collection of "prayers to various deities" that can be chanted by devotees at *devalayas*, especially when there are no *kapuralas* in attendance to do the chanting of a *yatikava* for them. These types of texts are often available on sale for a few rupees at pilgrimage sites, especially on *poya* days or during annual festivals. They provide more examples of how Visnu's profile continues to be maintained in the popular ritual context.

Below are two examples of these popular prayers, or better, invocations, which simply eulogize the deities, in this case Visnu. They are to be chanted or said in the context of making an offering of merit and a general request for good fortune. Both are simple and basic, but also contain rich allusions to motifs previously mentioned and discussed above. The first is in verse while the second is in prose. The first is written as a chant, while the second can be intoned in the general manner in which *kapuralas* chant their *yatika*.

O Visnu!

1.   Holding disc in right hand,
     Your body gleaming blue,
     Mounting *garuda vahana,*
     O Visnu, provide all of us with good fortune.

2.   Lord of Mount Vaikuntha
     Gazing on the four great *devalayas,*
     Accept our merit
     And bring wealth and good fortune within reach.

3.   Sri Lanka and the *Buddhasasana*
     Are under your care, Lord of Vaikuntha.
     O divine Sri Visnu, you provide
     Every good in every way.

4.   In water, on land, up, down or wherever,
     Plaints from the high, low, destitute vagrant or whoever,
     You have never forsaken any.
     O mighty *deva*, protect me as well!

5.   Offering sandal, camphor, oil and flowers,
     Mighty *deva*! We'll always plead to you.
     We offer our merit. Open your eyes
     And remove my sufferings.

6. Of the god named Maha Visnu
   There is great power and authority.
   If I have done anything wrong, forgive me!
   Accept our merit, and save us all.

To Visnu Deviyo

Prosperity!

O Visnu, supreme divine being, who for five thousand years will keep watch over Sri Lankadvipa, Jambudivipa, the four great islands, the eighteen countries, the *Buddhasasana*, the oceans, and the four great devales, supreme being known as *satta sila deva narayana,* Maha Visnu of the Asura clan dwelling at Vaikuntha, Half-Visnu for this *kalpa,* Sri Visnu, Demala Visnu, Full Visnu, you, known by all ten names above, who has appeared in the fourth *kali yuga* in ten avatars including Ravana, Varasara, Mal, Kirti, Demala, Gaja, Naga, Buddha, Sri Visnu, and Narasinha, you who appear in this world through ten avatars, will be the future Buddha. And if you crossed the human world in three great strides, and if you honored the Buddha, and if you are known as Dumartha Vijaya, O mighty god, destined to attain buddhahood in the future, may you consider the plaint I place before you. Pardon the thousands of errors committed by us intentionally or unintentionally. Partake of our merits, protect us, and accept these flowers and lamps. For your reign of five thousand years, prosperity! Prosperity! Prosperity!

Lord of heaven and the gods, Visnu, focus the gaze of your eyes on my plea; toss aside, like water on an *ola* leaf, all our perils and misfortunes caused by stars and planets.

Look upon me now, grant my pleas and bring me good fortune.

I have included these two plaints not only because of the fact that they are distinctive when compared to the *yatika* of the Visnu *devalaya kapuralas* in appendix 2, but because I think they are very widely used, given the fact that most small *devalayas* or images of Visnu are not attended by *kapuralas.* They exist in a kind of "self-service" capacity. These texts subsitute for a *kapurala*'s *yatika.* Moreover, in an interview with a senior monk at Kande Viharaya on the southwest coast, when I asked about how the *kapuralas* were recruited and trained for that temple's famous Visnu *devalaya,* I was told that pamphlets and books (such as the ones from which these two plaints have been drawn) can be found with the relevant *yatika* to be learned.[65] The two examples cited above clearly show the continuing influence of Hindu and Christian traditions at work, where motifs such as Visnu's three strides, his ten avatars, and asking for forgiveness of sins are found.

When I began to regularly attend the Visnu *devalaya* in Kandy in February 2000, I spent several days simply observing the ritual behavior of devotees, interviewing initially only the *basnayaka nilame* and *kapuralas*. I could see that the *devalaya* was much more busy on Wednesdays and Saturdays, the traditional *kemmura* days of the week when the deities are thought to be more responsive to entreaties, owing to the fact that these days are generally regarded as inauspicious times when people are more likely to find themselves in need of help. I began the process of interviewing individual devotees following the *pujas* or *yatika*-chanting performed on their behalf by the *kapuralas*. Sometimes, this led to long and animated conversations lasting up to forty-five minutes or an hour each, especially with devotees who had arrived alone at the *devalaya*. These are the questions uniformly asked of these first interviewees:

> Where do you live? Which deity [Visnu, Dadimunda, or Huniyam] have you come to petition and why? How often do you come to the *devalaya* (daily, weekly, monthly, annually)? Are you Buddhist? What do you think of Ven. Soma's contention that Buddhists should not worship the deities, but should seek to strengthen themselves through practicing *sila, panna*, and *samadhi*?

I managed to talk to about three or four people a day on this type of basis. Since most people arrive for the mid-morning *puja*, this was about all I could manage at the beginning, but these were also the most in-depth contacts I made. I learned that some people came to the *devalaya* very regularly, even daily, as part of their devotional religious lives. More often, I found that many came once every three months to renew their lives spiritually—a kind of ritual maintenance to make sure that they continued to be within the focused glance of the deities.

Others came in response to immediate troubles. Their stories were sometimes heart-wrenching, sometimes almost pathetic. Some women arrived because of husband or father troubles. Several had husbands who were having affairs with other women, or were angry or abusive to them or their children. One mother had a son seriously ill with fatal diseases that could not be cured by Western or Ayurvedic medicine. Another had a son possessed by a *bhuta* and had been told to take the boy to Alutnuvara, but he had refused to go. She had come to Visnu to help change his mind.[66]

Other women wanted to become or were already pregnant and had come to the Visnu *devalaya* to insure a successful gestation. Some were looking for good

matches for their daughters or for themselves. Some were hoping that their husbands would get promotions. One had been robbed and sought justice from
Dadimunda. Another wanted Visnu's blessing and permission to get help from
Dadimunda in keeping her son, who had assaulted a fifteen-year-old girl he had
wanted to marry, and was hiding from the police. Another wanted permission
to approach Huniyam to help evict tenants who, she said, were destroying her
house. One simply wanted blessings (*santiya*) from Visnu for a nice family va-
cation in Lanka (having returned from Switzerland with her Swiss husband).

One day, a middle-aged woman became so emotionally wrought in front of
the Huniyam shrine that she literally trembled in anger and stamped her feet
during the *kapurala*'s *yatikava*. She came to ask Huniyam to cause the woman
with whom her husband was having an affair to be plagued by the possession
of *yaksas*, to suffer from horrible nightmares, to go crazy, and then, as a result,
to commit suicide.

Men came for some of the same reasons, seeking health for sick members of
their families, promotions in their jobs, protection for their wives working in
the Middle East, for their sons serving in the Sri Lankan Army, etc.

Besides petitioning the deities for these specific types of assistance, many
devotees would also first come to the *bodhi* tree, light incense or lamps, chant
gathas (verses), or simply meditate, before proceeding to the *devalayas* proper
to offer their *pujas*. This they did to transfer merit to the deities as offerings in
exchange for help.

The cultic activity at the Visnu *devalaya* in Kandy was hectic on Wednesday
and Saturday mornings. By interviewing selected individual devotees, I felt
that while I was learning a lot about a number of specific reasons for devotees
to seek the help of Visnu and Dadimunda, I did not think that I was getting the
kind of information that might yield an understanding of general patterns.
Also, I found that people arriving in groups (almost always as families) were
unlikely to give me some of their time to answer questions after their *pujas*. I
also felt that I was increasingly becoming a distraction at the *devalaya* by continuing to conduct these types of interviews. Sometimes, crowds of people
would surround us in curiosity, some thinking that there was a queue to join,
to get interviewed next.

But in these conversations, I did learn that most of the devotees did not take
seriously Ven. Soma's exhortations to stop worshipping the deities to solve
their problems. In general, it was precisely because their problems were irre-
solvable by conventional means that they sought help from the deities in the
first place. Most said that Ven. Soma simply couldn't understand their plights
and didn't realize just how important the deities are for purposes of protection. Almost all mentioned that Visnu, in particular, was part of Buddhist tradition (since he was the protector of the *Buddhasasana* and would become a

buddha himself), so they were a bit perplexed that a famous monk would say that Visnu shouldn't be worshipped.

After a few weeks of these "qualitative" interviews based on the questions I have noted above, I designed a new two-pronged strategy aimed at generating data that were not simply incidental and could indicate in general how many and what types of people came to the *devalaya*, and for what purposes. So, I decided to pursue a more detailed case study on the one hand, and also to take a controlled "census" of devotees on the other.

In the first instance, I asked one of my assistants to spend a day with one of the female devotees who regularly came to the *devalaya*, an elderly woman who had been most obliging in response to our inquiries. My "census" data below, which profile the types of people visiting the *devalaya* and the reasons for their visits, reveal that middle-aged and elderly women form the age and gender group most frequently in attendance at the *devalaya*. For that reason, I selected Mrs. G. Wijeratne of Kandy as a case study to pursue in some detail. As it turned out, her story was certainly not typical of most devotees. It was extraordinary. But it addressed many of the salient issues with which I had become concerned. I reproduce it in full as it was recorded and then translated by my assistant[67] in May 2000.

I am originally from India. I was very small, around five or six years old when I came here. We had come because of our father's business. I am the seventh child in a family of sixteen children—eight boys and eight girls. Today, I am sixty-nine years of age and a widow. My husband died two years ago. I have two children. My daughter is married and my son lives with me.

I have been coming to this *devalaya* for forty years. I come here every Saturday without fail and sometime on Wednesdays too. When I come, I first go to the [Dalada] Maligava, and then to the *bodhi* tree here, then to the *devalayas*: Visnu, Dadimunda, and Huniyam. I tie a *panduru*, offer some betel and light an oil lamp, and have a *puja* performed when I can afford it. Those days, I used to have big *pujas* performed every day. That was when I was comfortably well off. Now I am not.

Even though we are originally Hindus, I consider myself as basically Buddhist. I do not see much if any distinction between the two religions because Buddhism also originated in India and is therefore basically Indian. I do not see any distinction between deity-worshipping and Buddhism either. It is the same in both cases—you go and ask for help. There are also gods in Buddhism like Visnu.

I know very well that I have the blessings [*santiya*] of the deities and the Buddha. In fact, I was born in *deva gana* [an auspicious time frame—

nakethe) because my grandmother made a vow before *Isvara deviyo* [Lord Siva] that I should be born as a girl and not a boy. I am a *deva daruwa* ["child of the gods"].[68] My birth has been very fortunate for my family. After my birth, the business flourished and the troubles ceased. Before that, my father had had many problems.

Because I am blessed by the deities (all the deities—Kataragama, Visnu, Dadimunda, Kali, Isvara, etc.), I'm never subjected to serious suffering. They look after me. If any troubles befall me, I always see them in my dreams. Deities, could be any deity, appear in my dreams and inform me. Sometimes they might suggest that I take some precautions.

I have many problems at present. My sister-in-law (the wife of one of my brothers) is trying to grab the entire family business along with my brother. They do not want to divide it among the other siblings. My father was a very successful businessman. He had a textile industry. We were one of the richest families in Kandy, those days, and owned many shops— Chandra Batiks, Chandra Textiles. Since my father's death, my greedy brother has been trying to grab everything. He has even killed three of my other brothers through *gurukam* and *Huniyam* and "black magic." He practices those arts to destroy me too. I was involved in the business with my father. But now since the shops have been forcibly taken over by my brother, I have lost all income. My eldest brother and one of my sisters support me. We have all filed a court case against my brother and it has been going on for twelve years now. I come here every week and pray to the deities for justice. I know they will grant it. My brother is still trying to destroy me through *Huniyams*. Sometimes deities appear and show me the places where charmed eggs, pots and other things have been buried in my premises to kill me. I actually find them. Another person would have been killed by such powerful charms. But I am protected by the deities and therefore am alive.

Sometimes, I get visions of the deities and also of the Buddha, who I have seen three or four times. I have seen the goddess Kali and Kataragama Deviyo many times in my dreams. They always tell me that they are there to protect me from the evil intentions of people. Visnu Deviyo appears in times that I have *apalas* [times of bad planetary influences]. Once he told me that I will have this bad period for thirty-one years, but that none can do me harm nevertheless.

I also go to Dadimunda and Huniyam. People say they are malicious. No deity is malicious. It is people who come and make vows to kill others who are malicious. But deities are not like that. They first judge if the intended punishment is just or not, if that person really deserves the punishment. If he or she does not, then the deities will not punish. Again, if you try to do something bad to others [by appealing to the deities], it will definitely come back at you some day. Also, if your karma is such, even the deities cannot help you. I also go the *kovil* [Ganesa temple] almost every week. All these gods here [Visnu, Dadimunda and Huniyam at the Maha (Visnu) Devalaya] are present there too.

I do not like it when people blame deities when their wishes do not come through. It doesn't have anything to do with the deities' powers, but has to do with their own karma. One day there was this man who had taken a big loan from someone and couldn't repay. He was failing and he blamed Visnu Deviyo in my presence. He really tried my nerves and so I hit him with my slipper. I told him not to talk such blasphemy, because the fault was his own *karma.*

I have a special attachment to Kataragama Deviyo. Twenty-five years ago when I went to Kataragama, I fell unconscious all of a sudden. Those days, I suffered from a disease (piles). When I regained consciousness, I was already feeling much better and I got a *disti*. The *kapu mahattaya* said that I had been gifted with a very powerful *disti*, but I didn't want to continue with it. My illness was cured. Since that day, I went to Kataragama [the cultic seat of this deity located to the far southeast of the island] each year for seventeen years. But I haven't been able to go for the past two or three years because of my financial problems and needing to look after my children. During those seventeen years, I have danced *kavadi* and walked on fire four times.

Those days, whenever I would hear drumming during the *puja*, I would always go into a trance. Now it does not happen that often, because my power has declined owing to the *gurukam* and *Huniyam* done against me. This is because deities do not like "black magic" and do not come very close if it is present. They will help only from afar. Even now, during the *vali yakuma* dance just after the *perahara*, I get possessed, but no more during the *pujas.*

I did not want to make use of my *disti* because I would have used it, like others, for my own selfish purposes, like making money. Those days, when I went to Kataragama, I used to offer curtains each time I went. It was something that my father used to do. I have offered curtains to this [Visnu] *devalaya*, as well as to the Pattini and Kataragama *devalayas*. Even today, it is my brother who offers clothing for elephants during the *perahara*. I cannot do these things any more because I have no money now. But I did it while I could. I have also offered Buddha statues to the [Dalada] Maligava.

I stopped donating curtains to Kataragama after a certain incident. One day, the *kapu mahattaya* asked me to give him some money if I wanted to have my curtains displayed at the *devalaya*. He was sort of asking me for a bribe. I was disgusted. I did not give him any money and did not go back there [the Kataragama Devalaya in Kandy].

One day I had a peculiar experience. I was going to Kataragama [the temple in the southeast] along with a friend. At night, the two of us decided to climb Vadahiti Kanda [a nearby hill famous in local myths about the deity] in Kataragama. It was so dark and we were not sure of the way. Then a white clad shadow of a man appeared with a dog and accompanied us to the place. When we reached the *devalaya* there, the shadow and the dog disappeared. It was some deity who had guided us. Because of my faith in Kataragama Deviyo, I would go to the Kataragama Devalaya in Kandy every day. It was a daily routine.

Today I am alive and well thanks to the blessings of the deities, despite all my problems and the evils that have been done to destroy me. All I ask of the deities is for justice. I have only them to rely upon. It is true that I have lost the luxurious life I once lived. Nevertheless, I am happy and have never spent a day starving, even without much income. When I really need money, I somehow get it as if by a miracle. If I have only fifty rupees, and if I by a lottery ticket, I will get at least five hundred or one thousand rupees. Because the deities are always by my side, I know that I will turn to them until the day I die.

Mrs. Wijeratne's account puts flesh and blood on what has been, until now, a somewhat abstract pursuit of central motifs constitutive of Sinhala Buddhist religious culture, as they are revealed in a study of the cult of Visnu at *devalayas* in Sri Lanka. In particular, her account embodies a number of orientations identified so far in this study: nonsectarian religious consciousness, the belief in auspicious times, how Visnu is related to planetary influences, the inexorable law of karmic retribution and its moral implications, the protective powers of deities, the practice of sorcery, the power of faith, and the experience of *disti*. Since I have previously discussed or referred to each of these phenomena, I will let Mrs. Wijeratne's account speak largely for itself as an illustration of what dynamics of power are assumed to operate in this dimension of Sinhala Buddhist religious culture. But I will elaborate on her references to "possession" now, as I found this type of religious experience to be common at Alutnuvara for a number of devotees in that context, and will have occasion to take it up in more depth in chapter 7.

It was uncommon to observe devotees in the grips of possession at the Kandy Visnu *devalaya*. On only two occasions did I or my assistants observe it. On the whole, *kapuralas* at both the Visnu *devalaya* in Kandy and at the adjoining Alutnuvara *devalaya* expressed much skepticism about the genuine nature of these experiences. Yet Mrs. Wijeratne's experiences illustrate clearly how *disti* is understood as a power that can be used either constructively or destructively. She is a perfect example of the types of devotees who were profiled by Obeyesekere in his famous article on the "The Fire-walkers of Kataragama" (1978).

What I want to emphasize is the ambivalent and potentially dangerous nature of this "gift." Mrs. Wijeratne notes that she decided not to pursue or further cultivate her power when it was authenticated by a Kataragama *kapurala*, because she feared she would only use it selfishly and for destructive purposes. What her comment indicates is how the constructive use of power has to be linked with moral inclinations in order to gain positive fruition. Otherwise, the same type of power that can be used constructively can also be used deleteriously, or in connection with sorcerous activities.

Mrs. Wijeratne's world teems with various types of powers—those emanating from the very context of time itself, from the deities, from the planetary deities, and also from those humans (in her case, her brother and sister-in-law, who have draped the doorways of the Visnu and Dadimunda *devalayas* in Kandy) who seek to cause harm. It is a world of danger and protection, of superior and inferior powers vying for domination.

Disti is a personal power that can be cultivated for either moral or for destructive designs. It is a sign of the presence of a deity's power within the individual. I interviewed another woman at the Kandy Visnu *devalaya*, in her early thirties, who claimed to have experienced *disti* frequently in her teens and early twenties. But though she still is "visited" on occasion, she has stopped seeking the experience, because it makes it difficult for her to find a suitable husband. Her comment, I think, reflects the general ambivalence with which this type of religious experience is regarded in Sri Lanka. The experience of power can easily lead one morally astray.

In Mrs. Wijeratne's case, she used her power almost exclusively as a defense to ward off machinations deployed by others. That is, Visnu's power (as well as the power of other deities) was invoked primarily as a deterrent. He functioned literally as a "minister of defense."

In order to obtain a more accurate sense of the types of people and the specific reasons for why they came to the Visnu *devalaya*, and thus to understand more precisely how Visnu's power was thought to operate in the lives of contemporary Sinhala Buddhists visiting the *devalaya*, I devised another plan for the field study. Quite simply, the previous method of interviewing individuals was too inefficient to be able to come to some kind of general conclusions, and I wanted more precise indications of who was attending and why.

With the permission of the *basnayaka nilame* and with the consent (and collusion) of the *kapuralas* of both the Visnu and Dadimunda *devalayas*, I stationed my two assistants within the *digges* of the respective *devalayas* as unobtrusively as possible, but within such a distance to the *kapurala* and arriving devotees that the specific requests that the devotees made to the *kapurala* were audible. I armed each of the assistants with a form (see appendix 3.b) that categorized the nature of requests that I anticipated, based upon the conversations I had previously elicited in individual interviews, and also one that registered the approximate ages and genders of the devotees. The form was designed to indicate the nature of requests by age and gender. But this proved too problematic to complete accurately, as many of the devotees arrived in mixed groups of male and female, old and young, at times very rapidly, one after another, so that it became impossible for my assistants to tabulate accurately under the time constraints and pressures. So, we made due with simply categorizing the number and nature of the requests.

Meanwhile, I positioned myself inconspicuously within the *devalaya* compound, so that I had a clear view of all four cultic venues (the *bodhi* tree, the Visnu, Dadimunda, and Huniyam *devalayas*). Armed with my own form (see appendix 3.a), I determined the number, age and gender of all devotees visiting each of the cultic areas. We undertook this census during five *kemmura* (Wednesdays and Saturdays) during late February and early March 2000, for a total of exactly twenty hours. The results appear in appendices 3.a and 3.b.

Of the 1,058 devotees who visited the Kandy Visnu *devalaya* compound during our twenty hours of controlled observations, 705 were female and 353 males, indicating that the cult of Visnu in particular, and probably the cult of the deities in general, is sustained predominantly by women in Sri Lanka, specifically those over eighteen years of age. From this, it could be surmised that adult women are either more likely to experience powerlessness or, more surely, to seek the protection and assistance of the deities when they do.

In terms of age, the largest number of both male and female devotees is drawn from the 18–35-year-old category, indicating that seeking assistance from deities is not a form of religion largely confined to older generations, or one that is dying out among the younger population, as some middle-class, urban Buddhists (supporters of Ven. Soma) might wish. Indeed, with the exception of older males (55+), I was surprised at the substantial representation of all age groups among the devotees who visited the *devalaya* compound. I was also surprised that about only about one half (508) of the total number of devotees (1,058) actually entered the Visnu *devalaya* per se, indicating that the compound is understood as a sacred place providing venues for purposes other than specific plaints made to Visnu alone. Two hundred and ten engaged in cultic activities at the *bodhi* tree, often conducting their own private *bodhi pujas*, 243 entered the Dadimunda *devalaya*, and 55 sought the powers of Huniyam. The greatest gender imbalance occurred at the *bodhi* tree, where only 43 males were found conducting *pujas* or engaged in meditation, in comparison to 176 females.

The survey of types of requests for help to Visnu and Dadimunda reflected in appendix 3.b shows how deeply Visnu is associated with planetary influences in Buddhist Sri Lanka. I divided the categories between a *specific* problem being experienced due to an immediate astrological condition and *general* plaints for well-being in relation to the planetary positionings. When these two categories are combined, they account for exactly half of all petitions made to Visnu (175) and Dadimunda (83). In other words, the most common reason for visiting the Kandy Visnu *devalaya* is to seek the blessing (*santiya*) of Visnu because of his perceived powers in ameliorating the conditions of existence as occasioned by planetary positionings. As I indicated earlier in the chapter, this is fundamentally and at base a problem of karma. The second most common reason had to do with various domestic issues occurring within the family context. More than twenty percent of the plaints we registered (103 of 508) were focused on family matters. Concerns about health, economic prosperity, and justice were also frequently articulated (59, 46, and 37 respectively), while sorcery accounted for just less than one percent (5).

The significance and relevance of some of these numbers need further explanation. In the first instance, it should be noted that I collected only 508 plaints from 1,058 devotees. There are obvious reasons for this discrepancy. First, many devotees arrived in groups when making their requests to the *kapurala*. Second, a few of the *devalaya*'s visitors simply performed *pujas* or engaged in meditation only at the *bodhi* tree, and never entered the shrines to the gods. On the other hand, I was also able to ascertain that, in some instances, devotees approached two, three, or all four of the cultic venues within the compound to get assistance for the same problem.

Finally, my categories meant to identify types of problems sometimes proved to be too clumsy, simply because some problems brought by devotees could not be categorized so easily. For instance, there is the case of a woman seeking help from Visnu because she was suffering physically and emotionally from the abuse of her husband, who was overly aggravated because of business reversals which had been foreseen by an earlier reading of his horoscope. Her "problem" could have been identified within no less than four different categories (health, planets, economic prosperity, and family).

So the categories within the appendices are by no means perfect indices. Yet they are helpful in registering in general what types of devotees may come to the Kandy Visnu *devalaya* and why they do so. The example of Mrs. Wijeratne is also such a pertinent one, because of the array of problems for which she seeks the help of the deities.

The Maha (Visnu) Devalaya in Kandy is a quiet venue in the city's "sacred square," where many Buddhists, mostly from Kandy, seek the protection of a deity perceived to reside near the apex of the religious culture's moral economy. It is likely that Visnu has not been the first stop in their quests for help, but rather only one source among many to whom appeals have been made. He does not seem to be a deity who commands an impassioned sacrifice, whose presence often generates an ecstatic religious experience, or who can be counted on to exact revenge on one's enemies. He is, rather, a somewhat distant yet compassionate presence, responsive to entreaties for fairness and justice.

His profile is decidedly mild and benign. In comparison to the images of Visnu articulated in the Puranas and bhakti Hinduism, it can be said that there is consistency: Visnu intercedes (not so spectacularly in the Buddhist context) in the affairs of the world to uphold the norms of what is dharmic. But there remains a fundamental difference: in the Buddhist contexts, Visnu is still mortal; he is not the dispenser of the means that assure attainment of the final religious goal. Instead, he is appealed to because, as a "minister of defense" of the *Buddhasasana*, who will one day become a Buddha himself, he is perceived to be a marker or symbol of positive karmic fruition. As such, his power is assuredly moral in nature, and his acts of benevolence expressive of his abundant compassion for those suffering the woes of samsaric existence. His appeal is deeper than the purely *laukika*.

The preceding discussion has provided a view of cultic life and variations of its religious meaning found on a regular basis at Visnu *devalayas* in the Kandy cultural area. I have concentrated on presenting the scenario as it normally unfolds on the weekly *kemmura* days. The most important rite germane to the public life of the Kandy Visnu *devalaya*, however, is the annual *asala perahara*. While the role of the Visnu *devalaya* in the *perahara* ritual is not necessarily distinctive in relation to the Natha, Pattini, and Kataragama *devalayas*, a related rite held immediately after the conclusion or "water-cutting" finale of the *perahara* definitely is: this is the *valiyaka natuma* or *mangalya*. It is on this important and distinctive ritual of the Kandy Visnu *devalaya* that attention must now be focused.

Appendix I
[The Gold Plated Sannasa of the Vishnu Devalaya, Kandy][69]
Transliterated Sinhala

Side A

Svasti Sri Paramapursottama Dasanana Kumbhakarna Somaka Balisura Rahktabija Madhukaitabha Kamsasura Hinanyadi nikara paramarapramathana Giri dhurandarayamana Khadhiradehali mahavatamsaka indranilamanikaya sri sarira sobhadharavu Sri Ramacandrayan vahanse karuna mot-sit pamudita bhavupagatava vadara taman vahanse visin bhara labana lada dasabaladhari vu Sarvagnayan vahasnsege pratipatti sasanaya saha Sri Lankadvipaya rak-

savaranayata samprapta vu maharajottamayananvahansge pautuparivar-
tanopakramadi sakalantaraya sarvopada ha anavihita apaksa apiramana dusta
durjana krodha bahulayak surya vikasayak dutu timira Skandayak putap-
atanaya vannaka men sarvaprakarayen dhuribhuta nivranayana kota suvaca
kikaru paksapata bhaktiprematibharavanatottama

Side B

[?]yan pirivara kota salasva usas teda yasas anavikum bala diga savusirin
abhivrddhidayaka kota raksa kara deva vadaranu pinisa sakavarsa ekvadahas
sasiya tis ek vaeni [?] virodhi nam vu me varsayehi durut masa pura tiyavak nam
tithiya lat senasurada me davasa Satarakoralen Algam dolosada ehi bada gevatu
gahakola godamada valvil arak aetuluva saramaru panduru dakva vadala
panatat e panatat sarvathamana prakarena siddhabhilostuh Sri Viraparakrama
Narendrasinha maharajottamayanan vahansege me karuna panatayi

Appendix II
Yatika to Visnu[70]

1. *Yatikava* from Maha (Visnu) Devalaya, Kandy (recorded in February 2000):

Lord Upulvan, *devaraja*, I pray to you who protect the Buddhasasana, and you
who live at various holy places in Sri Lanka including Devinuvara. Sri Visnu,
with your divine vision, please see if there are any enemies of this devotee who
has come here from Yatihelagala soliciting the support of *yaksas* such as Oddi
Huniyam. Protect him from those enemies who cause various difficulties and
discomforts. Please use your divine vision and divine hearing to protect this
devotee who has come here seeking your help, with the assistance of Huniyam
and Vadiga, attacking his enemies with thunderbolts balls of fires causing them
to be insane, tracing these criminals by the power of your divine vision wherever they happen to be. Cure the 98 diseases and 203 minor afflictions and accidents, epidemics, black magic, and evil caused by other forms of malevolent
magic spells, the malevolent effects of the evil eye and evil mouth. Make his job
and professions prosper. If it is true that your power exists at this place, if there
are any evil influences of planets or any impending fatal accidents and ob-
structions to be faced, ward them off and protect him. May you please fulfill
his wishes and punish robbers and enemies. I pray you lord, king of the gods.

2. *Yatikava* from Maha (Visnu) Devalaya, Kandy (recorded in February 2000):

May I have permission [to address you], lord, you have been waiting to become
Buddha for a long time, aiming for buddhahood, having come to this island of

Sri Lanka. If your power exists in the Himalayas, in the Vaikuntha mountain, in many other places including Devinuvara, and if at this central shrine your power exists truly, and if that is the truth, however many *devalayas* in which you now abide, if it is true that your glance is focused on this main shrine all the time, Utpalavanna, Dasarama, Parasurama, Mahakanthesvara, Vaikunthanatha, Upulvan *devaraja*, may you attain buddhahood. This gentleman who is from America, greeting you respectfully, offering you flowers, what he requests from you, all his diseases and all sorts of other problems and difficulties, ward off all such things if he is afflicted with problems caused by *yaksas*, *pretas*, and planets. Protect everyone who enters his house. Protect his trade, cattle and other property kindly making his requests come true. Protect him from back magic and evil charms, illnesses caused by going out at inauspicious times, the evil eye, enemy problems, and false allegations. Protect his body, all five parts. Protect him from diseases caused by planets, whatever the nature of any problem, listening to this prayer. Sri Visnu, with the four guardian gods, drive off all these illnesses, problems and fears. So be it lord who will become Buddha for five thousand years.

3. *Yatikava* at Maha (Visnu) Devalaya in Kandy (recorded in March 2000):

May I have your permission [to approach you]. For five thousand years, king of the gods, as long as the sun and the moon exist in this universe, you who will become a Buddha, protect the *sasana* of our Lord Buddha, you who will conquer the three worlds, glorious king of the gods Upulvan. You who have kindly come down to this island of Sri Lanka to protect the *sasana* of the Buddha, king of the gods, Sri Visnu, on this island of Sri Lanka, on the mountain peak Ramagiri, at Ramesvaram and Devundara, living in three hundred and ninety thousand places, protecting all deities and *kovils* and temples situated in those places, having come to this *devalaya* of yours, and having been offered *panduru* [coins], fragrant incense, camphor, flowers and betel leaves, this is what this person is petitioning you. May you see all of this with your divine eye, may you hear it with your divine ear, bringing him victory and curing him of all 98 *rogas* [diseases], the 108 *vyadhi* [serious diseases], the 203 minor ailments, and all epidemics, removing all these and further, if there is any *gurukam* [maledictive incantations], *huniyam* [sorcery] or evil eye or evil mouth, protect him well. Whatever his job or profession, make him prosper day by day. If there are any disturbances or dangers due to the inauspicious timings of planets, I plead with you, worshipping at your feet and praying, just as a mighty tusker pierces the trunk of a plaintain tree, make him victorious, protect his profession, protect him from the anger of kings or rulers. May you become a Buddha, my lord.

4. *Yatikava* from Maha (Visnu) Devalaya (recorded in March 2000):

May I beg your permission, lord, you who are waiting to be Buddha in 5,000 years; may I have your permission, from you who will be here for a very long time to come, you who will be there as long as earth and water shall last, please be kind enough to hear this plaint. Lord, you who are known by the epithets such as Shripati, Parakrama, Tilakasura, Tilokesvara, Jayanandana, Sri Upulvan, king of the gods, and Maha Visnu, these devotees having come to this main shrine of yours, you who have obtained the prophecy of the four Buddhas, Kakusanda, Konagamana, Kasyapa and Gautama, having offered you various objects and offerings of coins, further, having transferred merit to you, this is what they wish to petition from you after worshipping at your feet: ward off the 98 illnesses, the 99 *vyadhi*, and the 203 minor ailments, all ill effects caused by *yaksas* and *pretas*, and the effects of epidemics. Further, please fulfill all their wishes which they bear in their minds, just as a tusker with its tusks pierces a milky tree. Having fulfilled all their wishes and aspirations, helping them to be safe from all dangers from the planets and evil forces from the practice of *huniyam*, and making them prosper in their jobs and professions in which they are engaged daily, protect by your power all the children, kith and kin of their families, kindly bless them with protection, Lord. It is well, Lord, who will be a Buddha, my lord.

5. *Yatikava* at the Visnu Devalaya at Alutnuvara (recorded in April 2000):

May I have your permission [to approach] . . . For one hundred years, as long as the sun and moon last, for five thousand years, for a long, long time to come, may you attain Buddhahood, my lord. Beginning with Mount Udagiri up to Mount Amaragiri, and in three hundred and ninety-eight other places, King of the Gods, Maha Visnu, may I be granted permission [to approach . . . In the Himalayan peaks, the mansion of Vaikuntha, and at the four cardinal points of Mount Meru, all these places where your majestic power and glory prevail, and in all those abodes where your powers dominate, wherever you are at present in whatever heaven or assembly of the gods, these humble devotees, having visited the main *devalaya*, as well as the lower *devalaya*, coming here with offerings, gifts of money, scents and flowers, having offered them to you together with lamps, praying here to you, King of the Gods, please look at these devotees with your divine eyes casting divine glances. Focussing on these humble, devout patients, prevent all evil influences of the planets, all sickness and ailments, problems, difficulties and evils caused by poisons, kindly ward off all these evil influences if they are suffering—from nightmares, Maha Visnu, if they are the evil influence of any *yaksas, pretas, gurukam,* or *Huniyam,* or suffering from the consequences of staying outdoors at unsuitable times [going out alone at dawn or dusk].

Maha Visnu, in this shrine at Alutnuvara which was your abode, but now that great deity Dadmiunda Devata Bandara is occupying, we also pray to that might deity with this same *yatikava*. Having come to this Uggal Alutnuvara, by the power of the the god Visnu, that Dadimunda *deviyo* having brought here one hundred and fifty thousand *yaksas*, getting them to cut the granite rock in one night, now residing in the shrine built on that rock, great god Dadimunda Devata Bandara of Alutnuvara, please cure all diseases of these patients and ward off the influence of the possession of *yaksas* Huniyam, Kadawara, Devol and also Huniyam *devata*, and fulfilling the wishes of these humble devotees, in the mornings and the evenings and all times of the day, and causing them to prosper, may you too become a buddha.

6. *Yatikava* from Lankatilaka Visnu Devalaya (recorded in May 2000):

May I have your permission [to approach] . . . King of the gods, Sri Visnu, who is the guardian of the *buddhasasana*. Lord Kumara Bandara, I seek your permission too. Your power exists all over this Sri Lanka. And in this Sri Lanka, for all those who know of your majesty and power, and for all those who do not know, we pray at your feet to protect these people in all their jobs and work, and to protect them in all their travels and journeys, making their aspirations come true, improving daily, bringing them success and profit. Cure them of the 98 *rogas*, the 99 *vyadhis* which are caused by the imbalance of air, bile and phlegm, driving away the 203 dangers, removing all evil effects caused by the evil eye and evil mouth, warding off problems arising from the nine planetary gods. Sri Visnu and Kumara Bandara, may we be blessed with your divine compassion, and may we be protected by your divine power. May you become the Buddha in five thousand years!

7. *Yatikava* from Gadaladeniya Visnu Devalaya (recorded in May 2000):

May I have permission [to approach] . . . King of the gods, Maha Visnu, you who protect the *Buddhasana* and will be Buddha for 5,000 years. If there are offences committed unconsciously or consciously when we visit this *devalaya* of yours, if we breach the rules inadvertently, or if some people are oozing spittle from their mouths, please protect these bodies which are precious like golden weapons the, golden weapons that glisten in your bed chamber. Now they are here with what they had promised to offer when they made their vows, worshipping at your feet. This is what they want to say—protect everyone including those who are aware and those not—their villages, land and cattle, their jobs, their travels. Fulfill their hopes and wishes to make them prosper day by day, like the milk that boils over from the kettle. Make them successful and prosperous. Protect them from the 98 *rogas*, the 99 *vyadhis*, and the 203 dangers. If there are any contagious diseases or epidemics, please eradicate them, making even the sun that shines daily beneficial to them. Bless them with your divine compassion and divine protection. May you become Buddha for 5,000 years.

8. *Yatikava* from Devinuvara Visnu Devalaya (recorded in April 2000):

May I be given permission [to approach] Lord Sri Visnu, who is a *bodhisatva*, who has the power to remove all diseases and problems. I have worshipped you by kneeling, by joining palms to the head. Sri Visnu, Kadiradeva, Utpala Varna, Maha Visnu, known by various names such as Devanarayana, who possesses great power gained through such names, existing in ten *avataras*, you who reside here in this divine palace at Devinuvara, casting loving glances about it, to all these devotees who are gathered here to obtain protection and help from you, here I am presenting their appeals on their behalf, may you safeguard all their jobs and professions and make them prosperous as a result of this prayer that I chant, removing all diseases they are afflicted with, all illnesses caused by the 3 humors [*tun dos*], and the illnesses caused by the 5 elements, the 98 *rogas* and 203 minor ailments, deadly accidents, hazards caused by the 9 planets, warding off the curse of the leopard,

Removing the curse of *yaksas*, problems caused by *pretas*, curing the effects caused by the evil eye, evil mind, and improving their residential places, cattle, crops, and making them prosper in their jobs and professions, making this New Year and lucky and prosperous one to all of them. Bestow them with blessings to be successful and fruitful. May you live for 5 thousand years!

9. *Yatikava* at Visnu Devalaya at the *stupa* of the *viharaya* at Devinuvara:

May you hear, Sri Visnu, the Buddha-to-be, I have worshipped you standing, sitting, joined palms to the head, with the ten fingers. Utpalavarna, Sri Visnu, who is born of the Kadira *devi* clan, Siddha Visnu, Maha Visnu, being known to the world by ten names such as Sankha Sila and Devanarayana, complete in ten avatars, we are seeking refuge and help from you, king of the gods, who dwells here in the heavenly Devinuvara palace casting your loving glance about. These devout people, and the sick among them who are gathered here— all the diseases they suffer from, which they have contracted from others, all physical diseases, diseases caused by outraged humors, air, phlegm and bile— the 98 types of *rogas*, the 99 types of *vyadhis*, the 203 petty hazards, problems caused by the nine planets, deadly diseases and untimely dangers, evil caused by *yaksas* and *pretas*, effects of the evil eye, evil mind, evil words and jealousy, the evil darkness caused by *huniyam*, provide protection from these. Protect their houses and dwelling places together with their livestock, make them successful in their jobs and professions. For this New Year which has just dawned, may it be lucky to all these people and their friends and relations, may it be happy. May you have the blessings of the triple gem.

Appendix III. A
Age and Gender of Devotees Visiting Kandy Visnu *Devalaya*

A Controlled Census Based on 20 Hours of Observation
During Five *Kemmura* Days in February and March, 2001

	MALE				FEMALE			
AGE	−18	18–35	35–55	55+	−18	18–35	35–55	55+
Visnu *Devalaya*	39	85	74	15	47	117	87	76
Total by gender	213				327			
Total devotees (males and females): 540								
BO TREE	11	17	11	5	19	52	55	50
Total by gender	43				176			
Total devotees (males and females): 219								
Dalimunda *Devalaya*	30	23	17	7	31	47	44	44
Total by gender:	77				166			
Total devotees (males and females): 243								

	MALE				FEMALE			
Huniyam *Devalaya*	3	5	4	7	1	3	20	12
Total by gender:	19				36			
Total devotees (males and females): 55								

TOTAL AGES BY GENDER

MALE				FEMALE			
83	130	106	34	98	219	206	182

TOTAL AGES (MALE AND FEMALE COMBINED)

−18	18–35	35–55	55+
181	349	280	216

TOTAL BY GENDER

353 males   705 females

Appendix III. B
Types of Problems and Petitions Presented by Devotees

to the *Kapuralas* Serving the Visnu, Dadimunda and Huniyam *Devalayas* in
Kandy During 20 Hours of Controlled Census on Five *Kemmura* Days in
February and March 2001

"**Blessing**" (**santiya**) for general planetary problems: **201** (Visnu 128, Dadi-munda 73, Huniyam 4)

Family (fertility, marriage, domestic violence): 103 (Visnu 60, Dadimunda 43, Huniyam 2)

Health: 59 (Visnu 39, Dadimunda 20)

Planetary problems (specified): 57 (Visnu 47, Dadimunda 10)

Economic prosperity: 46 (Visnu 24, Dadimunda 22. Huniyam 2)

Sorcery (including *yaksa*s and *preta*s): **5** (Visnu 1, Dadimunda 1, Huniyam 3)

Vows for justice: 37 (Visnu 25, Dadimunda 12, Huniyam 6)

THE *VALIYAK MANGALYA*
The Curative Powers of the *Mala Raja*

In contrast to the last chapter's discussions centered on daily and weekly ritual life at Visnu's Maha Devalaya in Kandy on *kemmura* days, this brief chapter will examine aspects of an annual rite that is now, it would appear, unique to the cult of Visnu in Sinhala Buddhist religious culture. Indeed, the annual *valiyak mangalya* or *natuma*, which commences each year on the second night after the concluding early-morning "water-cutting" ceremony of Kandy's *asala perahara* pageant and continues for six nights with a concluding short afternoon ceremony on the seventh day, is performed only at the Maha Devalaya in Kandy and at no other venue in the country. My research assistants and I observed the *valiyak mangalya* in August of 2000 and 2001.

We begin with a very skeletal account of the proceedings of the seven-day rite.[1] The first night begins with drummers worshipping Visnu at the *devalaya* followed by the syncopations (*deva pada* and *pirima pada*) of their auspicious drumming. The chief *yakdessa* (the ritual dancer who functions as a priest during the ritual) then makes his appearance and begins to chant *kavi* (verses) in order to sacralize a *pirit* thread, thus alluding directly to Upulvan's primordial action sanctioning the practice of *pirith* among Vijaya's followers. Then follows the recitation of several *kavi* sacralizing sixteen ritual accoutrements to be placed at the sixteen angles of an elaborate geometric *yantra* then to be drawn. The *yantra* is first drawn by artfully and dexterously pouring three concentric line-circles of previously untouched rice from a *kotale*, a ritual vessel usually used for pouring water. An undulating swerve-line intersecting the cardinal points of the concentric circles is then drawn symmetrically. Five petals of the coconut flower, one at the center and four at the cardinal points are then placed within the inner circle, six are then placed symmetrically in the second circle and twelve are placed in the third. Two squares of lashed wooden spars are then placed around the circular designs of rice and coconut flowers and mounted, the second diagonally, so that when the second is placed on top of the first together they form an eight pronged star (and so sixteen angles protrude at the perimeter of the *yantra*). Then sixteen piles of beetle leaves, sixteen husked coconuts, sixteen oil lamps and sixteen *panduru*[2] are each placed at each of the angles of the star. Then four young sprouting coconuts are placed at the cardinal points of the base square and three white threads of string are tied around the eight points of the star. The result is stunning in appearance, but its function is simply to inaugurate the first night of the *valiyak mangalya* in an auspicious manner. The inaugural night session concludes after the chanting of *yatika* with the *yakdessa* then dismantling the *yantra*.

The second night session is also brief: auspicious drumming is followed by a recitation of the *mandurupaya* in which Pattini's presence is invited and invoked followed by a dance with the coconut flower. The third through the fifth nights follow the same basic liturgical scheme beginning with auspicious drumming, invocations to benevolent *yaksas*, invocations to the various companies of deities, the recitation and performance of the *Mala Raja Upata* and the offering of fruits (*palavala dane*). On the fifth night, after the *palavala dane*, *kavi* are recited to invite the *veddhas* to attend the rite (this segment of the night's proceedings also includes some good natured comedy at the *vaddhas'* expense). On the third through the fifth nights, *yatikas* are also chanted for anyone in attendance.[3] Except for the sixth all night session, the number of people attending on other nights amounted to no more than between twenty and forty. But perhaps as many as two hundred crowded the ritual arena under the portico of the Visnu *devalaya* proper on the sixth night of performance.

The sixth night, referred to as *maha yakun* to signal the fact that it constitutes the denouement of the *valiyak mangalya,* is an all night affair. In addition to the liturgy in place for the third through the fifth nights, it contains not only a fully rehearsed version of the extended *Kuveni Asna,* but a myriad of other invocations to the *veddhas,* the *kohomba* deities and several other genres of *kavi.* The drama of the rite climaxes with the frenzied dance pantomiming the *mala raja's* hunt of Rahu in the form of a boar.

The seventh and final session is held on the afternoon following the all night proceedings of the sixth session. It includes auspicious drumming, appeals to the benevolent *yaksas* and the *kohomba* deities, performances of the *mala naetima* ("flower dance"), the *mal pada* (to invoke the *mala raja's* blessing of the people in attendance), the special "elephant dance" by the specialist *yakdessas,* and finally the transfer of merit derived from the ritual to the deities.

As I now proceed, many of the details and their significance in these scenarios I have just described will come into sharper focus.

The *basnayaka nilame* of Visnu's Maha Devalaya in Kandy claimed that the *valiyak mangalya* was a ritual previously performed (and one that is still supposed to be held) at all of the other *devalayas* whose ritual participants take part in the annual Kandy *perahara.* Indeed, I also heard some vague indications to the same effect from the *devalaya kapuralas.* One of them speculated that *valiyak natuma* may have been held formerly at Alutnuvara, maybe even orig-inally so, as well as at Hanguranketa, Gadaladeniya and perhaps at other par-ticipating *perahara devalayas* too. But I could not confirm this in any written source.

Valiyak mangalya is also a ritual that seems to be on the verge of disappear-ing. Mudiyanse Dissanayake (2000),[4] who recently completed a detailed book-length study of the ritual after many years of research, has gone so far as to say that it is now on the verge of dying out.

Knox provides a tantalizing description of what may have been the *valiyak mangalya* in his description of Kandy's public religious life in the mid-seven-teenth century.[5] In addition, the mythic cycles that come into play within the rite are drawn from texts likely to date, according to Neville, to the seventeenth and eighteenth centuries. I have briefly discussed, for example, the *Ramayana*-derived *Palavala Dane* mythology in chapter four, a text that contains much of the narrative mythical material that is brought into play during *valiyak man-galya*. But the antiquity of the *valiyak mangalya* rite *per se*, specifically its rela-tion to the *asala perahara*, is difficult to establish with any great certainty. *Yakdessas*, the class of Kandyan dancers who perform the elaborate dramatiza-tions of myth as well as the various invocations and petitions of the *valiyak na-tuma* and the *kohomba kankariya* as well, did not begin participating in the processions of the *asala perahara* as *ves* dancers until 1916 (A. Senviratne 1984:49). So the *valiyak mangalya*'s connection to the *asala perahara* may be more recent than usually assumed, though this certainly does not rule out the possibility that the *valiyak natuma* was performed in other ritual contexts for other specific purposes well-before before the twentieth century, which seems to be the position taken by Dissanayake (2000). In any case, the *valiyak man-galya* is very closely related to the celebrated and complex series of rites known as *kohomba kankariya* and now has been integrated into the calendrical cycle of rites still performed at Visnu's Maha Devalaya in Kandy, as far back as any-one with a living memory can ascertain.

The formal purposes and cultural logic of the rite would seem to be of im-portance to all participants in the *perahara* proceedings. According to Dis-sanayake, the main reasons for performing the *valiyak mangalya* have been: 1) to remove the *vas dos* (especially the affects of "evil eye") that all ritual partic-ipants (including the *perahara* elephants[6]) might have incurred during their extensive "public exposure" in the nightly *perahara* processions that circum-ambulate the "sacred temple square" and parts of Kandy town; 2) to ask the deities to pardon any inadvertent ritual mistakes that may have occurred dur-ing the many days of the *perahara* rites; and 3) to transfer merit to the gods in gratitude for a successful performance of the *perahara*. As such, the *valiyak mangalya* would now seem to function as a kind ritual insurance premium for those participating in and executing the *perahara*. But it is also more than this, and the elements of myth and ritual that it shares with the *kohomba kankariya* reflect a more general purpose: to secure protection from any *vas dos* (not just the *dos* contracted from exposure during the *perahara*) and to insure fertility and prosperity in the future. As I am about to show through an examination of the ritual's mythic context, the elimination of *vas dos* is the central end purpose of the *valiyak mangalya*. As such, it adds another specific cultic dimension to cult of the "Buddhist Visnu" in Sri Lanka.

Categorically and quite substantially similar to the performance of the *kohomba kankariya*,[7] *valiyak mangalya* may have been, indeed, an important *shanthikarma*[8] rite in late-medieval Kandyan up-country *devalaya* ritual culture independent of the *asala perahara*. Dissanayake (2000) remarks that the *valiyak mangalya* can be understood as a concise version of the *kohomba kankariya*, as many of the dances and rites performed within the *kohomba kankariya* are also included within its proceedings.[9] P. B. Meegaskumbura also says that "it is obvious that the *valiyak* ritual and the *kohomba kankariya* are twin rituals sharing the same textual traditions."[10] According to Meegaskumbura, since there are mythic traditions in the *kohomba kankariya* that tell of the origins of the *kohomba* deities from the actions of the *valiyak* gods, and since the *kohomba kankariya* rites are far more elaborated and diverse than those of the *valiyak mangalya*, it is quite possible that the former evolved out of the latter. The elaboration of *kohomba kankariya* may be the result of a process whereby a ritual (*valiyak mangalya*) strictly held at a *devalaya* was appropriated and adapted for village or household contexts. He goes on to observe that the main differences between the two rites involve various degrees of emphases: 1) in the *valiyak mangalya*, the mythic birth of the *mala raja* ("flower king") or the three divine *valiyak* princes,[11] about whom we first read while discussing the *Palavala Dane* in chapter four, is one of the celebrated central events of the rite, while the creation of the *kohomba* deities is mentioned only in passing; 2) *vice versa*, in the *kohomba*, the three *valiyak* princes are regarded simply as human beings who were later transformed into benevolent *yaksas* rather than being regarded as a divine king, the *mala raja* or the three *valiyak* princes who figure so prominently in the *valiyak mangalya*;[12] 3) in the *valiyak mangalya*, Upulvan (Visnu/Rama) is regard as the father or ancestor of the three *valiyak* princes collectively known as *mala raja*; and 4), it is clear that the ritual performers of the *valiyak natuma* and *kohomba kankariya* constitute two separate schools of interpretive ritual dance performance. Related to Meegaskumbura's fourth point, Dissanayake (2000) adds:

> *Yakdessas* [ritual dancers] and drummers who participated in the *perahera* do not take part in *valiyak*. *Valiyak* dance was [itself a separate] *rajakariya*

within the feudal social system. As such, members of only two families said to be descending from the time of the kings are [now] involved. They were granted land in return. Even today only those who are descendents of these two families retain the right to participate in the ritual. These two families are from Mavanella and are affiliated with the Alutnuvara Devalaya. The *rajakariya* of *keela bandeema, kali yama,* and *gara yak* dance [celebrated on the climactic sixth night of the ritual] rest with one family with the closest [links] to [the] Alutnuvara Devalaya. *Gara yak* dance has to be performed by people of the Olee caste. Other dances are done by people of either *berava* or *nakethi* castes. . . . Although the ritual of *valiyak* takes place in the Visnu devale in Kandy, the *rajakariya* lies with these families connected to Alutnuvara. [brackets mine]

So not only are the ritual specialists of the *valiyak mangalya* separate from those who perform in the *asala perahara* and in the *kohombo kankariya,* there is also a clear assignment, indicated by caste status, about who will or can perform various specific dances within the extended *valiyak* rite itself. And just as the *kapuralas* of the Maha Devalaya Visnu shrine in Kandy perform their services in exchange for land grants in Alutnuvara, so too it is the case for these *yakdessas* who perform the *valiyak natuma.* It is very likely, then, that the *valiyak natuma* and its performers share the same heritage of ritual culture that I have described above in relation to the *kapuralas* of the Visnu's Maha Devalaya in Kandy. But these *yakdessas* are ritual specialists and participate only in the performance of *valiyak natuma.*[13] Just like the *devalaya kapuralas,* the current lead *yakdessa* of the *valiyak natuma,* Devanagala Saiman, claims to be of the Brahman caste and says his ancestors came from Devinuvara.

Meegaskumbura's comments about the main differences between *valiyak* and *kohomba* form an excellent point of departure for the ensuing analytical discussion of the ritual's mythic cycles. The first three points he makes point to specific details of the mythic traditions informing the *valiyak* and *kohomba* rites, mythic traditions that help to explain the provenance, function and general meaning of the *valiyak* rite in Kandy along the lines that have been mentioned by Dissanayaka above. The cycle of myths related to the performance of *valiyak mangalya* ultimately explain the origins and cure of *divi dos,* a disease that appears to be a condition of mental depression and physical atrophy brought about by a curse or ill-intentioned form of magic.

There are two myths, fragments of which have been referred to and discussed in chapters three and four, that form the main narrative of myth for the *valiyak mangalya.* The first explains the birth of *mala raja,* the composite divine king derived from the three *valiyak* princes who were born to Rama and Sita. It is thus a myth that forms an important segment of Sinhala *Ramayana* lore. A second myth, this one with its roots in the *Mahavamsa,* has been linked to the first to form the narrative background of the *valiyak mangalya* rite. Here the *mala raja* affects a cure for King Panduvas who suffers from *divi dos,* owing to his brother's (Vijaya's) betrayal of the *yakkini* queen, Kuveni. This *divi dos* that Panduvas suffers is Kuveni's revenge for Vijaya's decision to abrogate his liaison with Kuveni, a passionate relation that has produced two children, and marry a South Indian princess from Madurai out of his concern for the legitimization of his kingship. This second myth (the *Kuveni Asna*), as I have mentioned, is part of the Vijaya cycle of myths in the *Mahavamsa,* but also has been creatively and significantly extended within the *valiyak mangalya* and *kohomba kankariya* ritual contexts. Taken together, the combination of these two mythic cycles reflects the manner in which mythic traditions from the *Ramayana* and *Mahavamsa* have been blended creatively within the cult of the "Buddhist Visnu." Thus, their combination reflects one more significant instance in which Sinhala Buddhists of late-medieval Sri Lanka appropriated and transformed Visnu.

More specifically, the birth of *mala raja* (the "flower[14] king") is a consistent focus of the *valiyak mangalya* for four of the six nights of its performance. In chapter four, I briefly outlined its narrative while discussing the contents of the *Palavala Dane,* itself a remarkable poetic synthesis linking both of these two mythic cycles germane to the *valiyak mangalya.*[15] Since the dramatization of "the Birth of Mala Raja" forms such a significant segment of the ritual dance performance of *valiyak natuma* on the third through the sixth nights, I will provide two renditions of it, a detailed summary of the *Valiyak Upata* provided by Mudiyanse Dissanayake (2000:23–25)[16] and the second a performed and recited version of the *Mala Raja Upata*[17] as it has been recorded by Dissanayake. As I noted above, the latter is chanted and pantomimed on the third through the sixth nights.

VALIYAK UPATA

Lord Visnu, afflicted with *senasuru apala* [bad planetary influence of Saturn] escaped into the forest where he lived for 7 years taking the form of a tusker. After 6 years and 11 months and 23 days, Ravana abducted Visnu's wife Sita [just at the end of Visnu's sojourn as a tusker in the forest?]. Later on, Rama, Lakshmana and Hanuman took back Sita after a battle with Ravana. Some time later, Umayangana [Siva's spouse] asked Sita to describe Ravana. Sita drew a picture of Ravana on an *alu kesel patha* [banana leaf]. Seeing Rama approaching just at that moment, she hid the leaf under the *yahana* [bed]. Knowing nothing of this Rama lay down on the bed. At once the bed started to shake and heat up. As Rama searched for the cause of this wonder he came across the hidden image of Ravana. He was at once suspicious of Sita, thinking that she was in love with Ravana.[18] He ordered his brother Lakshmana to take the pregnant Sita to the jungle and to kill her. Instead of killing her Lakshman abandoned her in the forest and reported to Rama that he had killed her.

As she roamed alone in the jungle Sita came across a *rsi varaya* named Valmiki. He allowed her to remain in his *asapuwa* [abode]. After a few days she gave birth to a child. One day, she went out to gather food leaving the child on the bed. He fell off the bed. Thinking that it was not apt for him to touch the child and that Sita would be upset to find the empty bed on her return, the sage threw a lotus bloom on to the bed and made a wish, and created a second child. Unaware of the incident Sita returned, and as she took the child on the bed into her arms, she heard another child crying. She searched and found the other under the bed. Taking both she went to the sage, perplexed. She would not believe what the sage had to say. So he picked a piece of *kusa* grass and threw it onto the bed with a wish and created yet another child so as to convince her. These three children were named Kiristya, Malaya and Sandalindu. [Dissanayake: "The *mala raja tun kattuwa* referred to in *Kankari* and *Valiyak* are these three."]

During this time the goddess Pattini went into the forest to pick mangoes along with prince Palanga. As they picked mangoes with the aid of a stick forked at the end, their *kekka* (sticks) got tangled. Palanga made fun of Pattini who was unable to free her stick. She was ashamed. She saw the three children returning from school and pleaded with them to help her. At one *vali* (at one shot) the three of them drew the stick with such force that they even broke Palanga's stick. Since they were able to free the stick at one attempt (*ek valiyata*) Pattini commented that they were '*valiyata yakku*' and granted them *varam*. [brackets mine]

The second version of the birth of the *mala raja* is given in the verse form in which it is sung during four nights of the *valiyak mangalya*. As I have mentioned, it is a central focus of the third through the sixth night of the proceedings.

MALA RAJA UPATA

I shall recite how the 36 *valiyaks* came to be and how they arrived in Sri Lanka.

I shall recite the legend of the *mala raja*, his fascinating hunt in Hantana, and the legacy of his parentage.

Near a lake frequented by *munis* [ascetics] in the Himalayas stood a temple that belonged to Nagapatana the *muni*.

Munis would pick blue lilies (*nil utpala*) from a nearby pond for use in their sacrificial offerings.

They used these lilies for every rite. But one day no flowers were to be seen and so they kept a vigil.

Then seven heavenly [maidens] descended to the pond, picked the blue lilies, and wore them in their hair while enjoying their time bathing.

Two other people came to the pond eating luscious fruits. They watched the women and drew their bows to shoot.

They released their arrows and both flew at the same speed. One of the maidens was unable to retrieve her clothes and stayed behind bathing in the water.

The other six escaped from the water by putting on their magic clothes. Yet the seventh could not and on that day lost her magical power.

Bereft of her magic, she searched around and found a path to follow.

"Who are you? Where did you come from? What is your village? What calamity has brought you here?

"We are heavenly maidens, the seven of us who came here together. While enjoying our bathing, my clothes were lost and so I am now in this condition."

She was given a place to live and some sweet fruits to eat—a grass thatched temple and bed.

Rama became intoxicated with her and slept with her in her house at night.

Before a week was out, the queen was pregnant with child.

Born without a miss, there were no sorrows of regret. The object of great care, he was given an auspicious bath to be granted a long life.

"Coming from which direction? Standing on which pose? Keeping which hand down?" So the ceremonial almsgiving [*dana*] was announced.

"Coming from the north! Standing towards the south! Keeping the right hand down! That is how the *dana* will be auspicious!"

"First the auspicious *dana;* second the pregnancy *dana;* third the *dana* at the moment of death." Now I shall recite the *dana* at the birth of *mala raja.*

What is the beginning of *dana*? What is its middle? What is its end? What is the beginning of all three?

The beginning of *dana* is the stomach, the middle is the throat, and the end is the mouth. The beginning of all three is the tip of the tongue.

Garudas, pigeons and owls all fly high in the air. Partridges also do not walk the land.

Partridges fly with the *garudas*. In the same way do small boats accompany the big ships of sail.

Palms and *kitul* trees grow in the forest. And dwarf *kitul* plants grow there as well?

Amidst the houses of colored clay are there not simple mud huts too?

Don't those learned ones dwelling in the forest also enjoy poetic sentiments? What of the leopards and bears? Are those who cannot understand these verses not human?

Taking a banana leaf, she [Sita] drew a figure of his [Ravana's] beautiful body. Knowing the virtues of motherhood, she produced it with affection.

Two brother kings were summoned and a sword was issued for their use.

They were told to take the queen away and to slice her in two.

Without hesitation, they took the sword and marched Sitapati to the dense forest.

They anguished at the plight of pregnant Sita. Without creating suspicions for the king, they left her unharmed alone.

The queen sojourned towards a temple and pond, surveyed the environs and stood under a banyan tree.

There, she took some nurture from fruit and realized the nature of her condition.

The *Book of Signs* indicated that she was one month into pregnancy.

So the first month passed and the second, after the third came the fourth followed by the fifth and so the queen entered her sixth month.

After the sixth, so the seventh and the days of the eighth came to an end. In the ninth month, her womb was heavy and in the tenth she finally gave birth.

Sitapati, the mother, endured the pains of labor and the child, was a veritable gem, born into the hands of Ganga devi.

The child was happy, nourished with food and drink. Asleep on the bed, the handsome prince was guarded by the *muni*.

Leaving the prince on the bed, the queen went to gather fruit. The tired child in his sleep cried and fell off the bed.

When the ascetic went to see the child on the bed, the child was nowhere to be seen. The ascetic was very anxious at this.

"Was he carried away by an elephant in rut or by a hunting hawk? Or by a *yaksa* plodding about? Or was he bitten by a cobra? Where has this dear child gone?

"The mother who went to the jungle
Will soon return pining for the child.
Her breasts will be like mountains full of milk
That the child is accustomed to take.

"A high cliff blocks the wind!
Water magically created! And fire!

No doubt he has gone to the pond!
Oh what is the use of observing austerities?"

Taking a blue water lily (*nil utpala*)
He charmed with magical medicine
And heated it up in a jolly mood
So that a person was indeed created.

Figure to figure was thus made.
But then the other child also appeared.
The mother returned after her search.
Both were taken into her arms.

Carrying both, one on each hip,
The woman entered the temple
Showing both to the *muni.*
"These are two!" exclaimed the queen.

"O mother, the first child cried
Once the strange prince was conjured.
Don't bear me ill-will.
With unique powers I can create them.

The queen was astonished,
Bent down at his feet to venerate the *muni.*
"There are now two tender little ones.
Now explain this to me immediately!"

"When you went to the forest, the first child
Disappeared from my sight.
Then by charming a beautiful flower
I created the other child.

In distress, the queen said:
"If I see this myself today
I shall be relieved.
Make me another child."

Taking a blade of arrow-grass in hand,
He muttered his charm and handed it to the queen.
A gem-like child appeared.
All three then sprang to her hips.

"My two children have now become three.
They are fortunate to be born into wealth.
Now this event will become renowned," she said.
How did the three win her love?

The last born prince
Came to be called Kiristi.
The one born in the womb
Was named Prince Mala.[19]

She raised them affectionately
Feeding and nourishing them well.
Days passed smoothly
While they played in their own hut.

The prince born of the flower
Received his milk by hand.
He was as attractive as Kama
And grew day by day.

Not venturing very far
They entered nearby forests
And with their little bows
They hunted for many animals.

Rabbits, mongeese, mouse deer,
And many monkeys and apes,
As well as other bush-dwelling creatures
They would hunt.

Beautiful fan-tailed peacocks,
Parrots, pigeons and jungle-fowl,
And other types of jungle birds,
They would shoot to kill.

Seeing animals feeding together,
Such as deer and wild boar,
They would take aim, saying: "These animals are ours."
They would kill two or three with a single shot.

Elk, deer, and wild boar,
Spotted deer, tigers and bears,

Leopards and fierce buffaloes
They would chase after and kill.

Taking their small bows in hand,
They shot and collected game constantly.
Enjoying their environs as well as they could,
They followed the course of a stream.

An elephant furiously approached them
So they continued with great caution.
Cleverly they evaded him
And mounted him from the rear.

Seeing herds of elephants in rut,
They surrounded them as well.
With just one arrow shot,
They died right on the spot.

Having entered a very thick forest
Replete with banyan tree roots and creepers
And three layers of other scrub vegetation,
Still their arrows passed through like lightening.

Boars who were shot
Were brought on their backs.
But surviving young boars
Were brought to the temple to play.

"O children, never go to
Rama's pond."
To find out why,
Two of the brothers went.

So, they went to the pond,
Enjoyed sweet fruits,
Saw the crowds
And took guard with their bows.

They shot their bows
With equal vigor.
"Whose children are these?"
King Rama's acquaintances asked.

"We were born in the forest.
Our ancestor is Upulvan.[20]
We become one or we become three.
We never back down from the *asura*s.[21]

"When the *dasa bimbara* armies came,
Our bow was in our hands.
Who else could take such aim?
What *yaksa* could contend?[22]"

"From which country did you come?
What deities of this world gave you birth?
What is your clan [*gotra*] and who are your parents?
Answer clearly."

"Rama and Laksmana,
The two brothers are our fathers.
The *muni* is our grandfather,
And the one who gave us birth is Sita.

Sitapati is our mother.
The *muni* our teacher
And not our mother
But the father, though he did not give us birth.[23]

Our temple is vested with magical power.
Our lineage [*gotra*] has the blood of the *muni*[24]
Whose power has been displayed
The blood of the *muni* has ebbed [?].[25]

Scattering the blooming lotuses
Diving down and stirring up the mud
Swimming to the surface and throwing up sand
To make piles of mud.[26]

Kiristi, Sandalindu and Mala,
The trio got together[27]
For an audience with King Rama.
They shot [arrows] at him to no avail.

From a distance
A shaft was hurled

In the direction of the resolute princes.
And Rama entrusted them for war.

They were saved for the sake of their name and *gotra*.
In order to bring no offense
They related [their] story to Rama very carefully.
Then, without *a dieu*, they departed.

Born in the womb of powerful and beautiful Queen Sita,
The prince was left on the bed while the *muni* practiced his arts.
Maha Visnu made a mistake and the queen was exiled.
But through the power of merits, Sandalindu's name spread.

The queen in exile searched for fruit in the forest.
The *muni* discovers the prince is not on the bed.
The *muni* conjures the arrow-grass.
From its blade Prince Kiristi is made.

From hoards of merit in previous births,
When a blue lily [*nil utpala*] was placed in his [*muni's*] hand,
Just as if he was amidst his powerful retinue,
The prince born of the flower [*mala*] became Prince Malaya.

The deities witnessed all of this with their divine eyes
And protected them well to become warriors.
When the need arose for dispelling *divi dos*,
Sakra cast his glance at them.

In order to rid the *divi dos* afflicting King Panduvas,
The deities assembled and were put on alert.
Then Rahu took the guise of a monstrous boar
And came here warranted by Visnu.

While trapped by the assembly, the boar jumped above them,
Swam through the seven oceans and came ashore.
Mala Raja was given charmed sandalwood paste
To smear on the summoned Panduvas.

May there be long life [Ayubova!]!
May our ritual healing bear fruit!
May all ills be dispelled!
May fortune come from Sakra and Brahma!

Reciting these episodes by verse,
But not disclosing the twelve sections,
The deities take water from the river
And perform the ritual act of benevolence.

A close reading of both versions indicates slight but significantly different elements from the *Palavala Dane* version discussed by Neville (*Sinhala Kavi*:1:38) and previously noted in chapter four. The present *Valiyak Upata* as rendered by Dissanayaka begins with Visnu suffering from a condition of bad planetary influence (*dos*) himself and taking the form of an elephant to wade through his extended problematic period of inauspicious time. It is a substitution for the more conventional episode in the *Ramayana* when Rama is exiled from his kingdom and Sita is kidnapped by Ravana. Here, however, Visnu, rather than his avatar Rama, is predicated first in the story. So what the prelude accomplishes is a framework within the orbit of Visnu's divine and cosmologically ultimate form of existence for the events that are to follow. That is, the eventual birth of the *mala raja* (the "flower king" who becomes the central character(s)[28] or hero(es) later in the Kuveni saga, is understood ultimately as a consequence of Visnu's divine action. Therefore, both myths (the birth of the *mala raja* and the elaborated Kuveni saga) have been posited within Visnu's Puranic profile. The three sons who are miraculously "born" to Sita, are therefore Visnu's own children. Dissanayaka [2000] speculates that this is probably one of the primary reasons why the *valiyak mangalya* is performed at Visnu's Maha Devalaya in Kandy.

It is not until the sixth night, after the ritual has continued to unfold towards its climax, that the birth of the *mala raja* is linked to the *Kuveni Asna* portion of the extended and combined narrative. When that occurs, the most intense, even frenzied moments of the *valiyak mangalya* proceedings take place.

The *Valiyak Upata* also includes a role for the goddess Pattini. As I noted, Pattini is invited to the ritual proceedings of the *valiyak mangalya* on the second night and several *kavi* are chanted on her behalf. It is Pattini who gives the three princes their *valiyak* name. This detail would appear to be an addendum to the earlier forms that the myth has taken in the *Mala Raja Upata* and in the *Palavala Dane*. Nonetheless, it is an episode that has gathered some note, as indicated in the following verses translated as *The Legend of Three Valiyak Devi* by P. B. Meegaskumbura:[29]

Flags, umbrellas, fans and shields appear.
Light flanks a palanquin.

Golden belts glitter around his waist.
Valiyak Devi appears.

See the manner in which the three[30] stand
Near the shadow of the ant-hill
Surrounded by a coterie of friends.
Let us go see *ankeliya*.[31]

[Pattini] said: "Come here."
[They replied]: "Should we pull these ropes, we need to inspect them
    first!"
Saying as much, they approached the horns and stood
Before taking them in hand and breaking.

Then goddess Pattini, very pleased,
Came and sat down on a nearby rock.
"A single pull (*vali*) and the horn breaks!
So, you are hereby '*valiyak*.' And so their name since.

Sivili and *jata*[32] are both worn,
Above the center of the dance arena a *muva mala*[33] hangs,
Thousands of dances and dramas are performed.
Valiyak appears as a triad.

Make vows at flower altars and *devalayas*
To dispel all diseases afflicting this country.
Make parasols and weapons too.
May you benefit from the power of Valiyak.

Having experienced Pattini's power,
They came nearby to the *devalaya*
Where a decorated dwelling for them had been erected.
That is the *devalaya* at Badulla.

Flags, umbrellas, fans and shields were offered,
A blanket covered their palanquin.
An army of warriors on horses and elephants assembled.
This is how Valiyak appeared!

Behold! He rides a tusker
Adorned on the flanks with torches

And glittering goads.
I can see Valiyak *devi* going forth!

He first came ashore at Kataragama,
Saw a red-shield that pleased him.
"Why delay in what is to be done?"
He appeared at the doorway [?].[34]

Warranted so at Kataragama
After observing rites and offerings,
The power and majesty of Valiyak was apprised
And Valiyak Devi departed in style.

Across the jungle he sojourned,
Forded the Ma Oya and continued
Passing through Ratmal Vatiya[35]
Coming to rest under the shade at Kadawata.

To insure our prosperity
All in this country offer *pata panduru*
With no regret for the efforts we make.
May the Valiyak triad grant us good fortune.

What these verses signal is how various mythic and cultic traditions have been conflated within the *valiyak mangalya* and the *kohomba kankariya*. For instance, during the second night of the *valiyak mangalya*, Pattini is invited to take up her seat at the ritual and to bless all who have come in the *mandupur-aya*. This certainly widens the appeal of the rite as Pattini's auspicious presence enriches the panoply of deities who may be entreated. In addition, the allusions to Kataragama in the verses above implicate the presence of that powerful deity in the Valiyak cult as well, as it appears that the *valiyaks'* warrant for acting in the world is supplied by him. Moreover, there are various other invocations held each night for veritable companies of *yaksas* and *kohomba* deities asking them to be present to hear the plaints of those in attendance. While the myth of *mala raja* constitutes a consistent narrative thread throughout the ritual, there are many other dances and chants that have been appended to the mythic core of the rite.

The *Mala Raja Upata*, the second version of the birth of the *mala raja* that I have provided above, is probably a more fluid text, insofar as it is an oral tradition performed in dance. Obviously composed in the *yakdessa* tradition, the final verses establish a link to the *Kuveni Asna*, as it briefly refers to the famous episode of the boar hunt and the subsequent curing of Panduvas from his condition of *divi dos*. The mention of the *mala raja*'s hunting of the boar and the curing of Panduvas' *divi dos* at the end of performance of the *Mala Raja Upata* is but a harbinger for the recital and performance of the more elaborate version which occurs during the sixth and last night of the rite. But in general, the dance performance and recitation of the *Mala Raja Upata* is the staple of the *valiyak mangalya*. The lead *yakdessa* charms the audience with his *kavi* (verse) recitations, his miming of episodes, and his moments of free dance performed between some of the verses (perhaps when he trying to remember the precise verses to follow).

As I noted, the *Kuveni Asna* is an extension of the *Mahavamsa*'s Vijaya myth in which the exiled Sinhala progenitor king Vijaya and his retinue of seven hundred men arrive in Lanka and are received by Upulvan who administers *pirit* to them for their protection. The narrative is expanded greatly and presented in very ornate prose and verse in both the *Kuveni Asnaya* and *Maha Kuveni Asnaya* [Dissanayake 1991: 69–72 and 310–314; also cited by Neville at *Sinhala Kavi* 3: 178]. It is this part of the combined mythic narrative that is dramatically enacted as the climactic moment in both the *kohomba kankariya* and the *valiyak mangalya* during the sixth session of the rite, which is by far the longest of the serial seven ritual occasions lasting virtually throughout the night until the break of dawn. This is also the segment of the *valiyak mangalya* that comprised the moments of greatest cultic intensity. In 2000, some observers "dropped into *disti*" and almost upset the performance of the *yakdessas* in the process.

As the narrative in the *Kuveni Asna* is quite detailed, I will summarize its main episodes as translated from the Sinhala by P. B. Meegaskumbura from Dissanayaka's Sinhala version (1991) before providing relevant sections of its poetry.[36] I will pick up the story after Vijaya's encounter with Upulvan, who has just administered the archetypal *pirit* thread for the safety and protection of Vijaya's men.

Then Kuveni, queen of the *yakkhinis* took the form of a bitch and appeared before Vijaya. Seeing her, he thought that perhaps this meant the presence of a human habitat somewhere nearby. So he dispatched his seven hundred men in search of water, each in turn. When none of them returned,[37] he took out his sword and went in search himself only to find Kuveni, who had transformed herself into a beautiful young maiden under the shade of a banyan tree near a lotus pond. Vijaya pondered whether this woman might be the cause of his men's disappearance, so he seized Kuveni by her hair and raised his sword. Kuveni pleaded with Vijaya to spare her life and bargains that if he would make her his chief queen, she would release his seven hundred men and make him the undisputed ruler of Lanka. Vijaya accedes, his men are returned, and he begins to live intimately with Kuveni in a palace and city that she magically conjures for their conjugal bliss. Subsequently, Kuveni, fearing that her *yaksa* kin will regard her actions with Vijaya as a betrayal, assumes the form of a mare, enters the *yaka* city and devours all of her kind,[38] thus establishing the safety of the island for Vijaya and herself.[39] Soon, however, Vijaya understands that his kingship is not legitimate without a chief queen of proper birth, and upon hearing that a princess from Madurai had landed at the island's chief port, summons Kuveni and announces that it is not right for *yaksas* and humans to co-habitat. He tells her to go. Kuveni laments:[40]

"Bright full moon over eastern mountain
Appears as a red ball of smoldering iron.
Sandalwood fragrance on the breeze
Has become a cool fire instead.
Our bed covered with fragrant flowers
Is now a bed of thorns.
The passionate call of the cuckoo
Is now a spike struck in my ear.
In this plight, the god of love
Has arrived with five spears of war.
How could I bear this separation?
. . . .
How can I console my heart?
. . . .
O gods, where am I to go?"

At this verse, the poem shifts voice and continues to its denouement:

Pouring out her grief in tears
She took herself to the forest.
Prince Vijaya, the ruler,
Was consecrated after marrying the Madurai princess
Who had arrived with great pomp and retinue
And lived in great happiness.
On realizing the great betrayal
The *yakkhini* teemed with hatred,
Took the form of a leopard
And extended a diamond tongue four miles long
Which pierced the seven gateways of the city

And pointed directly at Vijaya's heart.
Then the *devaraja* [Upulvan?] with the tips of his nails
Severed that tongue
Causing great havoc and confusion.
Hoards of leopards rushed Vijaya,

Hoards of *devatas* protected him.
Dispelled are all forms of planetary *dos*, the monthly and the annual.

All *divi dos* have been dispelled on his [Vijaya's] account.
For five thousand years since that time
And for five thousand years hence,
May you be protected.
Daily, may you be victorious!
May you be victorious indeed.

The narrative, however, is not at an end here. It continues on to episodes of dramatic importance to the *valiyak manglaya* and to the *kohomba kankariya* as well.[41] A summary follows:

With *divi dos* dispelled, Vijaya lives in splendor for another twenty years and is succeeded by Panduvas who then, himself, becomes afflicted with *divi dos*. The cause of his illness is determined when a leopard appears on his bed during his sleep by a goddess who then reports the matter to Sakra. Sakra inquires of Visnu if he can send the Mala Raja to cure Panduvas of his *divi dos*. To entice the Mala Raja to Lanka, Rahu assumes the form of a giant boar who proceeds to ravish the Mala Raja's royal garden. The Mala Raja, in the form of Visnu's three sons, set out in hot pursuit of the giant boar throughout many kingdoms of India and finally to the shores of Lanka and through its various realms. Finally at Hantana, the mountainous realm above Kandy and Peradeniya, the boar is trapped. When the Mala Raja attempts to slice it in half, the boar turns into a stone. Overwhelmed with anger at the deception, the Mala Raja then learns from Sakra that the real reason he has been brought down to Lanka is that he is only person born of the blue water lily (*utpalavan*) who could dispel the *divi dos* that had struck Panduvas. Panduvas was then instructed to wear sixty-four ornaments[42] and cured of his illness, the *dos* dispelled for as long as the moon should shine.

The dramatization of the *Kuveni Asna* reveals the purpose and logic of the *valiyak manglaya* at Visnu's Maha Devalaya in Kandy in general. Just as the *mala raja* (the three *valiyaks* as they were so named by Pattini)[43] cured the *divi dos* of King Panduvas, so he (they) can be called upon to cure whatever kinds of *dos* that may afflict the *peraharas'* ritual participants. By extension, the *valiyaks* can also be appealed to by the *yakdessa* to cure the afflictions of all who attend the rite.[44] That is, the significance of this extended cycle of myths, beginning with Visnu/Upulvan Rama's meeting of Sita at the "blue lotus pond," Sita's pregnancy, her survival in exile, the birth of her three children as a result of the combination of her love for Rama and the conjuring of the *muni*, the children's transformation into the *mala raja* (or three *valiyaks*), the meeting of Vijaya with Upulvan and the giving of the *pirit* thread, the extended Kuveni episodes culminating in the *mala raja's* chase of Rahu disguised as a boar, and the final curing of King Panduvas, are all singularly telescoped to explain the legitimacy and function of the *valiyak mangalya* as a ritual of the *mala raja's* curative powers. Its ultimate referents of power, as we have seen, are Visnu/Upulvan/Rama as channeled through the offspring *mala raja*, Visnu's (Rama's) and Sita's divine progeny.[45] The chief *yakdessa* who performs the *valiyak mangalya*, represents the presence of the curative powers of the *mala raja*. The purpose and perceived function of *valiyak natuma*, then, is completely consonant with the substance and ethos of ritual life as it is has been outlined in the previous chapter. The *valiyak mangalya* is now simply a specialized rite aimed at protection from *dos* that might have been occasioned during the *asala perahara*, though its ultimate origins may be quite old.[46] Within the *valiyak mangalya*, the *yakdessa* functions as a type of *kapurala* as well, insofar as he chants *yatika* on behalf of all *perahara* participants and also for anyone attending the rite who makes an offering and a request.

The *valiyak mangalya*, therefore, seems to be the one ritual context in which a significant slice of the mythology germane to the late-medieval cult of the "Buddhist Visnu" is still sustained. It is also a composite mythology, insofar it as its sources derived from *Ramayana*, south Indian Tamil and Sinhala sources. As such, it is a fossil of what previously existed of the former formal cult patronized by Kandyan kings. If it atrophies and dies, a dimension of the cult of the "Buddhist Visnu" will probably die along with it.

While this aspect of the cult of the "Buddhist Visnu" may be in historical jeopardy, the legacy of many other elements has been sustained and modified in the cult of Alutnuvara Deviyo. That is the topic of the next chapter.

LEGACIES OF THE "BUDDHIST VISNU"
Myth and Cult at the Alutnuvara *Devalaya*

"Doubtless historical accidents always played some later part, but the original factor fixing the figure of the gods must always have been psychological. The deity to whom the prophets, seers, and devotees founded the particular cult bore witness to what was worth something to them personally. They could use him. He guided their imaginations, warranted their hopes, and controlled their wills,—or else they required him as a safeguard against the demon and a curber against other people's crimes. In other words, they chose him for the value of the fruits he seemed to them to yield. . . . The gods we stand by are the gods we need and use, the gods whose demands on us are reinforcements of our demands on ourselves and one another." —William James[1]

Sinhala religious culture has been assimilative historically. Its pliability and practicality has sustained its remarkable endurance for more than two millennia. Thus, change, or more specifically *transformation*, has been its ally or *modus vivendi*. I have argued that assimilations and transformations tend to occur through time if they are perceived as functionally efficacious and then determined to be teleologically or soteriologically relevant. In the case of Visnu, his incorporation was at first politically and socially expedient for Sinhala kingship. Since his mythic profile was then rationally linked to the soteriology of Buddhism, further abetted by means of his identification with the indigenous Upulvan, his assimilation has not only endured, but his presence has been religiously valorized according to bedrock principles of Sinhala Buddhist culture. As "minister of defense" and bodhisatva-in-the-making, Visnu acts in the interests of Sinhala people individually and collectively, on the basis of his embodiment within the moral economy of Sinhala Buddhist religious culture. I have also noted that assimilations of this nature periodically encounter resistance, and, in the next chapter, an especially relevant contemporary example of such resistance is examined at some length.

In this chapter, however, we examine one further important twist in the assimilation and transformation of the cult of the "Buddhist Visnu" in Sri Lanka: how a number of Visnu's mythic attributes as well as elements of his functional relevance have taken root, or, in turn, have been incorporated into the cult of Dadimunda Devata Bandara, also known as Alutnuvara Deviyo, and to a much lesser extent, into the cult of the *yaksa* Huniyam, who is also simultaneously, or alternatively, imagined as a part-time *devata*. In turn, this process has abetted the continued sustenance and prestige of the cult of Dadimunda and Huniyam as well. These assimilations are, I believe, largely a consequence of the fact that historically the venue of the Alutnuvara shrine has served as the chief seat for the cults of Visnu, Dadimunda, and even, to a lesser extent, for Huniyam as well. Proximity has bred conflation.

Gananath Obeyesekere (1984:319–21), in an interesting digression within his monumental study of the cult of the goddess Pattini, was the first scholar, to my knowledge, to refer to how "the myths of Upulvan-Visnu were transferred to [Devata Bandara]." Why and how this occurred, and what significance it has for contemporary Sinhala Buddhist religion, are the fundamental concerns of my limited inquiry that follows in this chapter.[2] In ferreting out the various vicissitudes of this problem, in order to determine its specific relevance for this study, I find it necessary to return to an examination of historical sources and mythic expressions within seventeenth- and eighteenth-century Kandyan Sinhala literature. In the process, I have also addressed the problem of how Visnu has come to figure in various popular forms of contemporary Sinhala religion now embodied within the ever-popular Alutnuvara cult, including possession, soothsaying, and healing. We will look at the historical context first, in order to determine how various understandings of history and myth, as least as these are known through Pali and Sinhala sources, help to understand the significance of Visnu's legacy in the cult of Dadimunda Devata Bandara.

A RETURN TO HISTORY

At various points in the discussion thus far, it has become clear that the cultic site of Alutnuvara has played a pivotal role in the dissemination of the cult of the "Buddhist Visnu." As I have noted previously, the cult of Upulvan seems to have spread from southern Devinuvara to the up-country regions of the island perhaps as early as the late-thirteenth century, during the reign of Parakramabahu II of Dambadeniya (1236–70C.E.). Moreover, it would appear that the chief cultic seat of Upulvan in the up-country region of the island from the thirteenth until the late-seventeenth century was located at Alutnuvara, some eleven miles, as Sri Lanka's many crows and bats fly, west of Kandy.

When I first visited the Alutnuvara Devalaya (see fig. 7.1) on a Saturday *kemmura* morning in April of 2000, I was somewhat overwhelmed by the large

FIGURE 7.1 Sketch of the Alutnuvara Devalaya (Kanchuka Dharmasiri)

numbers of pilgrims and devotees, approximately 700 of them, who were standing in a long serpentined queue under the hot sun, waiting patiently, usually for more than an hour, to gain entry to the *devalaya*, in order to make their offerings of fruit, betel leaves, incense, and cash before hearing the *kapurala*'s generic *yatikava*. It was a scene in complete juxtaposition to the subdued and reverent, almost meditative atmosphere of the Maha Devalaya in Kandy. The vast majority of the devotees at Alutnuvara were also decidedly rural or rural-village in orientation, in contrast to the middle-class background of most of those who visit the Kandy Visnu *devalaya*. Immediately, I knew quite clearly, because of the huge numbers of people visiting the *devalaya* (some 500 or so entering and leaving the *sanctum sanctorum* every hour), that the field-study methods I had deployed at the Kandy Visnu *devalaya* earlier would be impossible to use at Alutnuvara. There could be no "controlled census" here because the numbers of devotees were largely uncontrollable. There could be no ascertaining the specific reasons for their visits to the *devalaya* either, because with such large groups of people, about fifty entering the *sanctum* at the same time, the *kapuralas* could not practically solicit anyone's specific needs and intentions individually. Originally, we did our best at counting, and asking people where they had come from, but obtaining a more personal reading of their individual intentions was an impossible expectation under these circumstances.

Every ten minutes or so, a batch of fifty to sixty devotees were allowed into the *devalaya*, made their offerings, were given a very brief *darsan* (seeing—and being seen by—the deity) of the splendid bronze image of Dadimunda (see fig. 7.2), listened to the *kapurala*'s standard chant, and then were shuttled out of

FIGURE 7.2 Sketch of Dadimunda image in the sanctum sanctorum at Alutnuvara (Kanchuka Dharmasiri)

the sanctum in order to make room for the next batch in the queue. Every half an hour, large-sized containers bearing the fruits that had been offered to Alutnuvara Deviyo were carried away to be emptied. The entire area surrounding the *devalaya* reeked of rotting fruit. Dozens of roosters, given by various devotees to the *devalaya*, strutted about on the large green in front of the temple. Roosters are the *vahana* (vehicle) of Dadimunda. The whole scene was hectic, intense, bustling, and yet businesslike.

I had done considerable reading ahead of time about Alutnuvara and Dadimunda, so I knew that the complexity of the history and scope of the cult would be ethnographically exhaustive, beyond what I could possibly include in a study focused on the Buddhist transformation of Visnu. Thus, it took some time to develop an effective field-research strategy to find out exactly what I needed to know.

Initially, because of the confusing nature of that first of many visits over the next three months, and also during the months of the following spring (2001), I settled first on the prospect of interviewing just two people in particular: the chief monastic incumbent of the Ran Gal Lena ("Golden Stone Cave") Viharaya, located on the majestic jungle-covered hill just above and opposite the Alutnuvara Devalaya, and the chief *kapurala* of the *devalaya* per se.

Ven. Udawela Vipulasara Nayaka Thero was an 85-year-old *bhikkhu* of the Siyam Nikaya, who first came to Alutnuvara in 1928 and has been a monk in the Ran Gal Lena Viharaya ever since, for seventy-two years. He was completely lucid and gracious when I met him in the spring of 2000. On showing me around his temple, he was eager for me to see the *viharaya*'s recently and completely refurbished *buduge*, a project that had preoccupied him for much of his time over the past decade. It was, no doubt, his farewell project or gift to his temple.

On entering the cave *buduge*, I could see that on both sides and above the main door frame leading into the shrine were stone carvings, which appeared to date to the seventeenth or eighteenth century c.e., of the familiar sun-face circle to the left and the moon-rabbit circle to the right, symbols traditionally found on the flag of the *Sat Korale*s (the traditional name for a part of the modern province of Sabaragamuva) and now always found within symbolic ensembles for Dadimunda Devata Bandara. At one time, then, this was not a *viharaya buduge*, but rather a *devalaya* for Dadimunda. After I had interviewed Ven. Udawela Vipulasara and learned from him about the many changes that have occurred during the twentieth century in the cult of Alutnuvara,[3] we agreed that I would return on a later date to record a history of the *viharaya* as he could best reconstruct it. He viewed it as background for me to better understand the importance of his *buduge*. Here is a translation of his account as I later recorded it on tape on a subsequent visit:[4]

During the Dambadeniya period, King Parakramabahu reigned from 1236 until 1270. At one time, he suffered from a speech difficulty. Many treatments were tried, but all these were in vain. Eventually, the king decided to have a *puja* performed to the deity of the *devalaya* at Girihelapura [Devinuvara] in the hope of discovering the cause of his impediment. He sent his chief minister, Devapathiraja, with gifts and offerings to the Girihelapura *devalaya*, now known as the Devinuvara *devalaya*. Devapathiraja performed the *puja* as he had been instructed and went to bed that night. In his sleep, a white-clad *brahmana* figure appeared to him in a dream and told him: "Even if the stalk of the Keketiya flowers could be straightened, the stammering of the king could never be cured." Devapathiraja returned home and informed the king of this strange phenomenon with the message of the mysterious nocturnal figure. The king's reaction was that he could now understand that his problem was the result of his *karma* and he was pleased that the deity, in sympathy for his plight, had appeared himself to reveal the truth. Therefore, the king decided to hold more elaborate *pujas* to the deity.

He instructed his minister to go to Devinuvara again and to fetch the images of Visnu, Chandravathi, and Devata Bandara, along with their divine "weapons" which were then brought to Dambadeniya. While the images were being brought in a *perahera*, Queen Sunethra pleaded and persuaded the king to build a *devalaya* for the deity in her *biso pattu* [lands belonging to her as queen]. During that time, this region was known as Thilakapura, later on as Nava Thilaka Puraya before it was named Alutnuvara. This area was part of her *biso pattuwa* then. The king agreed to her request and the *perahera* turned toward Thilakapura away from Dambadeniya. When the images were brought at last, there was no place to keep them. So the king decided to keep them safely at Ran Gal Len Viharaya, which is here, with the consent of the monk who was residing here, Asvaddana Piriven Sami. They were kept here for a while, and all due rituals were performed. One day the deity appeared before the monk in his sleep and asked him to build a separate *devalaya*.

After this, a new *devalaya* was built in the premises of where the present *devalaya* is now located, and the images were transferred there. Meanwhile, King Kirti Sri Rajasimha decided to take the Visnu image to Kandy to complete the presence of the four *devalayas*. It is believed that this image is still in Kandy.

When the other images were removed from the Ran Gal Lena Viharaya, the deity again appeared in dreams to the monk and to the king and told them both not to leave the *viharaya* empty. So the king instructed that three new images should be carved. A huge *sapu* tree from Sapugastenne was felled and three life-sized images carved of Visnu, Chandravathi and Devata Bandara were kept at the *viharaya*. Now they are gone. It may be that they have been stolen by treasure hunters.

On yet another later visit to Alutnuvara, I found that Ven. Udawela's account was similar, with the omission of many of his details and some other minor differences,[5] to one written in Sinhala on a large prominently displayed sign board just opposite the contemporary Alutnuvara Devalaya, under a massive *sapu* tree purported to be a marker of the original site of the thirteenth-century Upulvan *devalaya*.

Later on that first day, after I had spoken to Ven. Udawela, when the crowds at the Dadimunda shrine had subsided a bit, I subsequently met a harried and wearied chief *kapurala* of the Alutnuvara Devalaya who, quite understandably, was still more preoccupied about crowd-control measures than with answering the questions of an inquiring foreign scholar. In anticipation of the types of questions I might ask, he handed over a four-page mimeographed document, claiming it to be the "*Sannasa* of the Alutnuvara *devalaya*." When I asked the *kapurala* about the text's content, he told me that the original *sannasa* is now in the British Museum. An English translation of the document is provided below:

"'SANNASA' OF ALUTNUVARA DEVALAYA"[6]

King Parakramabahu of Dambadeniya, pleased with the fact that he had recovered from a fatal illness after doing *pujas* to the deity of Devinuvara, decided to send *pandurus* and gifts to Devinuvara in thanks. He sent one of his officers, Devapathiraja, along with others to Devinuvara in a *pera-hera* with gifts, including a *sannasa* declaring the dedication of some villages to the *devalaya*: Paddawela Debage, Patunugama, Alapalawela and Dampalgoda from Mayadunu Korale, villages which belonged to Queen Sunethra's *pattuwa* [land]. The king instructed Devapathiraja to fulfil vows to the deity, to conduct *pujas* in his name and to see that an annual *asala perahera* was carried out on his behalf as a mark of veneration. He also assigned Seneviratne Bandara, Chandra Mohottala and *brahmanas* with the task of accompanying the *devaraja petikada* [cloth painting of the 'king of the gods'] with the *ran ayudha* [golden weapons] to Dambadeniya in a *perahera*, along with Dissanayaka *kapurala*, Ranabahu Rala of Devin-uvara, Handuru Gamarala, Kankani Gamarala and others. After the image was brought to Dambadeniya, a huge *deva mandiriya* [palace of the deity] was built where it [the *devaraja petikada*] was to be kept safely and where elaborate rites were performed.

Having done so, Handuru Gamarala and Kankani Gamarala came to report all details of the mission carried out to Queen Sunethra. They showed her the *sannasa* that was taken to Devinuvara, related in detail how the image of the deity had been brought to Dambadeniya in a *perahera*, and how land donated by her along with other gifts and *pandurus* had been properly given to the deity.

Thirty-three years later, Parakramabahu died. He was succeeded by King Bhuvanekabahu who set up his own capital in Yapahuva. During this time, a monk residing in Asvaddana Pirivena saw the Devinuvara deity appearing in his dreams, who requested him to build a *devalaya* for him in a particular place. The monk informed the king of the request.

The king consented to building the *devalaya*. After observing all the necessary rituals at an auspicious time, the building of the *devalaya* commenced under the leadership of Wijesundara *acariya*. Within twelve months, a *deva mandiraya* of the length and width of six *riyana*s, a *sandun kudama* of three *riyana*s and a *muluthan geya* of seven *riyana*s, were constructed. The *deva mandiraya* was decorated with ironwork, steel, ivory, gold, precious gems and paintings. This done, Wijeyasundara *achariya*, along with his followers and the monk from Asvaddana Pirivena went to the king to inform him of the completion of the building. The king then brought the *devaraja petikada* in a *perahara* along with the *ran ayudha* to the new abode, the Thalaga Maligava of Mahathanne near Ganethenna Nuwara, in the same way that way that it was brought from Devinuvara. Since that time, the image was kept here with *pujas* being performed and *murutan rajakariya* being offered. Since its presence, many miracles have been witnessed; after three years of suffering from total blindness, Adikari Rala of Makadawara regained his vision by making vows and performing *pujas* to the deity. Another time, floods without rain occurred in which a herd of cattle were threatened. It stopped after vows were made to the deity.

Seeing these wonders, the king decided to make images of Visnu and his wife Chandrawathi, and asked the sculptor Pathiraja to carry out the tasks. The images were beautifully carved and decorated. After, they were brought to the *deva mandiraya* in a procession in January during *mrgasheersha nakatha*. Then, all the rites performed in Devinuvara were carried out in similar fashion here. The previous name given to the *deva mandiraya* was abandoned and replaced by the name Alutnuvara ["New City"]. To the previously allocated lands, new ones were added along with *rajakariya* duties. The incumbent of Galathurmula was asked to supervise the place. In return, he was given four *amunu*s of paddy land, saffron robes, five hundred betel leaves, a *pirit pavada* and a temple to reside in.

Then the two *brahmana ralas* were made into *kapu ralas* of the *devalaya* and were given six *amunus* of paddy lands each. Dissanayaka *rala* was given the position of *vannaku* along with nine *amunus* of paddy lands in Kirihungampattiya, five *pala* of paddy lands in Kotakumbura in Alutnuvara, the Tibutte *hena*, the Maddegoda *hena* and six *amunus* of paddy lands in Karahampitigoda. Ranabahu *rala* was given the Meekumbure *devalaya*. Sumangala *thero*, a relation of Asvaddana *thero*, was named as the *vidane swami* and given responsibilities to administrate the *devalaya*. In this manner, the *sannasa* declares the offerings of gifts and lands to the deity along with the message from Bhuvaneka Bahu that all the kings who succeed him shall continue to uphold these duties.[7]

Soon after these first visits to Alutnuvara, and after I had an opportunity to study these two contemporary versions of the *devalaya's* "*sthalapurana*,"[8] I found the following substantial passage of relevance to the history of the Alutnuvara Devalaya in H. C. P. Bell's (1904:46–47) antiquarian *Report on the Kegalle District*. It contained another "*sthalapurana*" or *sannasa* type of document, similar in kind to the two I have presented above. In what follows, Bell first introduces the text before offering his own translation followed by a bit of his own commentary:

"Unlike most *dewales*, [this one] is dedicated to the *devatava*, or demi-god *Dedimunda Bandara*, otherwise styled *Wahala Bandara Deviyo*, a minister of Visnu. . . . The *dewale* has a definite history, carrying it back directly to the days of Kalikala Sahitya Sarvajna Pandita Parakramabahu [II] . . . and indirectly some centuries earlier, when the sacred image and cloth of Visnu were brought over from India. Particulars are gathered both from tradition and from a rare little *ola* manuscript discovered in the district:—

On the full moon day in Vesak, in the Saka year 712 (790 A.D.), a red-sandalwood image of Visnu was brought across the sea. King Dapulu Sen saw in a vision that the image had started, and would be landed at Girihelapura Magulwella; and it was told him that he must build a *dewavimanayak* in Devinuvara (Dondra). Accordingly, the king built the city of Devinuvara as ordered, and kept there the red-sandalwood image of Visnu, and in the month of Esala planted the sacred post (*kap-hitawanawa*) at a lucky hour as customary before the commencement of the *perahera*, and commenced the procession. In it the image of Maha Brahma was borne ahead; this was the origin of such processions in this Island. The place was called *Vimal Sri Dewunuwara*. The King Dapulu Sen granted lands to the Brahmins and others who accompanied the image of Visnu, the cloth in which Visnu's image was painted (*Dewa-raja-peti vahanse*), and the large gold weapon (*maha-ran-avudha*) and he bestowed on the chief Brahmin, Rama Chandra, two villages and many offices.

After that the King Pandita Parakrama Bahu who reigned at Dambadeniya, sent his Prime Minister Dewaprati Raja to Mahatota (Matara) to bring the *Dewa-raja-peti-kada* and the *maha-ran-avudha*, in order that they might be worshipped by the people of Pihiti [Rata] and Maya Rata. Two sons, Navaratna Bandara and Surya Bandara, had been born to King Dapulu Sen by the daughter of the Brahmin Rama Chandra. Surya Bandara, the youngest, married the younger sister of the chief Visidagama Buddhagosa and remained there. But the elder son, Navaratna Bandara, Disanayaka Kapurala, and others were sent with the minister Dewaprati Raja to bear the sacred cloth and the gold insignia to Dambadeni Nuwara. These were placed in the Gallena Vihare at a lucky hour on the 10th day of the waxing moon of Nikin, in the year of Buddha 1779 (1236 A.D.). Lands were given to the persons who accompanied them, and to Navaratna Bandara were granted two villages, Katugampola and Elabadagama in Seven Korales. He entered the service of the king.

When 183 years time had elapsed, the reigning prince besought the god Visnu, and was instructed in a vision to cut *lev* grass in the place where rushes were planted, and to build a house for the gods, and to have the marshy land asweedumized [sic], and an offering made once a year, of a *pingo* [*pangu?*] of *muluten* and a bunch of cocoanuts to the *dewale* (*dewa mandiraya*) of Sri Visnu Deviyo-raja at Alutnuwara called *Tilaka-navapura*. When this vision was made known to the King Mahalu Bhuvaneka Bahu, he confirmed the said grant.

After this, the same king, in the month of Vesak, caused a two-storied dewale to be built and had placed there [the] *Dewa-raja-peti-kada*, which had been brought from Devinuvara, and appointed the grandson of Navaratna Bandara to the office of Basnayake Nilame of the Visnu Dewale, bestowing on it 24 *amunams* of mud land from Galatara [brackets mine].

"Upon the order of a later king the images of the god Visnu and the *Dewa-raja-peti-kada* were transferred to Kandy and deposited in the Maha Dewale built to receive them. Offerings were ordered to be given to Alutnuwara Dewale in the name of Dadimunda and Malwatte Bandaras. After some time the sacred cloth was removed from Kandy to Hanguranketa, where a Dewale was erected, and only the sandalwood image [was] kept in Kandy. This transference and merging of the Maha Dewale of Kandy is supported by the fact that there are now no lands dedicated directly to Alutnuvara Dewale. These, with its administration, have passed to the Maha Dewale and the hands of the Basnayaka Nilame."

Directly related to these three accounts, I reviewed the little of what can be known about Devinuvara from the *Culavamsa*'s extensive narrative of Parakramabahu II's long thirteenth-century reign. The first passage figures in the *Culavamsa*'s account of Prince Virabahu's epical defeat of the displaced and invading prince Chandrabhanu (from Tamradipa, or what is now northern Malaysia) and his Javaka mercenaries, an important historical watershed that preserved Sinhala kingship in the thirteenth century:

> Going forth to the combat like Rama, Prince Virabahu slew numbers of Javakas, as Rama slew the Rakkhasas. The Veramba wind, namely Vira-bahu, possessed of great vehemence, shattered again and again the forest wilderness, namely the Javaka foes. After thus putting to flight the Javakas in combat, he freed the whole region of Lanka from the foe. Hereupon he betook himself to Devanagara [Devinuvara], worshipped there the lotus-hued god [Upulvan] and celebrated for him a divine sacrifice. [83.44; II,152; brackets mine]

Then, in further cataloging the manifold meritorious works attributed to Parakramabahu II and performed by the king on behalf of the *sasana* through-out his reign, the *Culavamsa* (85.85–89; II,167) includes this passage:

> Then when the Monarch [Parakramabahu II] learned that the sacred town of Devanagara which was a mine of meritorious works, the shrine long since erected to the lotus-hued god [Upulvan], the King of the gods [*de-varaja*], had now fallen into decay, he betook himself to the superb town and in rebuilding the dwelling of the King of the gods [Upulvan *devaraja*] like the heavenly mansion of the King of the gods [*devaraja* Indra or Sakra], he made it an abode of all riches. Then the best of men had the town filled with all splendours even as the beauteous city of the gods. Hereupon he determined to celebrate every year in the town an Asalhi [*asala*] festival for the god. [brackets mine]

Here are four traditions, four versions, and four emphases, each with its own agendas to establish, and each eventually impinging in its own way on an understanding of the emergent cult of Alutnuvara Deviyo. The narrative of my field-research efforts and the results that they yielded at Alutnuvara will be continued in a later section of this chapter. We now turn directly to an analysis of these pertinent accounts before examining related issues as they surface in ritual texts of the Alutnuvara cult.

All four sources agree that King Parakramabahu II of Dambadeniya recognized and celebrated the miraculous powers of *devaraja* Upulvan at Devinuvara, be they construed as those of a national guardian deity of the state or as a healer of disease and a revealer of truth, and that he played the decisive and salutary role in shifting the cultic seat of Upulvan to up-country Alutnuvara. It is clear that the cult of Upulvan was not only recognized as important to the Sinhala state, but it would also seem that Parakramabahu wanted its presence in up-country Sri Lanka, closer to his seat of power and accessible to peoples in the *Udarata* or *Mayarata* regions. From the *Culavamsa*'s long profile of this particularly important king, we also know that he was very much influenced by Brahmanical tradition, recognized as an accomplished Sanskrit scholar in his own right, and a great supporter of all literary activity—Sanskrit, Pali, and Sinhala. The comparison of his nephew's (Prince Virabahu's) victory over Candrabhanu to Rama's victory over Ravana, his nephew's subsequent visit to the shrine of Upulvan to give thanks, and the reconstruction of Devinuvara in the image of Indra's celestial city, all would seem to indicate the weighted presence in the *Culavamsa* of the Puranic and Vaisnava ideologies of kingship.

With the exception of the *Culavamsa* passage that credits Prince Virabahu as having made a pilgrimage of thanks to Devinuvara, each of the other accounts cites the king's prime minister, Devapathiraja, as the royal official who proceeded to Devinuvara on behalf of the king. All of these accounts agree that, in one fashion or another, a *perahara* was either established in Devinuvara, or that images and symbols of the Devinuvara deity were brought in a *perahera* either to Dambadeniya or to Alutnuvara, by the king's order, to his prime minister. Finally, with the exception of the skeletal references I have culled from the *Culavamsa*, each of the sources mentions the importance of visions or dreams of the deity connected to the setting up *devalayas* or in the construction of images. (In the three accounts, visions are mentioned no less than seven times.)

To be sure, there are many other very interesting and important details revealed in these texts, many of which I have anticipated in earlier contexts and some that will again surface in a consideration of the poems and ballads of the Dadimunda Devata Bandara cult. We may now simply note some of these more significant details in passing—those which are associated with issues raised before: the inclusion of, or grafting on, of yet another version of the red-sandalwood-image myth in Bell's *ola* manuscript (which has the effect of stressing the Brahmanic origins of the cult in India); the prerogatives of queens, likely of South Indian descent, and their role in providing lands for the support of the *devalaya* (signaling a continued interest, first seen in Polonnaruva days, of significant support for deities from this particular royal quarter); the Brahmanical background of the Alutnuvara shrine priests (including the Dissanayake *kapurala*, who is mentioned in both the second and third sources, and who was probably the progenitor of those *kapurala* namesakes serving Alutnuvara to this day) and their conversion from being *brahmana rala* to being *kapu ralas* (indicating the shift from Brahmanical Hindu to Sinhala-Buddhist ritual orientations); the cultic importance given to a *petikada* cloth tapestry (indeed, a very old one does remain to this very day in the Maha (Visnu) Devalaya at Hanguranketa) and the deity's "golden weapons" (*ran ayudha*, the ritual objects still paraded in the *perahara* processions); the general emphasis on the dissemination of the Devinuvara Upulvan cult into the *Mayarata* or *Udarata* (up-country), and the naming of Alutnuvara ("New City"), apparently to signify it as a successor to or being of parallel importance with Devinuvara ("City of the God"), etc.

While each of these details are of great interest, I want to emphasize (or reemphasize) specifically the significance of three others: 1) the royal and political significance of the Devinuvara deity (Upulvan/Visnu) in general; 2) the establishment of the *asala perahara* in Devinuvara and the prominence with which *peraheras* figure in all of these accounts; and 3) the importance attached to divine revelation through visions.

The political significance of Upulvan, and later the "Buddhist Visnu," as a deity of national importance to the state or kingship has been belabored in previous chapters of this study. I want to reemphasize it again in this context because Alutnuvara Deviyo, as a deity who inherits various mantels from the "Buddhist Visnu," remains a very significant political deity in Sri Lanka today, in a number of different ways.[9]

This political legacy is, in part, specifically derived from his associations with the "Buddhist Visnu;" that is, in his role as Visnu's "prime minister," and in the aspects of Upulvan/Visnu mythic profile that he inherits. In each of our accounts about the beginnings of the Alutnuvara Devalaya, the same pattern between the king, Parakramabahu II and his "prime minister," Devapathiraja, is emphasized. In the Sinhala classic, the *Pujavaliya*, written during Parakramabahu's reign, it is this same Devapathiraja, who is described as an aspirant for Buddhahood, who also urges the king himself to aspire for Buddhahood by means of perfecting the *paramitas* (H. D. J. Gunawardhana, *Pujavaliya*: 16–18). He is the figure in the *Pujavaliya* text who elicits the sermons descriptive of the various virtues of the Buddha that become the substance of this classic Sinhala Buddhist exposition. In our "*sthalapuranas*," it is this same "prime minister" who is the actual performer of *pujas*, the elicitor of divine power, and the figure who procures the divine images and divine weapons (symbols of the presence and power of the divine) for the up-country region on the king's behalf. He is the figure who actually does what is necessary to implement the king's or the queen's wishes, and makes possible the meritorious acts that accrue to them. In addition, he functions as a type of commander-in-chief under the king.

What I am suggesting is simply this: that in each of these stories of the *devalaya*'s origins, there is a pattern in which the prime minister is to his king what Dadimunda Devata Bandara is to Upulvan/Visnu (or to the Buddha in later folklore, soon to be examined). The accounts of the founding of the *devalaya* seem to emphasize this type of relationship between these two types of authority figures: There is a royal figure (Parakramabahu II and the *devaraja*, or the Buddha) on the one hand, and his commander-in-chief (Devapathiraja and Devata Bandara) on the other. That is, there is a clearly established hierarchy of political authority that is parallel to a relevant divine hierarchy of deities. In one of the "*sthalapuranas*" and in one of the important texts of the cult of Dadimunda to be examined shortly, it is claimed that the image of Devata Bandara was also brought from Devinuvara to Alutnuvara along with the images of Upulvan and his consort, as if the three images were part of the same cult. The effect of this detail is to link Dadimunda to Upulvan from the very beginning of the Alutnuvara's foundation in two ways: in relation to the royal directives that led to the establishment of the *devalaya*, and to the top of the divine hierarchy, as the pantheon of deities was understood at the time.

Though there are passages in the three ritual texts I am about to consider that belie the possibility of the Dadimunda's South Indian origins,[10] one of the reasons, among others, that the cult of Dadimunda is so ascendant in recent times is his currently unquestioned Sinhala Buddhist identity, an identity that now can be as political in significance as it is religious in nature. As I mentioned in chapter 5 and as Bell indicates in his comments (see above), the *basnayaka nilame* of the Visnu *devalaya* in Kandy is also simultaneously the *basnayaka nilame* of the Alutnuvara Devalaya. This may well have been the administrative arrangement since the seventeenth century, when the Visnu *devalaya* was shifted to Kandy by Senaret, Rajasimha II, or more likely by Vimaladharmasurya II (and probably not Kirti Sri Rajasimha). Recall that the current *basnayaka nilame*'s family, one that has dominated politics in post-independent Sri Lanka, has been intimately connected to both of these *devalayas* for a number of generations. Indeed, the current *basnayaka nilame*'s (and Sri Lanka's current president's) grandfather had his name inscribed (in 1924) in the foundation stones of the present *devalaya* building. Moreover, the *basnayaka nilame*'s brother, Deputy Minister of Defense during the time of my fieldwork, frequently performed *pujas* to Dadimunda at the Alutnuvara devalaya on his comings and goings between Kandy and Colombo.

I have already footnoted the conspicuous legacy of President Premadasa's regular visits to this venue. It was generally known that he was also a frequent and fervent patron of Dadimunda (and on one of his visits donated an elephant to the *devalaya*).[11] In this connection, I can report that when I asked *kapuralas* and members of their families about Ven. Soma's campaign to stop Buddhist laity from worshipping the gods, I was told more than once that Ven.

Soma's admonition did not apply to Dadimunda. The reason given for this was that, unlike the other deities in question, Dadimunda was purely a Sinhala Buddhist deity. (Other details will be added to the contemporary political significance of the Alutnuvara cult later in the chapter.)

While Visnu, in the last two centuries, has lost some of his luster as a deity of great political import, owing most certainly to the disestablishment of Sri Lankan kingship in the early nineteenth century, the more overt legacy of national political identity seems to have been sustained in the newer version of Alutnuvara Deviyo, that is, Dadimunda. The reasons for this may become clearer subsequently in my review of the cultic texts. But the transformation of this deity, clearly not born of Buddhistic origins, is as thorough as it is remarkable. Briefly, it will be seen that Dadimunda's cult was not only established through royal support, but that his mythic profile is dominated by images of martial power enlisted in support of Buddhism and the Sinhala political interests of the state. This is the first pattern of the "Buddhist Visnu's" legacy that I wish to emphasize.

With regard to the second pattern I wish to highlight within these accounts of the *devalaya*'s origins, the public performance of *peraheras* was also of considerable political significance in traditional medieval Sinhala Buddhist culture. Indeed, H. L. Seneviratne (1978:136–49) has underscored its continuing significance as an expression of political and social hegemony for the Kandyan and nationalist elites of modern Sinhala society. Elsewhere, I have argued that the *perahera* has become a primary ritual expression of Sinhala Buddhist "civil religion" in modern Sri Lanka (1982:23–40). I have also tried to show that in late-medieval times, *peraheras* functioned as ritual devices through which symbolic power centripetally and centrifugally radiated within and throughout the pulsating *mandalic* polity of the Kandyan kingdom (1991:171–201).

While performances of *peraheras* have now proliferated exponentially and are sponsored regularly by many major Buddhist monastic *viharayas* throughout all regions of Sinhala Sri Lanka, during the time of Kandyan kingship (and I suspect even before that), only kings sponsored these public processions of pomp and pageantry. Just when Kandyan kings began to sponsor *asala peraharas* annually, specifically the Mahanuvara (Kandy) *asala perahera*, is not known for certain. But when the Kandy *perahera* did come into vogue as an annual pageant, at least by Knox's seventeenth-century era, if not earlier, it was held only in connection with those *devalayas* that had been royally endowed and sponsored specifically by Sinhala kings.[12]

Contrary to popular belief, the presence of the *Dalada* (Tooth-Relic of the Buddha) in Kandy's *asala perahera* did not occur until the mid-eighteenth-century reign of the *nayakkar* king Kirti Sri Rajasimha. Before this time, *peraheras* were chiefly, and more simply, royally sponsored processions of the insignia of various deities.[13] What I am suggesting here is that the claim made in

Bell's "rare little *ola* manuscript," that the inauguration of the *asala perahara* in Devinuvara by Parakramabahu II "was the origin of such processions in this Island," is a claim that needs to be taken seriously. It seems to be completely supported by the *Mahavamsa* and *Culavamsa*, insofar as an "*asalhi* [*asala*] festival" per se is mentioned only in connection with the text's description of Parakramabahu II's establishment of the tradition at Devinuvara, and not in any other passages throughout the entire one hundred chapters of the *vamsa* text. That is, the ritual that has eventually become the nation's undisputed cultural pageant articulating traditional Sinhala up-country social, cultural, religious, and political identity may very well have had its origins in Parakramabahu's thirteenth-century rejuvenation of the cult of Upulvan at Devinuvara.

With the shift in the cultic venue of Upulvan from Devinuvara to Alutnuvara, and then finally to Mahanuvara (Kandy), it is not surprising that Knox would have known the supreme deity of the Sinhalas within their supreme public ritual as "Allout Neur Dio." It would appear that Upulvan or the "Buddhist Visnu" is the deity originally honored in the *asala perhara*, first at Devinuvara, then at Alutnuvara, and finally in Mahanuvara. It goes without saying that Alutnuvara continues to hold its own elaborate *perahera*, since it is claimed that whatever rites were performed in Devinuvara were continued at Alutnuvara. I observed the great pomp and vigor of the rite in Alutnuvara in July 2001 (see figs. 7.3–7.7). In addition, the reestablished cult of Visnu in

FIGURE 7.3 Scenes from the Aluthnuvara *perahara* in June/July 2001

FIGURE 7.4 Scenes from the Aluthnuvara *perahara* in June/July 2001

FIGURE 7.5 Scenes from the Aluthnuvara *perahara* in June/July 2001

FIGURE 7.6 Scenes from the Aluthnuvara *perahara* in
June/July 2001

Devinuvara holds its own *perahara* during the same time as Kandy's. The Devinuvara *asala perahara* will be described and discussed in the conclusion.

As for the third aspect that I wish to highlight, it will be seen in a subsequent
discussion in this chapter that visionary experiences are now not only central
to the cult of Alutnuvara Deviyo, but they have largely replaced exorcisms of
yaksas as the predominant form of esoteric cultic behavior to be observed at
Alutnuvara Devalaya. While Dadimunda Devata Bandara seems to have arisen
in fame owing, in part, to his purported control over *yaksas* as their "commander-in-chief," the experience of *disti*, which confirms *varamas* ("warrants") to begin one's own private practice of healing, predicting, or performing as a medium with the dead, is now far more prevalent by comparison.
Seeing the deity in a vision confirms the power to perform the miraculous, to
do the deity's will on the deity's behalf, and to become a vessel of divine power.

FIGURE 7.7 The *basnayaka nilame* and the Government of Sri Lanka Minister of Cultural Affairs at the Aluthnuvara *perahara*, 2001

Given the accounts of dreams and visions in our "*sthalapuranas*," it would appear that this dimension of the cult of Upulvan has been paradigmatic, and has been vigorously sustained in the contemporary Dadimunda cult.

PRIMARY TEXTS OF THE DADIMUNDA CULT

Within the primary texts of the cult of Dadimunda, the legacy of the "Buddhist Visnu" becomes readily apparent. I have collected three *kavi* that are especially transparent in this regard: *Galakappu Sahalla, Dadimunda Avataraya,* and *Alutnuvara Devale Saha Dadimunda Bandara Deviyange Vittiya*. Complete translations of these three *kavi* are presented for reading in appendix 1. (A quick reading of these texts will greatly assist the reader in the discussion that follows.)

In addition to these three texts, there are many more relevant sources and traditions about Dadimunda, particularly one cycle of *kavi* related to the Dadimunda cult as it is known at the Ambekke Devalaya near Lankatilaka and Gadaladeniya.[14] While these sources also contain references germane to the interests at hand, the present analysis will be limited to just these three texts, to maintain the focus on Alutnuvara and to avoid redundancy.

Each of our texts, as well as three others cited by Neville in his *Sinhala Kavi*,[15] contain Dadimunda's greatest claim to fame as a Sinhala Buddhist deity: his martial defense of the Buddha during the great night of awakening, a defense which earned him the name given to him by the Buddha as "*dadimunda*" ("the sturdy" or "the resolute"). As I noted in the fourth chapter, this is an earlier mythic event that was first attributed to Upulvan before it later became an important attribute of the "Buddhist Visnu." It is a legacy of the "Buddhist Visnu" that the cult of Dadimunda Devata Bandara probably appropriated when the chief seat of the "Buddhist Visnu" (then Alutnuvara Deviyo) was shifted from Alutnuvara to the royal capital of Mahanuvara (Kandy). In this regard and in others, the *Dadimunda Avataraya* goes further than either of the other two texts under review in emphasizing Dadimunda's connection to the Buddha and the *Buddhasasana*. Dadimunda not only protected the Buddha from Mara during the night of enlightenment, but he is also said, in this particular text, to have come to Lanka specifically to protect the *sasana* and Sri Lanka for five thousand years.

These are, again, the salient mythic motifs inherited or appropriated from the "Buddhist Visnu," ones that I have indicated remain particularly alive in the *yatika* of contemporary Visnu *kapuralas* in the Kandy cultural area. But taking matters even further, the *Dadimunda Avataraya* includes the prediction by the Buddha that Dadimunda will one day become a buddha in his own right. This is the most explicit and direct evidence I can possibly present that indicates the assimilation of a deity into Sinhala Buddhist culture according to the principles I have explained in my thesis, for Dadimunda is a deity with absolutely no Pali canonical or monastic-commentary provenance. His mythic profile is very similar to another Kandyan *bandara*-class deity, Pitiya Deviyo, whose origins also seem to have been South Indian, and whose power over *yaksas* is similarly, if not quite so spectacularly, emphasized.

Apart from the associations with the Buddha and the *Buddhasasana* that Dadimunda has inherited from the "Buddhist Visnu," it is clear that he is originally related to forms of popular religion and cult that lie completely beyond the purview of the Buddhist *sangha's* domain. For instance, the *Dambadeni Katikavata,* issued by Parakramabahu II to insure monastic discipline within the *sangha's* ranks, forbids *bhikkhus* from encouraging or participating in the exorcism of *yaksas*. Yet, the most consistent attribute of this deity is that he is "commander-in-chief" of the *yaksas*. These texts, then, present the head of *yaksas* as the protector of the Buddha.

This episode warrants a digression, for it raises the question of martial power in relation to Buddhist teachings of nonviolence. It needs to be pointed out that in every description of Dadimunda's protection of the Buddha, no physical violence actually takes place. Either Mara and his hordes are intimated by a show or threat of Dadimunda's power, or the Buddha himself is seen as defeating Mara by virtue of his perfection of the *paramitas*. In no case is Mara physically assaulted by Dadimunda. But he is clearly threatened with violence by him. While that may indeed be the case, that is, that the Sinhalas could not go so far as to insert an incident of actual physical violence into the moment that is celebrated as the apex of spiritual achievement in this world aeon, the martial presence of Dadimunda is palpable and is even given approval. This seems to be a mythic signal for the presence of a type of "just war" theory, an ideology very frequently appealed to or implied within the *Mahavamsa, Culavamsa, Rajavaliya, Nikaya Sangrahaya,* and other historically oriented texts. In defense of the Buddha, and in the defense of the *Buddhasasana,* violent action may be justified.[16]

The acceptance of this principle seems clear in the violence that Dadimunda perpetrates upon his *yaksa* foes or underlings, an action that becomes paradigmatic for the manner in which his *kapuralas* are known to beat the presence of *yaksas* out of women who are possessed by them. I have provided a particularly graphic nineteenth-century description of this violent phenomenon in appendix 3 to this chapter. Dadimunda's own coarse and violent nature is apparent in two other episodes detailed in various degrees in all three of these selected *kavi*: in the mythic accounts of his birth, and in his deployment and control of *yaksas* to break up the great rock that inhibited the construction of his *devalaya* at Alutnuvara. Those two events will be discussed shortly.

In addition to Dadimunda's explicit links to the Buddha and the *Buddhasasana,* he is clearly also related to and warranted by other deities of distinction and ethical repute in the Sinhala pantheon. While these three *kavi* mention warrants that he receives from Sakra (Indra), Vessamuni (Kuvera), and Saman, I am, of course, especially interested in highlighting the references to Dadimunda's relations with Upulvan and Visnu.

Both the *Galakappu Sahalla* (vs. 20) and the *Alutnuvara Devala . . . Vitti* (vs. 25) make references to Dadimunda having the sanctum sanctorum of his *devalaya* constructed out of sandalwood. As if this allusion would not be clear enough, the *Galakappu Sahalla* (vs. 13–14) also includes the following lines:

> In the guise of a sandalwood log
> Wafted by the waves, he [Dadimunda] came ashore,
> Assuming the form of a divine image.

Here, then, is a clear transfer of the myth of the sandalwood image from the mythic profile of Upulvan to the mythic characterization of Dadimunda. The divine arrival of Upulvan has become the divine arrival of Dadimunda.

The *Dadimunda Avataraya* contains even more graphic transfers of this nature, transfers that explicitly link Dadimunda's identity to the "Buddhist Visnu." I have already noted how Dadimunda is now celebrated as the divine protector of the Buddha, and that he is understood as the protector of the *Buddhasana* and the Sinhala state, but in this text his avatar links to Visnu and Upulvan are made in the following types of expression. Consider, for example, vs. 5:

> In this *kalpa*, the first incarnation was Upulvan.
> Next came Narayana to dispel fear.
> In Sri Lanka, there are ten famous incarnations.
> This *yaksa* I call Dadimunda *avataraya*.

This is a formulation completely unique to Sinhala Buddhist religion. Nowhere in Sanskrit literature could one expect find a being who is a *yaksa* and an avatar at the same time. The classes of supernatural beings remain wholly separate and in juxtaposition, since *yaksas* in Sinhala culture bear some similarities to the *asuras* of Puranic myth. But in this text, the conflation between *devata* and *yaksa* has been made quite obvious, a conflation that is to be discussed at some length later. For now, I want to emphasize that Dadimunda's appearance and function as a deity are set into the Vaisnava avatar lineage of Upulvan and Narayana (Narayana regarded here as one of the earlier appearances or forms of Visnu). Not only is Dadimunda here regarded as one of the ten avatars, but he is placed on the same high level of divinity as these renowned predecessors.[17]

This connection between Dadimunda and Visnu, as an avatar begotten of the former, is not simply a unique or arcane reference, but actually one that is fairly well-known in Sinhala folklore. In a later verse (40), Visnu's sanction of Dadimunda is strengthened even further when, after the Buddha has predicted future buddhahood for Dadimunda, Visnu, who has come into this world to attain buddhahood himself, confirms that "Dadimunda is Dadimunda indeed." By this, he refers to Dadimunda's own great and reliable resolve, one of the sine qua non virtues needed for this most supreme of spiritual attainments.

But perhaps the most salient and relevant reference to the transference of Upulvan's or the "Buddhist Visnu's" attributes to Dadimunda becomes apparent in verses 15 and 16 of the *Dadimunda Avataraya*:

> Wearing divine attire, having the golden bow and ornaments,
> His power was displayed when he destroyed the rock.
> So he went to Visnu and obtained his boon [*varama*]
> And received the golden bow from him too.
>
> With due respect he honored Narayana.
> By invoking Visnu he received the golden bow.

Without hesitating, he protected all the people.
By the mere tinkling of bells, diseases were dispelled.

In the fourth chapter, I discussed at some length the cycle of Sinhala *kavi* associated with Upulvan's and Visnu's golden bows, and how the golden bow was symbolic of the "Buddhist Visnu's" mythic prowess at dispelling diseases and expelling *yaksas*. The golden bow is, thus, a celebrated symbol of his this-worldly power. I also noted the signficance of the bow in relation to Upulvan in chapter 3: how perhaps a subsidiary cult of the "bow deity" (Dunu Devi) existed in thirteenth- through sixteenth-century Devinuvara, and how this possibility has led some scholars to link Rama more closely to the origins of Upulvan. In connection with that particular discussion, I indicated that Upulvan's associations with Rama became ever more prevalent in the later Kandyan period, and are very still clearly evinced or recalled in the contemporary expression of the *valiyak mangalya*. Specifically, as I have said, the golden bow represented a power of the "Buddhist Visnu" to dispel disease and to expel *yaksas*. In chapter 5, I also discussed how Visnu now seems somewhat removed from these functions, especially in relation to exorcism, though the literary evidence is clear that his cult was once quite deeply implicated in it.

What these two verses from the *Dadimunda Avataraya* might possibly reflect, then, is the transfer of this attribute from the "Buddhist Visnu" to Dadimunda, for exorcism became Dadimunda's most popular attribute; it became his niche within Sinhala religion. That the golden bow obtained from Visnu becomes emblematic of Dadimunda's power is seen in the *Dadimunda Avataraya* by the reference (vs. 29) to his use of it to threaten Mara.

The *Dadimunda Avataraya* is far more thoroughly Buddhistic in its presentation or characterization of Dadimunda than is either the *Galakappu Sahalla* or the *Alutnuvara Devala . . . Vitti*. These latter two *kavi*, while prominently mentioning the defense of the Buddha against Mara, give far more emphasis to Dadimunda's role as commander-in-chief of the *yaksas* and his breaking of the stone that impeded the construction of his *devalaya*. Indeed, the *Dadimunda Avataraya* would appear to be a Buddhist gloss on another form of Sinhala religion. As I have said, it perfectly illustrates the dynamics of transformation with which this study is concerned. To gain a deeper awareness of what has been transformed, we need to examine more closely the profile of Dadimunda as it is constructed in these two other *kavi*.

The *Dadimunda Avataraya*, the *Galakappu Sahalla*, and the *Alutnuvara Devala . . . Vitti* all refer to the princely birth of Dadimunda from a royal mother: Somavati, in the *Galakappu Sahalla*, and Erandati in the *Alutnuvara Devala . . . Vitti*, and in the *Dadimunda Avataraya*. But the *ADV* adds an extensive background scene to his birth through a series of verses (5–12) that describe how Purnaka, the famous *yaksa* of Hindu lore, won the princess Erandati through playing with the king in a gambling game. The *Galakappu Sahalla*'s version says that Somavati was cremated at the end of her pregnancy as Dadimunda was born "besmeared with ash" (vs. 12).[18]

When this motif is combined with the fact that in each of these three *kavi*, as well as in many other texts, Dadimunda is reported to have come ashore to Lanka by ship (usually in a stone boat) at either Devinuvara or at relatively nearby Sinigama, it seems quite clear that his origins are imagined as being South Indian. With a *yaksa* for a father, and a mother who was deceased, the resulting image is of a rather tragic figure, though no anterior story or karmic event is provided to explain his difficult origins or plight. His father's *yaksa* lineage and his mother's unseemly death, however, are harbingers of the darker side of this supernatural being. Indeed, his supernatural character seems to hover in ambivalence between the classification of *yaksa* and *devata*. His parentage is meant to reflect this split.

While all three texts, especially the *Dadimunda Avataraya*, extol his virtue in protecting the Buddha, the *Galakappu Sahalla* (vs. 18) and the *Alutnuvara Devala . . . Vitti* (vs. 23) report an episode that clearly refers to Dadimunda's part-sinister presence or power: how the milk of the royal cows turned to blood. Moreover, Dadimunda is portrayed in positively brutish terms, both in relation to how he threatens Mara (*Alutnuvara Devala . . . Vitti*, vs 17: "I shall beat you with my golden staff and break your body in two!") and with the scorn and punishments that he heaps on the *yaksas* who have just assisted him in breaking up the rock impeding the construction of his *devalaya* (*ADV*, vs. 39–41, 44–45; *GS*, vs. 31–34, 38, 40).

What is emphasized here is not a benign or kindly deity of compassionate action, but a rough-and-ready power that can be unleashed to exact severe punishment and destruction. In his mythic constructions, what makes Dadimunda a *devata* is not so much the intrinsic ethical nature of his actions (that is, his karma), but rather the association of his power with a just cause. Beyond the Mara episode, what justifies Dadimunda's force (his chief attribute being a cane that he uses to beat *yaksas*) is that it can be put to use to expel forces or powers that are positively demonic in nature. The reference in this instance is to how he is called upon to relieve the distress of women who are suffering from the possession of *yaksas*.

In this connection, it is interesting to observe that there is not the slightest reference or inference to Dadimunda's sexuality in these *kavi*, despite the fact that women are described as experiencing "intense burning pain in their loins" (*ADV*, vs. 43). Nowhere is there any mention of a consort or spouse. Dadimunda is a bachelor. Indeed, he is presented as rejecting the request of the *yaksas*, generated by their physical attraction to Sinhala women, to remain in Lanka. If anything, he appears to protect, rather than to exploit, their sexual welfare. This orientation within his cult seems to coincide with the emphases of *kapuralas* who make the avoidance of *kili* a major preoccupation. Hence, there is an ascetic, renunciatory dimension to this cult.

In all, the mythic figure that emerges from these three *kavi* is martial. Dadimunda is even credited with having defeated the Portuguese at Alutnuvara (*GS*, vs. 48) and at Ambekke (Barnett: 20). Dadimunda's power, and it can be a type of awful power, is enlisted only for what is regarded as a just cause. That is what distinguishes him from the *yaksas* per se, and the supernatural figures of Sinhala sorcery traditions. Yet it is the brute nature of his power that also makes him something of an ambivalent figure. Moreover, I think that ambivalence best characterizes the nature of exorcisms (again, see the nineteenth-century description in appendix 3) that women undergo at his shrine in Alutnuvara. On the one hand, there is great relief (akin to a sexual climax) when the cure has been effected, but the method of severely beating the *yaksa* out of the woman, and hence the brutal suffering she must endure in the process, exacts a terrific physical and painful price. On the surface, it would seem to be a type of sadism (on the part of the *kapurala*) and/or masochism (on the part of the *yaksa*-inflicted woman) enlisted for a higher spiritual cause.

LEGACIES OF VISNU IN THE RITUAL CULT OF DADIMUNDA

In this chapter, I have been demonstrating the various legacies of the "Buddhist Visnu" apparent in the history and myth of the Dadimunda cult. Some contemporary examples of cultic practice will further enhance this line of inquiry.

The *kapuralas* at Alutnuvara say that they still deal with one or two *yaksa* possessions every month. In all of my visits, I failed to see any instances of the phenomenon at all, much to my disappointment. The *kapuralas* also say that it is becoming more and more rare, and that the punishments they have to exact are quite benign compared to what they are known to have been in the past. Instead, they say, there is a rising instance of *disti*, among people claiming possession by a deity or by a *preta*.

With regard to possession by deities, all of the *kapuralas* expressed much skepticism at the rising frequency of this phenomenon and pointed out that, as a result, many people have begun to set up *devalayas* of their own as a way to make a living. They come to Alutnuvara to have their powers confirmed by Dadimunda. *Disti* is a manifestation of their warrants to conduct rites of healing and soothsaying at their own private *devalayas*. The *devalaya*, despite the skepticism of its *kapuralas*, however, does a good business of its own, selling *halambas* (a round anklet type of ornament) to those who wish to buy.

*Halamba*s are popularly regarded as the instrument through which the power of a deity is transferred to the possessed. One can "plug in" or "unplug" divine power by means of contact with the *halamba*.

The *kapuralas* all say that the number of visitors to the *devalaya* keeps increasing. This may be because of better transportation, or it may just be that the fame of the deity is spreading. In my informal attempts to determine the origins of visitors, it was clear that most people come from the up-country and Sabaragamuva province, but there are many from the North Central, Western, and Uva provinces, as well as many from the Colombo area and the South. It is clear that Alutnuvara is also on the "pilgrimage circuit" for many groups on their way to Sri Pada ("Adam's Peak"), to Sri Mahabodhi at Anuradhapura, or to the Dalada Maligava ("Temple of the Tooth-relic") in Kandy. It is also a widespread practice to bring children of three months' age to the *devalaya* to receive the protection of the deity.

So, though the *devalaya* is famous for its cases of *yaksa* possession, and the late-medieval Sinhala *kavi* also celebrate Dadimunda as the "commander-in-chief" of the *yaksas*, people are now coming for a broad array of reasons, and in steadily increasing numbers. The amount of money given on *puja* trays on *kemmura* days must be a staggering amount. The *devalaya* runs an extremely lucrative business.

Two families, both claiming to be descendants from the Dissanayaka *kapurala* brought by Parakramabahu II from Devinuvara, alternate every two years in serving the ritual duties at the *devalaya*. These families have grown very wealthy and politically influential locally. Each of them has a member who has been elected to the Central Provincial Council—one who was a member of the then ruling Peoples' Alliance (PA), the other a member of the then oppositional United National Party (UNP). One family has acquired vast lands (including tea and rubber estates) and has built truly palatial homes for virtually all of its members, including sons and daughters, several kilometers from Alutnuvara. The other operates a thriving transportation business that owns several passenger buses.

Like the Visnu *kapuralas* in Kandy, the Alutnuvara *kapuralas* are extremely mindful of *kili* and take elaborate measures to insure their purity, as well as the purity of the *devalaya*. This means avoidance of all funerals, as well as partaking in a vegetarian diet, during their two-year stints of ritual service. If there are any deaths or females coming of age within a specified territorial circumference that includes the village of Alutnuvara, the *devalaya*, in spite of the enormous cost, is closed for several days. All of the *kapuralas* insist that the power of the deity "to get things done" is entirely dependent upon maintaining their own states of purity. While they provided open access to the sanctum sanctorum during my visits, they steadfastly refused to allow me to tape-record any of their *yatika*.[19] Nor was I allowed to photograph the magnificent *dev-arupa* image of Dadimunda in the sanctum sanctorum.[20] Their decisions, which I had to respect, were made out of concern for *kili*.

The lineage of *kapuralas* is, of course, entirely patrilinear. In interviews with one of the *kapurala*'s wives, and in another interview with the daughter of another, both mentioned that just being born as a woman involves an inherent degree of *kili*, and that is why women are not allowed to become *kapuralas*. That is also another of the main reasons why *kapuralas* and their womenfolk are skeptical of women who come to the *devalaya* claiming to be possessed by deities and who have set up their own private *devalayas*. Both of these women whom I interviewed spoke proudly of their husband's and father's profession, indicating that it brought them local prestige. While the daughter of the *kapurala* is married to a successful provincial politician, both said that if it is possible, a *kapurala* would prefer to marry the daughter of another *kapurala*, though there is no set precedent or "rule" for this.

In 1988, the chief monastic incumbent of the Kirti Sri Raja Maha Viharaya, located just opposite the Alutnuvara Devalaya, and for all intents and purposes now a part of the greater Alutnuvara cultic context, opened a new Visnu *devalaya* located within the *sima* (sacred boundary) of his temple. It is also now a thriving cultic venue. When I interviewed the monastic incumbent, Ven. Talgaspitiye Nandasiri, he pointed out that his monastic ancestor, of the Asvaddana Pirivena, had originally received a vision to construct a Visnu *devalaya* in Alutnuvara during the reign of Parakramabahu II. Since Vimaladharmasurya II had shifted the *devalaya* to Kandy, along with all the lands attached to the *devalaya*, he saw no reason why he could not re-establish a Visnu *devalaya* at this site once again. He also stressed that there was a "historical connection" between Visnu and Dadimunda. He said that he has no plans to create a *kapurala* lineage at this new *devalaya*, and that providing *yatikas* was not difficult since they can be read in various publications.

When I asked the Alutnuvara Devalaya *kapuralas* about the new Visnu *devalaya* that had been constructed by the monk at the adjacent monastic *viharaya*, they shrugged, expressed some chagrin at the new "business venture," and pointed out that the new Visnu *devalaya kapurala* was just a boy working in the temple at odd jobs before he was appointed *kapurala* by the monk. But their reactions about this matter were, in fact, not very strong. And the monastic incumbent explained that he had not encountered any resistance to the opening of the Visnu *devalaya* from anyone connected to the Alutnuvara Devalaya. I sensed that there was a formal, yet healthy set of relations between the two institutions.

As in Kandy, none of the *kapuralas* would claim that they had experienced *disti* or had experienced an extraordinary revelation of any kind from the deities. But there was no shortage of devotees at their *devalaya* who seemed under an extraordinary influence. In late June (2001), on a Sunday (after we had been visiting regularly for two months, at all times of the day, on the Wednesday and Saturday *kemmuras*), we witnessed an especially striking outbreak of *disti.* Within the span of an hour, more than ten people broke out into a trance state. At least seven of these indicated that they were healers and soothsayers, but the most noteworthy was a young man in his thirties, with long matted hair, from Wattegama (some ten miles northeast of Kandy), who had offered his *puja* along with about twenty others from his town. He went into a frenzied trance as soon as the *devarupa* of Dadimunda was revealed from behind the sanctum sanctorum curtain. Following the *puja,* his entire group proceeded to the adjacent Huniyam *devalaya,* where another four lapsed into wild gyrations, bodies shaking, arms akimbo, with their leader chanting continuously the names of Pattini and Dadimunda (as *devaraja*). Each of the entranced four, assuming some composure, knelt down in front of the Huniyam shrine before their leader, who then blessed them. They all then proceeded with coconuts to the coconut-breaking, or vow-taking, area, where each of the twenty in the group, including the four entranced, appeared before the leader (still chanting and still in his own state of *disti*), and gave a coconut over to him, as he smashed each in turn.

At this moment, when each of their turns came, the four in *disti* were in especially mad frenzies. When we approached one of them following the conclusion of this remarkable scene, my two assistants were abruptly shouted at, and told that if they advanced any closer, they would be beaten! A few moments later, my assistants received profound apologies, and were told that it was the deity who had shouted at them and not the persons themselves. We learned that this group of twenty was a self-declared "religious elite" of Wattegama, who occasionally come to Alutnuvara to get "recharged." Some of them were *kiriammas,* while others claimed to be healers and soothsayers.

During the long stretch of time that it took for all their coconuts to be broken, the *kapuralas* at the *devalaya* were becoming increasingly agitated at the extended commotion, and finally requested that the group finish quickly so that others could make use of the vow-taking area. Afterwards, the *kapuralas* explained that such a scene was not unusual, and that they often have to make requests of certain groups not to monopolize the ritual areas. They further explained that *distis* seem to be of three types: 1) possession by *yaksas*; 2) possession by *pretas*; and 3) possession by *devatas,* though they doubted the authenticity of the last, the type that the members of this group had claimed for themselves.

Since I had no opportunity to witness the first type of possession, and since this form of cultic behavior seems to be of decreasing importance and frequency, I set out to learn more about the second and third types through de-tailed interviews and case studies. I found considerable overlap among these second and third types of "possessions," insofar as a deceased relation often is perceived to initiate the phenomenon of possession, and that deities are then thought to follow at the appropriate time. Two middle-aged to elderly women were particularly helpful in sharing their experiences with me in this regard. What they had to relate is indicative, I think, of how the power of Visnu is con-strued within this "*disti* dimension" of Sinhala religion.

Anula Rajapakse is a very strong-willed, confident, and articulate woman, 59 years old when I first came to know her in 1999. I interviewed her on several occasions, the last time in March 2001. She has been operating her own Suni-lagama Devalaya for nearly twenty years. She received her *varama* (warrant) originally at the Alutnuvara Devalaya and returns periodically to renew her power. Each week, she sees about eighty clients or so and tries to heal them of their afflictions. Many are from immediately surrounding villages, but others come from Colombo, Polonnaruva, Dambulla, and Kurunegala, on a fairly regular basis. Her father died when she was only three months old, and her own mother was a very religious devotee, insuring that she was raised in a con-text where her own religious consciousness was thoroughly nurtured. Her mother-in-law was also deeply religious, a devotee in particular to Visnu as well as Alutnuvara Deviyo. Mrs. Rajapakse claims to be possessed regularly by Visnu. Her narrative is quite compelling.

In a rural-village context located several miles from Kandy, I visited Mrs. Rajapakse on several occasions in her home, where her *devalaya* is located. On one of these occasions, she agreed to provide a narrative about how she ac-quired her power. Here is the full translation of that account.

ANULA RAJAPAKSE[21]

It is my late mother-in law who first awakened this power in me. She passed away twenty-three years ago. She was bed-ridden toward the end and there was nobody else to care for her, though she had seven sons. I am married to her youngest son, so I looked after her as best I could despite numerous difficulties. We were so poor then. We did not even have a proper house to live in. When it rained, water leaked in everywhere through the roof and the whole hut was in a pool of water. The rain fell even on the bed where my mother (in-law) was lying. I used to hang a piece of polyethylene like a canopy above the bed to prevent her from getting wet and collected the water in a bucket. Added to this were a lot of financial problems. We lived from hand to mouth. We were short of food, because this was in the 1970's when the whole country suffered from a lack of provisions.

It was under these conditions that I had to look after her. I had only two changes of clothes to dress her. When she wetted herself, I would wrap the clean cloth around her and wash the dirty cloth. Then I would wrap the washed one around me so that it would dry sooner, especially during the rainy season.

One day she wanted to drink a king coconut. There was no king coconut in the house and there was no one to climb the tree to get one. So, I did it myself. When I descended from the tree, there were bruises all over me. The scars are still visible. She asked me how I managed to get one and I told her I got someone to pick it from the tree. Then I fed her with a spoon.

The following day she wanted some milk. Again, there was no milk in the house and I had only ten cents with me. However, I bought a bit of milk from the kade and gave it to her. She loved me a lot and often told me that although she had nothing to give me for what I had done for her, she would be by my side even after her death.

We were so desperate that I went to a sooth-sayer to see what was going to happen next. He told me that my mother (in-law) would not survive long and that she would be dead by a certain date. I was upset. When I came home she told me that she wanted to sit up. So, I had a rope hanging from the roof and tied it to the bed so that she could sit up with some support. Sometimes, I would sit with her while she remained sitting against me.

Her condition soon became critical. She entered states of delirium and started muttering. I was frightened. She would often wet and dirty herself, and me in the process. One particular day, I went to the well to wash the dirty clothes. I told my children (I have four children), to keep an eye on her because I was worried she might fall out of the bed. While I was away, she had asked for some water. I had told my kids to give her water from the flask in case she asked for it. I told them not to boil the water and meddle with the fire, which they did anyway. My mother (in-law) did not like what they had done and asked them not to bother with the water. When I returned, she was already dead.

After her death, I began to see her constantly in my dreams. One night, I dreamt of her sitting on a bed in front of the house. She was dressed in white and had a bundle of money in her hand. I went and asked her to come in. She refused and said she had brought some money for me and that she would give it to me. The next moment, she vanished. I stopped seeing her in my dreams after that.

About three months later, I went to the nearby forest to collect faggots. I left home around 7 a.m., and was still searching for firewood at noon. I never seemed to be able to collect enough faggots. I was struggling with the firewood trying to tie it up. Each time I tied the rope, it broke. I was hungry, exhausted and felt desperate.

I have always had faith in the gods, particularly Visnu. So I pleaded with him to help me. At that moment, I noticed someone standing nearby. He was very fair. He carried a white knife in one hand and a bundle in the other. He approached and addressed me as "child." I thought he was Tamil and I called him Kankani and asked him where he was going. He said he was going to a nearby garden to pick a king coconut. I told him I had been starving since morning and asked him to bring me one too, if there were any to take. Then I asked him in which estate he was working because I thought he was a laborer. However, in my subconscious [*yatihita*], I felt he was someone exceptional.

He told me to move my bundle of firewood from where it was to another place and then to tie it up. Because the rope had been breaking and because I had placed the wood on top of a tomb, I did as he told me and I finally managed to tie up the bundle and returned home. Even though it was a small bundle, it was extremely heavy and stunk. Before I reached home, I had a raging fever.

Late that evening after I had prepared dinner, I went out to bring the bundle of firewood. When I bent down to take it, I felt as if someone was pushing me from behind, I couldn't straighten myself. I felt very giddy and a terrible pain shot through my back. I started to cry out in pain. My husband came and helped me to sit on the bench outside our hut.

Then I started talking to my husband, I remember myself saying: "Son, take me in. I cannot stay outside. I'm your mother." That was the first time that I became possessed [*avesa*] by my mother-in-law, and it was the first experience I had ever had of that type. "I came to protect my daughter-in-law. Don't let her go out alone. Don't let her go to the woods in search of faggots. Maha Sona *yaksa* is waiting to destroy her." Then I saw her giving me a knife. It was just a shadow. Then she vanished.

I was still in a trance [*disti*]. I started to relate how, when I went to the woods to collect firewood, I met Maha Sona *yaksa* in human guise, and how he had given me a king coconut to drink. If it had been someone else, he or she would definitely have been killed. But, he couldn't do anything to me because of the presence of my dead mother-in-law who had been following me everywhere I went. But I had suffered a severe stomach pain and fever due to that king coconut.

I remember telling my husband, "Son, I'm so hungry. I've been without food for almost one year since my death. Give me something to eat with meat." We didn't have any money to buy meat and offer a proper *dana*. However, someone owed us Rs. 75 for work we had done for him. We happened to get a hold of this money. And so we brought in a *gurunnanse*, an exorcist, and gave the offering for the dead one [mother-in-law as *preta*] who had possessed me. So, that night when they offered me the meal, I mixed the rice and applied it all over my body from head to foot. Because of her greediness, my mother-in-law had been reborn as a *preta atma*. Then, in a possessed state, I said to my husband: "Son, get me a bucket of water so that my daughter can wash away the food." When I had finished washing, I said: "Son, bring me one of your sarongs to wipe myself. This done, I again told him: "Do not think that you are bowing down to your wife. This is your mother in her. So come and sit before me [in a worshipping posture]."

Then when he sat before me, I put my hand on his head and blessed him, and I told him: "In one year's time, you and your wife will get a good piece of land and your troubles will end. At that time, I will bring Lord Visnu with me. Until then, be good to your wife and family. It is good for me to go now." Then I fell unconscious.

Since that incident, she continuously appeared in my dreams. She would inform me before hand of things that would happen in the future and warn me of impending trouble. Once my eldest daughter fell seriously ill. She had contracted yellow fever. My mother-in-law appeared in my dreams and told me to take her to the hospital before it was too late, and also to give her juice from the *kura* plant which she pointed out to me. This is an herbal plant about which I knew nothing at the time. The following day, I had no money to take my daughter to the hospital. Her condition had worsened. Nevertheless, I took her and started walking hoping to borrow some money. I noticed Rs. 12.50 lying on the road before me. This was just enough to go by bus and to come back.

After about one year, we came to know that the government was distributing land. In my mind, I wanted to have this same piece of land and this is what happened. About a week later, we started to clear the land. My mother-in-law appeared in my dreams one night and gave me an auspicious time to lay the foundation for the house. We followed her instructions and within two weeks we had already laid the foundation. She asked us to chant the *Karaniya Metta Sutta,* which we did. At the end of three months, we had already built the house and we shifted to the house during an auspicious *nakata*.

Around four months later, I started going into trances again. I started to act as a sooth-sayer. Many exorcists were brought but no one could explain what or why this happened to me. I started predicting through the power of Visnu. None of the *gurunanses* could stop this. I insisted that I be taken to Alutnuvara. No one took my request seriously. They brought another well-known and experienced exorcist. As he approached the house, I already knew of his presence, asked him not to come near me, but to sit at least at arm's length. Then I asked him if he knew who I was. I offered to make some predictions about him, how he had gone to a *tovil* house to perform a *tovil* in Anuradhapura where he had created a big hullabaloo. He had invited all of the gods to take up their places but had ignored Visnu. Thus, as a punishment, he was locked inside a room.

Again, I asked him if he knew who I am. He said no. I asked him what color I am. Again he didn't know. Then I showed him a piece of blue cloth, after which I entered into a frenzied trance. I told him that I am the powerful god Visnu who protects this whole island. The *gurunnanse* then asked why the god should be troubling this woman. Then I [Visnu] replied: "I trouble her because no one listens to me and does what I ask you to do." The exorcist wanted to know what should be done. I said: "I [Visnu] need to go to Alutnuvara. This woman is gifted with a powerful *varama* with the help of her late mother-in-law. To use it properly, she should go to Alutnuvara and get the blessings of that god [Alutnuvara Deviyo]. It is so powerful that she can even walk on fire and do many extraordinary things. So take her there."

Then I became seriously ill and many exorcists were solicited. I suffered from some sort of paralysis. It was Visnu who made me fall ill because I was not doing what he had asked to be done and the others were not listening to him.

It was only when this well-known exorcist suggested that I be taken to Alutnuvara that the others consented to do so.

To convince them of my power, I told them that I had acquired the ability to heal. The first time I did that was for a woman in our neighboring house who was very ill. I told her to bring me some rice and curry without any meat. When she brought that, I made three balls of rice and gave her one ball to offer to Visnu Deviyo with the aspiration that she should get well soon. Then I gave her a second one to eat. The third one I ate. The next day she came and told me that she felt better. This time I had asked her to bring a king coconut with a bit of sandalwood in it. I chanted something (I can't remember what) over it and gave it for her to drink. She began to feel even better. The third day I asked her to bring some coconut oil over which I chanted and told her to apply it all over her body.

So at last we decided to go to Alutnuvara, although my family was still frightened at the prospect. We were asked by Visnu to go in a vehicle. Visnu

told me not to worry and to set off on the journey after bathing for purifi-
cation, without stepping back into the house, and that I would find a vehicle. A group of six of us went. The sick woman from next door also went
with us. I was asked to go without letting any males touch me even slightly.
When we got into the bus, there was an empty seat for two where I sat with
the sick woman and thus avoided any males. When we got into the second
bus (we had to go in two buses), the same thing happened.

When we reached Alutnuvara, I climbed the flight of stairs by hopping
on one foot. I was in a trance [*disti*] again when we went into the inner
shrine and the *kapumahattaya* demanded Rs. 500 for the *halamba*. Meanwhile, the god [Alutnuvara Deviyo, Dadimunda] revealed that I could obtain it only if I managed to visit the Sakra Bhavana, Asura Bhavana and
Naga Bhavana. I was to collect seven limes from the Naga Lokaya, get seven
mantras from Sakra Bhavana, and a sword from the Asura Bhavana and
then step into the Manusya Lokaya [human world] to heal people. Only if
I accomplished this would I get the *halamba* and an oil lamp which I saw
appearing in the blue sky. Then the inner shrine at Alutnuvara appeared to
me as a paradise as I fulfilled these prerequisites. So, the god granted me
the *varama* and gave me the *halamba*. I saw my late mother-in-law standing beside me. Since I did not have Rs. 500, I got the *halamba* and oil lamp
for Rs. 125. I brought them home and since then I've had no probems and
I started curing people suffering from all kinds of illnesses. I do not do this
for money, but only to help the helpless.

I also perform certain rituals like *kavadi,* putting fire in my mouth (I
never got burnt), and hanging from ropes and pandals. We did these every
year on the first of January. But three years ago since the death of the village monk, we have stopped it because there is defilement [*kili*] in the
village.

I still have this power but I do not perform these rituals very often now
because I have a heart problem. Visnu has asked me not to go through any
surgery. No one else's blood can be transferred to me, except that of a goat.
I got this illness after I was poisoned by a *gurunnanse* out of jealousy. Consequently, the exorcist's own son, who doesn't have a *varama,* got possessed
and cursed him saying that he would be dead at the end of three months.
A lot of misfortunes befell him (he was bitten by a dog, fell and fractured
his arm, etc.) and he did, indeed, die after three months. Compared to previous times, my power has somewhat declined after I was poisoned by him.

I usually see beforehand certain troubles that this country suffers from.
During 1983, I saw the oncoming war. I [Visnu] was standing near the
door outside. I felt very upset. Then I saw an old man coming. I invited him
in. Then he said he came to set fire to my [Visnu's] *bata* [bamboo] forest.

After a moment, a rowdy-looking person with a beacon came along and gave me a torch. The whole country was covered with *bata* trees. I set fire to it. Then I asked the old man to help me eliminate the fire. He said there would be a time for that. Then I saw a tiger emerging from the hole that I set fire to. It tried to jump onto me. Then it went back into the hole. Then the old man and the one who brought the fire went away towards the West. I told my family that there would be a terrorist attack the next day. And there was: in Anuradhapura.[22]

Another time, while in *disti*, I saw Indira Gandhi giving me [Visnu] a *sannasa*. I told her I could not take it but to give it instead to J. R. Jayawardhana who was standing with Rajiv Gandhi. Prabhakaran was also there. He had a garland of *yaksa* heads around his neck and he went and put it around Rajiv Gandhi's neck.[23] Then someone came and gave me some seeds and asked me to sprinkle them over the country. I went into the sky above the country and did so. Then the one who gave me the seeds told me that very soon the island will blow into little pieces like those seeds.

Another time someone appeared before me and said that the country's leader would be killed. I put on my *halamba* and put my oil lamp into a bag and ran to see the leader who was going for a meeting. I came a long way to the foot of a mountain. I prayed to Visnu to help me get there on time. I climbed and hid my bag behind a bush and went to where J. R. was attending a meeting. He was just arriving. I went to one of the policemen and told him what they are doing is wrong, knowing that the leader was in danger. I went and stood behind him. Then I said that the enemy approaching and at that moment there was a blast. This was the bomb blast in the parliament that I saw.[24]

I saw several battles between elephants, humans, lions, tigers and a lot of other animals and the death of elephants in the battle, indicating the death of Premadasa.[25] Then I saw an emerging female hand. But there was fire beneath the hand. So I said there was going to be a woman leader, but a lot of trouble.[26] I do not have these visions any more because I was not suppose to discuss them with others, something which I did.

I see all these things in my dreams. It is through God Visnu's power that I work. I'm not suppose to do hard, physical work, I should meditate a lot and follow the *pansil* [five moral precepts] and other religious teachings of the path. For seventeen years, my husband and I have not lived as man and wife, even though he is my husband. We are like mother and daughter. I do not eat meat. No one else can use my belongings. God Visnu is born out of fire, not by the union of man and wife. Since I am devoted to this god, I cannot live with my husband. Hence, Visnu is very powerful and he does not easily grant any *varama* to anyone. Only a person with a lot of merit can hope to get it. It is even more difficult for a woman to obtain it. There are several Visnus: Maha Visnu, Sri Visnu, Demala Visnu, etc. Among them, Maha Visnu is the one responsible for protection of the *sasana*. Every god appears in twelve forms.

Because Visnu was born out of fire, he likes fire. Hence, when I am in *disti*, I can do anything with fire without getting burnt. I like blue very much. Hence, from the time I was small I would always wear something blue.

I also work through Kali. Then I wear red. It is Visnu who has given me the *varama* and he sometimes gets his work done through Kali. That is why I get possessed by Kali sometimes.

When I was very small, I saw an image of Visnu in the village temple. I did not know who it was then. I went and kissed the feet of that image. My mother told me not to do so, and that it was God Visnu. That was when I started to believe in him.

Each year during the third week of January, I [when possessed] attend *deva samagama* [meetings]. When we go there, Visnu asks if we have killed beings, if we have done meritorious activities, if we have sinned, if we have been charitable, how much we have earned. The *samagamas* are held separately for men and women.

Mrs. Rajapakse's world, like Mrs. Wijeratne's (see chapter 5) is dominated by the ebb and flow of supernatural power, some of which she feels privileged to channel constructively and some of which she attempts to fend off defensively. What I have found compelling in her account is the simple fact that she perceives the power and character of Visnu to be within her own possession. While I either encountered or learned of others in and around the Kandy culture area who make similar claims to possession by Visnu, Mrs. Rajapakse's account was by far the most coherent, rationalized, and clearly constructed of all that I collected. Her experiences, I think, are part and parcel of a growing religious phenomenon in Sri Lanka: the experience of *disti* or trance. That Visnu has been implicated in this dimension of religious practice is a further measure of his complete assimilation and enduring presence in Sinhala religious culture in general.

As I indicated at the outset, there seems to be overlap between the experiences of possession by dead relations (*preta*) and possession by *devata*. Mrs. Rajapakse was first possessed by her late mother-in-law, and thus began her practice of healing and making predictions before Visnu began to possess her. While there is virtually no historical or textual evidence for possession by Visnu in Sinhala Buddhist literary traditions, there is a minor anthology of the Pali canon, the *Petavatthu*, which contains, in the form of monastic sermons, stories of lay encounters with departed kin. It is an ancient legacy of occurrence that continues to be sustained in popular Sinhala religious culture. In Mrs. Rajapakse's case, the encounter with her dead mother-in-law served as a harbinger of her possession by Visnu. What seems to have occurred in instances like those typified by Mrs. Rajapakse is that the line between having a vision of a deity and being possessed by a deity has been crossed.

Unlike the case of Visnu Kalyani, another female practitioner with her own *devalaya*, about whom I will relate more below, Mrs. Rajapakse has not ventured into the practical orbit of functioning as a medium for those seeking contact with deceased kin. Rather, her primary work is as a healer, which she claims to accomplish through Visnu's power. In that respect, what she does for her clients is not categorically different from what *kapuralas* do at traditional Visnu *devalayas* when devotees come with health concerns. What is different, however, is the specific remedies she recommends, based upon her growing knowledge of Ayurvedic medicine.

It is evident from her account that she believes that various substances, from "king coconuts" (*tambili*) to different types of rice to various herbs and leaves, cause disease, the cure of disease, and extraordinary states of consciousness. That is, in her constructions, there is clearly a physical basis to what she and her clients experience. Hers is a type of hybrid practice, insofar as physical substances and physical conditions induce illness, health, and states of trance. Her account of encountering Mahasona, a notorious *yaksa* of great and fearsome power, who through a coconut tried to poison her, is a good example of how she understands the dynamics of power within her world. Moreover, her references to how another exorcist tried to poison her, an event which she believes has weakened her power, also confirms this understanding of a magical world of physical cause and effect. Her possessions by Visnu are the means by which knowledge is revealed to show how to defend against and how to positively channel supernatural power.

Mrs. Rajapakse, however, is insistent on how her power to heal and to predict is also dependent upon her practice of purity in avoiding *kili* and in her pursuit of an ethical life. Celibacy, vegetarianism, and avoidance of contact with men insures her state of purity. In addition, ethical conduct according to Buddhist principles is what also makes her a worthy conduit for the channeling of divine power into the world. But what I find so compelling in her account is the political nature of many of her clairvoyant visions.

In the course of her account, she has made reference to her foreknowledge of many of the remarkable events that have altered the contours of Sri Lanka's recent and unfortunate political history. In serial fashion, she claims to have been possessed by Visnu and consequently been made aware ahead of time of the 1983 conflagration between Sinhalas and Tamils that became the critical moment fueling the subsequent ethnic conflict that has beleaguered the country

ever since; the rise of the Liberation Tigers of Tamil Eelam; their murderous attack upon Buddhist religious devotees at Sri Mahabodhi in Anuradhapura in
1985; the 1987 Indo-Lanka accord signed by President J. R. Jayawardhana and
Indian Prime Minister Rajiv Gandhi; the assassination of Rajiv Gandhi by followers of the LTTE leader Prabhakaran; the bomb blast in Parliament; the assassination of President Premadasa; and the rise to power of today's President
Chandrika Bandaranaike Kumaratunga.

In this extraordinary example, the role of Visnu as protector of the state is
powerfully evoked in Mrs. Rajapaksa's visions of warning. This is a legacy of
the Visnu cult that has found its expression within a decidedly unusual religious context. Even here, he continues in his role as "minister of defense."

Visnu Kalyani

On one of my frequent visits to the Alutnuvara *Devalaya* (located about ten
miles southeast of modern Kegalle in the Kandyan culture area of up-country
Sri Lanka) during the spring of 2000, while I was researching the issue of
Visnu's legacy within the cult of Dadimunda Deviyo, I made the acquaintance
of a middle-aged woman and her husband who had come to the *devalaya* for
the 8 p.m. *puja*. She introduced herself to me as "Visnu Kalyani."[27] During the
subsequent *puja* to Dadimunda Deviyo, Visnu Kalyani fell into an ecstatic
trance during the *kapurala*'s *yatikava* ("petitionary prayer") as soon as the
deity's name was invoked, jerking herself wildly from side to side while simultaneously emitting a series of strident yelps—sounds that were entirely unintelligible but thoroughly emotive in nature. After the *puja* to Dadimunda, she
proceeded in an entranced state to the portico of the abutting Huniyam *devalaya*, where she began to chant her own *yatikava* in a frenzied Tamil voice. I
spoke with her shortly thereafter.

Her eyes were blurred and bloodshot, her body soaked in sweat, her hair
completely disheveled, and her breath rapid and panting. She had come to the
devalaya, she gasped in Sinhala, at "the behest of the god." The god in question
was Alutnuvara Deviyo (a.k.a. Dadimunda, Devata Bandara). She and her husband, she continued, were now offering a thanksgiving to Alutnuvara for the
new van they had just purchased, and she was also, more importantly, seeking
to get her warrant by the god "recharged." I learned that she operated her own
devalaya about fifteen miles outside of Kandy, and she invited me to come for
a visit in the near future. She gave me vague directions and said that I only
needed to proceed about ten kilometers down a given road and ask for her
whereabouts. People would tell me how to get there.

About a month later I set out in search of her *devalaya* with one of my research assistants. True to her word, we were easily guided by helpful villagers.

Indeed Visnu Kalyani was well known in this relatively remote village area and we had no trouble locating her *devalaya*, despite the fact that it was located about one kilometer off a secondary road on a winding trail that traversed the side of a mountain. In our first meeting, I had learned that she was considered mad for many years, that she had spent some of those years in forced confinement within mental hospitals, and that she claimed to function as a medium for family members wishing to communicate with departed kin (Sinhala: *preta*).

Her *devalaya* was a two-storied, well-constructed building adjacent to her similarly well-constructed house. Actually, her *devalaya* consisted of two *devalayas*, one on the first floor dedicated to the goddess Pattini, with a small shrine for Huniyam outside the sanctum. On the top floor, with separate stairs leading up, was another room containing images of Visnu, flanked on the left side by Kataragama Deviyo (holding a black head in one of his left hands) and Bhadra Kali on the right. Further to the right was a small effigy of Dadimunda. She made it explicit what the symbolism implied: Visnu was the chief deity who presided over the *devalaya*. Indeed, she said she was simply his "helper," though her power came directly from Dadimunda.

During the morning of this Saturday *kemmura* day, a milling crowd that ranged consistently of about seventy people was in attendance. About fifty of these were middle-aged women. They had generally come from the up-country region around Kandy, but there were also some people from Colombo, including four businessmen, who regaled us with stories about how Visnu Kalyani had facilitated many contacts with their various departed kin. The morning was taken up with *pujas* to the various deities, after which *prasad* was distributed to all. The priestess then engaged in sessions of soothsaying, predicting future events in the lives of her clients.

A prominently displayed sign announced fees of Rs. 105 for contact with the departed, but only if the departed had been dead for a minimum of three months or a maximum of ten years. The charge for a generic *puja* during which vows could be sworn or *santiya* ["blessing"] sought was Rs. 52.50. The minimum requirement of four separate fruits and a coconut (to be broken on a stone adjacent to the *devalaya*) was also specified. These items could be purchased in a small shop on the first floor of the *devalaya*, along with *tambili* ["King Coconut"], tea, Sprite, Fanta, and Coca-Cola.

At noon, the nature of activities changed, as did Visnu Kalyani's function. During the morning, clients had been issued numbers to determine the order of their engagement with the priestess. On this day, the list ran to twenty-four. (I saw that the list of the previous Wednesday *kemmura* was only seven.) The sessions began with the priestess adorning herself with her *halamba* (bangle), then chanting rhythmically for about three minutes before breaking into her familiar yelps. Later, she told us that her yelps indicate when the deceased are either entering her to possess her or when they are exiting from her body. We recorded the first four sessions on tape, and here, for reasons of brevity, I am providing a translation of just the first two. My comments on the significance of these sessions follow their presentation.

FIRST SESSION.[28]

DEAD FATHER (VISNU KALYANI): Is it you, son?

SON (AYURVEDIC PHYSICIAN): Yes, it's me.

F: Did my daughter come?

S: No she didn't.

F: And your children?

S: No.

F: Come and sit in front of me. I can't see you properly. Why did you ask me to come?

S: I want to know how you are doing and where you are.

F: I'm in Kataragama now, at Kirivehera. I'm born as a *deva* now.

S: I'm happy to know that. I know you did a lot of meritorious work while you were alive. We will come to Kataragama very soon.

F: If you come there, give alms to the beggars. You should acquire merits while you are still alive. As the Buddha says, this life and everything else is transient. I had a natural death. My funeral was done properly and I'm happy for it. I received my 7th day almsgiving, as well as the 3rd month and the 1st year ones. I came to see my dead body as it was lying in the coffin, and it was in good condition—not deformed. I intend to go to Isipathanaramaya in Dambadiwa. I do not intend to be born again. But I regret that I could not enter the *sangha*. So, I do feel like being born again to become a monk. But that will not happen yet. I will remain this way for a *kalpa* or so. Because if I am born in the human world again, I may get trapped in this hell of violence. Now they kill each other. My times were better and our generation was a well brought up one. This present generation is corrupted, addicted to alcohol. They reject religion. Thus, the deities are not in favor of them anymore. This period of the human world is in something of a vacuum. I will be born again in this world when there is a good time—that is when this world is blessed again with a Buddha. It will mark the debut of a new era, a new *kalpa*.

S: I came because my mother and others wanted to know how you are. Did you leave your body and home once you were dead?

F: No. I waited until the funeral and the almsgiving were over. After my death, I did not expect any more merits. I had already acquired enough. While I lived, I had the *varama* of the deity Ausadha (medicine). I cured many people. Who is continuing my profession now?

S: My elder brother.

F: It has been handed down through generations. I feel thirsty often. My arm chair that I used to sit in at home is still where it used to be, isn't it?

S: Yes.

F: I have never let my children go astray. I never drank. My children do not either. I always lived according to the *dharma*. I do not come to this human world often. But if I see any troubles befalling you, I will see to them and not let any troubles come upon you. I need to go now. It is difficult for me to be seated on the floor like this! [laughter] I never used to sit on the floor. You do not need to worry about me. I'm fine. I only want to know if all my children live in peace.

S: Yes they do. I need to know if we have ever done anything wrong to you. If we have, I hope you will forgive us.

F: No you have not. You always respected me. I will be leaving this place by *asala poya* to go to Isipathanaramaya along with Kataragama Deviyo. I think I'll leave now.

SECOND SESSION.

FATHER (VISNU KALYANI): *Loku duva* [elder daughter]?

DAUGHTER: It is me, *podi duva* [younger daughter].

F: Where is *loku duva*? Why didn't she come?

D: She is at home.

F: Why did you ask me to come? You are disturbing my sleep!

D: I need to know where you are and how you are.

F: Did you give my 1st year almsgiving?

D: Yes we did.

F: What about the 2nd year?

D: We will give it too.

F: Did Chuti also come?

D: Who is Chuti?

F: Why, my youngest daughter.

D: No, she couldn't. She had problems.

F: What problems?

D: Her daughter passed away.

F: How? What happened?

D: She met with an accident. She was run down by a train.

F: Who is at home now?

D: Mother and myself.

F: So why did you ask me to come?

D: I want to know if you are short of merits, and what we could do for you.

F: I have enough merits. Right now I am born as a *bhuta*, but soon I will quit this life. I used to come home until you held the 3rd month alms-giving. After that I stopped coming. Now I stay in Anuradhapura. That is where I get my merits. So, how is your mother? Is she well?

D: No, she is always ill. She has a continuous headache.

F: What about her pains in the joints?

D: Those are okay now.

F: What did the doctors say about her headaches? Didn't they tell you she has a weak vein? That is what she has, so the blood circulation is not proper. See to it. And she thinks too much about things. Tell her not to do so. At this stage, she should relax, do meritorious activities.

D: Do you know that your second son died?

F: No, what happened to him?

D: He died suddenly.

F: Did someone poison him?

D: No, nothing like that. He just died.

F: Did he suffer from any illness?

D: No.

F: Did he drink poison?

D: Of course not.

F: Then how did he die suddenly? I doubt it. Did they conduct a post mortem?

D: No, they didn't.

F: Then, just how did he die?

D: I don't know.

F: Then don't tell me about it. This just upsets me a lot now.

D: He died while you were still alive. Nine months before you died. We told you, but you were not conscious of it. You were not aware.

F: No, you never told me about it.

D: No, we did.

F: No you didn't. No one told me about it until this moment, until I am dead and gone. You shouldn't have told me about this now. I'm very upset. It must have been a previous *karma*. I still cannot believe he's dead. I'm going to seek his *atma* and go and see him. I was happy that I had a son who was a monk. But now I am upset.

D: We told you all about it, but you were so ill you didn't understand anything going on around you.

F: Yes, I had this terrible wound in my leg. Doctors said that my leg would have to be amputated, but I didn't like it, did I? They said I would have been alive if I allowed them to do so. It was a *huniyam* done to me. I do not know if they did the same thing to the monk, my son, since he is said to have died without a cause. Shall I leave now? I need to sleep. I cannot properly sleep because I suffer from a terrible headache. I suffered a lot on my death bed. I hope it will not be the same in the future.

Visnu Kalyani is a skilled actress who can change her disposition and presentation almost immediately on whatever cue she picks up. Her clients, at least the ones we met, expressed amazement at how she assumes the personalities and knows the personal details of their dead relations. She claims that Alutnuvara Deviyo (Dadimunda) has eighteen different avatars, and that these enable her to change herself in eighteen different ways, which correspond to the various personalities of the dead.

The substance and pattern of her communications between the living and the dead is consistent. Predictably, the basic reason her clients seek her out is to inquire into the well-being of their departed kin. She always anticipates this, and she always reciprocates by inquiring into the continued well-being of the family. That is the structure of the basic exchange. The substantial theme that surfaces throughout these exchanges is the power of karmic retribution, and how it determines everyone's well-being, now and in future rebirths. The advice that Visnu Kalyani consistently gives, therefore, is to gain merit to assure favorable future circumstances. It is the same advice rendered in the *Petavatthu*: gain merit now, and transfer it to the departed if they are in need.

But many of the inquiries about the well-being of deceased kin made by family members are not motivated entirely out of curiosity or compassion. In the second exchange noted above, it is clear that the surviving family has experienced some serious tragedies before and after the death of the father. Many of Visnu Kalyani's clients suffer similarly. They have come to her in order to determine if there is something specific that was done in the past that has provoked the anger of their departed kin, suspecting perhaps that it is the anger of the departed that is causing them to experience suffering now.

Acts of merit transfer, according to the *Petavatthu*, can assuage the suffering of departed kin. But within this context, it is clear that merit transfer is also a means to placate departed kin who might be wreaking havoc in anger or revenge. Even in the relatively smooth exchange of the first session recorded above, the inquiring son wants to know if anyone in his family had done anything wrong to the departed father.

Visnu Kalyani says departed kin reborn as *bhutas* or *pretas* are often re-sponsible for the misfortunes visited upon their surviving kin. In these cases, it is necessary to determine the exact or specific grievance that is annoying the departed relation. This is clearly the stated motive in the second example I have provided: the deceased's surviving daughter is quick to seek her father's for-giveness if it is needed. Unlike the first case, which could be characterized as amiable, the second exchange between the daughter and father was somewhat sharp and tense. Visnu Kalyani had assumed a scolding or rebuking stance, and the inquiring daughter was clearly nervous, and ill at ease. When the daughter asked if her father was short of merit, this was a way of attempting to deter-mine exactly what could be done to alter the present situation. Visnu Kalyani's probing questions about whether the almsgivings had been properly con-ducted were part of her attempt to find a suitable explanation for the family's misfortunes.

While Visnu Kalyani is able to make a productive living from the belief that *pretas* and *bhutas* may inflict harm on the living, it is also true that she believes in the powers of a moral universe. Her advice, more often than not, is for her clients to begin living the moral and therefore meritorious life. After I had spent many hours with her, I began to see the close parallel between the advice she dispensed and the ethic of the *Petavatthu*.[29]

Other motifs surfaced within the context of the occasions I observed that also deserve some comment. The first is that departed kin are almost always understood to be currently dwelling at places deemed sacred to Buddhists in Sri Lanka. In the two instances I have provided above, the departed locate themselves at Kataragama and Anuradhapura, two of the most important places of Lankan pilgrimage. During the long afternoon of our observances at her *devalaya*, we noted Kelaniya and Sri Pada (Adam's Peak) as other venues that were also frequently mentioned. These are sacred places whose inhabita-tion by the departed indicates an auspicious and favorable progress for them in the afterlife. But it also became clear that when the priestess didn't mention a sacred venue for the departed, it was an indication that the afterlife condition into which they had been reborn was not so favorable at all.

The second recurring element is Visnu Kalyani's skilled reading of the minds of her clients. She seems quite adept at sizing them up before she even begins to react to them. And she nimbly deflects the course of the exchange if she has turned it in the wrong direction. For instance, in the second instance above, it is clear that Visnu Kalyani was not aware of her client's brother's death. Yet she managed to manipulate the exchange to cover her error. And through observing linguistic conventions, she came to understand that the dead brother was a Buddhist monk. Clients are more than willing to help her in the process. In these instances, it is clearly the case, as William James once noted in one of his essays, that "faith in the fact helps create the fact."[30]

In addition to observing her work at her *devalaya*, I interviewed Visnu Kalyani on three other occasions. During one of those visits, her husband showed us her diary. With her permission, I borrowed it and had it translated by one of my assistants.

Just as her work as a medium seems to be dominated by concerns about karma, merit, and rebirth, so it is also with her "autobiography." As Visnu Kalyani recounts her life, she presents it as one of great disappointment and suffering, the consequence of bad karma that she was responsible for generating in a previous life. She says that it seems as if she was born into this present life to suffer and that the life she has been leading is primarily a means of repaying her debts from previous lives. By helping others at her *devalaya*, she is trying to accumulate merit that will pay off her debt in lives to come. Because she has suffered so much in this life, she has tried to commit suicide, and also entertains thoughts of becoming a *sil maniyo* (a saffron-robed, but lay Buddhist "sister") before her life comes to an end.

Visnu Kalyani's visions, like many of those experienced by the protagonists of the stories in the *Petavatthu*, started with the appearance of a dead relation in her dreams. In her case, it was her grandmother who first appeared, from which time *distis* (possessions) became very frequent. Quoting from her "autobiography," she says that her powers to practice came about in the following way:

At this time, Ruk Devi, in the form of a Buddhist monk from Bogahapitiya, gave me the full *varama* ["warrant" to practice]. Three births ago, Ruk Devi was my father. During the time of Dutugemenu [the second-century B.C.E. Buddhist hero-king], Ruk Devi was also my father and married to my *kiri amma* [literally "milk mother" but here referring here to her maternal grandmother]. They were high caste and high officials for the king. At that time, my husband was a servant. One day he abducted me because I owed him some pay. Now in this life I am paying off the debt. In fact, all these three past lives I have been with this husband. My work at the *devale* helps me pay off this debt. Ruk Devi told me about the origins of the village we were living in and helped me to get rid of a *yaksa* who was plaguing me due to the *huniyam* [sorcery] practiced by a neighbor. He dedicated me to Alutnuvara [Dadimunda] who was able to command the *yaksa* to leave. Alutnuvara can take the form of eighteen *avataras*, so he can change me in eighteen different ways that I now have learned to recognize. Ruk Devi stayed here for seven days and told me to go to the local *devale* each day. After that he told me to go straight to Alutnuvara with seven betel leaves, seven candles and oil. I got possessed at Alutnuvara and crawled inside the *devale* on hands and knees, writhing like a serpent. I got the *halamba* [bangle]. This was on the 27th of August, 1988. Only the deity understood my suffering for which reason I was given the *disti* [vision].

I was told to build a *devale* by Ruk Devi. Before this, the *devale* was inside of our small house for about a year. When I was asked to build the *devale*, I had no money to do so. The deity sent me to beg to find money for this. I had never known or learned to recite *kavi* [verses] before, but the deity taught me to sing *virindus* [a form of song accompanied by the small *rabana* drum] at little gatherings and on buses. Then he sent me from house to house like a gypsy singing *virindus*. In this way, I collected some money that I kept safely. Then I built a small *devale*.

When I first started predicting, I charged ten rupees. The deity guides me to make correct predictions. I obtained the *varama* first from Alutnuvara *Deviyo* and then from Kataragama. Then eventually I was given the *varama* by all twelve deities.

It was after a *yaksa* was exorcised at Alutnuvara that Visnu Kalyani began to work successfully as a medium between the living and the dead, and also as a soothsayer. She has cultivated a loyal following, despite the fact that her relations with neighboring villagers remain uneasy. Like other priestesses I came to know, she has been victimized by *huniyam* (sorcery) performed by rival practitioners, and has continued to have difficulties involving the police.

During one of our interviews, she offered a very pertinent way of categorizing the deities of Sri Lanka. At the highest level, in her view, Visnu reigns and rules over the planetary movements that can affect our lives. Visnu, however, does not possess human beings. She was insistent on this matter. But below Visnu are what she called the *mahesakhya* (very powerful) deities. These are worldly deities who were originally born as *yaksas*, but came to worship the Buddha and to learn of his *Buddhadharma*. They have received their *varamas*, or warrants to act in the world, directly from the Buddha. These include Kataragama, Pattini, Pitiye, Alutnuvara (Dadimunda Devata Bandara), and Kumara Bandara. They are the specific deities who have been transformed by the Buddha and his *dharma*. The deities on the next lower level are those who are in charge of particular areas of the country. They act as they do because they fear the power of the Buddha, and thus can be commanded. These include Ganga ("river") Bandara, Aiyannar, Kande ("hill") Bandara, and Gala ("rock") Bandara.

Visnu Kalyani's interpretive scheme of the Sinhala pantheon of deities is actually in rough accordance with the hierarchy as it is often portrayed in

Kandyan folk literature: an ethical hierarchy stratified on the basis of each deity's perceived proximity to the Buddha, a position derived from the amount of positive karma attributed to each. It is also a scheme that explains the transformation of supernaturals from *yaksa* to *devata* status. It parallels the manner in which *pretas* can be transformed into *devatas*, and it is the fundamental principle that she imparts in her advice to clients. Also, note that this principle shows up in relation to how and where she situates the afterlife residences of the deceased. If the rebirth is favorable, they dwell at a place associated with the power and *dharma* of the Buddha.

Visnu Kalyani's understanding of the nature of *yaksas* also turned out to be surprisingly similar to one developed by a well-known Sri Lankan scholar of Buddhist studies, M. J. Marasinghe,[31] who many years ago had been concerned to show how the "popular" meaning of *yaksa* had been construed in early Pali Buddhist literature. Marasinghe noted how the term was defined by Rhys Davids and Stede in their *Pali Text Society Pali Dictionary* (s.v.):

> Yaksa is the name of certain non-human beings, as spirits, ogres, dryads, ghosts, spooks. Their usual epithet and category of being is *amanussa*, i.e. not a human being (but not a sublime god either); being half deified and of great power as regards influencing people (partly helping, partly hurting . . .)[32]

Marasinghe was specifically interested in the problem that arises when *yaksas* are seen in various Pali *suttas* to be asking metaphysical questions of the Buddha while at the same time they were "not considered capable of any intellectual accomplishments as to understand an exposition of the *Dhamma*, or to ask questions which involve deeper thinking" (105). His answer to this problem was that

> Yaksas were not non-human beings, but were those from the yet uncultured tribes, whose presence was a doubtless reality at the time of the Buddha (108).

He says that this explanation renders references in the *Vinaya* proscribing "sexual intercourse with a female *yaksa* [as not being] anything other than a reference possibly to a vagrant tribeswoman" (109). Therefore, in relation to the various exchanges between the Buddha and *yaksas*, these figures "would have been at least respectable tribesmen, if not tribal chiefs" (112). He concludes that *yaksas* referred to

> in the early Buddhist texts were no more than mere tribesmen, who were of course mythologised at a time much later than that of these *suttas*. The

fact that they belonged to tribal societies also goes to explain their 'myste-rious' character, as has been observed about them in such early texts as the *Rgveda*" (116).

In short, *yaksas* were those human beings who had not yet been civilized either by the brahmans or, in this case, by the teachings of the Buddha. What brings them into the fold of civilization is an understanding of dharma, or Buddhist teachings.

This is precisely how Visnu Kalyani understood the transformation of deities of the second class, such as Alutnuvara Deviyo—beings who have suc-cessfully made the transition from *yaksa* to *devata*. It is also how she explained the manner in which the deceased can be assisted by the living. It is their rela-tion to and understanding of the Buddha and the dharma that transforms them. Moreover, what is implied by this principle is that Visnu, by virtue of his position among all of the deities in the pantheon with the possible exception of Natha, is the deity who is regarded as having the greatest understanding of the Buddha's dharma, and the greatest amount of merit.

Visnu Kalyani understands her own life according to this principle too. Born to suffer because of her karma, she labors, according to her understand-ing of the Buddha's teaching, to assuage the suffering of others. That much is very clear by the verses of *kavi* with which she concludes her autobiography:

I'm born to this world because of *karma*.
I've been pushed into this wretched life because of *karma*.

Why live without freedom?
What do I take with me when I die? Only merit and nothing else.

I do good for people before the deity in my *devale*.
I beseech you to help them, to ease their pain and grant them their needs.

The world of the "gone but not departed" in Buddhist Sri Lanka pivots on the dynamic power attributed to karma, whether generated by the living before they depart, or by the living for those who have already departed. Both the liv-ing and the dead inhabit a universe that changes (rises and passes qualitatively) according to the principles of a moral economy. Soteriological empowerment is generated, in part, according to moral observance, but power leading to suf-fering can also be generated by sorcery or the relative qualitative condition of time itself, measured in terms of proximity to the presence of a buddha and his dharma.

But perhaps the most important force characterizing the relation between the living and the dead is the desire on the part of the living to assist the well-being of the dead. Not only may this help to avert misfortune and suffering for both, but it sustains the bonds of the Sinhala familial pact. Therein lies the link I wish to stress in this particular consideration: the positive well-being and relative health of the extended family (among the living and the recently dead) is rendered dependent upon the transformation of the dharma as karmically realized. Morality and merit are the substance of familial religion. Visnu ultimately presides over this dimension of Sinhala religion as well.

THE LEGACY OF VISNU IN THE CULT OF HUNIYAM AT ALUTNUVARA

As I noted in the chapter five summary of Visnu *devalayas* in the Kandyan culture area, there are consistently three cultic venues, one each for Visnu, Dadimunda, and Huniyam, at each of the Visnu *devalayas* in Kandy, Hanguranketa, Gadaladeniya, and Lankatilaka. If the new Visnu *devalaya* within the monastic *viharaya* at Alutnuvara is included, the same arrangement now obtains at Aluthnuvara as well.

The spatial layouts at the Visnu *devalayas*, as I indicated before, reflect the divine hierarchy among these deities: Visnu's shrines are the main attractions, and the constructions that dominate the compounds (see figure 5.1). He is, of course, the "highest" of the deities: benign, compassionate, and well on his way to nirvana. As Visnu's "prime minister," Dadimunda's shrines are located to the side of the dominating Visnu *devalayas*, and are small, yet substantial and impressive *devalaya* structures (replete with *digges* and *sancta* containing iconic images). Huniyam, as one of the Kandy Visnu *kapuralas* has put it, is "Dadimunda's hit man."

In general, it seemed that devotees at Visnu *devalayas* did not like to draw much attention to their cultic activities in relation to Huniyam; some of them came at night when they would be less likely to be noticed. At the Kandy Visnu *devalaya*, Huniyam's shrine is little more than a cupboard or a shed located behind and slightly to the side of the Dadimunda *devalaya*. The *basnayaka nilame* said that he had arranged for the Huniyam set up when he took over the *devalaya's* administration just five years ago.

So Huniyam's presence in Kandy was new, and until recently deemed unnecessary at the Kandy Visnu *devalaya*, probably because a full-fledged *devalaya* for Gambara Deviyo (Huniyam as the village protective deity) is located just 150 yards away at the adjacent Natha *devalaya*. In the case of Hanguranketa, the Huniyam *devalaya* was so inconspicuously located behind the Dadimunda *devalaya* and so encroached upon by vegetation that I didn't notice its presence until my second visit! At Lankatilaka, the "shrine" consisted of little more than a small area on the ledge of the outside back wall of the Dadimunda *devalaya*. Gadaladeniya also has a marked area to the side of the Dadimunda *devalaya* for petitioning Huniyam, but no structure per se.

But at Alutnuvara, the shrine for Huniyam is a full-fledged *devalaya* construction complete with small *digge* and a *sanctum sanctorum* housing an image never revealed to the outside for fear of unleashing its ambivalent and therefore potentially dangerous power. When I asked one of the *kapuralas* if I could see it, he stared at me incredulously and asked if I was *pissu* ("crazy"). About twenty percent of the devotees who take *darsan* from Dadimunda and listen to the *kapurala's yatika* at the Alutnuvara *devalaya* proper (in its sanctum) continue on to the detached Huniyam *devalaya* for a plaint to that *yaksa/devata*. Some of those visiting Huniyam bring their malevolent sorcery, others fall into *disti*, while still others quietly light incense and hear a generic *yatikava*. Every *kemmura* night before the 8 p.m. *puja* held for Alutnuvara Deviyo, *kapuralas* solicit indications from those in the waiting crowd who would like to practice sorcery (*paligahanava*) at the Huniyam *devalaya*. A percentage of those gathered then proceed to the Huniyam *devalaya*, where their sorcerous plaints are made, before the Huniyam *kapurala* chants his generic *yatikava* (which he consistently refused to have tape-recorded).

Huniyam is a formidable presence in the lives of those who venerate him, a highly ambivalent power who can be benevolent at times and malevolent in relation to one's enemies. As a *yaksa*, Huniyam's fundamental characteristic is his brute strength, which is fearsomely and sometimes gruesomely expressed in Sinhala *kavi* and iconography (see fig. 7.8).

It is clear that these three deities (Visnu, Dadimunda, and Huniyam) have been linked in a hierarchy and corresponding "division of labor" that is karmically articulated and legitimated. They are seen to exist in a complementary relation to one another within the religious and ritual culture of these up-country *devalayas*. These links and relations, however, are not consistently found in other ritual venues within the Sinhala Buddhist culture areas of the country. There are many venues, particularly at the newer and larger pilgrimage stops, such as at Kande Viharaya in Aluthgama on the southwest coast, at the Visnu *devalaya* at Devinuvara itself, at Kataragama, or at Bellanvila Viharaya in Colombo, where there are shrines to so many different deities, all lined up in a row in "line houses," that the cultic mix defies any attempt at rational order.

Also, in many villages in the Kandyan area, it is more likely for the worship of Visnu to take place in front of an image of Visnu within the *viharaya buduge*, and a small *devalaya* for Huniyam may operate independently from another venue in the village, where he is more likely to be known primarily as Gambara Deviyo. But the links between these three (four if we count the Buddha) divine

FIGURE 7.8 Popular portrait of Huniyam

or supernatural characters are consistent in the limited context of the "Buddhist Visnu" *devalaya* religious culture that I have described.

There are some notices in Sinhala *kavi* that articulate these very links, reflecting a legacy of the "Buddhist Visnu" and a place in the moral economy for Huniyam, despite his *yaksa* origins.

There is, in fact, a fairly large literature in Sinhala *kavi* about Huniyam, in addition to abounding oral traditions easily elicited from almost anyone. In what follows, I have selected a relevant fragment of literary materials to illustrate the legacy of the "Buddhist Visnu" in Huniyam's cult. But there are several studies recently and not so recently undertaken that take a far more comprehensive view of Huniyam's significance than the one I am about to offer.[33]

Gombrich and Obeyesekere (1988) note that recently Huniyam has become an *ista devata* (personal or chosen deity) of many lower-class Colombo urban dwellers, and they surmise that the tradition of making Huniyam a personal deity (*ista devata*) probably began among ritual specialists—i.e., sorcerors themselves, who sought protection from other local sorcerors. In their consideration, Huniyam's perceived rising popularity among urban folk is explained as a consequence of the fact that a "pervasive fear of sorcery is endemic to crowded 'villages' and wards in and around Colombo," (121), a social condition that is the product of intense "urban anomie" (130), in turn produced by massive population shifts from village to city. In this struggling socioeconomic context, they argue, Huniyam has become an increasingly important protective deity, not only for sorcerors but for those minions finding it difficult to make a decent living, with powers perfectly suited to fend off enemies who seek to do harm through equally endemic jealousies in a social world of limited access to material wealth.[34]

But if Huniyam is a *yaksa*, as traditionally and predominantly understood in ritual literature, how can he be regarded as a *devata* or protective deity? According to Gombrich and Obeyesekere (122):

A protective deity is by definition benevolent to his devotee, but malevolent toward his enemies. It is, of course, difficult to reconcile *any* kind of benevolence with the traditional Huniyam Yaka (demon). Thus an ingenious theory has been invented in the city that Huniyam is *both* demon and *devata* (a "godling"): during the waxing (*pura*) of the moon, he is a *devata*, and during the waning (*ava*) a demon (*yaka*) . . . . [T]he needs of the devotee can also be resolved in this fashion: one can invoke Huniyam in his good form to give *pihita* ("help") and in his bad form to curse (*avalada*) or practice sorcery against one's enemies.

Earlier, I also noted that there is actually a good deal of overlap in general between the nonhuman categories of *devata* and *yaksa*. That ambivalence is also found to some extent in the cult of Dadimunda. But in the case of Huniyam, the *yaksa* side of the divide is ever more pronounced, and thus whatever attempts are made to elevate his status by his devotees (whether they are Colombo slum dwellers or middle-class Kandyans), they must be somewhat exaggerated in order to balance the scope and intensity of Huniyam's clearly fearful and malefic *yaksa* presence. Indeed, I think efforts to compensate for the *yaksa* profile, that is, to make a strong case for his simultaneous *devata* status and power, have stimulated his cultic devotees to associate (thereby legitimizing) Huniyam with the figures of the Buddha, Visnu, and Dadimunda, who, in turn, epitomize, in relatively positive degrees, the karmically determined hierarchy of a Sinhala Buddhist moral economy.

Obeyesekere (1986:213) has collected a remarkable contemporary myth about Huniyam from the village of Wellampitiya that illustrates precisely what I have just alluded to. Here is Obeyesekere's rephrasing:

Huniyam yaksa was born to the Oddisa [Orissa?] king during the lifetime of our Buddha. At his birth, astrologers predicted that his presence would be so inimical that he would eventually destroy the kingdom. On hearing this, the king hatched a plan to kill the *yaksa,* even though he was his son. But Huniyam fled to the jungle safely. There he became enamored with serpents, learning to eat them and to drape himself with them. Developing himself into a ferocious *yaksa*, he sought revenge for his pitiable condition by vowing to kill the Buddha. However, nearby people learned of his plan, he was captured and then tethered. The Buddha, knowing of good karma in Huniyam's past and knowing that eventually he would become a *paccekabuddha*, determined to subdue Huniyam in a manner of control. Unable to completely subdue Huniyam, the Buddha banished him to Sri Lanka where he encountered Visnu who, in his role of guardian deity, made him a commander of *yaksas* under the authority of Dadimunda. Huniyam then retreated to Sri Pada where he meditated and in the process became a *devata*. Visnu then asked him to become a protector of villages wherein he assumed the title of *Gambare deviyo*. Agreeing, Visnu bestowed on him divine sight and he assumed the responsibility of witnessing the good and bad activities of human beings and reports these to the gods. During the waxing moon he protects the good and during the waning he punishes the wicked. The Buddha also grants him lordship over magical acts as well.[35]

This remarkable myth locates Huniyam precisely in the same position within the hierarchy of moral economy that I found operating at the Visnu *devalayas* around Kandy and in Alutnuvara. Within this schematization, Huniyam is domesticated and situated to function positively, not as a bringer of disease and death, nor as a powerful agent of sorcerous intentions, but as a witness to karmic behavior and a protective guardian deity of villages. That is, this myth contains a complete makeover of Huniyam from his *yaksa* status to that of *devata*. He has been brought positively into the *devata* fold by means of his direct encounters with the Buddha and Visnu, the epitomes par excellence of the Sinhala Buddhist moral economy, and he has even made progress on the spiritual path by means of his practice of Buddhist meditation at a sacred Buddhist place of pilgrimage! That is, he has been *buddhacized*. Moreover, the myth also attempts to provide the rationale for why he has been given a moral authority and status as a *devata*.

While Kapferer may be correct in asserting that the forms of religion and magic in which Huniyam's cult plays a major role are experiencing something of a renaissance in contemporary Sinhala Buddhist culture, the assimilation of Huniyam and his fundamental ambivalence as *yaksa* and *devata* are probably centuries old. Indeed, the "problem" of *yaksa* and *devata* overlapping has been noticed in various ways within many strands of late-medieval Sinhala *kavi*. It is also within this late-medieval literature that we can find something of a legacy of the "Buddhist Visnu" being implanted into Huniyam's cult.

There are several lengthy tracts of Sinhala *kavi* that detail the birth, arrival, and "career" of Huniyam. That there are a number of mythic accounts of Huniyam's origins may betray the fact that there have been many various attempts aimed at explaining his ambivalent nature. In the *Kabala Patuna Hevath* (de Elaris 1929:1–5), a descriptive poem of some 42 verses in Telugu (the language from Andhra Pradesh in India) that is, sacred verses of power (*huniyam*) in the form of a book, which Kabala (Huniyam) comes to personify, are brought ashore at Devinuvara by brahmans. Kabala (Huniyam) impresses the king with his magical mantra-driven powers, and is granted lands in mid-country Sitavaka. Kabala then travels throughout many villages as far away as Munneswaram in the north where, in each case, his powerful presence is left behind to remain in the *kovils* he has visited, before he finally settles down at Kabalava. The poem concludes with an invitation to the *devata* to perform a frenzied dance on the prepared *mal yahan* (altar of flowers). It is followed by a twelve-verse addendum (5–6) celebrating Kabala (Huniyam) as Gambara Devi, protector of villages and their boundaries. The eighth verse specifically refers to his abode in Alutnuvara, while the ninth refers to his skin color as blue.

In short, this is a poem that, while not referring to Visnu and Dadimunda directly, locates Huniyam's origins at Brahmanic Devinuvara, and ends up by situating him as blue deity in Alutnuvara! A modeling on the mythic career of the "Buddhist Visnu" is quite transparent here. Huniyam becomes the power of magic transformed by divine sanction into a protective power to be tapped within the boundaries of villages. In general, this is also a myth that is an attempt to explain the dissemination of Huniyam's cult throughout Sinhala cultural areas in the western half of the country.

The *Kabalave Bandara Nohot Deviange Vittiya* (Pragnaloka 1952:40–42) contains an entirely different story, but one similar in form and substance to the *Huniyan Yak yadinna* (*Sinhala Kavi* I:11) and the *Huniyan yakunge kavi* (*Sinhala Kavi* III:330) collected by Neville. In this mythic cycle, during an epic battle between the *asuras* and *devas*, Huniyam is born as a mighty blast of poisonous smoke out of the nostil of Maha Gini Kala, a cosmic serpent who has wrapped himself around Mt. Meru and has thus bent the axis at the center of the world, which in turn has to be straightened by Upulvan, who dives into the cosmic sea to reach the mountain's base.

The *vittiya* version continues in much more detail about Kabalave Bandara's (Huniyam's) arrival in Lanka with two retinues of 500 *yaksas*, his wanton killing of human beings, and his drinking the blood of an elephant! He is finally subdued and subordinated by Vessamuni, and put in charge of *yaksas* under Dadimunda's power. Similar patterns of domestication and transformation from murderous *yaksa* to protective *devata* are found in the *Suniyam Kavi* (Pragnaloka 1952:118–20) and the *Kapun Sirasapadaya saha* (J. D. Fernando 1929:12–13). In the latter, Huniyam is said to be the *yaksa* son of King Panduvas and Queen Rankara, who can only be satiated by sacrifices of blood and by the power of Isvara (Siva).

There are two other versions of the birth of Huniyam that I want to cite, among a number of others that could be discussed as well. The first is from the *Oddisa Upata* (*Sinhala Kavi* I:89). Here the motif of royal associations of Huniyam is also noticed, as well as two confrontations with Mara. In the first instance, Mara attempted to prevent a noble named Kadirangara from giving alms to the Buddha by preparing a pit of fire in his path. Kadirangara passed through the fire pit, and it then turned into lotus blossoms. Mara predicted that Kadirangara would some day become a buddha.

The story continues with a minister (Oddisa/Huniyam) under Kadirangana vowing to become a *rsi*. At the beginning of this *kalpa*, he was so reborn while Kadirangana became Mahasammata. When Mara possessed Manikpala (Visnu's sister), the *rsi* came to her rescue after seven other *rsis* had fled in fear. He had been persuaded to do so by Visnu. The motifs here would seem to be a recasting for Huniyam of the Upulvan/Visnu/Dadimunda victory over Mara.

Finally, Neville briefly cites a remarkable poem (*Sinhala Kavi* II:229), which he says he collected in the Northwest Province, in which "Visnu *Devatavi* conceived and bore a son, and this son was Huniyan Devata." The sicknesses that he causes can be cured by appealing to various forms of Pattini.

In each of these mythic traditions, the fundamental pattern is the tension that exists between Huniyam's *yaksa* and *devata* profiles. In the versions I have selected, Visnu's function as a domesticating and moral presence is clear. Visnu has been domesticated and legitimated so thoroughly that he becomes a means by which later arrivals and assimilations into Sinhala Buddhist religious culture can be legitimated too. In relation to Huniyam, Dadimunda also seems to function precisely in this way. It is under his direct authority at Alutnuvara that Huniyam is allowed to operate.

In conclusion, I want to stress not only the legacy of the "Buddhist Visnu" as a legitimator of Huniyam's *devata* status within this culture's moral economy, but also that there is a danger in too clearly demarcating a boundary between *devata* and *yaksa*. The term *yaka* in contemporary Sinhala discourse remains notoriously ambiguous in meaning. For instance, on the social level it can be used derisively to convey a sense of "othering or otherness." On various occasions, I have heard myself being referred to (by Sinhalas who do not realize I understand their language) as a *sudu* ("white") *yaka*. In these contexts, references to me as a *sudu yaka* emphasize the fact that I do not belong or have not been welcomed—my presence is understood as being intrusive.

On the other hand, Sinhala friends may sometimes colloquially call each other *yaka* in a fashion that designates their intimacy: "We are all *yakas* here, don't you know!" So its usage is definitely pliable and not necessarily fixed categorically, even in colloquial parlance. And so it is with those denizens of the supernatural world in the traditional religious culture of Sinhala Buddhists. *Yaksas* may indeed be malevolent forces of great strength that need to be exorcised if they gain possession of a human being. However, one *yaksa*, in this case especially Huniyam, can be called upon to provide protection from the presence of another. Both Dadimunda and Huniyam have been variously referred to as "commanders" (*adikar*) of *yaksas*. They can, therefore, be called upon to control these potentially inimical forces precisely because they have been domesticated by the Buddha or have received their warrants for acting in this world from a morally enriched deity such as Visnu.

Finally, with specific regard to Huniyam, there are legions of stories in popular Sinhala culture in which Huniyam is understood more as a mysterious rather than malevolent figure. He is known, for instance, for talking daily walks in the villages or in the countryside during the twilight hours of the day, dressed always in white and carrying his cane by his side. Herein, he is not necessarily understood as being mischievous in his comings and goings or his encounters with unsuspecting human beings, but rather as miraculous in the signs that he leaves behind. That is, his presence (its ephemerality indicated by twilight) is a sign of supernatural power. How that power is channeled, or how it is reacted to, determines its constructive or destructive consequence. In its perceived interaction with Visnu, the consequence is therefore benevolent, such that at least within one mythic instance, Huniyam is even understood to have been conceived by Visnu.

In the first three chapters of part 2, my focus has been on the cult of Visnu and its legacy within more traditional segments of Sinhala Buddhist religious culture. But in the next chapter, my focus shifts to its contemporary political salience.

Appendix I:
Kavi of the Dadimunda Cult

Galakaeppu Sahalla[36]
(Breaking the Stone)

1. Great seer Siddhartha,
    The Dhamma he expounded to the world,
    The Sangha—to these three gems
    I bow my head in reverence.

2. When ten earth-loads of Mara's retinue
    Congregated to declare war,
    The gods all fled on sight
    Taking refuge beyond Mt. Meru.

3. [The Buddha,] his back against the Bodhi Tree,
    Sitting on the Diamond Throne, declared:
    "Even if Mara comes for war
    I shall not move before I am enlightened.

4. On that day, Vasavarti Mara
    Gathered together his battalions of death
    And tried to prevent Buddhahood's realization
    Surrounding the Buddha with his forces.

5. Abandoning the Buddha,
    The gods departed;
    But a strong-willed ["Dadi"] deity came forward
    And declared he was ready to fight:

6. "Without any weapon in hand
    And only a golden walking cane,
    I shall attack and sever them
    in combat," he told the Sage.

7.   Having provided the ten-fold gift
      By creating persons of the ten perfections [*paramitas*],
      The Buddha declared, "Wait, O Mara!
      I shall show you how to fight!"

8.   In surveying the six heavens
      The world of *naga*s, and the three worlds,
      There is none comparable to you
      Who received the epithet "Munda Daedi."

9.   Venerating the Buddha and setting forth,
      He saw Lord Vesamuni.
      Entrusted with the command over all *yaksas*,
      He went to see Upulvan deviyo.

10.   Having surveyed the surroundings,
      He descended to the Maya country.
      There it was commanded
      That a city be constructed for Devata Surindu.

11.   A child was conceived in Somavati's womb.
      After nine and half months,
      The mother died and was reduced to ashes
      As her house was set to flame.

12.   The child of that burnt woman
      Came out of her womb as a prince.
      In the morning the king and his ministers
      saw him besmeared with ash.

13.   In the middle of the ocean, rejoicing reigned
      Amidst the constant light of torches.
      In the guise of a sandal wood log
      Wafted by the waves, he came ashore,

14.   Assuming the form of a divine image.
      Two persons went mad
      Near the city of Maya.
      A mountain stream appeared.

15.   Having performed the *asala* festival,
      He ordered the various realms of his kingdom.

By charity and benevolence,
He protected his kingdom for twenty-five years.

16.   Then that king of the gods,
       Being fond of Udarata [the upcountry],
       According to ancient custom,
       Took a shine to the Satara Korale.

17.   (Daedimunda) went to Kirungandeniya
       To survey the environs
       And took the road
       That led to the Golden Stone Cave.

18.   He made the milk from the cows of the royal herd
       Turn into blood!
       The wise royal ministers
       Declared it as the work of his magical power.

19.   The king who had dreamt this
       Cleared an area of trees and stumps
       Where the golden walking cane had been planted.
       There he erected a three storey palace of pure gold.

20.   He built Alutnuwara with
       It's inner shrine ofsandalwood,
       A dancing chamber at its center
       And thirty-six halls.

21.   "In the descending path to the compound,
       There is a boulder obstructing.
       We cannot break it!"
       The plaint was made to Devata Surindu.

22.   Advised by his ministers, the king examined the situation
       Finding the difficulty of creating a flat ground.
       So he [Dadimunda] declared: "I shall manifest my power by
           employing the *yakkas*
       To smash this rock to make the ground flat for the
           compound.

23.   "Make *kavun* [oil cakes] and *kiri bath* [milk rice].
       Do not make these in small pieces.

Offer these to the *yakkas* so they will not tire.
May the *yakkas* blast this rock tonight!"

24.   Bedecked in sandal and smeared in cow-dung,
      Covered with coconut flowers and tender coconut leaves,
      Attended by coquettish and charming women,
      That place was filled with *kiri bath*.

25.   *Yakkas* from Bengal, Gauda, Malla countries,
      Yakkas from Kongani, Java, and Andhra countries,
      Yakkas from Kannadiga, Kaudi and Kaberi countries,
      All *yakkas* were summoned to Sri Lanka.

26.   "*Yakkas*, eat whatever you desire.
      Take spears, swords and iron cudgels.
      Take whatever weapon you please
      And smash this stone into tiny pieces."

27.   As a strike of thunder in the sky,
      As the earth rumbles in an earth quake,
      As the ground shakes when guns burst,
      They blasted that rock as if playing hand ball.

28.   Their languages varied according to their countries.
      The Tamil *yakkas* shouted loudly.
      In anger some attacked each other.
      The *yakkas* from the Sinhala country made little noise.

29.   Some break the stone just by chanting.
      Some show their strength in fighting each other.
      Some stay away after being beaten.
      Some shoulder the rocks and roll them down.

30.   So they broke the stone to make the ground flat.
      They filled the streams and canals in equal measure.
      They fixed stones for a breakwater in the tank.
      This they informed (to Daedimunda) and worshipped at
         his feet.

31.   "If we are allowed to stay in this country
      We shall perform all work asked of us by this king.

It is verily difficult to meet this god."
Saying so, they fell down at his feet.

32. These women full of charm are like golden images.
    They chatter in a lovely manner like the golden parrots.
    They tie their long hair bedecked with flowers and eschew wigs.
    Oh, how can we leave these lovely women behind?

33. "O *Yaksas*, you are ignorant of (our) Sinhala charms.
    (Our) *mantras* will bind and imprison you.
    (Our) *mantras* will punish you severely. You will stand on *yantras*,
    Be confined to a smoke-filled chamber, and sprayed by nasal
       unguents.

34. Do not sicken the women you encounter.
    (Leave us) without grief. Get away!
    Like a lake empties when the dam is burst,
    Each of you get back to your respective countries!

35. With the blasting of the rock being a display of great power,
    Group after group of people from towns and villages came
    To see (Dadimunda)
    And to worship him intimately.

36. They clean their teeth, wash their heads and bathe (their bodies).
    They wear clean clothes with pleats a plenty.
    They offer betel, coconut, rice and gifts,
    Worship him and happily leave.

37. They bring their women possessed by *yaksas*,
    Women with intense burning pain in their loins.
    (Women) dance vigorously in the (devale) compound.
    "We must leave!" the *yaksas* plead.

38. (*Yaksas*) are tied to trees, beaten and broken by canings.
    (*Yaksas*) are made to stand in the sun with stones on their heads.
    "Take a vow, go and do not lie!"
    "We shall go now not looking back on this country!"

39. All around the compound, silk-cotton poles were erected.
    The *Devol yaksas* were summoned from this (Sinhala) country,

Raised to silk-cotton poles and tethered.
"Leave! Out with your curses!" It is decreed.

40.   What punishments were meted to *Pilli* and *Suniyam yaksas*!
      They were summoned in groups and beaten mercilessly.
      Faces paled, they groveled for mercy at (Dadimunda's) feet.
      "*Pilli yaksas*! Leave or face further torment!"

41.   *Yaksas*! Don't you know the teachings of Gautama Buddha?
      Yaksas! Don't you know the commands of Lord Vesamuni?
      Yaksas! Don't you know that *yaksas* are afraid of the gods?
      Yaksas! Don't reckon with the power of Dadimunda! Leave now!

42.   *Davul, tammaettan, pataha*, and *morahu* drums are beaten.
      Dancer here and there wearing masks perform.
      Is anyone in the world superior in making war?
      Behold Dadimunda's display of martial arts!

43.   (Dadimunda) takes his bejewelled cane in hand.
      I take flowers, lamps, and gifts in a golden plate and offer them.
      Clothes, canopies, and curtains are hung for a week.
      There is no one on earth who compares to Devata Bandara of
          Aluthnuvara!

44.   It is Devata Bandara, commander of the *yaksas*,
      Who I worship and recite poetry pleasing to his ear.
      Proclaim his divine virtues so the three worlds may hear.
      See him and all diseases will be quelled forever.

45.   An elephant came to the devale compound and gave a mighty
          thrust at the *kitul* tree.
      By a single right handed blow to the body (the elephant's)
      Back was broken, (the elephant) paralyzed and crawled to its death.
      In these three worlds, there is no one tougher than you who dwells
          where the stone was broken.

46.   Some of you *yaksas*! Go into the country, spread disease and
          beget ritual offerings.
      Do not be rash! Accept ritual offerings and cure disease and
          affliction.

He is like the king of the cobras in exacting vengeance, poisonous
   to all, know this!
He is like the lord of the clouds, O *yaksas*, remember this too.

47. In breaking the rock, your arrival in Satara Korale was revealed.
     Go[ne] forth from [to?] all quarters, from[to?] all countries one
        after the other.
     The Gods of the Four Quarters, with their divine eyes, have seen
        (these) great courageous deeds.
     From then, the Sun and Moon flags of Satara Korale were raised
        and the people began to dance in joy.

48. The Portuguese who came here surrounded Sunuvela and
        Aluthnuvara.
     Challenging the god with abusive words, they tried to rob (our)
        treasures here.
     The *yaksas* were summoned and the Portuguese chased beyond the
        river at night.
     Only then did Devata Bandara's suzerainty over the *yaksas* become
        renowned.

Dadimunda Avataraya[37]
(The Incarnation of Dadimunda)

1. The fame of holy Dadimunda deviyo,
    Whose brilliance exceeds the sun's rays,
    Is renowned throughout Lanka
    And exceeds the splendor of Sakra's heaven.

2. Obtaining a boon from Sakra,
    Subjugating all vicious *yaksas* and *pisachas*,
    For his valor, he came to be known as Dadimunda
    And his power spread in no mean manner.

3. I worship that Dadimunda, the highest
    And foremost power in the world.
    His power and glory
    Surpass the brilliance of the sun and the moon.

4.   I worship at your feet with devotion.
For, your power is manifest throught the world
Just like the sun's rays
Protecting people as their needs arise.

5.   In this *kalpa*, the first incarnation was Upulvan.
Next came Narayana to dispel fear.
In Sri Lanka, there are ten famous incarnations.
This *yaksa* I call Dadimunda *avataraya*.

6.   Granted a boon to protect Lanka for five thousand years,
To protect the world and the *sasana* for five thousand years,
Having gathered all the gods headed by Isvara,
He was conceived in the womb of Queen Erandati.

7.   That princess was married to Purnaka,
A *yaksa* of enormous might, famous world-wide.
After a long lapse of time,
She conceived.

8.   In the womb of his mother he healthily grew
And after ten months the queen went into labor.
O wise ones! Dadimunda, the divine prince, was born,
Shining like a gleaming jewel.

9.   As the moon expands in its waxing phase,
His rays steadily spread throughout Lanka.
With vigor and zeal, he protected people in the world
And proceeded to the Mayavati country where he met god Kadira.

10.   Appearing like an image of solid gold,
Forehead glistening like the crescent moon,
Blue-hued locks of hair thick as a jungle,
He searches the ten directions with his bright blue eyes.

11.   Ears glittering like the petals of *kinihiri* flowers,
Lips like the *vada* [hibiscus] flower, teeth like white lilies,
Arms shaped like elephant trunks,
Breast and back as if cast in solid gold.

12.   Flanks and sides with *gomara* marks,
Chest glistening with gold dust,

A slender waist, as thin as a blue crystal bow,
And his forehead elongated like a half-moon forges the beauty of
   his face.

13.   Flower-like purple and blue specks
      On is his chest, white specks on arms and hands incite passion.
      Flower-like blooming specks shine
      On the body of this lord like blue flower creepers.

14.   With divine eyes, he perceived the Asuras' mansion.
      He stopped the sporting of the sun, moon, lightening and
         clouds.
      With the speed of an arrow, he swam across the ocean of milk.
      Thereafter he received the golden bow from Saman Deviyo.

15.   Wearing divine attire, having the golden bow and ornaments,
      His power was displayed when he destroyed the rock mansion.
      So he went to Visnu and obtained his boon
      And received the golden bow from him too.

16.   With due respect he honored Narayana,
      By invoking Visnu he received the golden bow.
      Without hesitating, he protected all people.
      By the mere tinkling of bells, diseases were dispelled.

17.   His hair is well-combed and bedecked with *champak* flowers.
      He wears a three-tiered collar with frills at the neck.
      He walks with pendulant hands like two garlands.
      His look is auspicious like sandal unguents.

18.   Glittering pearl necklace around his neck,
      A sash falling from his shoulder graces his holy body,
      Saying, "Stop!" He halted the sun and moon!
      His power was manifest when he removed that rock.

19.   Opening the golden curtain with his right hand,
      He rises through the air and walks elegantly in the sky.
      Seeing the golden mountain and admiring it,
      He goes to Saman Deviyo and receives his permission.

20.   He calculates the future
      Scorching and beating enemy *yaksas*.

Yaksas flee in with fearful groans
At the tinkling sound of the green cane.

21.   When holy enlightenment was gained by the Great Seer.
       Mara soon followed creating war's havoc.
       In confusion did the gods of this universe disappear.
       Dadimunda alone remained worshipping at the Buddha's feet.

22.   He remained with bow in hand taking aim.
       By the power of his ten *paramitas*, the Buddha
       Crushed Mara's hoards and their repeated attacks.
       He gave him the great name "Munda dadi."

23.   With folded hands, Dadimunda worshipped the Buddha
       And received his prediction that he would become a future Buddha.
       He stopped the ravages of the wind, rain, lightening and fire
       And from that moment protected the world's people from *yaksas*.

24.   Taking his iron mallet which gleans in the ten directions,
       Vesamuni comes out of Kubera's city and appears on top of Mount
           Meru.
       With flames shooting out of his hands, he scorches those *yaksas*.
       And bequeaths his assent to Dadimunda's emerging power.

25.   He, who has protected the Buddha Sasana for five thousand years,
       Whose cane is used ritually to beat back the *yaksas*,
       Has performed miraculously for the benefit of good,
       Commander-in-chief, prime minister, scorches the *yaksas*.

26.   Walking with majesty and pride
       Like golden Mt. Meru at sunrise, he subjugates the *yaksas*.
       And earthload of *ginikadavars* flank him on both sides.
       Bandara Devata carries a cane of fire in hand.

27.   Naga, bhuta, preta, Sinha and Kannadi,
       Raga, Nadam Gopalu, Pilli and Ginijal *yaksas*,
       Lavadi, Gini, Bradi and Malawara *yaksas*.
       And *yaksas* of Devol, Vatakumara and Mangara,

28.   Follow the arrival of Bandara.
       He goes to Uggalpura

To reward those *yaksas* who fulfil their tasks.
Truly he made the Meru-like rock disappear.

29.   When the gods fled wildly on the occasion
      When Mara's assembled his retinue, with his right foot firmly
         planted
      He fixed an arrow to that golden bow
      And the Buddha named him Dadimunda.

30.   In facing Mara, the Blameless One
      Cried: "Stop!" And Dadimunda withdrew his arrow.
      The Earth Goddess sprang from below
      And worshipped the lotus feet of the Great Seer.

31.   So he gained the favor of the Buddha, the teacher of the three
         worlds.
      This powerful lord of great fame, taking his cane,
      Dispells the calamities and misfortunes which people in the three
         worlds face—
      Madness, possession and sorcery—all afflictions caused by
         yaksas.

32.   Granted permission from Vesamuni perfectly,
      Taking the blue colored cane perfectly,
      Cutting the stone at Alutnuvara perfectly,
      What power and majesty can compare to Dadimunda!

33.   His retinue is a hoard of *yaksas.*
      He wears pleated Kavani cloth and a blue turban.
      He takes his cane and shouts "Stop!"
      Lord Dadimunda supreme, give me boons.

34.   Like incessant lightning flashes above the earth,
      Like ocean waves dashing against a mountain side,
      How his power and victories are apparent!
      Dadimunda? Give me refuge!

35.   You gained victory over Mara's army
      And there is none comparable to you in the three worlds.
      As you wished, twenty-eight *yaksas* form your retinue.
      Accordingly, "Dadimunda" was given as a name.

36.   Wearing sleek clothes, ornaments and jeweled crown,
       Holding a jewel-encrusted cane as a weapon,
       Sweet floral bodily scent pervades all directions,
       O Dadimunda of Alutnuvara fame!

37.   Within a beautiful flower garden
       Is your mansion made of gold and silver.
       Don't bend to the will of malevolent *yaksas*.
       Dadimunda is lord of this island.

38.   As powerful as the rays of the sun,
       Wearing sleek clothes, ornaments and jeweled crown,
       Nobly attired and jewel-encrusted cane in hand.
       You are indeed Alutnuvara Deviyo!

39.   Soundly crush those ruthless *raksasas*
       And be victorious ten times over!
       The Great Buddha abstained from violent acts—
       You are Devata Bandara, Munda dadi, indeed!

40.   Having considered the Buddha's words,
       Upendra [Visnu] came to this world for Buddhahood.
       He bestowed prosperity and declared:
       "That Dadimunda is Dadimunda indeed!"

41.   By flames you display power and majesty to the world
       Prevailing among the gods as commander-in-chief of *yaksas*.
       You who incurably cure the afflictions of people,
       I worship you, Dadimunda, and receive rewards.

42.   O people! Stand silently then make your pleas;
       See the majestic power of Devata Surindu.
       May his universal rule be sustained.
       Dadimunda Deviyo is indeed fit to rule the *yaksas*.

                          Alutnuvara Devala Saha
                   Dadimunda Bandara Deviyange Vittiya[38]
                (The Vitti of Alutnuvara Devale and Dadimunda Devi)

1.   Dadimunda deviyo, renown and respected,
       Prayed to for prosperity and wealth,

Has power that extends like the sun's rays
Spreading throughout all of Sri Lanka.

2.   With a boon granted by the king of the gods,
       Powerful Dadimunda
       Checked the fiercest *yaksas* and *pisacas*
       By manifesting his valor.

3.   Chief in this world,
       Strong as the sun god,
       Glorious as the moon's rays,
       I worship Dadimunda as supreme.

4.   Your power is displayed to the world,
       Like sun rays it has
       Protected people in need.
       In Sinhala, I will relate what you have done.

5.   In Dambadiva [India] in days of yore,
       There dwelt a certain king
       In the city of Indipat
       In the country of Koravya.

6.   The famous pandit Vidura
       Was his minister,
       Serving the king
       And happily living in that city.

7.   Decreed:
       Whoever can provide the heart of Vidura
       To satisfy Queen Vimala's pregancy cravings
       Will receive the hand of Erandati.[39]

8.   Then *yaksa* Purnaka
       Went to Indipat city
       And in order to get the pundit Vidura
       Told this to the king:

9.   "From many countries, people have come to
          gamble.
       Many kings have lost and gone.

Should I lose too, take this precious gem and my horse."
So came Purnaka the *yaksa*.

10.   He gambled with the king
        Who placed the country at stake.
        The enraged Purnaka scowled at the parasol goddess[40]
        And played out the losing king.

11.   "In exchange for the country I have won, give me the Pandit!
        I will take him to Vimala
        To satiate her craving.
        And give me your daughter in marriage."

12.   The princess was married to Purnaka,
        That *yaksa* of enormous worldly power.
        After a long lapse of time
        She conceived.

13.   Having been given a boon to protect Lanka for five thousand years,
        To protect the world and the Sasana for five thousand years,
        When all *suras* including Isvara had assembled,
        He was conceived in Erandati's womb.

14.   Growing healthily in his mother's womb,
        After ten months, the queen went into labor.
        O wise ones! Dadimunda, the divine prince was born,
        Shining like the rays from a gleaming gem.

15.   As he grew to be sixteen years old,
        He carried a golden walking staff in hand.
        When Vasavarti Mara declared war,
        He remained near the Buddha and said:

16.   "Leave the Buddha alone!
        Other gods have fled,
        But I am stubborn
        And I will fight!

17.   "Not taking another weapon in hand,
        I shall beat you with my golden staff
        And break your body in two!"
        So he exclaimed in verse to Mara.

18. The Buddha surveyed the six heavens,
     The Naga world and the three worlds
     Finding none equal to him.
     "This is a sturdy [dadi] one." And so he was named.

19. Worshipping the Buddha and then departing,
     He met with King Vesamuni,[41]
     Took charge of the *yaksas*
     And met with Upulvan Deviyo.

20. He surveyed the country
     And reached the Maya region
     Where he requested Devata Bandara[42]
     To build a city.

21. Then that king of the gods,
     Being fond of the upcountry,
     According to ancient custom,
     Took a shine to Satara Korale.[43]

22. He went to Kirungandeniya
     To survey that locale
     And took the road
     That led to the Golden Stone Cave.

23. When the milk of the royal cows
     Turned to blood,
     Wise royal counselors
     Declared his magical powers.

24. The king who had dreamt of this
     Then cleared an area of trees and stumps.
     There a golden walking staff was planted
     and a three-storied palace of pure gold built.

25. He built Alutnuwara with
     It's inner shrine of sandal wood,
     A dancing chamber at its center
     And thirty-six halls.

26. "In the descending path to the compound,
     There is a boulder obstructing.

We cannot break it!"
The plaint was made to Devata Surindu.

27. Advised by his ministers, the king examined the situation
     Finding the difficulty of creating a flat ground.
     So he declared: "I shall manifest my power by employing the
          yaksas
     To smash this rock to make the ground flat for the compound.

28. "Make *kavun* [oil cakes] and *kiri bath* [milk rice].
     Do not make these in small pieces.
     Offer these to the *yakkas* so they will not tire.
     May the *yakkas* blast this rock tonight!"

29. Bedecked in sandal and smeared in cow-dung,
     Covered with coconut flowers and tender coconut leaves,
     Attended by coquettish and charming women,
     That place was filled with *kiri bath*.

30. *Yakkas* from Bengal, Gauda , Malla countries,
     Yakkas from Kongani, Java, and Andhra countries,
     Yakkas from Kannadiga, Kaudi and Kaberi countries,
     All *yakkas* were summoned to Sri Lanka.

31. "*Yaksas*, eat whatever you desire.
     Take spears, swords and iron cudgels.
     Take whatever weapon you please
     And smash this stone into tiny pieces."

32. As a strike of thunder in the sky,
     As the earth rumbles in an earth quake,
     As the ground shakes when guns burst,
     They blasted that rock as if playing hand ball.

33. Some cut the with thorney canes,
     Some used sledge hammers to crush the boulder.
     Hoards of *yaksas* worked for that righteous Dadimunda
     Following his instructions without fail.

34. Their languages varied according to their countries.
     The Tamil *yakkas* shouted loudly.

In anger some attacked each other.
The *yakkas* from the Sinhala country made little noise.

35.   Some break the stone just by chanting.
Some show their strength in fighting each other.
Some stay away after being beaten.
Some shoulder the rocks and roll them down.

36.   So they broke the stone to make the ground flat.
They filled the streams and canals in equal measure.
They fixed stones for a breakwater in the tank.
This they informed (to Daedimunda) and worshipped at his feet.

37.   "If we are allowed to stay in this country
We shall perform all work asked of us by this king.
It is verily difficult to meet this god."
Saying so, they fell down at his feet.

38.   These women full of charm are like golden images.
Their lovely chatter is like the golden parrots.
They tie their long hair bedeecked with flowers and eschew wigs.
Oh, how can we leave these lovely women behind?

39.   "O *Yaksas*, you are ignorant of (our) Sinhala charms.
(Our) *mantras* will bind and imprison you.
(Our) *mantras* will punish you severely. You will stand on *yantras*,
Be confined to a smoke-filled chamber, and sprayed by nasal
    unguents.

40.   Do not sicken the women you encounter.
(Leave us) without grief. Get away!
Like a lake empties when the dam is burst,
Each of you get back to your respective countries!

41.   With the blasting of the rock being a display of great power,
Group after group of people from towns and villages came
To see (Dadimunda)
And to worship him intimately.

42.   They clean their teeth, wash their heads and bathe (their bodies).
They wear clean clothes with pleats a plenty.

They offer betel, coconut, rice and gifts,
Worship him and happily leave.

43.   They bring their women possessed by *yaksas,*
       Women with intense burning pain in their intestines [?] [loins?]
       (Women) dance vigorously in the (devale) compound.
       "We must leave!" the *yaksas* plead.

44.   (*Yaksas*) are tied to trees, beaten and broken by canings.
       (*Yaksas*) are made to stand in the sun with stones on their heads.
       "Take a vow, go and do not lie!"
       "We shall go now not looking back on this country!"

45.   All around the compound, silk-cotton poles were erected.
       The *Devol yaksas* were summoned from this (Sinhala) country,
       Raised to silk-cotton poles and tethered.
       "Leave! Out with your curses!" It is decreed.

46.   "If we are not given permission to stay,
       We won't see this god any more.
       In the name of the god they lamented
       And departed to their own countries.

Appendix II:
Liturgies of the Dadimunda Cult

Invocation to God Dadimunda Bandara,
Lord of Alut-nuvara[44]

O God Dadimunda of Alut-nuvara we do humbly proclaim that thou wert
the invincible victor in the wars against the Asuras, against Ravana, and
against Mara, the Evil One. Thou were begotten of Purnaka, the leader of
the hosts of Yakshas, and wert conceived in the womb of Erundati, the
Mother of the Nagas. Thou camest to Devundara, from whence thou didst
make entry into Uggal Alut-nuvara. And there espying a sugar-cane field,
you turned that plantation into stone and thenceforth that place came to
be known as Uggal Alut-nuvara. Thou didst summon the Damila Yakshas
from Vadiga-desa and caused them to break with thy cane the rock that ob-
structed the way. Thou did cause the erection of an upper courtyard and a
lower courtyard, and the construction of of an Uda Vidiya (upper road-

way) and Dik Vidiya (lower roadway), and thou didst cultivate the field
with sixty yalas of paddy. O Thou Lord of Alut-nuvara, who art known by
the name Seneviratne Adikaram to the *Yaksas* and Yakkhinis of Sri Lanka,
thou doest await happily the celebration of a Murutan Feast in thy honour.
O Lord we implore thee, and mayest thou harken to our supplication with
sympathy, and succour us out of thy charity.

And O Lord Natha. . . .

And O God Vibhisana. . . .

And O mighty God Manik Bandara. . . .

And O God Devol. . . .

And we do implore the Four guardian Gods of the Universe, Dhratarastra,
Virudha, Virupaksa and Vaisravana . . . .

And O God siddha Suniyan who presides over the Shrine of Kabalava casting they benign vigil over the entire island of Sri lanka, including its sacred
Kovilas or shrines numbering one lakh and forty thousand; we do implore
the and mayest thou harken to our humble prayer.

And to all these gods we make adoration with our hands clasped in conventional form of salutation, offering sheaves of betel, "panduru," altars of
flowers with betel leaves and offerings of lights, camphor, musk, sandal,
rose-water and garlands of scented flowers. And we humbly supplicate and
pray thus. It is not for the proud to boast of a foreign ship reaching the
shores of this land; not for the prowess of our hands, nor the might of our
forces, but our prayer, O Ye Gods, is concerned with diseases overwhelming the human body. If these maladies afflicting our supplicators are due
to your divine wrath, or do to some evil darkness cast by your attendant
deities or due to some evil charm or nailing of a human effigy, or due to
some malignant curse prounounced in a Devale or over a "punava vessel,"
may ye be pleased to relieve the afflicted supplicators from those malefic
effects; or if such afflictions are due to obsession by some demon or de-
moness or "kumbanda" casting their evil effects on the ailing supplicators
at some waysie corner or two-way junction, or three-way junction, or at
some deserted village, or at a place of undressing and dressing a garment,
or at the bereavement of a relation, for the purpose of drinking human

blood, then O Gods, may you be pleased to command those malignant spirits to accept our "dola offerings" and depart to their dark abodes. Save for the effrects of sunshine falling from above, and the winds blowing from around, O Gods, let not any exctraneous evil befall these supplicators and may ye accept these offerings of floral altars, be pleased to protect and succour them out of your bounty and charity. O Gods! May your fame and glory last for 5,000 years and may you be pleased to shower your blessings of long life on these, thy humble supplicators.

Invocation to Dadimunda
(From *Sarva Deva Kannalavva*)

O Dadimunda Deviyo, king of the gods, replete with power, destined to possess divine wisdom for five thousand years, who after winning the battle with the *asuras*, spread the sound of victory throughout, and who lives in the palace of Alutnuvara not lacking in valour, vigor and power, I humbly ask in salutation, with hands to my head, that you consider my plaint with compassion and fulfil all the hopes of these helpless human beings.

Divine king, born of the womb of Erandati, the *naga* queen married to Purnaka who was commander-in-chief of the *yaksas*, you who went to Devundara and from there to Uggal Alutnuvara where you saw a chena of sugar cane and petrified it, you who brought down those *yaksas* from the Vaduga country and cut the rock with thorney creepers and established the sections of *uda maluva* ("upper terrace"), *palle maluva* ("lower terrace"), *uda vidiya* ("upper street"), *palle vidiya* ("lower street"), *dik vidiya* ("short street"), *kota vidiya* ("short street"), you who prepared and cultivated paddy lands producing sixty cart loads of sown grains, you who came to known as the commander-in-chief and prime minister of the Lanka *yaksas*, you who also established the *murutan* rite and live in prosperity here as Alutnuvara Deviyo, hear our plaint compassionately, fulfill our hopes, remove, dark clouds of afflictions every day, every hour and every minute, and restore us to prosperity. Help us in our quests for merit and share in this merit. May you prevail for five thousand years!

Chief of the *yaksas* in the land of Lanka
Dadimunda, who conquers enemies, open your divine eyes
And remove all perils caused by the planets.
Be my refuge and protect me for a hundred years.

Appendix III:
Cases of Possession and Cure

A Late Nineteenth-Century Description[45]

Pilgrims from every part of the island repair to this temple during all seasons of the year, hoping to get relief from some demon influence, with which they suppose themselves to be afflicted, and which appears to them to be irremovable by any other means. This is especially the case with those persons, most frequently women, who are supposed to be possessed by a demon. Dancing, singing, shouting without cause, trembling and shaking of the limbs, or frequent and prolonged fainting fits are considered the most ordinary symptoms of possession by a demon. Some women, under this imaginary influence, attempt to run away from their homes, often using foul language, and sometimes biting and tearing their hair and flesh. The fit does not generally last more than an hour at a time; sometimes one fit succeeds another at short intervals; sometimes it only comes upon a woman on Wednesdays and Saturdays, or once every three or four months; but always invariably during the performance of any demon ceremony.

On these occasions, temporary relief is obtained by the incantations of the *Kattadiya*; but when it appears that no incantations can effect a permanent cure, the only remaining rememdy is to to *Gala-kepu Dewale*, where the following scene takes place. When the woman is within two or three miles of the temple, the demon influence is suppose to come on her, and she walks in a wild, hurried, desperate manner towards the temple. When in this mood, no one can stop her; if any attempt it, she will tear herself to pieces rather than be stopped. She walks faster and faster, as she comes nearer and nearer to the holy place, until at last, on reaching it, she either creeps into a corner and sits there, crying and trembling, or remains quite speechless and senseless, as if overpowered by extreme fear, until the *Kapuwa* begins the exorcism. Sometimes she walks very quietly to the temple without any apparent influences of the demon on her, and that influence only seems to come upon her once the exorcism begins.

The principal room of the temple is partitioned off by curtains into three divisions, the middle one of which is the *sanctum sanctorum* of the god, as the demon chief is generally called. The *Kapuwa* stands outside the outermost curtain with the woman opposite him. After the offerings of money, betel leaves, and silver ornaments have been devoutly and ceremoniously laid in a sort of small box opposite the *Kapuwa*, he tells the god, as if he was actually sitting beind the curtain at the time, in a loud and conversational tone, and not in the singing oranmental style of invocations made to other gods and demons, that ____ (the woman) has come all the way from ____ (the village) ____ situated in ____ (the korale or district) to this temple for the purpose of comlaining to his godhip of a certain demon or demons, who have been afflicting here for the past ____ years; that she has made certain offerings to the temple, and that she prays most humbly that his godship may be graciously pleased to exorcise the demon, and order him never to molest her again. In this way he makes a long speech, curing which time the woman continues shaking and trembling in the most violent manner, sometimes uttering loud shouts. Presently, the *Kapuwa* puts to her the question: "Wilt thou demon quit this woman instantly, or shall I punish thee for thy impudence?" To this she sometimes replies, still trembling and shaking as before, "yes I will leave her forever;" but more generally she at first refuses; when this happens, the *Kapuwa* graps in hi right hand a good stout cane and beats her mercilessly, repeating at this same time his question and threats. At last, after many blows have been inflicted, the woman replies, "yes, I will leave her this instant;" she then ceases to tremble and shake, and soon recovers her reason, if indeed she had ever lost it. So she and her friends return home congratulating themselves on the happy result of their journey—a result which is invariably the same in the case of every pilgrim to the temple.

We know thirty or forty women who have made this pilgrimage, only two of whom have ever again shown any of the symptons of the return of demon possession. It is said thirty or forty years ago , especially during the time of the Kandyan Kings, four bundles of canes were left at the temple by the *Kapuwa* every evening before he returned home; that during the night loud shouts and cries were heard proceeding from the temple, and that the next morning, instead of bundles of canes, there were only small bits of them found dispersed here and ther in the presmises, as if the canes had been broken in flogging disobedient demons.

Visnu Kalyani[46]

My name is Wijekoon Mudiyanselage Anulawathi Manike. I was born in Paragoda on January 31, 1960. My father is W. M. Muthu Banda and my mother is A. B. Bandara Manike. They are both alive and well.

I'm writing all of this to ease my mind. I remember the events of my life from the time I was 3 years of age. When I was 3 years old, I was sent to my *kiri amma* [grandmother] in Wela Gedera. She was the one who took me to school. I went to Daluwela School when I was five, but by the time I was 10 I had stopped school because there was no one to encourage me though I had the ability to do well. My grandparents, being illiterate, had no idea of the necessity of education. We also had no money to buy the required text books. Not like these days, one had to even buy text books those days. Added to this was the load of household chores that I had to attend every day. This also made it difficult for me to cope with school. It would have been better if my parents had not sent me away from home and had found a way for me to continue with my studies.

By 12, I attained age. From this time, I have lived a wretched life. I had to work in the paddy fields and my *kiri amma* forced me to run so many errands for her. Every day, I had to fetch 80 buckets of water from the well to fill the big tank for my grandfather to bathe. My parents should have never sent me away.

As a result, I am not so much attached to them nor them to me. My brothers and sisters do not love me either. I think it was all my parents' fault. Even today I feel as if I have no one to turn to.

By 15, I was still with my grandparents which resulted in a lot of problems. So I was taken to my other grandparents place under the pretext of looking after them. There, I met another boy who my grandparents were caring for. He was my cousin and older than me. He was more like an elder brother to me, like the one I never had. (I have an elder sister, two younger brothers and two younger sisters.) But he did not treat me like a younger sister. The result is that I ended up having an affair. When my parents came to know about this (when I was 16), they took me back home with them.

Ultimately, I was the one who suffered. I was the one who was left with nothing. I was so unhappy about having dropped out of school, so my father helped me to get into another school where I studied for a while. Again, the problems started. This time my mother wanted me to stop studying to work in the field and to do household chores. So I did, as did my younger brother. About the same time, my father had an argument with my mother and finally left us.

I was getting ever more depressed. Then my cousin started frequenting our house. Since he was my cross cousin, my grandmother tried to negotiate between our two families and announced her consent that we could be married. The horoscopes were matched, arrangements were made when, at the eleventh hour, my father vehemently opposed the marriage. He swore that he would not let us marry even if he was killed. I did not know what to do. My cousin suggested that we elope. I refused because I did not want to cause further scandal. He got angry and left me. I obeyed my parents. My father said he would shoot us if we ran away. My cousin married someone else. I was 17 at the time.

I feel that my grandmother was responsible for the problems I encountered. We were not on good terms after this event. I swore I'd never marry.

But my grandmother was insistent. She said she wanted to see me married somehow before she died. So she arranged a marriage proposal with a family in Aluthgama. I did not like the idea, nor did my father. However, she was insistent that I finally gave in, and within ten days of the proposal, I was married. I thought that this was the result of my bad karma that I had entered into the prison of a forced marriage. I then had to suffer a lot at the hands of my mother-in-law. It seemed as if I had been born to suffer. As I expected, I had no solace in this marriage and I felt like killing myself.

We had no place to stay on our own. We had to live with the in-laws. There was no means of earning an independent living and I was not used to taking odd jobs outside of the house. I became further depressed.

At 18, I had my first child (a daughter). Now that I had become a mother, I decided that I had to put up with everything for the sake of the child. Later on, we put up a small hut and moved into it. My parents never thought to help me in my misery. We lived pathetically, in sheer penury.

However, my husband and I had no problems between us. He worked as a wage laborer. I used to cry at night when I saw how hard he tried to keep us alive then. When I was 21, I had my second daughter, which put even more of a burden on me and my husband. Then things started to go wrong. I had not brought any dowry with me when I got married. Under my in-laws influence, my husband now demanded it and started harassing me. I had treated my grandmother well when she was alive, but she had not left me anything when she died.

When she died, I could not even attend her funeral as I was expecting my third child (a son). I was 23. After his birth, I came down with a very serious illness. This was during the time we had a severe draught. We did not have enough water. We had been taking water from a nearby well. One day when I was going to the well to fetch water, I noticed that the whole place was in a disgusting condition. There was garbage and filth all around the well. I told my husband that I couldn't bring water from that well again, and I suggested that we dig our own, which we did. But when we had finished the digging, I fell seriously ill. I contracted a high fever and had severe stomach pains. I was taken to the Kandy hospital. I recovered. However, something else had happened to me. I was always afraid, frequently in a panic and running around in a frenzy. Then it turned into a kind of madness which lasted for some five years. We performed many *thovils* and *balis* and everything we could think of to get rid of it, to no avail. Finally, I was admitted to the Kurunegala *Ayurvedic* Hospital for mental illness and then was transferred to the University of Peradeniya Hospital. My hands and legs were tied to the bed. My family had to spend everything we had to cure me. My father-in-law tried to help financially. My children suffered as their educations collapsed. We didn't even have a proper place to live. I was locked inside a room and was never allowed to come out. I was given food through a window. At that time my husband was working as a care-taker on a small estate. One day, the body of a dead woman was found on the estate. Everyone accused my husband of the murder. On this day, my grandmother appeared to me in a dream. She told me to make a vow to Alutnuvara, after which we would not have to worry, and that she would not allow any injustices to happen to us. From this day, I began to have *distis* (visions).

At this time. Ruk Devi, in the form of a Buddhist monk from Bogahapitiya gave me the full *varama*. [Three births ago, Ruk Devi was my father. During the time of Dutugemenu, Ruk Devi was also my father and married to my *kiri amma*. They were high caste and high officials for the king. At that time, my husband was a servant. One day he abducted me because I owed him some pay. Now in this life I am paying off the debt. In fact, all these three past lives I have been with this husband. My work at the *devale* helps me pay off this debt.] Ruk Devi told me about the origins of the village we were living in and helped me to get rid of a *yaksa* that was plaguing me due to the *suniyam* practiced by a neighbor. He dedicated me to Alutnuvara who was able to command the *yaksa* to leave. Alutnuvara can take the form of eighteen *avataras,* so he can change me in eighteen different ways which I now have learned to recognize. Ruk Devi stayed here for seven days and told me to go to the local *devale* each day. After that he told me to go straight to Alutnuvara with seven betel leaves, seven candles and oil. I got possessed at Alutnuvara and crawled inside the *devale* on hands and knees writhing like a serpent. I got the *halamba* (bangle)]. This was on the 27th of August, 1988. Only the deity understood my suffering for which reason I was given the vision.

I was told to build a *devale* by Ruk Devi. Before this, the *devale* was inside of our small house for about a year. When I was asked to build the *devale,* I had no money to do so. The deity sent me to beg to find money for this. I had never known or learned to recite *kavi* before, but the deity taught me to sing *virindus* (a form of song accompanied by the small *rabana* drum) at little gatherings and on buses. Then he sent me from house to house like a gypsy singing *virundus.* In this way, I collected some money which I kept safe. Then I built a small *devale.*

When I first started predicting, I charged ten rupees. The deity guides me to make correct predictions. I obtained the *varama* first from Alutnuvara *Deviyo* and then from Kataragama. Then I was given the *varama* by all twelve deities.

[The deities are divided into three categories. The first, including Visnu who is in charge of the planets, do not possess. The *maheshakakya* deities are the second. These are worldly deities like Kataragama, Pattini, Pitiye, Alutnuvara, and Kumara Bandara. These are the deities who were born as *yaksas* but who worshipped the Buddha and the *Buddhadharma*. So they received *varama*s directly from the Buddha. The third category includes Ganga Bandara, Aiyannar, Kande Bandara, and Gala Bandara. These are deities who are in charge of particular areas. They fear the Buddha.]

The deity then instructed me to build a permanent *devale*. He helped me to find the money necessary to build it. He said that there has to be a name for the *devale* and thus asked me to name it *Bagale Kanda Devale*. He also made me change my name from Anulawathie to Visnu Kalyani.

There have been many conspiracies to destroy me and my *varama*. I had a "soul" enemy, a woman named Soma. The whole village fears her big mouth. One day she barged into my *devale* and almost destroyed the pedestal on which the images are set, battered me, and threatened that she would not allow me to continue with the *devale*. The following day when I went to the *kade*, she attacked me and tried to kill me. I went to the police. They were not bothered. She and other villagers started to laugh and make fun of the people who came to my *devale*, saying that they were going to a mad woman to seek solace. Every time I went out I was abused by foul language. They blocked the path to the *devale* by putting huge branches across it to prevent the people from coming.

I couldn't take it anymore. I pleaded to the deity and told him that I would leave this village because it was intolerable. But he told me to be patient and wait, and that things would be better. Later, someone on the path tried to kill me with a sword but I escaped. The deity chased this person from the village. After that, my troubles were less.

The woman who harassed me remained my enemy for eleven years. She and other villagers had planned to stone me and the *devale* but I came to know of this ahead of time through another villager. So one night while I was performing *pujas*, I heard stones showering on the roof. Tiles were broken and I knew very well who was doing this. I went to the police again. Someone had already gone there and had complained that I was inviting all kinds of thieves to the village through the *devale*.

During the time of my madness, I roamed the village and people used to lock themselves up inside if they saw me coming. But after I got the *disti*, they all became jealous of me. Three times the villagers came to throw stones at my *devale*. After the third time, the deity appeared and told me to put up a concrete slab. I was so depressed and frustrated at the things that were happening to me that I tried to commit suicide.

It must have been my bad *karma*. I never hated anyone, but terrible things were always happening to me. My mother-in-law went to the police and complained that I was planning to run away with the drummer in the *devale*. The police came to ask my husband about this and were assured that there was no truth in this.

Eventually the entire village turned against me. Even my husband started hating me and even started to batter me because of the rumor of my involvement with the drummer. The drummer was only a teenager who stayed with us for eight years. Sometimes my husband would shatter and break everything in the house. However, I tolerated him and did not rush into a divorce. Whenever I couldn't take it, I just went back to my parents. . . .

If I am happy, it is whenever I think of the deity; it is when I am able to help the helpless who come to me. I have been doing this now for eleven years. Thanks to the deity, I built a proper house, bought funiture and was able to give my two daughters away in marriage properly. I feel that I no longer owe anything to anyone. I have vowed at Anuradhapura, Kataragama, Munneswaram and Alutnuvara never to break my trust in the deity and to serve him until the day I die.

Sometimes I feel like leaving all of this to become a *sil maniyo*. But the deity has told me to continue with the *devale* until I reach 50. My *varama* will last for twenty years. . . .

If I ever become a *sil maniyo*, I would do it without telling anyone. This is my only solace since I have no one to turn to and I do not expect that my children will take care of me in old age. Even my husband does not bother to understand my feelings, what I suffer, or that I will not stay with him all my life. I will definitely leave and no one will ever know where I am.

Even the Buddha and the deity cannot protect us from *karma*. This is why I suffer . . . sometimes I feel like taking poison and killing myself as the only way out. . . . I don't know what will happen to me when I lose my *varama*. Then the deity will leave me alone. I do not think I can bear it. I hope that he will take me with him. . . .

I'm born to this world because of *karma*.
I've been pushed into this wretched life because of *karma*.

Why live without freedom?
What do I take with me when I die? Only merit and nothing else.

I do good to people before the deity in my *devale*.
I beseech you to help them, to ease their pain and grant them their
   wishes.

Appendix V:
A Liturgic Plaint of the Huniyam Cult

Invocation
(From *Sarva Deva Kannalavva*)[47]

You who live contentedly on the Ajasatta Mountain in the Hiranda forest; you, Oddi Vadiga Siddha Suniyam, lord of the gods; you, who wear a white turban on your head which has thirteen matted locks of hair, thirteen vipers, a face of a *raksasa* on your belly, two cobras around your waist, four *krate nagas* on one shoulder, a *vadiga* sword in the right hand, a fire pot in the left, a bora around your neck and two more cobras draped head to foot; you, who wear a leopard skin and have a blue body; you, who goes about on a blue horse and appear in ten *avataras* such as *yaksa*, *raksa*, or a prince; you, who are renown and truthful; you, who fixes your gaze on one hundred and forty thousand *kovils* and reside in Kabalave; the appeal I make to you should be heard by your divine ear with compassion. Accept these offerings of incense, flowers, and lamps. Cast away all dark dangers of sorcery that afflict these afflicted humans. Throw your benevolent glance upon them. Chase away immediately all *yaksas*, *bhutas*, *pretas*, *kumbhandas* who cling to them wreaking havoc and weakness. Bring them prosperity, remove all illness, and grant them all a long life. May you be victorious!

You who wear the white turban and white cloth, who rides a horse,
O Suniyam *devata* of the ten powers who shines on Sri Lanka with thousands of rays of glory,
Bear with us, accept our merits, remove all malafflictions caused by the planets.
Hear me, grant my wishes, and bring about prosperity!

MINISTER OF DEFENSE?
The Politics of Deification in Contemporary Sri Lanka

*"I am aware that Westernized Sinhalese and many sophisticated nation-
alists treat their folk culture with contempt, and are ashamed to admit it
as a part of their greater culture."*
—Martin Wickramasinghe[1]

Throughout the course of this study, it has become apparent that Hinduism
has made an indelible impact on Sinhala Buddhist religious culture historically. In the process, patterns of Hindu religious culture have been transformed, or better, *conformed* to a different cultural regime rooted in Buddhist
values. While it is evident from a study of the cult of the "Buddhist Visnu" that
the Hindu presence and its transformation is now a historical legacy, it is also
something of a continuously unfolding reality.

In Sri Lanka today, about one in ten people are self-consciously Hindu in religious orientation. This general figure, of course, consists of an overwhelming
percentage of the Sri Lankan Tamil population on the island. In addition to the
ubiquitous Buddhist *viharayas* and *devalayas* throughout Sinhala cultural
areas, large Hindu temples can be found in most good-sized Sri Lankan towns,
inside or outside predominantly Sinhala areas. Many Sri Lankan Tamils live
amidst the Sinhalese, and have done so for centuries. This, of course, is one of
the sources of continuing Hindu influence and its continuing transformation
among the Sinhalas.

In addition, with the late twentieth-century revolution in communication
technologies (especially satellite television), both the religious and secular cultural flow from India is intensifying among the Sinhala urbanized middle and
upper classes, affecting many aspects of Sri Lanka's changing culture—from
cuisine, dress, dance, and music to religion, politics, and business. Thus the
continuing influence of contemporary Indian culture and society on Sri Lanka
is palpable: "Bollywood" Hindi films, the Bajaj family's famous "tuk-tuks"
("three-wheeler" taxis), and the cult of Sai Baba, as immediate examples

among innumerable others, are very much a part of the contemporary Sri Lankan scene.

Sinhala regard for India in general, however, is highly ambivalent.[2] On the one hand, while India is recognized as the birthplace of the Buddha and the dharma, as well as a host of other Indian cultural constructions now valued as part and parcel of Sinhala life, there is also a general and recurrent political suspicion or distrust of India among many Sinhalese people. This suspicion, a type of lightly buffeted antipathy, is rooted deeply in Sinhala historical consciousness, and has been reinvigorated by some recent political events dating primarily to the 1980s when: 1) after the ethnic riots of 1983, Indian Prime Minister Indira Gandhi nurtured, on Indian soil, Tamil militants who were bent on forging by force an independent Tamil state of Eelam in northeast Sri Lanka, and exacting a violent revenge on the Sri Lankan state for its collusion in the terrible 1983 Sinhala pogrom against Tamil peoples; and 2) when Mrs. Gandhi's son, Prime Minister Rajiv Gandhi, prevailed upon then-president of Sri Lanka J. R. Jayawardene in 1987 to allow Indian troops to occupy the north and east of the island to enforce the stipulations of the Indo-Lanka accord.[3]

Sri Lanka's massive political neighbor to the north, therefore, is presently regarded warily. Historical memories of invasions from ancient and medieval times, as well as recollections of the recent interventions, are not far beneath the surface and can be awakened easily.[4] This wariness is disclosed in any number of ways. Coming and going between the two countries has not been made easy because of the dynamics of the recent political climate.[5]

While I have noted above that the continued social and cultural influence of India (and Hinduism) upon the urban Sinhala middle and upper classes is palpable, the physical isolation between the two countries, coupled with the recent sour political dynamic, has simultaneously contributed to a type of psychological distancing process between the vast majority of Sinhalese and their Indian neighbors, especially the non-middle and non-upper classes, which account for at least three-fourths of the Sinhala population.

Related to this process of distancing is the fact that Sinhalas remain very proud of their historical political independence from India, as well as their distinctive cultural character, which derives in part from their sustained heritage of Buddhist culture. When middle-class Sinhalas travel abroad, particularly to Western countries, they are often mistaken for Indians. Try as they may to educate Western acquaintances about their distinctive Sri Lankan identity, the problem is persistent and irritating, much in the same way that Canadians endure the "slur" of sometimes being dubbed Americans, or New Zealanders as Australians, etc. That is, while Sinhalas recognize their close ties to India and affirm proudly their general South Asian identity, they would rather be known first as Sri Lankans, or alternatively, as Buddhists.

There are, at least, two other practical reasons for this current and general ambivalence of regard for India and its culture. The first is due to the fact that almost all Sinhalas, despite the fact that India is but twenty-two miles from Sri Lanka's northwest coast, have never been there. It is a contemporary *terra incognita* for them. The ferry service between Talaimannar (northwest Sri Lanka) and Ramesvaram in Tamilnadu has been closed, due to security concerns, since the mid-1980s, making affordable travel between the two countries impossible for almost all.[6] Consequently, the only convenient mode of transportation between the two countries is by airplane. This alone has guaranteed that, for the past generation, only the middle and upper classes have been able to afford a journey to India and to gain, thereby, a firsthand experience of its culture. That is, the forced physical separation due to strained political relations between the countries has led, concomitantly, to an increasing loss of shared cultural intimacy. So it is one thing for the middle or upper class to take *darsan* of (i.e., absorb) India's culture by satellite TV, but it is quite another matter for most Sinhalas to be shut off from immediate personal exposure.

The second reason follows from the first. Ironically, despite the fact that contemporary Sri Lanka is located adjacent to India and therefore shares many aspects of life more closely with her neighbor to the north than with any other culture, there are now, no doubt due to economic and educational opportunities, many more Sinhalas who have traveled to Middle Eastern countries, the U.K., Australia, and the U.S.A., than to India. In the case of the Middle East, this has contributed to an intensification of fundamentalist Islamic influence in the Sinhala Muslim community.[7] In the case of Western countries, it has meant that some Sinhalas are identifying increasingly with social, political, cultural, religious, and economic values other than those traditionally held in South Asia.[8] (While India itself is also bombarded increasingly with popular aspects of Western culture, Sri Lanka, perhaps because of its size and the fact that it was much more intensively colonized by European powers, seems comparatively much more affected by "globalization.")

Consequently, Sinhala images of India are often more imaginary than based upon personal experience. One such image, for example, consists of India as a struggling and impoverished nation (which I think is derived in part from Western stereotypes generated through media coverage).[9] Another image conjures up India as a kind of giant Tamilnadu perched nearby and ready to pounce, an alien power that needs to be kept at bay if it is not to swallow little Lanka. This latter image was cultivated and exploited politically by a number of self-serving politicos in the late 1980s, including the Janata Vimukti Peramuna (JVP) movement, which sought to mobilize mass Sinhala political opinion to save and "protect the mother land," when the IPKF (Indian Peace Keeping Forces) were present in the north and east as a result of the 1987 Indo-Lanka accord.

There are, without question, many other reasons that can be identified as contributing to the ambivalence that many Sinhalas feel toward India and its culture. As I have indicated at the outset, contemporary political agendas are quick to exploit the antipathetic side of this ambivalence. But as I have alluded to throughout this study, political agendas and economic forces have also been salient in fostering significant religious transformations of Hindu constructs throughout Sri Lanka's history. These accommodations within Sinhala Buddhist culture express the dominance of an empathetic penchant, historically.

In this chapter we will look at the manner in which the practice of Buddhists worshiping Visnu in Sri Lanka has become a contemporary controversy that is part and parcel of the antipathetic side of the ambivalent divide cited here and in the chapter 2, where I noted monastic criticism of laity worshiping the gods in the thirteenth through fifteenth centuries, as well as in the nineteenth.

The issue of worshiping gods within the practice of Buddhism has been rather dramatically brought to the general public's attention by the monastic and charismatic television personality, Venerable Gangodawila Soma Thera. In the late 1990s, Ven. Soma became one of the most popular and highly visible monks in Sri Lanka, frequently making the rounds of Colombo-based television talk shows, hosting his own air time on various TV channels, and consequently becoming an eagerly sought-after source of publishable quotes, including comments critical of the government and the religious establishment, by Colombo newspaper columnists.

Ven. Soma's style of argument and presentation was widely acclaimed and appreciated by his Sinhala Sri Lankan audiences, even more so than Ralph Buultjens, who charmed the country on the radio with his "*dharma*-talks" in the mid- to late 1980s. Ven. Soma was quietly frank, and delightfully so for many. His criticisms of government policies, and the political dynamics occurring between the government and the opposition party, were often witty and pointed, and resonated with a significant segment of the Sinhala population that has grown wary and cynical of its political leadership.. He was a highly recruited public speaker and toured the country, preaching at many town and village temple venues. His rise to prominence was meteoric, and the issue upon which he rode to fame was his biting criticism of Buddhist laity who worship deities, especially those gods of Hindu origins.

His other favorite topic was what he labeled "the Christian insurgency." When he died quite unexpectedly of heart failure on a tour to Russia in December of 2003, where he was to receive an honorary degree, his death sparked a welter of conspiracy theories in the Sri Lankan press and in sections of the *sangha*, theories postulating that Soma had been murdered at the hands of evangelical Christians for his outspoken stance against them.[10] While consideration of this last issue would lead to a fascinating analysis of the now explosive issue within India and Sri Lanka surrounding the ethics of religious conversion, an issue that is giving rise to the formulation of new laws prohibiting the scope of Christian missionary work in these countries, I want to keep the focus of this discussion trained on the question of deity veneration within Buddhist tradition and how it reflects the manner in which politics shapes religious reform.

Ven. Soma made many controversial public statements on various other issues as well. Ascertaining his general political views helps to place into perspective (or, as I would contend, even explain) his criticism of deity veneration. He was continuously outspoken about how Muslims and Tamils do not practice birth control and that, as a result, population demographics will lead to the inevitable domination of these communities over the Sinhalese in Sri Lanka.[10] He campaigned for the return of Buddhist temple lands distributed by the colonial British to Muslims around the sacred site of Dighavapi, in the extreme southeast quadrant of the island, an area that has been for many centuries and remains predominantly Muslim.[12] He chided both the government and the opposition for being bankrupt in relation to the *pancasila* (the five cardinal moral principles of Buddhism), especially the policies of taxing alcohol and cigarettes, which, he argued, gave the government an interest in promoting these vices.[13]

Ven. Soma was extremely well known, respected in many quarters while somewhat feared in others, owing to the nature of his biting criticisms. The People's Alliance government soon came to regard him warily, and eventually restricted his access to Rupavahini, the government-controlled television channel. Newspaper columnists generally critical of the Sri Lankan government's economic and political policies during the past twenty-five years— policies that have brought about rapid social and cultural change—applauded Ven. Soma's positions as a champion of Sinhala Buddhist causes. Here is how one columnist hailed the impact of Soma's now widely disseminated views and rising popularity among Colombo's youth:

> Young people whose heroes are Madonna, Michael Jackson, Maduri Dixit and Sachin Tendulkar started listening to Ven. Soma Thero on TV. Devotees flocked in thousands to the temples to listen to his bana [sermons]. While the gods were displaced in homes, the nation and the religion were energized anew in importance. Every kind of question was asked, 'Is there a creator god? How does science look at these problems? Are the Sinhalese becoming extinct because of population control? Can the Buddhists eliminate terrorism?[14] [brackets mine]

The widely-read author of this column, Kumbakarana (an alias) cites the fact that Ven. Soma appeals to modern, educated, professional and urban people and has suggested pointedly, on the eve of presidential and then parliamentary elections of 1999 and 2000, that these same people should consider uniting behind Ven. Soma in a new political initiative independent of the established Sinhala political parties. As a columnist, Kumbakarana is known for his defense of Sinhala Buddhist interests, and he saw in Ven. Soma a leader with the potential to galvanize them anew.

Soma also seems to have appealed to Sinhala nationalists who believe that the *sangha* should act as guardians of the country. In the 1990s, the chief prelate, or *mahanayaka*, of the Asgiriya chapter of the Siyam Nikaya, who along with his counterpart in Kandy at the Malwatta chapter is one of the most powerful *bhikkhus* in the country, proposed a "supervisory council" to the president to help oversee the political affairs of the country. These two monks of this historically prestigious *nikaya*, which understands its own provenance as the successor to the Mahavihara fraternity of the Anuradhapura and Polonnaruva eras, remain very important political voices in the contemporary context, and they clearly understand their roles as guardians of the country—at least its Buddhist interests. Ven Soma's advice to the Sinhala Buddhist public must be seen against the backdrop of this kind of view, espoused by some Sinhalas with respect to the role of the monastic *sangha*.

Kumbakarana's less communal but nonetheless sympathetic columnist colleague at the *Sunday Times*, Rajpal Abeyanayake, also similarly acclaimed the rising popularity of Ven. Soma:

> Ven. Soma striking at the core weakness of Lankan mentality [worship of the gods] has placed him[self] in a unique position. The man is on the tube. From that vantage point, once he has captured the imagination of the audience, he becomes a superstar and like Michael Jackson he becomes a god.[15] [brackets mine]

Ven. Soma's political views and the manner in which his presence has been hailed are also to be found in a number of statements that he issued directly to the media. Here, for example, is what he said in an interview to the oppositional newspaper, *The Sunday Leader*,[16] about the developing political situation in the spring of 2000—that is, after government forces had lost the *Vanni* (the far north central region of the island) in November 1999, to the Liberation Tigers of Tamil Eelam; Chandrika Kumaratunga had been reelected president in December 1999; the Sri Lankan Army was retreating from an LTTE attack on the northern Jaffna peninsula; and the government and opposition were in the midst of talks regarding a constitutional package that would de-

volve more power to the provincial level, in the hope that it would meet the political aspirations of the moderate segment of the Tamil minority:

> The choice between the UNP [the chief oppositional United National
> Party] and PA [the People's Alliance coalition of parties led by Chandrika
> Kumaratunga and the Sri Lanka Freedom Party, the coalition then holding
> parliamentary power] is like choosing between an insecticide and pesticide
> to commit suicide with. One party won and the other collected more votes
> than usual. In this sense the people approve of both so they have to put up
> with both. [brackets mine]

Here, Ven. Soma seems disappointed that the electorate had not followed his
call to spoil ballots in the December 19, 1999, presidential election contested
chiefly between the People's Alliance candidate Chandrika Kumaratunga[17] and
the United National Party candidate Ranil Wickremesinghe.[18] Soma saw both
leaders and their parties as being too interested in caving in to the demands of
militant Tamils.

> Now the two have got together to discuss how to give Eelam [a separate
> wholly independent Tamil state]. Prabhakaran [the military-political
> leader of the Liberation Tigers of Tamil Eelam or LTTE] will not settle for
> anything less. How can you hold talks with someone who is not willing to
> negotiate? The only option is war under the circumstances. [brackets
> mine]

On this issue, the Sinhala polity, ever fractious, has been divided between a ne-
gotiated or a military strategy for ending the almost twenty years of civil war.
Ven. Soma was among those hard-line Sinhala voices who have seen little hope
in negotiation, arguing that the only realistic solution to the problem of ethnic
strife in Sri Lanka is a total military victory over Prabhakaran and his LTTE
forces. In this, the monastic prelates of the Siyam Nikaya publicly concurred on
many occasions.[19] The phrase "give Eelam" would be especially galling to both
the PA and the UNP, given how much has been sacrificed and lost by both sides
in the conflict since 1983. With specific regard to initiatives aimed at renewing
discussions through third-party mediation provided by Norway, Soma said:

> I do not think we need foreign intervention to solve a national problem.
> Besides, Norway has always supported the LTTE. In the first place they
> don't treat the minority group in their own country properly so I can't see
> how they could help us solve our problem. This is all a ploy to spread their
> religion here.

In the spring of 2000, the Norwegian government agreed to mediate talks between the LTTE and the Sri Lankan government, and those talks, aimed at negotiating an end of the conflict within the a united Sri Lanka, continued into April, 2003, before they were suspended. But Ven. Soma's comment was a good example of the kind of cynicism Norway's initiative generated in Colombo among Sinhala hard-liners, who saw a conspiracy rather than diplomacy in Norway's initiative. A series of venomous articles appeared in various newspapers, attacking the sincerity of the Norwegians. One even went so far as to ridicule Norway's constitutional monarchy as medieval, and another tried to scandalize the public by revealing that the chief Norwegian mediator/facilitator was a "playboy." In the summer of 2003, just before this book was to be published, mass demonstrations by Buddhist monks protesting Norway's involvement in the peace process were being held in Colombo. Ven. Soma continued to articulate suspicions about the Norwegians wanting to spread their religion in Sri Lanka, a view that seemed to reflect his antipathy for any religion other than Buddhism. It also plays to a Sinhala penchant for conspiracy theories. The conclusion to Soma's interview in the *Sunday Observer* contains a rather chilling suggestion that the military might best be called upon to run the affairs of the country.

> The war is now a game on which the kings dine. Everyone is just interested in clinging on to power and are [sic] willing to do whatever it takes to stay there at the cost of the community and country. It should be handled by those who know how to fight and not by ministers or members of parliament who do not know the art of winning a war.

This last parting shot was aimed not directly at President Chandrika Kumaratunga, though it is she who then held the government defense ministry portfolio. Rather, the more pointed target was her uncle,[20] Gen. Anuruddha Ratwatte, who was an outspoken Deputy Minister of Defense—and brother of the *basnayake nilame* of the Maha (Visnu) Devalaya in Kandy—whose advocacy of a military solution and celebration of past temporary successes looked increasingly problematic following the government's massive military setbacks in late 1999 and in the spring of 2000.

Indeed, there are other reasons, including specifically the issue of venerating deities, to explain why Ven. Soma would want to target Gen. Ratwatte. As I pointed out in chapter 5, members of the Ratwatte family (i.e., President Chandrika Kumaratunga's mother's side) are ardent supporters and patrons of the cult of Visnu,[21] the very contested issue which brought Soma to contemporary public fame.

Soma's position in relation to deity veneration, the issue that he rode to prominence through the media, was usually couched first in doctrinal terms in an attempt to establish its veracity among his Buddhist listeners. He talked much about karma. But he also frequently appealed to ethnic sentiments. Until recently, his fundamental position was that "the idea of the gods is totally unacceptable to Buddhism."[22] However, in late October of 1999, he published a column in *The Sunday Times* which indicated a distinction he then wanted to draw between Christian, Hindu, and Muslim conceptions of the gods, on the one hand, and Buddhist conceptions on the other. Here is what he said (with my own critical comments on Soma's statement interspersed):

> Every other religion in the world is founded upon the belief that God created the world, that the world is composed of *nithya* (permanence), *sukha* (happiness) and *athma* (self) and that belief in God will help you.

Soma seems to have confused the tenets of "every other religion in the world" with those of an essentialized and misunderstood Hinduism.

> According to Buddhism, if the gods possess power, that too was gained through *kamma* and can be changed by no being and therefore there was [sic] no powerful being. The concept of gods in Buddhism teaches that there is no all powerful being. Gods are just another group of beings whose bodies are more beautiful, sensitive and radiant than human beings.

Here Ven. Soma rightly asserts the ontological primacy of karmic retribution. This is his major appeal to Buddhist doctrine, and it should be noted that he is, in general, correct in the assertion that the Sinhala Buddhist conception of deities is dependent upon the assumption of cosmic karmic retribution. Since Soma's style of public speaking is *bana* (preaching), he refers often to particular scriptural passages to warrant his assertions. But it is also somewhat apparent that the "Buddhism" Soma refers to is always a decontextualized or simply textual reality. It is an abstract and yet essentialized understanding. It is clear that by "Buddhism," Soma does not have in mind Sinhala Buddhist religious culture as it has developed historically over the past two millennia. Indeed, he frequently laments that "pure Theravada Buddhism" is not practiced by most people in Sri Lanka. Rather, "what the Buddhists in Sri Lanka practice is a mixture, a concoction of Buddhism, Hinduism and Christianity."[23] To return to his desiderata:

> Humans are not governed by gods. However, good comes to people who receive the blessings of the gods. Not everyone can receive the blessings of the gods. To receive blessings a person must have an inherent fear and shame of committing sin. Thus gods love people who refrain from sin and

are humane. There is a scientific basis to this too. Those who avoid com-
mitting sin, and follow the five precepts and other forms of righteousness
and possess compassion and loving kindness [sic], have serene and con-
tented minds. When the mind is happy, the hormones will be activated and
the power of hormones which are linked to the blood cells will cause a special power and purity in the blood. The aura generated by a good person's
body possesses magnetism. The gods who see this virtuous person's be-
havioral patterns are drawn to bless this person. Then as the blessings of
the gods encircle him he becomes a person liked by others, a charismatic
person even non-human.[24]

Ven Soma often appealed to science in his presentations, as he has done here.
His "scientific" appeals conformed to a trajectory of argument regarding the
scientific nature of Buddhism that has been articulated consistently since the
early 19th century. It assisted Soma in appealing to the urbanized and educated
professional constituency of Colombo, who are unable to identify very much
with the residual, traditional religious culture of the rural village. For them,
Soma has styled himself appealingly as the "modern monk" who has emerged
from a tradition that has allowed itself to become immersed in superstition.
Soma's references to science were often regularly combined with his appeals to
the fundamental five ethical precepts (*pancasila*), to rationality, and to logic.[25]
But what passes for his scientific view regarding such topics as hormones,
blood, auras, magnetism, and charisma, etc. reflects, unfortunately, the absence of basic science as one of his own fields of sustained study.

   While Ven. Soma was clearly anti-Christian and clashed in a publicly tele-
vised debate with a leading Muslim member of parliament who was a member
of the government's cabinet, he and his fellow columnists at the *Sunday Times*
saved their most virulent attacks for Hindus and Hinduism. In the following
extract,[26] Ven. Soma is quoted at length by Rajpal Abeyanayake on how he understands the concept of the divine in Hindu tradition. Here, Soma is trying to
distance Hindu from Buddhist understandings and chastises Buddhists for
venerating deities of Hindu origin. The degree of Soma's understanding of the
Hindu worldview is self-evident in what follows.

   Whenever a great son is born to humankind in India, it's a practice of the
   Hindus to call him a reincarnation of Vishnu—it's a tradition. For exam-
   ple, they say Sai Baba is a reincarnation of Vishnu. Now we know that
   Sai Baba is not an *avatharaya* (apparition) [sic!] and that he is a good
   man. . . . The Hindus say that the Buddha is a reincarnation [sic] of
   Vishnu. Are we prepared to accept Buddha as a reincarnation of Vishnu?
   Not me! I know that the Buddha descended from a clan of Indian kings, he

is no apparition or incarnation. Even Sai Baba, if you touch him nicely, would not feel to the touch as an apparition because he is a good man.

The Hindus know their religion is the polar opposite of Buddhist philosophy. The Buddha says the world is the result of causal phenomena, but the Hindus say Brahma created the world. So they don't try to match their religion with ours. In which case, why do Buddhists try to match Buddhism with theirs? . . .

When a Buddhist worships various imaginary gods [Visnu and Skanda] and other [Hindu] gods, he must be suffering from some mental condition! [brackets mine]

Quite apart from Soma's confusion over what is signified by *avatara*, reincarnation, and apparition, the political significance of the final sentence cannot be lost when it is known that the then leader of the opposition in parliament (Ranil Wickremesinghe) and the then current deputy minister of defense (Anuruddha Ratwatte) were both engaged at that very time in high-profile, media-saturated campaigns, in which they had ritually requested the assistance of the gods Visnu and Skanda to help to find a way out of the deteriorating military situation. Smarting perhaps from Ven. Soma's criticisms of the deputy defense minister (which are detailed below), the political columnist, Lucien Rajakarunanayake, of the government newspaper *The Sunday Observer*, actually co-opted Ven. Soma's increasingly popular perspective to the advantage of the government when he wrote this in response to the fact that opposition leader Ranil Wickremesinghe had undertaken a highly publicized pilgrimage with many UNP followers to the town of Kataragama to invoke the blessings of Kataragama Deviyo (a.k.a. Murugan, or Skanda) to help find an end to the ethnic conflict:

It seems time for all those individuals, secular and religious organizations, members of the Maha Sangha, sections of the media, political parties, and all others who were opposed to the Indo-Lanka Accord, the arrival and stay of the IPKF here, and the 13th amendment, to make a collective apology to India for the manner in which our closest neighbour who came to assist us on the last occasion was treated.

This is a sarcastic reference to the fact that Sri Lanka asked for India's military assistance in the spring of 2000 as the government's situation on the northern Jaffna peninsula worsened, after Sri Lankans had reacted so negatively to the previous Indian military presence on the northeast of the island between 1987 and 1993—an occupation which ended only when then-President Premadasa (UNP) actually colluded with the LTTE before finally asking the Indians to leave. Rajakarunanayake continues:

One does not know what Ven. Gangodawila Soma Thera will have to say about the UNP leader making a special political pilgrimage to Kataragama, to plead with the deity there and all other deities to save the country at this hour of crisis. With all his opposition to the worship of deities, we have not heard a word from him about the UNP's pleadings at Kataragama. Whatever Ven. Gangodawila Soma Thera, who is on BBC record saying "We must fight!" has to say about the UNP seeking the aid of Kataragama to fight Prabhakaran, it would appear that the first apology for the previous ugly treatment of India should come from the UNP and Mr. Ranil Wickremesinghe. Breaking all the coconuts possible at Kataragama, and offering the richest "pooja vattiya" cannot make up for his silence at the time Premadasa ordered the IPKF out, and his continued silence about that shamed act even today. It is difficult to see the UNP genuinely seeking the blessings of the Kataragama deity for the success of Sri Lanka in the current war, because such success would mean even further defeat for the UNP. However, to give the devil its due let's believe that's what they have done. But do they really think that Skanda, whose shrine Kataragama is, would listen much to the pleadings of the UNP that carried out so many attacks on Tamil Hindus in Sri Lanka during its 17 years in power? Would not Skanda lend at least a little more ear if the pleas for assistance come from Velupillai Prabhakaran, not because Skanda likes terror, but because the Tiger leader at least comes from the people who were barbecued alive, and had their homes and shops torched by the thugs of the UNP.[27]

The Sunday Observer, at the time, was a veritable mouthpiece for president Chandrika Kumaratnga's PA government, and this article is ripe for much discussion, but here I would simply note how Ven. Soma, a noted critic of the government, is here co-opted by the very government he criticizes. Note also that the author uses the Sanskrit "Skanda," rather than the more familiar Sinhala reference to "Kataragama Deviyo," to indicate the Indian origins of the god, though the Tamil "Murugan" would have been more appropriate for the point that the columnist is making. That is, just as Ven. Soma might say, Rajakarunanayake is pointing out that this god is of Hindu origins and, as such, is more likely to show favor for the Tamil community in their times of suffering. The columnist is more generally asking as well: Why is the UNP doing falling over itself worshiping a Hindu deity, particularly in light of its sorry history of relations with India? The barbed reference to Soma's silence is elicited by the fact that the popular monk has been so vocally critical of how PA government ministers participated in and supported the cult of the gods, particularly Visnu.

In early June of 1999, *The Sunday Times* (the independent newspaper that Soma wrote a column for, and the one containing the columns written by

Abeyanayake and Kumbhakarana), in one of its "special assignments," published a highly polemical exposé[28] of plans to build a multireligious complex, including a Visnu temple, just north of Colombo in Muthurajawela. Adversarial in strategy, style, and substance, the exposé identified the deputy minister of defense, the minister of Buddha Sasana, and the president, among others, as backing the project, which would require Rs. 600,000,000 ($8,000,000) to complete.

> Grasping at straws and blaming external factors for the war that is raging in Sri Lanka, the two ministers have made the extraordinary request for funds on the advice of some South Indian priests who say that a Vishnu temple in Tiruchchirapalli has malefic effects on Sri Lanka. But religious elders and businessmen who have been approached for funds feel the scheme is based on some religious belief or some attempt to blame the whole ethnic crisis on supernatural forces instead of facing reality and taking responsibility . . . This temple, according to these priests, is facing Sri Lanka, thus casting evil effects. They believe it is largely responsible for the turmoil in the country.

The article goes on to state that a large Visnu image will be sea-freighted to Sri Lanka from South India at great expense, and that the entire project is "shrouded in secrecy." Much space is then given to solicited reactions from such figures as the Roman Catholic bishop of Mannar, well-known Buddhist prelates and laymen in Colombo, the president of the Hindu Cultural Council, etc., all of whom express their "shock and amazement" at how two cabinet ministers could be heading a project based on "mere superstition."

"From the sublime to the ridiculous," "waste of brick and mortar," and "total fabrication" are but a few of the phrases attributed to the reactions of these well-known religious leaders. Two weeks later, *The Sunday Times* columnist Rajpal Abeyanayake added Ven. Soma's reaction:

> It is imbecilic to construct a Hindu Kovil to deflect a curse on this island bestowed on it by Lord Vishnu.[29]

In the wake of this publication, I held more conversations with Mr. Denis Ratwatte, the *basnayake nilame* of the Maha (Visnu) Devalaya in Kandy, in which we discussed at length the contents of this particular story. The *basnayaka nilame*, I then learned, was a trustee on the committee formed to oversee the funding and building of the multireligious complex in question. As I noted in chapter 5, he is also the brother of the then deputy minister of defense, and an uncle of President Chandrika Kumaratunga.

The *basnayaka nilame* had been quoted in the *Sunday Times* exposé as say-ing, "It was not Lord Vishnu who was looking upon Sri Lanka unfavorably, but his benevolent view was being blocked by a building 35' above sea level." He complained that even though he had tried to explain that the matter was a prob-lem of *darsan* and not sorcery, the writer of the article kept referring to curses and malefics instead, and that this is how the rationale for the project had been presented (in what he regarded as an extremely distorted fashion) to the reli-gious and lay officials who had reacted so negatively to the idea, as quoted in the exposé. Mr. Ratwatte explained that M. G. Ramachandran, a Tamil movie star turned politician, whose native home was Kandy, who was a key early supporter in arming the LTTE, as well as, at the time (1983), the chief minister of Tamil-nadu, had built a *gopuram* at the famous Tirupati temple in Andhra Pradesh (not the Sri Rangam temple in Trichy noted within the exposé) in front of Visnu's gaze. The obstruction of Visnu's gaze had corresponded with the terri-ble riots of July 1983, and Tirupati priests had expressed the view to his brother, the deputy defense minister, that the loss of Visnu's benevolent gaze may be why Sri Lanka's experience since 1983 had been so problematic.[30]

Mr. Ratwatte explained that, although building the Visnu temple had been the original plan, he and his fellow trustees had decided that what the country needed at this time was a broad vision, and so they planned to build a church, and a mosque, as well as Buddhist and Hindu temples, in a complex that could come to symbolize the multireligious character of Sri Lanka. He added that "the story had blown the Visnu aspect way out of proportion."[31]

Finally, he noted with frustration that the cost of the project had been esti-mated at Rs, 60,000,000 ($800,000) and not Rs. 600,000,000 ($8,000,000), as sensationally reported by the *Sunday Times*. He was particularly upset that such a well-intentioned plan could be so misconstrued for blatantly political reasons. To him, this was politics at its worse intruding into religious affairs.

But perhaps the most vituperative attack upon those who worship the gods, and Visnu in particular, occurred two months later, again in the *Sunday Times,* in a column by Soma's ardent well-wisher and colleague, Kumbakarana. The column was entitled: "Sanctioned by Religion, Killing Goes On."[32] The core paragraph recorded below again speaks for itself and requires little commen-tary for the reader to understand its political significance and its distortions of Hindu thought:

According to a dialogue between Krishna (Vishnu) and Arjuna, the taking of one's life and that of another is endorsed by religious belief. Under the Hindu concept of an unchanging soul transmigrating from life to life, death does not end life, and life does not end with death. Krishna tells Arjuna that there is no sin in taking one's own life. So suicide and killing others is justified by religion. Sections of the Defense authorities who are falling over each other to build Hindu kovils would do well to realize the newest sustenance of the Tiger killers is the Hindu atman concept. With great foresight, the LTTE is publicizing a video which shows Black Tigers performing Vishnu pujas before their departure to kill their targets and themselves. The Christian missionaries supporting the LTTE and propagating their religion will soon meet the reincarnation of Vishnu, in the Wanni and the East.

Unfortunately, this reading of the *Bhagavad Gita* reflects the depths of confusion and hostility that can be evoked when religious ideas are interpreted through the passions of ethnic sentiments, and within the context of an emotionally wrenching civil war. Here, unfortunately, it becomes quite clear how politics can transform religious understanding.

With this brief attempt to indicate something of the substance of the contemporary Sri Lankan controversy about Buddhists worshiping the gods, and Visnu in particular, the problem would appear to be a classic doctrinal debate between those claiming purity in adherence to the Buddha's "original" teachings and those who have assimilated popular aspects of South Asian religious culture. But, as I have tried to demonstrate, abstract analyses, without benefit of historical analysis, can be incomplete in the attempt to ascertain what is driving the issue at hand.

The contemporary controversy about Buddhists worshiping gods of Hindu origins is driven by an ethos of exclusivity among some sections of the Sinhala Buddhist community, which have been made to believe their future is under siege. In fact, the deep-rooted concern here is really less with Buddhist doctrine than it is with political and economic well-being. That is, the catalyst for the current controversy is based on fears, real or not, experienced by a largely urban, educated, middle-class, and "modern" segment of the Sinhala Buddhist community, who are feeling uncertain about the future: precisely those who are ardent supporters and share the religio-political views of Ven. Soma.[33]

Nalin de Silva is a good example of a Sinhala Buddhist layman who represents this segment of the Sinhala populace. He is a former mathematics professor turned political gadfly, and an effective spokesman for the *jathika cintanya*—an ideological movement that seeks to preserve and promote "people's thinking" or "indigenous thinking" in Sri Lanka. *Jathika cintanya* is a school of thought often allied with the Sinhala nationalists, insofar as it shares the types of fears for the future of Sinhala culture I have noted above and seeks to sustain a cultural survival apart from the globalization process.

Nalin de Silva is intelligent, articulate, and precisely the type of Sinhala Buddhist layman who envisages a special place for Buddhist monks in the political life of the country. He is unabashedly critical of the Christian presence in Sri

Lanka, especially of the Christian clergy who seek a peacemaking role between the LTTE and the government. He also harbors resentments towards the "intellectual NGO types." He responds sharply to criticism that Buddhist monks are urging war while Christian priests are urging peace.

> The impression given by [some] people . . . is that the Bishops of the Catholic Church as well as the Church of Ceylon are for peace and their activities are purely religious, while the Maha Sangha act with political intentions. Nobody denies that when the Maha Sangha want[s] the unitary state to be preserved and the significance of the Sinhala Buddhist culture [to] be accepted [that] they are taking a political stand. That has been the tradition in this country so far as the Bhikkhus are concerned and their advice has been accepted in general except under the colonial rule when the Bishops had access to the European governors.[34]

Nalin de Silva's point about the important political role of the *sangha*, that Sinhala nationalists understand this role as a historical and entitled legacy, is even more pointedly expressed in relation to the dynamics of the current ethnic conflict:

> If the Tamils are prepared to accept the significance of the Sinhala Buddhist culture symbolized by the Maha Sangha then the problem is solved. However, Tamil racists have stolen the key from the Maha Sangha by refusing to accept that significance.[35]

Nalin de Silva's perspective on the rightful place of Buddhist monks, as symbols of Sinhala Buddhist culture, to represent themselves politically in the national dynamic, is part of an ancient and ongoing conversation within Buddhist tradition about what constitutes the true vocation of the Buddhist monk. On the one hand, there are those within the *sangha* and the laity who have believed that ideals of Buddhist monasticism and monastic renunciation are compromised by overt political involvement. Others have contended that it is the responsibility of the monk to "wander for the welfare of the many"; insofar as "the welfare of the many" includes their political well-being, *bhikkhus* should be primarily concerned with this aspect of social life.[36]

    In the conclusion to his recent study of Sinhala Buddhist monasticism and its political activism in twentieth-century Sri Lanka, H. L. Seneviratne has provided some insights that help to put into perspective why it is the case that some Buddhist monks, such as Ven. Soma, and others who would support him, would oppose the practice of deity veneration among the laity. Seneviratne's book, on the whole, is a devastating albeit controversial critique of the role of the political monk in modern Sri Lanka. It is also a vehement lamentation by a deeply concerned Buddhist layman. In the following passage, he seems to have anticipated Nalin de Silva's comments (cited above):

> Related to the monkhood's lack of broad social and human concern is the warmongering propaganda of the elite monks and the theory that a military victory alone would solve Sri Lanka's ethnic conflict when it is perfectly clear that, had the monkhood taken a firm stand for peace, the question would have been easily solved. The warlike stand and its obverse, the opposition to devolution, in addition to illustrating the lack of humanism and compassion, is telling of the ignorance of the monkhood of its own social organization, which is one of the most extreme decentralizations imaginable. [1999:324]

While the sardonic title (*The Work of Kings*) and several important passages in Seneviratne's book indicate that his signature analysis identifies a modern proclivity on the part of contemporary political monks in Sri Lanka to assume the role of disestablished Buddhist kingship, he also introduces the issue of "guardian deities" to his concluding discussion. While considering the impoverished state of monastic scholasticism, the *sangha*'s moral poverty, and the worldliness of the politically militant Buddhist monk, he adds:

> The most frequent label these monks now give themselves is that they are the "guardian deities" (*muradevatavo*) of the nation, a self-description of the Brahmanic attempt to call themselves gods on earth. However, no one except a religious purist can quarrel with monks for determining what they want to do with themselves. If that task is playing guardian deity to the nation, the monks are entitled to do so, but the nation in turn is entitled to expect that they are properly equipped to do so. For this they must acquire a minimum of basic knowledge in the areas of government, the economy, planning, nationhood, urbanism, public health, the arts, the sciences, ethnicity, human rights, rule of law, procedural justice, to name a few. It is one of the stark facts of the contemporary elite monastic scene in Sri Lanka that we do not have a single monk who would fit the basic requirements to qualify as an urbane, cosmopolitan intellectual who alone would be qualified to play the role of "guardian deity." [339]

Decrying the deteriorated state of the *sangha* "especially in the post-1977, post-'open economy' era," Seneviratne continues:

It is then no surprise that merit making rituals enjoy a supreme place in Sri Lankan Buddhism, and monks are still most valued for their ritual role rather than for any social service they allegedly render, or as some divinized force that guards and guides the nation as suggested in their self-representation as guardian deities. [348]

I have quoted from Seneviratne's book enough to give some sense of why some, like Ven Soma, insist on taking such a hard stand against the lay worship of deities. On the one hand, their views are politically inspired within the context of the current ethnic conflict. They appeal to the age-old and yet current antipathetic dimension of ambivalence for things Hindu among Sinhala Buddhists. Visnu is understood as being Hindu in this particular context. But Seneviratne's discussion also provides another reason: Not only do some of these politically inspired monks wish to articulate a "new Buddhism in Sri Lanka" that is the "work of kings," but they also wish to assume the role of "guardian deities." That being the case, they want to play the role traditionally that was historically ascribed to Upulvan in the medieval period of history, and later to the "Buddhist Visnu." They wish to displace the literal conception of "guardian deities" by their own symbolic self-references as such.

This view, embraced by this section of the Sinhala Buddhist community is not, however, necessarily indicative of the community's views in general. Over several months of fieldwork at Visnu *devalayas* in Sri Lanka, collecting materials for the previous chapters of this book, I directly asked scores of *kapuralas* and lay devotees for their reactions to Ven. Soma's views regarding the worship of gods, especially Visnu, in Buddhism. As I have noted previously, I realized that what I was doing might be compared to asking church-going Catholics outside of the Vatican whether or not they believed in the authority of the Pope. But I asked anyway, just to get a sense of what might be a Buddhist cultural response to Soma's politically inspired Buddhist critique, or to see if my interviewees were aware of the class and ethnic factors driving this doctrinal aspect of his critique.

Responses to Ven. Soma's position on venerating Visnu were uniformly very personal in character and varied from the polite to the agitated. While most said that worshiping the gods was a matter of personal religious discretion, part of the heritage of Sinhala religious culture, or that gods, especially Visnu, protected the Buddhist *sasana*, the more extreme responses included charges that Ven. Soma was a liar, and actually a Catholic sent to destroy Buddhism, or was not aware of the damage he was doing to Buddhism. These last were among the more visceral reactions.

But perhaps the most thoughtful response was given by a *kapurala* at the Maha (Visnu) Devalaya in Kandy, who said this to me: "Ven. Soma doesn't have a wife. He doesn't have children. So he doesn't have family. He doesn't have property to look after, doesn't need to worry about his food and seems to be in good health. If Ven. Soma had any of these problems, like the people who come to this *devalaya*, he would also come to worship Visnu Deviyo and to seek his help."

While I have intimated that the recent attack on the practice of Buddhists worshiping the gods has been driven by an ethos of exclusivity bred by ethnic and class consciousness, the *kapurala*'s response yielded an existential indication of why Sinhala Buddhists will probably continue to worship the gods. They don't seem to do it consciously for ethnic or politico-economic reasons, though these may be the social and historical forces that led to the introduction of these practices. And these forces seem to lie behind the real reasons that they are being asked to stop worshiping the gods by Ven. Soma and his followers. Rather, most of them do it to express some hope that the current problems they encounter might be recognized by *someone*, and that some compassionate force in the cosmos will respond to their entreaties for help.

Ven. Soma persuasively argues that people ought to solve their own problems rather laying them at the altar of deities. What he may have overlooked, and what perhaps his monastic ancestors overlooked too, is that some people may not be in a position to solve their problems by themselves in rational, disciplined, and "scientific" ways. They haven't had access to resources that might engender such a method for solving or perceiving the nature of their problems. They recognize that they need some extraordinary kind of help in their current plights, and so they appeal to the deities for their miraculous assistance.

Here are three examples of these appeals for divine protection and assistance that indicate why the deities continue to have appeal among Sinhala Buddhists.

It is not uncommon to see young families, especially mothers with infants, ask the *kapurala* at Visnu *devalayas* for the deity's *santiya* ("general well-being," "blessing," "peace") for their children. Young children, especially infants, are not yet equipped to handle whatever life might be ready to serve up to them. Moreover, it is customary in Sinhala Buddhist culture to bring a newborn infant to receive the blessings of the deities at the age of three months. Worshiping the gods on these occasions, then, is a recognition that life is full of unpredictable occasions, that in some circumstances, at least until children become adults, all can use some help and protection in finding their way. Asking for Visnu's protection does not imply that parents will cease to look after their children's well-being as best as they know how. Rather, worshiping provides parents with a psychological reassurance, or a feeling that as parents they have done whatever they can for their children, including asking for divine protection. Upulvan sprinkled *pirit* water on Vijaya's newly arrived men. Mothers ask Visnu to protect their children and look after their well-being in life.

The second example may be more to the point. Many people making *pujas* in *devalayas* are seeking justice of one sort or another. It may be that neighbors are stealing coconuts, someone is practicing sorcery against them, or that a more powerful landowner has filed a court case against them. Anyone living in Sri Lanka for the past generation knows that the police, the politicians, the courts, and businessmen can often act in capricious ways. Justice can be elusive, and no amount of calculated self-effort or rationalized methodology is going to change that.[37]

Visnu is particularly relevant in this type of context. Unlike other deities who exist on the lower rungs of the pantheon's hierarchy, Visnu is never invoked to undertake any actions that might be regarded as unethical. His Buddhistic bodhisatva status is not congruent with such behavior, and his mythic profile is entirely benign. He can only be petitioned to perform actions that are intrinsically good (healing the sick, protecting against planetary imbalances, etc.) and ethically just. What he represents to those who call for his intervention is a hope for the existence of benign, responsive, and protective justice in this world. Without this hope, or without deities who embody these hopes, existence can give way to dejection

Finally, a third example is a direct answer to Ven. Soma's campaign. Over months of fieldwork at Visnu *devalayas* in up-country Sri Lanka, many devotees made *pujas* to the deities because their sons, brothers, and husbands were currently serving in the government's security forces, fighting the civil war with the LTTE. They were frightened and concerned for the safety of their loved ones, and they came to *devalayas* for the obvious reason that they were seeking the protection of the deities, especially Visnu, the "minister of defense." Most of these devotees were not urban, educated, and professional, because almost all the young men serving in Sri Lanka's armed forces are from the rural areas of the country. The matter is put bluntly by some who say that "village boys are fighting Colombo's war." Once this is understood, it can then be seen that not only did Ven. Soma and his supporters want villagers to fight their war, but they also wanted to relieve them of one source of their family's hopes that they would survive the carnage: that is, *santiya*, the protective blessings of the gods, the divine force which the Buddhist Visnu is best known for embodying and imparting.

Conclusion

During the final days of my two years of field research in Sri Lanka, I returned to the southern tip of the island, to Devinuvara, to observe the Visnu *devalaya*'s annual *perahara*, the ritual descendant of what may have been the first *perahara* held for a *deva* in Sri Lanka. I had spent only a few days in Devinuvara during the first spring of my fieldwork in order to do an initial survey of the religio-cultural context of the its famous Visnu *devalaya*. At that time, I had engaged in some interesting conversations with the *kapuralas* at the many subsidiary *devalayas*[1] in the city that has now become a full-scale pilgrimage site. They had told me about how cultic life had changed in the past thirty to forty years, since the days before the "open economy" and the ethnic conflict. In short, they had said that there were far fewer traditional rites (*bali, tovil,* etc.) in demand these days, but the *devalaya* (meaning the Visnu *devalaya* and the adjacent *viharayâ*) "had become a big business."

I had also collected two interesting *yatikas* from Visnu *kapuralas* at that time.[2] Further, I had thought that a consideration of the Devinuvara Visnu *devalaya*'s *perahara* would make for a fitting conclusion to my fieldwork experiences, owing in part to the fact that Devinuvara had been so historically germane to the origins of cult of the "Buddhist Visnu," having been probably the site where the myth of the sandalwood image had been spawned, and where Upulvan had risen to fame, from the thirteenth through sixteenth centuries. In addition, Obeyesekere had once written that Devinuvara was now regarded as the chief cultic seat for Visnu on the island.[3]

Moreover, I also had thought that observing the ritual performances of the Devinuvara *perahara* might be especially relevant for consideration in the concluding remarks of this study, since there is some reason to believe that the very first *perahara*, at least in the basic ritual form in which it has come down to us, was celebrated here under the auspices of Parakramabahu II in the thirteenth century. And finally, I was very much aware that virtually all of my fieldwork observations were drawn from the *udarata,* the Kandyan up-country cultural region, and I wanted to at least gain some familiarity with the cult of Visnu in the Sinhala low country, especially since many people had also told me about the great wealth and popularity of Kande Vihara in Alutgama, where a famous Visnu *devalaya* is also to be found. So my plan had been to write about Devinuvara and Alutgama in the first part of my conclusion, as an initial foray into the conditions of the popular cult of Visnu in contemporary "low country" Sri Lanka. I have done that, but not with the kinds of results that I had expected or anticipated at the outset.

DEVINUVARA

The secretary of the Devinuvara Visnu *devalaya*, Mr. P. S. Hewage, and the *basnayaka nilame*, Mr. Bandula Wijesinghe, a prominent Colombo lawyer from nearby Beliatta, proudly informed me that the *devalaya* was now (in 2001) celebrating its 745th annual *asala perahara*. Since my previous studies had led me to understand the significance of the *asala perahara* in Kandy as a remarkably symbolic procession that, in addition to its archaic function as a rainmaking rite and a symbolic military capture of the capital city, continues to articulate the hierarchies of the social structure and the divine pantheon of the socio-cosmos that constitutes the traditional Kandyan "world view," I eagerly anticipated the daily *perahara* performances in Devinuvara in hopes of coming to a nuanced understanding of this "southern Sri Lankan", Sinhala cultural display. On each of the first three days of my observance, I was struck by significant differences between the Devinuvara *perahara* and the Kandyan.

The *asala perahara* in Kandy follows a regimen in which members of all castes in traditional Kandyan Sinhala society are represented. At Devinuvara, it is said that caste is not a criteria for inclusion in the processions. The only prerequisite, according to the chief *kapurala* and the *basnayaka nilame*, is that participants are Buddhists and that they come from the Southern Province of the country. Both *basnayake nilame* and the chief *kapurala* were keen to emphasize that "their" *perahara* was only an expression of "southern Sri Lankan culture." They proudly noted that only with the exception of representatives from four *karava* ("fisher folk") families indigenous to Devinuvara (see fig. 9.1), who are said to have participated in every *perahara* since its inception, caste was not the slightest consideration in this *perahara*. They were quite intent on juxtaposing "their" *perahara* with Kandy's in this regard.

In Kandy, each of the main four *devalayas* of the four great "warrant deities" (Natha, Visnu, Pattini, and Kataragama), together with *basnayaka nilame*s and *kapuralas* representing subsidiary *devalayas* throughout the Kandyan region that are affiliated with these four *devalayas*, form the fundamental ritual contingents of the processions, along with the contingent of ritual performers representing the Dalada Maligava ("Temple of the Tooth-Relic"). The order of their appearances in the *perahara* symbolizes their rank within the social and

FIGURE 9.1 The four *karava* (fisher-folk caste) leading the procession of the Devinuvara *perahara* in 2001

cosmic hierarchy. The sheer numbers of elephants in the Kandy processions, usually from seventy to ninety, creates an ambience of great strength and power.

In Devinuvara, there are no such contingents representing the other minor *devalayas* within the Devinuvara complex, a fact that would seem to correspond to the egalitarian ethos of the rite that the *basnayake nilame* and *kapurala* had inferred. In Kandy, most of the participants, including the dancing troupes and drummers, are seasoned and even famous ritual specialists, many of whom are also now advancing in age. In Devinuvara, during all but the final day of the *perahara*, most of the dancers are young, school-aged children (see figs. 9.2–9.5); women (see fig. 9.6) are allowed to participate as drummers (impossible in Kandy); and there is no traditional order assigned to the various contingents, except for the *basnayaka nilame* and the head *kapurala*, who, along with their ritual attendants, form the concluding segments of the procession (see figs. 9.7–9.8). In addition, costumed participants representing various types of *yaksas*, including the *sanni yaksas* and others (see figs. 9.9–9.14)—representations never found in Kandy—play a very conspicuous and even dominant role. They lend a comedic presence to the processions.

Unlike the Kandy processions that circumambulate the downtown area of the old capital city, the Devinuvara procession proceeds from the *devalaya* proper down a narrow lane to a *sinhasana* ("Lion-throne"), much in the same

FIGURE 9.2 School children participating in the Devinuvara *perahara*, 2001

manner as village *peraharas* proceed in the up-country Kandyan culture area.[4] The *sinhasana*, which was constructed in the 1950s when the *devalaya* was last rebuilt, is regarded locally as the site where the sandalwood image of Visnu, or Upulvan, first arrived on Lanka's shores.

In light of these observations, the question was: Aside from the egalitarianism that the *basnayaka nilame* and other temple officials wanted me to see, what are the various and specific meanings of this "southern Sri Lankan" cultural display? How can this *perahara* be read as "an expression of southern Sri Lankan" culture?

On the day before the final *perahara*, I again interviewed both the chief *kapurala* and *basnayaka nilame* of the Devinuvara Visnu Devalaya at some length, in an effort to answer this basic question. I was aware that the royally endowed *rajakariya* services for the *devalaya* had been disrupted by the Por-

FIGURE 9.3 School children participating in the Devinuvara
perahara, 2001

tuguese destruction and desecration in the sixteenth century. In addition to
the obvious consequences of that locally infamous occasion, I also wanted to
know about other basic matters pertaining to the continuing sustainability of
the *devalaya* and its ritual. I learned that the *kapurala* understood that the *devalaya* had been restored in 1718 C.E., and that his family, *karava* (fisher folk),
had served the *devalaya* ritually since that time. Like the Kandyan *goyigama kapuralas*, he too observed elaborate prohibitions to protect himself from *kili.*
He also reported that instances of *disti* were very much on the rise, and that the
requests that devotees bring to Visnu were increasingly mundane or even
strictly commercial in nature. He also said that before the ethnic conflict arose
in the early 1980s, a significant number of Tamil devotees from south India or
the northern Jaffna peninsula of the island would frequent the *devalaya*, but
they had now stopped visiting almost completely.

FIGURE 9.4 School children participating in the Devinuvara *perahara*, 2001

FIGURE 9.5 School children participating in the Devinuvara *perahara*, 2001

FIGURE 9.6 Female drummer participating in the Devinuvara
perahara, 2001

He acknowledged that Visnu was understood quite differently in the Hindu
tradition as a creator deity with many avatars, but that he and the people of
Devinuvara regarded Visnu (rather than Natha, as held in Kandy and elsewhere), as the next Buddha-in-the-making. While the Devinuvara *devalaya*
was his chief abode, Visnu, he said, was also the chief protector of Sri Mahabodhi in Anuradhapura and the Dalada Maligava in Kandy. He said that the
nearby *galge* (see fig. 3.2) was not the site of the original Upulvan *devalaya,* as
Paranavitana had argued, but was instead the place where Rama had killed Ravana; and so it was simply a memorial to Ravana as a Lankan hero of the past.
He said he had no doubt that his son would carry on the family legacy of tending ritually to the needs of the *devalaya.* And finally, he requested that I send
him a copy of my book, when finished.

FIGURE 9.7 The *basnayaka nilame* of the Devinuvara Visnu *devalaya* participating in *perahara*, 2001

FIGURE 9.8 The chief *kapurala* of the Devinuvara Visnu *devalaya* participating in the *perahara*, 2001

FIGURE 9.9 Costumed *yaksa* participating in the Devinuvara
perahara, 2001

From the *basnayaka nilame*, I learned that he had been elected to a five-year
term by 650 *grama sevakas* (village headmen) and, as such, had to canvass or
campaign widely and intensively in order to win enough votes for election
within a competitive and politically charged atmosphere. This seemed to be
one of the reasons for his descriptions of the Devinuvara *perahara* being populist in nature. He consistently stressed the southern provenance of the *devalaya*'s *perahara*, and somewhat defensively argued, "My *perahara* represented
southern Sinhala Buddhist interests," as opposed to the up-country orientation of Kandy's and that it was, indeed, a traditional expression of his
provinces' social and cultural values.

He related that it had cost some Rs. 1.8 million (@$20,000) to stage the *pera-
hara* this year, that he was personally responsible for raising the bulk of it, but
that in the end he had to spend about Rs. 500,000 to Rs. 600,000 (@$6,000 to

FIGURE 9.10 Costumed *yaksa*s participating in the Devinuvara *perahara*, 2001

FIGURE 9.11 Costumed *yaksa*s participating in the Devinuvara *perahara*, 2001

FIGURE 9.12 Costumed *yaksa*s participating in the Devinuvara *perahara*, 2001

$7,000) of his own money each year to fund the expenses. He doubted that the *perahara* could be held much longer in its current fashion, owing to its great expense and the effort it took each year to manage the cost and to oversee its administration. He said that finding the funding for the *perahara* was his greatest challenge as a *basnayaka nilame*, and he stressed that while there were thirteen *basnayaka nilames* in Kandy, he had to do all the work and provide for all the expenses in Devinuvara himself.

The *devalaya*, he said, owns only twenty acres of land, and that it had been donated by President Premadasa in the early 1990s as a means to support the feeding needs of the elephant that he had also donated. President Chandrika Bandaranaike Kumaratunga had recently donated a second elephant. The one other elephant (for a total of three) in the *perahara* had to be brought down from Kandy (see figure 9.15) at an expense of Rs. 40,000 (@$500).

When I asked the *basnayaka nilame* who decided which ritual troupes would be included in the *perahara*, he said that he personally made those decisions. The *devalaya* had a registry of various dance and music groups, he would solicit those on his list, and choose from those who responded with interest in participating. None volunteered their services; all had to be paid. The *basnayaka nilame* presented himself as a harried yet exceedingly proud sponsor of the rite. He was keen to convey what he regarded as the populist spirit of "his" *perahara*, in contrast to what he regarded as the elitism of Kandy's.

FIGURE 9.13 Costumed *yaksas* participating in the Devinuvara *perahara*, 2001

The final day of the *perahara*, to which the *devalaya* officials refer as the
randoli perahara,[5] witnessed a spectacular influx of visitors to Devinuvara.
Tens of thousands attended and crowded into what became an even narrower
and more severely clogged lane linking the *devalaya* to the *sinhasana*. While
many of the dance troupes consisting of schoolchildren were still present from
previous days, along with the comical presence of several groups of costumed
yaksas, on this final day no less than twenty groups of *baila* "musicians" and
"dancers" also participated in the procession—which took nearly three hours
to pass.

Baila troupes constituted nearly every third or fourth contingent, and the seriously off-key, disharmonious din of their trumpets and trombones succeeded
in drowning out the drummers' cadences for all of the other dance troupes. The
effect was largely disruptive, for the schoolchildren consequently could not hear

FIGURE 9.14 Costumed *yaksa*s participating in the Devinuvara *perahara*, 2001

the drummed cadences to keep their rhythms. Many of the children wore bewildered faces and meandered through their dance steps tentatively.

Some of the *baila* "dancers" and "musicians," all bare-chested, wearing
gaudy bright-colored and matching sarongs, gold chains hanging around their
necks, gold earrings from their ears, their backs stenciled with sparkling and
flecked renderings of the names of their fishing boats or of their girl friends,
were seriously inebriated with *arrack*, the coconut-distilled liquor of choice in
Sri Lanka. Members of the *baila* troupes passed around their bottles of booze
openly, shouted mightily at the sky, leered tauntingly at young women in the
crowd, and lewdly grabbed their crotches with one hand while they rhythmically swiveled their hips and raised the fists of their other hands into the air. It
was a stunning and raucous social display of "testerone consciousness," as I interpreted it.

FIGURE 9.15 Elephant from Kandy showers himself in front of the Devinuvara Visnu *devalaya*

About two hours into this scene, with my patience waning and my disappointment mounting, one extremely drunk and probably drugged *baila* dancer appeared in the procession with an American flag draped around his shoulders while he repeatedly swung it between his legs, in a manner indicating that he was using the flag to wipe himself after defecation. I was appalled. And so were many others.

In the hours and days that followed, before my departure from Sri Lanka, I reflected long and hard upon the proceedings of the Devinuvara *perahara* in general. On our way back to Kandy, my research assistant and I talked about the drunken displays and vulgar forms of behavior we had seen that last day in Devinuvara; and I mulled the incident over for weeks thereafter. The character of the final day of the Devinuvara *perahara* had a profound effect on me.

Back in Kandy, I spoke to a number of my good friends at the university about what had transpired in Devinuvara . Every one of them winced at my description, but expressed no surprise at hearing of the "*baila* factor" in the *perahara*. Two of my colleagues complained at length to me about the growing specter of thuggery and intimidation in public life in contemporary Sri Lanka, a form of social behavior that, unfortunately, has come to play a role in so much of public political behavior in Sri Lanka during the past two decades as well. Now, they said, it was also creeping into ritual life. I had no choice but to agree that, at least under the supervision of this *basnayaka nilame*, the authority who personally chooses what is and what is not to be included in the Devinuvara *perahara*, that the cult of Visnu, traditionally the religion's, the people's, and the island's "minister of defense," had deteriorated publicly, at least within the context of "a southern Sri Lankan cultural expression," into a sociopolitical statement reflective of goon-empowered politics on the one hand, and a class-based public expression of male dominance on the other. I could understand and accept the incipient anti-Americanism I had witnessed, but I was dejected that public ritual life at the old and venerable Devinuvara site had degenerated into such a raucous, uncouth spectacle.

Having been counseled by my friends back in Peradeniya, I began to step back from my immediate reactions to reflect more peacefully on what had occurred. Ironically and unexpectedly, however, I came to the conclusion that the nature and character of the contemporary Devinwara *perahara* once again seemed to prove the veracity of my thesis; that is, social and political forces, rather than doctrinal rationalizations, are often responsible for the transformations of religious culture. Devinuvara was no longer the chief ritual center of the Visnu cult I had been studying, but rather a fossil of the past, whose basic form was now implanted within the ethos of an emerging Sri Lankan public sociopolitical culture. Indeed, the Devinuvara *perahara* was something of a *vox populi*. But it was also a statement in form and substance that I had not come to expect.

The same case, in theory of course, can be made in principle about the service of public ritual in Kandy, either historically or in the present.[6] Nonetheless, even a casual observer can perceive that the ethos of Kandy's *perahara* (though growing increasingly commercialized by the tourist industry in Sri Lanka) has managed to retain a sense of its relation to what is regarded as a sacred past, even if that "sacred past" is largely remembered through nationalist-inspired memory.

In my own mind, I drew this distinction after observing the Devinuvara *perahara*, as well as the nightly performances of the *valiyak mangalya* in Kandy, within a span of two weeks' time. In the former, my mind kept encountering and comparing those images of thuggish young *baila* dancers at Devinuvara with the dignified old men who are the *yakdessas* performing the "Birth of Mala Raja" and the *Kuveni Asna* in Kandy. I could only conclude, and rather wistfully at that, that the demolition of Devinuvara's religious culture by the Portuguese in the sixteenth century had been rather complete then, and few signs of the old cultic life remained even in fossilized form. Politics often has a sustained deleterious effect on religion.

KANDE VIHARAYA

Kande Viharaya is located in Alutgama, about sixty kilometers south of Colombo and about one hundred kilometers north of Devinuvara, on the main-trunk coastal road running from Colombo to Galle. In addition to the famous Kalutara Bodhiya located about fifteen kilometers to its north, and the Visnu *devalaya* in far-south Devinuvara, Kande Viharaya is one of the most highly frequented Buddhist cultic sites in the south and west of Sri Lanka's low country. But like Devinuvara, it was not a *rajamahaviharaya* (royally endowed monastery). There is a very well-known Visnu *devalaya* within this *viharaya*, located adjacent to and within the same building as a large *buduge* hall. There is no doubt that the *viharaya* has gained its status and its wealth because of the great popularity of the Visnu *devalaya*. This temple is now reputed to be one of the wealthiest and most heavily endowed in Sri Lanka.

Ven. Yatadolawatte Ariyawansa, a monastic incumbent of the *Siyam Nikaya* at the *viharaya* for more than forty years, since 1960, explained that the *viharaya* and its *devalayas* are open from 5 a.m. to 9 p.m., 365 days a year. This is a very different arrangement from the time when he was a young monk in the 1960s. At that time the Visnu *devalaya* was open only on Wednesdays and Saturdays until noon. He estimates that today approximately 5,000 people pass through the premises daily. The *viharaya* also houses a monastic *pirivena*, a kind of seminary for monastic novices. When the number of *samaneras* is combined with the number of fully ordained *bhikkhus* in residence, the number of monks at the *viharaya* numbers nearly one hundred, an impressive number by any standard in Sri Lanka.

In January of 2001, the President of Sri Lanka, Chandrika Bandaranaike Kumaratunga, donated a young elephant tusker to the *viharaya* in a high-profile media event. This created a lot of local excitement. Ven. Yatadolawatte told me of the subsequent plans being developed at the *viharaya* to begin a *perahara* of its own within the next year or so. Many of the graduates of the *pirivena*, as well as other fully ordained *bhikkhus* of the *viharaya*, have traveled abroad to Australia, the U.K. and the U.S.A. The *viharaya* was active in various schemes to send Buddhist missionaries to the West.

When I asked Ven. Yatadolawatte if he thought that worship of Visnu was on the decline, as some scholars have asserted, or if Visnu was losing ground to the very popular Kataragama Deviyo, as others have claimed, he said, "Certainly not here!" To the contrary, he said, the numbers of Visnu devotees seems very much to be on the increase.

In interviewing Ven. Yatadolawatte, I was interested in determining if there were any ritual links between Devinuvara and Kande Viharaya, and if, by chance, the *kapuralas* at the Kande Viharaya Visnu *devalaya* were related to those at Devinuvara, or even more remotely by chance, to the *kapuralas* in the up-country region. There were no known links of any kind, he said. Indeed, all of the *kapuralas* serving the various *devalayas* within Kande Viharaya had been recruited from small *devalayas* in nearby village areas, or were simply lay Buddhists from Alutgama, employees of the *viharaya* receiving a monthly salary.

They were taught the *yatikas* to Visnu that were readily available in the types of publications mentioned in chapter 5. They could be from any caste, not just the *goyigama*, and all of the money that they collected for chanting *yatika* in the various *devalayas* for the ceaselessly attending devotees was handed over to the *viharaya*.

I visited the Visnu *devalaya* at Kande Viharaya in the spring of 2000 and the summer of 2001, since, during the course of my field studies, many people in the up-country had referred to this Visnu *devalaya* as a famous cultic venue. As I mentioned earlier, since my field research had been almost entirely confined to the Kandyan culture area, I felt that I needed to become familiar with patterns of the Visnu cult in the "low country" as well—particularly because the Visnu *devalaya* at Devinuvara, at the southernmost point of the island, had experienced a renaissance in popularity in post-independence Sri Lanka. I was also hoping to find links of a cultic or kinship nature between the *udarata* Visnu *devalayas* and the traditions of Devinuvara and/or Kande Viharaya. While the historical weight and political significance of Visnu was to be known from an examination of its cultic provenance in up-country Kandy, its contemporary venues of note in the south and west could not ignored.

I had also been told by a university colleague about oral traditions linking Visnu to the origins of the *salagama* caste, a community heavily represented in this southern coastal region of the country. Despite persistent inquiries regarding this lead and a scouring of historical sources, I found no individuals familiar in Alutgama with this specific tradition, nor could I find any references to it in any of the potentially relevant literary materials I examined. But what I did ascertain at Kande Viharaya, and then again at Devinuvara, provided me with more depth of perspective for understanding the cult of the "Buddhist Visnu" in particular, and Sinhala religious culture in general, in contemporary Sri Lanka.

Kande Viharaya, as I have mentioned, is now a thriving religious cultic complex. While the presence of the Visnu *devalaya* is its main claim to fame, owing to oral traditions which allege that the cultic seat of Visnu was shifted here after the demise of the old Upulvan *devalaya* in Devinuvara by the Portuguese in the late sixteenth century C.E., Kande Viharaya is now a veritable religious multiplex that reflects the general patterns and trajectories of contemporary Sinhala Buddhist religious culture. Like the Bellanvila Viharaya in southeast Colombo, it has achieved enormous regional importance, and the sheer number and variety of *devalayas* within its boundaries have made it a kind of functional surrogate for those who cannot find the time, inclination, or means to go on pilgrimage to the major and distant cultic seats of several deities.

This monastic *devalaya* site is now an expanding campus with various new buildings and shrines in the midst of construction, including two brand-new abodes of worship for Ganesa and Kali. Within the walls of the original temple complex, there is a free-standing *devalaya* for Kataragama under the sprawl of a massive *bodhi* tree, in front and slightly to the left of the main *buduge* and Visnu *devalaya* structure. To the left and running parallel to the *buduge* is a 1950s "line house" building containing four small *devalayas* dedicated respectively to two sets or combinations of deities (the first to the goddesses Pattini, Sarasvati, and Lakshmi; and the second to Natha and Saman), and then two others dedicated individually to Siva and Huniyam.

In front and to the right of the *buduge* stands the oldest and most interesting structure within the old *viharaya* walls: a hexagonal *buduge* dating to 1730 c.e. and containing the remnants of mid- to late eighteenth-century paintings of the Kandyan school.[7] However, the most outstanding features of the Kande Viharaya complex are the façade and porticos of the *buduge* built in 1886, constructed in impeccable Iberian style (see figure 9.16). At very first sight, one could immediately mistake this building for a small Roman Catholic church.

The architectural style of the *buduge* was a harbinger of the style of cultic activity I then found within the famous Visnu *devalaya*. Rather than one *kapurala*, two on either side of a large square table were chanting *yatikas* to the devotees, who had lined up in two queues to make their offerings. The two *kapuralas* were not dressed in the traditional white garb of the Kandyan shrine priests, but rather in blue-colored shirts and sarongs, with blue vestment

FIGURE 9.16 Iberian façade of the *buduge* and Visnu *devalaya* at Kande Viharaya

shawls draped around there necks, vestments unmistakably made in the style of those worn by Protestant Christian clerics of "high church" liturgical traditions (Anglican or Lutheran, for instance).

Yatikas were not chanted on behalf of devotees within a sanctum sanctorum, but instead were chanted while facing the devotee with one palm resting on the top of the devotee's head. This bestowal of *santiya* was done, therefore, in a form corresponding to how a Christian minister administers a blessing.

Remarkably, in the small sanctum behind the *kapuralas*—a sanctum dominated by a large blue Visnu *devarupa,* visible from only the chest up and crowded with a number of other small, recently rendered images of the deity— there was a recently cast, eighteen-inch, standing Visnu figure made of plaster, but with two arms held out in the manner of "the good shepherd." The Christian assimilations at the Visnu *devalaya* at Kande *Viharaya* were palpable indeed. Visnu's image and the manner in which his power is envisaged and ritually channeled had been transfigured at Kande Viharaya as a consequence of low-country Sri Lanka's extended historical experience of domination by European Christian colonial hegemony. Again, my thesis about how political forces of history transform the character of religious culture seemed to be confirmed by what I saw at Kande Viharaya.

In light of my experiences in low-country Devinuvara and Kande Viharaya, I gained new perspectives for the ritual traditions still sustained in Kandy. There is still a sense, at the Visnu *devalayas* in the *udarata,* that a moral economy based on karma continues to operate, and that Visnu is a marker and index to that reality. His identity has been understood within a mythically imagined but ethically warranted hierarchy. Moreover, there is little hint at Kandy, Hanguranketa, Alutnuvara, Lankatilaka, or Gadaladeniya that the cult of the "Buddhist Visnu" is becoming seriously Christianized in any significant way. Somehow, those cultic venues have largely deflected what Randy Newman had once sung about, as the march of the "great nations of Europe coming through." For now, while old men born of previous generations seem to be the guardians of traditions, those traditions can still be sustained and understood with some clarity. Herein, Visnu continues to epitomize a moral possibility within the dynamic flux of samsaric existence, spanning the *laukika*—focused and *lokottara*-oriented.

Throughout this study, it may have been apparent at times that I have offered a subtle apology for the manner in which the cult of Visnu has been constructed in previous centuries of Sinhala Buddhist religious culture. Indeed, I have done so for a variety of reasons. First, the religious meaning of this particular dimension of Sinhala Buddhist religious culture has been rarely articulated in juxtaposition to the modern Sinhala Buddhist critiques delivered by

the likes of such erstwhile twentieth-century reformers as Anagarika Dharmapala or Ven. Soma, who have given so much of their energies to attack it.

As my inquiry has unfolded, I have simply sought to point out, as best as I
can, and in concert with devotees who constitute the cult of the "Buddhist
Visnu," that their religiosity is not simply a corruption of Buddhist tradition
that needs to be excised or expurgated, but rather that it is rooted within and
exemplifies the ethical depths and principles of an operative Buddhist moral
economy, and that it is genuinely expressive of religious existential and soteriological hope.

Second, I have done so in the hope that this study can help to widen the
scope in which Buddhist culture is understood, not simply as an attractive option to be considered in the spiritual supermarkets of the West, but as an indication of the type of religiosity engaged in by most Buddhists in south and
southeast Asia, particularly those outside modern urban circles.[8]

Third, and formally, I have argued consistently that political forces, rather
than doctrinal niceties, often shape the changing trajectories of religious cultures, and that assimilations are not usually and simply matters of happy syncretistic happenstance.

Sri Lanka, more specifically Sinhala Buddhist religious culture, has been the
site of many remarkable cultural crosscurrents and metamorphoses, owing to
the pressures of political forces, throughout its history. Consequently, one of
the legacies of its past, and one of the realities of its present, is that it remains
an evolving sociocultural mosaic. How Buddhist Sri Lankans respond to that
legacy remains a pressing political question of the day.[9] Recognizing that Sri
Lanka's political history has bequeathed a multireligious culture, and a multi-
ethnic society, may continue to generate lamentations about an imagined pristine past now compromised in the present. Perhaps such a pattern of antipathy, given the provenance of its own historical legacy, is inevitable in some
quarters, particularly from those monks who are unequivocal in their political
inspiration. In turn, the articulation of that antipathy will guarantee a more
general societal ambivalence about past assimilations and transformations in
Sinhala Buddhist religious culture.

On the other hand, historical awareness of change in religious culture can
also foster perspectives that respect difference and affirm its presence within
the larger sociocultural whole. Indeed, it is remarkable to think that most Sinhala Buddhists still venerate Visnu, and that their religious culture has secured
a place for him as a "minister of defense" within the parameters and principles
of a Buddhist-inspired moral economy.

Notes

Part 1

Introduction: The Historical and Theoretical Problems

1. *Aspects of Sinhalese Culture*, 4th ed. (1952; reprint, Dehiwala, Sri Lanka: Tisara Prakasakayo, 1992), 11.

2. *Buddha in the Crown* (1991).

3. See especially the studies by Tu Wei-ming, *Neo-Confucian Thought-in-action: Wang Yang Ming's Youth (1472–1509)* (1976) and Julia Ching, *The Religious Thought of Chu Hsi* (2000).

4. Charles Wei-shun Fu, "Chu Hsi on Buddhism" (1986).

5. For a brief discussion of these issues, see H. A. R. Gibb, *Mohammedanism: An Historical Survey* (1970:30–32).

1. The "Hindu Buddha" and the "Buddhist Visnu"

1. *Aspects of Sinhalese Culture* (1992:120).

2. There are a number of solid, yet now somewhat dated sources that examine the relationship between *sramana* movements, including Buddhism and the Brahmanical tradition. Among these, P. S. Jaini's "Sramanas: Their Conflict with Brahmanical Society" (1970:39–81) remains a standard and accessible discussion which, when combined with the preceding chapter in the same volume by J. A. B. van Buitenen on the Vedic and Upanisadic bases of Indian civilization, provides a fine general introduction. Especially useful in determining pre-Buddhist heterodox teachings which may have influenced the development of Buddhist thought per se is Benimadhab Barua, *A History of Pre-Buddhist Indian Philosophy* (1970). Nalinaksa Dutt in his "Brahminism and Buddhism" in *Bulletin of Tibetology* 7 (1970:7–11), discusses concisely the manner in which key concepts in the Upanisads were understood in Pali sources. For more detailed, sophisticated, and highly rewarding treatments of a similar nature, see especially K. N. Jayatilleke, *Early Buddhist Theory of Knowledge* (1963:21–276), wherein the epistemologies of the Vedic, Upanisadic, materialist, skeptic, Ajivaka, and Jain worldviews are admirably elucidated, and J. W. de Jong's "The Background of Early Buddhism" in *Journal of Indian and Buddhist Studies* 12 (1964:34–47), in which the author sees Buddhism as a creative synthesis between Aryan

and non-Aryan conceptions. Complementary studies which examine specific aspects of the relationship between the emerging Buddhist tradition and its Vedic and non-Vedic contemporary rivals are Fedor I. Stcherbatsky, *Buddhist Logic* (1962; vol. 1: 15–27), and V. P. Varma, "The Vedic Religion and the Origins of Buddhism," in *Journal of the Bihar Research Society* 46 (1960:276–308). For an interesting comparative study between the Upanisads and the Pali *Nikayas* relating to the issues of personal gods, self and non-self, karma and rebirth, the problem of evil, the symbolism of the wheel, and epistemology in general, see Sanjay G. Deodikar, *Upanisads and Early Buddhism* (1992).

3. *Naradiya Purana* I.15.50–52.

4. Lal Mani Joshi, *Discerning the Buddha* (1983:xvii).

5. For an extensive study of the relationship between Buddhist epistemology and metaphysics and their partial incorporation within the *Bhagavad Gita*, see Kashi Nath Upadhyaya, *Early Buddhism and the Bhagavadgita* (1971).

6. See especially the third chapter of the *Bhagavad Gita* wherein the teaching of karma yoga and the realization of nirvana are presented as a means and goal of the disciplined spiritual path. Herein, it is important to note that nirvana, rather than *moksa*, is the term used to designate the ultimate summum bonum of the religious quest, thus incorporating the terminology usually employed by Buddhists.

7. P. V. Kane, *History of Dharmsastra* (1962; 5:913ff).

8. J. C. Heesterman ("The Conundrum of the King's Authority"; 1998:22), citing the *Mahabharata*, notes the tradition of the first king being Visnu's "mental son." Thus, though the actual historical and political "replacement" of the Buddha in favor of Visnu and Siva occurs largely in the eighth century, the theory of such kingships must have been very ancient indeed.

9. *Varaha Purana* 4.2; *Matsya Purana* 285.6–7; *Agni Purana* 49.8; *Bhagavata Purana* X.40.22 and I.3.

10. Krishna Sastri, *Memoirs of the Archaeological Survey of India* 26 (1945:5ff.).

11. The temple sculptures I refer to probably date to the time of Vijayanagar recovery from Muslim Turkic invasions of South India in the fourteenth century C.E. See Burton Stein (1989:18) and Richard H. Davis (1997:114–115).

12. See the introduction to Cornelia Dimmitt and J. A. B. van Buitenen, *Classical Hindu Mythology* (1978:3–13).

13. For an excellent explanation of the substance and history of Vaisnava theology from a thoroughgoing Vaisnava persepective, see S. M. Srinivasa Chari, *Vaisnavism: Its Philosophy, Theology and Religious Discipline* (1994). See especially pp. 49–65 and 131–56 for discussions regarding Visnu as the ultimate reality.

14. *Rg Veda* I.154.

15. See George Dumezil, *The Destiny of the Warrior* and *The Destiny of a King*, both translated by Alf Hiltebeitel for the University of Chicago Press in 1970 and 1973 respectively.

16. For an excellent discussion of how the footprint becomes an aniconic (nonanthropomorphic) symbol for both Visnu and the Buddha, see Jacob Kinnard, "The Polyvalent *Padas* of Visnu and the Buddha," *History of Religions* 40- (2000:32–57).

17. In addition to the Puranas cited above in note 8, where the number of Visnu's avatars is said to be ten, the *Markandeya Purana* (4:44–58) lists twelve, while *Matsya Purana* (47:32–52) lists twenty-two.

18. David Kinsley, *The Sword and the Flute* (1975), especially the first chapter.

19. Joshi (1983:xviii) notes that even in the sixteenth-century *Ramacaritamanasa* by Tulsi Das, and in the *Satyarthaprakasa* by Swami Dayananda Sarasvati, this popular Puranic view of the Buddha was sustained. He notes that Buddhist pilgrims to India, including those such as the Chinese pilgrim Hsuan-tsang who knew Sanskrit, must have been shocked by the Brahmanical Hindu formula of homage to the Buddha: *namo Buddhaya Suddhaya daitya danava mohine* ("Adoration to the Enlightened One, the Immaculate One, who enchanted [or deceived] the demons and devils.")

20. Particularly valuable sources for understanding and situating Vivekananda in relation to emergent Indian nationalism are Amitya Sen, *Swami Vivekananda* (2000); Anantanand Rambachan, *The Limits of Scripture* (1994); and many of the essays in William Radice, ed., *Swami Vivekananda and the Modernization of Hinduism* (1998).

21. Some recent scholars have argued that Ramakrsna's religious orientation was not necessary or exclusively *bhakti*, but may have been predominantly tantric. See, for instance, Jeffrey Kripal, *Kali's Child* (1996), which not only raises this issue but also attempts to explore what he argues is the homoerotic nature of Ramakrsna's religious experiences.

22. For a summary of Vivekanda's understanding of the Buddha as publicly articulated, see Joshi (1983:58–73).

23. Vivekananda, *Complete Works* (1971–73;I: 117–18) Swami Sivananda also regarded the Buddha as a karma yogi. See David Miller, "Swami Sivananda and the Bhagavadgita," in Robert Minor, ed., *Modern Interpreters of the* Bhagavad Gita (1986:173–99).

24. Vivekananda, *Complete Works* (VII: 59).

25. C. D. Sharma, *A Critical Survey of Indian Philosophy* (1960:318). For a detailed analysis of the manner in which Mahayana ideas have exercised a profound effect upon, or were a heritage for, Sankara, see S. G. Mudgal, *Advaita Vedanta of Sankara: Impact of Buddhism and Samkhya on Sankara's Thought* (1975).

26. Mudgal, *Advaita Vedanta* (1975:173–188).

27. Quoted in Joshi, *Discerning the Buddha* (1983:64), who in turn quotes A. Aiyappan and P. R. Srinivasan, *Story of Buddhism with Special Reference to South India* (1960:5).

28. Sarvapalli Radhakrishnan, *Eastern and Western Religious Thought* (1940:330).

29. Cited in Pathmanathan (1986:79) as originally coming from the foreword of P. V. Bapat, ed., *2500 Years of Buddhism* (1956). What is especially interesting about this passage is that it completely reverses the significance of the Buddha-as- avatar doctrine formulated in the Puranas. There the Buddha was sent to further delude the wicked. Here, according to Radhakrishnan, he purifies Brahmanical religion of its own abuses and delusions.

30. Jawaharlal Nehru, *The Discovery of India* (1956:121, 109).

31. D. C. Sircar, *Inscriptions of Asoka* (1956:3).

32. For a study of this dramatic mass conversion, see Eleanor Zelliot, *Dr. Ambedkar and the Mahar Movement* (1969).

33. How "religious revivalism" at the turn of the century evolved into a fervent nationalism is explored superbly by Shamita Basu, *Religious Revivalism as National Discourse* (2002).

34. *Mahasamaya Suttanta* in *Digha Nikaya* ("book" ii, "section" 253; vol. 2: p. 290).

35. Wilhelm Geiger, among others, has identified Visnu with the indigenous deity Up-ulvan, who, in the seminal *Mahavamsa* myth recounting the first migration of "Sinhalese" to the island, is appointed by Sakka (Indra), who was in turn appointed by the Tathagata, to protect the Sinhalese and their religion on this island where the *dhamma* will flourish. See Geiger, *The Mahavamsa* (ch. 7: vs. 1–8; p. 55).

36. Here it is interesting to remember how Durkheim, in his opening "book" (part 1) of *The Elementary Forms of Religious Life* (1965:45–49), pointed out that definitions of re-ligion dependent upon the notion of "belief in God" had to be called into question be-cause Theravada Buddhism is obviously a religion yet does not assert "belief in god." What Durkheim's discussion demands is a definition of religion that goes beyond the issue of belief in god as a determining criterion. For a startling example of the perspec-tive I am referring to in the contemporary context, see the article entitled "Is Buddhism Being Betrayed in Sri Lanka?" in the July 5, 2001, edition of the (Colombo) *Daily News*. Here, a British convert to Buddhism with the kind of understanding of the religion I have just indicated reports that he recently visited Sri Lanka for the first time and proceeds to ask Sri Lankan Sinhala Buddhists to explain to him how they can consider themselves as Buddhists when they continue to engage in such "unBuddhistic" practices as stupa ven-eration, *bodhi puja*, deity propitiation, etc.

37. Martin Southwold, in his *Buddhism in Life* (1983), has discussed extensively the problem of defining religion and Buddhism as a matter of "belief." He argues persuasively to the contrary that Buddhists have always stressed the importance of action. Buddhism has not been primarily credal but ethical.

38. A good example is M. M. J. Marasinghe, *Gods in Early Buddhism* (1974).

39. See the opening chapter of his widely used *What the Buddha Taught* (1959), in which he stresses that the Buddha is nothing more than a human being.

40. Peter Masefield, *Divine Revelation in Pali Buddhism* (1986:xvi); see also the dis-cussion of von Glassenapp (1970:30ff), in which he argues, on the basis of studying the Pali *Nikaya*s, that the "Buddha and all his adherents believed in the concrete existence of these gods, just as do most Buddhists even today. It is an unpardonable mistake for a his-torian to assume that only later tradition has incorporated them into the teaching to pan-der to the masses."

41. See, for instance, Heinrich Zimmer's wonderful retelling of "Indra and the Parade of Ants," from the *Visnu Purana*, in his *Myth and Symbol in Indian Art and Civilization* (1972:3–11).

42. For a study of karma and the origin and nature of *petas* ("departed kin"), as these are known in the *Petavatthu*, see my "Assisting the Dead by Venerating the Living: Merit Transfer in Early Buddhism" (1981).

43. See *Encyclopaedia of Buddhism* 4 (Fascicle 3): 413–18) for a Pali *Tipitaka*–based discussion of the nature of deities.

44. Charles Hallisey, "Roads Taken and Roads Not Taken in the Study of Theravada Buddhism," in Donald Lopez, ed., *Curators of the Buddha* (1995:31–61), notes how Sri Lankan scholars embraced Western scholarly analyses, particularly those of T. W. Rhys Davids, in the late nineteenth and early twentieth centuries.

45. See, for instance, F. L. Woodward, trans., *Udana: Verses of Uplift and Itivuttaka: As It Was Said* (1935:9); V. Trenckner, ed., *The Majjhima Nikaya* (1888; 1:39) and K. R. Nor-man, trans., *Theragatha* (1961), especially vol. 1.

46. The *Sigalovada Suttanta* of the *Digha Nikaya* is a particularly apt example in terms of the manner in which the Buddha advises lay followers to abandon efforts aimed at worshipping the gods of the four directions and the zenith and nadir, in favor of cultivating wholesome social relations with various sets of people, including family, teachers, etc. For a powerful argument asserting the superiority of a religion without God as its focus, see Gunapala Dharmasiri, *A Buddhist Critique of the Christian Concept of God* (1988).

47. Ariyapala (1956:185) notes how the thirteenth-century *Saddharma Ratnavaliya* admonishes the people to give up worship of Visnu and Siva. Vidagama Maitreya Thera, an eminent royal preceptor in the fifteenth century, was a famous rival and critic of Sri Rahula Thera, the great grammarian and poet, who is recognized as having sanctioned the worship of the gods and the practice of ritual magic. Kitsiri Malalgoda's brief account in *Buddhism in Sinhalese Society 1750–1900* (1976:169–70) describes how an anti-Visnu sentiment accompanied the formative years of the Ramanna monastic sect of the *sangha* in Sri Lanka.

48. Though Dharmakirti seems to have been "imbued with Mahayana ideals," Godakumbura notes that "one also sees in him a profound hatred towards the Saivites who have been gaining power in the country and spreading their ways of life and religious practices." C. E. Godakumbura, *Sinhalese Literature* (1955:91–92).

49. See Ariyapala (1956:182–83).

50. In the spring of 2000, a new Sinhala political party, the Sihala Urumaya, was founded to protect the interests of the Sinhalese community from being overrun by the Tamils. Buddhist monks have been deeply involved in the establishment of this new political party. The Ven. Gangodawila Soma, profiled in the eighth chapter as the leading spokesperson of the current anti–Hindu deity campaign, joined this party in 2002.

51. The clarion call in June 2001 by Sri Lanka's then prime minister, Ratnasiri Wickramanayaka, for Sinhala Buddhists to produce more male children to fight as soldiers in the war and to become Buddhist monks is a perfect illustration of this disposition.

2. "Unceasing Waves": Brahmanical and Hindu Influences on Medieval Sinhala Buddhist Culture in Sri Lanka

1. *Aspects of Sinhalese Culture* (1992:21).

2. For a general historical description of Sri Lanka's variegated religious culture, see my *Buddha in the Crown* (1991:4–11).

3. An equally remarkable pattern, one that I believe merits serious analytical investigation, is the manner in which Hindu patterns of religious practice in Sri Lanka per se (as opposed to the Hindu patterns of absorption) seem to have remained singularly unaffected, or largely uninfluenced, by the concomitant presence of Buddhism in Sri Lanka. What I am indicating here—and I realize that this could be a controversial statement within the highly charged political context of contemporary Sri Lanka—is that historically, the Buddhist Sinhala community seems to have been far more inclusive than the Hindu Tamil, if we consider the substance and structures of these respective religions as they are practiced in Sri Lanka today.

4. Roberts's (1995) study of the *karava* caste is one of the most lucid accounts of the manner in which arriving immigrants found their cultural and social niches in an increasingly variegated Sri Lankan social milieu.

5. For an account of the reasons why Kataragama remains such an important deity for Sinhalas, see the best study of this deity to date, by Gananath Obeysekere (1978). His study also provides a relevant bibliography for further reading and research.

6. The earlier formulation of the four guardian deities included Saman, Vibhisana, Upulvan, and Skanda, a selection that seems somewhat dependent upon the vicissitudes of the epic *Ramayana*.

7. Obeyesekere's discussion (1984:50–70) of the dynamics of change within the Sinhala Buddhist pantheon of deities is an excellent account of the principles and hierarchies at work in relation to deities, their functions, and their roles relative to one another.

8. For a discussion of the religious and social significance of the *asala perahara*, see H. L. Seneviratne (1978:136–70) and my *Buddha in the Crown* (1991: 176–201). For a study of Kirti Sri's reorganization of public ritual and Buddhist monasticism, see my *The Religious World of Kirti Sri* (1996:15–40).

9. For an illuminating discussion of this relationship, see Bardwell L. Smith, "Kingship, the Sangha and the Process of Legitimation in Anuradhapura Ceylon: An Interpretive Essay," in Smith, ed. (1978:73–95).

10. Just when Sri Lankan royalty can be identified as "Sinhala" royalty per se, or more generally when a genuine self-conscious Sinhala identity emerges historically, has been the subject of a spirited debate between R. A. L. H. Gunawardana and K. N. O. Dharmadasa. Gunawardana (1990:45–86) argues that such an identity cannot, without precision, antedate the 12th century C.E. More precisely, his argument is much more subtle than what I have rather baldly inferred. In his conclusion, he states: "The nature of Sinhala identity as well as the relationship between the group brought together by this identity and the other groupings based on religion, ritual status and language varied in different periods of history. Thus all these groupings represented historically variable, intersecting social divisions. Identities based on ritual status and religion can be traced back to the most ancient documents available in Sri Lanka. The Sinhala identity in its earliest historical form bears the imprint of its origin in the period of state formation, in association with the ruling dynasty and its immediate socio-political base. It is only by about the twelfth century that the Sinhala grouping could have been considered identical with the linguistic grouping. The relationship between the Sinhala and Buddhist identities is even more complex. There is a close association between the two identities, but at no period do they appear to have coincided exactly to denote the self-same group of people" (78). Dharmadasa (1992) has written an extensive and detailed critique of Gunawardana's argument, the conclusion of which is: "The phenomenon we have discussed—the vision of the Sinhala identity embodied in the *Dipavamsa* and in the *Mahavamsa* and the commentary of the latter, the *Vamsatthappakasini*, the political activities in the cause of Sinhala ethnicity by some sections of the Kandyan elite, the strivings of James de Alwis with the Sinhala language as a nationalist focus—all can be considered as periodic expressions of a continuous ideological position. Certain salient themes in it can be easily recognized, the most prominent being the Sinhaladvipa concept" (55), which Dharmadasa finds articulated at least four or five centuries before the twelfth. This is a very instructive debate about the issues involved and the strategies deployed in determining the natures of ethnic and religious identities.

11. The first section is generally attributed to the Theravada monk Mahanama in fifth-century C.E. Anuradhapura, the second to the monk Dhammakitti in the twelfth century,

during the Polonnaruva reign of Parakramabahu I, the third to yet another Dhammakitti Thera, during the fourteenth-century reign of Parakramabaha IV at Kurunegala; and finally, the fourth installment was written by Tibbotuvave Buddharakkhita from Ridigama Vihara, during the eighteenth-century reign of Kirti Sri Rajasimha in Kandy. Kemper (1992:42–43) has noted traditions regarding both of the Dhammakittis that allege that they were foreign monks, possibly from the Tamil Cola country of India.

12. Not including references to *nagas, raksasas, yaksas, gandharvas, kinnaras, pretas, bhutas,* etc.)

13. One of the best sources for gaining an effective overview of the religious, artistic, political, and social aspects of culture in the Polonnaruva period remains Saparamadu, *The Polonnaruva Period* (1973); for the general reader, see the beautifully illustrated *Polonnaruva: Medieval Capital of Sri Lanka* by Anuradha Seneviratne (1998).

14. See O. H. De A. Wijesekera, "Pali and Sanskrit in the Polonnaruva Period" (1973).

15. It is difficult to overemphasize the historical importance of Parakramabahu's reign for the history of Theravada fortunes and for Sinhala Buddhist culture in general. Not only was the *bhikkhusangha* reconstituted according to the principles of the Pali *Vinaya,* but the *bhikkhunisangha* (the female monastic order) was not reconstituted at all. In terms of political history, the preceding three to four centuries in India had witnessed a complete shift away from Buddhist ideology in the manner in which kingship had been envisaged. The conversion to Hindu or Purana-related imagery and Kautilyan (relating to Kautilya, author of the *Arthasastra*) models of statecraft had been almost complete. In the twelfth century, on the eve of Muslim invasions, it had reached its zenith in prevalence. The Sinhala recovery and reestablishment of a Buddhist kingship at Polonnaruva following the Cola invasions was, therefore, an extraordinary development that resisted the larger tides of political and cultural change on the Indian subcontinent. Indeed, unless Tibet is regarded as part of the subcontinent, the Sinhalas were the only Buddhist peoples in South Asia to retain a Buddhist lineage of royalty.

16. Von Schroeder (1990:671, 676) provides a very brief discussion of two, and a blueprint plan for one of five Visnu "devales" (sic) whose remains are still found at Polonnaruva. There are some seven Siva "devales" and a temple to Kali which have been archeologically surveyed.

17. Prematilleke, however, describes a burial site within the monastic complex that precedes the construction of the monastery. He writes: "The practice of burying bones in earthen pots was an accepted convention in tribal society specially [sic] of the megalithic phase current in the Indian Sub-continent. Evidently, this practice had continued down to the middle ages. Prior to the re-establishment of Sinhalese rule in Polonnaruva, the city was a province of the Chola kingdom and it is probable that the site of the Alahana Parivena had been used as a cemetary [sic] even before the monastery was founded by Parakramabahu I in the 12th century" (1981:13).

18. See Frank Reynolds (1972) and S. J. Tambiah (1976) for detailed analyses explicating the Buddhist nuances of understanding this critically important term.

19. I have tried to show in my *Religious World of Kirti Sri,* (1996:15–40) that Kandyan kings in the later 18th century *nayakkar* period deployed not only these conceptions but that of the bodhisatva as well.

20. *Epigraphia Zeylonica* 2:215–16; also cited in Pathmanathan (1982).

21. Ibid., 3:323–24.

22. P. B. Meegaskumbura points out (in a private communication) that pure Sinhala was used by Gurulugomi for the "narrative elegance of creative writing," but also that Gurulugomi culled material for the *Amavatura* from the *Atthakatha*s, such that the *Amavatura* can be regarded really as more of a work of editing and translation than as a truly creative work.

23. Hallisey (2003:697–98), in writing about the relations between Sinhala literary culture and the political context of this time writes: "In contrast to elsewhere in South Asia and Southeast Asia, there is a notable absence of Sanskrit in the public discourse found in Sri Lankan inscriptions, with Sinhala—admittedly often a highly Sanskritized Sinhala almost always preferred. This absence challenges us to consider just how it was that elites in medieval Sri Lanka simultaneously participated in and resisted absorption in the 'Sanksrit cosmopolis,' that symbolic network created in the first instance by the presence of a similar kind of discourse in a similar language deploying at similar idiom and style to make similar kinds of claims about the nature and aesthetics of polity."

24. Lynn de Silva (1974:21).

25. Here is part of the *Culavamsa*'s account of Rajasinha's conversion to the cult of Siva: "But one day the King, after he had brought a gift of alms, asked the Grand Theras full of anxiety: 'How can I undo the crime of my father's murder?' Then the wise Theras expounded to him the doctrine, but could not win over the wicked mind of this fool. They spake: 'To undo this crime is impossible.' Full of fury like some terrible poisonous snake which had been struck with a stick, he asked the adherents of Siva. The answer they gave him that it was possible, he received like ambrosia, he smeared his body with ash and adopted the religion of Siva" (II:225–26; 93.6–10).

While the focus of my inquiry is especially directed to Visnu, it is clear that during this time frame significant Saiva forces made their presence felt, especially in coastal towns, but also in the dynastic capitals as well. Sri Rahulas's *Salalihini Sandesaya* (C. Reynolds: 286) contains explicit references to a Siva temple and rituals performed therein. It is also known that Siva temples existed in Munnesvaram and Devinuwara (Pathmanathan 1986:85–86).

26. See chapter 2 of my *Religious World of Kirti Sri* (1996).

27. For a brief account of this important historical battle, see my *Buddha in the Crown* (1991:95–98).

28. It is interesting to note that Bhuvanekabahu VII of Kotte (1521–51 C.E.), who was the last of the Sinhala kings before Dharmapala converted to the Roman Catholicism of the Portuguese, signed all of his official proclamations in Tamil. I have learned this from a private communication with Alan Strathern, who is writing his doctoral dissertation on Bhuvanekabahu VII at Trinity College, Oxford, U.K.

29. Hallisey (2003) also discusses the impact of Sanskrit and the facility with Tamil among important Sinhala writers of this period. In relation to the impact of Sanskrit he writes: "The impact of Sanskrit went far beyond morphological developments, however. Sanskrit discourse had a pervasive effect on the prose Sinhala of the period, particularly in Buddhist scholastic works . . . where the language is full of Sanskrit loanwords and derivatives . . . as well as 'Sanskritic' modes of thinking. Certain moral values of Sanskrit literary culture, such as prowess, valor, and prestige, also became part of Sinhala literary

culture as did Sanskritic literary values such as selectivity, homogeneity, and conservatism" [697]. In regard to the presence of Tamil among Sinhala writers, he notes: "Sinhala authors in the fifteenth century . . . commonly knew Tamil and sometimes referred to Tamil words, while authors who were ethnically Tamil sometimes wrote in Sinhala" [694].

30. Pathmanathan continues (1986:109). "In the Gadaladeniya temple, which is mostly of stone construction, Hindu influences are found to be overwhelming. In architectural design, the arrangement of subsidiary shrines dedicated (to the gods) and the order of its pillars exhibits the characteristic features of a Hindu temple of the Dravidian style. The main shrine, like the Dravidian monuments, has as its principal components the *garbha grha, antarala* and *mandapa*. The moulded base, *adhisthana*, rising from the plinth which provides a level ground for it, has the chamfered torus characteristic of Dravidian buildings. The exterior face of the building is ornamented with pilasters which are carried through the two upper mouldings of the bases and have capitals and corbels of the late Pandya and early Vijayanagara type. Besides, as in Dravidian monuments, the *sikhara* rises above the *garbha grha* and *antarala*."

31. See Agarwal (1994:168–79).

32. See Roberts (1995:22–23) for maps that illustrate the types of boats and the routes they traversed between Sri Lanka and India and along the Indian coasts.

33. See the Sagama rock inscription of 1380 C.E. in *Epigraphia Zeylonica* (4:310–11; for a brief overview of the Alakesvaras role in the political dynamics of the late fourteenth and early fifteenth centuries, see my *Buddha in the Crown* (1991:102–103, 109–110); see also the *Alakesvara Yuddhaya*, ed. A. V. Suravira (1962).

34. Somaratne (1984:3) cites the *Nikayasamgraha* reference to the four guardian deities as Kihirali, Saman, Vibhisana, and Skanda Kumara, whose respective *devalayas* were located at the four corners of the rampart of the fortress at the Kotte capital of Jayavardhanapura, and were ritually attended to by Brahmans who were provided with accommodation within the royal fort.

35. Following the widespread implications of Obeyesekere's discussions, I have also attempted, previously, to analyze "colonization myths" within the context of the cult of a regional Sinhala deity, Pitiye, and his mythic conflict with Natha (Avalokitesvara) Deviyo in the Dumbara region of Kandy (1992:125–150), while Roberts (1995:18–32) has analyzed how migration myths (or "myths of origins") of the *karava* caste and others (including the *durava*s and *salagama*s) reflect community conceptions of identity within a newly adopted milieu.

36. Originally recounted in the commentary of the *Ratana Sutta*.

37. This is a theme also explored in the conclusion of H. L. Seneviratne's *The Work of Kings* (1999:333–48).

38. Ariyapala (1956:185) amplifies: "The *Saddharmaratnavaliya* admonishes the people to give up faith in Visnu and Mahesvara and take refuge in the Triple Gem: '*sujanayan visin visnu mahesvaradi bhakti nativa tunuruvanhi ma bhakti ativa*' (516). The *Saddhamaratnavaliya* affords definite evidence regarding the prevalence of these cults. . . . The Pandaranga story in this book relates the doings of some followers of Isvara at Magama in Rohana. The story relates that the ministers in this province wanted to give alms, when a certain Saiva praised the virtues of a *paribbajaka* who lived in the cemetery.

He described him thus: 'Isvara is the creator of the whole world. Any good or evil that can befall man is due to him. There lives in the cemetery a follower of his. He applies ashes to his body. His mouth is covered with his moustache and his beard covers his chest. He wears a turban and is dressed in a dirty rag. . . . When people went to see him with alms they found that he had misconducted himself with a woman the previous night and had drunk toddy, and at this time he was found fishing'" (Sdhlk, p. 689). This is just one example of the type of unfortunate polemics that can be found throughout Ariyapala's work.

3. The Sandalwood Image: Upulvan Deviyo and the Origins of the Visnu Cult in Sinhala Buddhist Sri Lanka

1. *Aspects of Sinhalese Culture* (1992:21).

2. Indeed, a Sinhala translation of the *Mahavamsa* was not available to read in Ceylon for many years after the appearance of Geiger's English translation.

3. See, for instances, many of the essays in Bardwell Smith (1978).

4. Walpola Rahula's *History of Buddhism in Ceylon* (1956), for instance, is based almost exclusively on this source. E. W. Adhikaram's *Early History of Buddhism in Ceylon* (1946) is also very heavily dependent on it.

5. See the Sri Lankan national newspapers in English and Sinhala any year about the time of Poson *poya* (June full moon) or Vesak *poya* (May full moon).

6. Kemper's *The Presence of the Past* (1992) is the best source for understanding this practice at work.

7. See, for instance, H. L. Seneviratne (1978:12), David Scott (1994:41), Bruce Kapferer (1983 and 1997), and Charles Hallisey (2003:716). This may be because basic sources like Lawrie (1898), Bell (1904), Barnett (1916), and Neville (1954) assume that Upulvan was just an epithet for Visnu—or Upulvan *was* "Visnu." Barnett's "Alphabetical Guide to Sinhalese Folklore" based on Nevill's catalogue of Sinhala *kavi*, for instance, simply says "See Visnu" under its entry for Upulvan.

8. See especially Richard Gombrich (1991:208), who says: "Professor Paranavitana questions whether Upulvan really was Vishnu, but as the two have been popularly equated the question is purely academic. Vishnu's traditional character is benevolent and colourless; his character as *fidei defensor* is his only salient characteristic." Analysis shows that his character, following Upulvan's mythic profile, has more salience than this comment would indicate. Gombrich also says that the name Upulvan means "having the colour of a blue lotus." Following Pathmanathan (2000), I think the insertion of "blue" in the translation is part of the confusion leading to the conflation of Upulvan with Visnu.

9. H. L Seneviratne (1978:102–8) notes that this well-known mythic story is still recited as part of the Valiyak rites held every year following the conclusion of the *asala perahera* at the Maha Devalaya in Kandy. This subject is addressed specifically in chapter 6.

10. Yet the well-known nationalist historian G. C. Mendis (1965) was making it clear by the early 1960s that the Vijaya story was purely myth, with little historical value except for the fact that it is a clear instance of a people's historicization of myth.

11. These include mythic episodes in the *Mahavamsa* that describe the conversion to Buddhism of the Sri Lankan king, Devanampiya Tissa, who then articulates a model of

Asokan Buddhist kingship that becomes paradigmatic for ensuing centuries (two millennia), the arrival of the *dhamma* and *sangha* in the persons of Asoka's own children, Mahinda and Sanghamitta, who establish the *bhikkhu* and *bhikkuni sanghas*, propagate the *dhamma*, and herald the arrival of the *Sri Mahabodhi* (a sapling believed to be a graft from the original tree of enlightenment in Bodhgaya, India). Other myths explain the arrival of bodily relics of the Buddha to inaugurate the beginnings of festivals, such as the *perahera*, the legitimization of the Mahavihara monastery, the consecration of a boundary around the holy city and royal capital of Anuradhapura, etc. See Geiger, *Mahavamsa* (1912:3–135).

12. The myth of Vijaya and the establishment of kingship is found in chapters 6 through 10 of the *Mahavamsa* (51–76).

13. The British claimed he was from a low-caste village five miles out of Colombo and had been duped by Kandyan chiefs into leading the insurrection. A very detailed account of the entire insurrection from beginning to end that is constructed from official sources is found in Appuhamy (1995:421–95).

14. For the rather dramatic details of this event, taken from court testimony on record in Kandy from the mid-nineteenth century, see Archibald Lawrie (1898 2:127–29).

15. For a discussion of this modern identification of Natha Deviyo with Bodhisatva Maitreya, see the concluding chapter, entitled "Maitreya-in-the-Making," in my *Buddha in the Crown* (1991:214–25).

16. This remarkable turn of political events is described in detail in Paranavitana and Nicholas (1961:306–307).

17. The specific version that Bell has recorded and von Schroeder has alluded to is linked to the founding of the Alutnuvara *devalaya* and the spread of the Visnu cult to Kandy and Hanguranketa, not Dambulla.

18. Scott tells the story to illustrate how the power of sight has been valorized in the cultic context of *yaktovil*, or ritual sacrifices to channel or deflect the power of *yakkhas*. See his chapter entitled "Malign Glances" in Scott (1994:38–66). Anuradha Seneviratne (1984b:51) refers to this myth in passing in his treatment of the cave at Dambulla in which this image is ensconced. But Wanaratana (1972:105) adds significantly to the discussion: "Because of the strong glare of the gems fixed in the eyes of the statue, many navigators were led astray at night, being unable to gauge the proximity of the land, and met many accidents. Therefore, with the king's consent, the statue was taken elsewhere. . . . Another myth holds that some navigators bribed a goldsmith to cut off the feet of the statue to lower its gaze. As a result, the goldsmith could no longer live in this area in peace. It is also said that a painter altered the gaze of the statue. However, the mystery of the sandalwood image still remains" (translated from the Sinhala by Kanchuka Dharmasiri); I collected the same story, almost verbatim, from Mr. W. Dayananda, the long-time *kapurala* of the Kataragama Devalaya at the Devinuvara Visnu ritual complex, in April 2000.

19. Godakumbura (1955:222–224) says that the *Parakumba Sirita* is largely an erotic poem, which he thinks was written metrically so that it could be danced rhythmically by dancers in the king's court.

20. The inclusion of Seenigama as a possible venue for the arrival of the sandalwood image would seem to link the cult of Visnu somehow with the cult of Devol Deviyo, whose introduction to the island at Seenigama is, as Obeyesekere (1983:306–312) argues, a reflection of historical migrations of merchant communities from South India to the

west coast of Sri Lanka. Obeyesekere provides an interesting analysis of how the myth of Devol's coming onshore reflects the ambivalent Sinhala process of first excluding and then including a "foreign deity," similar to the patterns and processes of initiation rites. These patterns and processes, in turn, are reflective of sociocultural assimilation. He has observed this ambivalent process within the performances of many folk dramas.

21. Wanaratana is clearly appealing to the popularly understood significance of the well-known mythic story of the "Kustarajagala" bodhisatva image located in nearby Weligama. The myth of Kustaraja has to do with the arrival of a foreign king who suffered from a skin disease and was cured by a steady diet of coconut milk (see my *Buddha in the Crown*, p. 164 and plate 8). Paranavitana (1928) originally believed the image was of Avalokitesvara and, as of this writing, there is still a prominent sign at the site created by the Sri Lanka government Department of Archaeology indicating that this is indeed the case. Wanaratana would know this. Prematilleke (1978:172–75) argues that the image is a confusing cross between the iconography of the Mahayana bodhisatvas Samantabhadra and Avalokitesvara, thus refining the thesis that had been previously suggested by van Lohuizen-de Leeuw (1965)—that the image is one of "the Adi-Buddha Samantabhadra in his Dharmakaya aspect."

22. I cannot locate the original 1970 publication in which this article appeared. However, it was reprinted as a pamphlet: A. D. T. Edward Perera, *The Enigma of the Man and Horse at Isurumuniya, Sri Lanka* (1978); see my *Buddha in the Crown*, 81–82, for a critical comment on Perera's speculation, and plate 19 for a photo of the sculptural relief in question.

23. Jon Walters points out that the *Mahavamsa* commentary, the *Vamsatthappakassini* (2:407) identifies this site as Kassapagiri Vihara, and that the *Culavamsa* (1:43, *n.* 7) refers to the main monastery at Isurumuniya as *bodhi-uppalavanna-kassapa-giri rajamahavihara*. Walters also notes inscriptional evidence for this name in *Epigraphia Zeylonica* I:33, but doubts that the naming of the monastery has anything to do with Kassapa's daughter; instead, he suggests that perhaps it is named after one of the prominent nuns in *apadana* literature (private communication).

24. For a summary description of the historical and cultural significance of this victory over the invader from Southeast Asia, see my *Buddha in the Crown*, 94–99; for an extensive discussion of the problems involved in reconstructing the political nature and significance of the *Javaka* invasion led by Chandrabhanu, see Amaradasa Liyanagamage, *The Decline of Polonnaruwa and the Rise of Dambadeniya* (1968:133–59) and W. M. Sirisena, *Sri Lanka and Southeast Asia* (1978:36–57).

25. The *Culavamsa* (90:100; 2:209–210) credits Parakramabahu IV (1302–46) with constructing "a long temple consisting of two stories" and "in the district of Mayadhanu a new town with fine walls and gate towers. There he had a fair temple erected to the gods with lofty spires and two stories, placed there a glorious statue of the lotus-hued King of the gods (Visnu) and celebrated a great sacrificial festival."

26. I have discussed this story at some length in *Buddha in the Crown*, 49–51, as it appears in the *Avalokitesvara Guna Karandavyuha Sutra*. Variants of the myth are found in the *Divyavadana, Mahavastu,* and the *Jatakas.*

27. See pp. 62–90 of my *Buddha in the Crown* for an overview of Mahayana in the Anuradhapura period and a discussion of the iconography of Avalokitesvara in Sri Lanka from its earliest appearance to the present.

28. Neither is Upulvan mentioned in any Sanskrit literature.

29. See note 17 above.

30. Since Sri Lanka's independence, the nationalists' agenda for archeology has been apparent in any number of projects undertaken by the government's Department of Archaeology. The complete renovation of the Devinuvara Visnu *devalaya*, celebrating the country's "minister of defense" in the immediate aftermath of independence from Britain, was, therefore, a "natural" project to undertake at this time.

31. See *Epigraphia Zeylonica* I:132.

32. *Culavamsa* 60.59; 2:220.

33. Indeed, a separate shrine for Upulvan is located in the surrounding *devalaya* section of the temple, while Visnu is seen only in the constellation of deities above the *makara torana* of the *buduge*.

34. Within the lengthy quoted text below, I have cited page numbers in Paranavitana's monograph that contain various discussions relevant to the conclusions that he draws. These are given within brackets, so that the reader interested in examining Paranavitana's conclusions more comprehensively may do so directly.

35. Not only is there no material, cultural, or literary evidence for the presence of Sanskrit epic literature in Sri Lanka's Buddhist culture before the sixth century of the first millennium C.E.—see Hallisey (2003:690), the conventional dating of these texts is anywhere from the second century B.C.E. to the second century C.E.

36. I have presented only a part of Obeyesekere's analysis of Upulvan. The remainder will be applied to later discussions.

37. For instance, the seventeenth- or eighteenth-century *Ran-dunu Paralaya* ("The Inspiration of the Golden Bow") and the *Randunu Mangalle* ("Ode to the Golden Bow"), and the early nineteenth-century *Ramasandesa* and *Ahalepola Varnanava*.

38. Buddhist *vamsa* literature is somewhat analogous to Old Testament biblical literature that would include *Exodus*, I and II *Chronicles*, and I and II *Kings*.

39. It is possible, but not certain by any means, that the Vijaya story, and hence the role of Upulvan, was not inserted into the *Mahavamsa* narrative until a much later time than Mahanama's compilation. I am suggesting this possibility because of the nature of the myth of the sandalwood image. It functions, as I have said, as a myth of origins for the cult of Upulvan. Its first literary reference is in the fifteenth century, but it alleges to describe events during the eighth century. Aside from Upulvan's brief reference within the Vijaya story, there is no mention of Upulvan in the *Mahavamsa-Culvamsa* until Prince Virabahu's post-victory pilgrimage to Devinuvara after his defeat of Chandrabhanu in the thirteenth century. It is difficult to explain why there is no mention of Upulvan or his cult for eight hundred years if his recognized function was the protection of the Sinhala state during this time. If the *Mahavamsa-Culavamsa* was updated or expanded during the reign of Parakramabahu I (1153–86 C.E.) at Polonnaruva and again during the reign of Parakramabahu IV (early fourteenth century) at Kurunegala, it is possible that the Vijaya myth, or at least the reference within it to Upulvan's definitive role, was not inserted until one of these redactions. Since Upulvan's popularity as the guardian deity of the state seems to reach its zenith in the fourteenth and fifteenth centuries, given the evidence of *sandesa* literature, it is possible that either the Vijaya story, or at least Upulvan's role within it, was included within the recension of *Mahavamsa-Culavamsa* in the early fourteenth century during the reign of Parakramabahu IV—in effect, reading

back into tradition an understanding of his important role as it was then popularly understood.

40. The *Sinhala Encyclopaedia* (1970:4:728–32) article on Upulvan suggests, on the basis of references in the *Pujavaliya and Rajavaliya* that the town was first established by Aggabodhi IV (667–83 c.e.).

41. Wanaratana (1971:16ff).

42. Wanaratana (1971:16 ff.) mentions that even today there are people living in Devinuvara whose family name is Thenuwara.

43. See note 37 above.

44. There is more to this account of Parakramabahu's connection to Devinuvara, which is associated with the founding of the Alutnuvara *devalaya*, a mythic extension discussed in chapter 7.

45. The inscription is translated by Paranavitana (1953:69–70).

46. K. A. Nilakantha Sastri (1939:275–76), cited in Pathmanathan (2000:4–5); see also Albert Gray, *Ibn Batuta in the Malidives and Ceylon* (Madras: Asian Educational Services, 1996).

47. As a reference for this, Pathmanathan simply notes one Dipankara Thera, who is quoted in Ariyapala (1956:189).

48. While Queryoz's account is compelling, Tennent (1977: 2:637–38), having read other Portuguese sources as well, offers this summary description: "Dondra Head, the Sunium [?] of Ceylon, and the southern extremity of the island, is covered with the ruins of a temple, which was once one of the most celebrated in Ceylon. The headland itself has been the resort of devotees and pilgrims, from the most remote ages;—Ptolemy describes it as *Dagana*, 'sacred to the Moon,' and the Buddhists constructed there one of their earliest dagobas, the restoration of which was the care of successive sovereigns. But the most important temple was a shrine which in very early times had been erected by the Hindus in honour of Vishnu. It was in the height of its splendour, when, in 1587, the place was devastated in the course of the marauding expedition by which De Souza d'Arronches sought to creat a diversion, during the siege of Colombo by Raja Singha II [here Tennent has confused Rajasimha I (1581–93 c.e.) and Rajasimha II (1635–87 c.e.)]. The historians of the period state at that time Dondra was the most renowned place of pilgrimage in Ceylon; Adam's Peak scarcely excepted. The temple, they say, was so vast, that from sea it had the appearance of a city. The pagoda was raised on vaulted arches, richly decorated, and roofed with plates of gilded copper. It was encompassed by a quadrangular cloister, opening under verandahs, upon a terrace and gardens with odiferous shrubs and trees, whose flowers were gathered by the priests for processions. De Souza entered the gates without resistance; and his soldiers tore down the statues, which were more than a thousand in number. The temple and its buildings were overthrown, its arches and its colonnades were demolished, and its gates and towers leveled to the ground. The plunder was immense, in ivory, gems, jewels, sandal-wood, and ornaments of gold. As the last indignity that could be offered to the sacred place, cows were slaughtered in the courts, and the cars of the idol, with other combustible materials, being fired, the shrine was reduced to ashes. A stone doorway exquisitely carved, and a small building, whose extraordinary strength resisted the violence of the destroyers, are all that now remain standing; but the ground for a considerable distance is strewn with ruins, conspicuous among which are

numbers of finely cut columns of granite. The dagoba which stood on the crown of the hill, is a mound of shapeless debris."

49. The full text of this *sannasa* translated privately for me by Prof. P. B. Meegaskumbura of the Dept. of Sinhala at the University of Peradeniya is given as an appendix to chapter 5.

50. It is very interesting to note here that Queryoz's (1992: 1:9 ff.) stated rationale for the labor of love that took him seventeen years to write, that is, his *Spiritual and Temporal Conquest of Ceilao,* was to critique and condemn the behavior of the Portuguese armed forces in Sri Lanka, a behavior he found adverse to creating conditions receptive to the Christian gospel. From Queryoz's point of view, the expulsion of the Portuguese from Ceilao a decade earlier was a sign of God's displeasure.

51. The sacking of Devinuvara is usually reported by historians as a kind of diversionary maneuver on the part of the Portuguese during the time when they were under a severe pressure within the Colombo Fort owing to the concerted siege mounted by Rajasina I. Indeed, it very well may have been. But the symbolic significance of attacking Devinuvara also needs to be mentioned. By destroying the central cultic shrine of the most politically significant deity of the era, the lead guardian deity of Lanka, the Portuguese were declaring that the Lankan state, despite its temporary position of advantage, was not inviolate. Their strike on Devinuvara was a thrust to the heart of medieval Lankan political legitimization. It is interesting that within five years of this event, another claim to Sinhala kingship had been established in Kandy which was far more Buddhist-oriented in its rhetorical and symbolic claims to legitimacy, insofar as the *Dalada* (tooth-relic of the Buddha) and the reestablishment of the *sangha* were emphasized as Vimaladharmasuriya I's chief objects of patronage.

4. Transformed Deity: The "Buddhist Visnu" in Sinhala Literature and Liturgy

1. *Aspects of Sinhalese Culture* (1992:8).

2. In the up-country at Kandy, Hanguranketa, Gadaladeniya, Lankatilaka, Alutnuvara, and at the southernmost tip of the island, Devinuvara.

3. Translated privately by P. B. Meegaskumbura, Dept of Sinhalese, University of Peradeniya, from J. E. Sedaraman (1967:86–87).

4. The fourteen are those objects listed in the third and fourth verses which were procured by Visnu when he stirred the Ocean of Milk.

5. Referring to the thirty-three gods of traditional Vedic lore.

6. A ninth verse has been added:

These eight verses which are extremely auspicious and which destroy the ocean
    of evil
Have been composed by that virtuous poet Kalidasa.
If one conjures a singular focus of the mind while contemplating Mahesvara and
    then recites them,
As the Ganga reaches the ocean, so too would merits flow.

7. Ibid., 91.

8. For a cogent resume of the relationship between Sinhala and Sanskrit, as well the Sinhala literary relationship to South Indian vernaculars, see Hallisey (2003:689–746).

9. Verses 133–36 translated privately by Prof. U. P. Meddegama, Dept.of Sinhalese, University of Peradeniya, from Siri Tilakasiri, ed., *Tisara Sandesa* (1996); minor adaptations are mine.

10. Translated privately by Prof. P. B. Meegaskumbura, Dept. of Sinhalese, University of Peradeniya, from Gunawardhana (1949); minor adaptations are mine.

11. This is the same important monk I mentioned in the first chapter, who became critical of the worship of the gods.

12. Here we also see Alagonakkara, the de facto military defender of Sinhala interests, mentioned prominently as well.

13. Translated by Prof. U. P. Meddegama, from W. F. Gunawardhana (1952).

14. Translated by P. B. Meegaskumbura, from K. D. Endiris de Silva (1927:15–16).

15. This tenth verse is in Sanskrit.

16. The final verse constitutes a mantra.

17. Cited as "Text 6" of the "Ritual Torch of Time," a *yadinna*, or invocation to Visnu, in Obeyesekere (1984:103–105).

18. Here Obeyesekere indicates that these last three lines in brackets were not sung in his tape-recorded version, but are found in a written text from Sinigama on the southwest coast.

19. Visnu as the cosmic creator is certainly known in the popular lore of Lanka. Early in the twentieth century, Henry Parker (I:39–41) recorded a myth from the Northwest Province about how Rahu (here understood as the chief *asura*) and Visnu collaborated in the re-creation of the world in this last of the *yugas*, the *Kali*. Among the interesting details in this story is that, unlike its telling in the Brahmanical *Visnu Purana*, this Sinhalese version has the chief *asura* cooperating with Visnu to create the world, rather than impeding it, and Saman Deviyo assisting in the creation of men and then women. There is another creation myth, the *Loka Uppattiya* (*Sinhala Kavi* 3:279), in which Visnu figures. According to Neville, it was chanted when *govi* women attained full age. It contains the interesting detail that Mahasammata, the first and primordial king, was married to Visnu's sister, Manikpala. The couple ask Visnu to build the Mahasammata palace.

20. See especially Sree Padma, "Serpent Symbolism in the Mythology of Andhra Folk Goddesses" (1998).

21. Obeyesekere (1984:141–56) provides several textual traditions of the myth of Devol Deviyo and his powers.

22. This particular rite of exorcism has been studied in great depth by Kapferer (1997). The rather minor role played by Visnu in this context is indicated on pp. 127–28.

23. Translated privately by Prof. P. B. Meegaskumbura, Dept. of Sinhalese, University of Peradeniya, from Nimal Prematillake, ed. (Bandaragama, Sri Lanka: Sisira Printers, 1987:9–10).

24. The *garuda* is a mythical eagle, which serves as the vehicle upon which Visnu rides.

25. P. B. Meegaskumbura suggests that this may be the Kaustubha gem found in the "ocean of milk."

26. Verses 14 and 15 are in Sanskrit.

27. "Venu" is the literary Sinhala form of Visnu.

28. Frank Reynolds (1994:60) has said, in relation to the fact that the *Ramayana*'s significance has not been studied much, if at all, by scholars interested in Theravada Buddhism: "In part, this serious lacuna in Theravada scholarship can be traced to some very influential Buddhologists, who have concluded from the seeming paucity of classical Rama traditions in Sri Lanka that these traditions do not play a significant role in Theravada culture as a whole."

I think Reynolds is very right here. While I would hesitate to identify the Rama traditions examined as "classical" in nature, I think they are much more important than what Richard Gombrich (1985:427–37) has indicated. On the other hand, the Sri Lankan sources are not nearly as important as the Rama traditions in the traditional Thai-Lao historical and cultural contexts that Reynolds has studied.

29. For an excellent study of the many various "crystalizations" of the *Ramayana* in various Indian and Southeast Asian contexts, see Paula Richman, ed., *Many Ramayanas* (1994), especially the articles by A. K. Ramanujan, "Three Hundred Ramayanas: Five Examples and Three Thoughts on Translation [pp. 22–49]," and Frank Reynolds, "*Ramayana, Rama Jataka,* and *Ramkien: A Comparative Study of Hindu and Buddhist Traditions*" [pp. 50–63]. Ramanujan points out that there are some 25 Sanskrit recensions, in addition to a legion of other versions in diverse languages, from Central Asia to the Indonesian archipelago. The variations in substance and in didactic intention are so great that Ramanujan is finally forced to illustrate the issue by referring to "Aristotle's jack knife." "When the philosopher asked an old carpenter how long he had had his knife, the latter said, 'Oh, I've had it for thirty years. I've changed the blade a few times and the handle a few times, but it's still the same knife'" [p. 44].

30. The *Dasaratha Jataka* (Cowell 4:78–82) in Pali confirms the fact that the *Ramayana*, at least in part, goes back to possibly the later centuries of the first millennium B.C.E. Its adaptation here stresses the Buddhist virtues of detachment and awareness of change, as the major focus is upon how Rama-pandita responds to the news of his royal father's death. There is no mention of Ravana, Lanka, or Ravana's abduction of Sita, and Sita is simply known as the younger sister of Rama and Lakkhana (Laksmana). The conclusion to the *jataka* adds that the Buddha was Rama in this former life, "Rahula's mother" was Sita, and Ananda was Bharata, Rama's half brother whose mother had tried to claim the royal throne for Bharata when it rightfully belonged to Rama. Rather than Ayodhya, the setting is Benares. A summary of the story is given below in relation to the *Rajavaliya*'s account of Rama.

31. In Valmiki's *Ramayana*, Dasaratha is king of Ayodhya, and Rama and Laksman (and his twin Satrughna who is not mentioned in this *jataka*) are born of separate mothers. Sita, of course, is not Rama's sister but the bride he wins by stringing his enormous divine bow.

32. In Valmiki's account, it is Dasaratha's youngest queen, Kaikeyi, previously having saved King Dasaratha's life and consequently having been rewarded with two boons, who gives birth to Bharata. Fearing Rama, she first requests that he be banished to the forest for fourteen years, and that Bharata become the heir apparent to rule in the meantime. Rama accepts these conditions, and departs with Sita and Laksmana, but Bharata has misgivings and pursues Rama in the vain hope of persuading him to return; he doesn't, because of his loyalty to his father King Dasaratha's wishes. Bharata says he will reign only

until Rama returns, and in the meantime places Rama's slippers on the throne as a symbolic gesture of the true kingship.

33. The identification of Saman with Laksmana in this story lends more support to the assertion that the first formulation of the "four guardian deities" of Lanka was drawn from the *Ramayana* epic.

34. This very question is raised and explored at some length in Kathleen Erndl's "The Mutilation of Surparnakha," in Richman (1994). It would seem that the question is even more sharply focussed in the Sinhala context, insofar as it is Rama, rather than Laksmana, who mutilates Surpanakha. Neville (1954, 3:98–99) also makes a lengthy comment on this episode, but focuses instead on Surpanakha's "unmaidenly conduct." Here is part of it: "I think this is important and an ancient and intentional feature. It probably reflects the contempt felt by the people of Northern India, for the ancient and matriarchal custom still kept up by the Nairs and others, in southern India, by which the wife has full authority over her affairs, selects her own husband, and gives her son the right of inheritance to her mother's brother's estate. A connected custom exists among the Sinhalese, called a *binna* marriage, under which the woman selects and discards her husband at her will."

Neville's explanation of *binna* marriages is a bit overwrought, but I think his point in general about some tension between northern and southern, or Aryan and Dravidian, custom has an element of merit in it. In addition to the more favorable way that the Sinhalas depict Ravana, some communities in Tamilnad even today understand Ravana as a great culture hero. For an extended example, see Richman (1994:175–201).

35. Translated by Prof. P. B. Meegaskumbura, Dept of Sinhalese, University of Peradeniya. The original text, supplied to me by Prof. Jon Walters, Dept. of Religion, Whitman College, is found in Dhammaloka, ed., *Siri Rama Sandesa* (1950).

36. Until at least the late 1980s, the government-owned television station, Rupavahini, every night at around 6 p.m., used to broadcast "Homage to the Triple Gem," a fifteen-minute chant led by Buddhist monks. Within that chant, several verses referred to each of the four guardian deities. Some of those verses were extracted from this particular *kavi* and modified.

37. Henry Parker (1981:156–58) collected another and more extended version of this myth early in the century. In Parker's version, among the various differences, the seventh and eldest child is Kadavara.

38. Visnu's role as a progenitor of deities, or as a god providing their warrant, is also seen in myths related to the cult of Aiyanar. Aiyanar seems to have been worshipped in Lanka since at least the time of *Kokila Sandesa* (vs. 203), which refers to his shrine at Mannar. Ilangasinha says that Aiyanar may have come to Lanka with the "Aryans" who migrated to the Kandy region during the Gampola reign of Bhuvanekabahu IV (1335–41 C.E.). He wonders if the worship of the god had something to do with the emergent power of the Jaffna *aryacakravarti* at that time. What is interesting here is that the *Ayyanayaka Devi Kavi* (Barnett: 7), another Sinhala folk ballad, notes that Aiyanar came to Lanka after having been born from the right side of his mother by virtue of the power of Upulvan, and that it was Upulvan who granted him permission to come to Lanka (Ilangasinha 371).

39. See Shulman (1980:275–85) for his extensive discussion of the Murukan/Valli myth, elements of which he describes as being very ancient. In the Tamil rendition he

presents, one that is quite similar in detail to the version just presented, Valli is born "to a deer impregnated by the lustful glance of Sivamuni" (276), thus indicating that Siva is her father.

5. Seeking Protection: Cultic Life at the *Udarata* Visnu *Devalayas*

1. Knox (1985:72).

2. According to local lore recorded on a public sign posted in the middle of the Alutnuvara Devalaya complex, the shift to Kandy was made by King Senaret [1604–35 c.e.], but the date is erroneously given as 1714. Bhikkhu Thalgaspitiye Thero, incumbent of the Kirti Sri Rajamahavihara opposite the Alutnuvara Devalaya, says that Senaret made the move in 1643, again a problematic date. The dating of the move from Alutnuvara to Kandy is a difficult problem to resolve with any certainty. Duncan says (72): "In 1748 Kirti Sri had the image of the god Visnu brought from Alutnuvara to Kandy. A temple for Visnu was built to the northwest of the palace where a temple for the local godling, Devata Bandara, had been. The image of Devata Bandara was removed to Alutnuvara and a small *devale* for a smaller image of Devata Bandara was built next to the new one for Visnu in Kandy. Devata Bandara, who was also known as Dedimunda, remained in Kandy as Visnu's chief *adikar* and commander in chief."

H. L. Seneviratne (1978:12) says this: "According to the Sinhalese work of the Kandyan period, the *Lanka Puvata*, it was in the early seventeenth century that he [Visnu] was brought to Kandy, and Robert Knox (1681) refers to him as 'the god of Alutnuvara,' an allusion to the town where to this day the most famous shrine dedicated to him is located, and from which he was ceremonially brought to Kandy."

Neither Duncan's nor Seneviratne's statements are exactly correct. With regard to Duncan's statement, the *devalaya sannasa* I shall present and discuss below clearly indicates the presence of the Visnu *devalaya* in Kandy in 1709. With regard to the uncharacteristic mistakes in Seneviratne's statement, the *Lanka Puvata* actually refers to the insignia of the warrant gods being brought to Kandy during the reign of Vimaladharmasuriya II [1687–1707 c.e.], which makes the dating of that text at least late seventeenth century or early eighteenth century. And further, Alutnuvara is not known "to this day" as the location of the most famous shrine to Visnu. Rather, it is known instead as the cultic seat of Dadimunda, who is also now known as "Alutnuvara Deviyo." There is a rather newly constructed Visnu *devalaya* now located within the Kirti Sri Rajamahaviharaya, adjacent to the present Alutnuvara Devalaya, but it was built in 1985, seven years after the publication of Seneviratne's study, and therefore its presence cannot account for Seneviratne's confusion.

3. Another, less well-known but significant example is Ridigama Deviyo.

4. See Obeyesekere (1984:66–70) and Gombrich (1991:210–11).

5. In the hierarchy of the Kandyan Sinhala pantheon of deities, the Buddha, of course, occupies the apex and, as such, is sometimes referred to as *devatideva* ("the deity beyond the deities.") Beneath the Buddha are the "four warrant deities," or gods of national significance; below these the more regionally oriented *bandaras*; and finally, a series of various supernatural agents, including strictly village deities—*yaksas*, *bhutas*, *pretas*, etc.—all within a hierarchy graded by ethical considerations.

6. This means that Duncan's assertion that Kirti Sri shifted Visnu's seat to Kandy in 1748 is in error.

7. Translated from the early eighteenth-century Sinhala by Prof. P. B. Meegaskumbura, Department of Sinhalese, University of Peradeniya, Sri Lanka; edited by Prof. John Clifford Holt, Department of Religion, Bowdoin College, USA; authenticity confirmed by Mr. Denis Ratwatte, Basnayaka Nilame, Maha Devalaya, Kandy, Sri Lanka, in May 2000. There is no title affixed to the *sannasa*. Footnotes 8–17 below are contributed by Prof. Meegaskumbura.

8. *Girihela: Devundara. Girihela* is the original name of the place before it came to be known as *Devinuvara* ("City of the Deity"). The deity at *Devinuvara*, as discussed in chapter 3, was Upulvan, later identified as Visnu.

9. Literally "body of *Khadhira* (modern Sinhala: *Kihiri*) wood;" a reference to the sandalwood-image myth about the image of Upulvan being carved out of a sandalwood log by the god *Visvakarma* in the presence of King Dappula.

10. *Dasanana,* an epithet of *Ravana.*

11. Doubtful term.

12. An *asura*; literally, "born of a drop of blood."

13. Name of a demon.

14. Evil uncle of *Krsna* in the *Harivamsa.*

15. Vishnu's demonical antagonist in his *Narasimha avatar.*

16. December–January.

17. 1709 C.E.

18. An area in modern-day Sri Lanka located to the south of the 45-kilometer post on the present Kandy–Colombo road.

19. Ananda Coomaraswamy has included a plate (XL, no. 7) of the ivory casket of the Algama *sannasa* in his *Mediaeval Sinhalese Art* (1956). Erroneously, he (206) ascribes the dedication of the *sannasa* to King Rajadhi Rajasimha (1782–98 C.E.] "after a victory over the Dutch at Gurubebile."

20. See Duncan (42–58) for his elucidation of what he calls the "Sakran discourse," which refers to elements of Hindu myth which were accommodated by Sinhala kings in the construction of "narrative landscapes." The other major discourse discussed at length by Duncan is the "Asokan discourse," based on the model of kingship attributed to the Indian emperor Asoka in the third century B.C.E.. For a full discussion of various discourses of Kandyan kingship, see my *Religious World of Kirti Sri* (1996:15–39).

21. Indeed, the royal consecration was a multi-ritual affair. We know that the *abhiseka* or "anointing" ritual inspired by Hindu practice took place at the Kandy Visnu Devalaya in 1798 C.E. for the last of the Kandyan kings, and we know that kings received their formal names at the Natha Devalaya at the time of Kirti Sri's 1751 coronation. As for the idea of the king first marching like a *cakravartin* to the north, I think this observation is a bit strained. If the Visnu *devalaya* was the first stop in the ritual procedures, the direction of the march would have been west, given the location of the king's quarters within the royal complex. Moreover, I think there is more obvious symbolism attached to the fact that the king looked out from his venue to the west, between the Visnu *devalaya* closely located on his right and the Natha *devalaya* closely located on his left. Further in the direction of town, but still within the precincts of a designated sacred area, was the Pattini *devalaya*.

Two blocks to the west and within the hub of Kandyan commerce was (and is) the Kataragama *devalaya*. The symbolism of this arrangement expresses the closeness of Natha and Visnu to the concerns of kingship and to the *Dalada*, indicating simultaneously the importance of their guardian-deity status and their progress toward *nibbana*. Pattini's and Kataragama's venues indicate their more thoroughly involved action in the concerns of the common human world.

22. In the spring of 2000, I met a well-known university professor at the Alutnuvara Devalaya, seeking help in his court case to secure a coveted academic chair in his department. In the spring of 2001, I observed an obvious VIP in the presence of a well-known Buddhist monk making a petition to Dadimunda at Alutnuvara. I later learned that the VIP was actually the Major General, Chief of Staff of the Sri Lankan Army, seeking Dadimunda's help. The following weekend, I read on page 1 of the *Sunday Times* (April 15, 2001) that, contrary to the accepted policy of being forced to retire at age 55, the major general had received a special dispensation from the president of the country to continue in service for one more year.

23. See the detailed study by Desmond Mallikarachchi, *Religious, Ritual and Ceremonial Practices of Sinhala Buddhist Traders in the City of Kandy* (1998:136–37).

24. See Obeyeskere (1963), Ames (1964), Halvorson (1978), Scott (1994), Gombrich (1991), etc.

25. See Malalgoda (1976:191–255).

26. For a recent critical discussion of Dharmapala's legacy for the Sinhala Buddhist tradition, both monastic and lay, see H. L. Seneviratne (1999:25–55).

27. Dharmapala is sometimes given more credit for "reforms" than he deserves. Throughout this study, it has been clear that deity veneration is an issue that has surfaced within the Buddhist *sangha* periodically since at least the thirteenth-century *Amavatura* and *Butsarana*. The urge to depreciate deity veneration and *devalaya* ritual practice in the twentieth century probably owes its origins, more precisely, to a controversy known as "Devapuja Vadaya," which brewed in the 1870s and for several more decades, owing in part to the origins of the Ramanna fraternity and its attempt to establish a more rational Buddhism devoid of what it regarded as superstitions and cultural accretions. See Malalgoda (169–70) for specific references in Sinhala pamphlets of the time that discuss the substantial, relevant, and attendant details.

28. See especially, for instance, Terence Day, *The Great and Little Tradition in Theravada Buddhist Studies* (1988).

29. In the abstract, this is the structure of Weber's argument that is articulated in *The Protestant Ethic and Spirit of Capitalism*. See Weber (1976).

30. Sometimes it is the case that *yaksas* are the karmic consequence of society's injustices or undue punishments. Their malevolent presence in this world is what society deserves for its deviance from moral rectitude. P. B. Meegaskumbura, private communication. See also my *Buddha in the Crown* (1991:133–37).

31. See, for examples, the direct discussions of the issue as they are articulated in the *Vinayapitaka* (I.1.8), the *Dhammapada* (vs. 32, 57, 87, 253, 272), *Samyutta Nikaya* (39.1), among many others that can be cited.

32. *Samyutta Nikaya* 56.11.

33. See *Buddha in the Crown* (1991:19–26).

34. Carter, s.v. "lokottara."

35. Most of the lesser deities (*devata*) receive their warrants directly from the higher gods such as Visnu, Natha, or Kataragama. As indicated in earlier discussions, even Upulvan received his charge from Sakra, and not directly from the Buddha.

36. The best sources remain H. L. Seneviratne (1978) and Godakumbura (1970); see also my discussion and analysis of the *perahara* symbolism in village contexts where Natha *devalayas* are located (1991: 190–201).

37. These include *Karti, Alut Avurudda,* etc.

38. In addition to the four *devalayas* in Kandy, the thirteen include Lankatilaka (Visnu), Gadaladeniya (Visnu), Pasgama (Natha), Vallahagoda (Pattini), Ganegoda (Kataragama), Ambekke (Kataragama), Dodanwela (Natha), Vegiriya (Natha), and Alawatugoda (Saman). For a picture of the group of *basnayaka nilames* together with President Chandrika Kumaratunga Bandaranaike in 2000, see figure 5.3.

39. *Goyigamas* are the land-owning farmer caste, and the highest-ranking within the hierarchy of caste as it has been configured among the Sinhalas. Differently from the well-known Brahmanical scheme, there exist no *dvija* or "twice born" *varnas* (Brahmans, *ksatriyans,* and *vaisyas*). For an overview of social stratification in traditional Kandyan society, see L. S. Dewaraja, "The Social and Economic Conditions of the The Kandyan Kingdom in the Seventeenth and Eighteenth Centuries" (1995); for more in-depth studies of caste in traditional Sinhala society, see Ralph Pieris, *Sinhalese Social Organization* (1956), and Bryce Ryan, *Caste in Modern Ceylon* (1993); for a consideration of caste issues arising in relation to Buddhism, see Gombrich (1992: 343–71).

40. In 1983–85, I had learned that the Natha *devalaya* in Kandy had been endowed with 10,000 acres. Thus, the Visnu *devalaya* owns more than three times that amount of land, a sign of its prestige among the former kings of Kandy.

41. *Rajakariya* literally means "service to the king." It connotes a ritual obligation or duty levied by the Kandyan kings, on behalf of *devalayas* and *viharayas*, on castes or families. In exchange for cultivating the lands donated by the king for the endowment of *devalayas* and *viharayas*, these castes or families are expected either to perform ritual service (such as drumming, providing linen, or sweeping the sacred compounds) or make a payment in lieu of such services. For specific examples of types of *rajakariya* duties assigned by kings at various *devalayas* and *viharayas*, see Lawrie (1898).

42. A keeper and trainer.

43. To understand the magnitude of these costs, it is helpful to remember that the current *per capita* income of Sri Lanka is about US $850 per year.

44. For an excellent discussion of the nature of royal endowments made on behalf of Kandyan kings for *viharayas* and *devalayas*, see L. S. Dewaraja, *The Kandyan Kingdom of Sri Lanka (1707–1782)*, pp. 176–88; for a discussion of how this system was impacted by colonial powers, see K. M. de Silva (1981:212–16; 243–48).

45. The LTTE allegedly bombed the Dalada Maligava in January 1998, by having suicide bombers drive a truck filled with explosives to the temple's entrance. Since that time, the entire "sacred square" area has been fenced off, one of the major arteries of traffic in Kandy has been indefinitely closed, and all who enter the area are subject to a careful (and sometimes intrusive) physical body search. On one random day, I counted more than 65 army or police personnel on duty within the "sacred area."

46. For a diagram of the *devalaya* compound, see figure 5.1.

47. Indeed, I found that attitudes about photographing images of deities were quite different from those I had encountered in the 1980s. At that time, when I was trying to write about the iconography of Avalokitesvara (Natha Deviyo), I was given unrestricted access by *kapuralas*, enabling me to photograph the images in question. It proved impossible this time around. Therefore, I have had to leave the discussion of iconography aside in this study, much to my regret. A drawing of the image by Kanchuka Dharmasiri is found in figure 5.4.

48. See, for example, figure 5.5. In this example, however, the traditional attributes of Visnu are plainly seen: the conch, the mace, the disc, the empty right front hand in *abhaya* ("fear not") *mudra*, with the deity seated on *Garuda*, his well-known *vahana* ("vehicle").

49. I unsuccessfully tried to interview this woman, as well as her husband, on several occasions.. But they claimed to be Kataragama devotees and said I should talk to someone else. On this business woman devotee, see the account of Mrs. Wijeratne below.

50. At Gadaladeniya, as at every other Visnu cultic venue, my request to photograph was denied. But I was granted permission for a brief viewing of the image of Visnu inside the sanctum sanctorum at Gadaladeniya. It is an extraordinary image, quite unlike any other deity image I have seen in Sri Lanka. Whatever the substance of its physical core, it is now plastered but rapidly deteriorating. It is a seated figure with two arms, about four feet in height, and holding the remnants of a lotus in the left hand. The right arm is badly decayed. It wears a crown. I could identify no more iconographic traits associated with Visnu. What is so unique about the image is that its head doesn't simply sit on its shoulders, as is the case with so many images of deities of late-medieval or South Indian origins. This one has a narrow neck supporting a narrow (rather than full) face, with facial lines etched on the forehead and around the eyes. While I did not get a chance to study it carefully, my impression is that its origin is not South Indian or Sri Lankan. Moreover, if I had to guess, which I do not like to do in these matters, I would surmise that the image is of Chinese cultural origin, given the general lines of its bodily design. For information about Gadaladeniya's royal endowments and *rajakariya* services, see Lawrie (1898:234–40).

51. An excellent study focused largely on the political economy of Lankatilaka, but describing many other aspects of ritual and social organization, is Evers, *Monks, Priests and Peasants* (1972). Indeed, Evers's study contains a three-page description (41–44) of the current *kapurala* that reconfirms much of what I was told (thirty years later), and a description (55–60) of weekly rites.

52. Evers (1972:30–31) reports the same, and provides a local myth about the origins of this deity, one very similar to what I recorded about Pitiye Deviyo in the 1980s. See also my *Buddha in the Crown* (1991:125–50).

53. On the significance of the *petikada*, see chapter 7.

54. I have detailed some of the frustrations I experienced in trying to gain credible information on the Hanguranketa Visnu *devalaya* in note 58 below.

55. The earliest reference I can find to the *devalaya* in Kandy is, as I indicated earlier, from either the late seventeenth or early eighteenth century.

56. I asked these questions first in English, and followed this with a Sinhala translation provided by one of my two field assistants. Some of the *kapuralas* were minimally con-

versant in English, but the bulk of our conversations were in Sinhala. I usually deployed one assistant to actively translate, while the second recorded the conversation in writing.

57. Whenever I approached *kapuralas* to ask if I could hear (and record) their *yatikas*, I stated simply that I was requesting *santiya* (a blessing), trying to be as innocuous as possible. This may have somewhat skewed my sample, because each *kapurala* may know several different *yatikas*. The Dadimunda *kapurala* in Kandy told me that he knows three different types of *yatikas:* those that result in punishment for enemies, those that help with solving health and vocation problems, and those that provide *santiya*.

58. At present, there seems to be considerable confusion at the Visnu *devalaya* in Hanguranketa. The current *kapurala*, who serves for both the Visnu and Dadimunda *devalayas*, is new to the profession and humbly apologized for his inability to provide me with much in the way of details about the history or ritual life of the *devalaya*. He seemed unsure about the contents of the *yatikava* himself, having recently learned it from his "uncle." In my efforts to learn more about the *devalaya*, I interviewed the brother of the current *basnayaka nilame*, himself a former *basnayaka nilame* of the *devalaya*. I also searched the lands registry in Kandy for information about *devalaya* holdings, but to no avail, after I had been told by the *diyawadana nilame* of the Dalada Maligava that the temple did not have the Hanguranketa *sannasa*, a "fact" imparted to me by both the Hanguranketa *kapurala*, its former *basnayaka nilame*, and the monastic incumbent of the *viharaya* adjacent to the *devalaya*. I also spent a day, after long and profound bureaucratic wrangling with the government Ministry of Buddha Sasana and the government Department of Archaeology, foraging through the collection of palm-leaf manuscripts at the library of the Hangaranketa Rajamahaviharaya, with Prof. Meegaskumbura from the Department of Sinhala at the University of Peradeniya, looking for texts that might contain the *devalaya*'s history, or references to it. This was also to no avail. I found only one individual somehow connected to the *devalaya* who was willing to speak, and somewhat forthcoming, about the *devalaya* and its history. He was the former (now displaced) *kapurala* of the *devalaya*, who was tracked down for an interview in a remote village with some difficulty. From him, I only confirmed what I had gleaned from secondary sources: that the Hanguranketa Visnu *devalaya* had been established and maintained by Kandyan kings, probably first by Kirti Sri Rajasimha in the middle of the eighteenth century, as a kind of "*devalaya* in reserve" to the Maha Devalaya in Kandy; that Hanguranketa was a site where many Kandyan kings would retreat in the face of military pressure from the Dutch; that the sandalwood image had been brought here from Kandy; that the lineage of *kapuralas* originated in Devinuvara; and that the most famous artifact in the *devalaya* was the *petikada* cloth painting. The dispossessed *kapurala* had presented this outline recently to a local-school cultural celebration, and the substance of his presentation had been published in a local newsletter that my assistants then translated for me.

59. The nine planetary deities are Ravi (sun), Candra (moon), Kuja (Mars), Buda (Mercury), Guru (Jupiter), Kivi (Venus), Sani (Saturn), Rahu (Dragon's head), and Ketu (Dragon's tail).

60. See Gooneratne (1998), Wirz (1954), Kapferer (1983), and Scott (1994).

61. See Kapferer's brief references (1997:125–28) to how Visnu is invoked within the preliminary liturgical portions of the elaborated *Huniyama* rite that he has detailed from

his observances in the deep south of the country. See also Kapferer's reference (1983:116) to how Visnu is sometimes configured as a *raksa* in *bali* rites.

62. Scott (1994) does not not even refer to Visnu in his study of the southern "*yak tovil*" traditions. His index entry for Visnu simply says, in reverse of Barnett (1916), "see Uppalavanna." His references to Upulvan are limited to the oral version of the myth of the sandalwood image, told to him by an accommodating *kapurala* at the Devinuvara complex. Somewhat inexplicable is the fact that Dadimunda, the "chief of the *yaksas*," is nowhere mentioned at all in Scott's study about Sinhala and colonial "discourses" of "*yak tovil*," despite the fact that there is a Dadimunda *devalaya* within the premises of the Visnu *devalaya* in Devinuvara, where Scott's chief informant is a *kapurala* for another deity.

63. It is said that Asoka's missionary son, Mahinda, preached the *Petavatthu* and *Vimanavatthu* in his third sermon after having arrived in Lanka. For a study of the significance of the *Petavatthu* in relation to Buddhist conceptions of karma and the afterlife, see my "Assisting the Dead by Venerating the Living" (1981).

64. Contrary to Scott's experiences at Devinuvara, I found *disti* to be a term referring to a visionary type of possession that can occur, a type of trance indicating possession of a divine presence and power. The devotee whose story I have recounted below provides an excellent example of the mechanics and functions of *disti*, as I found it to be understood in Kandy.

65. As will be noted in the conclusion, I found the ritual and symbolic expressions at Kande Vihara to be heavily reinfluenced by Hindu, but especially Christian, motifs.

66. Again this is anecdotal evidence for how Dadimunda, rather than Visnu, is much more intimately related to the cult of possession by external agents. Here, Visnu is asked only to help change the disposition of the boy, so that his mother can take him to the best source of help at Alutnuvara.

67. Tape-recorded in May 2000, and translated from the Sinhala, by Vindya Eriyagama, Department of Sociology, University of Peradeniya.

68. There are three *ganas* under which people are born: *deva* (divine), *manusya* (human), and *raksa* (demonic).

69. Transliterated by Prof. P. B. Meegaskumbura, Department of Sinhalese, University of Peradeniya.

70. Translated from the recorded Sinhala by Prof. Udaya Meddegama, Department of Sinhalese, University of Peradeniya.

6. The *Valiyak Mangalya*: The Curative Powers of the *Mala Raja*

1. Sinhala readers can consult Dissanayake (2000) for many relevant details.

2. A coin wrapped in a silk cloth, the traditional offering made at the *valiyak mangalya* at the conclusion of every session. It is also the form of traditional tribute that used to be the custom at the Alutnuvara Devalaya.

3. For some in attendance, the performance of *valiyak mangalya* seems to have become just another occasion to petition the gods for whatever needs they may have. During 2001, we observed people asking for assistance from the *yakdessa* to chant a *yatikava* to the gods for help in locating their stolen vehicle. In these instances each night, the *yakdessa* was only too happy to receive more than the traditional *panduru* as payment.

4. Pages 1–43 and 61–73 of Dissanayake's *Valiyak Mangalya Wimasuma* were translated privately from the Sinhala to the English by Vindya Eriyagama and P. B. Meesga-
skumbura respectively. I have not correlated Mudiyanse's pagination with those of my
translations, so my indebtedness to Dissanayaka will have to be made generally and not
so precisely noted.

5. "At this time they have a Superstition, which lasteth six or seven days, too foolish to
write; it consists in Dancing, Singing and Juggling. The reason of which is, lest the eyes of
the People, or the Power of the *Jacco*'s [*yaksas*], or Infernal Spirits, might any way prove
prejudicial to the aforesaid Gods in their Progress abroad. During the Celebration of this
great Festival, there are no Drums allowed to be beaten to any particular Gods at any private Sacrifice" [Knox: 80; brackets mine].

6. According to Dissanayaka (2000): "Sri Lankans believe that it is a bad omen for a
crow to sit on the back of an elephant. A *garayak* dance (a *santikarma*) is held in such an
instance to rid the elephant of any *vas dos*. Thus it is believed that initially, *valiyak* formed
part of the *garayak* ritual, and that later, it emerged separately out of the combination of
the *garayak* and *valiyak pelapalis* (rituals), according to Devanagala Saiman *yakdessa*."
Gara dancing occurs on the final day of the *valiyak*.

7. For a resume of the central myth, extensive preparations for the ritual and the performances of various dances of the *kohomba kankariya*, see Raghavan (1967:117–25) and
A. Seneviratne (1984c:29–33).

8. "Procuring peace" literally, but in general seeking the protective and curative blessing of the deities.

9. The *kohomba kankariya* is the most elaborate and extensive of all Sinhala folk rites.
Preparations begin up to three months in advance for what becomes a week of serial proceedings consisting of invocatory offerings, dramatic and pantomimed dances re-enact-
ing mythic episodes drawn from related cycles of myths, and specific petitionary plaints.

10. Private communication. Dissanayake (2000) says: "It is true that certain rituals
from *kankariya* are adopted in *valiyak*, but it also contains rituals which are totally different from those of *kankariya*. There is no special *kap situweema* [ritual planting of part
of a tree trunk to indicate that the auspicious time for the ritual to begin] in *valiyak* as in
kankariya. In *valiyak* it is a coconut flower but in *kankariya* it is a banana tree and the banana flower used in the ritual. In *kankariya* the flower is felled by piercing it with a bow
and arrow while in *valiyak* this does not exist. In *kankariya* the flower is thrown away but
in *valiyak* people struggle to secure parts of it which are safely kept as sacred objects"
[brackets mine]. Indeed, these seem like minor differences reflecting two different ritual
rather than textual traditions.

11. As we shall see in the literature to be reviewed in this chapter, the *mala raja* is a
composite character constituted by the three sons of Rama named by Pattini as
"*valiyaka*."

12. Neville (*Sinhala Kavi* 2:118) describes the contents of the *Valiyak Kavi* in which a
very different focus is given, evidence of yet another mythic cycle related to the cult of the
valiyaks. This is what he says: "This is an incantation to be sung at ceremonies to Wali yak.
It relates that Wali yaka obtained leave from Upulwan Deva or Vishnu, before exercising
his powers. Rama Surindu or Vishnu was placed in charge of Laka or Ceylon by Mundi
or Buddha. Vishnu therefore formed an abode at Devundara (Dondra), whence he

blessed Laka. The poem then alludes to Sitapati's birth from the blood of an ascetic, an allusion I do not understand. It then states that Wali yaka stopped the jingling of Pattini's anklets, but again the allusion is not explained. Pattini and Saman also gave their authority to Wali yaka. Wali Yaka possessed the prince, son of Waelihela Gamarala, and he became a yaka, and was known as Kosambha. He and wali yaka receive offerings to relieve the sufferings of mankind and the halamba bangle of Pattini was given to him." As Neville has noted, this saga contains some tantalizing allusions. It would seem to be a song sung at *kohombo kankariya* proceedings, since the *valiyak* seems much more *yaksa* oriented than in the cycle of myths I examine below. Moreover, there is an explicit reference to the *kohomba* deity and how he shares with the *valiyaks* the propensity to relieve suffering. This poem also recognizes Visnu's or Upulvan's abode at Devundara, which make provide a clue as to its antiquity.

13. The current *yakdessa*, Devanagala Saiman, is now more than seventy-five years old and has been performing the *valiyak* for more than sixty years. His son, now in his late thirties or early forties, also performs with him, along with a younger nephew in his early twenties.

14. Here, the flower that dominates the ritual proceedings in the *valiyak* is the coconut flower, as opposed to the banana plant in the *kohomba kankariya*, as Dissanayake (2000) has noted.

15. Given the fact that *Palavala Dane* cited by Neville is so inclusive of the *valiyak* myths, it is possible that it was a text either specifically written for or derived from the *valiyak* performance.

16. Translation by Vindya Eriyagama.

17. Translated privately for me by Prof. P. B. Meegaskumbura, Dept of Sinhalese, University of Peradeniya.

18. In other versions of this story that Neville notes (*Sinhala Kavi* 1:38 and 2:323), the conflated Visnu/Upulvan/Rama finds that the blue water lilies (*utpala*) of his pond are mysteriously disappearing. He discovers that seven heavenly maidens periodically descend to the pond and pick them. One day, he sees the maidens in the pond and hides the clothes of one of them. Without her clothes, she has lost her magical power to reascend to heaven. Upulvan is enamored with her, takes her to his Vaikuntha palace in the Himalayas and within a week she is pregnant with the first child of the myth who eventually becomes one of the *valiyak* trio who become the *mala raja*.

19. There is some confusion here. The prince from the womb could not be Prince Mala ("Flower"). "Mala" is generic for "flower" and thus would refer to the prince born of the lotus (*utpala*).

20. This clarifies their lineage insofar as Rama would here be understood as an avatar of Visnu/Upulvan..

21. Thus indicating their *deva* propensities. In traditional Vedic lore, the *devas* are in constant battle with the *asuras* trying to uphold the norms of order.

22. This is an allusion to the defense of the Buddha against Mara and his retinue during the night of enlightenment. This allusion thus joins those of the same nature attributed in various mythic scenarios to Upulvan, Visnu, Dadimunda and Huniyam. Clearly, the intention at this point in the verses is to link the three princes (*mala raja*) to Upulvan.

23. Here the verse is trying to say that the ascetic is the father yet not a biological father.

24. This may mean that like the Buddha (here taken as *muni*), Rama and Sita share his *ksatriya* lineage, or it may mean a link to the conjuring ascetic who created two of them.

25. The text seems corrupt here as any translation would be quite stilted.

26. Here the three act mischievously in the face of being warned not to disturb the pond.

27. The text is not clear whether this means that they formed one prince (Mala Raja) or that they got together to approach Rama in a unified stance.

28. While the Mala Raja is referred to in singular form, it is understood that "Mala Raja" also refers to all three of Sita's children at once.

29. Translated from Pragnaloka [1952:66–67].

30. Referring to how Valiyak is really the three divine princes who comprise the *mala raja.*

31. *Ankeliya* is the "horn-sport" usually celebrated during the New Year in April. It is a kind of ritual "tug-of-war" between the forces of Pattini and her erstwhile husband, Palanga. According to the *Valiyak Upata* cited above, it was during the *ankeliya,* when the three prince's intervened within the contest, that Pattini gave them the name *valiyak.* For an extended discussion of *ankeliya,* see Obeyesekere (1983:382–423).

32. Dissanayaka (2000) provides a discussion of the significance of the *sivili* head dress as follows: "Valyak has to be performed wearing a special crown/headdress called *siviliya.* The myth has it that the *siviliya* was the crown of King Malaya, a mythic figure associated with the birth of *santhikarmas* such as *valiyak* and *kohomba kankariya.* The dancers (*yakdessa*) believe that wearing the crown could even bring many calamities (*vas vedeema*). It is reported that certain predecessors who danced wearing the *siviliya* were doomed to die within a few days of the ritual. Due to this reason, today dancers do not wear this headdress in performing *valiyak.* Instead they merely bring out the *siviliya* to the stage all 7 days where the ritual takes place. It is wrapped in a blue cloth." A *jata* is simply a ritual turban. Translated from the Sinhala by Vindya Eriyagama.

33. This means that a coconut flower, rather than the usual banana flower, is used as the auspicious flower of the rite.

34. Of the Kataragama *devalaya*?

35. *Ma Oya* "great river" and *Ratmal Vatiya* "Red Flower Place."

36. As I have noted, in addition to the *Mahavamsa* (1:55–61), the legend of Kuveni is found in a number of different sources including the *Kuveni Asnaya* and *Helu Kuveni Asnaya* (*Sinhala Kavi* 3:178 and 180–81). Neville is of the view that these sources are very old, dating perhaps to the thirteenth-century Dambadeniya period of Parakramabahu II's reign.

37. The *Mahavamsa* version stresses that though they were captured by Kuveni, they were not harmed owing to the protection of *pirit* thread.

38. In the *Mahavamsa* version, Vijaya actually slays the *yakkhas* with his sword with Kuveni's assistance.

39. In the *Mahavamsa's* version of the Kuveni legend (1:55–61; VII:1–74), when Kuveni is sent away by Vijaya, she takes her son and daughter by Vijaya back to the *yakkhini* city where she is taken for a spy and killed immediately. Her uncle (mother's brother) tells the children to flee immediately, which they do, to Sumanakuta (Adam's Peak). The brother eventually takes his sister as his wife and they become the progenitors of the "Pulinda" (often assumed to be the *Veddhas*).

40. Kuveni's lament and the remainder of the poem translated here is drawn from Dissanayake (2000:69–73).

41. This part of the *Kuveni Asnaya* is wholly unknown to the *Mahavamsa* narrative.

42. Kandyan kings were known to adorn sixty-four ornaments on formal occasions. This number corresponds to the enumerated sixty-four sacred places of the Kandyan kingdom. See my *Buddha in the Crown* (1991:179–82). What is of further interest here is that sixty-four ornaments worn by *ves* dancers "comprise the royal costume of the Malaya King. In fact, the master of the [*kohomba* and *valiyak*] ceremony takes on the guise [*Ves*] of the king" (A. Seneviratne 1984c:49).

43. Thus linking the *valiyaks* to the *ankeliya* rite as well.

44. This is done by means of formulating *yatikas* to be chanted at the end of each night's proceedings. A "*maha yatikawa*" for this purpose has been recorded by Dissanayaka (2000:40–41).

45. H. L Seneviratne (1978:102–108) also interprets the *valiyak* as a ritual essentially as a matter of mimetic magic.

46. The *Ramayana* origins of the mythic episodes relating to birth of the *mala raja* are undeniable. When they were fused to the cycles of Kuveni myth is a very interesting question. Given the historical background of *ves* as a form of dance, it may be that some impetus for the fusion occurred during the reign of Narendra Sinha (1707–1739) when, according to A. Seneviratne (1984c:36–50), various forms of dance from Kerala, including those that eventuated in the *kathakali* (which still heavily emphasizes *Ramayana* episodes), were introduced to the Kandyan court at the behest of Nayakkar queens.

7. Legacies of the "Buddhist Visnu": Myth and Cult at the Alutnuvara *Devalaya*

1. James, *The Varieties of Religious Experience* (1958:280–81).

2. It is not possible for me to mount a full-scale study of the cult of Dadimunda within this context. Given the scope and complexity of the cult, that would necessitate the writing of a separate and lengthy monograph.

3. One of the most significant observations offered by Ven. Udawela was how the worship of Dadimunda at Alutnuvara had changed so significantly in the twentieth century. Of course, many more people come to the *devalaya* these days. But there are far fewer *yaksa* possessions and more claims for the experience of *disti*. Further, devotees now make offerings primarily of fruits, in the manner traditionally accorded Hindu deities. The shops in the vicinity of the *devalaya* compound have sprung up to take advantage of the thriving business. It used to be the case that offerings were simply *pandurus*—coins tied especially in a cloth and offered to the *kapuralas* before the *yatikava* was chanted.

4. Translated from a tape-recording made privately by Vindya Eriyagama, Department of Sociology, University of Peradeniya.

5. There are three prominent explanatory signboards erected within the *devalaya* compound. The first is the one I have just referred to that purports to give the ancient history of the compound. The second is placed beneath the *pattirippuva,* a wooden pentagonal-shaped structure on top of a large bolder on the side of a hill adjacent to the modern *devalaya*. It is identified as the *devalaya* built for Dadimunda after the Visnu *devalaya* was transferred to Kandy by King Senaret (1604–35 C.E.). The sign goes on to say

that the boulder on which the *devalaya* was built is what remains of the rock that was dashed by the *yaksas* summoned by Dadimunda, a central event in the mythic profile of Devata Bandara, repeated thrice in the *Dadimunda Avataraya,* the *Galakaeppu Sahalla* ("Breaking of the Stone"), and the *Alutnuvara Devalaya Saha Dadimunda Deviyange Vittiya* ("The *Vitti* of *Alutnuvara Devalaya* and *Dadimunda Devi*"). For a full translation of each of these texts, see appendix 1. The third is a sign erected by President Ranasinghe Premadasa in 1989, a souvenir of his presidential declaration making Alutnuvara a *puja bhumi.* During his twelve years as prime minister and five years as president, Premadasa relentlessly made various declarations and dedications throughout the Sinhala Buddhist–culture areas of the country at many sacred places such as this.

6. Mimeographed sheets distributed by the chief *kapurala* at the Alutnuwara *Devalaya* in April 2001. Translated privately by Vindya Eriyagama, Dept. of Sociology, University of Peradeniya, and amended by P. B. Meegaskumbura, Dept. of Sinhala, University of Peradeniya.

7. My sense is that the so-called *sannasa* distributed by the *devalaya kapurala* is quite possibly a recent adaptation and summary of an *ola*-leaf manuscript known as the *Alutnuvara Devale Karavima* ("The Building-up of Alutnuvara Devalaya"), now in the British Museum in London. Ilangasinha (329–30), who seems to have thoroughly examined the manuscript, summarizes its contents as follows: "According to the work, when Parakramabahu was afflicted by an incurable disease, it was to Upulvan that the prime minister of the king, Devapatiraja, was sent in supplication. It was on an *Asala* Full Moon Day that the minister prayed to the deity on behalf of his master; this coincided with the annual Asala festival of the *devalaya.* The document adds that the god was so impressed by the fervent devotion of the minister that he manifested himself in the night in the guise of a *brahmin* attired in white robes, but with no beneficent effect on the king, for what the deity could do was only to assert that it was useless trying to cure him. However, the disappointment caused by this divine revelation seems not to have ended the devotion of the king to the god, for, according to the document, the king honoured his pledge made before by the grant of some productive lands to the shrine of Upulvan at Devinuvara."

This is almost a perfect match of the events in the story revealed by the *kapurala*'s *sannasa.* Further, Ilangasinha (113) also reports "that there was a monastery attached to that devalaya; and it was one of the duties of the incumbent of the monastery to chant *pirit* in front of Upulvan every day." He also says (137) that "The *Alutnuvara Devale Karavima* . . . records that there were thirteen successive *ganas* [monastic incumbents] . . . of the monastery attached to the Upulvan *devalaya* at Alutnuvara from the Dambadeni period to the date of the composition of the work" [late-seventeenth century] [brackets mine] and that Rajasimha I (1581–93 C.E.), often cited by nationalist historians for being a traitor to the country because of his conversion to Hinduism, "gave substantial benefactions to the Upulvan *Devalaya* at Alutnuvara and the monastery attached to it" [202]. The only other reference to this particular text that I could find comes from Liyanagamage (1968:28,96,151,172) who says that it is not to be found in Sri Lanka and that the only copy is located in the British Museum, where it consists of twelve leaves. He says that it is probably a seventeenth-century text, which basically reports, in addition to the story of Prince Virabahu's holding of the *asala* festival in honor of Upulvan following his victory over the Javakas, the story of Parakramabahu's attempt to cure himself of his speech defect and the consequent founding of the *devalaya* at Alutnuvara.

8. In Hindu Indian contexts, Sanskrit *sthalapurana* refers to a story or a myth of origins about a sacred place. It is often about how a deity came to take up its seat at the local shrine, or how some miraculous divine action sanctified the place. While there is no perfect equivalent for these in Sinhala Buddhist literature, there are texts and accounts like the ones I am citing that are very clearly the functional equivalent.

9. Ovitagedera (2001:33–50) refers to several strands of myth that link Dadimunda to the fortunes of the Sinhala state. Of particular interest is one tradition that assigns a definitive role to Dadimunda in assisting the second-century B.C.E. King Dutugamunu in his epic defeat of the Tamil King Elara. Dutugamunu, of course, becomes one of the primary paradigms of Sinhala kingship, his mythic profile gradually gaining force and scope throughout history as the quintessential warrior-king of the Sinhalas. Still, the best treatment of the religious and ethical problems involved in reconciling the values and orientation of this warrior-king (or any other warrior-king) with the moral economy of the *Buddhasasana*, is Greenwald (1978).

10. Obeyesekere (1984:213–214) also speculates on the Dravidian origins of Dadimunda because of the non-Sinhala basis of *munda* and the fact that in his cult the numerology deployed "is not found elsewhere in Sinhala mythology."

11. Ovitagedera (2001:97) reports the following from the current Diyavadana Nilame (chief custodian) of the Temple of the Tooth-Relic, Mr. Neranjan Wijeratna: "Former President Mr. Premadasa, when he was still the Prime Minister, informed me that he was coming to worship at the Maligava on the first of January. The secretary of the Prime Minister's office called in the morning and asked if there was anything to be done for the Maligava. I informed him that the monkeys had destroyed the roof of the temple and he expressed his desire for getting it repaired. It needed about 20 lakhs. After worshipping at the temple, Mr. Premadasa had a small gathering and donated a cheque for Rs. 20 lakhs in order to start the constructure of a new roof . . . . Mr. Premadasa visited the temple again a few days later and before leaving came into the Diyavadana Nilame's office. "Neranjan, something strange happened to me. When I went to sleep on the first of January after coming here, I saw this strange person in my dreams. He was wearing a Kandyan costume and I didn't see his face. He told me firmly: "Do it from Sevana! Do it from Sevana." That's why I came again. The temple was sheltered by funds from the Sevana lottery." [Translated from the Sinhala by Kanchuka Dharmasiri.]

Indeed, at that time, a new and rather garish gold-colored roof came to adorn the relic chamber of the Dalada Maligava. Another popular tradition reported by Ovitagedera is that Dadimunda is said to be in charge of protecting the golden casket containing the Dalada ("Tooth-Relic").

12. Rajasinha II cancelled the *asala perahera* in 1664, perhaps because he feared a rebellion during this time. The rebellion occurred anyway, and he fled to Hanguranketa as a result. I mention this because this historical incident indicates that it was the king's prerogative to sponsor the *perahera* or not. By doing so, he expressed his kinship with the deities as their this-worldly counterpart.

13. In Sri Lanka, it is popularly understood that the Kandy *asala perahera* is an ancient ritual that has been performed annually since the early Anuradhapura period. This idea has been promoted by various nationalist historians and politicians. It can be supported largely on the basis of Fa Hien's account (Legge:105–107) of witnessing a royally sponsored procession of the relic on the back of an elephant to the Abhyagiriya *viharaya* dur-

ing the third month of the year. But Fa Hien's description reveals a very different signifi-cance to the ritual in comparison with what it has come to mean many centuries later. In his time, it was a ninety-day ritual performed largely by monks within the *viharayas* and recalled the various births of the Buddha as known through the *Jatakas*. It is thus, very clearly, an entirely separate ritual than the one practiced in Kandy. Further, Fa Hien never uses "*perahera*" in referring to the rite he has observed.

The *Mahavamsa* does contain an account of a royal procession headed by King Dut-thagamini, leading to the enshrinement of relics of the Buddha (31.36–44; p. 212), and the *Culavamsa* (74.224–227; I:41–42) contains an account of Parakramabahu I mounting an elephant and receiving the Tooth and Bowl relics which legitimated his kingship, but these are the only references to what might possibly be construed as *perahara* processions involving the *Dalada*. Again, "*perahera*" is not used to describe these accounts either. Only Fa Hien's reference would seem to indicate the possibility of such a ritual being held on an annual basis. And this, as I have just observed, is a very different ritual. It is true, ac-cording to the fourteenth-century *Dalada Sirita*, written during the Kurunegala period, that there was an annual *puja* involving the public displaying of the tooth-relic accom-panied by music and dancing, thus containing the basic elements of what has become Kandy'a *asala perahara* today. Nonetheless, the relic's inclusion in the Kandy rite does not seem to predate the eighteenth century.

14. See, in particular, the resume and sources provided by Barnett (1916:15–16), as well as Neville's *Sinhala Kavi* (1954:1:40; 2:5; and 3:2–5).

15. The *Dadimunda Upata* (1:40), the *Dadimunda Pralaya* (3:4), and the *Dadimunda Kavi* (3:2).

16. For an excellent discussion of the issue of royal violence and the teachings of the Buddha in relation to the *Mahavamsa*'s account of King Dutthagamani, see Greenwald (1978); for a thorough discussion of just-war theory in relation to Buddhism in Sri Lanka based on textual, historical, and anthropological readings, see Bartholomeusz (2002).

17. As described by Neville (3:2), the *Dadimunda Kavi*, after describing the Mara episode and Dadimunda's arrival in Lanka with the powers of Upulvan, also explicitly refers to Dadimunda as an avatar of Visnu.

18. According to Neville (3:5): the *Dadimunda Warama* has a different and yet another very interesting version of this mythic episode: "When Somavati Devi was cremated, being pregnant, the child was formed again by Dadimunda from her ashes, and was named Dapulu. He became king of Devinuvara. The gods afterwards landed at Sinigama, and went to Uggal Nuwara, and then to Dambadeni Nuwara, and resided at Raja-giri cave . . . and Dapula placed an image of Visnu at the Ran-deni gala lena" ("Golden Stone Cave"). Thus, this text links the ninth-century C.E. king Dapula, who founded Devinu-vara and worshipped Upulvan, with Dadimunda!

19. Because I was not able to tape-record the *yatika* of the Alutnuvara *kapuralas*, I have provided the translation of two *yatikas* that were printed elsewhere (in Sinhala). These can be read in appendix 2 to this chapter.

20. Instead, see the drawings of the Dadimunda *devarupa* and *devalaya sanctum sanc-torum* by Kanchuka Dharmasiri.

21. Tape-recorded in April 2000, and translated privately by Vindya Eriyagama, Dept. of Sociology, University of Peradeniya.

22. Here, Mrs. Rajapakse is first referring to the 1983 Sinhala pogrom against the Tamil people in which many Tamil homes and businesses were set ablaze. The tiger coming out of its hole refers to the emergence of the revolutionary Liberation Tigers of Tamil Eelam (LTTE). The reference to the terrorist attack at Anuradhapura refers to the 1985 massacre at Sri Mahabodhi in which over 130 defenseless people, including many *dasa sil matas* (Buddhist "nuns") were shot and killed by attacking cadres from the Liberation Tigers of Tamil Eelam (LTTE), who were armed with AK-47 assault weapons.

23. This seems to be an allusion to the assassination of Indian Prime Minister Rajiv Gandhi.

24. The assassination attempt on Sri Lankan President J. R. Jayawawardhana occurred in 1986.

25. Sri Lankan President Ranasinghe Premadasa was assassinated on May 1, 1993.

26. The "emerging female hand" is a reference to the election of President Chandrika Bandaranaike Kumaratunga, and the "lot of trouble" is the deepening civil war that broke out when peace talks between President Kumaratunga and the LTTE collapsed in 1995.

27. This is an obvious alias, a kind of stage name. Sinhala parents would most likely not select this kind of name for their child.

28. The Sinhala translations that follow were provided by Vindya Eriyagama.

29. For a detailed explication of the ethic of the *Petavatthu*, see my "Assisting the Living by Venerating the Dead" (1981).

30. William James, "The Will to Believe." In Aubrey Castell, ed., *Essays in Pragmatism* (New York: Hafner, 1969), pp. 88–109.

31 M. J. Marasinghe, "The 'Yakkhas' in Early Buddhist Literature," *Journal of the Vidyanlankara University of Ceylon* 1:103–118.

31. Dandris de Silva Gunaratna (1998:71–81) wrote extensively about Huniyam in his nineteenth-century classic ethnography; Gombrich and Obeyesekere (1988:107–132) have also conducted research on the cult of Huniyam in urban Colombo; and Bruce Kapferer (1997) has written an extensive monograph focused specifically on Huniyam in exorcism and sorcery in southern Sri Lanka near the regional city of Galle, so there is considerable secondary interpretive literature about this particularly fascinating deity. Gombrich and Obeyesekere have provided a resume of many of the important mythic and lierary notices of significance to Huniyam and his cult (one of which I will cite in detail below). There is no need here to rehearse all of the details they have discussed in their presentation.

32. Kapferer has also argued, somewhat along the same lines but on different bases than Gombrich and Obeyesekere, that sorcery, and therefore the cult of Huniyam, is making a strong comeback in Sinhala culture. He says: "In Sri Lanka, before more recent nationalist reevaluations, traditional practices such as exorcism were disregarded by elements within Sinhalese bourgeois elites. To these elites they exemplified the decline of Buddhist values and institutions. In many respects exorcisms and other folk practices were viewed by these elites much as the Dutch and later British colonial rulers viewed them: as demonic and primitive practices in a Western Christian and rationalist sense. The English educated members of local and national elites were ideologically connected with the Sinhala Buddhist reformation (which aimed to purify Buddhism of its alien influences but at the same time was highly rationalist) and resistant to colonial rule. Exor-

cism, especially episodes of its drama, and other elements of the folk tradition have been positively revalued in recent times. This is related to the acute cultural reaffirmations among Sinhalese in the circumstances of the Tamil-Sinhala ethnic war . . . ." (1997:18).

Kapferer continues by making the observation that a new class of Sinhalese have come to wield power since 1977, primarily businessmen who are not English-educated, but Sinhala-educated, Sinhala-speaking people, who maintain "strong connections with the peasantry and urban poor."

33. Schonthal (1999) has drawn my attention to this myth.

34. Translated privately by Prof. P. B. Meegaskumbura, Dept. of Sinhalese, University of Peradeniya, from Charles Dias, ed., *Galakaeppu Sahalla* (Colombo: Samayawardhana Press, 1926).

35. Translated privately by Prof. P. B. Meegaskumbura, Dept. of Sinhalese, University of Peradeniya from Charles Dias, ed., *Galakaeppu Sahalla* (Colombo: Samayawardhana Press, 1926).

36. Translated privately by Prof. P. B. Meegaskumbura, Dept. of Sinhalese, University of Peradeniya from Ven H. U, Pragnaloka, ed, *Purana Sivupada Sangrahava* (Colombo, SL: Government Press, 1952), pp. 24–30. Obeyesekere (1984:214–20) has translated a very similar version which he says was edited by N. J. Cooray, but he gives no further bibliographical information for his text.

37. Vimala was the wife of a Naga king and Erandati their daughter.

38. The goddess was regarded as the king's lucky gaming power.

39. Vaisravana in Sanskrit literature. In Lankan Sinhala literature, Vesamuni is one of the lords of the four quarters and the king of the *yaksas.*

40. A curious passage in that Devata Bandara becomes an epithet for Dadimunda once he is established as Alutnuvara Deviyo.

41. The up-country region in modern Sri Lanka surrounding Kegalle and environs.

42. Cited in C. M. A. de Silva (1969:336–37). De Silva says he translated this piece after he "extracted [it] from an old printed text of Malyahan Kavi published in 1893, a copy of which is available at the Colombo Museum Library" (334).

43. Recorded from the 1880s diary of a Mr. R. W. Ievers by H. C. P. Bell (1904:48).

44. Translated privately by Vindya Eriyagama, Dept. of Sociology, University of Peradeniya. This text is a translation of Visnu Kalyani's autobiography, plus relevant excerpts I have inserted from an interview which followed my reading of her autobiography. The excerpts from the interview are indicated by brackets. Parentheses are mine.

45. Translated privately for me by P. B. Meegaskumbura, Department of Sinhalese, University of Peradeniya.

8. Minister of Defense? The Politics of Deification in Contemporary Sri Lanka

1. *Aspects of Sinhalese Culture* (1992:9).

2. As a contemporary example of this ambivalence, Carl Muller, the popular Sri Lankan novelist based in Kandy, has recently written: "Our people are now totally enamored of Hindi films, Hindi songs and Hindi dance, and swarm to see and listen to visiting Hindi artists. Bollywood needn't worry about its canned rubbish which consists of sex-charged dances and hick actors and actresses swarming up and down slopes and

around trees screaming their sentiments at each other. There's always a market for this junk in Sri Lanka. . . . Even Sinhalese singers and actors are now proud of the fact that they can also sing Hindi songs and swivel their hips and send Morse code with their pudenda as the Hindi dancers do. It's all this mania to imitate that makes our prize idiots think it's a new art pinnacle to ape everything Bollywood tosses our way. "Don't Let Cultural Nerve Gas Destroy Sinhala Culture." *The Island*, March 24, 2001, p. 15.

3. Two lucid and detailed studies of recent and relevant political history have been written by K. M. de Silva (1996 and 1998).

4. One of the most obvious instances of antipathy is evident immediately upon arrival in Sri Lanka, when individuals negotiate formal procedures with government customs and immigration officials. Most Westerners, upon arrival in Sri Lanka, are automatically issued visas *in situ* for at least a month (in some cases three months), while arriving Indian neighbors are required to have in hand a restricted visa issued only by Sri Lankan diplomatic missions abroad. So while Westerners may sail through the official process and are admitted without any undue delays, Indians, even though they have completed formalities at Sri Lankan diplomatic missions in India, are sometimes detained and scrutinized. (In turn, Sri Lankans must endure long queues in the hot sun and polluted air of Colombo's Galle Road, in order to secure visas from the Indian High Commission for travel to India.) In the spring of 2002, this situation was finally changed after more than fifteen years of practice.

5. Recently, relations between the two governments have improved, due to the assassination of Rajiv Gandhi by the LTTE. India has officially proscribed the LTTE and issued a warrant of arrest for Vellupillai Prabhakaran, the militant leader of the LTTE. These legal moves were welcomed by Colombo in the late 1990s.

6. In the summer of 2002, Indian and Sri Lankan transportation officials began to consider the possibility of reopening ferry service, but this time between Tuticorin and Colombo. Unfortunately, the Indian cabinet vetoed plans for the ferry service in September of 2003.

7. On this phenomenon, see Victor C. de Munck, "Sufi and Reformist Designs: Muslim Identity in Sri Lanka" (1998:110–32).

8. Steven Kemper, in his *Buying and Believing* (2001:32, n.36), points out that imports and exports with India amount to only three percent of Sri Lanka's volume of trade.

9. Kemper (2001:67) has also encountered this Sinhala image of "India as a land poverty" and has also taken note of how India evokes ambivalent responses.

10. An avalanche of media coverage, newspaper articles, and editorials, as well as television program specials, followed in the wake of Ven. Soma's demise and funeral—a funeral held on Christmas Eve, 2004, and attended by hundreds of thousands, perhaps even millions of mourners. The outpouring of emotion lionizing Soma as a symbol of Sinhala Buddhist social, political, and cultural aspirations was, according to many observers, unprecedented in the history of modern Sri Lanka. What follows is a very brief summary of the sensation as it was articulated in four instances.

In "Ven. Soma, beacon of hope for Buddhists," *The Island* (December 20, 2003), p. 11, Sisira Wijesinghe had this to say: "Ven. Gangodawila Soma Thera, the embodiment of Buddhist morality and paragon of virtue, emerged as the champion of the Sinhala-Buddhist cause and as the most outstanding and controversial religious [leader] in the last

decade. . . . His erudition, enriched with scientific psycho-analytical perspectives continued to be a beacon of hope for the common masses [and] his ocean of knowledge on
Buddhist canons, scriptures and literature remained unchallenged, well-respected and
thoroughly logical. [He was] quite identical to the 19th century Buddhist revivalist, Anagarika Dharmapala, who inspired and aroused Sri Lankan Buddhists from apathy and led
them towards socio-political awareness, highlighting the importance of preserving archaeological ruins, a nation's heritage and places of Buddhist worship . . . His epoch-
making assertions, particularly against public worship of assortments of deities, among
many other issues he raised, evoked enthusiasm and wrath from some sections, but Ven.
Soma Thera, true to his convictions was defiant and went against the beliefs of the high
and mighty of the land. Self-confidence taught in Buddhism was the only 'God' for
him. . . ."

Here is what Nalin de Silva, ardent champion of *jatika chintanya*, or "indigenous
thinking," had to say in his article "Soma Hamuduruwo and Sinhala Buddhism," *The Island Midweek Review* (December 31, 2003), p. II: "Hundreds of thousands of people who
flocked . . . to pay their respects to Ven. Gangodawila Thera . . . should have reminded
those in the fourth estate and other pundits who know only to vomit the so called theories that they had learnt from their masters and mistresses in the Christian west that this
country is foremost Sinhala Buddhist. . . . The Sinhala Buddhists suspect foul play with
respect to the death of Soma Hamuduruwo. Whether these suspicions are well founded
or not, the question could be asked as to why people suspect. The answer is simple. The
west has not hesitated to kill people and make sure that the general public get the impression that these killings are due to 'natural causes,' in order to maintain their hegemony in the world. The west rules the world not only through politics and economics but
also, I would say mainly, through their knowledge system consisting of theories created
in Greek Judaic Christian Chinthanaya. In this country the Sinhala Buddhists are mainly
suppressed by the use of western Christian concepts such as the secular state, pluralism
and objectivity of knowledge, meaning of course western knowledge."

In a similar vein, consider the following from Malinda Seneviratne in his "Buddha
Sasana: time to act on the Act," *The Island* (December 28, 2003), p. 8: "Ven. Gangodawila
Soma Thero is no more. And yet, he still lives among us in his words, his actions, example and most of all his teachings, which include among other things a concerned effort to
regain the *Dharmadvipaya* that was this island. At his funeral, Ven. Ellawala Medananda
Thero made some very pertinent observations. He made a strong case for a Presidential
Commission to probe the circumstances of Ven. Soma Thero's demise. His concerns are
not unfounded . . . . It is clear that very little attention has been paid to matters of security from predatory forces with respect to Ven. Soma's life. In fact, it is probably true, that
the entire Buddhist community is under serious threat. Ven. Soma had clearly understood
this. Almost as if he was inspired by a premonition of his own demise, three months ago,
September 23 to be exact, speaking at the Annual Convention of the Jathika Sangha Sam-
menlanaya, Ven. Soma Thero pointed out that legislative protection is absolutely and ur-
gently necessary to protect Buddhists and the Buddha Sasana. He was specifically referring to proselytization [sic] by deceitful means. . . . The strong sentiments expressed on
the issue [of protection of the Sinhala Buddhists] at the funeral and the unprecedented
and untrammeled flow of sympathy and sorrow evidenced since the news of Ven. Soma

Thero's death trickled in, in fact constitutes a referendum, on the injustices caused to the Buddha Sasana."

Finally, the following passage from *The Island*'s lead editorial on December 26, 2003 (p. 10), summarizes precisely how the death of Soma occasioned a process in which he was transformed into something much larger than himself: "The monk's message was this: Sri Lanka is the home to all religions and races but this undoubtedly is a Sinhala-Buddhist country. This may be an anathema to most of those who since the early eighties have been preaching the doctrine of multi-lingual, multi-racial and multi-religious composition of the country. . . . Colombo's anglicized elite may consider Soma Thera a representative of the 'lumpen proletariat.' To one such choirboy in the state media, Soma Thera was a 'totemic figure.' . . . To some fundamentalists, anyone not in their pantheon is a 'totem' that deserves to be smashed to smithereens. Judging from the island-wide grief and mourning and the massive show of sympathy shown at Independence Square, Soma Thera is indeed an indestructible 'totem.'"

11. Rajpal Abeyanayake, "He Cuts Down Gods, Real and Imagined," *The Sunday Times,* January 17, 1999, p. 5.

12. *Ibid.,* October 10, 1999, p. 6. In this interview, Ven. Soma charges that someone is hiding an inscription by King Saddhatissa which grants these lands to the Sinhalese temple. He says the land grant was last seen in the 1920s, and that when it is rediscovered it will prove who really owns those lands.

13. *Ibid.,* November 14, p. 15.

14. Kumbhakarana (an alias), *The Sunday Times* (September 5, 1999), p. 12.

15. *Sunday Times,* June 20, 1999, p. 14. I doubt that Abeyanayake is aware of the irony of his last sentence! It is very interesting to note that in the months following the articles by Kumbakarana and Abeyanayake that the *Sunday Times* enlisted Ven. Soma to write his own column, entitled "Reflections." These columns ran for about two months before they were stopped. Most of them were simply excerpts from dharma talks, and contained little of controversy on political issues.

16. April 16, 2000, p. 5. The *Sunday Leader* was closed down in late May, 2000, for allegedly violating the government's draconian censorship laws, which were put into effect as the war situation on the Jaffna peninsula deteriorated in April.

17. Her mother is Sirima Ratwatte Bandaranaike (the world's first woman prime minister in 1960) and her father, S. W. R. D. Bandaranaike, was elected prime minister by a resounding vote in 1956 (on a platform of "Sinhala-only" and Buddhism as the religion of the nation), only to be assassinated in 1959 by a Buddhist monk.

18. The nephew of J. R. Jaywardene, president of Sri Lanka from 1977 to 1989.

19. After the LTTE announced (in the spring of 2002) that they would accept "autonomy within a united Sri Lanka," the *mahanayakas* agreed to support the UNF (UNP–dominated) peace talks with the LTTE.

20. Anuruddha Ratwatte was a first cousin to Sirima Ratwatte Bandaranaike, the world's first woman prime minister and the mother of current president Chandrika Bandaranaike Kumaratunga. The president's great-grandfather and the grandfather of Anuradha and Denis Ratwatte (*basnayaka nilame* of the Maha [Visnu] Devalaya in Kandy), were one and the same. He was also the *basnayake nilame* of the Maha (Visnu) Devalaya and the Alutnuvara Devalaya.

21. President Kumaratunga's grandfather was the long-time *basnayake nilame* of the Maha (Visnu) Devalaya in Kandy and the Alutnuvara (Dadimunda) Devale. The post is currently held by Mr. Denis Ratwatte, the president's uncle and Deputy Minister of Defense General Anuruddha Ratwatte's older brother.

22. Ven. Soma, "Reflections . . . ," *The Sunday Times,* November 7, 1999, p. 14.

23. *Ibid.,* August 22, 1999, p. 13.

24. *Ibid.,* October 31, 1999, p. 15.

25. See footnote 10 above.

26. *Ibid.,* January 17, 1999, p. 5.

27. Lucien Rajakarunanayake, *The Sunday Observer,* June 4, 2000, p. 5.

28. Ruth Jansz, "Religious Star Wars," *The Sunday Times,* June 6, 1999.

29. Rajpal Abeynayake, "TV Demi-God and the Star-Crossed Leaders,"*The Sunday Times,* June 20, p. 14.

30. Denis Ratwatte's version of the story is corroborated by the manner in which the story was reported by *India Today* in its January 17, 2000 issue.

31. During the course of fieldwork at the Maha (Visnu) Devalaya in Kandy and at the Alutnuvara Devalaya, I came to learn that the deputy defense minister is indeed an ardent patron and frequent visitor to both *devalayas,* which is not surprising, owing to the fact that his family has been deeply involved in the administration of both places for generations. He and his two sons were arrested in the spring of 2002 for their alleged complicity in the murders of ten Muslims during the December 2001 general elections. They are currently, as of January, 2004, free on bail.

32. *Sunday Times,* August 15, 1999, p. 15.

33. Here, I do not mean to suggest that Soma's sympathizers were entirely limited to the urban educated. At the time of his funeral, it became clear that Soma had attracted the affection of many village people as well, especially as he was being transfigured into a general symbol of Sinhala Buddhist nationalist sentiment.

34. Nalin de Silva, "The Political Bishops." *The Island.* February 21, 2000, p. 17.

35. In a fascinating aside within this same article, Nalin de Silva talks about how it is precisely because Hindu gods, especially Visnu, have been transformed into "Sinhala Buddhist Gods" that they have found a legitimate place in Sinhala culture. His understanding of history and Hindu theology is badly distorted, yet his insights about the process of religio-cultural transformation are basically correct: "The Sinhala nation that came into being during the time of Pandukabhaya, whose teacher incidentally was a Brahmin by the name of Pandula, who would have been versed with the Vedic Suthras [sic] inherited not only the Vedic Gods but indigenous gods such as Upulvan, Mahasena and Sumana (Saman). When the Sinhalas as a nation became Buddhists during the reign of Devanampiya Tissa these gods were not thrown away. They became Gods within Sinhala Buddhism, the Gods themselves becoming Buddhists. In other words, the gods were assimilated into Sinhala Buddhist culture. The pantheon of 'Sinhala Buddhist Gods' pay homage to the Buddha. Even if the God Vishnu was introduced to Sinhala Buddhism later from Hinduism and merged with the God Upulvan, the God Vishnu of Sinhala Buddhism is not the same as the God Vishnu of Hinduism. Hindu God Vishnu has gone through a kind of metamorphism before the God Vishnu of Sinhala Buddhism. In Sinhala Buddhism all these gods are mortal beings and not eternal. The God Vishnu is a

Bodhisathva [sic] who would become a Buddha in the future . . . and is not an avathar [sic] of Brahman. . . ." Given the comments I have quoted above about how Nalin de Silva seems to think that the the Tamils must recognize the position of Buddhist monks as symbols of Sinhala Buddhist culture, it would seem that the two processes (political and religious) are mirror images of one another.

36. Three recent studies that examine this issue directly and historically are Martin Southwold, *Buddhism in Life* (1983), S. J. Tambiah, *Buddhism Betrayed* (1992), and H. L. Seneviratne, *The Work of Kings* (1999).

37. Ronnie de Mel, one of Sri Lanka's most senior politicians, who has served in governments from both sides of the political divide since 1977, has said this recently (in April 2001): "Over the years law and order has deteriorated in this country and the system of justice and our legal system which was one of the best in our part of the world in earlier times has all but collapsed so far as the ordinary man is concerned." Quoted in an interview with Wilson Gnanadass, "The Lack of a Speaker's Will," *The Sunday Leader,* April 15, 2001, p. 5.

Conclusion

1. The contemporary Devinuvara complex underwent major changes in the early 1950s, just at the time that Paranavitana was publishing his study *The Shrine of Upulvan.* Not only was the very impressive *devalaya* structure (see figure 9.16) rebuilt at this time, but another building (a "line house") with provisions for several other subsidiary *devalayas* was constructed as well. Consequently, since that time, pilgrims and devotees have also been afforded the opportunity to take vows or conduct *pujas* for Kataragama Deviyo, Pattini, Dadimunda, etc., in addition to Visnu.

2. See chapter 5, appendix II.

3. Obeyesekere (1984:23).

4. See my *Buddha in the Crown,* pp. 195–98, for a discussion of the *sinhasana* and its symbolism.

5. *Randoli* is a misnomer, because the *devalaya* does not have a *randoli* , or "queen's palanquin," nor does it possess any *ran ayudha* ("golden weapons" of the deity) to put into a *randoli.*

6. See the last two chapters of H. L. Seneviratne (1978).

7. For an overview and discussion, along with color photo illustrations, of the fundamental patterns and religious symbolism of Kandyan Buddhist-temple wall paintings of this nature, see my *Religious World of Kirti Sri* (1996:41–72). Within this *buduge,* one painting within the hexagon contains the figure of a Dutch soldier, thereby suggesting its eighteenth-century origins.

8. To a certain extent, I find the studies of Martin Southwold (1983) among Sinhala villagers near Kurunegala, the work of Kamala Tiyavanich (1997) about twentieth-century Thai forest monks, and the insights of Nicola Tannebaum (1995) among the Shan people of Myanmar very compatible with my own approach.

9. For a discussion of how contemporary Sinhala politicians implicate Buddhist history within the discourse of nationalism, see my "The Persistence of Political Buddhism" (1998) and Kemper, *The Presence of the Past* (1991).

Bibliography

Adhikaram, E. W. *Early History of Buddhism in Ceylon.* Colombo: D. S. Puswella, 1946.

Agarwal, Bina. *A Field of One's Own: Gender and Land Rights in South Asia.* Cambridge, U.K.: Cambridge University Press, 1996.

Ames, Michael. "Magical Animism and Buddhism: a Structural Analysis." In E. B. Harper, ed., *Religion in South Asia.* Seattle: University of Washington Press, 1964.

Ameresekere, H. E. "Vimal Sri Devinuwara." *Ceylon Literary Register* 1 (Third Series): 199–204 and 279–83.

Appuhamy, M. A. Durand. *The Kandyans' Last Stand Against the British.* Colombo: M. D. Gunasena, 1995.

Ariyapala. M. B. *Society in Medieval Ceylon.* Colombo: Department of Cultural Affairs, 1956.

Babb, Lawrence A. *Absent Lord: Ascetics and Kings in a Jain Ritual Culture.* Berkeley, Calif.: University of California Press, 1996.

Barnett, L. D. "Alphabetical Guide to Sinhalese Folklore from Ballad Sources." *Indian Antiquary* 29 (Supplement), 1916.

Bartholomeusz, Tessa J. *In Defense of Dharma: Just-war Ideology in Buddhist Sri Lanka.* New York: Routledge/Curzon, 2002.

Barua, Benimadhab. *A History of Pre-Buddhist Indian Philosophy.* Delhi: Motilal Banarsidass, 1970.

Basu, Shamita. *Religious Revivalism as National Discourse: Swami Vivekananda and New Hinduism in Nineteenth Century Bengal.* New Delhi: Oxford University Press, 2002.

Bechert, Heinz, ed. *Buddhism in Ceylon and Studies on Religious Syncretism in Buddhist Countries.* Gottingen: Vandenoeck and Ruprecht, 1978.

Bell, H. C. P. *Report on the Kegalla District of Sabaragamuwa.* Colombo: George J. A. Skeen, Government Printer, 1904.

Carter, Charles. *A Sinhalese-English Dictionary.* Colombo: M. D. Gunasena (first published, Baptist Missionary Society, 1924), 1970.

Chari, S. M. Srinivasa. *Vaisnavism: Its Philosophy, Theology and Religious Discipline.* Delhi: Motilal Banarsidass, 1994.

Ching, Julia. *The Religious Thought of Chu Hsi.* New York: Oxford University Press, 2000.

Clough, B. *Sinhala English Dictionary.* 2nd ed. New Delhi: Asian Educational Services (first published, Kolupitiya: Wesleyan Missionary Press, 1892), 1999.

Coomaraswamy, Ananda. *Medieval Sinhalese Art.* 2nd ed. New York: Pantheon, 1956.

Cowell, E. B. *The Jataka.* New Delhi: Munshiram Manoharlal. 4: 78–82.

Davis, Richard H. *Lives of Indian Images.* Princeton, N.J.: Princeton University Press, 1997.

Day, Terence. *The Great Tradition and Little Tradition in Theravada Buddhist Studies.* Lewiston, N.Y.: Edwin Mellen Press, 1988.

de Elaris, R. P., ed. *Suniyam Devatavunge Kavi.* Colombo: Sastraloka Press, 1929.

de Jong, J. W. "The Background of Early Buddhism." *Journal of Indian and Buddhist Studies* 12 (1964): 34–47.

De Lanerolle, S. D. *Purana Parsi Adhirajyaya.* Colombo: M. D. Gunasena, 1964.

De Munck, Victor C. "Sufi and Reformist Designs: Muslim Identity in Sri Lanka." In Tessa J. Bartholomeusz and Chandra R. de Silva, *Buddhist Fundamentalism and Minority Identity in Sri Lanka,* pp. 110–132. Albany, N.Y.: State University of New York Press, 1998.

Deodikar, Sanjay G. *Upanisads and Early Buddhism.* Delhi: Eastern Book Linkers, 1992.

de Silva, C. M. Austin. "The Ancient Shrine of Alut-Nuvara." *Spolia Zeylonica* 31 (1969): 329–44.

de Silva, K. D. Endiris, ed. *Vadiga Tantraya* (Part I). Kegalle, S.L.: Vidyakalpa Press, 1927.

de Silva, K. M. *Regional Powers and Small State Security: India and Sri Lanka.* Baltimore, Md.: Johns Hopkins University Press, 1996.

de Silva, K. M. *Reaping the Whirlwind: Ethnic Conflict, Ethnic Politics in Sri Lanka.* New Delhi: Penguin, 1998.

de Silva, K. M. *A History of Sri Lanka.* Berkeley, Calif.: University of California Press, 1981.

De Silva, Lynn. *Buddhism: Beliefs and Practices in Sri Lanka.* Colombo: Wesley Press, 1974.

Dewaraja, L. S. "The Social and Economic Conditions of the Kandyan Kingdom in the Seventeenth and Eighteenth Centuries." In K. M. de Silva, ed., *University of Peradeniya History of Sri Lanka,* vol. 2: 375–97. Colombo: Sridevi, 1995.

Dewaraja, L. S. *The Kandyan Kingdom of Sri Lanka (1707–1782).* 2nd ed. Colombo: Lake House, 1988.

Dharmadasa, K. N. O. "The People of the Lion: Ethnic Identity, Ideology and Historical Revisionism in Contemporary Sri Lanka." *Ethnic Studies Report* 9 (1992): 37–59.

Dharmadasa, K. N. O. *Sinhala Deva Puranaya.* Colombo: Government Press, 1994.

Dharmasiri, Gunapala. *A Buddhist Critique of the Christian Concept of God.* Antioch, Calif.: Golden Leaves, 1988.

Dias, Charles, ed. *Galakaeppu Sahalla.* Colombo: Samayawardhana Press, 1926.

Dimmitt, Cornelia and J. A. B.van Buitenen. *Classical Hindu Mythology.* Philadelphia: Temple University Press, 1978.

Dissanayake, Mudiyanse. *Valiyak Mangalya Wimasuma.* Colombo: Godage Brothers, 2000.

Dissanayake, Mudiyanse. *Kankarigita Sahitya.* Colombo: Godage Brothers, 1991.

Dumezil, George. *The Destiny of the Warrior.* Alf Hiltebeitel, trans. Chicago: University of Chicago Press, 1970.

Dumezil, George. *The Destiny of a King.* Alf Hiltebeitel, trans. Chicago: University of Chicago Press, 1973.

Duncan, James. *The City as Text: The Politics of Landscape Interpretation in the Kandyan Kingdom.* Cambridge, U.K.: Cambridge University Press, 1990.

Durkheim, Emile. *The Elementary Forms of Religious Life.* New York: Macmillan (first published, George Allen & Unwin, 1915), 1965.

Dutt, Nalinaksa. "Brahminism and Buddhism." *Bulletin of Tibetology* 7 (1970): 7–11.

Eck, Diana L. "Dialogue and Method: Reconstructing the Study of Religion." In Kimberley C. Patton and Benjamin C. Ray, eds., *A Magic Still Dwells: Comparative Religion in the Postmodern Age,* pp. 131–49. Berkeley, Calif.: University of California Press, 2000.

Encyclopaedia of Buddhism. (4 vols. to date.) Colombo: Government of Sri Lanka Press, 1959.

Epigraphia Zeylonica (7 vols. to date.) Oxford, U.K.: Oxford University Press, 1904.

Erndl, Kathleen. "The Mutilation of Suparnakha." In Paula Richman, ed., *Many Ramayanas: the Diversity of Narrative Tradition in South Asia,* pp. 67–88. New Delhi: Oxford University Press, 1994.

Evers, Hans-Dieter. *Monks, Priests and Peasants: A Study of Buddhism and Social Structure in Central Ceylon.* Leiden: E. J. Brill, 1972.

Fernando, J. D., ed. *Manikpala Santiya.* Colombo: Granthaprakasa Press, 1929.

Fernando, P. E. E. "Tantric Influence on the Sculptures at Gal Vihara, Polonnaruva," *University of Ceylon Review* 18 (1960): 50–66.

Fu, Charles, Wei hsun. "Chu Hsi on Buddhism." In Wing-tsit Chen, ed., *Chu His and Neo-Confucianism,* pp. 377–407. Honolulu: University of Hawaii Press, 1986.

Geiger, Wilhelm. *The Mahavamsa or The Great Chronicle of Ceylon.* Colombo: Ceylon Government Department of Information (first published, London: Pali Text Society, 1912), 1950.

Geiger, Wilhelm. *Culavamsa.* (2 vols.) Colombo: Ceylon Government Department of Information, 1953.

Geiger, Wilhelm. *Culture of Ceylon in Medieval Times.* Heinz Bechert, ed. Wiesbaden: Otto Harrasowitz, 1970.

Gibb, H. A. R., ed. and trans. *Ibn Batuta: Travels in Asia and Africa (1354–58).* London: Routledge, 1929.

Gibb, H. A. R.. *Mohammedanism: An Historical Survey.* 2nd ed. New York: Oxford University Press, 1970.

Glassenapp, Helmuth von. *Buddhism: A Non-Theistic Religion?* London: George Allen & Unwin. 1970.

Godakumbura, G. C.. "Sinhalese Festivals: Their Symbolism, Origins and Proceedings." *Journal of the Royal Asiatic Society (Ceylon Branch),* n.s., 14 (1970): 91–134.

Godakumbura, G. C.. *Sinhalese Literature* (Colombo: Colombo Apothecaries, 1955).

Gombrich, Richard. *Buddhist Precept and Practice: Traditional Buddhism in the Rural Highlands of Ceylon.* Delhi: Motilal Banarsidass (first published, Oxford University Press, 1971), 1991.

Gombrich, Richard. "The Vessantara Jataka, the Ramayana and the Dasaratha Jataka." *Journal of the American Oriental Society* 105 (1985): 427–37.

Gombrich, Richard and Obeyesekere, Gananath. *Buddhism Transformed: Religious Change in Sri Lanka.* Princeton, N.J.: Princeton University Press, 1985.

Gooneratne, Dandris de Silva. *On Demonology and Witchcraft in Ceylon.* New Delhi: Asian Educational Services (first published in *Journal of the Royal Asiatic Society* (Ceylon Branch) Vol. 5, No. 13, 1–122, 1865), 1998.

Gray, Albert. *Ibn Batuta in the Maldives and Ceylon.* Madras: Asian Educational Services (first published as special issue of *Journal of the Ceylon Branch of the Royal Asiatic Society*, 1882), 1996.

Greenwald, Alice. "The Relic on the Spear." In Bardwell L. Smith, ed., Religion *and the Legitimation of Power in Sri Lanka.* Chambersburg, Pa.: Anima Books, 1978.

Gunasekere, B. *The Rajavaliya.* Colombo: George J. A. Skeen, 1900.

Gunawardana, R. A. L. H. *Robe and Plough: Monasticism and Economic Interest in Early Medieval Sri Lanka.*Tucson, Ariz.: University of Arizona Press, 1979.

Gunawardana, R. A. L. H. "Seaways to Sielediba: Changing Patterns of Navigation in the Indian Ocean and their Impact on Precolonial Sri Lanka." *Kalyani: Journal of Humanities and Social Sciences of the University of Kelaniya* 5 and 6 (1986): 1–33.

Gunawardana, R. A. L. H. "The People of the Lion: the Sinhala Identity and Ideology in History and Historiography." In Jonathan Spencer, ed., *Sri Lanka: History and Roots of Conflict.* London: Routledge, 1990.

Gunawardhana, H. D. J. *Pujavaliya* (Part I). Colombo: Department of Cultural Affairs, 2000.

Gunawardhana, W. F., ed. *Kokila Sandesaya,* 2nd ed. Colombo: Peramuna Press, 1925.

Gunawardhana, W. F., ed. *Mayura Sandesaya.* Colombo: M. D. Gunasena, 1949.

Hallisey, Charles. "Roads Taken and Roads Not Taken in the Study of Theravada Buddhism." In Donald Lopez, ed., *Curators of the Buddha.* Chicago: University of Chicago Press, 1995, pp. 31–61.

Hallisey, Charles. "Works and Persons in Sinhala Literary Culture." In Sheldon Pollock, ed., *Literary Cultures in History: Reconstructions from South Asia.* Berkeley, Calif.: University of California Press, 2003, pp. 689–746.

Haldar, J. R.. *Early Buddhist Mythology.* New Delhi: Manohar Book Service, 1970.

Halvorson, John. "Religion and Psychosocial Development in Sinhalese Buddhism." *Journal of Asian Studies* 37 (1978): 221–32.

Heesterman, J. C. "The Conundrum of the King's Authority." In J. F. Richards, ed., *Kingship and Authority in South Asia.* Delhi: Oxford University Press, pp. 1–13.

Hodgson, Marshall G. S. *The Venture of Islam.* (3 vols.) Chicago: University of Chicago Press. 1974.

Holt, John Clifford. "Assisting the Living by Venerating the Dead: Merit Transfer in Early Buddhist Tradition." *Numen* 27 (1981): 1–28.

Holt, John Clifford. "Pilgrimage and the Structure of Sinhalese Buddhism." *Journal of the International Association of Buddhist Studies* 5 (1982): 23–40.

Holt, John Clifford. *Buddha in the Crown: Avalokitesvara in the Buddhist Traditions of Sri Lanka.* New York and Oxford: Oxford University Press, 1991.

Holt, John Clifford. *The Religious World of Kirti Sri: Buddhism, Art and Politics in Late Medieval Sri Lanka.* New York and Oxford: Oxford University Press, 1996.

Holt, John Clifford. "The Persistence of Political Buddhism." In Tessa J. Bartholomeusz and Chandra R. de Silva, eds., *Buddhist Fundamentalism and Minority Identity in Sri Lanka.* Albany, N.Y:. State University of New York Press, 1998, pp. 186–95.

Horner, I. B., ed. and trans., *The Book of Discipline (Vinaya-pitaka),* vol. I (*Suttavibhanga*). London: for Pali Text Society by Luzac and Co. (first published, Oxford University Press, 1938), 1970

Hutchins, Francis G. *Young Krisna: Translated from the Sanskrit* 'Harivamsa, trans. West Franklin, N.H.: Amarta Press, 1980.

Ilangasinha, H. B. M. *A Study of Buddhism in Ceylon in the Fifteenth and Sixteenth Centuries (Circa 1400–1600)*. Ph.D. Thesis, School of Oriental and African Studies, University of London, 1972; subsequently published as *Buddhism in Medieval Sri Lanka*. Delhi: Sri Satguru, 1992.

Inden, Ronald. "Ritual, Authority, and Cycle Time in Hindu Kingship." In J. F. Richards, ed., *Kingship and Authority in South Asia*. New Delhi: Oxford University Press, 1998, pp. 41–91.

Jaini, P. S. "Sramanas: Their Conflict with Brahmanical Society." In Joseph W. Elder, ed., *Chapters in Indian Civilization*. Dubuque, Iowa: Kendall Hunt, 1970, pp. 39–81.

James, William. *The Varieties of Religious Experience*. New York: Penguin Books (first published, Longmans, Green, 1902), 1958.

Jayatilaka, D. B., ed.. *Tisara-sandesaya*. Colombo: 1935.

Jayatilleke, K. N.. *Early Buddhist Theory of Knowledge*. London: George Allen & Unwin, 1963.

Joshi, Lal Mani. *Discerning the Buddha*. New Delhi: Munshiram Manoharlal, 1983.

Kane, P. V. *History of Dharmsastra*, vol. 5. Poona: Bandarkar Oriental Research Institute, 1962.

Kapferer, Bruce. *A Celebration of Demons*. Bloomington, Ind.: Indiana University Press, 1983.

Kapferer, Bruce. *Legends of People, Myths of State*. Washington, D.C.: Smithsonian Institution Press, 1988.

Kapferer, Bruce. *The Feast of the Sorcerer: Practices of Consciousness and Power*. Chicago: University of Chicago Press, 1997.

Kemper, Steven. *The Presence of the Past: Chronicles, Politics and Culture in Sinhala Life*. Ithaca, N.Y.: Cornell University Press, 1991.

Kemper, Steven. *Buying and Believing: Sri Lankan Advertising and Consumers in a Transnational World*. Chicago: University of Chicago Press, 2001.

Kinnard, Jacob. "The Polyvalent *Pada*s of Visnu and the Buddha." *History of Religions* 40 (2000): 32–57.

Kinsley, David. *The Sword and the Flute*. Berkeley, Calif.: University of California Press, 1975.

Knox, Robert. *Historical Relation of the Island Ceylon*. Introduction by H. A. I. Goonetileke. New Delhi: Navrang (first published, London: Robert Chiswell, 1681), 1984.

Kripal, Jeffrey. *Kali's Child*. Chicago: University of Chicago Press, 1996.

La Fleur, William R.. *Liquid Life: Abortion and Buddhism in Japan*. Princeton, N.J.: Princeton University Press, 1992.

Lawrie, Archibald. *A Gazeteer of the Central Province*. (2 vols.) Colombo: George J. A. Skeen (Government Printer), 1898.

Legge, James. *A Record of Buddhist Kingdoms*. New Delhi: Asian Educational Services (first published, Oxford University Press, 1886), 1993.

Liyanagamage, Amaradasa. "Keralas in Medieval Sri Lankan History: a Study of Two Contrasting Roles." *Kalyani: Journal of the Humanities and Social Sciences of the University of Kelaniya* 5 and 6 (1986): 61–77.

Liyanagamage, Amaradasa. *The Decline of Polonnaruwa and the Rise of Dambadeniya (circa 1180–1270 A.D.)*. Colombo: Department of Cultural Affairs (Government Press), 1968.

Lohuizen de Leeuw, J. E. van. "The Kustarajagala Image—and Identification." In *Paranavitana Felicitation Volume*, N. A. Jayawickrama ed. Colombo: M. D. Gunasena, 1965.

Malalasekera, G. P.. *The Pali Literature of Ceylon*. Colombo: M. D. Gunasena, 1928.

Malalgoda, Kitsiri. *Buddhism in Sinhalese Society: 1750–1900*. Berkeley, Calif.: University of California Press, 1976.

Mallikarachchi, Desmond. *Religious, Ritual and Commercial Practices of the Sinhalese Buddhist Traders in the City of Kandy*. Ph.D. Thesis. University of London, 1998.

Marasinghe, M. M. J.. "The 'Yakkhas' in Early Buddhist Literature." *Journal of the Vidyalankara University of Ceylon* 1 (1972): 103–118.

Marasinghe, M. M. J. *Gods in Early Buddhism: A Study in Their Social and Mythological Milieu as Depicted in the Nikayas of the Pali Canon*. Kelaniya, S.L.: University of Sri Lanka Vidyankara Campus Press, 1974.

Masefield, Peter. *Divine Revelation in Pali Buddhism*. Boston: George Allen & Unwin, 1986.

Mendis, G. C. "The Vijaya Legend," in N. A. Jayawickrama, ed., *Paranavitana Felicitation Volume*. Colombo: M. D. Gunasena, 1965, pp. 263–92.

Miller, David. "Swami Sivananda and the *Bhagavadgita*," in Robert Minor, ed., *Modern Interpreters of the* Bhagavad Gita. Albany, N.Y.: State University of New York Press, 1986.

Mudgal, S. G.. *Advaita Vedanta of Sankara: Impact of Buddhism and Samkhya on Sankara's Thought*. Delhi: Motilal Banarsidass, 1975.

Mudiyanse, Nandasena *Mahayana Monuments of Ceylon*. Colombo: M. D. Gunasena, 1967.

Nehru, Jawaharlal. *The Discovery of India*. London: Rider, 1956.

Nevil, Hugh, trans. *Sinhala Verse (Kavi)*. (3 vols.) P. E. P. Deraniyagala ed., Colombo: Ceylon National Museums Manuscript Series, vols. 4–6., 1954.

Norman, K. R., trans. *Theragatha*. London: Pali Text Society, 1970.

Obeyeskere, Gananath. "The Great Tradition and the Little in the Perspective of Sinhala Buddhism." *Journal of Asian Studies* 22 (1963): 139–53.

Obeyesekere, Gananath. "The Fire-walkers of Kataragama: The Rising Tide of Bhakti Religiosity in Buddhist Sri Lanka." *Journal of Asian Studies* 37 (1978): 457–78.

Obeyesekere, Gananath. *The Cult of the Goddess Pattini*. Chicago: University of Chicago Press, 1984.

Obeyesekere, Gananath. "The Cult of Huniyam: A New Religious Movement in Sri Lanka." In James A. Beckford, ed., *New Religious Movements and Rapid Social Change*. Thousand Oaks, Calif.: Sage, 1986.

Ovitagedera, Sinila *Aluthnuwara Devalaya Saha Vathpiliveth Vimarshanaya*. Colombo: Tharangi, 2001.

Padma, Sree. "From Village to City: Transforming Goddesses in Urban Andhra Pradesh." In Tracy Pintchman, ed., *Seeking Mahadevi*. Albany, N.Y.: State University of New York Press, pp. 115–143.

Padma, Sree. "Serpent Symbolism in the Mythology of Andhra Goddesses." Paper presented at 50th Annual Meeting of Association for Asian Studies. Washington, D.C., 1998.

Paranavitana, S. "Mahayanism in Ceylon." *Ceylon Journal of Science*, sec. G, pt. 2 (1928): 35–71.

Paranavitana, S. *The Shrine of Upulvan at Devundara.* Oxford, U.K.: Oxford University Press, 1953.

Paranavitana, S. and C. W. Nicholas, *A Concise History of Ceylon: From the Earliest Times to the Arrival of the Portuguese.* Colombo: Ceylon University Press, 1961.

Parker, H. *Ancient Ceylon.* New Delhi: Asian Educational Services (first published, London: Luzac, 1909), 1981.

Parker, H. *Village Folk Tales of Ceylon.* (3 vols.) Dehiwala, S.L.: Tisara Prakasakayo(first published, London: Luzac, 1910), 1971.

Pathmanathan, S. "Kingship in Sri Lanka: A.D. 1070–1270," *Sri Lanka Journal of the Humanities* 8 (1982): 120–45.

Pathmanathan, S. "Buddhism and Hinduism in Sri Lanka: Some Points of Contact between Two Religious Traditions *circa* A.D. 1300–1600." *Kalyani: Journal of Humanities and Social Sciences of the University of Kelaniya* 5 and 6 (1986): 78–112.

Pathmanathan, S. "The Temples of Devinuwara: Trade, Urbanization and Multiculturalism." Unpublished manuscript text for lecture to Ramakrishna Math Mission, in Wellawatte, Colombo, March 2000.

Perera, A. D. T. E. *The Enigma of the Man and the Horse at Isurumuniya.* Moratuwa, S.L.: Cultural Research Publications, 1978.

Perera, A. D. T. E. "Upulvan, the Patron God of the Sinhalese," *Vidyodya Journal of Arts, Science and Letters* 4 (1971): 88–104.

Pieris, P. E. "The Destruction of Devi Nuwara." *Ceylon National Review* 1 (1906): 81–83.

Pieris, P. E. *Ceylon: The Portuguese Era.* Colombo: Colombo Apothecaries, 1913.

Pieris, Ralph. *Sinhalese Social Organization: The Kandyan Period.* Colombo: Ceylon University Press Board, 1956.

Pollock, Sheldon. "Divine King in the Indian Epic." *Journal of the American Oriental Society* 104 (1984): 505–528.

Pragnaloka, Ven. H. U. *Purana Sivupada Sangrahava.* Colombo: Government Publications, 1952.

Prematilleke, P. L. "The Kustharajagala Image at Valigama, Sri Lanka." In *Senarat Paranavitana Commemoration Volume.* Leiden: E. J. Brill, 1978, pp. 172–80.

Prematilleke, P. L. *The Alahana Parivena Polonnaruva Archaeological Excavation Report (April–September 1981).* Colombo: Ministry of Cultural Affairs, 1981.

Queyroz, Fernao de. *The Spiritual and Temporal Conquest of Ceylon.* (3 vols.) S. G. Perera, trans. New Dehli: Asian Educational Services, Government Printer, (first written 1688), 1992.

Radhakrishnan, Sarvepalli. *Eastern and Western Religious Thought.* 2nd ed. Oxford, U.K.: Oxford University Press, 1940.

Radice, William, ed. *Swami Vivekananda and the Modernization of Hinduism.* Delhi: Oxford University Press, 1998.

Raghavan, M. D. *Sinhala Natum.* Colombo: M. D. Gunasena, 1967.

Rahula, Walpola. *What the Buddha Taught.* New York: Grove Press, 1959.

Ramanujan, A. K. "Three Hundred *Ramayanas*: Five Translations and Three Thoughts." In Paula Richman, ed., *Many Ramayanas.* New Delhi: Oxford University Press, 1959, pp. 22–49.

Rambachan, Anantanand. *The Limits of Scripture: Vivekananda's Reinterpretation of the Vedas.* Honolulu: University of Hawaii Press, 1994.

Ratnayake, C. N. R. *Glimpses of the Social, Religious, Economic and Political Conditions of Ceylon from the Sandesaya*s. Master's Thesis. Department of History, University of Peradeniya, 1949.

Ray, Benjamin C. "Discourse about Difference: Understanding African Ritual Language." In Kimberley C. Patton and Benjamin C. Ray, eds., *A Magic Still Dwells: Comparative Religion in the Postmodern Age.* Berkeley, Calif.: University of California Press, 2000, pp. 101–116.

Reynolds, Christopher, ed. *An Anthology of Sinhalese Literature up to 1815.* Battaramulla, S.L.: Sri Lanka National Commission for UNESCO. 1970.

Reynolds, Frank E. "*Ramayana, Rama Jataka,* and *Ramakien*: A Comparative Study of Hindu and Buddhist Traditions." In Paula Richman, ed., *Many Ramayanas: The Diversity of a Narrative Tradition in South Asia.* Delhi: Oxford University Press, 1994, pp. 50–63.

Reynolds, Frank E. "The Two Wheels of Dhamma: a Study of Early Buddhism." In *The Two Wheels of Dhamma,* Bardwell L. Smith. ed. Chambersburg, Pa.: American Academy of Religion; *AAR Studies in Religion* (1972), no. 3.

Rhys Davids, T. W. "The Inscription at Dondra." *Journal of the Ceylon Branch of the Royal Asiatic Society* 5 (1870): 57–66.

Rhys Davids, T. W. and Rhys Davids, C. A. F., eds. and trans. *Dialogues of the Buddha* (Digha Nikaya*).* (3 vols.) London: Pali Text Society. 1921.

Roberts, Michael. *Caste Conflict and Elite Formation: The Rise of a Karava Elite in Sri Lanka, 1500–1931.* New Dehli: Navrang, 1995.

Richman, Paula, ed. *Many Ramayanas: The Diversity of a Narrative Tradition in South Asia.* New Delhi: Oxford University Press, 1994.

Ryan, Bryce. *Caste in Modern Ceylon: The Sinhalese System in Transition.* New Delhi: Navrang (first published, Rutgers University Press, 1953), 1993

Saparamadu, S. D., ed. *The Polonnaruva Period.* Dehiwala, S.L.: Tisara Prakasakayo (first published as special issue of *The Ceylon Historical Journal,* 1955), 1973.

Sastri, H. Krishna. *Memoirs of the Archaeological Survey of India.* Delhi: Archaeological Survey of India, vol. 26, 1945.

Sastri, K. A. Nilakanta. "Saivism in Ancient Ceylon." In N. A. Jayawickrama, ed., *Paranvitana Felicitation Volume.* Colombo: M. D. Gunasena, pp. 305–312.

Sastri, K. A. Nilakanta. *Foreign Notices of South India.* Madras: University of Madras, 1939.

Schonthal, Benjamin *Managing Ambivalence: The Moon-Huniyam Metaphor in Contemporary Sinhala Buddhism.* Honors Thesis. Department of Religion, Bowdoin College (Maine), 1999.

Scott, David. *Formations of Ritual: Colonial and Anthropological Discourses on the Sinhala Yaktovil.* Minneapolis, Minn.: University of Minnesota Press, 1994.

Sedaraman, J. E. *Lanka Bali Upata.* Colombo: M. D. Gunasena, 1967.

Sen, Amiya P. *Swami Vivekananda.*Delhi: Oxford University Press, 2000.

Seneviratne, Anuradha. "Rama and Ravana: History, Legend and Belief in Sri Lanka." *Ancient Ceylon* 5 (1984a): 221–36.

Seneviratne, Anuradha. *The Golden Rock Temple of Dambulla.* Colombo, S.L.: Ministry of Cultural Affairs; Publication No. 14, 1984b.

Seneviratne, Anuradha. *Traditional Dance of Sri Lanka.* Colombo: Ministry of Cultural Affairs, 1984c.

Seneviratne, Anuradha. *Polonnaruva: Medieval Capital of Sri Lanka.* Colombo: Archaeological Survey Department, 1998.

Seneviratne, H. I... *Rituals of the Kandyan State.* Cambridge, U.K.: Cambridge University Press, 1978.

Seneviratne, H. L. *The Work of Kings: The New Buddhism of Sri Lanka.* Chicago: University of Chicago Press, 1999.

Sharma, C. D. *A Critical Survey of Indian Philosophy.* London: Rider, 1960.

Shulman, David. *Tamil Temple Myths: Sacrifice and Divine Marriage in the South India Saiva Tradition.* Princeton, N.J.: Princeton University Press, 1980.

Sinhala Encyclopaedia. D. E. Hettiaratchi, ed.. (4 vols.) Colombo: Government Press, 1970.

Sircar, D. C. *Inscriptions of Asoka.* Delhi: Ministry of Information, Government of India, 1957.

Sirisena, W. M. *Sri Lanka and Southeast Asia: Political, Religious and Cultural Relations from A.D. c. 1000 to c. 1500.* Leiden: E. J. Brill, 1978.

Smith, Bardwell, ed. *Religion and the Legitimation of Power in Sri Lanka.* Chambersburg, Pa.: Anima, 1978.

Somaratne, G. P. V. "Jayawardhanapura: the Capital of the Kingdom of Sri Lanka c. 1400–1565." *Sri Lanka Archives* 2 (1984): 1–6.

Southwold, Martin. *Buddhism in Life.* Manchester, U.K.: University of Manchester Press, 1983.

Stcherbatsky, Fedor I. *Buddhist Logic,* vol. 1. New York: Dover (first published, Leningrad, 1930), 1962.

Stein, Burton. *Vijayanagara.* In *The New Cambridge History of India.*vol. 1, pt. 2. Cambridge, U.K.: Cambridge University Press, 1989.

Sugatapala, T., ed. *Gira-sandesaya.* Alutgama, S.L., 1925.

Suravira, A. V., ed. *Alakesvara Yuddhaya.* Colombo: Ratna, 1962.

Suzuki, M. "Rituals of Rural Highland Villages in Southern Sri Lanka," in K. Iwata and Y. Ikari, eds. *Religion and Cultures in Sri Lanka and South Asia.* Osaka, Japan: National Museum of Ethnology, pp. 67–98.

Tambiah, S. J. *World Conqueror, World Renouncer.* Cambridge, U.K: Cambridge University Press, 1976.

Tambiah, S. J. *Buddhism Betrayed.* Chicago: University of Chicago Press, 1992.

Tannenbaum, Nicola. *Who Can Compete Against the World? Power Protection and Buddhism in Shan Worldview.* Ann Arbor, Mich.: Association for Asian Studies, 1992.

Tennent, James Emerson. *Ceylon: An Account of the Island.* (2 vols., 6th ed.) Dehiwala, S.L.: Tisara Prakasakayo (first published, London: Longman, Green, Longman and Roberts, 1859), 1977.

Thera, Kunkunawe Sumangala. Ven. Welivita Dhammaloka, ed. *Siri Rama Sandesaya.* Maradana, S.L.: Sri Lankodaya Press, 1950.

Tiyavanich, Kamala. *Forest Recollections: Wandering Monks in Twentieth Century Thailand.* Honolulu: University of Hawaii Press, 1997.

Trenckner, V., ed. *The Majjhima Nikaya*. London: Pali Text Society, 1954.

Tu, Wei-ming. *Neo-Confucian Thought in Action: Wang Yang-ming's Youth (1472–1509)*. Berkeley, Calif.: University of California Press, 1976.

Tweed, Thomas. "On Moving Across: Translocative Religion and the Interpreter's Position." In *Journal of the American Academy of Religion* 70 (2002): 253–77.

Upadhyaya, Kashi Nath. *Early Buddhism and the* Bhagavadgita. Delhi: Motilal Banarsidass, 1971.

van der Veer, Peter. "The Moral State: Religion, Nation and Empire in Victorian Britain and British India." In Peter van der Veer and Hartmut Lehman, eds., *Nation and Religion: Perspectives on Europe and Asia*. Princeton, N.J.: Princeton University Press, 1999, pp. 15–43.

Varma, V. P. "The Vedic Religion and the Origins of Buddhism." *Journal of the Bihar Research Society* 46 (1960): 276–308.

Vitharana, V. *Sun and Moon in Sinhala Culture*. Colombo: Educational Publications Department, 1993.

Vivenkanda, Swami. *Complete Works*, vol. I. Calcutta: Advaita Ashrama, 1971–73.

von Schroeder, Ulrich. *Buddhist Sculptures of Sri Lanka*. Hong Kong: Visual Dharma Publications. 1990.

Walters, Jonathan. "Communal Karma and Karmic Community in Theravada Buddhist History." In John Clifford Holt, Jacob Kinnard, and Jonathan Walters, eds., *Constituting Communities: Theravada Buddhism and the Religious Cultures of South and Southeast Asia*. Albany, N.Y.: State University of New York Press, 2003, pp. 9–40.

Walters, Jonathan. *The History of Kelaniya*. Colombo: Social Scientists' Association, 1996.

Warder, A. K.. *Indian Buddhism*. 2nd ed. Delhi: Motilal Banarsidass,1980.

Waharatana, Kamburupitiye. *Matara Pura Vidyatmaka Itihasaya*. Tihagoda, Sri Lanka: Siri Ratana Joti Pirivena, 1994.

Weber, Max. *The Protestant Ethic and the Spirit of Capitalism*. Talcott Parsons, trans. New York: Scribner's, (first published in English, London: G. Allen & Unwin, 1905), 1958.

Weber, Max. *The Religion of India*. Glencoe, Ill.: Free Press, 1958.

Wickramasinghe, Martin. *Aspects of Sinhalese Culture*. 4th ed. Dehiwala, S.L.: Tisara Prakasakayo (first published 1952), 1992.

Woodward, F. L., trans. *Udana: Verses of Uplift and Itivuttaka: As It Was Said*. London: Pali Text Society, 1935.

Wijesekera, N. de S., ed. *The Selahini Sandesaya of Totagamuve Sri Rahula*. Colombo: M. D. Gunasena, 1934.

Wijesekera, O. H. De A. "Pali and Sanskrit in the Polonnaruva Period," in S. D. Saparamadu, ed., *The Polonnaruva Period*. Dehiwala, S.L.: Tisara Prakasakayo, 1973, pp. 102–109.

Wirz, Paul. *Exorcism and the Art of Healing in Ceylon*. Leiden: E. J. Brill, 1954.

Zelliot, Eleanor. *Dr. Ambedkar and the Mahar Movement*. Philadelphia: University of Pennsylvania Press, 1969.

Zimmer, Heinrich. *Myths and Symbols in Indian Art and Civilization*. Joseph Campbell, ed. Princeton, N.J.: Princeton University Press (first published, Washington, D.C.: Bollingen Foundation, 1946).

Index of Place Names

Index of
Sinhala (snh), Pali (p), Sanskrit (skt) and Tamil (t) Texts
(translated or cited)

Subject Index

Italic page numbers refer to illustrations.

Abeyanayake, Rajpal, 336, 340, 343, 407*n*15
Agbo (king), 75
Age, of devotees, 215, 223
Ahura Mazda, 68, 91–92
Aiyanar, 148, 150, 388*n*38
Alahana Parivena, 40, 377*n*17
Alakesvara family, 52, 53–54, 55
Alutgama, 352, 365–370
Alutnuvara Devalaya: *asala perahara* of, 262, *262–265*; and *basnayaka nilame*, 180, 189; and Christianity, 369; and Dadimunda, 171, 248, 389*n*2; Dadimunda image in, 250, *250*, 273, 274; and Devinuvara, 259; and devotees, 205, 272; and *disti*, 271–272; history of, 251–260; and Huniyam, 248, 300; and Huniyam *devalaya*, 296; and *kapuralas*, 192, 194, 195; Maha Devalaya compared to, 249–251; Maha Devalaya connected with, 137, 158, 191–192, 256, 389*n*2; *sannasa* of, 253–256, 400*n*7; sketch of, *249*; and Upulvan, 80, 248, 257–258, 262; and *valiyak mangalya*, 227, 229; and visionary experiences, 264; and Visnu, 99, 158, 162, 248, 252, 253, 254; and *yaksa* possession, 193; and *yatikas*, 198, 220–221
Alutnuvara Devale Saha Dadimunda Bandara Deviyange Vittiya, 265, 267, 269–270, 314–320
Alutnuvara Deviyo: cult of, 257; Dadimunda as, 132, 162, 163, 186, 248, 261, 389*n*2;

devalayas of, 186; and hierarchy of deities, 292; Knox on, 162; offerings to, 251; political significance of, 259, 261; and protection of Buddha, 102; and Upulvan identity, 92; and visions, 264; and Visnu, 124, 128, 132; and *yaksa/devata* transition, 294
Alwis, James de, 376*n*10
Amavatura, 44, 58, 60
Ambedkar, B. R., 22
Ambekke Devalaya, 265
Anti-Americanism, 364, 365
Anuradhapura, 281, 284, 357, 403*n*22
Anuradhapura era, 46, 107
Architectural monuments, 51–52, 60, 88
Ariyapala, M. B., 59, 88–90, 379–380*n*38
Arthasastra, 42, 44
Asala peraharas: of Alutnuvara Devalaya, 262, *262–265*; and *basanayaka nilames*, 182, *183*; and Dalada Maligava, 163, 182, 261, 352, 402*n*13; in Devinuvara, 259, 262, 264, 351–365, *353–363*; and four guardian deities, 145, 163; function of, 34, 261; and Gajabahu myth, 56; and Hanguranketa, 192; history of, 261–262, 401–402*n*13; in Kandy, 140, 352–353, 359, 365; Knox on, 161, 163; and Parakramabahu II, 76, 253, 262, 351; political significance of, 261; and sandalwood image myth, 74; television coverage of, 182; and Upulvan, 262, 400*n*7; and *valiyak mangalya*, 158, 225, 227–228, 229; and Vijaya myth, 64; and Visnu *devalayas*, 192, 217

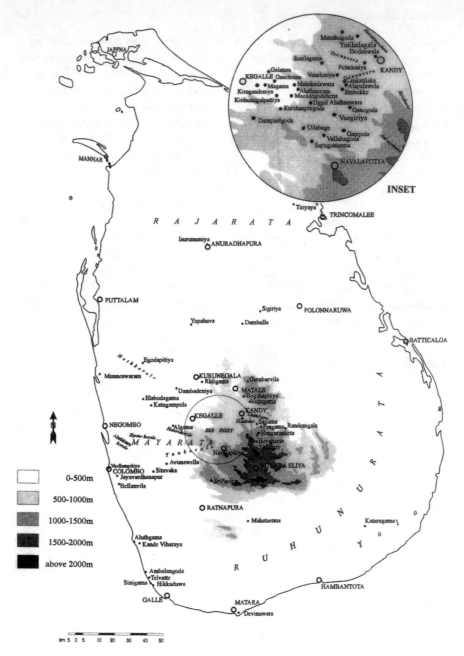

INSET

MAP   Sri Lanka (with upcountry inset)